LUTHER'S LIVES

MANCHESTER
UNIVERSITY PRESS

for Lowell and Marla

Be thou an example of the believers,
in word, in conversation, in charity, in spirit,
in faith.

1 Timothy 4: 12

Luther's lives

*Two contemporary accounts
of Martin Luther*

*translated and annotated
by Elizabeth Vandiver, Ralph Keen
and Thomas D. Frazel*

MANCHESTER UNIVERSITY PRESS
Manchester and New York

distributed exclusively in the USA by Palgrave

Luther's lives

*Two contemporary accounts
of Martin Luther*

*translated and annotated
by Elizabeth Vandiver, Ralph Keen
and Thomas D. Frazel*

MANCHESTER UNIVERSITY PRESS
Manchester and New York

distributed exclusively in the USA by Palgrave

Copyright © The Sohmer-Hall Foundation 2002

Published by Manchester University Press
Oxford Road, Manchester M13 9NR, UK
and Room 400, 175 Fifth Avenue, New York, NY 10010, USA
http:///www.manchesteruniversitypress.co.uk

Distributed exclusively in the USA by
Palgrave, 175 Fifth Avenue, New York, NY 10010, USA

Distributed exclusively in Canada by
UBC Press, University of British Columbia, 2029 West Mall,
Vancouver, BC, Canada, V6T 1Z2

British Library Cataloguing-in-Publication Data
A catalogue record is available from the British Library

Library of Congress Cataloging-in-Publication Data applied for

ISBN 0 7190 6104 0 hardback
ISBN 0 7190 6802 9 paperback

First published 2002
First published in paperback 2003

10 09 08 07 06 05 04 03   10 9 8 7 6 5 4 3 2 1

Typeset in Monotype Bell by Carnegie Publishing Ltd, Lancaster
Printed in Great Britain
by Biddles Ltd, *www.biddles.co.uk*

Contents

Scholars

Elizabeth Vandiver earned her MA and PhD at the University of Texas (Austin). Her areas of concentration are ancient historiography (Herodotus, Livy), elegy (particularly Catullus), and ancient drama and stagecraft. She taught at Northwestern University and the University of Maryland, where she is presently the Director of the Honors Humanities Program. Her publications include Heroes in Herodotus: The Interaction of Myth and History, *Studien zur klassischen Philologie*, 56, series editor Michael von Albrecht (Frankfurt, 1991); 'Hot Springs, Cool Rivers, and Hidden Fires: Heracles in Catullus 68.51–66,' in *Classical Philology* 95 (2000); 'Millions of the Mouthless Dead: Charles Hamilton Sorley and Wilfred Owen in Homer's Hades', in the *International Journal of the Classical Tradition* 5.3 (1999); and 'The Founding Mothers of Livy's Rome: The Sabine Women and Lucretia,' in Richard F. Moorton, Jr, and Frances B. Titchener (eds), *The Eye Expanded: Life and the Arts in Greco-Roman Antiquity* (Berkeley, Los Angeles, London, 1999).

Ralph Keen was born in Philadelphia and received a BA in Greek from Columbia in 1979. He coupled graduate studies in Classics at Yale with several years as assistant research editor of the *Complete Works of St Thomas More*, published by Yale University Press. He earned his PhD in the History of Christianity at University of Chicago. He taught at Alaska Pacific University (Anchorage), and at the University of Iowa, where he is now Associate Professor of Religion. His publications include critical editions of two Latin works by Cochlaeus, *Responsio ad Johannem Bugenhagium Pomeranum* (Nieuwkoop, 1988) and *Philippicae I-VII*, 2 vols (Nieuwkoop, 1995–6), and *Divine and Human Authority in Reformation Thought* (Nieuwkoop, 1997), a study of the political philosophies of Lutheran, Catholic, and Anabaptist theologians. He lives in Iowa City with his wife and daughter.

Thomas D. Frazel was educated at the University of Chicago and the University of California (Los Angeles). He is currently Visiting Assistant Professor in the Department of Classics at Tulane University. His scholarly interests focus primarily on Latin literature of the classical period, ancient rhetoric (in particular Cicero), and Roman intellectual history.

Abbreviations

Clemen   *Luthers Werke in Auswahl*, ed. Otto Clemen, 8 vols (Berlin, 1930) and numerous reprints.

CR   Corpus Reformatorum, ed. C. G. Bretschneider and H. E. Bindseil [edition of Melanchthon's writings], 28 vols (Halle, 1834–60).

Herte, *Lutherkommentare*   Adolf Herte, *Die Lutherkommentare des Johannes Cochlaeus: Kritische Studie zur Geschichtschreibung im Zeitalter der Glaubensspaltung* Reformationsgeschichtliche Studien und Texte, vol. 3 (Münster, 1935).

LW   *Luther's Works*, American edition, ed. J. Pelikan and H. T. Lehmann, 55 vols (Philadelphia, 1955–86).

OER   *Oxford Encyclopaedia of the Reformation*, ed. Hans Hillerbrand, 4 vols (Oxford, 1996).

Spahn   Martin Spahn, *Johannes Cochläus: Ein Lebensbild aus der Zeit der Kirchenspaltung* (Berlin, 1898; rpt Nieuwkoop, 1964).

StA   *Melanchthons Werke in Auswahl*, ed. Robert Stupperich *et al.*, 8 vols (Gütersloh, 1951–78).

WA   *D. Martin Luthers Werke*, 89 vols, including separate series of correspondence (Briefwechsel) (Weimar, 1883–1986).

In general, sources are cited in English versions whenever possible; the headnotes in *LW* provide references to original texts in *WA*. When no English version is available, the most authoritative modern edition is cited; when these are lacking, references are to original editions.

Introduction

We have only two substantial eyewitness accounts of the life of Martin Luther. Best known is a 9,000-word Latin memoir by Philip Melanchthon published in Latin at Heidelberg in 1548, two years after the Reformer's death.[1] In 1561, 'Henry Bennet, Callesian' translated this pamphlet into English; the martyrologist John Foxe adopted Bennet's text into his *Memorials* verbatim, including a number of the Englisher's mistranslations. For example, where Melanchthon wrote that Luther nailed his 95 Theses to the door of the Castle Church in Wittenberg *'pridie festi omnium Sanctorum'* – that is, 'on the day before the feast of All Saints' (31 October 1517) – Bennet mistranslated *pridie* as 'after' and wrote, 'the morrowe *after* the feast of all Saynctes, the year. 1517.'[2] Since every English church was obliged to own a copy of Foxe, Elizabethans – including William Shakespeare – believed Luther's Reformation began on 2 November. The present volume corrects this and other Bennet/Foxe errors, and provides an authoritative English edition of Melanchthon's *Historia de Vita et Actis Reverendiss. Viri D. Mart. Lutheri*, the first new translation in English to appear in print in many years.[3]

But the other substantial *vita* of Luther – at 175,000 words by far the longest and most detailed eyewitness account of the Reformer – has never been published in English. Recorded contemporaneously over the first twenty-five years of the Reformation by Luther's lifelong antagonist Johannes Cochlaeus, the *Commentaria de Actis et Scriptis Martini Lutheri* was published in Latin at Mainz in 1549. Perhaps because of Cochlaeus's unabashed antagonism for the Reformation – and his virulent attacks on Luther, his ideals, and his fellow reformers – the *Commentary* has remained untranslated for more than 450 years. In the present volume this colossal work makes its first appearance in print in English – and its debut is timely. At a moment of *rapprochement* among the divisions of Christianity, Cochlaeus's first-person account of Luther and the turbulent birth of Protestanism is a tale of profound and enduring interest both to the general reader and to students of the Reformation.

Johannes Cochlaeus (1479–1552) was born Johannes Dobeneck (or Dobneck) in Wendelstein in the region of Nuremberg, Germany. A thoroughly educated humanist and pedagogue, Cochlaeus was also an ordained Catholic priest. Conservative, zealous, and personally ambitious, he placed himself in the forefront of the early Catholic reaction against Luther and the reformers. In 1520, Cochlaeus entered the fray with responses to Luther's *Address to the Nobility of the German Nation* and *The Babylonian Captivity of the Church*. On 18 April 1521, Cochlaeus was present in the great hall at the Diet of Worms when Luther made his famous declaration before Emperor Charles V: 'Here I stand. I can do no other. God help me. Amen.' Afterward, Cochlaeus sought out Luther, met him, and debated with him. Luther recalled their confrontation with patience; he wrote of Cochlaeus, 'may God long preserve this most pious man, born to guard and teach the Gospel for His church, together with His word, Amen.'[4] But the encounter left Cochlaeus deeply embittered, and convinced that Luther was an impious and malevolent man. When Luther published his September Bible (1522) and gave the Germans the New Testament in verna-cular language, Cochlaeus bristled that

> even shoemakers and women and every kind of unlearned person ... read it most eagerly as the font of all truth. And by reading and rereading it they committed it to memory and so carried the book around with them in their bosoms. Because of this, in a few months they attributed so much learning to themselves that they did not blush to dispute about the faith and the Gospel, not only with laypeople of the Catholic party, but also with priests and monks, and furthermore, even with Masters and Doctors of Sacred Theology.

Cochlaeus was horrified when Luther encouraged women to take an active role in the life of the church:

> Lutheran women, with all womanly shame set aside, proceeded to such a point of audacity that they even usurped for themselves the right and office of teaching publicly in the Church, despite the fact that Paul openly speaks against this and prohibits it. Nor were they lacking defenders among the Lutheran men, who said that Paul forbade the right of teaching to women only in so far as there were sufficient men who knew how to teach and were able to do so. But where men were lacking or neglectful, there it was most permissible for women to teach. And Luther himself had long before taught that women too were true Christian priests, and what is more, that whoever crept out of Baptism was truly Pope, Bishop, and Priest ...

Cochlaeus deplored Luther's marriage in 1525 to a former nun: 'Katharine von Bora, was – so please the Heavenly powers! – made the wife of Luther, just as soon as the Elector Duke Frederick died. A nun married to a monk; a damned woman to a damned man; an infamous woman to an infamous man ... "They have damnation, because they have made their first faith void."'[5]

Throughout his life Cochlaeus remained an enthusiastic persecutor of heresy wherever he found it. With unconcealed pleasure he chronicles the decline and fall of the short-lived Anabaptist 'kingdom of a thousand year' at Münster (1534–5) – from the excesses of its tailor-turned-king, John of Leiden, to the massacre of his followers. Cochlaeus prides himself on directing the authorities to the clandestine printing press in Cologne where William Tyndale was preparing the first English translation of the New Testament in 1525, and describes the flight up the Rhine of Tyndale and his collaborator, William Roy, to the Lutheran sanctuary of Worms where they finally completed their monumental work.

Cochlaeus was an eyewitness when the Diets of Nuremberg (1522–3) abrogated the Emperor's edict suppressing the reformers and demanded a national German council. At the outbreak of the Peasants' War in 1524–5 Cochlaeus barely escaped with his life; his account of the savagery on both sides is still harrowing. In 1526 he was present when the Diet of Speyer laid the foundation for reformed German churches (*Landeskirchen*) independent of the authority of the pope. At the Diet of Augsburg (1530) Cochlaeus was a member of a Catholic delegation determined to debate, defeat, and humiliate Philip Melanchthon and the Lutherans. But the confrontation ended with a decisive defeat for Cochlaeus and the Catholic side, and the publication of Melanchthon's *Augsburg Confession* became a defining moment in the Reformation.

After Augsburg the tide of reform swept Cochlaeus aside. He spent his latter years scrabbling for funds to publish his anti-Lutheran polemics. But he remained a keen observer of affairs, both on the Continent and in England. In 1535, Cochlaeus published a pamphlet attacking the divorce of King Henry VIII of England – an impolitic act that cost him his post as chaplain to Duke George of Saxony. But in the *Commentary* Cochlaeus records with pleasure Henry's reactionary Six Articles (1536–9) which ended any hope of communion between his English church and the Lutherans. Toward the end of his life Cochlaeus served as canon at Breslau. He died there in 1552.

Cochlaeus's *Commentary* provides a fascinating perspective on Luther's struggle with his contemporary Catholic opponents. Vividly Cochlaeus captures the intensity and ardor on both sides of the Reformation dispute – a public battle for hearts and minds which had become possible only after the Gutenberg revolution. A prodigious reader, Cochlaeus punctuates his narrative with lively citations – many from documents little known or lost – which distill the ferocity and vitriol of the Reformation debate. Cochlaeus cites Thomas More writing in a most unsaintly tone about Luther, declaring the Reformer seeks only

> a most absurd kind of immortality for himself, and that he has already begun to enjoy it fully, and entirely to exist, to act, and to live in the sensation and titillation of this kind of tiny glory, which he presumes is going to last several thousand years after this present time – that men will remember and will recount that once, in some previous age, there lived a certain rascal whose name was Luther, who because he had outstripped the very devils themselves in impiety, surpassed magpies in his garrulousness, pimps in his dishonesty, prostitutes in his obscenity, and all buffoons in his buffoonery, so that he might adorn his sect with worthy emblems.

In a footnote to the text of his *Commentary* Cochlaeus recalls that most of his book had been written at Meissen by the year 1534. Then he recounts how, at the urging of Dr Jerome Verall, Archbishop of Rochester and Apostolic Nuncio, he added the brief chapters covering the years 1535–47 at Regensberg and published the *Commentary* in 1549. But Cochlaeus's real cue to update and publish his fifteen-year-old manuscript may have been the appearance in 1548 of Melanchthon's *vita* of Luther. After the Reformer's death a rumor was bruited among Catholics that demons had seized Luther on his death-bed and dragged him off to Hell. There was also a long-standing slur (attributed to Cochlaeus) which held that Luther's mother had been an attendant in a bathhouse, and the Reformer's birth was the result of her coupling with a demon. Indeed, Luther's birth was widely suspected to be illegitimate; perhaps to refute that allegation Melanchthon offers the evasive testimony of Luther's mother, Margarethe, who protests that she can remember the day of Martin's birth but not the year. In response to the slander that demons dragged the dying Luther to Hell, Melanchthon supplies an exhaustive (and patently embroidered) account of the reformer's last moments.

But the best evidence that Cochlaeus completed and published his book as a response to Melanchthon's *vita Lutheri* appears near the end of the *Commentary*. Cochlaeus records that

> Many people are writing many things about his [Luther's] death. The Catholics in the neighboring areas tell the story and write in one way; the Lutherans speak and write of it in another. For they are producing, in hordes, many pamphlets in German, to persuade everyone of how holy a death that most holy (as they say) father of them all died. The writings of three of his colleagues in particular are being circulated, namely of Jonas Cocus, who falsely calls himself 'Justus,' of Philip Melanchthon, and of Johannes Apel ...

In the present volume Melanchthon's *vita* and Cochlaeus's *Commentary* finally achieve their long-postponed confrontation. Read against each other, the rival texts rekindle the colossal crossfire of faith-against-faith that animated and illuminated the Reformation. Our modern sensibilities may favor Melanchthon's restrained, understated style. But the erudition, intelligence, and passion of Cochlaeus make electrifying reading. His unique insider's account of the Catholic establishment's efforts to suppress the first Reformers provides a rare insight into the beginnings of the Counter-Reformation. Most importantly, Cochlaeus's account of the birth of Protestantism isn't based on hearsay. He was present at the creation. *He was there.* For the modern reader Cochlaeus's chronicle is the best kind of history book. His eyewitness testimony brings the actors and the times vividly alive.

Cochlaeus's *Commentary* was translated for this edition by Professor Elizabeth Vandiver of the Classics Faculty at the University of Maryland. The scholarly apparatus for this text and the introduction to the life and work of Johannes Cochlaeus were compiled by Professor Ralph Keen of the University of Iowa. Philip Melanchthon's *vita* of Luther was translated into English by Thomas D. Frazel, Visiting Assistant Professor in the Classics Department at Tulane University. Professor Keen prepared the introductory essay and notes for Melanchthon's text.

The Sohmer-Hall Foundation is honored to be associated with these distinguished scholars, and privileged to make these documents available in perpetuity to English-speaking readers.

The Sohmer-Hall Foundation
Deidre Hall, Chair
Bel Air, California
The Sohmer-Hall Foundation is a non-sectarian, non-profit endowment for the study of the Renaissance and Reformation.

1

Philip Melanchthon
and the historical Luther

by Ralph Keen

'Isaiah ... John the Baptist ... Paul ... Augustine ... Luther': with these five names Philip Melanchthon identified the points of descent in the transmission of the true faith of the church.[1] The occasion was Luther's funeral, at which Melanchthon, the eulogist, would describe the Wittenberg community as being like orphans bereft of an excellent and faithful father.[2] The combination of reverence and affection for the great Reformer reflected in these comments has cast all of Luther's Protestant contemporaries in his shadow. If Luther remains a figure of heroic proportions, it is due as much to the work of his admirers as to his own efforts. And Philip Melanchthon, Luther's closest colleague, was so successful in creating a legendary Luther that his own role in Reformation history has been regarded as less substantial and influential than it actually was.

Born in 1497 in Bretten, a town north of Pforzheim, and educated at Heidelberg (BA 1511) and Tübingen (MA 1513), Melanchthon was very much a product of the southwestern German regions. His grandfather was mayor of Bretten; a great-uncle by marriage was the humanist Johann Reuchlin; and his father, who died when Philip was eleven, was an armorer for the Heidelberg court. Placed under Reuchlin's care after his father's death, Melanchthon attended the Latin School at Pforzheim, where he excelled at Greek, Latin, and Hebrew, and went on to the arts program at Heidelberg. Here he received as thorough a grounding in the classics as was possible in Germany at the time, and acquired some familiarity with theology and natural science as well.[3]

In 1518 Melanchthon was called to Wittenberg to take up a newly instituted professorship of Greek. It was the second such position in Germany (Leipzig had the first) and Melanchthon was the second choice (Leipzig's incumbent was the preferred candidate). Melanchthon, although only twenty-one, was well trained and showed potential for making Wittenberg a center of humanism like Heidelberg, Tübingen – or Leipzig. Saxony had been divided in the preceding century, and the electoral, or Ernestine, branch wished to build a center of culture comparable to Leipzig, in the rival Albertine branch. The political division between the two branches would become a bitter religious conflict by the 1520s.

Humanism would not, however, be the movement that brought Wittenberg its fame. The preceding fall the university's biblical scholar, a pious Augustinian and an influential preacher, had identified a number of theological issues that he felt should be placed under critical scrutiny. The ninety-five issues that Martin Luther listed as debatable struck at the heart of Catholic practice. They also served as articles in an indictment of traditional ecclesiastical authority. Within a year Luther would become the pole around which, negatively or positively, Western Christendom would orientate itself. Within three years Luther himself would be condemned and excommunicated by the Roman church; and before his death the dividing lines that demarcate the Western confessions to this day would be firmly in place.

To 1530

One of the more fascinating historical questions is whether the youthful Greek instructor knew enough about Luther to want to join him in his work in Wittenberg. Records from Melanchthon's time in Tübingen are tantalizingly scarce, and speculating achieves little. What is undeniable is that Melanchthon found plenty of work at Wittenberg, for Luther needed the services of an energetic Hellenist. Luther's illuminating insight had rested on discovering the meaning of certain passages in the epistles of Paul, and the recovery of the original meaning of scriptural revelation demanded a higher order of philo-logical ability than Luther possessed. Melanchthon proved a capable ally, placing his teaching and humanistic work in the service of the new religious movement. Much of the progress of Lutheran thought in its first dozen years is in fact Melanchthon's work.[4]

From the start of his Wittenberg teaching career, Melanchthon studied the early Christian canon as carefully as he had the pagan authors of classical antiquity. From his lectures on the Pauline epistles came commentaries on Romans and Colossians; from courses on the gospels came expositions of John and Matthew. These were some of the first Protestant commentaries to appear, and they helped set the tone and method for later efforts.[5] With sensitivity to the meaning of the Greek, as well as careful understanding of doctrinal issues, Melanchthon crafted interpretations of book after book, each successive com-mentary a next step in the construction of a comprehensive new exegetical theology. This was both a return to the biblical sources and a retrieval of the Patristic tradition, in the Reformers' view the last body of theological writing that recognized the power of the scriptures.

A modest handbook of theological concepts that appeared in 1521 would prove Melanchthon's most enduring monument. The book was called *Theo-logical Outlines*, though for later editions it was renamed *Loci communes*, in English, *Commonplaces*. This work was a comprehensive treatment of the the-ological positions recognized from the evangelical perspective, but without the elaborate philosophical structure found in the scholastic summas of the preced-ing centuries. As such, it bridged the gap between the scholastic treatise and the biblical commentary.[6]

Melanchthon's ability to conceptualize and arrange the components of Protestant thought was as instrumental in the implementation of religious reform
as it was in its formulation. Beginning in 1527, the Wittenberg theologians
together with secular magistrates began a process of visitations throughout a
number of German territories. These were inspections of parish life with an
eye to evaluating the quality of pastoral care. Melanchthon prepared the manual
for these visitations, and in so doing he both adopted a procedure of the Roman
church and anticipated some of the pastoral initiatives of the Council of Trent.[7]

Visitation protocols were only one way in which the young Melanchthon
sought to extend evangelical principles to everyday life in society. Another
was through education; and this was the work that earned Melanchthon a
reputation as an architect of German education and the label 'Preceptor of
Germany.'[8] This activity began with efforts to re-establish the Nuremberg
Latin school, an institution that had prospered under the patronage of an
educated patrician class, and continued through the reorganization of a number
of higher institutions that would acquire and hold prominence for centuries.
No individual before the nineteenth century was as influential in the history
of German education as Melanchthon. However, Melanchthon's educational
work gave him a place in secular cultural history that ignores important
connections between his view of culture and his religious convictions. His work
as an educator and humanist is carefully controlled by his theological program.[9]

Melanchthon's educational efforts represent more than an attempt to reclaim,
within the secular realm, something that until then had been the almost
exclusive province of the Catholic church. For Melanchthon, as for much of
the Christian tradition before him, the worldly realm is a product of divine
ordering, and thus no more 'secular' than the church itself. Moreover, in
Melanchthon's view the refinement of manners and speech that classical studies
could bring was an essential component of a complete Christian society. A
well-ordered people is one that clearly discerns the difference between the
godly and worldly realms (and thus avoids having the church control worldly
affairs) and benefits from classical culture as the most perfect products of the
worldly imagination.[10]

With the formal 'Protest' issued by the evangelical states at Speyer in 1529,
the Reformation, already well under way, received the name that would identify
it as a rival to Catholicism. The formation of the Schmalkald Federation in the
same year marked a solidification of political boundaries between Catholic and
Protestant states, a division that would bring bloody conflict in coming decades.
Catholic court theologians like Johannes Cochlaeus set about defining the
responsibilities of a Christian ruler in matters of religion. Melanchthon and his
Wittenberg colleagues labored to clarify for Protestant rulers the points of
difference from the Roman religion, and to specify the rulers' duty to institute
and protect Evangelical worship in their lands.

1530–46

In 1530 Charles V, recently crowned Holy Roman Emperor, set the Protestant question at the forefront of his political program, and called a diet to address matters in dispute. As Speyer had demonstrated, it was not unusual for significant political developments to arise from debates about religious issues. Charles had sworn an oath to protect the interests of the Roman church, and was therefore obligated to address problems in religious matters. But the stability of his secular realm was also at stake.

The Diet of Augsburg in 1530 was a decisive moment for the Protestant interests, clerical and political alike. The Confession presented by Melanchthon represented both a comprehensive statement of Wittenberg theology and a challenge to the Empire on behalf of the Protestant territories. Rather than suppressing the Reformation, the Diet helped consolidate the movement, as the Confession became a statement to which more and more of the German nobility subscribed.[11]

With the growth of the Reformation came more controversy, increasing in frequency and ferocity. Hopes for a resolution of religious differences ran high after the accession of the new pope in 1534. When Paul III called for a general council of the church, Protestant and Catholic interests alike began preparing their positions. Rulers convoked colloquies in which opposing theological points could be resolved if possible and clarified if not. Indeed, even those theologians who may have questioned the authority of a papally convened council welcomed the opportunity to propound and defend their convictions. Melanchthon was the most visible representative of Wittenberg theology at a number of these meetings, and he was the ideal choice for the role. Eloquent, logical, and erudite, Melanchthon was a powerful advocate of Reformation thought and (usually) an amiable adversary of his Catholic opponents.[12] Never ordained, he escaped some of the attacks that Luther and other former priests drew; but his lay status also led to dismissive comments about his 'amateur' status as a theologian.

As much as any of his writings, Melanchthon's participation in these discussions helped shape his reputation, both among his contemporaries and for later generations. Two aspects of his reputation, mutually contradictory and both inaccurate, emerged from his work in the colloquies. The first quality associated with Melanchthon was that he was a reluctant participant, a humanist only grudgingly engaged in theological debate. This is at best a half truth. Melanchthon may have been averse to controversy, but he did not shy away from it. Indeed, his participation in the ecumenical debates of his time serves as evidence of his dedication to dialogue and mutual understanding.[13] And to say that he was a humanist only pressed into the service of the church by others is to ignore Melanchthon's voluminous production of dogmatic work. Melanchthon's correspondence from the 1530s and 1540s bears this out.

The second quality that became associated with Melanchthon in the wake of his participation in confessional debates is irenicism.[14] He certainly seems to have been committed to dialogue; and his activities have been taken as signs of a desire for harmony in the church at all costs, but nothing could be less true. Like most theologians of his time, Melanchthon longed for peace in the church, aware of the adverse effects of discord on popular piety. But he resolutely refused to compromise on doctrine in the interest of such harmony. We come closer to the true Melanchthon if we see a polite but stubborn advocate of evangelical principles rather than the gentle and conciliatory compromiser of historical legend.[15] In the second half of the last century Melanchthon became a hero of ecumenically minded scholars, advocates of conciliation who saw a sympathetic spirit in the Wittenberg humanist. In recent years it has become clear that other theologians, notably the erstwhile Dominican Martin Bucer, better fit the irenical model.

In point of fact, the Melanchthon who emerges from the religious colloquies of the 1530s, as well as from developments in the larger political sphere, is a determined opponent of compromise in matters of religion. He reserved his sharpest invective for 'Erasmians' like Georg Witzel (1501–73), who appeared to some to represent a return to the apostolic ideal, and Julius Pflug (1499–1564), a conciliator in principle and politics, and agent of imperial ecclesiastical policies.[16] Taking up lines of thought initiated by Luther, Melanchthon developed a theory of secular rule that underscored the ruler's duty to protect religion in a territory. This duty might call for the expulsion of Catholic clergy, the establishment of evangelical worship, and the creation of secular agencies to take up disciplinary tasks previously performed by the Catholic church. Melanchthon's program of polity presented a heavy burden of pastoral responsibility to princes who may have wanted nothing more from Protestantism than freedom from the Roman church and the Holy Roman Empire.

1546–60

With the death of Luther in 1546 the Wittenberg movement entered a period of instability. The Schmalkald War pitted the Empire against the Protestant forces of the Schmalkald League, who were defeated at the Battle of Mühlberg in 1548. Charles V, out of desire to establish uniformity in religious practice, imposed a series of measures intended to mediate Roman and Lutheran practice. Such a middle way was anathema to Melanchthon and his fellow evangelicals, since it included practices the Protestants had for decades condemned as idolatrous. It was equally repugnant to conservative Catholic theologians, such as Cochlaeus, who rejected on principle any form of conciliation with critics of Roman ecclesiastical authority.

The disputes that followed tested Melanchthon severely. His opposition to the conciliation effort remained strong.[17] Indeed, his convictions may have been strengthened in the wake of the defeat of Protestant forces. The Reformation was at its most vulnerable, and Melanchthon recognized that wavering could spell the end of the movement. On the other hand, the political theory that had granted the ruler the right to impose religious reform seemed to give the Emperor sufficient authority to impose the Interim.[18] It was a dilemma that demanded either resistance or capitulation. Melanchthon chose the latter, responding to the Interim with reservations and qualifications. Not doing so would have further imperiled the cause of religion.[19]

In the view of many of his fellow Protestants, this was the wrong choice. A faction claiming fidelity to Luther undertook a polemical campaign against the Interims and any of its defenders, whether Catholic or Protestant. Melanchthon wsa accused of weakness, of giving in to Catholic interests (and thus being a crypto-Romanist), and of betraying the cause he was supposed to have led after Luther's death. The antagonism created a schism within the Lutheran church, with Melanchthon's supporters calling themselves 'Philippists' and partisans of Luther calling themselves the 'genuine Lutherans', or *gnesiolutherani*, using the Greek word for 'authentic' in their name. The feuding continued through the final decade of Melanchthon's life and for most of the next two decades. Only with the Formula of Concord in 1577 was harmony restored to the Lutheran ranks.[20]

The last dozen years of Melanchthon's life were a time of tumult and uncertainty, in which divisions among Evangelicals multiplied and became more pronounced, just as the Roman church in Trent was consolidating its position against the Reformation in all its forms. To the end a committed defender of the doctrines he and Luther had begun formulating in the early years of the Reform, Melanchthon collected his most important writings into a *Corpus of Christian Doctrine*. On his sixty-third birthday he prepared a preface which identified those texts as his theological last will and testament. He died two months later.[21] His colleagues and students gave him a funeral equaling Luther's in praises of his work and expressions of grief, and buried him opposite Luther in the Wittenberg Castle Church where, according to the legend for which Melanchthon is our only source, the Reformation began in October 1517.[22]

Melanchthon's *Life of Luther*

Their close collaboration over almost thirty years made Melanchthon an ideal custodian of Luther's legacy after his death in February 1546. The eulogy he delivered in Wittenberg was printed quickly and circulated broadly.[23] A collection of the Reformer's major works, assembled by Melanchthon, followed shortly afterward. In preparing these volumes for the press Melanchthon prepared a life of Luther, to introduce the author to future readers and to correct false reports about Luther's life and character.

Just as Melanchthon had served as the arranger and systematizer of Luther's theology, so he presents Luther's life in a noticeably Melanchthonian fashion: clearly and straightforwardly. Melanchthon's orderly mind, ever averse to ambiguity, creates a Luther who rises heroically from the dregs of late medieval Catholicism, and with prophetic zeal restores the piety of the ancient church.

It is evident from the *Life* that Melanchthon saw Luther as a prophet, and depicted him as one, with as little stylistic embellishment as the genre and theme would permit. Melanchthon had identified Luther as a prophet in his funeral oration in 1546,[24] and implied it in his 1548 oration on Luther and the ages of the church.[25] Casting Luther in such a role separated him from all the Bugenhagens, Jonases – and Melanchthons – in his circle, setting them among the followers rather than the agents of the movement.

Just as the prophetic narratives serve a theological purpose in the biblical canon, and just as the lives of great figures play a pedagogical role in humanism, so should Melanchthon's depiction of Luther be seen as an integral part of his larger work of elucidating the salient qualities of the Christian life. The Melanchthon who wrote encomiums of Aristotle, Galen, and Erasmus, praising their usefulness for learning, would not have been complete in his life's work without some record of Luther's life and praise of his contribution to piety.

Melanchthon's interest in history was extensive and genuine. Describing it as philosophy taught by examples, Melanchthon saw the record of human events as an essential component of culture. Moreover, the Protestant theological enterprise called for a certain measure of historical argumentation. In contrast to their Catholic contemporaries, Protestant theologians needed to articulate a vision of history that accounted for the deterioration of religion over time and its restoration in their own day. From his first years in Wittenberg, Melanchthon stressed the purity of the distant past over the corruption of recent times.[26] The heroic figure was the one who could restore ancient thought, practice, and piety. The contrast of a heroic antiquity with a decadent modernity is a prominent theme of Melanchthon's work.

Nevertheless, the *Life of Luther* is structured strangely, and one would be tempted to dismiss it as an incomplete work. Melanchthon's part of the narrative stops at 1521. It is followed by the official account of the proceedings of the Diet of Worms, and that is in turn followed by a eulogy Melanchthon delivered before an academic assembly. Instead of dismissing this arrangement of texts as a poor substitute for a continuous narrative, we might see the use of the Worms narrative as a record that accentuates the heroic character of Luther's stand before the Empire. Like a Passion narrative from the New Testament or one of the ubiquitous hagiographies of the later Middle Ages, the record of Luther's trial presents in a factual manner a steadfastness that is larger than life. The episode is so dramatic that to present this with rhetorical embellishments is actually to undermine the record. The facts speak for themselves, and they do so more eloquently than even Melanchthon, a master of Latin style and a literary mentor, could. Hence the transition from Melanchthon's narrative to the transcript of the proceedings at Worms is a rhetorically effective change of tone.

The eulogistic piece at the end of the *Life of Luther* is not the third part of a three-part work, but a concluding text for a two-part essay. The piety recorded in the 1546 text echoes the stolid faith of a quarter century earlier. The centerpiece of this final passage is Luther's prayer, which like the Worms testimony serves as a witness in the Reformer's own words. By withdrawing from the authorial stage and allowing Luther's words to stand out as they do, Melanchthon preserves an element of Luther's personality, an echo of a majestic presence recently departed from the stage of history.

2

Philip Melanchthon's *History of the Life and Acts of Dr Martin Luther*

translated by Thomas D. Frazel
and annotated by Ralph Keen

HISTORY OF THE LIFE AND ACTS OF THE MOST REVEREND DR MARTIN Luther, Dr of true Theology, written in good faith by Philip Melanchthon

Certain poems have been added by John Policarius [1] on the blessings which God through Luther bestowed upon the whole world. Including several distichs on the Acts of Luther, which were recounted in this same year. 1548.

Reverend Martin Luther gave us hope that he would relate the course of his life and the occasions of his struggles, and he would have done so if he had not been called from this mortal life into the everlasting converse of God and the heavenly Church. But a lucidly written contemplation of his own private life would have been useful, for it was full of lessons which would have been useful in strengthening piety in good minds, as well as a recitation of events which could have made known to posterity about many things, and it would also have refuted the slanders of those who, either incited by princes or others, fictitiously accuse him of destroying the dignity of the Bishops, or that, inflamed by private lust, he broke the bonds of Monastic servitude.

He would have published these things, wholly and copiously set forth and commemorated by himself. For even if evilwishers were to reproach with that common saying, *He himself blows his own pipe*, nevertheless we know there was so much seriousness in him that he would have related the Account with the utmost fidelity. And many good wise men are still living, to whom it would have been ridiculous for another account to be mixed in, as sometimes happens in poems, since he knew they were aware of the order of these events. But because his day of death turned aside the publication of so important an account, we shall recite in good faith about the same matters those things which partly we heard from the man himself, partly those which we ourselves saw.

There is an old family, with many descendants of moderate men, by the name Luther, in the district of the famed Counts of Mansfeld. The parents of Martin Luther first made their home in the town of Eisleben, where Martin Luther was born, then they moved to the town of Mansfeld, where his father, Johannes Luther, acted as Magistrate and was most cherished by all good men because of his integrity.

In his mother, Margarita, the wife of Johannes Luther, since all the other virtues of an honest Matron were seen coming together – modesty, fear of God, and prayer especially shown forth – the other honest women looked to her as an example of virtues. She answered me as I asked several times about the time of her son's birth that she remembered the day and hour exactly, but she was uncertain of the year. However she affirmed that he was born the night of 10 November after eleven o'clock, and the name Martin was given to the infant, because the next day, on which the infant was brought into the Church of God through Baptism, had been dedicated to Martin.[2] But his brother Jacob, an honest and upright man, said the family believed that the year of his birth was AD 1483.

After he was at the age capable of learning, his parents had diligently accustomed their son Martin to the knowledge and fear of God and to the duties of the other virtues by domestic instruction, and as is the custom of honorable men, they saw to it that he learned to read, and his father brought him, even as a quite young boy, to the elementary school of George Aemilius, who can be a witness to this story because he is still living.[3]

At that time, however, Grammar Schools in Saxon towns were of middling quality, so when Martin reached his fourteenth year, he was sent to Magdeburg along with Johannes Reineck, whose virtue was later so outstanding that he had great authority in these Regions.[4] There was exceptional mutual kindness between these two, Luther and Reineck, whether by some concord of nature or whether rising from that companionship of boyhood studies; nevertheless, Luther did not remain in Magdeburg longer than a year.

Next in the school at Eisenach he studied for four years with a praeceptor who taught Grammar more correctly and skillfully than others; for I remember Luther praised his intelligence. He was sent to that city because his mother had been born of an honest and old family in those parts; here he completed grammatical study, and since the power of his intelligence was the most keen, and especially suited for eloquence, he quickly surpassed his coevals and easily surpassed the rest of the youths in the school, both in acquiring vocabulary and fluency in diction, as well as in the writing of prose and verse.

Therefore, having tasted the sweetness of literature, by nature burning with the desire for learning, he sought out the Academy, as the source of all learning. So great a power of intelligence would have been able to grasp all the arts in order, if he had found suitable Doctors, and perhaps both the gentler studies of Philosophy and attention in forming speech would have benefited in softening the vehemence of his nature. But at Erfurt he encountered the crabbed Dialectic of that age and quickly seized it, since by the sagacity of his intelligence he grasped the causes and sources of the precepts better than the rest of the boys.[5]

And since his mind was eager for learning, he sought more and better things, and he himself read the many writings of the ancient Latin writers, Cicero, Virgil, Livy, and others. He read these, not as boys do, picking out the words only, but as the teaching of human life, or, since he looked at the counsels and sayings of these men more closely, and as he had a faithful and firm memory and read and heard many authors, the images were in sight and before his eyes. Thus he was therefore outstanding among the youth, so that Luther's intelligence was a thing of wonder to the whole Academy.

Decorated therefore with the degree of Master of Philosophy at the age of twenty, on the advice of his relatives, who judged that so great a power of intelligence and fluency should be brought forth into the light and for the Republic, he began the study of law.[6] But a short time later, when he was twenty-one, suddenly, against the opinion of his parents and relatives, he went to the College of Augustinian Monks at Erfurt, and sought to be admitted.[7] Once admitted, he soon learned the teaching of the Church not only by the most intense study, but he himself also gained self-mastery by the greatest severity of discipline, and he far surpassed the others in all the exercises of readings, disputes, fasts, and prayers. He was, however, by nature something I often marveled at, neither small nor weak in body, though he ate and drank little; I saw him on four consecutive days neither eat nor drink a thing the entire time, yet he remained completely strong; I often saw that on many other days he was content with a tiny bit of bread and fish per day.

This was the occasion of his starting in on that manner of life which he reckoned more suitable for piety and studies of the doctrine about God, as he himself told and many know. Often great terrors so suddenly terrified him as he thought more intently on the anger of God or the awesome examples of punishments that he almost went out of his mind. And I myself saw him, when he was overcome by tension in a certain debate about doctrine, go to bed in the neighboring cell, and when he repeatedly mixed that recollected idea with a prayer, he counted it all as sin, so that he would be forgiven for all. He felt those terrors either from the beginning, or most sharply in that year because he lost his companion who was killed in some sort of mishap.

Therefore not poverty but eagerness for virtue led him into this mode of monastic life, in which even if he daily learned the customary learning in the schools, and read the *Sententiarii*,[8] and in public debates eloquently explained to amazed crowds labyrinths inexplicable to others, nevertheless, because he sought the nutriments of piety in that type of life, not renown for his intelligence, he put his hand to these studies as if they were a side interest, and he easily grasped those scholastic methods. Meanwhile he himself avidly read the sources of heavenly doctrine, namely the writings of the Prophets and the Apostles, in order to educate his mind about the will of God, and by faithful witnesses to nourish his fear and faith. He was moved by his own sorrows and fears to seek out this study more.

And he told that he was often encouraged by the conversations of a certain old man in the Augustinian College at Erfurt, when he set forth his worries to him. He heard the old man discuss much about faith, and he said that he was led to the Creed, in which it is said, I believe in the forgiveness of sins. That old man had interpreted this Article so that it should be believed not only in general, i.e. forgiven by some persons or others, as they believe Demons are forgiven by David or Peter, but that it was a commandment of God that each one of us individually believe his sins are forgiven. And he said that this interpretation was confirmed by a saying of Bernard, and then he pointed to a place in his sermon on the Annunciation, where there are these words, But you should also believe what is given to you in your sin, namely the testimony that the Holy Spirit puts in your heart, saying 'Your sins are forgiven.' For the Apostle thinks thus, that man is gratuitously justified through faith.[9]

Luther said he was not only strengthened by this statement, but even forcibly reminded of the whole passage of Paul, who so often hammers home this saying, that we are justified by Faith. When he had read many treatises about justification, and then applied himself to Bernard's sermons and *On Consolation of the Mind*, he recognized the emptiness of the interpretations that he then held in his hands. Little by little, as he read and compared the sayings and lessons recorded in the Prophets and Apostles, and as he kindled his faith in daily prayer, he acquired more illumination.

Then he also began to read the works of Augustine, where he found many clear statements, in both the *Commentary on the Psalms* and the *On the Spirit and the Letter*, which confirmed this doctrine concerning faith, and he found consolation, which had burned in his own heart.[10] Still he did not completely abandon the *Sententiarii*; he was able to recite Gabriel[11] and D'Ailly[12] by memory almost word for word. He read for a long time and thoroughly the writings of Occam,[13] whose perspicacity he preferred to that of Thomas and Scotus. He also carefully read Gerson,[14] but he read all the works of Augustine frequently, and remembered them the best.

He began this most intense study at Erfurt, where he stayed for four years at the Augustinian College.

At this time, because Reverend Staupitz,[15] who had helped the beginnings of the Academy of Wittenberg, was eager to stimulate the study of Theology in the new Academy, and since he had had confidence in Luther's intelligence and learning, he brought him to Wittenberg in 1508 when Luther was already twenty-six. Here, amidst the daily exercises and lectures of the School, his intelligence began to shine even more. And since wise men, Dr Martin Mellerstadt[16] and others, would listen to him attentively, Mellerstadt often said that there was so great a power of intelligence in that man, that he plainly foresaw that he would change the common form of learning, which was the only one being transmitted in the Schools at that time.

Here he first commented on Aristotle's *Dialectic and Physics*, yet all the while not dropping that eagerness of his for reading Theological writings. After three years he set out for Rome, because of controversy among the Monks, when

he returned that same year, at the expense of Duke Frederick, the Elector of
Saxony, in the usual manner of scholars he was adorned with the rank of
Doctor, as we customarily say. For he had heard Luther debating, and had
marveled at the power of his intelligence, the powers of his speech, and
excellence of his explications of matters in debates. And so that you might see
that the rank of Dr was conferred on him for a certain maturity of judgment,
you should know that this was the thirtieth year of Luther's life. He himself
used to tell that Staupitz ordered him, when he was running away and refusing,
to let himself be adorned with this rank, and that Staupitz jokingly said that
God had a lot of work to do in the church, and would be able to use Luther's
help. This statement, even if it was said jokingly, nevertheless was true, as it
presaged many changes.

Afterwards he began to comment on the *Epistle to the Romans*,[17]next the
Psalms;[18] he so illuminated these writings that, as light after a long, dark night,
so new doctrine seemed to appear, by the judgment of all pious and prudent
men. Here he pointed out the essential point of the Law and the Gospel, there
he refuted the error, which held sway at that time in the Schools and in debates,
which taught that men merited forgiveness of sins by their own works, and
that men were justified before God by discipline, as the Pharisees taught.
Accordingly Luther called the minds of men back to the son of God, and, like
the Baptist, he showed that the lamb of God, who took away our sins, freely
forgives sins on account of the Son of God, and therefore this favor must be
accepted by faith. He also explained other parts of ecclesiastical doctrine.

These beginnings of the greatest things gave him great authority, especially
since the teacher's character was one with his teachings, and his speech seemed
born, not on his lips, but in his heart. This admiration of his life produced
great changes in the minds of his audience, so that as even the Ancients said,
His character was, almost, so to speak, the strongest proof. Wherefore, when he later
on changed certain accepted rites, honorable men who knew him were less
vehemently opposed, and, in those statements in which they saw, with great
sadness, the world torn apart, they gave assent to him on account of his
authority, which he had previously acquired by the illustration of good things
and by the sanctity of his morals.

Neither did Luther back then change anything in the rites – rather he was
a severe guardian of discipline – nor did he have anything to do with the
harsh opinions then current. But he was more and more explaining that
universal and absolutely necessary doctrine to all, about penitence, the remission
of sins, faith, and the true consolations in the cross. By the sweetness of this
pious doctrine all were strongly won over, and what was pleasing to the learned,
as if Christ, the Prophets, and Apostles were led out of darkness, jail, and
squalor, the essential point of the Law, and the Evangelists, the promises of
the Law, and the promises of the Gospel, of Philosophy and the Evangelists,
became apparent, [and] something certainly not found in Thomas, Scotus, and
others like them, the essential point of spiritual righteousness and political
affairs.

He approached the understanding of Latin and Greek, to which the studies of his youth had already been invited by the writings of Erasmus,[19] wherefore, since the gentler type of his doctrine had been shown, many men endowed with good and free minds began to abhor the barbaric and Sophistical doctrine of the Monks.

Luther himself began to give himself to the studies of Greek and Hebrew, so that having learned the peculiar quality of the language and the diction, and doctrine drawn from its sources, he might be able to judge more skillfully.

When Luther was in this course of study, venal indulgences were circulated in these regions by Tetzel the Dominican, a most shameless sycophant.[20] Luther, angered by Tetzel's impious and execrable debates and burning with the eagerness of piety, published *Propositions concerning indulgences,*[21] which are extant in the first volume of his writings, and he publicly attached these to the church attached to Wittenberg Castle, on the day before the feast of All Saints, 1517. This Tetzel, true to his character, and also hoping he would obtain favor before the Roman Pontiff, calls his Senate, a few Monks and Theologians lightly imbued in some way or other with his own Sophistry, and orders them to cobble something together against Luther. Meanwhile Tetzel himself, so that he would not be a 'silent actor,' brandishes not just Public Debates, but thunderbolts, cries aloud everywhere that this Heretic must be condemned to fire, even publicly hurls Luther's *Propositions* and *Debate concerning indulgences* into flames.[22] These ravings of Tetzel and his Henchmen place the necessity on Luther of more expansively discussing these matters and of preserving the truth.

These were the beginnings of this controversy, in which Luther, as yet suspecting or dreaming nothing about the future change of rites, was not certainly not completely getting rid of indulgences themselves, but only urging moderation. Wherefore they falsely accuse him when they say that he began for a praiseworthy reason, so that afterwards he could change the State and seek power either for himself or for others.

And he was so removed that, suborned or incited by princes, just as the Duke of Braunschweig wrote, that even Duke Frederick, looking far ahead, lamented that struggles were set in motion, although the beginning was about a praiseworthy matter, nevertheless little by little this flame would wander wider, as is said in Homer about the Quarrel, *From small fear at first,* soon it lifted itself into the upper air.

Since Frederick was the one Prince of our era both the most fond of public tranquility and the least selfish, and since he was especially accustomed to set forth plans for the common well-being of the world, it can be seen from many matters [that] he was neither an instigator nor an applauder of Luther, and he often made known his own distress, which he continually proclaimed, fearing greater dissensions.

But, not only following profane judgments, which bid that the gentle beginnings of all changes be most quickly suppressed, but also employing the divine precept in decision, which bids the Gospel to be heard, and which forbids opposing the known truth, and calls blasphemy horribly damned and condemned by God, a stubborn adversary to the truth, the wise man did what many other pious and learned men did: he yielded to God, and carefully read those things which were written, and those which he judged to be true, he did not want to do away with.

For I know that he often ascertained the opinions of the erudite and learned about these very matters, and in that Convention that the Emperor Charles V held in the city of Cologne after his coronation, affectionately bade Erasmus of Rotterdam to say freely whether he reckoned Luther was wrong in these controversies about which he had especially discoursed. Then Erasmus clearly said that he thought Luther was correct, but that he wanted mildness in the man. Wherefore, when Duke Frederick afterward wrote to Luther with the greatest seriousness, he strongly encouraged him to lighten the harshness of his pen.

It is agreed that Luther would have promised Cardinal Cajetan [23] that he would be silent, if he had also enjoined silence on his opponents. From which it can clearly be seen that indeed at that time he had not yet shown that he would in turn set other struggles in motion, but that he was desirous of tranquility, but little by little he was dragged into other subjects, with the uneducated challenging him on all sides with the Scriptures.

Therefore Debates followed concerning the difference between divine and human laws, concerning the abominable profanation of the Supper of the Lord in its sale and application for others (i.e. offering masses for other people). Here the entire theory of Sacrifice was set forth and the use of the Sacraments was shown. And when pious men in the Monasteries now heard that they must flee from Idols, they began to depart from their impious servitude.

Therefore Luther added to the explanation of the doctrines on penance, the remission of sins, faith, and indulgences, also these topics: the difference between divine and human laws, the doctrine on the use of the Supper of the Lord and the other Sacraments, and concerning Prayers. And these were the principal points of contention. Eck proposed an investigation of the power of the Roman Bishop, for no other reason than to fire up the hatred of the Pontiff and the Kings against Luther.[24]

He kept the Apostolic, Nicene, and Athanasian Creeds [as the] most pure, next he fully explained in many writings what should be changed in human rites and traditions, and why; and it is clear what he wanted to be kept and what form of doctrine and administration of the Sacraments he approved of from the Confession which Duke Johannes Elector of Saxony, and Prince Philip Landgraf of Hesse and others presented at the Diet of Augsburg to Emperor Charles V in 1530. The same is clear from the very rites of the Church in this city, and from the Doctrine which sounds forth in our Church, whose principal matter is manifestly expressed in the Confession. I therefore make mention of the Confession again not only for the pious to contemplate which errors Luther reproached and which Idols he removed, but also so that they might understand that it embraces a universal, necessary teaching of the Church, that he restored purity in the rites, and that he taught Examples for renewing the Church to the pious. And it is useful for posterity to know what Luther approved.

I do not want to recollect in this place those who first publicly offered both parts of the Lord's Supper, and those who first ceased saying private Masses when the Monasteries were first abandoned. For Luther had discussed only a few things about these matters before the Diet which was in the city Worms in 1521. He himself did not change the rites, but when he was not there, Karlstadt and others changed the rites:[25] and since Karlstadt did certain things more tumultuously, when Luther returned, he declared what he approved or disapproved with clear testimonies of his opinion.[26]

We know that political men vehemently detest all changes, and it must be admitted that even when upheavals are set into motion by the most just causes, something evil is always to be lamented in this sad disorder of human life. But nevertheless in the Church it is necessary that the command of God is to be preferred to all human things. The Eternal Father said this statement about his Son: *This is my beloved Son, listen to this man*, and he threatens everlasting wrath against blasphemers, that is, against those who endeavor to obliterate the known truth. Wherefore Luther's pious and necessary duty was, especially since he taught the Church of God, to reproach destructive errors which Epicureans were heaping up with even new shamelessness, and it was necessary for those who heard to give assent to the one teaching correctly. If change is truly hateful, if there are many discomforts in discord, as we see with great sadness that there are, the blame is on those who in the beginning spread the errors, as well on the men who now defend those errors with a diabolic hatred.

I recall these things not only to defend Luther and his followers, but also so that pious minds might ponder at this point in time and hereafter what is and always was the governance of the true Church of God, how God through the word of the Gospel selects the eternal Church for himself out from that mass of sin, that is from the great dregs of men, among whom the Gospel shines forth like a spark in the darkness. Just as in the time of the Pharisees Zacharias, Elizabeth, Mary, and many others were guardians of the true doctrine, so even before these times there were many, who, duly calling upon God, were more clearly keeping the doctrine of the Gospel, while others were less so. Such was also that old man, about whom I spoke, who often encouraged Luther as he was contending with fears, and who, in another way, was a teacher to him in doctrine and faith. Just as we should pray God with fervent prayers that he successively save the light of the Gospel in many men, so Isaiah prays for those his followers, *Seal the law in my disciples.* This remembrance then shows that counterfeit superstitions are not lasting but are rooted out by divine providence. Since this is the reason for the changes, care must be taken that errors are not taught in the Church.

But I return to Luther, just as he entered upon this cause without desire for private gain, even if his nature was ardent and irascible, nevertheless he was ever mindful of his own function – he only battled by teaching and avoided taking up arms, and he wisely distinguished the conflicting duties of a Bishop teaching the Church of God, and of Magistrates, who restrain the multitude by the sword.

Wherefore, since at different times the Devil, who is eager to destroy the Church with scandals and to insult God, and as he is *The evil one showing malignant joy*, takes pleasure from the sins and downfall of pitiable men, [and] has inflamed factious natures to foment disturbances, such as Müntzer and those like him,[27] he most vehemently condemned those ragings, and he not only adorned the dignity and all the bonds of the political order but also defended it. When, however, I ponder how many great men in the Church have often wandered in mind in this matter, I am of the distinct opinion that his heart was governed by not only human earnestness but also by a divine light, because he stayed so firmly within the boundaries of his office.

Accordingly he cursed not only the factious Doctors of this age, Müntzer and the Anabaptists, but also those Bishops of Rome, who most boldly and shamelessly asseverate in the Decrees they had written that not only was the duty of teaching the Gospel enjoined on Peter but Imperial politics were even handed over to him.

Accordingly he was an exhorter to all to give to God the things of God, to Caesar the things of Caesar, that is, to worship God with true penance, with the recognition and propagation of true doctrine, with true prayer, and with the responsibilities of a good conscience. Indeed let each man respectfully obey his own state in all civil duties on account of God. And Luther himself was in fact of such a kind: he gave to God the things of God, he taught properly, he called on God properly, he had also the other necessary virtues in a man which are pleasing to God, and finally, in political custom he most consistently avoided all factious plans. I judge that these virtues are so seemly that greater ones cannot be wished for in this life.

And although the virtue of the man himself who reverently used the gifts of God is praiseworthy, nevertheless it is especially necessary to give thanks to God, because through him He restored the light of the Gospel to us and the memory of its doctrine was preserved and propagated. Nor am I disturbed by the shouts of Epicureans or Hypocrites who either laugh at or curse the obvious truth, but I declare as true that this very doctrine which sounds out in our Churches is the uninterrupted concord of the Universal Church of God and that prayer and life are governed by the requisite admission of this doctrine. Accordingly [I say] that this is the very doctrine about which the Son of God speaks, *If any man loves me, he will keep my word, and my Father will love him, and we shall come to him and build a dwelling in his house.* For I am speaking of the highest Doctrine as it is understood and explained in our Churches by the pious and learned. For even if some men at times explain something more properly and elegantly while other men explain less so, or one man speaks sometimes in a less refined manner than another, nevertheless there is agreement among the pious and educated about matters of the greatest importance.

And as I often think hard about the doctrine of all times [handed down] by the Apostles uninterruptedly from that time, after the initial purity four prominent changes of doctrine seemed to have followed. First is the age of Origen.[28] However many there were who taught correctly, still I single out Methodius for condemning the decisions of Origen, who turned the gospel into philosophy in the minds of many, pouring out his conviction that moderate mental training earns forgiveness of sins, and that this is the righteousness about which the verse 'The righteous will live by his faith' speaks. This age almost completely lost the essential point of the Law and the Gospel and gave up the Apostolic teaching. For it did not keep the natural meaning in the words 'letter,' 'spirit,' 'righteousness,' 'faith.' And having lost the peculiar nature of words which are the signs of things, it is necessary to fabricate other things. Pelagius's error, which spread widely, arose from these seeds. And since the Apostles had given the pure doctrine or the pellucid and most health-giving sources of the Church, Origen filled the sources with a great deal of mud.

So that the errors of this age would be corrected from at least some part, God roused up Augustine,[29] who moderately cleaned the sources again; nor do I doubt, if this man would have been the Judge of the disputes of this age, that we would be reckoned straight away by the same vote. He clearly thought precisely as we do about the gratuitous remission of sins, justification by faith, the use of the Sacraments, and the indifferent things. However, even if here he explained more eloquently or properly what he wanted, there less so, nevertheless if a Reader would bring brilliancy and skill in judging him, he perceives that he thinks as we do. For the fact that our adversaries sometimes cite Augustine against us after having picked out sayings from him, and that they make an appeal to the fathers with a great shout, does not mean they do this out of eagerness for the truth and antiquity, but they deceitfully manufacture the authority of the ancients with the idols before them, those idols which had been unknown until a later age.

But nevertheless it is certain that the seeds of superstitions existed in that age of the Fathers. On that account Augustine decided certain things about prayers, even if he spoke less uncouthly about these than others did. However, the pollutions of one's own age always sprinkle some of the follies with even individuals' goods, because just as we are well disposed to our country, so to the rites at hand on which we were brought up, and that saying of Euripides is absolutely correct, *Everything familiar is pleasant.* Would that all those who boast that they follow Augustine actually return to the uninterrupted idea, and, if I may put it this way, the heart of Augustine, and not merely deceitfully twist mutilated sayings into their own beliefs.

And light having been restored to the writings of Augustine, it benefited posterity, for thereafter Prosper, Maximus, Hugo, and others like them who direct studies, even to the age of Bernard, follow the principle of Augustine. Meanwhile nevertheless the Empires and wealth of the Bishops were growing, and just as the age of the Titans followed, profane and uneducated men reign in the Church, some of whom had been refined in the arts of the Roman court or in the doctrine of the law court.

So Dominicans and Franciscans arose, who, when they saw the luxury and wealth of the Bishops, loathed profane morals, set up a simpler way of life and shut themselves up as if in the jails of discipline. But at first their inexperience increased the superstitions, then, when they saw that the studies of the men in the Schools were turned solely toward forensic doctrine, because already at Rome lawsuits were increasing the power and wealth for many, they themselves endeavored to call men back to theological studies but they lacked a plan. Albert and those like him who had given themselves over to the doctrine of Aristotle began to transform the doctrine of the Church into philosophy. And this fourth age poured not only mud but moreover poisons into the Gospel's sources by approving ideas – plain idols – and there is so great a labyrinth and false opinions in Thomas, Scotus, and those similar that sounder theologians have always wanted another simpler and purer kind of doctrine.

Nor can it be said without remarkable shamelessness that there was no need for the change of this doctrine, since it was evident that the great part of the Sophisms in those public debates were in no way grasped by those who grew old in that kind of doctrine. Then the *idolmania* is openly confirmed when they teach that the eucharistic sacrifice is efficacious simply by being performed, when they excuse the invocations of statues, when they deny that sins are gratuitously forgiven by faith, when out of human Ceremonies they make those of good conscience into an executioner, and finally there are many other things more loathsome and *blasphemous*, which, when I think about them, I shudder with my whole body.

Therefore let us give thanks to God the eternal Father of our Lord Jesus Christ, who wanted the dirt and poisons to be driven out again from the Gospel sources by his servant Martin Luther, and he restored the pure doctrine of the Church, wherefore it is proper for all pious thinking men in the whole world to join prayers and lamentations together and to beg with burning hearts that God strengthen that which he has done among us on account of his holy temple. This is your word and promise, O living and true God, the eternal Father of our Lord Jesus Christ, creator of all things and of the Church, *On account of my name I shall pity ye, on account of me, On account of me I shall not be reproached.* I pray You with my whole heart on account of your glory and the glory of your Son always to unite to you the eternal Church also among us by the word of your Gospel, and on account of your Son our Lord Jesus Christ crucified for us and resurrected, *intercessor and suppliant,* and to guide our hearts by the holy Spirit, so that we may truly call upon you and fulfill the duties pleasing to you.

Guide also the studies of doctrine and govern and preserve these governments and their order, which are the homes of your Church and disciples, since you created the human race for this reason, so that you be known and invoked by men, wherefore you also made yourself known by brilliant witnesses, may you not allow these battles in which your doctrine sounds forth to be destroyed. And since your Son our Lord Jesus Christ, as he was about to undergo his trial, prayed for us: *Father, sanctify them in truth,* your Word is truth. We join our prayers to the plea of this our Priest and we beg together with him that your doctrine may ever shine out in the human race, and that he govern us. We heard Luther also daily praying these, and during these prayers his soul was calmly called from his mortal body, when he had already completed his sixty-third year.

Posterity has many monuments of the man's teaching and piety. He published *Teachings* in which he embraced the saving doctrine and the necessity for men instructing good minds about penance, faith, the true fruits of faith, the use of the Sacraments, the essential point of the Law and the Gospel, the dignity of the political order, and finally the principal Articles of doctrine which must of necessity be present in the Church. Next he added *Cross-examinations* in which he refuted many destructive errors among men. He published *Interpretations* as well, that is, many commentaries on the Prophetic and Apostolic writings, in which genre even his opponents admit that he surpassed the extant commentaries of all.

All pious minds see that these merits are great, but indeed, the translation of the old and new Testament equaled these works in usefulness and labor, in which there is such great clarity that instead of a Commentary the very German reading itself can exist, which does not, however, stand alone, but has the most learned notes added to it, and the summaries of individual sections which teach the most important part of the heavenly doctrine and which educate the Reader about the kind of style, so that from the very sources themselves good minds would be able to take solid witnesses of doctrine. For Luther did not want to detain them in his own writings but to lead forth the minds of all to the sources. He wanted us to hear the word of God itself, and by this way he wanted true faith and prayer to be kindled in many, so that God be truly worshiped and many men be made inheritors of everlasting life.

It is fitting to publish with thankful mind this purpose and these labours so great, and to remember them as an example so that each of us also for our own sake will be eager to adorn the Church. For the whole of life and all the studies and plans of life must be especially referred to these two ends: first so that we embellish the glory of God; next that we benefit the Church. About the one of which Paul says, *Do ye all for the glory of God.* About the other Psalm 122, *Ask ye peace for Jerusalem.* And the most pleasing promise is added in the same verse, *Those who love the Church will be happy and blessed.* May these heavenly commands and these promises invite all men to learn the teaching of the Church correctly, may they love the ministers of the Gospel and the beneficial Doctors, and may they bring eagerness and dedication to spreading the true doctrine and to preserving the harmony of the true Church.

The deeds

of Reverend Father Dr Martin Luther in the Assemblies of Princes at Worms before the Emperor Charles V, the Princes, Electors, and the nobility of the Empire follow.

In the Year of Our Salvation 1521, on the Tuesday after *Misericordia Domini*

Sunday (Second Sunday after Easter), Dr Martin Luther entered Worms, called
by Emperor Charles, he the fifth King of the Spaniards of [that] name,
Archduke of Austria, etc., who in the first year of his Reign celebrated the first
gathering of Princes in that royal city.[30]

However, three years before, when Dr Martin had presented at Wittenberg
in Saxony certain paradoxes against the tyranny of the Roman Bishop to be
debated (which nevertheless meanwhile were censured, condemned, and burned
in different ways by the papists, yet refuted by no one either by Scriptures or
by logical arguments), the matter began to incline toward a disturbance, as
the people watched the cause of the Gospel against the Clerics. And for this
reason it seemed good, with the Roman Legates stirring things up, that Luther
himself be summoned by the Imperial Herald, and he was led in this by the
Emperor and the princes, who gave letters of safe passage. He was summoned,
he came, and he stopped at the Senate of the soldiers of Rhodes, or [as] they
are called, of the German order, where he stayed in an inn and was greeted
and sought after even late into the night by many Counts, Barons, honored
Cavalry Officers, and Nobles, Priests and Laymen.

But to many men both of the opposing party and to others his arrival
happened completely contrary to opinion, for even though he had been summoned by Imperial messenger and by letters given for public safety,
nevertheless because, a few days before he came, his books were condemned
by letters posted publicly and privately, no one thought that he would arrive
if he had already been condemned by this judgment.

And when in the neighboring town of Oppenheim, where Luther first learned
these things, a deliberation was held by his friends and many of them concluded
that he should not expose himself to danger, since he saw that these beginnings
were done against a given promise, with all listening, he himself responded
with a courageous spirit, 'Because I was called, truly it was decreed and is
right for me to enter the city in the name of the Lord Jesus Christ, even if I
know that as many Devils are opposed against me as there tiles in all the
houses of the entire world, etc.'

On the next day after his arrival, Wednesday, a nobleman, Master of the
Imperial cavalry, Ulrich von Pappenheim,[31] having been sent by the Emperor,
came before luncheon, showing to Dr Martin the command of Emperor Charles
that at the fourth afternoon hour he present himself before the Imperial Majesty,
Princes, Electors, Dukes and the remaining Orders of the Empire, where he
would hear to what he was summoned, which Dr Martin, as he ought, accepted.

And immediately after the fourth hour of this day, Ulrich von Pappenheim
and Caspar Sturm, Imperial Herald, through Germany, came[32] (this Sturm was
the Truce-Officer by which Dr Martin had been called forth from Wittenberg
and brought down to Worms) to accompany the very one called forth through
the garden of the Rhodians' Senate, into the lodging of the Counts of the
Palatinate. And so that Luther would not be exposed to the crowd which was
great in the road to the Imperial house, he was led down through some hidden
steps in the Auditorium. Nevertheless he was not hidden to many, who were

barely prevented by force from entering, and many fell to blows in eagerness to see Luther.

When therefore he stood in the sight of the Imperial Majesty, the Princes, Electors, and Dukes, in short of every one of the Empire's orders who then attended on the Emperor, Dr Martin was at first admonished by Ulrich von Pappenheim not to say anything unless asked.

Then the Orator of the Imperial Majesty, Johannes Eck, of the general Official of the Bishop of Trier, in a loud and intelligible voice, first in Latin, then in German, by the order of the Emperor spoke and moved the following resolution against the man, or one similar in effect to it, which follows its manner.

'Martin Luther, the Sacred and unconquered Imperial majesty, on the advice of all Ranks of the Holy Roman Empire, orders you to be called hither to the seat of his Majesty, so that I may interrogate you about these two points: first, do you confess that these books before me (a bundle of his books in Latin and his writings in German had been displayed) which circulate under your name are yours, and will you acknowledge them as yours or not? And second, do you want to retract and renounce them and their contents or rather cling to them even more and acknowledge them?'

Here, before Luther responded, Dr Jerome Schurff,[33] who was standing quite near Dr Martin, shouted out, 'Let the books be given a name.' This Official of Trier read out by name from the books of Dr Martin Luther those which were all issued at Basel, among which also were counted the *Commentaries on the Psalter*, the *Treatise on good works*, the *Commentary on the Lord's prayer*, and, in addition to these, other non-disputatious Christian treatises.

After these and to these Dr Martin gave these answers back in Latin and German: 'By the Imperial Majesty two things are proposed to me: first, whether I wish to acknowledge as mine all the books having my name; second, whether I wish to defend or in fact to denounce something from those writings which were written and published up to this point by me. To which I shall respond as briefly and correctly as I can.

To begin with, I cannot help but embrace as my own the books already named and I shall never indeed deny anything of them.

Next, so that I may set forth what follows, whether I want to defend everything in an equal degree or to renounce, because the investigation is about faith and the salvation of souls, and because it concerns the divine word than which nothing is greater in heaven as on earth, which we should all rightly revere, it would have been bold and hazardous as well if I published something unconsidered, since I might say either more than the truth or less, and thus come under the judgment of Christ when he said, *"Who denies me before men, I shall also deny him before my Father who is in the heavens."* [34] Therefore I ask, and especially humbly, of the Imperial Majesty for time for deliberating about this case, so that I may satisfy the interrogator without injury to the divine word and danger to my soul.'

From that a deliberation of the Princes began, which the Official of Trier reported thus: 'Even if now you, Martin Luther, were able to perceive sufficiently from the Imperial order to what you have been summoned, even though you are unworthy to receive a long delay for thinking about this case, nevertheless, out of inborn clemency, the Imperial Majesty grants one day for your contemplation, in order that tomorrow at the same hour you may appear in person and not set forth your thought in writing but relate it orally.'

After these words Dr Martin was brought back to his inn by the Herald. In which matter, in order that something not be omitted, between going to hear the Emperor's order and when Luther was already in the very assembly of nobles, he was strongly reminded by others in other words to be brave, to act manfully, and not to fear those who were able merely to kill his body, but were not able to kill his soul, but rather to fear that one who could send both his soul and body into hell. Also: When you stand before Kings, do not ponder what you say, for it will be given to you at that hour, etc.

On the following Thursday, after four in the afternoon, the Herald came and, taking Dr Martin, led him into the Palace of the Emperor, where he remained until six because the Princes were occupied, anticipating a large crowd of men, with himself spending time before the throng. And when all were assembled and Dr Martin stood before them, the Official sent forth these words.

'Martin Luther, yesterday evening the Imperial Majesty told you this hour, since you indeed openly acknowledged the books which we identified yesterday as yours. But to the question, "Do you want something of yours to be considered null and void, or do you approve everything which you acknowledge?", you sought deliberation, which is now at its end, even if by law you ought not have demanded more time for thinking, since you knew all along why you were called. And it was agreed by all that the business of faith is so certain that each one having been summoned at whatever time could give back his sure and unchanging explanation, much more should you, so great and so well-trained a professor of Theology. Come, at least answer the Emperor's demand, whose liberality you enjoyed in having time for thinking. Do you want to admit that all the books are yours? Or do you want to retract something?' The Official said these things in Latin and German.

Dr Martin himself responded in both Latin and German, albeit humbly, not clamorously, and modestly, nevertheless not without Christian ardor and steadfastness, and in such a way that his opponents desired a speech and a spirit more disheartened. But much more eagerly they awaited a Retraction, which a few had come to expect after the extra time for deliberating.

Then he replied in this way.

'Most Serene Lord Emperor, Most Distinguished Princes, Most Merciful Lords, obeying the limit determined for me yesterday evening I appear, beseeching through the mercy of God, that your most serene Majesty, and your most distinguished Lordships deign to hear mercifully this case, as I hope, in justice and truth. And if through my inexperience I have not given worthy titles to someone or I have erred in some way or other in courtly manners and actions, kindly forgive since I am a man experienced not in Palaces but in the corners of Monks, who is able to testify nothing else about myself than that by that ingenuousness of soul I have learned and written only this; that I should look only to the glory of God and the genuine education of the faithful of Christ.

'Most serene Emperor, Most distinguished Princes, Most Merciful Lords, to those two Articles proposed to me yesterday through your Most serene Majesty, namely, Whether I acknowledge the books examined and published under my name as mine and whether I want to persist in these defenses or to retract, I gave my prepared and clear answer, concerning the previous Article, in which I continue steadfastly, and I shall continue into eternity, that those books are manifestly mine and published under my name by me, unless perhaps in the meantime it happened that either by the cunning of rivals or by churlish wisdom something in them was changed or was perversely excerpted. For clearly I do not acknowledge anything else, only that which is mine only and written by me alone, without any other person's interpretation. To the second I would respond; I ask that your Most serene Majesty and your Lordships deign to turn your attention. My books are not all of the same type: For there are some in which I handled the piety of faith and morals so directly and Evangelically that my Opponents themselves are forced to admit that those books are useful, blameless, and clearly worthy of a Christian reading. But the Bull, although harsh and cruel, declares some of my books harmless, but then also condemns others with an absolutely monstrous judgment. And so if I were to begin to retract those, I beseech you, what would I do, unless I were the one man of all mortals to condemn that truth, which Friends and Enemies equally acknowledge, the only man of all fighting against a united acknowledgment?

There is another type (of my writing) which attacks the Pope and the doctrine of the papists, just as against those who by their own doctrines and worst examples have desolated the Christian world in both directions by an evil of the soul and the body. For no one can either deny or dissemble this, since the witnesses are the experiences of everyone and the complaints of all men that not only have the consciences of the faithful been most terribly entrapped, harassed, and tortured through the laws of the Pope and the doctrines of men, but in particular the money and properties, especially in this glorious nation of Germany, have been devoured by an unbelievable Tyranny, and are devoured to this day without end and in shameful ways: since nevertheless they themselves by their very own laws (as in *distinctio* 9 and 25, *quaestio* 1 and 2)[35] take care that laws of the Pope and doctrines contrary to the Gospel or the sayings of the Fathers are to be reckoned erroneous and false.

If I then retracted these books I would be doing nothing other than strengthening this tyranny and letting godlessness in through the windows and doors, giving it even more room and freedom for destruction. And the enemy would become rich and powerful, for all his evil could roam wider and with more impunity than it even dared up to this point, in a manner all the more intolerable to the poor multitude, for they would believe that my retraction, like a public proclamation, bolstered and strengthened him, especially if he boasted that he had been made that way by me on the authority of your severe majesty and the whole Roman Empire. O good God, how great a cover for wickedness and Tyranny I would then be. There is a third type of them, which I wrote against some private and individual (as they call [them]) persons, against those naturally who endeavored to defend the Roman Tyranny and to destroy the piety taught by me.

Against those men I admit that I was harsher than is fitting for my religion or calling, but I am not making myself some kind of saint, and I am not discussing my life but the teaching of Christ.

Nor is it honest for me to retract those, because by this retraction it would again happen that Tyranny and impiety would reign by my patronage and rage more violently against the people of God than they ever reigned.

Nevertheless, because I am a Man and not God, I am not able to support my books by another patronage than my Lord himself Jesus Christ supported his own doctrine, who, when he was before Annas and was asked about his doctrine and received a blow from the officer, said: *If I have spoken badly, produce the evidence about the evil.* If the Lord himself, who knew that he was not able to sin, did not refuse to hear evidence against his own doctrine, even from the most worthless servant, so much more should I, who am a piece of dirt and unable to do anything but sin, seek out and ask if anyone wishes to offer evidence against my doctrine. And so I ask through the mercy of God, Most Serene Majesty and your Most Exalted Lords, for someone finally, either the highest [ranked] or the lowest be able to give evidence, refute the errors, gain the upper hand by the Prophetical and Apostolic writings, for I will be the most prepared, if I shall have been taught, whatever error to retract, and I will be the first to cast my books into the fire.

From these I reckon that it is made clear that I have considered and reflected on the risks and dangers enough, or on the passions and disagreements stirred up in the world on the occasion of my doctrine, about which I was gravely and forcefully warned yesterday. Clearly that condition in matters is the most pleasing of all to me, to see on account of the word of God passions and disagreements brought about, for He is the way, the outcome and result of the word: For he said, *I did not come to bring peace but a sword, For I came to divide man against father, etc.*[36]

Accordingly we must ponder, since our God is wonderful and terrible in his counsels, lest by chance that which is attempted in such great studies, if we begin from the condemned word of God, turns afterwards rather into an intolerable flood of evils, and what must be avoided lest the Reign of this best Youth Prince Charles (in whom after God there is much hope) be made misfortunate and inauspicious.

'I would have been able to demonstrate the matter more fully by Examples from scripture, about Pharaoh, the King of Babylon, and the Kings of Israel, who back then most especially destroyed themselves, even though they were eager to pacify and stabilize their Reigns by the wisest counsels. For it is he himself who grasps the crafty in his cunning, and he overturns mountains before they know. And so the work of God is to fear.

I do not say these things because there is need either for my doctrine or my warning in these whirlwinds so great, but because I ought not to turn aside the obedience owed my Germany. And I entrust myself to these your Powers and to your most Serene Majesty, humbly asking that they not permit me to be rendered hateful to them by the efforts of my Adversaries without cause. I HAVE SPOKEN.'

To these words, the Orator of the Empire scornfully said that Luther did not respond to the point, nor ought be called into question things which long ago in Councils had been condemned and defined. For that reason a simple and not complicated response was asked of him: Whether he wanted to retract or not?

Here Luther said: 'Since your most Serene Majesty and your Powers seek a simple response, I will give that, neither sophistical nor pointed in this way: Unless I shall be refuted by the testimonies of the scriptures or by manifest reason (for I believe neither in the Pope nor in the Councils alone, since it is agreed that they have rather frequently erred and have contradicted themselves), I am defeated by the writings prompted by me, and my conscience has been caught in the words of God; I am not able to retract nor do I want to do anything that goes against my conscience, no matter how safe or complete it may be.

Here I stand. I can do nothing else. God help me. Amen.'

The Princes took this oration delivered by Dr Martin into deliberation. The official of Trier began to attack the examination in this way.

'Martin, you have responded more impudently than befits your person, and moreover not to the proposition, you divide the Books in different ways, but in such a way that they all contribute nothing to the investigation. The fact is that if you would have recanted those in which the great part of your errors is, without a doubt the Imperial Majesty and his inborn clemency would not tolerate the persecution of the rest of them which are good. However you revive what the universal Council of Constance, assembled from the entire German nation, condemned, and you want to be defeated through scripture, in which you violently rant. For what does it matter to make known a new Controversy about matter condemned for so many ages by the Church and the Council? Unless by chance an explanation must be rendered to anyone about anything whatsoever. The fact is if he carried his point once that he must be refuted by scriptures, whoever contradicts the Councils and the ideas of the Church, we shall have nothing sure or fixed in Christianity. And this is the reason why the Imperial majesty asked of you a simple and plain response, either negative or affirmative. Do you wish to support all your writings as for the Church? Or to in fact retract something from them?'

Then Dr Martin asked that the Imperial Majesty allow him, led and protected by sacred scriptures, not to be forced to reply against his conscience without the manifest arguments of his opponents. The response sought was not sophistical, but simple and straightforward. He had nothing else than what he had given before: If the adversaries could not, by valid arguments, release his conscience from the errors (as they called them) to which it was captive, he would remain so entwined that he could never extricate himself. What the Councils have decreed is not completely true. On the contrary, the Councils have been mistaken and have often defined things contrary to themselves, therefore the argument of his opponents does not carry weight. He was able to point out that the Councils have gone wrong, he was not able to retract what was carefully plainly represented in scripture.

To which the official answered nothing, unless in the littlest points, no doubt, was he able to show that the Council had gone wrong. Dr Martin promised to show truly that he was able and willing.

When, however, darkness covered the entire auditorium each accordingly went home to his own home. A good part of the Spaniards followed after the man of God, Luther, as he was departing from the Imperial Majesty and Tribunal, with yells and mocking gestures in a great roar.

On Friday after *Misericordia Domini,* when the Princes, Electors, Dukes, and the remaining Ranks who were accustomed to be present at consultations had convened, the Emperor sent a Decree into the Senate containing the following: 'Our ANCESTORS and the Christian Princes themselves, were in no way less obedient to the Roman Church than now Dr Martin Luther attacks it, and because he has taken it into his heart not to depart even a hair's width from his errors, we are not able deviate from the dignified Example of our Ancestors in defending the ancient faith and by bringing aid to the Roman seat: Martin Luther himself and his followers we charge with excommunication, and by other ways if they appear for the extinguishing [of Luther and his followers]. Nevertheless we are unwilling to violate the given and received security, rather we are about to take pains that he return preserved to the place whence he was summoned.'

This statement of Emperor Charles, the leading Electors, Dukes, society of the Empire, turned over through the entire Friday afternoon, even an entire Saturday followed, in this way, that Dr Martin as yet received no response from the Imperial Majesty.

In the meantime he was seen and visited by many Princes, Counts, Barons, Knights, Priests, religious and lay, nor can I say [how many] from the number of the commons; these ever occupied the senate nor were they able to get their fill by seeing. Two broadsides were even put up, one against Dr Luther, the other, as it seemed, for the Doctor. Though by a great many intelligent men, this very deed was craftily reckoned by his Enemies so that an occasion would be employed for annulling the given safe conduct, which the Roman legates were actively seeking.

The Monday after *Jubilate* Sunday (Third Sunday after Easter), before dinner, the Archbishop of Trier declared to Dr Martin that he should prepare to appear before him four days at the sixth hour before lunch, having again appointed a place. On St Gregory's Day, shortly before lunch, one of the clergy of the

Archbishop of Trier returned to Luther, with the order of his Prince, seeking that on the next day at the hour recently designated he appear at the inn of his lord.

On Wednesday after the birth of St George, complying with the agreement, Dr Martin entered the inn of the Archbishop of Trier, led in by his Priest and the Imperial Herald, with those following him who traveled with him from Saxony and Thuringia as he came here, and some other close friends besides, where before the Archbishop of Trier [were] Joachim the Marquis of Brandenburg, Duke George of Saxony, the Bishops of Augsburg and Brandenburg, Count George, master of the Teutonic Order, Johann Bock of Strasbourg, and Drs Werdheymer and Peutinger.

Dr Vehus, from the clerics of the Marquis of Baden,[37] began to speak and protested that Luther himself was not called in this, so that they would consult with him as if in a public debate or dispute, but only out of Christian charity and a certain mercy, the Princes obtained from the Imperial Majesty that they be permitted to encourage him mercifully and affectionately.

Then he said: 'The councils, even if they have decreed contradictory things, have not nevertheless decreed contrary things, Because if they had erred in the highest degree, if you will, on that account nevertheless they have not overthrown their authority, merely so much as anybody would want to strive against those things by his own sense.'

Inferring much from the Centurion and Zaccheus, even from human arrangements, from Religious ceremonial decrees, confirming that all those things were sanctified to restrain changes, according to the nature and change of the times, neither are the changes, according to the nature and change of the times, nor is the Church able to be without human arrangements. [He said that] the tree is known by its fruits. Nevertheless many good things are said to arise from laws. The fact is that St Martin, St Nicholas and many other saints attended councils.

Next, [he said that] Luther's books would rouse up tremendous disturbances and unbelievable uproars, because the common people misuse his book *On Christian Freedom* to cast off the yoke and lead disobedient lives. It has a very different meaning, namely that in believers there is one heart and one soul. Thus law and order are necessary.

Besides it must be considered that although he had written many good works, and without a doubt in good spirit, e.g. *Concerning the Threefold Justice*, and others, the Devil still works through hidden ambushes, so that all his works should be condemned for eternity. For one can judge rightly by the books he wrote most recently, just a one knows a tree by its fruits rather than its flowers.

Then he added words about the mid-day Devil and the work by walking in darkness and the flying arrow. The entire speech was exhortatory, full of rhetorical commonplaces about honesty, the utility of Laws, and conscience from the region of dangers, and communal and individual salvation. At the beginning, the middle, and the end he repeatedly stressed that this admonition was made with the most well-disposed will and a certain exceptional mercy by the Princes. Concluding, he added warnings in the Epilogue, saying that if he were to persist in the proposition, the Emperor would proceed to expel him from the Empire, admonishing him to reflect and weigh out these and the remaining things.

Dr Martin replied: 'Most Merciful and Illustrious Princes and Lords, Concerning that most merciful and kindly will, from which this admonition began, I thank you as humbly as I can. For I realize that I am a little man, not worthy of being warned by Princes so great.'

Then he boldly proclaimed that he did not reproach all the Councils but only the Council of Constance,[38] for this reason above all: because it condemned the word of God, which Jan Hus made manifest in the Article condemned there, that the Church of Christ is the company of the predestined. It is certain that the Council of Constance condemned this Article and thus consequently this Article of our faith: *I believe in the holy Church, Universal.* Accordingly he said that he was not able to recant and threaten his life and blood, therefore he was not now reduced to being forced to retract the evident word of God. For in this defending he ought to obey God rather than men.

And he said he was not able to avoid the Scandal of faith on this occasion, for the Scandal was twofold, of charity and of faith.

Of Charity, because it consists of morals and life, of Faith or, in truth, of doctrine, because it consists of the word of God, and he was not now able to avoid this, for it was not in his power to keep Christ from being the rock of scandal.

If the sheep of Christ were fed by the pure food of the Gospels, the faith of Christ truly preached, and the ecclesiastical Magistrates were truly good and pious, who would faithfully do their duty, there would be no need to burden the Church with human traditions etc. He knew that Magistrates and ones in power must be obeyed even though they lived evilly and unjustly. He knew that it must be yielded to one's own sense, and he taught this in his writings, and he would most obediently maintain all these, only he would not be driven to deny the word of God.

After Dr Martin left, the Princes discussed what they should answer to the man. Accordingly he was recalled into the dining-room; the Dr of Baden sought the earlier matters again, admonishing that he submit his own writings to the judgment of the Emperor and the Empire.

Dr Martin replied humbly and modestly that he neither allowed nor would he allow that he be said to have run away from the judgment of the Emperor, Nobles, and Ranks of the Empire. For he was so far from avoiding their examination through fear that he would allow his own [writings] to be weighed most exactly rather by the least [qualified], only let this be done by the authority of the divine word and sacred scripture. However, the word of God was so clearly in his favor that he could not waver unless he were instructed even better by the word of God. For St Augustine wrote that he had learned that this honor holds only in those books which are called *Canonical,* so he [said he] would believe the true ones; the Other Doctors in truth would be valued for ever so great sanctity or doctrine, if they wrote true things – [he said] only then would he believe them: On these points St Paul wrote to the Thessalonians, *Examine everything, keep what is good.*[39] And to the Galatians: *Even if an Angel comes from heaven and preaches something different, let him be anathema, and so he must not be believed:*[40] For that reason he humbly asked that they not urge his conscience bound by the chains of scripture and the divine word to deny the word of God so clear and [he asked] that they consider him committed and that they especially bring about before the Imperial majesty that he not be forced to do anything in this matter against his conscience, otherwise he would do everything most obediently.

As he was saying these things the Marquis of Brandenburg, Elector Joachim, asked him whether he had said that he would not yield unless refuted by sacred scripture.

Dr Martin replied: 'Even, most merciful Lord, by the clearest and evident proofs possible.' So when this Meeting was adjourned, while the rest of the Princes set out into the Senate, the Archbishop of Trier summoned Dr Martin to his own Dining-room, with Johannes Eck his official and Cochlaeus joining him:[41] Dr Jerome Schurff and Nicholas Amsdorff[42] were standing by Dr Martin Luther. There the Official then began to adduce proof just as a Sophist and a Canon Lawyer, defending the case of the Pope. [He said] heresies almost always arose from sacred writings, as Arianism from this passage of the Gospel: *Joseph did not know his wife, until she bore his first-born.*[43] Next having progressed so far, in order to strive to tear loose this proposition, that the Church universal is the company of the Saints, he even dared to make wheat from tare, and limbs from the excrements of bodies. After making public these and similar ridiculous and worthless ideas, Dr Martin and Dr Jerome Schurff reproved them, soberly nevertheless, as having nothing to do with the matter itself. Johannes Cochlaeus sometimes making noise in the midst of this, tried to persuade Dr Luther to desist from what he began and to abstain completely from writing and teaching thereafter. At length they departed.

Around evening of the same day, the Archbishop of Trier announced to Dr Martin, through his agent Amsdorff, that the safe conduct was extended by the Emperor into two days, so that he would meanwhile be able to talk with him.

So on this next day, Dr Peutinger[44] and Dr Baden would come to him and he himself would talk with him.

Therefore on Thursday, St Mark's Day, before Noon, Peutinger and Baden attempted to persuade Dr Martin to accept without reservation and completely the judgment by the Emperor and the Empire of his own writings.

He replied: He would do and allow everything if only they relied on the authority of sacred scripture: For otherwise he would commit to nothing. For God spoke through the Prophet, *Do not trust in princes, in the sons of men, in whom there is no salvation.*[45] The same: *Accursed is he who trusts in man.*[46] To the more vehement urgings he replied that nothing less should be allowed to the judgment of men than the word of God. So they went away saying that they would return before lunch so that he could deliberate how he would reply better.

After lunch they returned; they attempted in vain the same thing which [they had attempted] before Noon. They begged that he submit his writings at the least to the judgment of a future Council. Luther allowed this, but on this condition: that they themselves should show the excerpted Articles from his own books which would be submitted to the Council, but in such a way that they draw their view of these from the Scriptures and that they prove the contrary from the same testimonies.

And so after those men left Dr Martin, they told the Archbishop of Trier that Martin promised that he would commit his writings to the Council, in some Articles, and meanwhile he would be silent about them. Which Dr Martin had never considered, he who could never be persuaded either by any warnings or threats to want either to renounce his Books or submit them to the judgment of men, books which he had fortified by clear and evident Scriptural testimonies, unless it were proven incontestably by sacred writings and plain arguments that he had erred.

So it happened by a singular gift of God that the Archbishop of Trier personally summoned Dr Martin, wishing to speak to him face to face. When, since he had perceived a contradiction which Peutinger and Baden had said, he asserted that he would not undertake a costly case, unless he had listened to him: For otherwise he was about to approach the Emperor at once and would say what the Doctors had reported.

The Archbishop of Trier in fact acted most mercifully toward Dr Martin, first, by removing all the witnesses, both from the Emperor and the Empire and in particular from the court of the Council. Dr Martin concealed nothing from Trier in this conversation, maintaining that it would hardly be safe to entrust so great a matter to those men who, after attacking with new commands the one called forth under the protection of safe conduct, condemned his own opinion and approved the Bull of the Pope.

Then after his friend was admitted, the Archbishop of Trier asked for remedies from Dr Martin with which he would be able to answer this case. Luther replied: 'There are not better remedies than about which Gamaliel in Acts 5 has said, according to St Luke, *If this need the counsel of men, let it be dissolved, If in truth it is from God, ye will not be able to dissolve it.*[47] The Emperor and the ranks of the Empire can write to the Roman Pontiff that they know for certain that if this proposition of his is not from God, it will perish of its own accord within three, nay, two years.'

When Trier said what would he do, if the Articles were taken to be submitted to the council, Luther replied: 'Provided they are not those which the Council of Constance condemned.' The Archbishop of Trier said that he indeed feared that those very ones would be submitted. Yet Luther said: 'I am neither able nor willing to be silent about such a thing, as I am certain that the word of God was condemned by those Decrees. Accordingly I would rather lose my life and head than abandon such a clear word of the Lord.'

The Archbishop of Trier, seeing that Dr Martin would by no means submit the word of God to the judgment of men, dismissed him mercifully, and he replied to him asking to obtain a merciful leave for himself from the Imperial Majesty: 'I will properly take care of the thing and I will carry back word of it.'

And so not much after, the Official of Trier, in the presence of chancellor Maximilian, Secretary to the Emperor, told Dr Martin in his own lodging, by the command of the Emperor, that because he had been admonished so many times by the Imperial Majesty, Electors, Princes, and the Orders of the Empire, in vain, and did not want to restore himself to sense and wholeness, it remains for the Emperor (as Advocate of the Catholic faith) to proceed. So the command of the Emperor is that he return within twenty-one days hence, to remain in his own care under the protection of the safe passage and not to upset the commons on the way by neither preaching or writing.

When he heard this, Dr Martin most modestly replied, 'Just as it was pleasing to the Lord, so this was done, Let the name of the Lord be praised.' Then he added that first of all, he, a suppliant, gave thanks to the Most Serene Imperial Majesty, Princes, and remaining Orders of the Empire, as greatly as he could for so kind and tolerant a hearing, and for the safe conduct both for coming and going. For he neither desired anything in them, except the reformation through sacred scripture that he so greatly called for. Otherwise he would suffer everything for the Imperial Majesty and the Empire, life and death, fame and ill repute, retaining absolutely nothing for himself, except the unique free word of the Lord in order to confess and bear witness for that: Finally, most humbly commending himself to the Imperial Majesty and the entire Empire and subjecting himself to it.

So the next day, that is, the Friday after Jubilate, on the 26th day of April, after he said goodbye to his Patrons and friends, who had most frequently visited him, and had breakfast, he departed at the tenth hour before noon, accompanied by those who had set out with him on his way there, whom Caspar Sturm the Herald after some hours following found at Oppenheim, Sturm pursuing according to the spoken command of the Emperor Charles.

The usual daily PRAYER of Luther:
Strengthen God that in us which you have worked and complete your work which you have begun in us, for your glory, Amen.

Philip Melan[ch]thon To the Students of the School at Wittenberg, in the Year 1546. On the death of Luther.

Dr Philip Melanchthon publicly recited these following words at the ninth hour before lunch, when we had assembled for a reading of Paul's *Epistle to the Romans*, remembering that he did this on the advice of other Lords, for this reason, so that reminded about the truth of the matter we would not embrace those fictions being scattered (because they knew that many tales were circulating here and there about the death of Luther).

O Best Young Men, you know that we have undertaken to comment on the grammatical explication of the *Epistle to the Romans*, in which is contained the true doctrine about the Son of God, which God with singular benefit revealed at this time to us through our most beloved Reverend Father and Teacher Dr Martin Luther.

But on this day, the writings are so sad they have so increased my grief, that I do not know whether I am able to continue hereafter in these scholastic endeavors here: However, I therefore wish to recall these to you on the advice of other Lords, so that you may know how the matter truly is, so that you yourselves neither spread falsehoods about this death nor have faith in other tales spread here and there (as is accustomed to be done).

On the day of Mercury (Wednesday), which was 17 February, Lord Doctor, a little before dinner, began to labor under the customary illness, namely, the pressure of humors in the orifice of the stomach (under which I remember he also labored several times); this sickness recurred after dinner, with which when he struggled, he sought solitude in the nearest bedroom: And, he slept there for close to two hours, until the pains increased. And since Dr Jonas[48] was sleeping along with him in the same room, Lord Dr Martin called and woke him, and told him to get up and make sure that Ambrose, Pedagogue of the Children, heat the room since he would go in there.

Soon Albert, Count from the nobles of Mansfeld, came there along with his wife and many others, whose names have not been mentioned in this writing on account of the haste.

At last when he sensed that the end of his life was present, before the fourth hour of the following 18 February he commended himself to God with this prayer.

Mein Himlischer Vater ewiger Barmhertziger Gott Du hast mir deinen lieben Sohn unsern HERREN *Ihesum Christum oVenbaret den hab ich gelert, den hab ich bekandt den liebe ich, und den ehre ich für meinen lieben Heylandt und Erlöser, Welchen die Gottlosen verfolgen, schenden und schelten. Nim meine Seele zu dir. Inn dem redet er inn die drey mal: In manus tuas commendo Spiritum meum, redemisti me Deus veritatis. Unso hat Gott die welt geliebet x.*

[My Heavenly Father, eternal Compassionate God, you have revealed to me your beloved Son our LORD Jesus Christ whom I have known, of whom I have acquaintance, whom I love, and whom I honor as my beloved Savior and Redeemer, whom the Godless persecute, dissipate, and reproach. Take my Soul to you. This he said three times: 'Into your hands I commend my Spirit, you have redeemed me God of truth. And God so loved the world, etc.']

After repeating these prayers several times, he was called by God into the everlasting School and into everlasting joys, in which he enjoyed the company of the Father, Son, Holy Spirit, and of all the Prophets and Apostles.

Ach! the Charioteer and the chariot Israel died, who guided the Church in this last age of the world: for the doctrine of the Remission of sins and the pledge of the Son of God was not apprehended by human sagacity, It was revealed by God through this man, Whom we saw was roused even by God.

Accordingly let us cherish the memory of this Man and the type of Doctrine handed down by himself and let us be modest and let us consider the enormous calamities and great changes which followed this death.

I pray You O Son of God, Emanuel crucified for us and resurrected, guide, preserve, and protect your Church, Amen.[49]

3

Johannes Cochlaeus: an introduction to his life and work

by Ralph Keen

Johannes Cochlaeus stands among the prominent members of the Catholic reaction to the Reformation during its first three decades. His work serves as valuable evidence for scholars of the division of western Christianity that took place in the sixteenth century. But two qualities give him a special place among the early Catholic respondents to Protestantism: the volume of his work and the rhetorical ferocity of his reaction to the beginnings of Protestantism. He was the most prolific and most acerbic of the Catholic polemicists, and both of these qualities in tandem give him a historical importance that is only now being recognized. While the *Commentary on the Life of Luther* has long been acknowledged to be Cochlaeus's most important work, Cochlaeus himself and his other works remain largely unknown, especially in the English-speaking world.[1]

The early stage of Cochlaeus's career was one in which correcting errors in biblical interpretation seemed sufficient response to the new attacks on the old faith. But after the Diet of Augsburg of 1530, Cochlaeus's writings pursue a new theme. Whereas the preceding decade was focused on religious issues, in the 1530s the Reformers had drawn their princes' support to their cause, and in the eyes of Romanists like Cochlaeus the matter became a political as well as a theological one. From 1530 to 1539 Cochlaeus combined religious argument with political exhortation, impressing upon Catholic secular authorities the importance of recognizing the danger of tolerating the Protestants. Cochlaeus stands out among the controversialists in his combination of political and religious rhetoric. There is an obvious biographical reason for this. From 1528 he served as court chaplain to Duke George of Saxony, one of the most relentless opponents of reform among the German nobility. With the creation of political alliances like the Schmalkald Federation in 1529, the Reformation became an issue for public counsel. Cochlaeus, who as court chaplain had the ear of his duke, becomes through his writings of this period the theological counselor to the Catholic nobility throughout Europe.

This survey offers the reader of the *Commentary* an introduction to the main events of Cochlaeus's career and an assessment of his treatment of Luther. His career falls into three periods: from his youth to the beginning of his work as chaplain to the Duke of Saxony; the years in Meissen, when he was at his most powerful as an opponent of the Reformation; and his final years in Breslau, during which he completed a program of writing intended to accomplish with books what he was unable to do as an individual. The lasting monument of this period, and indeed of his whole career, is the *Commentary*, a work that demands some introductory remarks as well.

1479–1527

Three things about Cochlaeus set him apart from his contemporaries and help account for his early work: his humble origins, his secular status, and his humanist interests. Cochlaeus's early career is a chronicle of an intellectual rising from the most inauspicious circumstances to highly auspicious ones at the turn of the sixteenth century. Born Johann Dobneck of humble parents in Wendelstein, a small town outside of Nuremberg, the young Cochlaeus (the name is a Latinization of Wendelstein) was entrusted, in the manner of the age, to his uncle Johann Hirspeck, a parish priest, for his early education. In 1504 Cochlaeus proceeded to the University of Cologne, where he received the baccalaureate in 1505 and the master's degree in 1507. He remained in Cologne to study theology and earned the title of professor.

Cochlaeus's training and inclination suited him well for the life of the humanist scholar, and he secured a position as rector of the St Lorenz School in Nuremberg, one of the thriving centers of Renaissance humanism north of the Alps. In Nuremberg, Cochlaeus prepared a Latin grammar, an introduction to music, an edition of the *Cosmography* of the first century CE geographer Pomponius Mela, and an edition, with his own commentary, of Jacques Lefèvre d'Etaples's Latin paraphrase of Aristotle's *Meteorology*, all within a two-year period.[2] He proved sufficiently trustworthy that Willibald Pirckheimer, Nuremberg's foremost example of the patrician humanist, sent him to Bologna as tutor and chaperon of his two nephews. While in Italy Cochlaeus pursued the study of law and of Greek, and received a doctorate in theology from Ferrara in 1517.[3] His legal studies were more successful than his care of his young charges, for Pirckheimer broke off all contact with him later that year, displeased with Cochlaeus's restlessness and suspicious that he had used the boys' funds to pay for his travel expenses.[4] He nevertheless made good use of his travels, and was ordained to the priesthood in Rome in 1518.

The circumstances surrounding Cochlaeus's entry into theological battle remain clouded by incomplete, ambiguous evidence. Investigations of a century ago suggested that Cochlaeus received his first pastoral assignment with the charge to attack Luther, and that his ferocity was, at least in part, motivated by desire for additional support from his patrons, who may have included the influential Fugger family from Augsburg.[5] Cochlaeus was a deacon in Frankfurt, his first clerical position, when the Diet of Worms was held in 1521. He attended as an assistant to Crown Prince Richard von Greifenklau, and had his own debate with Luther – possibly by tracking him down at the inn where he was staying – the proceedings of which he published in 1540.[6] It matters little who antagonized whom at first; but it is certain that Cochlaeus's hatred of Luther stems from this encounter.[7] Just as Luther was banned from the church by a papal bull in 1521, Cochlaeus was subsequently banned by the papal nuncio from entering into disputation with Luther. Cochlaeus ignored his ban as freely as Luther did; and his *Colloquy with Luther* later joined the Reformer's works on the Index of Forbidden Books.[8]

Cochlaeus found his métier in polemical work: to be on the attack against enemies of a great cause animated him, and being at the center of controversy was a source of satisfaction. His interest in vituperative rhetoric probably began before the outbreak of the Reformation, for in early 1517 he was polishing his Latin style by imitating the acerbic Verrine orations of Cicero.[9] From the beginning, Cochlaeus displayed a tendency to magnify his own role in the course of events. In 1521, in the wake of the Diet of Worms, he boasts that the Lutherans have composed a collection of '*Acta Cochlaei,*' in which Cochlaeus stands up against Luther and responds forcefully to every heretical statement.[10] Enjoyment of the support and companionship of the influential, which he first tasted in the Pirckheimer circle in Nuremberg, returned with heady intensity in the early years of the Reformation. 'I have never been busier,' he told Frederick Nausea, the Bishop of Vienna, in 1524; 'tomorrow I see the Cardinal of Mainz, and have many places to go after that.'[11] Among the places that drew him were Leipzig, where he participated in one of the first great colloquies of the Reformation, and Augsburg, where he was one of the so-called 'four evangelists' (with Nausea, Johann Eck, and Johann Fabri) commissioned to compose a Catholic response to the Lutherans' Confession. Toward the end of his life he did all he could to participate in the Council of Trent, but that was not to happen.[12]

The first decade of Reformation polemics is the period in which Cochlaeus most ardently defends the teachings of the Catholic tradition. A characteristic work of this decade is his defense of the idea that St Peter had lived and taught in Rome.[13] Luther had questioned the Apostle's connection with Rome in the hope of deflating the Petrine claims that gave the Bishop of Rome primacy of honor and jurisdiction. In this work Cochlaeus is an historian rebuking a revisionist doctrine: the theologian and humanist scholar are one and the same here. Similarly, Cochlaeus serves both learning and dogma by providing editions of the decrees of early councils and statements by the first popes.[14] Although motivated by apologetic interests, these works were honorable contributions to the return to the sources that marked the Christian humanism of northern Europe in the early sixteenth century. For the early Cochlaeus, the charges of the Reformers could be refuted by more complete understanding of the history of the early church.

Though ostensibly composed in the service of Christian humanism, Cochlaeus's writings were all too obviously designed to antagonize the Lutherans, and Cochlaeus himself antagonized his own clerical patrons with his zeal. Soon after the appearance of the tract on St Peter, Cardinal Aleander reproached Cochlaeus for his harsh rhetoric. Aleander felt that the Lutherans' cause was fueled by popular anticlericalism, which would only be intensified if Cochlaeus continued his intemperate writing.[15] Rather than softening his rhetoric in response to such threats, Cochlaeus grew more defiant and acerbic in his polemical writing, and would later taunt Aleander for wanting to make peace with the Reformers. News that Cardinal Aleander was moving in the direction of peace was scandalous enough to be part of his 1532 gossip with Frederick Nausea; and the moderating tendency of Nausea's own theology a decade later elicited Cochlaeus's scornful comment that 'I'd think you were now for peace.'[16] No such suspicion would ever surround Cochlaeus.

1527–39, Meissen

Hieronymus Emser, a leader of the early Catholic reaction and an early target of Luther's scorn, was court chaplain to Duke George of Saxony when he died in 1527. Cochlaeus was his successor and strove to carry forward a program of steadfast defense of the Roman faith. The work involved preparing the writings of others for the press, sometimes at his own expense, as well as continuing to compose his own polemical works.[17] His own writings included the occasional extended treatise, but more often during this period consisted of series of controversial statements and passages drawn from the Reformers' works, with refutations of each. *The Fascicle of Calumnies, Ravings and Illusions of Martin Luther against Bishops and Clerics* is typical of the genre.[18] In this work Cochlaeus painstakingly classifies dozens of statements by Luther into these three outlandish categories, demonstrating why they are calumnies, ravings, or illusions, and indicating the offending statements' deviation from the Catholic faith. To this period also belongs Cochlaeus's best-known work behind the *Commentary* on Luther, the *Seven-Headed Luther*.[19] The seven 'heads' are the various personalities Luther appears to have exhibited in his works: Doctor, fanatic, fool, church visitor, churchman, criminal, and Barabbas. In Cochlaeus's work the different 'Luthers' take part in a series of dialogues about various matters of doctrine and practice, each quoting passages from Luther's works – no two of which, however, seem to be in agreement. Convinced that Luther's own incoherence, if proved, will undermine his authority even among his followers, Cochlaeus presents an absurd collage of statements that do indeed reveal a maddeningly inconsistent Luther.[20] This work and the *Fascicle* are among the compilations from this period that served as sourcebooks for the polemical writings of the later Cochlaeus – and for the *Commentary* itself. There are few, if any, quotations from Luther's writing that do not match passages in these early efforts to have Luther refute himself with his own words.[21]

Cochlaeus's intention in these compilations is to let the Reformers refute themselves by proving to be unreliable guides in anything concerning the faith. He is unconcerned about context, development of thought, or later revisions of earlier statements made by any Protestant thinker. The fact that all the major Reformers amplify and refine their works is grist to the mill; what may have been nothing more than an author's clarification of a point is presented as a self-contradiction. The effect is to shock the reader into recognizing that the Reformers are advocates not of sound doctrine but of inconsistencies. He wants to show that each Protestant theologian is both internally incoherent and in disagreement, in some point or another, with all the others. In contrast, his publications of Catholic works both ancient and recent are intended to show that the Roman church has taught the same essentials over time and is uniform in its teachings in the sixteenth century.

With the Diet of Augsburg Cochlaeus shifts his dominant theme. Cochlaeus was present at the Diet, and helped draft the Response that was suppressed on orders of the Emperor for being too harsh.[22] If the Diet of Worms revealed Luther to be an obstinate heretic, Augsburg exposed the danger to the Empire posed by the Protestant Estates that presented their Confession. In Cochlaeus's mind, Protestant princes had been lured from the Catholic faith by the heretical theologians within their territories. Like the intended readers of works like *Seven-Headed Luther*, these princes would recognize the instability of the Reformers' teachings if it were revealed to them. Cochlaeus assumed this responsibility; and his works from 1530 onward make much of the disobedience of the Reformers. Works like *A Faithful and Peaceful Warning by Johannes Cochlaeus against the Faithless and Seditious Warning by Martin Luther to the Germans* attempt to reveal the duplicity and unrest lurking in Luther's counsel.[23] These works are supplemented by more editions of authoritative works by others, most of them contemporary rather than ancient, and disciplinary rather than theoretical.[24] If the posture of the early Cochlaeus toward the Reformers was that of one Christian humanist trying to correct another with sources that both acknowledged as legitimate, the stance of Cochlaeus in the 1530s was that of the defender of orthodoxy warning his superiors, secular and ecclesiastical, of the heretical and subversive character of the new religious ideas. The fact that from Augsburg onward the Protestants are in open opposition to the Roman church and Empire makes Cochlaeus's job a relatively easy one. If one presupposes a unified political and ecclesiastical realm, then it is a matter of simple logic that neither schismatics nor revolutionaries can be tolerated.

Cochlaeus had a gift for making enemies. But he was equally endowed with a gift for making friends. The intensity of his commitment won him influential allies. In the second stage of his career as a polemicist Cochlaeus forged strong relations among like-minded clergy, and attempted to create a powerful reactionary front among German Catholics. The movement included theologians like Johann Eck, patrons like the Polish archbishop Peter Tomicki and Duke George of Saxony, and printers like Cochlaeus's nephew, Nicolaus Wolrab. But lack of funds and moral support, as well as the conversion to Lutheranism of some of his partners (Wolrab in particular[25]), kept the conservative wing from acquiring the strength its visionary imagined. And preparations elsewhere for the general council that would be held at Trent seemed to diminish the need for a definitive regional response.

Cochlaeus did his own part in preparing for the Council. Although a defender of the primacy of the papacy, and someone who believed that the Reformers refuted themselves with their own contradictions, he felt that a general council was the only competent authority in matters concerning the church as a whole.[26] In 1535 he congratulated the new pope, Paul III, on his election, and recommended that he call a council.[27] But whereas other theologians in Germany prepared for the Council by meeting and seeking concord or at least recognition of irreconcilable differences, Cochlaeus felt that the task of the assembled hierarchy should be the condemnation of Protestantism and the restoration of Roman piety. Thus the 'elimination of discord' which all sought meant, for Cochlaeus, the elimination of the Reformers as the source of discord.[28] In his private writings as well, Cochlaeus strove to tarnish and darken the Reformers' reputations, bringing vernacular attacks on the papacy to the attention of his Italian correspondents.[29] During these years, when he is perhaps at the peak of his influence, he also begins an aggressive campaign to win an invitation to the Council.[30]

1539–52, Breslau

For Cochlaeus personally, the most important event of the Reformation was the succession of Henry the Pious as Duke of Albertine Saxony in 1539. Henry was as weak as Duke George was strong, and as Lutheran as George was Catholic. For Cochlaeus, the fall of Albertine Saxony to the Reformation meant the loss of Germany's strongest bastion of the old religion. It also meant Cochlaeus's own exile from a center of Saxon power to the Silesian city of Wroclaw (then Breslau), in the eastern hinterlands that he had held in such contempt when satirizing Wittenberg. With the exception of some trips to participate in regional colloquies and a short stay in Eichstätt, not far from where he was born, Cochlaeus spent his last years in a city where, as his letters repeatedly reflect, he felt himself an outsider. It seemed an ignominious end to a career of service to his church.

The 1540s were certainly a time of troubles for Cochlaeus. By manipulating his patrons' sympathies he acquired a post as canon at the cathedral in Wroclaw. But he continued to struggle for support throughout the decade. He remained convinced that the conservative wing of the church would prevail, and was determined to serve the cause in any way possible. Such service had been made more difficult, however, by the move to Silesia (where he had few allies and little support from his bishop) and by increasing difficulty in finding printers for his work. Protestant and moderate Catholic literature had become far more profitable for the printing industry; polemical invective of the sort Cochlaeus excelled in had become too unpopular for printers to produce without subsidy from the author. In letters expressing abject and urgent need, Cochlaeus appealed to past and potential supporters for funds to buy paper and ink, hire typesetters, and pay for all other labor involved in producing defenses of the Catholic church. The fact that the reactionary wing had lost momentum in Germany was for Cochlaeus a sign that efforts needed to be augmented; at no point was Cochlaeus willing to capitulate to the interests of moderation. Their dominance even among Catholic prelates meant, in Cochlaeus's view, that the Reformers' rhetoric was proving increasingly devious and influential.

Convinced that his view would be vindicated at the Council, Cochlaeus devoted much of the decade to defending the duty of councils to prosecute and punish heretics. He returned to his early interests and studies in law, drawing on everything from the earliest fragments of canon law to its most recent theorists, to insist that discipline rather than conciliation was the path that needed to be taken with those who had deviated from obedience to the church. And in order to ensure that all Protestants were included in the Council's proceedings, he expanded his canon of adversaries beyond Luther and Melanchthon to include men such as Martin Bucer and Heinrich Bullinger.[31]

If the period 1530–9 was one for territorial rulers like Duke George of Saxony to come to the aid of the Roman church, the 1540s were time for action at the imperial level. Cochlaeus accordingly devoted his dozen years in exile to making imperial and papal powers aware of the disaster that would result if Protestantism continued to be tolerated. It was in this final stage that Cochlaeus achieved his full potential for reactionary rhetoric. In part, no doubt, because his own life was deeply affected by the political history of the Reformation, Cochlaeus tended to see the dangers of Protestantism as social and political and not as religious only. In Cochlaeus's mind, the difference between Catholic and Protestant was the difference between order and disorder; and his task was to make that difference so obvious that no rational person, and perforce no responsible Christian ruler, could choose disorder over order.

The Peasants' War gave the first indications that the danger posed by the Reformers' teachings extended beyond religious practice. For Cochlaeus, as for other polemicists, it hardly mattered that the person they held responsible for the Reformation was not directly the instigator of the 1525 rebellion.[32] Luther was widely depicted as the patron of disobedience, and his repudiation of the peasants' insurrection seemed all the greater proof of his responsibility. And the horrific casualty figures of the Peasants' War were only a minor foretaste of the carnage that still awaited.[33]

The Schmalkald War of 1547 fulfilled Cochlaeus's expectations. In contrast to the motley band of peasants and their opponents in 1525, the Schmalkald War was between the federation of Protestant territories and the Empire: it symbolized Reformation and Catholicism in their most organized forms. Moreover, the fact that the imperial forces of Charles V defeated the Protestant states indicated to Cochlaeus that the Catholics would prevail, that the Reformers would be utterly vanquished, and that the princes the Reformers had deceived would return with their subjects to the ancient faith. As Cochlaeus saw it, the late 1540s were no time for compromise, for complete victory was closer than it had been since the outbreak of troubles.[34]

The introduction of the Reformation into Albertine Saxony, and his own subsequent move to Wroclaw, convinced Cochlaeus even further that the Reformation was an evil needing complete eradication, no matter how harsh the measures taken to achieve that end may seem. Thus it fitted well into his intention to depict Luther even more demonically than he had in the previous two decades. To Luther's intellectual incoherence and defiance of tradition, the themes of the 1520s and 1530s, was now added an almost diabolical obstinacy, an inability to accede to reason, church discipline, or the threat of punishment by civil powers. Cochlaeus seems to have felt that only force would be able to compel him. In an exhortation to the German princes supposedly written in 1522 but published in 1545, Cochlaeus described Luther as worse than the universally feared Turk:

> Luther no longer wants to celebrate Mass, chant the canonical hours, or to have vigils, matins, saints' feast days, exequies for the dead, anniversaries, Lenten fasts, works of penance, or pilgrimages. What, by immortal God, could the most barbarous Turk do that could be worse to our religion? Who of the pagans has ever been so foreign to all divine praise and worship than Luther? Or what nation has ever been so barbarous as never to have any sacred things or priests? [35]

In order to appreciate the portrait of Luther in the *Commentary*, it is necessary to recognize how earnestly and consistently Cochlaeus held the view that the Reformer was a person of colossal wickedness and impiety.

At the end of his life Cochlaeus was concerned that the moderating parties among the Romanists, who had prevailed since the Diet of Augsburg, would continue to seek unity with the Protestants. The imperial Interim issued at Augsburg in 1548 posed a dilemma for Cochlaeus. On the one hand, the Empire appeared to be acting in the best interests of the Catholic church: the Interim promised peace on Catholic terms. On the other, it recognized as valid a number of Protestant critiques of liturgical practice. Conciliation with the Protestants, in Cochlaeus's view, was tantamount to capitulating to those factions intent on destroying the church. In a letter to the poet Heinrich Glareanus, Cochlaeus states his fear that the Interim will become an 'iterum,' a repetition of the same sort of turmoil already suffered.[36] Unity and tranquility held only a specious attractiveness. In his most generous view of them, the religious moderates were the victims of the Reformers' siren call of consensus with the Catholic tradition. With rare pertinacity, Cochlaeus adhered to the view that Protestant appeals to unity and harmony were rhetorical lures intended to entrap the faithful, who would recognize the duplicity of the Reformers' professions only after the church was fatally compromised. From beginning to end, the Reformation was the work of the Devil acting through Wittenberg theologians together with their allies and princes; and it was Cochlaeus's self-imposed duty to expose this fact.[37]

Some, indeed most, Protestant theologians rebelled against the Interim, and for a number of reasons. It was, first of all, an attempt to impose imperial law on sovereign territories, and thus an illegitimate incursion into the rule of the Protestant princes. Second, in seeking to steer a middle way between the rich liturgical life of the Catholic church, with its vestments, candles, relics, and shrines, and the severe rites of the Reformation churches, the Interim inevitably displeased those Reformers who themselves felt that any inclusion of Romanist 'idolatry' was corrupting to piety. Theologians like Andreas Osiander, Matthias Flacius, Philip Melanchthon, and John Calvin all responded, with varying degrees of harshness, to the Interim, and thereby gave Cochlaeus material for the final battle of his life.[38] Although he himself remained opposed to the Interim, he was able to attack the Protestants' rejections of it as being one more instance of their disobedience and obstinate persistence in erroneous positions. In his attack on Calvin's response to the Interim, Cochlaeus denounced the 'nefarious and seditious preachers and leaders of sects, despisers of all powers ... who vomit and excrete impious and notorious books in German, mostly in Thuringian and Saxon towns, against that ordinance issued with Imperial authority that they call the Interim.'[39] Neither acceptance nor rejection of the Interim could satisfy him.

Old and ill, exhausted by his efforts for the church and hurt by their lack of recognition, Cochlaeus spent his final years trying to serve his cause with books. Between 1545 and his death in 1552 Cochlaeus strove to publish everything he had written, a body of work of extraordinary volume and range. Collections of occasional tracts like the *Miscellanies on the Cause of Religion*, the massive *History of the Hussites*, and the present *Commentary on the Life of Luther* appeared during these years.[40] And to remind his contemporaries of his efforts since the beginning of the Reformation, he issued a bibliography of his works, the whole corpus separated into German and Latin and listed chronologically. At the end are listed five titles from his early juristic and humanistic studies, and eighteen polemical works 'written in German and never published'; all are apparently lost.[41]

The *Commentary*

Although most of it was written by 1534, as he tells his readers at the end of that year's chronicle, the *Commentary* on Luther is the monument of the final stage of Cochlaeus's career.[42] He boasted to Cardinal Marcello Cervini (who would become pope in 1555 as Marcellus II) that many have been pleased with it, and he intended to translate it into German.[43] Sending a copy to Cardinal Alessandro Farnese, grandson of Pope Paul III, Cochlaeus described his work as being 'not temerarious or without cause, but by necessity, especially because the majority of persons living today think, by the crudest of errors, that Luther was a good man and his gospel was a holy one.'[44] The publication of the *Commentary* was Cochlaeus's attempt to keep the memory of the 'real' Luther alive and to counteract tendencies to ignore faults and over time to idolize the man. It is at the same time a chronicle of Cochlaeus's work of thirty years, an effort to preserve, after his own death, a record of his efforts to combat Luther and his influence. What Cochlaeus could not achieve while Luther was alive, the posthumous Cochlaeus might be able to accomplish against the memory of the departed Luther.

Cochlaeus's hopes for this book were fulfilled abundantly. Four centuries of

Catholic historiography reproduced the image of Luther delineated in the *Commentary*.[45] No Catholic scholars between the sixteenth century and the great mid-twentieth-century theologians Joseph Lortz and Erwin Iserloh knew Luther's work as intimately as Cochlaeus did; and only in recent decades has there been a desire to return to the disputes of the Reformation era and scrutinize the sources. For historical information and theological insight from a neglected viewpoint, as well as the occasional rhetorical barb, few texts of the sixteenth century call for historical recovery more than the *Commentary*.

Cochlaeus's *Commentary* is unique and original in its contribution to the Luther heresiography.[46] If a hagiographer's task is to record his subject's virtuous life, miracles, and piety in order to convince the reader of his subject's sanctity, the author of a heresiography sets about to present his subject's errors, vices, and dangers in order to reveal his sinister character. But anyone who chooses to attack Cochlaeus on purely technical grounds, and argue that he is careless with the evidence available to him, will have a difficult task. Cochlaeus exploits his opponents' texts and historical tradition with scrupulous accuracy in his quoting both bodies of material. He knew, as the hagiographer knows, that the account loses validity if it is factually inaccurate.

Cochlaeus is the heresiographer *par excellence* among Reformation-era Catholic controversialists. He differs from many of his contemporaries in the importance he gives to the lives of his antagonists. Heresy for him is not a set of erroneous ideas to which the unwary might be exposed, but a tool in the hands of wicked persons who seek to corrupt others. Thus the heretic takes on as much importance as the heresy itself in Cochlaeus's work. His historical and biographical interests go back to his early excerpt from the Hussite chronicle of Albert Krantz, and continue through to the *History of the Hussites*.[47] Luther was the perfect figure for this sort of treatment, not simply because of the notoriety of his teachings or the scandalousness of his life, but also because of the strength of his personality. Luther did not shrink from the public eye; in fact he put parts of his own life on view. In his public boldness and in drawing the world's attention to certain aspects of his private life, Luther virtually invites his opponents to attack him personally.

Since, for Cochlaeus, the Reformation is a conflict of divine and diabolical elements, he tends to depict its leaders in heroic terms. Jan Hus and his accomplices are portrayed as larger-than-life enemies of religion in Cochlaeus's *History of the Hussites*. Likewise, Cochlaeus depicts Luther as a colossal figure, a person uniquely able to wreak havoc in the social and ecclesiastical realms.[48] By presenting the deeds and teachings of heretics in the most sinister light possible, Cochlaeus is able to demonstrate the complete unacceptability of their work as guides for doctrine. One senses when reading the *Commentary* that Cochlaeus writes from a close knowledge of Luther and his works. Moreover, Cochlaeus sets Luther within a context with which he was intimately familiar: the world of the colloquies, diets, and religious disputes formal and informal that mark the stages of the development of Protestantism in its first decades. Cochlaeus's *Commentary*, because of its thoroughness and accuracy, is in fact a uniquely valuable source for historians of Reformation-era Catholicism. As with hagiography, heresiography must be grounded in detailed and absolutely certain knowledge of the subject being described.

In addition to being an exposé of Luther's teachings and a chronicle of efforts to suppress it, the *Commentary* provides an unusually thorough account of Luther's life before 1534, especially when we recognize how little of the private Luther Cochlaeus would have known. Luther's life and character are as important as his thought and writings for Cochlaeus. In Cochlaeus's view, the moral worth of persons and the value of their teachings are connected, and connected so closely that would be impossible, almost by definition, for a wicked person to have a legitimate thought. Observations about the personal character of most of his opponents loom large in Cochlaeus's work and supply much of his polemical armament. The Reformers' rejection of clerical celibacy he saw not as a theological point but as an indication of their moral values; and repudiation of vows of celibacy for marriage stood as proof of their weakness of the flesh. Thus, although one may at first be tempted to see Cochlaeus's preoccupation with the lives of his opponents as an irrelevance unrelated to his theological argument, in Cochlaeus's mind the morality of his adversaries automatically undermines their teachings. It is not for nothing that Cochlaeus regularly contrasts Luther with the chaste and temperate lives of his clerical colleagues. The refutations of specific arguments that one finds in Cochlaeus's works are almost redundant reinforcements of the principal thrust of his rhetoric.

Yet there is theological exposition and refutation here; the work is after all a polemical account of a thinker's teachings. Although Cochlaeus may himself have been outmatched in theological dexterity by his Protestant adversaries, he still felt superior to them in learning. He delights in exposing gaffes in logic or biblical interpretation by his adversaries. And throughout the *Commentary* as well as in his other works he contrasts the Reformers' obtuseness with the erudition of his fellow Catholic theologians. Thus Cochlaeus's Catholic contemporaries stand in contrast to Luther and his colleagues not only in purity of life but in learning and intellectual subtlety as well. Cochlaeus delights in the stark contrast; and, either implicitly or explicitly, a pious and erudite counterpart to Luther is present at every stage of the *Commentary*.

In presenting the contrast between the impious Luther and his own pious and learned colleagues, Cochlaeus hopes the reader will recognize the absurdity of the juxtaposition and reject Luther's example and teachings. But the polemical goal of the *Commentary* can only be achieved if the reader feels that Luther is being presented honestly, fairly, and objectively. The merest hint of theological persuasion would undermine the work as a whole. The *Commentary* is thus, in the end, a work of delicious irony: a work covertly serving the most extreme polemical ends, while ostensibly a balanced and factual account of the life of a profoundly influential religious leader.

As much as modern scholarly sensibilities may recoil from the image of polemic being presented as objective biography, we must recognize that there was no strict separation of fact and judgment in the minds of Reformation-era historians. The conjunction of these two categories is seen nowhere more clearly than in Conrad Braun's essay on writing history, which appears as one of the prefatory documents to Cochlaeus's *Commentary*.[49] Braun, a priest and a jurist, was the author of several weighty treatises on heresy and sedition, and Cochlaeus was instrumental in publishing them.[50] History, according to Braun, teaches one to compare past with present and to draw conjectures that may help in predicting the future; it is thus most useful as a moral guide in the political realm.[51] In order to preserve peace and stability, ecclesiastical and secular authorities need the guidance of history in identifying heresy and extirpating it; and just as the historical record offers help in doing this, so does it reveal the dire consequences of failing to eliminate heresy.[52] For Braun, the chief value of history in his own day is its ability to reveal the similarities between Jan Hus and Martin Luther, similarities which will convince all loyal Catholics that the Lutherans are to be dealt with in the same way as the Hussites had been: condemned and rendered disordered and leaderless, their master executed as heretical and seditious.[53] Unfashionable as it proved to be in the middle decades of the century, that radical treatment was the prescription unfolded in Braun's juristic work. As a result, in Braun's view we should see the *Commentary* and Cochlaeus's twelve-book *History of the Hussites* as the twin panels of a diptych, together forming a thousand-page brief to the authorities against the dangers of Protestantism.[54] The absence in the *Commentary* of sustained rhetorical denunciation, which Cochlaeus's other writings lead one to expect, is understood once one recognizes that the *Commentary* is the presentation of factual evidence rather than concluding judgment. The judgment is drawn from the larger body of works by Braun and Cochlaeus from 1548–9.[55]

Cochlaeus makes this point in a letter to Ercole d'Este, Duke of Ferarra, that accompanies Braun's essay and introduces the *Commentary*. Recalling his own student days at Ferarra (and appending the citation of his doctoral degree), Cochlaeus tells his noble patron that he has left the judgment of Luther to the reader.

> My concern was to report truthfully the things that would allow the present age to understand how far from the limits of Evangelical teaching, from obligatory obedience, and from the unity of the church Luther and his accomplices have conducted themselves, written, and preached against the law of charity and against the most certain precepts of Christ and Paul his apostle; with nefarious plots and subterfuge and with no concern for consequences they have disrupted the entire world with discord and the most horrifying doubts about the Christian faith and religion... And may pious posterity learn from this to resist new dissensions of this sort quickly when they occur, to capture the predators when they are still small, before they become strong and aided by sedition, when they cannot be caught without great harm or calamity.[56]

Perhaps the most eloquent evidence of the purpose of the *Commentary* is found at the end of the 1549 edition. The Edict of Worms, with which the new Emperor, Charles V, condemned Luther in 1521, is reproduced at the end of Cochlaeus's massive tome, supplemented only by marginal notes pointing out Luther's criminality and impiety.[57] For Cochlaeus the Edict represented imperial business still pending, an emergency measure, taken for the sake of the people, whose urgency had increased rather than diminished in the intervening years – as the *Commentary* sought to demonstrate.[58]

The fact that the *Commentary*, taken without its highly charged peripheral matter, may have been intended as a presentation of factual evidence in a case against Luther gives it a readability that more overtly polemical works, by Cochlaeus and others, do not possess. Whatever Cochlaeus's intentions, one learns much about Luther – about his works, his life, his public deeds – from this biography. The narrative after 1534, in which Cochlaeus limits himself to listing Luther's writings, is an astonishingly impressive picture of heroic energy applied to a daunting cause.[59] And Cochlaeus's record of his own efforts to combat Luther and his influence strikes the modern reader with almost as much force. If Cochlaeus fails to emerge in this chronicle as Luther's equal, it is surely due in part to Cochlaeus's own larger-than-life portrayal of the Reformer. The three first decades of the Reformation come across in these pages as a period of titanic struggle for the souls of Christian believers; and the *Commentary*, possibly more than any other work by a Catholic author, stands as an eloquent record of that struggle.

4

The deeds and writings of Martin Luther from the year of the Lord 1517 to the year 1546 related chronologically to all posterity by Johannes Cochlaeus

for the first time translated into English by Elizabeth Vandiver and annotated by Ralph Keen

The Year of the Lord 1517

Martin Luther, who was born in the year of the Lord 1483 in Eisleben in Saxony, under the Counts of Mansfeld, had plebeian parents from the Luder family.[1] His father was named Johannes, his mother Margarita. He received the name 'Martinus' in baptism through ancient and ancestral custom, because he was born at night on the tenth day of November, the eve of the festival of Holy Martin.[2] But although for many years, according to ancient custom, he was called by the surname 'Luder' — which he himself also used in his letters, even to the pre-eminent theologian Dr Johannes Eck — nevertheless he later preferred to be called 'Luther' rather than 'Luder,' perhaps because among the Germans 'Luder' seems a less than respectable word.

After his infancy, when he had passed his boyhood at home (since by his parents' careful attention he was imbued with the rudiments of his letters in the school of his hometown), he was sent from there to Magdeburg, where he remained for one year. From there he progressed to Eisenach, a town of Thuringia, where he found a more congenial teacher and remained for years. Afterwards he went to Erfurt, a famous, large town of Thuringia, where there was a celebrated Academy. In his twentieth year he attained the rank of Master in the study of Philosophy, and certainly he was among the first-ranked students, since he surpassed many of his peers in talent and zeal.

From there he moved on to the study of law. But when he was in the country, either because he was terrified and prostrated by a bolt of lightning, as is commonly said, or because he was overwhelmed with grief at the death of a companion, through contempt of this world he suddenly — to the astonishment of many — entered the Monastery of the brothers of St Augustine, who are commonly called the Hermits. After a year's probation, his profession of that order was made legitimate, and there in his studies and spiritual exercises he fought strenuously for God for four years. However, he appeared to the brothers to have a certain amount of peculiarity, either from some secret commerce with a Demon, or (according to certain other indications) from the disease of epilepsy. They thought this especially, because several times in the Choir, when during the Mass the passage from the Evangelist about the ejection of the deaf and mute Demon was read, he suddenly fell down, crying 'It is not I, it is not I.'[3] And thus it is the opinion of many, that he enjoyed an occult familiarity with some demon, since he himself sometimes wrote such things about himself as were able to engender a suspicion in the reader of this kind of commerce and nefarious association. For he says in a certain sermon addressed to the people, that he knows the Devil well, and is in turn well known by him, and that he has eaten more than one grain of salt with him. And furthermore he published his own book in German, *About the 'Corner' Mass* (as he calls it),[4] where he remembers a disputation against the Mass that the Devil held with him at night. There are other pieces of evidence about this matter as well, and not trivial ones, since he was even seen by certain people to keep company bodily with the Devil.

In the year of the Lord 1508 he was moved from Erfurt to Wittenberg into another monastery of the same institute, where he publicly lectured on the Dialectic and Physics of Aristotle; for an Academy or public University of studies had recently been established there, by the Elector of Saxony Duke Frederick.[5] Moreover, when after three years a disagreement arose among the brothers of his order – since seven monasteries in Germany differed in certain matters from the Vicar General – he was chosen by those monasteries as the agent for their dispute, and he went to Rome, since he was keen in intellect, and bold and vehement in debate.

When that case between the disputing parties had been settled and concluded by some sort of transactions, and he had returned to Wittenberg, he was made a Doctor in Theology with the usual celebration, either by the order and administration of Frederick, Duke of Saxony, the Elector Prince, or through the funding of a certain matron who had fraudulently embezzled church moneys, since she cut off a certain sum of money, which was intended for the subsidy of another brother's promotion to the Doctorate at Nuremberg. For this reason it came about that when that brother discovered the fraud and the fact that the money had been taken away from him, he fled away secretly because of his sorrow and indignation, and no one knows to this day where he went.

But since Luther, who was adorned with the title of Doctor and prefect of the Ordinary Reading[6] in Theology, was an extremely keen debater and desirous of vainglory, he wished to be pre-eminent not among the learned of Wittenberg alone. He also went to Heidelberg, where he sought renown for his intellect and learning in debating, whenever he proposed new themes.[7] There it happened, in the year of the Lord 1517, that Pope Leo X published new indulgences throughout the world, on the occasion of the new building of the Cathedral of St Peter in Rome, which his preceder Pope Julius II had begun with the most sumptuous magnificence. But Julius was prevented by death and was not able to complete this work of such great magnificence. Indeed Constantine, the most powerful Emperor (whom we call 'the Great' but the ancients called 'the Greatest'[8]) had filled up that church (like many others) with religious artifacts and very sumptuous and marvelous work: especially noteworthy was the way it was supported by a varied series of enormous columns (such as are not made in our day). But this church had decayed (as is natural) through the passage of time. When it began obviously to gape open in many of its sections and to threaten ruin, Pope Julius II, a high-minded man, did not so much strive to repair the parts that had collapsed through age or to remake its patched buildings (would that he had so preferred!), but rather began to rebuild it anew, in the greatest and most astonishing size. That size can be seen today in the foundations laid by him, and in the lofty arches and vaults and columns, as large as the highest towers, lifted on high and extending into the sky. No doubt he acted on this consideration, that just as the Roman Church is pre-eminent among and outshines all other churches in the world in power and dignity, through the word of Christ and the principate of Peter, so also the Church of Peter should outstrip all others in the size of its structure and the magnificence of its work, and should be the most conspicuous among them.

But Pope Leo X, a generous man, and more given to paying out (I will not say to squandering) funds than to collecting and seeking them, since he was unequal to the expense of such an edifice, and could not continue a work of such cost from his own resources, gave out indulgences – a thing that often been done before him – in order that he might acquire the helping hands of many in pious relief.

Moreover, there was at that time among the ecclesiastical Prelates of Germany a most eminent man, both for the height of his dignity and the splendor of his birth, the Most Reverend Father and Most Illustrious Prince Albert, the Archbishop of Mainz and Magdeburg, Priest and Cardinal of the Holy Roman Church, Primate of Germany, and Elector Prince of the Holy Roman Empire, Margrave of Brandenburg, etc.[9] Therefore, Pope Leo X laid a special commission on him for the business of publishing the indulgences in Germany. And following the advice and opinion of many, he would have taken as assistants in this business the Brothers of the Order of St Augustine of the Hermits – who had earlier performed the most strenuous work in this matter for the Apostolic See, not only by declaring it to the people but also by writing and distributing books (such as, for example, the 'Mine of Heaven' and its supplement) – had not Johannes Tetzel, a Brother of the Order of the Preachers, seemed more suitable to certain people, especially because the memory of his sermons about indulgences was then recent. In these sermons he had acquired ample money for the Brothers of Holy Mary of the Military Order of the Teutonic Lords in Livonia, who were being hard pressed by the Muscovites and other nearby enemies. But the Augustinian Brothers took this as badly as possible, especially Johannes Staupitz (a man of noble family and famous for his facility and learning, and their Vicar General in Germany) and Martin Luther, Doctor of Theology, Ordinary of Wittenberg – as though these two were the two head rams of their flock, celebrated for their reputation and authority, and outstanding before the others.[10]

Staupitz was not only from a noble family and for that reason more beloved than the other Dukes of Saxony (to whom he feigned a blood relationship) and more well known on account of familiarity; but he was also versatile in intellect, and remarkable for the beauty and stature of his body, and moreover shrewd and practical in managing business, and so he had much influence through favor and grace with the Most Illustrious Prince Elector, the Duke of Saxony, Frederick, who surpassed many other princes in authority, wealth, power, generosity, and magnificence. Indeed, Frederick had recently instituted the Academy at Wittenberg at great expense, and he provided for its growth through a large endowment, and by means of ample salaries he summoned learned and intelligent men from all parts, whom he had noted on account of their fame. He also erected a new College of Canons, in which he made Jonas the Head and Karlstadt the Archdeacon.[11] [12] He called the church itself the Church of All the Saints. And in this church he collected from all regions very many bones of the saints and venerable relics of all kinds, most lavishly adorned with gold, silver, and gems, which he took care should be exhibited to the public on set days in their magnificent adornment. Thus, when it appeared to the Highest Pontiff how religious and pious were his generosity and greatness, he easily conceded to the Duke whatever privilege he sought, both for the new University and for the new College of Canons.

Therefore Staupitz worked his way in as a familiar to this Prince, instilling frequent abuses of indulgences into his breast, and scandals of Quaestors and Commissaries, so that they – through avarice for favors and through the pretext of grace – might plunder Germany and seek the things that were theirs, not the things of Jesus Christ. But Luther was of a more ardent nature, and more impatient of his injuries. He seized his pen and soon wrote an indignant letter to the abovementioned Albert, Primate of Germany. Indeed, in this letter, shortly after the preface asking for a blessing, he burst into these words:

'Papal indulgences are being hawked about' (he said) 'under your most illustrious title, for the building of St Peter's. In these matters I do not so much accuse the announcements of the Priests, which I have not heard, but I am grieved by the extremely false impressions the people have gotten from these things, impressions which are bandied about commonly, everywhere: namely, that they believe – unhappy souls! – that if they buy Letters of Indulgence, then they are safe as regards their salvation. Or again, that souls immediately fly out of Purgatory, when they throw their contribution into the chest.' And a little further on he wrote, 'It was not possible to be silent any longer about these things. For a man is not made secure concerning his salvation by any gift of a Bishop, when he is not made secure by the grace of God poured out over him. But the Apostle orders us always in fear and trembling to work at our salvation. And the just (says Peter) shall scarcely be saved. Then indeed, so narrow is the road that leads to life, as the Lord said through the prophets Amos and Zacharia (whom Torres calls worthy of salvation, snatched from the fire). And everywhere the Lord declares the difficulty of salvation. Why therefore do the announcers of these false stories and promises of favor use them to make the people secure and without fear? In short, with these indulgences they confer nothing of any use at all for Salvation or Sanctity to the people's souls, but merely bring them a foreign tax, which formerly used to be imposed by the Church.'[13]

These things and more of this sort Luther wrote then, from Wittenberg, on the Eve of All Saints, in the year of the Lord 1517. We recount these things for this reason, so that the reader may know that this letter was written by Luther not so much because of the opinion of his mind, as from the livid effect of envy: since no other person's doctrine made the people so secure concerning salvation and so slow and negligent toward good works as would Luther's new doctrine. For as he wrote publicly in the preface to his *Babylonian Captivity*, 'The Christian man is so rich that he could not lose his salvation, even if he wished to, unless he chose not to believe; nor can any sins damn him, since all sins are quickly absorbed and removed through the faith in the promise which was made for or by him at his baptism, provided only that he believe and consider that he has been baptized.' [14] Moreover, he was not content to have sent this letter privately; but also he publicly announced ninety-five theses (although in the first draft he had written ninety-seven), by which he attacked the common and received opinion and the doctrine of the Church concerning indulgences.

Tetzel was living in Frankfurt on the Oder River (where the most Illustrious Elector Prince, Joachim, Margrave of Brandenburg, had about that same time opened a University for scholars).[15] Since he was the Reporting Priest for indulgences, and the Apostolic Commissary, and also an Inquisitor of heretical depravity, and was fierce in his intellect and strong in his body, when he saw these Propositions, he bore Luther's outrageous audacity badly, and in order that equal might answer to equal he published 106 theses, in which he explained the contrary opinion. For example, Luther began as follows: 'Our Lord and Teacher Jesus Christ, by saying "Make your repentance, etc.," wished the whole life of a believer to be one of penance. That cannot be understood as concerning the penitential Sacrament of Confession and Reparation, which is celebrated by the ministry of a priest. For it does not refer only to inner repentance; indeed the inner is nothing unless it is manifested externally through various mortifications of the flesh, etc.' But against this opinion of his, Tetzel began as follows: 'Our Lord Jesus Christ not only desired everyone to be bound by the Sacraments of the New Law after his passion and ascension; he also desired to teach these Sacraments to all before his passion, through his extremely pointed preaching. He is in error, therefore, whoever says that Christ, when he preached "Make your repentance," taught interior repentance and exterior mortification of the flesh, but that he did not also wish to teach and to imply at the same time the Sacrament of Penitence and its parts of Confession and Reparation, although they are obligatory. For indeed there is no benefit at all, even if the inner suffering produces outer mortification, unless there be present also, in fact or vow, Confession and Reparation, etc.'

And so through publishing propositions of divergent and contrary opinions, the controversy of turbulent disagreement between these two antagonists [Tetzel and Luther] appeared to be waged so publicly that in the following year it broke out into an open fire – by which the peace and unity of the Church, to the greatest scandal of the weak and detriment of souls, was overthrown and dissolved. Luther trusted in his own intellect and learning, and also in the power and favor of his protector, Duke Frederick the Elector, and in the councils and practices of his wily Staupitz. But Tetzel considered it unworthy to cede to Luther, since he himself was renowned for the fame of his preachings, and was supported both by the commission and authority of the Apostolic See, and also by the office of the Inquisition.

1518

Therefore Luther, relying on the advice of his associates, published a Latin book, to which he gave this title: *Resolutions of the Arguments Concerning the Virtue of Indulgences, Etc.* [16] And in that book, he declared ninety-five Conclusions in accordance with his new reputation, not – to be sure – so that he might reconcile the Pope and his adversaries to himself, or succeed in placating them, whom he attacked most bitterly and extensively in this book itself; but rather so that he might enlist the reader on his own side, simulating a wonderful humility, submission, and reverence toward the Roman Pontiff. By this he was cunningly seeking both the reader's sympathy toward himself and hatred towards his adversaries. For he feigned that he was snatched and dragged into public view, entirely reluctant and unwilling, by his adversaries' wickedness. For he said, in the preface addressed to Leo X, 'Unwillingly I come into public, who am especially unlearned, and stupid in my wits, and devoid of learning. But necessity drives me to squawk as a goose among swans. And so, in order that I may soften my adversaries themselves and may fulfill the desire of many, behold – I publish my trifles.' And below he said, 'Therefore, Most Holy Father, I offer myself prostrate at your most holy feet, with all that I am and all that I have. Give life, kill; call, recall; approve, disapprove; as it will please you. I recognize your voice as the voice of Christ, presiding and speaking in you. If I have deserved death, I will not refuse to die.' [17]

And so by this cunning, as he complained that he was unjustly pressed by his adversaries and driven into public, he soon gained the greatest favor for himself, not just among the simple people, who easily believe and freely open their wide-spread, itching ears to every novelty; but also among many grave, learned men, who believing in his words through genuine simplicity, thought that the Monk sought nothing else, other than defense of the truth against the Seekers of indulgences, who (so Luther kept on accusing) appeared more zealous for money than for souls. And so that he might deflect all suspicion of heresy from himself on to his adversaries, he joined a certain solemn protestation to the book, after his complaints to Staupitz and his letters to Pope Leo. In it he deferred not only to the Holy Scriptures, but also to the holy Canonical and Pontifical decrees and the Church Fathers; moreover, he desired to consider the judgment of his superiors sound in all matters. [18]

Then a learned body of poets and rhetoricians, who were also driven by hatred for his adversaries, pitied Luther, and argued diligently for him by tongue and pen, and made his cause attractive to the laity, and by various cavils and insults struck out at the prelates and theologians of the Church, accusing them of avarice, pride, envy, barbarous behavior, and ignorance: [they alleged that] these churchmen persecuted the innocent Luther for no reason other than his doctrine, which seemed to them – and was – more learned, and more conducive to speaking the truth, than the impostures and tricks of the hypocrites. All in all, the poets and rhetoricians were so strong not only in their intellect and their acrimony, but also in the elegance of their language, be it in speaking or in writing, that they easily drew the minds of the laity into favor and commiseration with Luther, as one who was being harried for the sake of truth and justice by the jealous, greedy, and unlearned Churchmen, while the Churchmen lived in leisure and luxury and extorted money from the simple people by exciting their superstitions.

Thus the authority of Tetzel, who earlier had been a collector of moneys because of his frequent sermons supporting indulgences, decreased more and more day by day among the populace due to these sorts of complaints and accusations by both Luther and the poets and rhetoricians. The devotion of the people to indulgences was diminished, the Pardoners and Commissaries were made hateful, the bands of bribe-givers grew smaller. But for Luther, on the other hand, authority, favor, trust, esteem, fame were all increasing, since he appeared to be so generous and keen an assertor of the truth against the deceits of the Pardoners and the empty promises of amulets, which the Commissaries of indulgences did not give freely, but sold for money. Meanwhile, at Rome a Citation was procured by Luther's enemies, by which Luther was called to trial before the Pope's Treasury. The judges appointed for that trial were Jerome de Genutii, Bishop of Ascoli, Auditor of the Chamber, and Sylvester Prierias, Theologian and Magistrate of the Holy Palace. But Luther complained about plots, which meant that he could never rest in safety, and about the judges, whom he suspected. Moreover, putting forth the pretext of his poverty and the weakness of his body, he begged through Frederick, Duke of Saxony, Elector Prince, that the case might be entrusted to the regions. It was therefore entrusted to Thomas de Vio Cajetan, Cardinal of S. Sixtus, who at that time was in Germany as a Legate at large of the Apostolic See. Although this judge as well was extremely displeasing to Luther, because he was a Thomist and of the Dominican Order, nevertheless – lest he seem entirely stubborn and rebellious – Luther appeared before him in Augsburg.

Luther came to Augsburg, therefore, in the month of October, having indeed brought with him letters and commendations from his protector Frederick the Elector, Duke of Saxony, but nevertheless without the public trust or safe conduct of the Emperor Maximilian. And so, kindly admitted into the presence and conversation of the Cardinal Legate, and paternally admonished, he was bidden to be answerable for three things, at the Pope's mandate. First, that he return to his senses, and renounce his errors. Second, that he promise that in future he would abstain from those errors. Third, that he would restrain himself from all things by which the Church might be disturbed. But since he did not wish to acknowledge any errors, after many speeches had been given and listened to on both sides in the conference, he asked for some time for deliberation. Therefore he returned on another day, when four men were present who were of the highest rank and were among the Emperor's Counselors, and in order to remove every suspicion of heresy from their minds, he personally read his protest before the Legate and recited it in these words, written on a piece of paper which he held in his hands. 'I, Martin Luther, an Augustinian brother, protest that I revere and follow the Holy Roman Church in all my words and deeds, present, past, and future. If anything has been or shall be said to the contrary or otherwise, I wish to hold it and have it held as not having been said.' [19]

But the Legate, a most learned man, knowing well that Luther had uttered many things about indulgences and the power of the Pope that were different from what the Church believed, not only in his resolutions but also in the recent conference, insisted again that he affirm those three things which he had heard by the Pope's mandate on the previous day. But Luther further protested that he was not conscious in himself of having said anything that was against Sacred Scripture, against the Church fathers, against the Decrees of the Pontiff, or against right reason. Nevertheless, since he was a human being who was able to err, he wished to submit himself to the judgment and determination of the Lawful, Holy Church, and to all those of better discernment. But in particular he wished to submit to the judgment of the Doctors of the illustrious Imperial Universities of Basel, Freiburg, and Louvain, or – if this were not enough – even of Paris, which he said was the parent of learned studies, and always most Christian from ancient times, and most flourishing in theology – although shortly thereafter he thought and wrote very differently about it.[20] But when the Legate persisted in his early opinion, Luther asked that a written answer (as he said) be accepted. When this was accepted, it included many arguments against the extravagance of Clement VI, about indulgences, against the Decretal authority of the Roman Pontificate, against the merits of the Saints, against the Depository of indulgences, and against the merits of good works, arguing haughtily about the One Faith.

From these things the Legate easily understood that Luther answered solely in words but held his mind fixed in its errors and opinions. Therefore the Legate said to him that, unless he recanted, he would be given to the censors, at the Pope's command, to be bound. But Luther had heard that the Legate had a mandate for seizing and incarcerating both him and his comrade Staupitz. For this reason he was full of anxiety. Since Luther was forbidden to return into the Legate's sight unless he recanted, he began secretly to solicit through friends, who were members of the Imperial household, for getting a safe conduct. When this was accomplished, supported by the advice of his friend Staupitz, he wrote an appeal, challenging the Legate to inform the Pope better; which appeal he ordered to be hung up publicly, when he had secretly left Augsburg, for the purpose of stirring up more envy in the people of the Pope and his Legate and more hatred among the laity. Nevertheless, however, he kept saying many things to the Legate, both in person to his face and through letters when he was absent, wickedly deceiving and deluding the good man by them. And even when he was about to leave Augsburg, he wrote flatteringly to the Legate, both thanking him for the clemency he had exhibited toward himself and excusing the necessity for an appeal, not only because his friends had bidden him to do thus, but also because he knew that an appeal would be much more pleasing to his Prince than a resummoning.[21] Beyond this, he added that an appeal did not seem necessary to him, since he would submit everything to the judgment of the Church, nor did he desire anything other than the Legate's opinion.

But when he had returned home, he wrote again much more flatteringly, pointing out and praising the Legate's clemency, gentleness, and wisdom, because although he was able to act through force, he had preferred to act through Staupitz, who was such and so great a man in Luther's eyes that there was no one in the world to whom he would more gladly listen and with whom he would more gladly agree. And where he admitted his fault, both of too much vehemence and of too much irreverence against the Pope, just there he begged for pardon, sorrowing and penitent as though purely and from his heart. And he promised that he would proclaim this in all his addresses to the people, and that he would see to the matter, that henceforward he would be different and would speak differently than before. He sought one thing zealously, that he might be able to hear the voice of the bride, as surely as to hear the voice of the groom.[22]

These things, and many others of this sort, he wrote in an honorable fashion to the Legate himself. But to others he wrote very differently, not only in private letters, but also publicly: very seriously accusing the Legate of tyranny, pride, infidelity, ignorance, and so forth. For thus he wrote in his *Acts*: 'I see' (he said) 'that books have been published, and various rumors spread, about my actions in Augsburg. But in truth I did nothing there, except that I lost both time and money. Unless the following made it worth the trouble, that I there heard a new Latin language: that is, that to teach the truth is the same thing as to throw the Church into disorder. But to flatter, and to deny Christ, that is to pacify and exalt the Church.'[23]

In his second appeal, he said that the Legate was too greatly moved by his brothers against Luther's cause, and that he had put on an appearance of iniquity, and that he had used dire and most cruel threats, and that he held in contempt the sheep of Christ, who was seeking humbly to be taught the truth and to be led back from error. The same thing, in his preface to Galatians: 'Cardinal Cajetan' (he said) 'farmed himself out everywhere in Germany on behalf of the Roman Church, feigning – under the name of its *Brevia Apostolica* – to be very learned.'[24] Finally, in his second letter to Leo X, he most seriously and at the same time most maliciously accused the Legate when he said: 'I think it is known to you what your Legate, the Cardinal of S. Sixtus (an ignorant, unhappy and, in fact, faithless man) did with me. When through reverence of your name I placed myself and all my goods in his hands, he did not act in such a way as to establish peace, which he could easily have established with one little word, when I promised him silence, and that I would make an end of my cause, if he would order the same thing to be done by my adversaries. But this man of glory, not content with that agreement, began to justify my adversaries, and to lay bare his power, and to order a recantation from me, which, in a word, he did not have in his orders. And so clearly, when the case was in the best place, it came into a worse one by far due to the cruel tyranny of this man. Therefore, whatever happened after these things, the fault is entirely the Cardinal's, not Luther's, since he would not allow me to be silent and to become inactive – which I then sought with all my powers; what more could I have done?' [25]

Therefore, both so that he might appear victor over the Legate, and that he might acquire for himself greater fame and trust and authority, Luther wrote in his *Acts* that the Legate had never produced any syllable from the Sacred Scriptures against himself, nor could he, even if he desired to as greatly as possible. On the contrary, when Luther brought out Scripture, the Legate brought out his explanations from memory, according to the long tradition of the Roman Curia. 'It is for this reason that, when the Holy Scriptures have been left to one side and the traditions and words of human beings have been accepted, the Church of Christ is fed neither by a measure of wheat nor by the word of Christ. Rather, it is controlled by the not uncommon boldness and willfulness of some completely unlearned flatterer, and the magnitude of our unhappiness has reached that point at which they begin to compel us to the renunciation and abnegation of the Christian faith and of the most holy Scripture.' [26]

Luther increased his own favor and reputation in the eyes of many by this sort of complaint, and he increased the hatred and contempt toward his adversaries. And so he even dared, through the authority of his Protector and Prince, to issue a public written challenge in Wittenberg to certain Inquisitors of heretical wickedness, that any persons who believed they could eat iron and break stones should come there to dispute with him, and that they would not only have safe conduct but would even have free hospitality and provisions from his Prince. Tossing about these things and many others of this sort, and claiming that his own knowledge of the Scriptures was superior to all others', he drew many over to his side: charging that not only the learned Theologians, but also the Pope himself and his Decretals, did violence to the Scriptures, and distorted them, and interpreted them improperly and abusively. And he often exclaimed about those who wished that the Scriptures be interpreted otherwise than he wished, that they were a hundredfold worse than Turks: since they wickedly reduced the Word of God, which sanctifies everything, into nothing. And indeed at that time he feigned modesty, humility, and obedience by very soothing words, so that he might render his faction larger and more agreeable; but his heart was always filled with sharpness, pride, and rebellion, as he himself made abundantly clear in various places.

For he says to the Reader, in his *Acts*: 'Even if I gave my later response with great reverence, and as though I relied on the judgment of the Highest Pontiff, nevertheless do not believe that I did this because I felt doubt about the matter itself, or that I would ever change the opinion of my mind, but because it was necessary to respect the reverence of the man who was performing the office of the Highest Pontiff.' [27] However, he had said in the Response that his soul was completely prepared to yield, to change, to retract everything, when once it had been taught that things should be understood differently; but how could he be taught, who would never change the opinion of his mind?

Who scorned not only the Legate (a man of the highest learning in all respects, whom Luther himself admitted was endowed with outstanding talents, above all in sharpness of judgment), but also the Pope of Rome, Leo X? Who showed the most vehement contempt for Sylvester Prieras, the Magistrate of the Sacred Palace, together with S. Thomas? Slanders on all sides, which depended on words alone, without Scripture, without the Fathers, without the Canons, finally without any reasons. Therefore, he was only mouthing words when he promised that he would recant.

1519

However, the year of the Lord 1519 was already in progress. After the Emperor Maximilian – a Prince especially noteworthy both in arms and in piety – was removed from human affairs, Luther began to become more and more haughty daily. He began to attack his adversaries more seriously with insults and accusations, and to rebel from the Supreme Pontiff with greater contempt. Indeed he rebelled so much more ferociously that, in his second letter to Leo X, he even made the repeated claim that Charles von Miltitz, the Apostolic Nuncio, while running to and fro on various matters after Cajetan, and omitting nothing that pertained to repairing the state of the legal case (which Cajetan had troubled obstinately and proudly) nevertheless scarcely managed, even with the help of the Most Illustrious Prince Elector Frederick, to speak with Luther even once or twice in a friendly fashion. An astounding insolence and pride indeed, in a not yet uncowled monk, who was then appearing as defendant before the Highest Pontiff, his supreme judge on earth, on account of his reprehensible and heretical dogma, and furthermore on account of the disturbed peace of the Church, and the wounded authority – sacrosanct according to every law – of the Apostolic See! Insolence to such a degree that he himself wrote privately to Cajetan in these words: 'Most Reverend Father in Christ, I confess, as I have confessed elsewhere, that indeed I have been overly indiscreet – as my enemies themselves say – vehement and irreverent against the office of the Pontiff. And although I was certainly vehemently provoked to irreverence of this sort, nevertheless I now understand that it was befitting for me to treat this matter modestly, humbly, and reverently, and not to respond to a fool in such a way that I would seem similar to him. All of which now sincerely grieves me, and I beg for pardon.'[28]

In the same way, although he was a defendant who had neither been absolved nor granted a delay, but very gravely accused and in fact condemned in the city for his stubbornness, so great was his rebellion and his pride shortly afterwards that, as though it were rather a matter of high treason by an enemy conspirator or an Emperor than of a defendant or a Monk, he began to praise his own rank, no longer seeking pardon for any sin, but comparing his own cowl to the sacred headgear of the Highest Pontiff. Indeed he preferred (so he bragged most arrogantly) his own rank to that of the Apostolic Nuncio – a nobleman born of the famous Miltitz family of Meissen – who had constantly run to and fro in much labor, and had at length scarcely managed, by the aid of the Prince Elector, to be admitted once or twice into familiar conversation, because of the state of the case, which had been disturbed by Cajetan. Indeed, what Emperor – either of the Greeks or the Latins or the Germans – was ever said to have repelled Apostolic Nuncios with such disdain from a conference, as (so he boasted) this Monk had done, who was still cowled and a defendant, and one who only a few days earlier had appealed from the Legate to the Apostolic Ruler himself? And he boasted further, that in that Conference he had again yielded to the name of Leo X, because he was prepared to be silent, accepting as a judge either the Archbishop of Trier or the Bishop of Nuremberg, and so it had been done and effected. But while these things were being carried out in good hope, he said that another, greater enemy of the Pontiff – namely Eck – had arisen, through the disputation of Leipzig, which the Pope had instituted against Dr Karlstadt, and this new enemy had completely overthrown that council of peace. For now Luther seemed so great to himself, that he considered it a great boon and beneficence, and wished it to be called agreeable on his part, as though it were in some degree an exceedingly great gift, if he should grant peace to the Pontiff and his emissary, and be silent.

Dr Johannes Eck,[29] a most greatly learned man, had come to Leipzig by agreement to debate with Andreas Karlstadt. But when indeed Eck added one theme, concerning the prerogative and the power of the Roman Church, to Luther's twelve propositions that were going to be debated there, Luther – who was a most shameless hater and detractor of the Roman Church – thought that this had been done as an injury to himself (for he would quickly consider anyone who disagreed with him as an enemy), and of his own accord injected himself into that debate, although he had been neither invited nor summoned. At that time Luther and Karlstadt were the greatest friends, although they later became equally great enemies. Karlstadt was the Archdeacon of Wittenberg; Luther the *Praelector Ordinarius* of Theology; each one trusted very greatly in himself, and considered himself the most erudite of anyone in the world, and continually sought the glory of reputation through debating. Both of them envied Eck, who was a Professor of Theology at Ingolstadt and had gained the prestigious title of Disputator at Freiburg, Tubingen, Ingolstadt, Vienna, and even at Bologna, and desired to take praise away from him.

Moreover, an occasion for debate was taken from certain of the 'Obelisks' (that is, refuting annotations) which Eck had written privately concerning Luther's first propositions about indulgences, when a certain friend had asked him what he thought about the propositions. Karlstadt wrote against Eck in order to avenge that injury. But Eck, unafraid, ran boldly to meet the attacker. And so the matter began with skirmishes of books; an appropriate site for the battle and place for debate was sought; finally, by agreement both parties consented to Leipzig (a town famous, certainly, for its market and its University, but much more notable for the virtue and integrity of its Prince, namely the most Illustrious Duke George of Saxony).[30] On a certain day which was agreed upon by the consent of both parties, they came together there for debate, although this was vehemently displeasing to the Bishop of Merseburg, who was serving in the place of the Ordinary, and to the Theologians of Leipzig, who would have preferred that such a debate be prohibited and omitted.

But before that day dawned, there was a certain friendly contest between those two luminaries of Wittenberg, which they had already carried out in published books, in their exceedingly great contempt for Eck. Luther, on the one hand, wished to fight on Karlstadt's behalf for the sake of humility, since Eck was not worthy that a man of such dignity and eminence as the Archdeacon of Wittenberg should meet him in battle. But Karlstadt, for his part, challenged Eck for the purpose of championing Luther because of Eck's 'Obelisks.' In addition, Luther wrote in his Preface to the reader that Eck, the execration of the Apostolic See, used the words of the Scriptures and the Fathers as though they were the elements of Anaxagoras: and that, concerning the Apostle, Eck understood neither what was said nor what things the Apostle affirmed.[31] 'But' (he wrote) 'Karlstadt, who for a long time had been victor over the error of Eck, was going to appear not as a fugitive soldier, but would surely leave Eck as a dead lion,[32] prostrate before him.[33] Truly,' (Luther said), 'he himself feared in this matter neither the Pope nor the name of the Pope, much less these old men and dolls.'[34]

Therefore, on the appointed day (which was 27 June), the Wittenbergers came to Leipzig with great pomp. There were not only many comrades, but also they brought with them books as reserve troops – as though there were no books in Leipzig, if there should be any need of them. But Eck, who had to fear not only thieves and robbers but also the swords and tricks of Luther's adherents who were gnashing their teeth at him, came to Leipzig accompanied by only one servant, an unknown man among unknown men, traveling a much longer road than they did, since Ingolstadt is forty German miles distant from Leipzig, but Wittenberg only seven. They were all received with both friendship and honor, not only by the Senate and the University, but even by the Prince and Lord of the city, George Duke of Saxony. He not only enjoined his Counselors to maintain the equality of either side, but even allowed a place in his own citadel to the disputants, lest any disturbance arise, and furthermore honored the debate with his personal presence. And he warned the disputants kindly, through his own seriousness and prudence, that they should beware of any bitterness in their words or any stumbling block for the weaker people, and that they should have truth alone before their eyes.

Therefore, Eck and Karlstadt met first, to debate about man's Free Will; both solemnly protested that they never wished to depart so much as a finger's breadth from the Catholic Church, nor to go beyond the judgment of the learned, nor to prejudge the authority of the Universities. But Karlstadt did not find a dead lion there in Eck, as Luther had boasted, but a man far more energetic in intellect and quickness than Karlstadt was himself: in fact, in the remarkably good vivacity of his memory, he exceeded Luther himself, and in learning and the acuteness of his intellect he yielded nothing to either of them. Certainly Karlstadt, fighting it out with him over several days, gained more labor than praise. For he was greatly inferior to Dr Eck in everything. Luther bore this badly, and on the feast of the Apostles Peter and Paul he preached a sermon to the people in the chapel of the Citadel.[35] And indeed in that sermon, since he had a numerous audience, he openly and bitterly attacked both the authority of the Pope and the power of the keys, not without giving offense to many. Whence it happened that shortly thereafter Dr Eck publicly reproached this sermon of Luther's (which was also made public by the typesetters) when on the second day of July, in the festival of the Visitation of Mary, he addressed the people in the Parish Church of St Nicholas.

Luther succeeded Karlstadt, who was already worn out and exhausted by the debate, in the battle from the 4th to the 13th day of July. But there was a long discussion between the Counselors of Prince George and Luther, before he entered into debate with Eck. For he hesitated for a long time to submit himself to certain judges; for he greatly preferred the judgment of the common and confused multitude to that of Doctors in the University. When, however, he was not able to refuse honestly on any pretext, at length he agreed (although unwilling and angry) to judges from Paris and from the Theological faculty of Erfurt. Certainly among these judges he found greater familiarity and favor than did Eck, since he (Luther) had been educated in letters among them. Truly, he hoped to find among them judges who would approve the attacker, since they had recently been offended by the Pope in the case of Reuchlin and in the privileges of the French clergy, rather than those who would take the part of the defender of the Roman Church. However, he would have preferred to have poets, mockers of theologians, and the common people, who hate the clergy, as judges of his case instead of any theologians at all.

And so, when the Counselors of Duke George saw his wrathful face, they admonished him that he should do nothing through anger, but everything modestly, lest he be made a scandal to his listeners. Then he, overcome by anger, burst out into the open confession of his worst secret, saying 'This matter was not begun because of God, nor shall it be finished because of God.' But they ignored this statement, so that this debate which had been announced to the world should not become a laughing-stock, and they soothed his mind, so that he would dispute with Eck according to his promise. And so they debated, both bitterly and at length, first about the power and primacy of the Roman Church, then about Purgatory, about indulgences, about Penitence and about the Absolution of the priest. But at that time both Luther's mind (unless he dissembled everything) and his speech were very different concerning these matters than shortly afterward. For he, too, approved and embraced the declaration which the other two had made, and he spoke much more reverently about the Roman Church than he did afterwards: to such an extent that, declaring his opinion not only in Latin but also in German, he said that he would not attack the primacy and obedience of the Roman Church, nor could it be attacked by anyone in a Christian fashion; nor would he deprive the Pontiff of anything that was owing to him.

And since during the debate he had been suspected, from his words, of being a supporter and patron of the Bohemian schismatics, as Dr Eck openly accused him, he himself quickly exclaimed angrily, in German, that this was a lie. Then in responding more seasonably, rejecting this same thing as though it were a grave insult to him, he said the following: 'No evil schism that the Bohemians make has ever pleased me or will ever please me; because they, by their own authority, separate themselves from our unity, just as if a divine law were set up on their behalf, when the supreme divine law is charity and unity of the spirit.'[36] Therefore he asked of Eck that he not hurl such an insult at him, making him out to be a Bohemian, since they had always been hateful to him because they dissented from unity. Finally, although he also said strange and scandalous things about Purgatory, as for instance that there was nothing concerning it in the Scriptures, for which reason he was suspected of the heresy of the Greeks and Beghards (who deny Purgatory), for the purpose of removing that suspicion from himself, he said publicly:

'I, who strongly believe, indeed I dare say I *know* that Purgatory exists, am easily persuaded that there is mention of it made in the Scriptures: As this, which Gregory mentions in his Dialogue on Matthew: It shall not be pardoned, either in this age, nor in the future — signifying that certain sins are pardoned in Purgatory. I admit also this passage of 2 Machabees: It is a holy and wholesome thought, to pray for the dead, etc.'[37]

When Luther had at length been worn out, the intrepid and indefatigable Eck once again confronted Karlstadt who returned into the arena on the 14th day of July. Eck was summoned there by Karlstadt at the same hour that Luther had withdrawn, so that even if Eck (a pilgrim separated both from his books and from his well-known friends in a foreign region) could not be conquered by arguments, he might at least leave the arena, worn out by labor and by distaste for insults, and might display an appearance of having been conquered. Therefore, the argument returned to the question of man's free will. And that adversary added this to the paradox: 'That a just man sins in every good deed.' But this disputation lasted only a few days. For it was soon brought to an end, on the 15th day of July, and the whole case was referred to the Judges.

And so the Wittenbergers returned home. They had been honored exceedingly when they came to Leipzig, but they returned to Wittenberg with far less glory than they had hoped. For they had not believed that Eck would be such a man as they had found him. Therefore, since they had little trust in the outcome of the oral disputation, they took refuge in books, quickly publishing as though their position were victorious, before they knew what the Judges, chosen by each side, would rule — although it had been established at Leipzig that no one would publish about this disputation before the opinion of the Judges was known. Now, about the Erfurters and how they would rule, nothing was clearly known. But it was not possible to doubt that the Parisians would judge for Eck's side, since they not long before condemned Luther's 104 propositions in a criminal judgment, and published open testimony. But Luther published a letter, full of spleen and complaints, written to his friend Spalatin, who was a confidential advisor to Frederick, the Duke Elector, in matters sacred and secular, and who had performed many services for him secretly. In this letter Luther of course wrote many things that were very far from the truth, just as Eck demonstrated in his answer. The letter's beginning was as follows. 'My dearest Spalatin, you wish to know the story of this famous disputation which we had at Leipzig.' [38] He says that the disputation was a waste of time, not an inquiry into the truth; and however much there was in Eck, he had in no way touched upon his goal. Or if it was touched upon, it was not argued by anything except the most well-known and well-worn arguments. Then Luther began to assault the Leipzigers, saying: 'Let them attribute it to themselves, not to me, if they themselves are affected, whom an equal desire for glory and an unrestrained, long-established envy drove to scheme evil schemes against us on Eck's behalf.' [39] However, he did admit that he owed nothing to that excellent University except all honor and all duty, although the envy of certain people was displeasing to him. But nevertheless he praised Duke George, because truly the clemency and munificence of that Prince omitted nothing which could tend toward the most happy outcome of that debate, since he was on his guard toward everything and warned the participants that the debate should be carried on modestly and with zeal for seeking the truth. Still, Luther added many things that amounted to insults and complaints against the Duke's Counselors.

'For first,' he said, 'the pact was broken, by which it had been agreed between Eck and us that the matter would be freely discussed and that excerpts made by Notaries would be published for the public judgment of the whole world. But the Counselors decreed that the excerpts would not be published unless offered by judges who had been elected in common and by name, and unless they themselves accepted the ruling – as though the judgment of the world and of whatsoever best man you wish was insufficient.' He said that there was another scheme: When Karlstadt brought books with him, at Eck's will they set up a statute, that books must be left at home, and that the debate must be held through the strength and freedom of memory alone, orally. But when the objection was made to him that publishing the debate before the judges' decree neither complied with the pact nor saved the treaty, he answered thus: 'As if they themselves ever obeyed any pact made with us!' And he added that he had agreed that the debate which was excerpted by the hand of Notaries not be published, but that he had not promised that he himself would write no further. Once again, praising Duke George, he said that the Duke, chastising both sides most prudently, had said 'Whether it is so by divine law or by human law, the Roman Pontiff is and remains the Highest Pontiff.' He had spoken in this way truthfully and not lightly, and reproached their useless debate with this notable sobriety. Therefore when Luther, who considered the applause of the multitude the highest good, sensed that his disputation was less plausible to the people of Leipzig, he poured out all his anger against Eck (who was on everyone's lips as the victor, or certainly as Luther's equal and Karlstadt's superior), attacking him with innumerable insults through many varied pamphlets and letters. He even dared to complain of Eck openly and most seriously to Leo X, as though everything everywhere were disturbed and wounded by the lies, deceits, and tricks of Eck. 'Here is that enemy of yours, my Leo,' he said, 'or rather of your Curia, who preferring trouble to power, so long as he may snatch furiously at his own glory, reveals Rome's shame to the whole world. By the example of this one man we can learn' (he said) 'that there is no enemy more harmful than a flatterer. For what does he accomplish by his flattery, except an evil which no king was ever able to accomplish? Today the name of the Roman Curia stinks throughout the world, and the authority of the Pope weakens, and is in ill repute due to infamous ignorance – none of which we would hear, if Eck had not disturbed my and Charles von Miltitz's council about peace.'[40]

Jerome Emser, a man who was both exceedingly eloquent and exceedingly learned, wrote a certain letter about this disputation, to Dr Johannes Zack, the Administrator of the Church of Prague, when he heard that the Bohemians were boasting that Luther had defended their viewpoint. And truly in that letter, which investigated the truth of the matter most soberly and equally, setting aside every insult and detraction by Luther, he asserted that he had not defended the side of the Bohemians, but had openly spoken against them; but Eck, a most powerful Theologian, had keenly defended their propositions. However, Luther, whether because in the meantime he had obtained books by Jan Hus (whom he greatly esteemed) from Bohemia, or whether he was considering his own shame that Eck had been called 'a most powerful Theologian,' soon wrote – most petulantly – *A certain Hunting-Expedition against Emser the Goat-Horned* (for Emser had this symbol on his arms, inherited from his elders).[41] This letter was so exuberant in its insults, so biting in its scoffing, so bitter in its calumnies, that Emser – who only a short time before had received Luther with honor at a banquet in Dresden – appeared to have been buried rather than merely attacked. Luther certainly used this as a precaution, so that he might endeavor to terrify his adversaries by the bitter reiteration and clamor of his insults, and offer them as laughing-stocks before everyone. For he spoke as follows to Leo X: 'Concerning this very matter I am in such an uproar, with so great a spirit, that I may suppress those whom I perceived to be greatly unequal to me, more by the magnitude and force of many words than by my spirit.'

But he did not drive that mighty 'goat-horned' man[42] into either flight or hiding by this stratagem of his; rather, Emser answered that hearty hunter, the Saxon Nimrod, and struck back, putting many other objections against Luther very seriously and the following most seriously of all: that when he himself was elected by Duke George to the Counselors of Leipzig, he had heard from Luther's mouth 'This matter was not begun because of God, nor shall it be finished because of God.' Certainly Luther's reputation among good people was seriously wounded by this blow, especially since Luther remained silent about it for so long, his defendant's conscience neither contradicting it nor even complaining, but cleverly dissembling for twenty months. However, there was another struggle between him and Emser in the meantime, through published pamphlets. For he responded to none of his adversaries more frequently than to him. At length, when he was very frequently urged by his friends to make a statement that would repel so heavy a mark of suspicion from himself, he wrote a certain pamphlet in German, in which he tried to convict Eck of lying, but did so by pure deceits and trifles, not by any solid argument, but by the empty jangling of rhetorical exclamations. Soon, therefore, Eck refuted his trifles with certain proofs, and gravely checked his futile mockery in a manuscript[43] addressed to Tetzel and in other reproaches, and drove this Monk, as verbose as he had been before then, to be silent.

When the dispute was finished, Charles von Miltitz, so that he might bear the praise of bringing peace from his country to Rome, once more tried to reduce Luther to silence. But Luther boasted thus about this matter to Leo X: 'While we' (he said) 'were doing nothing to promote this dispute, apart from the greater confusion of the Roman case, now for the third time Charles von Miltitz comes before the fathers of the Order, assembled in the Chapter; he seeks advice about composing his case, which was already most disturbed and dangerous. Some of the most famous men among them are sent here to me, since (for God is gracious) there is no hope of attacking me by force. These men request that I at least honor Your Holiness's rank, and that I excuse both your innocence and mine in letters of humility: the matter is not yet at the final pitch of desperation, if Leo X, through his innate goodness, will set his hand to it.' And a little later, the rebel monk dared to prescribe the laws of peace to the highest Pontiff. He added, 'No one should assume, Most Holy Father, that I will hereafter make a recantation, unless he wishes to involve his cause in a still greater storm. Furthermore, I will not endure laws for interpreting the word of God, since it is proper that the word of God, which teaches the liberty of all other things, should itself be unfettered. Excepting these two things, there is nothing which I cannot do or suffer, and so I would most heartily wish. I hate quarrels, I will challenge no one, but I do not wish to be challenged in return. Moreover, when once I have been challenged, with Christ as my teacher I will not be voiceless.'[44]

Meanwhile the Elector Princes of Frankfurt were gathered in Mainz, since the Emperor Maximilian had died. They happily elected in his place his grandson, the most powerful Prince of many realms and provinces, Charles V. He was then passing his time far away in the realms of Spain. And certainly, since he was still a youth, many occasions were sought, on various pretexts, of approaching him and drawing him into Luther's camp: to such an extent, that the Lutherans persuaded themselves with the utmost certainty that Charles would be a wholehearted Lutheran. The deserts of Frederick the Elector, Duke of Saxony, were bandied about; accusations were cast at the Roman Pontiff and his Legate, that they had desired the King of France to be elected and had denounced Charles, both in secret and openly. Insults and well-known pamphlets against the Pope and against certain bishops and theologians were published. Then Luther himself, urged on by the advice of his associates, wrote a letter to the same Charles in feigned humility, minutely filled with hateful complaints against his adversaries. He even added an offering or declaration, none the less false and malicious for being pleasing to him. He aroused the hatred of the Emperor, his courtiers, and indeed of the whole people toward the Pope and the theologians, by publishing books of this sort.

Therefore he says in that letter, after seeking Charles's benevolence through flattery: 'Several books have been published by me, through which I brought down upon myself the envy and indignation of many great men, when I should have been safe through a double guard. First, because I came unwillingly into the public eye, nor would I have written whatever I wrote had I not been betrayed by the force and tricks of others. For I was always seeking, by the greatest devotions, nothing other than to hide myself in my corner. Second, because I testify according to my conscience, and according to the judgment of the best men I was zealous to publish nothing except the Gospel truth, as opposed to the superstitious opinions of human tradition. For this reason the third year is now almost ended, during which I continually suffer wrath, insults, dangers, and whatever evil people are able to think up. In vain I seek pardon, in vain I offer silence, in vain I propose conditions of peace, in vain I seek to be instructed in better things. One thing alone is prepared against me – that I should be destroyed, along with the universal Gospel. However, when I had tried everything in vain, at length it seemed good to me, following the example of St Athanasius, to call upon the Imperial Majesty, if by chance the Lord would deign, through that Majesty, to help his own cause.'[45]

And in his declaration he says: 'But I did not even accomplish this, which I had offered frequently, readily, and in many ways (as a suppliant and obedient son of the Holy Catholic Church – as which, with the best and greatest God as my helper, I hope to die), that I would be silent, if it were permitted by my adversaries, and that I would endure the examination and sentence of all Universities that were not suspect, before unsuspect judges, both sacred and profane, under proper and sufficient public faith, with free conduct; and that I would prepare myself freely and humbly, and that I would accept their examination and judgment.'[46]

Many complaints of this type were strewn through the crowd, not only by Luther himself, but also by his confederates, especially by numerous poets and rhetoricians, who were troublesome to the theologians and monks in the town, not only on Luther's account, but also because of Johann Reuchlin and Erasmus of Rotterdam – truly most learned men, and magnificently accomplished in letters and languages, who had grounds for discussion and disagreement with the poets and rhetoricians. And not a few lawyers and courtiers, who were distinguished for their riches, authority, and grace, did many things on Luther's behalf against the churchmen. They worked not so much through printed books as in letters and speech, sometimes secretly in the Princes' ears and sometimes openly before the people; and as the hatred of the laypeople toward the clerics grew, they continued cleverly increasing it by their slanders. And the German knight Ulrich Hutten, a man of both a noble lineage and of the keenest wit, most of all enflamed the minds not only of the princes and nobles, but also of the townsfolk and the rustics. For previously, even before Luther's name was known throughout the world, Hutten had written many things concerning the liberty of Germany, arguing against the seeking of pensions and the annoyances of summonses, by which the Roman Curia appeared to weigh Germany down. He was vigorous and keen not only in legal formulae, but also in common speech. He then had published the *Roman Triad*, certainly a slight book, but wonderfully witty and sufficiently plausible and acceptable to the laity due to the argument of its ingenious originality. Certainly he ensured, by means of this book, that nothing was equally hateful to most Germans as the name of the Roman Curia and its officials.

1520

Luther seized that opportunity and began to write a certain *Reformation* in German, addressed to Charles V who had just then been elected Emperor, and to the Christian nobility of Germany.[47] And in it, obviously in order to alienate everyone's mind from the Roman Pontiff and from his Curia and jurisdiction, he renounced as strongly as possible the Roman Curia's ostentation and abuses, most hatefully ridiculing whatever either was reprehensible in it or was able at least to appear reprehensible. And in addition, he further added slanders, neither trivial nor few, against the Roman Popes. Along with other things, he made mention of many things which the Popes had done in opposition to the [Holy] Roman Emperors and other Princes, since they had engendered wars out of wars, and had everywhere sown disagreements among Kings and Princes, through which disagreements they might increase their own power, since the Kings would be exhausted, impoverished, and reduced to extremes by the provisions of war and the expense.

And so that he might inspire the new Emperor, who was still young, to show greater hostility toward the Roman Pope and all clergy, he busied himself in proving, with many reasons and arguments from the Holy Scriptures, that the sword of the Emperor had free power over everyone, not only laity but clergy as well, without any impediment. For there was not any difference between laity and Clergy except a fictitious one, saving a difference in office, since we are all consecrated as priests by baptism; with the result that anyone at all who has received baptism is able to claim that he is already priest, bishop, and Pope; it is permissible for anyone, not only those for whom it is appropriate, to exercise that office. Made more bold by this argument, he openly advised rebellion from the Pope, saying: 'Therefore the Papal power ought not to be submitted to, but rather resisted with our bodies, our substance, and with all the strengths of which we are capable. Let us therefore be vigilant, O dear Germans, lest we become equally responsible for all unhappy souls, which have perished through this wicked and diabolical regimen of the Romans.'[48]

By these writings and many others of this sort, although exceedingly harshly written, he put forward an appearance of piety. And he placed the healing name of Jesus on individual pages in the front of the book, so that the reader might believe that all these things had been suggested to him by the spirit of Christ and were tending toward the best result. So he first subjected the Pope and the Bishops to the sword of the Emperor in this *Reformation*. Then he took away the authority of the Pope both to interpret the sacred Scripture and to appoint a general council. Having tried these things by varied deceit, drawn both from Scriptures and reason, he then began to inveigh bitterly against the morals and practices of the Roman Curia, criticizing each matter separately and, through slanders, presenting everything in the worst light. Therefore he exclaimed that it was a shameful thing that the Pope wore a triple crown, when the highest kings bore a single one; that he was the vicar of the crucified Christ, not of the exalted Christ; that his Cardinals were a useless, nay rather a harmful people, who sucked Italy and Germany dry. From the Papal household, he said, one hundredth part should be retained, and ninety-nine parts of it abolished; the first-year fruits [49] of bishoprics should be abolished, and the Papal Months; confirmations of Bishops should be thrown out, as should the Archbishops' robes. The house of the Papal Chancery was a brothel beyond all brothels. The Pope had no right to be compared to the kingdom of Naples and Sicily – everything which he possessed was force and plunder; the Roman Excommunication, together with its letters and tokens, should be plunged into a cold bath; the Canon Law, from the first letters to the very last, should be utterly destroyed, above all the Decretal Law, and so forth.

And so when he perceived that this book also was not only being read with calm minds by his friends among the laity, but was also being accepted and attended to with approval, he was made even more bold. He attempted and even accomplished an outrage that was certainly extremely bold, and unheard of throughout all previous ages; namely, he publicly condemned to the fire and burned the sacred canons, and the decrees of the holy fathers, and all the Pontifical law together with the Papal Bulls, and the letters and signs of indulgences, and of other Papal favors.

And he even published a book about this great crime, boasting about himself, so that the fame of the deed should be spread further. In this book, wishing to give a reason for the burning, he recounted thirty articles collected from the volume of the Decrees, which he considered absurd and impious. Twisting them into the worst sense by misrepresentations, he scourged them with many taunts and insults, and at last added these words: 'In these articles and others of this type, of which there are an uncountable number, but all of them arguing that the Pope is superior both to God and to all human beings, and that he alone is subject to no mortal, but all other beings, even God and the Angels, are subject to him.[50] So the disciples of the Pope say that the Pope is a marvelous thing: that he is not God, but he is not a man; perhaps he is the Devil and Satan himself.' [51] Later on he says, 'This is the sum and summation [52] of the whole Canon law: that the Pope is God on earth, the superior of all heavenly, terrestrial, spiritual and secular beings, and that all things are appropriate for the Pope, to whom no one dares say, What are you doing?' [53]

But Ambrosius Catharinus of Italy, obviously a very learned man, who had earlier refuted his errors and undertakings most keenly in five books, responded to him, so seriously and truly, in these words: 'Truly this is the sum and summation of all your follies, since you have displayed nothing but falsehoods and lies, to which it would be most foolish to respond. For if you persuade your mob of these things, setting aside any contradiction, surely there exists nothing so discordant or so absurd that you would not be able to persuade them of it also. For who could believe that in the Decrees the Pope is said to be superior to God, or to the Scripture, or to all heavenly things? What pious ears could receive this most cruel blasphemy, that the Papacy is the government of the Antichrist? In that case, were so many holy, proven men leaders in the Antichrist's government – Gregory, Leo, and their predecessors,[54] men full of knowledge and the spirit of God? O world, truly resting upon evil! The most malignant serpent heaps insults and pours his venom out, not only upon the rank or evil character of the Pope, but upon the office, the See, the Majesty that was appointed and immovably founded by God, etc.'[55]

And so Luther, already secure in popular opinion, and propped up by the favor of certain nobles, and trusting in the praises and defenses of the rhetoricians and the poets, proceeded most boldly to all imaginable misdeeds. He renewed before the Council his appeal against the Pope, as though it were against the Antichrist and one who denied the Scriptures. He pursued the Director of the Sacred Palace with dire curses and insults, because of an Epitome the Director had published – indeed, he even publicly summoned him to arms. 'Truly it seems to me' (he said) 'that if the madness of the Romanists continues thus, no remedy will be left except that the Emperor, Kings, and Princes, girded with strength and arms, should attack these plagues of the entire earth, and decide the matter not with words, but with the sword. For what do these lost men – who lack even common sense – babble, except that which it was foretold the Antichrist would do? If we punish thieves with the fork, robbers with the sword, heretics with fire, why do we not all the more, with all available weapons, fall upon these teachers of perdition, these Cardinals, these Popes, and all that conflux of the Roman Sodom, which continually corrupts the Church of God? Why do we not wash our hands in their blood?'[56]

This defendant proclaimed these things, and many others of this sort, as fiercely as possible against his judges. The Director of the Sacred Palace was present among them as a delegate; the Pope was supreme. And when the theologians of Louvain condemned several of Luther's propositions, books and sermons by name in a certain doctrinal criticism, and the theologians of Cologne followed them, and published a very similar condemnation, Luther was quickly incited by rage and inveighed against them with insults and misrepresentations. 'It is said' (he wrote) 'that the Gospel of Christ may not be proclaimed before the Turks. But if, among these doctrinal damnation-mongers, the Bull corresponds to their confidence and their great arrogance, what tyranny of the Turks could be compared with it?' And below he wrote, 'First, therefore, the trust of pronouncing judgments must be taken from our Directors, whether

they are true ones or feigned; and it must be demonstrated how much need
there is of mainstays in whom one might trust, when these have rarely judged
well, but have frequently – indeed almost always – judged badly. Nay, since
someone who is evil once should be presumed evil always, according to the
rule of law, then we must not trust any of our Directors at all, in any place
whatsoever, on any occasion whatsoever, concerning any thing whatsoever.
For it is certain that their judgment has already for many years been not only
capricious and hasty, but also erroneous, heretical, bold, and blind – such that
no one should trust in it securely, except for someone whom a wrathful God
decrees shall be deceived by the workings of error.' [57]

To support this matter he added certain examples, namely, that they had
unjustly condemned William Occam, without doubt the prince of all learned
scholastics (he said), and a man of keenest intellect; and they had unjustly
condemned Giovanni Pico, Count of Mirandola, and Lorenzo Valla, whom he
called either the last spark of the Primitive Church or a new tinder. And after
these, they had condemned Johannes Reuchlin, from whom, he said, the Theologians of the five Universities learned what they knew, what they understood,
what they sought. And so that he might further weaken the Directors' authority,
he often mocked them in other pamphlets as well with insults and slanders,
adding everywhere in the margin of the book, if something appeared to him
to have been said unskillfully, these ridiculous adverbs which he had invented
himself: Louvainly, Colognely, Nostraly, etc., so that through contempt and
scurrilous insults he might take away from them their authority as students
of literature and their reputation for doctrine in the eyes of the common people
and the youth – although in August he had respectfully requested men from
Louvain as his judges.

But against both Dr Johannes Eck and the Augustine brother Alveld (a pious
and erudite man, who belonged to the Franciscan order), he published most
bitter pamphlets in German, by which he rendered his cause more agreeable
to the people. In writing about Eck, in fact, he used this beginning: 'That Dr
Eck has returned to Rome is made clear to me by trustworthy signs. From
these it is most certain that just as earlier in Bavaria, Switzerland, Austria, the
Rhineland, Rome, and Bologna, now also in Meissen and Saxony, he is recognized and denounced as a false man who lies and deceives in whatever he
speaks, writes, and does, just as many learned, serious men have demonstrated
about him before now in "Unlearned Canons" and "Eck Hewn Down." ' (These
were two books published against Eck). 'But now he has wished to declare
openly his Roman protection, and has declared that he himself has conquered
lies. For Rome now produces such men, and no others.' [58]

But against Alveld he wrote thus in his preface. 'If Leipzig produced such
giants, it is fitting for that land to have a rich ground. Listen so that you may
understand what I want. Sylvester, Cajetan, Eck, Emser, and now the people
of Cologne and Louvain, displayed their extraordinary and warlike misdeeds
against me, and followed honor and glory according to their own worth. They
defended the cause of the Pope and of indulgences against me thus, because

they considered that it would turn out better for them. And at length several men planned to attack me, as the Pharisees attacked Christ, etc.' [59]

Therefore, when Pope Leo X, a most kind man in every respect, saw that the Church was being disturbed on every side by the unholy and seditious writings of Luther, and that the disagreement was increasing daily, and that Luther grew always worse, rejecting all admonitions no matter how pious, at length he bestirred himself against the exceedingly proud importunities of the rebellious Monk. First, he proposed that Luther's writings should be very carefully examined by certain most learned theologians. Then, when the Cardinals had been called into assembly, supported by their council, he proceeded to the rigor of judgment, since he had accomplished nothing by being lenient and working through Legates and Nuncios. Nevertheless, he used such moderation that, when forty-one false articles had been reviewed, in pronouncing his sentence he condemned only the books; but the author of the books he urged in a fatherly manner to recover his senses. He had earlier most kindly summoned Luther to Rome, offering him both a safe conduct and expenses for the journey; thus he also fixed in his Bull a limit of sixty days for him, in which to recant his errors; and then he added another sixty days for him to achieve the appropriate obedience to the Apostolic See and the correction of his errors, once again offering him a safe conduct, with the fullest trust. For it very greatly grieved the pious Pontiff that the German nation was incited by Luther to rebellion against the Roman Church, since the church always had embraced that nation before others in its loving heart; the Roman Empire had been transferred from the Greeks to Germany by Pope Leo III, the beloved of God, who presented Charles, surnamed the Great, with the Imperial Crown of Rome in the year of Christ's birth 801.

But before Luther received the published Bull of Leo X, he had, through the secret machinations of some of his Augustinian brethren, obtained from Bohemia books by Wycliff the Englishman and Hus the Bohemian, who were rebellious heretics and enemies of the Roman Church. He borrowed many things from these books, which seemed to support his rebellion. Therefore, he published a book against the Seven Sacraments that the Church uses for the sake of salvation. He gave this book the title *Concerning the Babylonian Captivity of the Church, a preliminary work of Martin Luther*. And in it he openly justified the Bohemians, and insulted the Catholic Church most ferociously, saying: 'Arise, then, here and now, in one body, all you flatterers of the Pope, make yourselves busy, and defend yourselves against charges of impiety, tyranny, treason against the Gospel, and the injury of brotherly dishonor: you who denounce as heretics those who do not follow the mere dream out of your own head, but who on the contrary are manifest [60] and powerful and know the Scriptures. If there are any who should be called heretics and schismatics, it is not the Bohemians, not the Greeks (who rely upon the Gospels) – but you Romans are heretics and impious schismatics, who take for granted only your own invention, contrary to the clear Scriptures of God. Men, wash yourselves clean of these things!' [61] And at the end of this book he added: 'I hear a rumor, that Bulls and Papistic threats are once again prepared against me, in which I am urged to a response, or I will be declared a heretic. If these things are true, then I want this pamphlet to be part of my future response, so that they may not complain that their tyranny was puffed up to no purpose. The remaining part I will quickly publish, Christ willing, which will be of such a sort as the Roman See has not seen or heard until this time. I will give abundant witness of my obedience.' [62]

Finally, he added this sacred verse:

Impious enemy, Herod, why do you fear for Christ to come?
He who gives heavenly kingdoms does not snatch away
*   mortal possessions.*[63]

Through this he was hinting to the reader that the Roman Pontiff was similar to Herod and was persecuting heretics for the sake of earthly power. But, on the contrary, it was for the Gospel of Christ.

The remaining part of his response, about which he threatened there, he published later, against Ambrosius Catharinus, concerning the vision of Daniel. In it he represented twelve aspects of the Roman Pontiff in such a way that through them he turned every reverence done to God in the church into a laughing-stock. And later, when he saw the Bull of Leo X that was published against his books, his wrath soon boiled up to so great an extent that he seemed, due to the savagery of his attacking, to rage rather than to write. First he published a pamphlet, which he gave this title: *Against the Execrable Bull of the Antichrist.* This entire book overflowed with pure attacks and false accusations, designed to stir up defection and sedition against the Apostolic See. He said: 'Whoever may have been the author of this Bull, I hold him to be the Antichrist. And in the first place I protest, that I dissent with my whole heart from the condemnation contained in this Bull, which I both curse and execrate as a sacrilegious and blasphemous enemy to Christ, the Son of God. Then secondly, I affirm by the entire pledge of my soul the articles condemned in the Bull, and I declare that they must be affirmed by all Christians on pain of eternal damnation, and that whoever agrees with this Bull must be held as Antichrists, whom by these writings I also consider as Pagans, and avoid as such.' [64] And further: 'Are you not afraid, you Bullated Antichrists, that stones and wood will pour out blood, at this most horrific sight of your impiety and blasphemy?' [65] And further: 'Where are you now, Charles, best of Emperors? Where are you, Christian Kings and Princes? You received the name of Christ in baptism; can you then bear these Hellish voices of the Antichrist?' [66] And further: 'And where does this thing that I have discovered come from, namely, that there are deposited in Germany, with those moneychangers whom they call a Bank, certain hundredweights of gold coins, which might destroy Luther? For the Holy Apostolic See, the teacher of the Faith and the mother of Churches, today fights, reigns, triumphs against these arguments and against Scripture – a See that is undoubtedly Antichristian, and convicted of heresy twice seven times, if it has fought against the sword of the Spirit, that is, the word of God.

Since it is not ignorant of this fact, and lest it may at some time be driven into danger on account of this fact, thus it rages in the Christian world with wars, slaughters, bloodshed, death, and devastation, overwhelming and destroying everything.'[67]

Now Charles V, the Emperor-elect, had come by sea from Spain into Flanders and Brabant, hereditary lands of his, to celebrate the Imperial Diet at Worms. When he learned from the Apostolic Nuntios Marino Caracciolo and Jerome Aleander that a Bull of Pope Leo X had been published against Luther's books, bearing in mind his Titles (for he was called – and was – the Catholic King of Spain and the Emperor of the Romans) he soon gave the most certain indications of his religious faith, his piety, and his obedience by commanding sternly that Martin Luther's books, which had been condemned by the Apostolic See, should be publicly burned. And so they were burned by executioners and butchers both in the towns of Brabant and in cities of the Empire, Cologne, Mainz, etc. And since Luther could not avenge this injury with the sword, he decided, aflame with rage, to avenge it with the pen. And furthermore, lest the eminence and authority of the Supreme Heads, the Pope and the Emperor, should make his books at the very least ambiguous and suspect to the people, if not entirely worthy of condemnation and execrable, with serpentine cunning Luther disregarded everything which the Pope and the Emperor had ordered or done publicly, and attributed all that was being done at their command to the envy of the theologians: when the theologians could accomplish nothing against him either by citing the Scriptures or through arguments, they incited the Pope and the Emperor through false accusations, so that they might overcome through force and power him whom they had been unable to conquer by law and in the court case.

Therefore, he published an assertion of all his articles, which Leo X had condemned in his Bull. Moreover, he published it not only in Latin, but also in German, and he was so puffed up by a spirit of pride that for his own single sake he condemned not only all the scholastic Doctors, as he had been accustomed to do previously, but he even wished that the Church Fathers, the Roman Popes, and the General Councils be believed less than he, one man though he was. Therefore he impudently laid claim to skill in the Scriptures for himself before all others. Furthermore, due to hatred for the Pope and the Theologians, he embellished everything, overwhelming the ears of the people and the mind and eyes of the reader with shameful accusations, taunts, and slanders; and indeed he did this even more frequently and more ferociously in the German version than in the Latin. For these were the words of the title in German: *The Foundation and Reason of all the Articles of Dr Martin Luther, which were Unjustly Condemned by the Roman Bull.*[68] Then he inserted the sweet name of Jesus among all his bitter abuses, with this salutation: 'To all good Christians, who will read or hear this little book, Grace and Peace from God. Amen.'[69]

Afterwards, beginning his preface, he tried to claim good will for himself (due to the laity's praise) and faith and authority (due to the blindness of the

Clergy). And he ascribed the matter to the Divine Goodness, which had so blinded certain Tyrants of Christianity, and had entangled them by the spirit of confusion in errors, that they had published a Bull to their own greatest disgrace and to their own noteworthy and irrecoverable weakening, in which they condemned the manifest truth to such an extent that the very stones and logs almost cried out against them. And further: 'I do not say' (he wrote) 'that I am a prophet. But I say to them that this — that I might be a prophet — is more greatly to be feared, the more they condemn me and the more highly they think of themselves. If I am not a prophet, nevertheless I am certain in my own mind that the Word of God is with me, and not with them. For I have the Scripture on my side, and they have only their own personal doctrine.'[70]

He wrote these things and many other things of this sort in the prologue, for the purpose of inciting the fierce people of Germany against the Pope and every member of the Clergy. But in what followed, so great was the petulance of his words, the scurrility of his insults, and his pride in condemnation, that it would have been a shameful thing to address even camp-followers and washer women in such a fashion. But in the Latin book, lest he should seem to the learned to be utterly raving through wrath and self-love, he displayed a certain amount of modesty; although in truth he was exceedingly immodest. The title was: *The Assertion of All the Articles,* etc.[71] *A Letter to the German Knights* followed this, in which he removed the spirit of judgment and of understanding of the Scriptures from the Clergy and handed it over it to the laity.[72] He added that God had delivered us clergy into an evil mode of thinking, so that we might condemn the truth which the laity embrace; and they who are not priests might become priests, and they who are not laymen might become laymen. 'For this reason' (he said) 'it seemed good to me to write to you laymen, a new race of Clerics, etc.'

After the letter was a fairly extended prologue, in which first he protested that he absolutely wished to be compelled by the authority of no pope whatsoever, however holy, except insofar as he was examined according to the judgment of the divine scriptures. And he added, after many other comments, that many errors are found in the writings of all the Fathers, and that they often fight among themselves, often disagree with one another, and twist the Scriptures. Augustine often only argues, and decides nothing; Jerome asserts almost nothing in his *Commentaries.* For the rest, he said that up until this time he had appealed from the Scholastic Doctors to the Church officials, not because he considered all their opinions true, but because they appeared closer to the truth than the Scholastics, who had almost no remnant of the truth. In the course of the book, he rejected even the Council proudly and insultingly, saying: 'Therefore whether the Pope or a party, whether the Council thinks thus or thus, no one should prejudge those matters which are not necessary for salvation, but each one should rely on his own opinion. For we are called into liberty.'

1521

Before the Emperor Charles V began the most splendid and famous Diet at Worms, Luther published a great many books, both in Latin and in German. Since he was aiming at the fame of piety and erudition, and at influence not only among the common people, and he was also hoping to gain the good will of the Princes, in these books he mixed many good things – both in explaining the Scriptures and in exhorting and rebuking the people – with his worst tricks; to such an extent that very many men, even of the greatest authority, believed that this was done both through zeal for virtue and in accordance with the spirit of God, to remove the abuses of hypocrites, to reform the habits and pursuits of the Clergy, and to direct the minds of mortals towards the love and honor of God.

The following were among these books: *An Exposition of the Ten Commandments; About Christian Liberty; Fourteen Consolations; An Explanation of the Lord's Prayer; A Commentary on Paul's Epistle to the Galatians; Expositions of the Epistles and Gospels by the Lord's Appearances; Offerings on Twenty Psalms; Exposition of the Seven Penitential Psalms.* And further on the Psalms: *On the Thirty-Sixth, the Sixty-Seventh, and the Hundred and Ninth; Exposition of the Song of Mary, the Magnificat; About the Good Works of Johannes, Duke of Saxony, Brother of Frederick the Elector;* and other little works of this sort, which seemed to display an appearance of both doctrine and piety. Afterwards, however, when that very great Diet was begun at Worms, the Papal Nuncio Jerome Aleander (who later was made Archbishop of Brindisi, and then a Cardinal), a man quite learned and skilled in tongues, began to accuse Luther most gravely with many speeches in the very crowded gathering of Princes, Prelates, and Representatives of the Empire. He accused him not only of disobedience and heresy, but also of sedition, rebellion, impiety, and blasphemy.

But since in the opinion of many Aleander seemed to be stirred up against Luther more from envy and a desire for vengeance than by zeal for piety, and since he accomplished or managed very little through his orations, be they however frequent and vehement, then finally he excerpted about forty Articles from Luther's book *About the Babylonian Captivity,* which had then recently been published.[73] In these articles Luther had dared to reject, trample upon, and condemn not only the rites and sacraments of the Church, but even the laws of the Princes and any and all governmental arrangements of human beings. These were among the articles: 'That the Seven Sacraments must be denied, and only three accepted for the time being; that Transubstantiation at the altar must be considered a human fiction, since it is based upon nothing in Scripture or in reason. That it is a manifest and impious error to offer or apply Mass for sins, for reparations, for the dead, or for any necessities of one's own or of others. That only they who have sad, afflicted, disturbed, and sin-filled consciences are worthy to communicate.[74] That Baptism justifies no one, nor is of any use; but faith in the word of the promise justifies, and Baptism is added to that. That neither Pope, nor Bishop, nor any human being at all has the right to determine a single syllable concerning a Christian person, unless it is done with the consent of that person. For this truly amounts to making people slaves of other people, subjects to statutes and their tyrannical laws. That no law can be imposed on Christians by any right, except insofar as they wish it, since they are free from all, etc.'

Therefore, when Aleander had read out these articles of Luther's, and many other impious and seditions ones of their sort, from the paper, and had exclaimed with oratorical fervor against them, then the Princes, who had not yet read this just-published book and had not suspected Luther of anything of this sort, were completely terrified and in an uproar, and looked one upon the other and began to murmur against Luther and his protectors. When Duke Frederick of Saxony, the Elector Prince, perceived this, in order to deflect their odium he said, 'These articles are not by Luther, but they were feigned by his adversaries because of their hatred of him.' And so an argument arose, in which some said that the articles were Luther's and others that they were not. And it seemed wise to the Princes that Luther himself should be summoned, so that he might declare from his own lips which books were his and which were supposititious. Then there arose a long consultation and a difficult dispute among the nobles of the Empire concerning by what security and with what conditions he should be brought before them. For to Luther's patrons, the public oath of the Emperor alone, given with whatsoever holy vow and confirmed with letters and seals, did not seem sufficient. For they feared that perhaps, when he had come, he would be betrayed by the Emperor into the hands of the Roman Pope, or that the Emperor would himself give him over to the ultimate punishment as a heretic, thinking that no sworn faith must be kept with a faithless heretic. But to many others it seemed an outrageously shameful thing that any other thing should be requested beyond the Emperor's sworn faith for the safe conduct of one Monk.

However, since a great disturbance in the people's minds against the clergy had been stirred up throughout almost all Germany by Luther's books, so that the situation seemed but little distant from mutiny and sedition, the Emperor permitted him to have safe conduct for going and returning, and several of the Princes also gave their oath to Luther. The Emperor added this condition, however, that Luther might not ever preach or write on the journey, lest he stir the people up more. And so Caspar Sturm, an Imperial Diplomat, was sent from Worms to Wittenberg, so that he might escort Luther on his outward and return journeys under public trust.

Meanwhile, however, other matters of state were being carried out at this Diet, since it was the first Diet the Emperor had held. Many of the Princes received their feudal rights from the Emperor, as the recently elected, true, and supreme Lord of the provinces, in a most splendid ceremony in which they paid him the appropriate homage.

When Sturm came to Wittenberg, that is from the Rhine to the Elbe, he brought both public and private letters to Luther, from which Luther learned of his complete security; his patron, in whom he trusted before all others and at whose expense he would undertake his journey, had thus provided for him with the greatest care. And so a coach was prepared for him, in the form of a shaded litter, provided against all the injuries of the sky; and as companions he had learned men – Jonas the Abbot, Schurff, an Ordinary of Laws, Amsdorf the theologian, and so forth. Whatever road they took, there was a thick crowd of people, due to their eagerness to see Luther. In the inns they found many a toast, cheerful drinking-parties, music, and enjoyments; to such an extent that Luther himself drew all eyes to himself in some places by playing songs on a lyre, as though he were a kind of Orpheus, but a shaven and cowled one, and for that reason more marvelous.

But although the Emperor had given him a safe conduct on the condition that he neither preach nor write on his journey, nevertheless he (famous scoffer at human law that he was) preached publicly in Erfurt on Low Sunday, and ordered that sermon to be published in type. And in this sermon, he said very many things against the virtue of good works and against human laws. For thus he spoke: 'One builds churches, another makes a pilgrimage to St James or St Peter. A third fasts or prays; puts on the cap, or walks barefoot, or does something else.[75] Works of this sort are absolutely nothing, and should be destroyed from the roots up. For whatever comes from the Pope, says, "Da Da,[76] if you don't do this, you are of the Devil." The matter would be a trivial one, if people were only being defrauded; but this is the greatest evil – alas! – that can be in the world, that people are directed in this way, [to think] that bodily works can save or justify.' And further: 'There are three thousand priests, among whom not four upright ones can be found – alas! And if ever they should be considered upright preachers, the Gospel is preached only superficially.' Next there was a certain fable from ancient times, from the *Vessel* or the *History* of Theoderic of Verona.[77]

But since Sturm, too, was secretly a supporter of Luther's party, he neither refused him any of these things nor made them known to the Emperor. Moreover, Luther himself described whatever was done at Worms with him, but hardly in good faith; rather, since he was most desirous of praise, he turned everything toward his own glory, mixing false things with true. However, so that he might seem a less shameless praiser of himself, he assumed the third person in speaking and recounting everything. But sometimes, preoccupied with too great a desire for praise, he would forgo the third person, and say 'I am the one ...'[78] For instance, he said: 'The Speaker for the Empire said that I had not responded to the case, etc.' Certainly from these words a reader who was not altogether stupid would easily understand that these *Acts* had been written by Luther himself, and indeed the style and the secret counsels of the man which were narrated therein plainly indicated the same thing.

And so Luther came to Worms on the 16th day of April, and remained there ten days. On the 26th day of the same month he left there. Therefore he himself says in his *Acts*: 'On the third day after Misericordia Domini Sunday, Dr Martin Luther, an Augustinian by profession, rode into Worms, in the year 1521, having been called there by the Emperor Charles, Fifth of that name. Dr Martin Luther had, three years earlier, put forward certain paradoxes to be discussed in Wittenberg, a town of Saxony, against the tyranny of the Roman Bishop. Although these paradoxes were, from time to time, torn up and burned by various people, nevertheless they were refuted by nothing from either the Scriptures or arguments from reason. The matter began to tend toward an uprising, since the common people supported the cause of the Gospel against the Clergy. And on this account it seemed wise, at the instigation of the Roman Legates, that the man should be called before the Imperial Negotiator, once letters of safe conduct had been given to him by the Emperor and the Princes. He is summoned, he comes, and he turns aside into the Curia of the Rhodians, where he is received with hospitality and greeted and sought for deep into the night by many Counts, Barons, armored knights, nobles, priests, and laypeople.' Luther wrote these things about himself in the introduction to his *Acts*.

On the next day at the fourth hour after noon, Luther was conducted by a nobleman, Lord Ulrich von Pappenheim, and by the abovementioned Sturm into the sight of the Imperial Majesty and of other Princes and Officials of the Holy Roman Empire. He was warned by them not to speak about anything on which he was not questioned. And so the Emperor's Spokesman, Johannes Eck, an eloquent man and one experienced in the law, who was the General Official of the Prince Elector Archbishop of Trier, spoke to Luther in the following fashion, first in Latin and then in German. 'The Imperial Majesty summons you here, Martin Luther, for these two causes. First, that you should openly acknowledge the books that have been published under your name up until this time, if they are yours. Secondly, that you should declare, concerning the books which have already been acknowledged as yours, whether you wish all of them to be held as yours or whether you wish to recant any of them.' [79] At these things, one of Luther's companions on the journey, a lawyer named Dr Jerome Schurff, exclaimed, 'Let the books be named!' [80] Therefore the spokesman listed many of his books, which had been published both at Basel and elsewhere.

Luther responded to these things as follows. 'The books which have been named,' he said, 'I am unable not to embrace as mine, and I will never deny any of them. However, concerning what follows, whether I should affirm or indeed recant those books, it would be foolhardy and dangerous for me to offer anything that had not been carefully considered, since the question concerns the faith and salvation of souls and the word of God, than which we have nothing greater. For this reason, I humbly beg an interval of time to deliberate whether I may satisfy this interrogation without injury to the Divine Word and peril to my soul.' [81] At this point a deliberation began among the Princes, until the Imperial Spokesman replied as follows: 'Although, Martin, you could have understood sufficiently from the Emperor's mandate for what purpose you were summoned here, and for that reason you do not deserve that a longer delay be given you for thinking; nevertheless His Imperial Majesty, through his own inborn clemency, concedes one day to your meditation, so that you shall appear here openly tomorrow at this same hour. On this condition: that you do not put your opinion forward in writing, but that you deliver it orally.' [82]

After this exchange, Luther returned to his inn. Here Luther mentions several voices of his supporters, which were raised in his praise; among them he makes note of one which said 'Blessed is the womb that bore you.'[83] But on the next day, when he had been led back at the same time by the negotiators and was in the palace, because of the Princes' business he waited outside the door until the sixth hour. But afterwards the Emperor and the Princes came secretly out of their conclave and took their seats in public, in the midst of a large crowd. Then the Emperor's spokesman said to Luther, again in Latin and German, 'The time for deliberation, which he asked for yesterday and which he should not have obtained, since he has known for so long why he was summoned, is now at an end. Therefore, let him now respond, whether he will uphold all the books which he acknowledges his, or indeed whether he wishes to retract anything.'[84]

Luther says that he responded to these things submissively, quietly, and modestly, although not without Christian pride. However, his adversaries had drawn not a little hope of his recantation from his request for time to deliberate. But since he did not respond to the principal article, but rather – in long digressions and extended speech, now flattering the Princes, now terrifying them with examples drawn at length from the Scriptures and concerning the kings of Egypt, Babylon, and Israel – noted an intricate distinction between three types of his books, when the summer day had already drawn to evening the Emperor's spokesman told him to respond to the matter at hand, and to give a simple answer, not a sophistical one:[85] Would he recant or not? Luther affirms that he responded thus to these things: 'Since your Holy Majesty and your Lordships seek a simple answer, I will give it, neither horned nor toothed, in this manner.[86] Unless I shall have been refuted by the testimony of the Scriptures, or by evident reason (for I do not trust in the Pope nor in Councils alone, since it is known that they have been wrong rather frequently, and have disagreed among themselves), I am convinced, by the Scriptures that I have brought forward and by my conscience which is bound by the word of God, that I neither can nor wish to recant anything, since to act against my conscience is neither safe nor honest. *Got Helff mir.*[87] Amen.'[88]

After this response, the Princes spoke with one another and, after deliberating and consulting, ordered the Imperial spokesman to answer Luther in these words: 'You, Martin, have responded more impudently than befits your rank. For if you had recanted those books in which the large part of your error is, it can scarcely be doubted that His Imperial Majesty, through his own inborn clemency, would not have tolerated the persecution of the remainder of your books, which are good. But you revive matters which the Universal Council of Constance, drawn together from the entire German nation, has condemned, and you wish to be proven wrong from the Scriptures. In this, clearly, you are completely out of your wits. For what is the use of holding a new disputation concerning matters which have been condemned through so many centuries by the Church and the Council?'[89]

But Luther, citing his captive conscience as a cause, was not able to withdraw from the nets in which he was caught; he kept on saying that he could not recant. Therefore, when shadows covered the entire hall, the meeting was broken up, and the Princes withdrew, each one into his own lodgings. They were bidden to return early on the following day, so that they might hear the Emperor's opinion. Therefore, on the sixth day after Misericordia Domini Sunday, the Emperor sent a paper written in his own hand, composed by himself in the Burgundian tongue, into the Senate of the Empire. Translated into Latin, it contained the following decision: 'It is known to you that my descent is from the most Christian Emperors, from the noble German nation, from the Catholic Kings of Spain, from the Archdukes of Austria, from the Dukes of Burgundy; all of whom remained faithful children of the Roman Church until death and always stood out as defenders of the Catholic faith, of its sacred ceremonies, decrees, ordinances, and its holy customs, for the honor of God, the increasing of the faith, and the health of souls. And indeed, when these suffered death, they left to us, by the arrangement of nature and by hereditary right itself, the holy Catholic rites which we have mentioned, rites passed down, as it were, by hand – in order that we might live according to their example, and that we might die in those rites. And thus we, inasmuch as we are true imitators of our forebears, have lived until this very day in this same course, with Divine Grace favoring us. And so for this reason I have decreed that everything should be guarded, which my predecessors themselves honored, or which I have honored up until this present time; but especially, before all else, that which was decreed and ratified by my predecessors, both in the Council of Constance and in others. But now, since it is well known that one single monk is hallucinating and is deceived by a certain opinion of his own, which is contrary to the opinion of all Christendom, both of those who preceded us in time gone by for over one thousand years, and of those who now live (for according to the revelation of his opinion, forsooth, the entire Christian family would seem always to have been turned about in error), on account of these things I have wholly resolved to lay out all my dominions, my Empire, my power, my friends, body, and blood, my life and my soul, that this evil beginning not spread further; for that would impute great dishonor to me, and also to you, who belong to the noble and most celebrated nation of Germany. To you and to me, for our honor, authority, and privilege, this has been granted by charter, that we should be considered as keen preservers of justice, and as defenders and protectors of the Catholic faith. And therefore, it would be an unending reproach to us in the eyes of our successors, if in our time any heresy should be left in the hearts of the people – not only any heresy, but even any suspicion of heresy, or any lessening of the Christian religion. And so, now that this obstinate response, which Luther gave out yesterday in sight of us all, has been heard, I announce to you my sworn sentence, and I regret the delay and the fact that for so long I postponed proceeding against Luther himself and his false doctrine; and I have determined that I will by no means listen any longer to the man or to whatever he is going to say. And I order that he be escorted home as soon as possible, in accordance with the custom of the charge, and that he himself take care, according to the conditions attached to his safe conduct, not to call together public gatherings nor to teach the people his false doctrine any further. Finally, let him take care not to engage in any action that might ever excite any sort of political innovation or might cause commotion. And as I have said before, I have determined to gird myself for proceeding against him, since it is proper to proceed against a notorious heretic. And at the same time I charge you, that as good Christians you decide as you should in a case of this sort, and as you have promised me to do. These things were written by my hand, on the 19th day of April 1521.'[90]

This judgment of so pious and Catholic an Emperor was read not only in Worms before all the Princes and Officials of the Empire, but was also later read in Rome, on the 10th day of May – the next month – in the public consistory, before the noble Senate of Cardinals. This was done at the order of Pope Leo X, in the ninth year of his pontificate. And the Emperor's constancy in the faith was praised beyond common measure by both branches of the Senate, as were the zeal of his young breast for piety and ancestral religion. But to whatever degree these good, grave, and pious men were praising the Emperor, so to the same degree the Lutherans were muttering against him and denouncing him in secret. They said that he was a boy, who was dragged by the nods and flatteries of the papists and the Bishops in whatever direction they wished.

Two German poets were especially irritated and gnashed their teeth in threats and complaints. These two men, Ulrich Hutten the Franconian and Hermann Busch the Westphalian, were descended from noble families and were famous for their intellect; but both were of extremely defiant mind. Busch was already a longtime enemy of the Scholastic Theologians and the monks, as Hutten was an enemy of the Courtiers and Nuncios of the Roman Curia. And so this saying was written up at night on doors throughout the city streets: 'Woe to that land, whose king is a child.' And furthermore, a hostile document was attached to the doors of the Mayor, in which it was claimed that 400 German knights were declaring war on the Cardinal and Archbishop of Mainz. (This Archbishop, in Germany, is Dean among the Elector Princes of the Empire, a position next in place and dignity to that of the Emperor.) However, not a single knight's name had been written on the document. In addition, this seditious German saying was read, placed at the end of the threatening document: *Buntschuch, Buntschuch, Buntschuch.* This word means 'popular alliance,' or, better, 'conspiracy against one's betters.'

And that the Catholics might be inspired with greater terror, that noble and powerful man, Franz von Sickingen, did not stay away from Worms for long. He had gained great renown for his military career, since he had undertaken war on his own behalf against both the Landgrave of Hesse and against the city of Metz, and had inflicted heavy losses upon both these enemies. And it was rumored that he had stationed himself nearby in his castle, which he kept heavily fortified, that he had collected a military band of knights, and that he was waiting to see the outcome of the Lutheran case, since he supported Luther most vehemently. The Princes and other Orders of the Roman Empire saw that there was turmoil and muttering among the common people not only in the city of Worms, where they themselves were, but outside the city as well, and not just in nearby areas, but even in far-away cities of Germany, and that the minds even of most of the nobles too were inclining toward Luther. Therefore, when they saw these things, although they had praised the constancy and piety of the Emperor, they now prayed him that he would graciously permit them to select certain representatives from the Orders of the Empire who would earnestly put to the test whether they could persuade Luther to recant those Articles that had been condemned by the Holy See.

In the meantime, Luther had done nothing publicly for three whole days. In private, however, he gathered together and incited a more sufficient group of restless men. On the 22nd day of April, the Emperor responded to the Princes and Officials of the Empire that he would permit some of them to confer with Luther and to put to the test whether he would be willing to recant the condemned articles. But the Emperor permitted this on the condition that the meeting take place quickly, and that Luther remain in Worms for no more than three days. Nonetheless, the Emperor would persist in his judgment, of which they had seen the manuscript on the Friday, however long Luther persisted in his stubborn willfulness.

Therefore, when the Emperor's permission had been obtained, with the agreement of the others the Archbishop of Trier, the Elector Prince, sent two priests from his own household to Luther, on the Monday after Jubilation Sunday, which was the 22nd day of April, around the dinner hour, so that they might bid him appear on the Wednesday, at the sixth hour of the morning, in a certain place which would be indicated to him. When he agreed to this, certain men were chosen from the Orders of the Empire, who would confer with him. These men included two Electors, the Archbishop of Trier and the Margrave of Brandenburg; also two Bishops, of Augsburg and of Brandenburg; George, Duke of Saxony and Master of the Teutonic Order. To these were added George Count of Wurtheim, Lord Bock of Strasbourg, and Dr Peutinger of Augsburg; and finally Dr Jerome Vehus, Chancellor of Baden, who would speak on behalf of all the others.

On the 23rd day of April, which was the holy day of St George the Martyr, the Emperor celebrated the feast with all due solemnity, because he himself was also a member of the Society of St George, as are many other kings and princes. The Abbot of Fulda, the Emperor's Ordinary Chaplain, celebrated the Mass with his attendants in the most solemn fashion, together with a Prince of the Empire, Lord Hartmann, Count of Kirchberg. He was indeed a most sagacious man, but at that time was an exile, having been banished by his subordinates. (The Emperor later reconciled him to his people by giving him an annual pension, which allowed him to live privately in Mainz in his own canonry, with the administration of his affairs entrusted to one of the Counts of Henneberg.) On that day nothing was done in secular cases, due to the veneration of St George. On the 24th day of April, which was the Wednesday

after Jubilation Sunday, the abovementioned delegation from the Princes and
Orders of the Empire gathered in the court and household of Lord Richard,
Archbishop of Trier. Luther too arrived at the prescribed time, which was the
sixth hour before dinner. Thus, when Princes and Orders had met in Assembly,
Dr Vehus (since he is a man both very eloquent and very learned) began to
exhort Luther in a long speech not to depend upon his own way of thinking
and to persevere in his own premise, nor so to denounce and reject the Councils
as he had done before the Emperor's Majesty. For the Councils did not enact
contradictory measures, as he had accused them of, but rather different measures
in accordance with the differences of persons, times, and places. Moreover, a
great many good things had come about because of the Councils: there was a
need for human laws, and the scandals of schismatics must be guarded against,
lest the seamless garment of Christ be divided. The Princes had procured this
meeting with him from the Emperor's Majesty for this reason – not, certainly,
to dispute with him, but rather so that they might exhort him, kindly and
gently, that he should not cling stubbornly to his own mode of thinking. They
made this exhortation because of the very numerous, extremely serious scandals
and dangers that would result if he did not desist from his obstinacy.

When Luther had heard these words, first he thanked the Princes, for so
kind and gentle an exhortation, of which he was not worthy. Then, he answered
the objections regarding his statements about Councils, that he had not censured
all Councils, but only the Council of Constance. He had censured it chiefly
because it had condemned the Word of God, as is clearly evident from this
Article of Jan Hus, which was condemned there: 'That the Church of Christ is
the whole community of the Predestined.' The Council of Constance had
condemned this statement, and so also the Article of the Faith: 'I believe in
the Holy Catholic Church.' But concerning scandals he said that there were
two scandals, the one of Charity, and the other of Faith. The first one concerned
Charity, because it had to do with morals and way of life; the second concerned
Faith or Doctrine, because it could not be avoided in the Word of God. For
in itself it could not be promised, that Christ would not be a stone for scandal.[91]
He knew, therefore, that rulers ought to be obeyed, even bad, evil-living rulers.
Moreover, he knew that he should yield to the common opinion. Nevertheless,
he begged that he might not be compelled to deny the Word of God; in all
other matters he pledged that he would be most obedient.[92]

And so on this pretext of the Word of God , in the same manner as he had
done from the start and as he would do at all times, Luther thrust forward,
hawked about, and inculcated the condemned errors of the Waldensians, the
Wycliffites, and the Hussites, and persuaded many of the Germans. And in this
matter many people think that the Emperor and the Princes did not act with
enough reflection when they called Luther before them but did not call any
theologians who might reveal his false pretexts and deceits. Certainly the pious
and learned bishop John Fisher, the Bishop of Rochester in England, shortly
thereafter showed very clearly and abundantly in a long volume that none of
Luther's articles which Pope Leo X had condemned in his Bull were contained

in Scripture or were the Word of God. Neither was it true that this Article of Johannes Hus (that the Church of Christ is the whole community of the Predestined) is the Word of God, especially not in that sense which the heretics pretended: that evil prelates and damnable sinners, although they are baptized and Christian, are not of the Church of Christ, nor are they members of the Church Militant. Indeed, this opinion is so clearly not the Word of God, nor in the Sacred Scripture, that the contrary can be proven from very many passages of Scripture; and most clearly, from the Parables of Christ, about the wheat and the tares in the same field; and about the net cast into the sea, and gathering all kinds of fish; and about the Ten Virgins, of whom five were wise and five foolish; and so forth.

Johannes Cochlaeus was present then in Worms, the Dean of the Church of the Blessed Virgin in Frankfurt-am-Main. This man followed Luther when he passed by there, and had come to him privately and on his own accord, summoned by no one.[93] He had come for no other cause than that he might expose and submit his body and his life to the utmost danger, if there were need, for the faith and honor of the Church. For he was burning with a great zeal, both for the sacraments of the Church, which Luther, in his *Babylonian Captivity*, had either entirely rejected or had profaned by evil alteration; and for the religion of his ancestors, which he grieved to see condemned and hostilely attacked by that man. And he had already written three books – which he brought with him – in support of the venerable Sacrament of the Eucharist, in refutation of Luther's *Babylonian Captivity*. Now Luther had already been made aware of these matters by Wilhelm Nesen, a Frankfurtian poet and schoolmaster who later died most pitiably at Wittenberg in the Elbe river.

Therefore, when Cochlaeus arrived in Worms, accompanied by only one boy, his own sister's son, he came first to Wolfgang Capito, who was certainly a learned and eloquent man, but extremely cunning with a more than vulpine skill.[94] Capito was then a counselor to the Cardinal and Archbishop of Mainz, and he most craftily dissembled the Lutheranism which he secretly nourished in his breast. He introduced Cochlaeus to Jerome Aleander, the Nuncio of Leo X, to whom Cochlaeus was already known through letters. In this way it happened that on the day on which the selected Princes were going to confer with Luther separately, Aleander called Cochlaeus to himself early in the morning, at the fourth hour, bidding him to wait in the court of the Archbishop of Trier until he should be called into a conversation with Luther. However, he earnestly enjoined him that he should by no means enter into disputation with Luther, but should only listen, so that he would be able to recount accurately how Luther was dealt with.

Cochlaeus did this, and later, after dinner, he entered into a private conversation with Luther in Luther's inn, at times debating with him and at times conversing in turn in a friendly manner; just as Cochlaeus himself has related at length in a small book written particularly about this matter.[95] But from that time the Lutherans were always enraged at Cochlaeus. They did not wait until he published something against Luther, but soon they were rising against him on all sides with various slanders, curses, tricks, and calumnies. And they even spread about the rumor that Cochlaeus had been secretly instructed by the papists for this reason, that he might induce Luther, by a trick, to renounce his safe conduct, and thus hand him over to the hangman. Moreover, they published songs, or to speak more truly, accusations and slanders, which they sent out into other cities so quickly that these songs arrived in Nuremberg and Wittenberg before Cochlaeus had returned to Frankfurt. These songs began: 'O Cochlaean ravings, new stories about Luther, record of jesters, most noteworthy for cowardice. They should be explained in verses, they should be depicted with horns, they should be smeared with shit, they should be rubbed down with lime,' etc. And above these they affixed German songs, which mocked Cochlaeus.

Cochlaeus learned from Capito early on the following day that this rumor was being spread about him. When by chance Cochlaeus met Jonas, the Provost from Wittenberg, on the road, he rebuked Jonas regarding this matter. For Jonas had been present at the conversation, and had spoken in this way to Capito. But Jonas denied everything to Cochlaeus's face; however, he warned Cochlaeus not to publish anything against Luther. For there were forty men who would sharpen their styluses to attack him, if he published anything. But Cochlaeus answered that not only injurious styluses but even Death should be held in contempt in order to uphold the faith of the Church.

The Princes of the Empire, lest they leave anything untried, obtained an interval of two more days for Luther from the Emperor, so that there could be further discussion with him. And so two Doctors of Law, Peutinger and Vehus, came to him on the next day, which was the feast of St Mark. They requested him to submit his books and writings to the Emperor's Majesty and to the Princes and Orders of the Empire for judgment. For in this way the best provision would be made, both for his books, so that whatever was good in them might remain, and for the public tranquility which this judgment would produce. And Luther said that he was prepared to do and to endure all things, provided only that they were supported by the authority of the Holy Scriptures. For the rest, he would nevertheless maintain his stance. For God had said through the prophet: 'Do not trust in Princes, in the sons of men, in whom there is no health.' And further, He had said, 'Cursed is he who trusts in man.' And when the Princes urged him more vehemently, Luther answered: 'Nothing is less worthy to be surrendered to the judgment of men, than the Word of God.' [96]

They left him, bidding him to consider better, and when they came back from dinner they asked him that he would at least submit his writings to the judgment of the future Council. He agreed to this, but on this condition, that the several articles about which the Council would give its opinion, according to the testimony of Scripture and the Divine Word, would be excerpted with his knowledge. But in his *Acts*, which were published both in Latin and in German, Luther reprimands these good and famous men for falsehood, because they said to the Archbishop of Trier that Luther had promised that he would submit his writings to the Council in several articles, when he intended to pass these things over in silence. In fact he had never said this, nor even thought it.

And so, summoned before the Archbishop himself, and admonished by him in the judges' absence, both about the judgment of the Emperor and the Empire, and about that of the Council, Luther answered that it would scarcely be safe for him to submit so great a matter to those who attacked with new charges one who had been summoned under imperial protection and condemned him, while they approved the opinion and the Bull of the Pope. Then the Archbishop requested that Luther himself propose some means by which it would be possible for the case to be answered. And Luther said that there were none better than those about which Gamaliel spoke in *Acts* 5: 'If this counsel or work is of men, it will be disbanded; but if it is truly from God, you will not be able to disband it.' [97] Again the Archbishop asked, 'What if those articles are excerpted, which must be submitted to the Council?' Luther answered, 'So long as they are not those that were condemned by the Council of Constance.' [98] Trier answered that he feared they would be precisely those ones. 'And so,' said Luther, 'about this matter I neither can be silent nor wish to be, since certainly the Word of God was condemned by that decree.' [99] When he had said these things, he was dismissed.

Luther himself, in his *Acts*, wrote the following things about himself, disguising his obstinacy throughout by the pretext of the Word of God, and tossing his own praises about unrestrainedly. For writing about Cochlaeus, he says: 'But Dr Martin, because of his incredible gentleness and probity, considered the man kindly.' [100] And at the end of the book he says, 'The most Christian father, responding extremely modestly, thus began.' [101] Further: 'Therefore, may God long preserve this most pious man, born to guard and teach the Gospel, for His church, together with His word, Amen.' [102]

And so when the Emperor saw that the man was made ever more and more stubborn by pious and merciful admonitions, he sent to him on the following day the Officer of Trier, and the Chancellor of Austria, and his own Secretary. They were instructed to say to Luther that since he refused to return to his senses and to the community, when he had been solemnly warned so many times, in vain, by the Emperor, the Elector Princes, and the Orders of the Holy Roman Empire, it remained for the Emperor, as the Advocate of the Catholic Faith, to proceed. It was the Emperor's command, therefore, that within twenty-one days Luther depart hence for his own safety, under free and public conduct; and that he take heed not to stir up the people on his journey either by preaching or by writing. Luther says that he answered these words as follows: 'As it has pleased the Lord, so was it done; Blessed be the name of the Lord.' [103] Then he thanked the Emperor and the Princes for such kind and merciful audiences, and for the free conduct which had been and would be observed for him. However, elsewhere he wrote the contrary.

On the next day, therefore, that is on 16 April,[104] the Friday after Jubilation Sunday, Luther left Worms with his comrades. Sturm, the Herald and Diplomatic Negotiator of the Emperor, had rejoined him to conduct him safely wherever he wished. But although the Emperor had commanded Luther neither to speak publicly nor to write on his journey, nevertheless, either forgetting this command or contemptuous of it, he wrote back to the Princes from Freiburg, and he publicly preached in the town of Eisenach. But he wrote letters that were very favorable and flattering, to gain approval for himself and to incite hatred of the Emperor and the Clergy among the people. For soon a letter in which Luther recounted everything he had done at Worms (and disguised his stubbornness throughout under the pretext of the Word of God) was reproduced by printers and dispersed among the people. He claimed that he had made no other reservation, except this only, which he had not been able to obtain: requiring that the Word of God be free, and not bound. And on the third day of the journey he sent the herald or negotiator of the Emperor back from Freiburg, where he had also written that letter; he feared no violence whatsoever, so secure was he under the protection of so many nobles. Besides, it seemed to him that the herald might be an impediment to his more secret councils, if he were not sent away. For after he had come to Eisenach, a town of his Prince and protector, and there had preached publicly on 3 May (the day of the Invention of the Sacred Cross) in defiance of the Emperor's command, when he had gone a little way out of the town he was with the utmost secrecy intercepted on purpose by his friends, who were pretending to be his enemies.

Soon the rumor was spread far and wide that Luther had been captured, and that his imperial protection had been violated and his safe conduct broken. And indeed, this malicious plan had been so secret that even the companions of his journey were ignorant of it and thought that he had been captured and abducted by enemies. Therefore many messengers were sent out, who announced through the cities of Germany how cruelly Luther had been captured, seized, and abducted while under safe conduct. And so that there would be greater sympathy for him and greater indignation at the Emperor and the Princes, the rumor was embellished by the messengers to say that his hands had been so cruelly bound, and that he had been dragged on his way on foot among hastening horsemen at such a speed that blood had spurted from his fingers. And this Holy Gospel was proclaimed even at Worms, so that the greatest possible muttering against the Emperor would arise, and not only among the people but even among the Princes, until the matter was investigated more carefully and was found to be a figment of wickedness.

And so throughout the cities the Lutherans raged because of the captured Luther, and ground their teeth at the clergy, and said that they would avenge Luther's death (for the rumor even claimed that he had been killed); for they suspected that the waylayers had been suborned by papists. But nowhere was there greater danger from mutinous men than at Worms. For even the Elector of Saxony complained among his friends that it was a shameful thing and unworthy of the Empire's Majesty that a man should be thus intercepted while under royal protection, and should be held captive. And among the common people the most seditious complaints were bandied about by many, but most bitterly and vehemently by the two poets who have already been mentioned,

Ulrich Hutten and Hermann Busch. The latter was present in the city and filled everything up with noises and complaints; while the former, who was not far away from Worms in the citadel of Franz (a nobleman), sent from there a most scurrilous letter against all Bishops and Clerics. For this reason nothing was more certainly expected than a serious and bloody revolt against the Emperor and all the clergy. But the Emperor's youth and goodness, and the diligence of the Princes, restrained those minds that were inclined to sedition.

But Luther went as soon as possible into territory that was allotted to his Prince (they say that this was a town of Thuringia, Allstedt by name, in which Müntzer later preached most seditiously). Although he lay hidden safe and sound in the citadel, nevertheless he was not able to be quiet in his spirit, which panted for the revolt of the people and the slaughter of the clergy. In that retreat he wrote many books, so that he might wholly move the minds of the Germans to defection from the Apostolic See and into hatred of all clergy. To this end he first wrote a book in German, addressed to Franz von Sickingen: *On Private Confession, and Whether the Pope May Command It.*[105] In the preface to this book he set together the Pope, the Bishops and every cleric with the people of Canaan, who did not wish to surrender of their own will but were battled down with the sword by Joshua (Kings 31). Then he threatened them, that if they did not change their customs, there would be someone who would teach them other customs, not by letters and words, as Luther did, but by deeds and arms. Moreover, he gave thanks, first to God, that the terror of the Roman See had been diminished, and that the heading in decrees, 'If anyone, with the Devil persuading him,' would deceive people no longer. Second, he thanked Franz himself, because he had in many ways and frequently consoled him, and had laid himself open to many things. Finally, he commended Ulrich Hutten and Martin Bucer to Franz, of whom the latter was an Apostate from the preachers, and the former an enemy of the courtiers. He wrote this preface on the 1st day of June.[106]

Shortly thereafter he wrote another book, about Dr Jakob Latomus, a Theologian of Louvain. In its preface he said: 'A monster of Rome sits in the middle of the Church, and hawks itself in God's place. The Bishops fawn on it, the Sophists obey it, and there is nothing that the hypocrites do not do for its sake. Meanwhile, Hell extends its spirit and opens its mouth endlessly, and Satan makes sport with the perdition of souls.'[107] And when he wrote the preface to Jonas, the Provost of Wittenberg, he warned him that he should not promote the most pestilential Decrees of the Antichrist, which he had been ordered to teach, for any other reason except to teach his students that they must forget these things which he taught, and that they should know that whatever things the Pope and the papists decree or believe should be avoided as deadly. And in the end of the book he says, 'From these things I think it has been sufficiently shown, that Scholastic Theology is nothing other than ignorance of the truth, and a scandal placed close by the Scriptures. In truth I have given my advice, that a young man should avoid Philosophy and Scholastic Theology, as the death of his soul. Thomas [Aquinas] wrote many

heretical things, and is the originator of the reign of Aristotle, the destroyer
of pious doctrine. What is it to me, that the Bishop of Bulls canonized him?
Therefore, in my opinion, he who flies from [scholasticism] will be safe. I do
what I should, and again I warn, with the Apostle. Watch lest anyone deceive
you through philosophy and empty artifice (for this is what I interpret scholastic
theology to be, strongly and with faith), according to the traditions of men
and the elements of this world (the laws about Bulls are among these, as is
whatever else has been ordained in the Church apart from the Scriptures), and
not according to Christ.' [108] Finally he added the following: 'And why does not
some one of you respond to the remaining things? Either you or Andreas
Karlstadt? Is Amsdorf completely idle? Should not the glory of the Gospel be
equally championed by all of you? I have destroyed the serpent's head; why
cannot you trample its body?' [109]

But his malice and impiety was most outstanding when he maligned St
Jerome as a favorer of Arius, because he did not want to admit the doctrine
of consubstantiality,[110] as if some poison lay hidden in its letters and syllables.
However, Jerome did not write about consubstantiality, but about substance.[111] Luther wrote another book, *About the Abrogation of the Private Mass,*
to his Augustinian brothers in the Wittenberg monastery.[112] In its preface, so
that he might strengthen his brothers (who were the first to annul Masses) in
his own insolence, he bade them to be strong in persisting against the accusations of conscience, since even he himself had scarcely yet made his own
conscience firm, with however many powerful and clear Scriptures, when he
dared – one individual though he was – to contradict the Pope and to believe
that he was the Antichrist; that the Bishops were his Apostles; and that the
Academies were brothels. He said that his trembling heart often quivered and
rebuked him, objecting: 'Are you the only one who is wise? Is everyone else
– so great a number! – in error? Have so many centuries been in ignorance?
What if you are mistaken, and drag so many people into error with you, who
must be eternally damned?' But he adds, that Christ at last confirms him, with
His certain and trustworthy words. But he did not disclose in what precise
words he was confirmed by Christ. And he says that those brothers should
maintain with certainty and confidence that which they had already assented
to: 'that not only should we regard the judgments of the whole world as fragile
leaves and chaff, but we should be armed for death, against the Gates of Hell.'
Nay, rather, he should have said to fight against the judgment of God who
tests us, and with Jacob to prevail against God. And as though the whole world
would be convulsed by that book, he wrote in the frontispiece: 'The lion will
roar, who will not be afraid?' [113]

Then he wrote a fourth book in Latin in the same place, addressed to his
father (a layman and unlearned), about monastic vows. In its preface he recounts
that he had become a monk in the twenty-second year of his age, and had
remained one for sixteen years.[114] But he became a monk, not through his own
desire, nor for the sake of the belly, but because he had been suddenly walled
in by terror from the sky and the agony of death and had vowed a forced and

unavoidable vow.[115] And he strove to prove by the testimony of his father that this had been an illusion and a deceit. And at the end of this preface he adds these words: 'What can it matter if the Pope kills me, or damns me to the limits of Hell? He cannot resurrect the dead, to kill me more than once. Truly, I wish to be condemned by him, so that he may never absolve me.' [116] He wrote this preface on the 21st day of November.

And so for six months he lay hidden in solitude – not a wild solitude, however, but a well-fortified one, which through an arrogant comparison and an overly proud imitation, he called his Patmos, as though he were a second John the Evangelist, banished by the Emperor to an island on the most malicious of pretexts; when in point of fact, the Emperor did not even know where he was hiding. He also called it his Hermitage and the place of his pilgrimage, so that by the wicked pretense of captivity he might claim for himself an appearance of great sanctity. And with the same falsehood, in the same place, he wrote his opinion about Vows, to the Bishops and Deacons of the Church in Wittenberg. But in reality, there was no Bishop there. And although that pamphlet was very short, nevertheless he divided it into two parts, the first of which contained 140 propositions, the second 139. He explained his reason for dividing them as follows: 'These first propositions' (he said) 'I want to be argued in such a manner that they may be held to be certain and true; those which follow, I simply put forward to be discussed and inquired about.'

Since Luther had previously requested a judgment from the Parisian theologians, both at Augsburg before Cardinal Caietanus and at Leipzig before the Counselors of Duke George, because he thought that the Parisians had been offended by the Pope, and since he had said that the University of Paris was the parent of all studies, and most Christian from antiquity, and most flourishing in Theology, therefore the Lutherans awaited the judgment of the Parisians with great expectation. In fact, they awaited it with such great confidence, that not a few of them in Worms (where Luther's cause was being entertained to the greatest extent) affirmed that the Parisians had approved thirty-eight of Luther's articles from the Papal Bull, and had left only two of them as questionable. But during these very days those theologians, solemnly convened and bound by oath, publicly gave out their judgment, which the Lutherans found odious and execrable, since it was far contrary to their expectation. 'We have carefully and fully examined,' they said, 'the entire doctrine which goes by the name "Lutheran," and have discussed it at length. We have found and have judged that it abounds in accursed errors, which touch most powerfully on the Faith and on morals. And we find that it is seductive to the simple people, injurious to all the learned, impiously disparaging of the Church's power and Hierarchical Order; openly schismatic, contrary to and distorting of the Sacred Scripture, and blasphemous against the Holy Spirit. And therefore we decree that it is destructive to the Christian Commonwealth, and should be altogether exterminated, and openly committed to the avenging flames. And its founder should be compelled, by all legal means, to public recantation.' [117] This judgment of theirs was published on the 15th day of April. However,

Luther came to Worms on 16 April, when the Lutherans were not yet able to know what the Parisians had decided. But after a few months, when certain printed copies of this opinion arrived in Germany, all the Lutherans changed their minds and began to accuse those whom before they had praised. And in order that their contempt toward the Parisians because of this verdict might seem greater, Philip Melanchthon, as a fervent defender of Luther, edited that same opinion about them, by which he augmented his Latin *Apology for Luther*, with this title: *Against the Insane Decree of the Parisian Theologians*, etc.[118] However, he wrote that Sophists ruled there in the place of Theologians, and slanderers in the place of Christian doctors, and that profane scholasticism had been born from Paris. Once that was acknowledged, nothing remained: the Gospel was obscured, the faith extinguished, the doctrine of works received. And he even charged that the remaining schools of Europe had accepted Scholastic Theology from them as if by force, so that the earth might be filled once more with Idols. And he reproached them as bitterly as possible with many sayings of this sort.

But nevertheless, Luther thought Melanchthon had dealt with them too gently. Therefore he himself translated both the pamphlet of the Parisians and the *Apology* of his ally Philip into German, and interspersed his opinion among them. In this book he offered this opinion, in German, concerning the French Theologians, for the sake of revenge and of paying them back in kind. He said, 'In its highest part, which is called the Faculty of Theology, the Academy of Paris is from its head to its feet a pure, snow-white leprosy of the true, most recent Anti-Christianity and of deadly heresy. It is the mother of all errors in Christianity, the greatest spiritual harlot that the sun ever saw, and a true backdoor into Hell. It was prophesied that in the time of the Antichrist all heresies which ever existed would gather together in one area, and would damn the world. God willing, I intend' (he said) 'to demonstrate this about the Parisians, that they are the foremost bedchamber of fornication of the Pope, the true Antichrist; and to prove that they are worse than the Montanists, the Ebionites, and all other heretics whatsoever whom they have written about. They are the ones, whom I have already desired for a long time.'[119] He wrote these things in German to the people, whom he was concerned to inspire against the judgment of the Parisians and to keep in his own faction. Nevertheless, he wrote nothing afterwards about the Parisians, except occasional brief complaints, like a biting dog which, not daring to attack one stronger than itself, barks fiercely from far away.

For the rest, Luther's allies published a ridiculous book, with their own names suppressed, and attributed it to the faculty of Theology of the Parisians. In this book, first a certain opinion is recounted concerning the *Apology* of Melanchthon, in weak and disordered barbarisms. Then is given the rationale of the prior opinion. And certain rules for understanding the scriptures are most inelegantly added, at great length. This was done so that men of the Gospel would be persuaded by this obvious fiction that the Parisian theologians knew nothing about the sacred Scripture. And so they say, after the tenth and last rule in that book, 'This kindly faculty alone has elucidated everything, first the Scriptures, after that the Fathers, writing for the final time, and it is not able to be mistaken. For the liripipe [120] and the canon's fur cape are infallible signs. Therefore they act wickedly, who follow the naked Scriptures; worse, who follow the naked Fathers; worst of all, those who in their writings proceed from obscurity into obscurity. Therefore, let them set these things aside and listen to the kindly Faculty, and cling firmly to the liripipe, since there is the light of the world, and the rules of the faith, and the infallible wall, etc.' [121]

1522

Luther and his adherents, on their own account, condemned every ecclesiastical judgment, and were rebels not only against their own Priors and Ordinaries as judges, but even against the loftiest heights of the Church, the Pope and the Emperor. So puffed up were they with the pride of contempt that they did not even wish to submit their doctrines (which they held for Gospel) to the Universal Council; and they had already forced the matter very close to the point of popular insurrection and sedition. Because of all this, King Henry of England, the Eighth of that name, who was most renowned for his piety, pitied and suffered with the German nation and in an extraordinarily rare example of devotion, and one that deserves to be admired throughout all centuries, descended from his royal height into the literary arena, to fight it out with the cursed Apostate of the mendicant Friars. And so King Henry wrote his *Affirmation of the Seven Sacraments*, in response to Luther's *Babylonian Captivity*, and addressed it to Pope Leo X. [122] Truly, he wrote it so eloquently, learnedly, and abundantly, that for this labor he merited, in the judgment of the Pope himself and all the Cardinals, the Title of perpetual praise, which he was given later by public assent, of 'Defender of the Faith.' In truth, how great this King's friendliness toward the Apostolic See was, how great his devotion to the Church, how great his modesty despite his enormous energy of intellect and his rare learning, and finally how great his zeal for defending the faith against his adversary, can most clearly be understood from his own words, which he addressed to the reader in his preface.

For he says: 'Moved by faithfulness and piety, although there is neither eloquence nor great store of learning in me, nevertheless I am driven to defend my Mother, the Bride of Christ, lest I be stained by ingratitude. Would that my skill were as great as my desire to do this. But although others are able to fulfill this task more richly and fully, nevertheless I considered it my duty, no matter how trifling my learning, that I myself should protect the Church with whatever arguments I could and that I should throw myself against the poisoned weapons of the enemy who attacks her. The very time and the present state of affairs entreat me to do this. For in earlier times, when no one was attacking the Church, there was no need for anyone to defend her. But now, when an enemy has arisen, than whom none more evil ever could arise, an enemy who under the incitement of the Devil alleges charity, and driven by wrath and hatred vomits out his viperish poison against both the Church and the Catholic faith, then it is necessary that all the servants of Christ, of all ages, of both sexes, of all ranks, should rise together against the common enemy of the Christian faith. Let those who are not strong in their powers at least bear witness to their duty by their keen feeling. And therefore now it is proper, that we fortify ourselves with a double armor – that is, with a heavenly one and an earthly one. Heavenly, so that he who by a feigned charity both damns others and is himself damned, may be won over by true charity and so win others; and he who fights by means of a false doctrine, may be conquered by the true doctrine. And an earthly armor, so that if he is of such stubborn malice that he spurns holy counsels, and condemns pious chastisement, then let him be forced by deserved punishment, so that he who refuses to do good may at least cease from doing evil, and he who has harmed others by the word of his malice may profit them through the example of his punishment.' [123]

These things the King himself said in his preface. And indeed in the course of the book he everywhere fortified and affirmed the opinion and doctrine of the Church both with close-set logical arguments and with citations from the Holy Scripture, and he so clearly laid bare the false pretexts and falsified subtleties of his opponent and so keenly refuted them, that within a few months his book had been published in many thousand copies by many printers and had filled the entire Christian world with joy and admiration. Nor was it enough for the Catholics in Germany to have read his book in Latin, although it had been most eloquently written in that language; but it was even translated into the German language, so that the laity as well, who were ignorant of the Latin language, might understand that there was nothing sound in Luther's new doctrine. And so it is permissible to recount here some few of the King's words against a certain haughty and inflated argument of Luther's concerning the sacrifice of the Mass, which he said was a promise, not a deed. 'It is a wonder' (said the King) 'how after he suffered for so long in childbed, he gave birth to nothing except pure wind, and that he, who wishes to appear so strong that he can move mountains, to me in fact seems so weak that he could not set a reed into motion. For if you take away the convolutions of the words in which he decks out his absurd subject-matter (like an ape in purple); if you take away those exclamations in which – as though the matter were already most clearly proven – he so frequently raves against the whole Church, and rejoices as though he were a fierce victor, although his army has not yet been mustered; you will see that nothing remains other than a naked and pitiable sophistry.' [124]

That new Evangelist had already returned to Wittenberg from his Patmos, and although he had earlier publicly praised his brothers greatly for their abolition of the Mass in a published book, nevertheless, since this had not been done by his bidding and under his authority, when he returned home he publicly disapproved of this matter in an address to the people on the first Sunday in Lent. 'Everyone' (he said) 'was mistaken, who cooperated in and agreed to the abolition of the Mass, not because this was not a good thing, but because it was not done in an orderly fashion. But you will say' (he said), 'that this is just, according to the Scripture. I too admit that; but what has become of order, since this was done out of heedlessness, without any due order and with scandal to one's neighbor? And were not the Mass so evil a thing, I would wish to restore it. I know the purpose of you all, and I do not know how to avert it. I would know well how to fight against the papists and other insane minds, but in the presence of the Devil I do not know how to hold up.'[125] In the same way he reproved other reckless acts of his followers, some barbaric, some sinful and impious, which they had put into action according to his words and following his doctrine while he was absent. Among these were: the destruction of sacred images; the throwing off of religious dress; the handling of the Body of Christ in the Sacrament by profane hands; etc. Even though he wished all these matters to be open to the people, and ascribed their present state to foolish laws of the Pope, he nevertheless reproved his followers, because these things had been attempted while he was absent. Nevertheless he wished that all the images in the whole world were abolished, because of their abuse, and he wanted all monks and nuns to desert their monasteries so that all such institutions might perish throughout the whole world. And about the venerable Sacrament he said, 'Although they had not sinned by touching it, neither however had they done a good work in this; since God cannot endure mockery as the saints can. However, if anyone is so impudent that he wishes by all means to handle the Sacrament with his own hands, let him see to it that the Sacrament is brought to him in his house, and there he may handle it until he is satiated; but not before the multitude.'[126] And so with sermons of this sort he maliciously restrained and repressed the audacity of other men – especially Andreas Karlstadt – who wanted to amount to something themselves, lest Luther alone should be all things to all people.

Furthermore, Luther attacked Pope Leo X's Bull, 'About the Lord's Supper,' very bitterly. This Bull had been published at Rome before Luther had come to Worms. For although according to ancient custom, all heretics had been excommunicated and anathematized in it, and by name the Gazari, the Patarenes, the Paupers of Lyon, the Arnoldists, the Speronists, the Wycliffites, the Hussites, and last of all Martin Luther together with all his allies and supporters, nevertheless this Bull had come to Luther's hands rather slowly. This was how it came about that after his return he prepared a certain German pamphlet against this Bull, which he sent to the Apostolic See as a New Year's gift. Therefore, he began as follows: 'Martin Luther to the most Holy Roman See and all its Court; first, my thanks and greetings. Most Holy See, make much ado about this greeting, but do not fall apart on account of it, in which I put my name in the first and last place, and forget the kissings of your feet, etc.'[127] Then, after restating the Bull, in response to it he said, 'Moreover, I say this to the Pope and to the threats of this Bull. Whoever dies because of threats, will be driven into his grave by winds breaking from the belly.'[128] But when he had come to the Sixth Article, in which everyone who would supply or sell swords or arms of war to Turks or Saracens was excommunicated, he found fault with this and said, 'What does it serve, to restrain the Turk bodily?

What evil does the Turk do? He occupies his provinces and governs them seasonably. It would be proper for us to experience the same thing from the Pope, who despoils us of body and life, which the Turk does not do. And what is more, the Turk permits each individual to remain in his own faith, which the Pope does not do. Rather, he drives the entire world from the faith of Christ to his own diabolical lies, so that the reign of the Pope, over body, goods, and soul, is undoubtedly ten times worse than that of the Turk. And if we wish to fight against the Turk, we should begin by fighting against the Pope.' [129]

But he attacked the King of England by far the most viciously, in defiance of all human shame, after he learned that esteem for Luther had been diminished to a large extent by the King's book, even among the Germans, once it had been translated into the German language by Jerome Emser. Indeed no slanders which the worst mind and the most evil mouth could invent seemed either too harmful or scurrilous to him. Whatever came into his mouth, he vomited out without any shame – insanely scorning the law of nations, by which a King's dignity ought to be deferred to, and every dictate of religion. And among his slanders he frequently interposed his own monstrous arrogance and contempt, while he falsely based himself on the word of God. 'In truth,' (he said), 'against the words of the fathers, of men, of angels, of demons, I place not ancient custom, not a multitude of people, but the word of the one Eternal Majesty, the Gospel, which they themselves are bound to approve. Here I stand, here I rest, here I remain, here I glory, here I triumph, here I assault the Papist, the Thomists, the Henryists, the Sophists, and all the gates of Hell – and much more the words of men, however holy, or fallacious custom. The Word of God is above all; the Divine Majesty has so taken my part, that I care not at all if a thousand Augustines, a thousand Cyprians, a thousand churches of Henry, should stand against me. God cannot err or be mistaken; Augustine and Cyprian, like all the elect, could err – and did so.' [130] And later: 'If we are Christ's alone, who is this dull-witted king who labors with his lies to make us the Pope's? We are not the Pope's, but the Pope is ours. It is our business, not to be judged by him, but to judge him. For the spiritual is judged by no one, but itself judges everyone. Since this is true, everything is yours, even the Pope; how much more those bits of filth and stains of humankind, the Thomists and the Henries.' [131] And later: 'And so we ripped away the Mass, and we triumph over the advocate of the Sacraments. And indeed, now that the Mass has been conquered, I think that we have triumphed over the entire Papacy. For on the Mass, as on a rock, the whole Papacy is founded, with its Monasteries, Episcopates, Colleges, altars, ministers, and doctrines; and indeed, with its entire belly. And it must happen that all of these will fall into ruin, when once their sacrilegious and abominable Mass has fallen.' [132]

And truly, is not this a shameless and monstrous taunt and boast of his, where he says: 'If for the sake of Christ I have trampled upon the Idol of the Roman abomination, which had set itself up in the place of God, and had made itself the ruler of Kings and of the whole world, who is this Henry, this new

Thomist, a faithful disciple of so cowardly a monster, that I should honor his virulent blasphemies? Granted, he is a defender of the Church, but of that very Church which he supports and guards in such a large book; that is to say, of a purple-robed and drunken whore, the mother of fornication. I consider both his Church and the defender himself as the same thing, and I will attack both of them in one rush, and with Christ as my leader I will prevail. For I am certain that I have my doctrines from Heaven, doctrines by which I was triumphant even against one who has more of virtue and wisdom in his smallest fingernail than all the Popes and Kings and Doctors. Thus, they who cast these Bulls of names and titles against me and who hawk pamphlets about under royal signatures accomplish nothing. My doctrines will stand, and the Pope will fall, despite all the gates of Hell, and the powers of the air, and the land, and the sea. They have called me out to war, therefore they will have war; they scorned peace when it was offered, therefore they will have no peace. God will see which of us shall fail first from exhaustion, the Pope or Luther. For the death of the abominable Papacy is at hand; its ineluctable fate presses on it, and (as Daniel says) it approaches its end, and no one will help it.'

Not content with all these things, and with a great many other frothings and threats of insane boasting of the same kind, he added falsehoods and deceits of the most savage kind, not only against the Pope and the King of England, but also against the Princes of Germany. And he expressed these much more ferociously in the German version than in the Latin, doubtless so that he could incite the people against the Princes more readily. Therefore he said: 'I have already appeared before them three times. At length I entered into Worms, even though I knew that the public trust granted to me had been violated by the Emperor. For the Princes of Germany, who belong to a nation that was of old most praised for its faith but is now in thrall to the Roman idol, have learned nothing more than to despise the faith, to the everlasting shame of their Nation.' [133] And later: 'These are the weapons by which heretics are conquered today: the fire and insanity of the stupidest asses and Thomist pigs. But let those pigs proceed, and if they dare, let them burn me. Here I am, and I will await them; in my very ashes, even if scattered over a thousand seas, I will follow that abominable crowd, and I will wear them out.' [134] Finally, 'While I live, I will be the Papacy's foe; if I am burned, I will be twice the foe. Thomist pigs, do what you can; you will have Luther as a she-bear in your road, as a lioness in your footpath. Everywhere, he will run against you and will not allow you to have peace, until he has worn down your iron necks and your brazen foreheads, either into salvation or into perdition.' [135] And again in the German version he said: 'The more things they wrote, the more insanely, stupidly, and shamelessly they kept on lying, until at length it became evident, through extremely clear Scriptures – by the grace of God – that the Papacy, the Episcopate, the Colleges, the Monasteries, the Academies, together with every priest, monk, nun, mass, and ceremony of God, are all nothing but damned factions of the Devil. For that crowd has this intention, that it should act before God by works, and not by unadorned faith: but through that kind

of action, clearly, Christ is denied and faith is extinguished.' [136] Again: 'The
Pope and Henry of England are rightly joined together. The former holds his
Papacy with as clear a conscience as the latter his kingdom, and so they scratch
each other, as mules are accustomed to do.' [137]

But in the same year Luther wrote far more savagely and more rebelliously
than this against every ecclesiastical estate, under this title: *Against the Spiritual
Estate of the Pope and the Bishops, Falsely So Called.* But he called himself a
Preacher [138] by the grace of God, and added that if he even called himself an
Evangelist by the grace of God he would be able to prove this more easily
than any of the Bishops could prove his own title. In truth, he was certain
that Christ himself called him thus, and so considered him; since Christ was
the teacher of this doctrine, and would be a witness in the last day that clearly
this doctrine was not Luther's, but was the pure Gospel of Christ. Therefore
he says, in the preface to the book: 'Through these words I certainly assure
you that henceforth I will no longer do you the honor of submitting myself
either to you or even to any angel from heaven, for the purpose of having my
doctrine either judged or examined. For there was enough of foolish humility,
for the third time already, at Worms, and yet it profited nothing. But I wish
to be heard, and – according to the doctrine of St Peter – to display the reason
and foundation of my doctrine before the whole world, and to keep it unjudged
by anyone whatsoever, even by all the angels. For since I am certain about
my doctrine, I wish on its account to be your judge and the judge of the angels
also (as Paul says), since anyone who does not accept my doctrine cannot be
saved. For it is God's, not mine; and concerning it, my judgment is not mine,
but is God's.' [139] And later he says, 'But if they should say, "Rebellion against
Church officials must be feared," then I answer, "But surely the Word of God
should not be neglected, nor should all the world perish, on that account?" Is
it just that all souls should perish eternally, while the worldly pomp of these
specters remains undisturbed? It would be better that all Bishops should be
killed, that every College and Monastery should be eradicated from the foundations up, than that one single soul should perish – I will not even say, than
that all souls should perish – for the sake of these useless specters and
dolls.[140] What purpose do they serve, except to indulge their desires through
the sweat and labor of others, and to impede the Word of God? Moreover, if
they do not wish to hear the Word of God, but babble insanely and rage with
their excommunications, their fires, their slaughters, and every evil; then what
could more justly happen to them, than some strong rebellion, which would
exterminate them from the world? And if this happens, it should be only a
cause for laughter; as the Divine Wisdom says in Proverbs 1.' [141]

These things he wrote in the preface. Truly, with what slanders, abuses,
grimaces, taunts, shameful names, bitter words, deceits, blasphemies, and curses
did he rave against every ecclesiastical Order, but most especially against the
Bishops, throughout that German book. No one could represent or judge him
better, than that book itself. Here it will be enough to repeat his Bull, which
appears in the approximate middle of the book, in these very words:

'The Bull and the Reformation of Dr Martin Luther. All those who bring aid, and devote body, goods, and reputation to this end, that the Episcopate should be destroyed, and the rule of the Bishops extinguished, these are the beloved sons of God, and true Christians, who observe the precepts of God and fight against the arrangements of the Devil. Or if they cannot do this, let them at least condemn and shun that system of rule. But in contrast, all those who support the rule of Bishops, and give them voluntary obedience, these men are the Devil's own ministers, and fight against the ordinances and the law of God.' [142] Now in this Bull, in order to persuade the people of Germany, he added many citations from the Scriptures, which he turned forcibly and twisted against the Bishops. And the laity agreed with these the more easily, and considered them to be correctly quoted, the more inimical they were to the abuses and tricks of avarice which (the Lutherans shouted) were extended publicly in the halls and courts of the Bishops, through the greediness of the Officials and the Procurators, which greediness Luther prettily described in his book.

And so this brawler began his boldest and most seditious crime by far, which most greatly disturbed Germany, not only through deceitful pamphlets, but also through the very Gospel of Peace. Just as Judas the Betrayer once did, to whom the Lord said, 'Judas, do you betray the Son of Man with a kiss?' (for a kiss is the symbol of peace and friendship) – thus, surely, Luther plunged Germany into war and rebellions by means of the Gospel of Peace. And in this matter, it was not only a case of city rising against city in obstinate hatred, people against people, province against province; but in every city, the common folk plotted wars and seditions against the Senate, the people against their Prince, and the Princes against their Emperor. And the more each one bandied about the Gospel and desired to appear as an Evangelist surpassing all others, the more he strove for revolution. Why was this so? Because Luther persuaded them that a Gospel was more true, the more revolution it produced. For long before, in Worms, in the presence of the Emperor, before all the Princes and Orders of the Empire, he had dared to say openly that this was to him by far the most delightful of all sights in the world, that he should see factions and dissensions being made concerning the Word of God. For this was obviously the course, the subject, and the outcome of the Word of God, as it says: 'I came to bring not peace, but a sword.'

But the King of England, of whom a mention was made above, cautiously foreseeing where this artifice was tending, warned the most Illustrious Princes the Dukes of Saxony, Frederick, Johannes, and George. He warned them very faithfully and as a friend, but late and too slowly, because of the distance of their locations. For before his letters reached them, already Luther's new German translation [143] was published far and wide throughout all Germany. Nevertheless, it is allowable to quote here the pious warning of that King.

'As I was about to seal these letters' (he said) 'it came into my memory that Luther, in his dirges against me, excused himself for responding so slightly to the remainder of what I had said, by claiming that he was busy with translating the Bible. It seemed good to me, therefore, to urge you, that you make this of all things the matter of your greatest attention: that he not be permitted to do so. For although I do not deny that it is a good thing to read the Sacred Scripture in whatever language, it is certainly dangerous that, in a translation done by this man whose bad faith inspires confidence in everyone, his true desire should be that he pervert the good Scripture by evilly twisting it; [144]so that the people will think they have read in Sacred Scripture things which an accursed man has derived from equally accursed heresies.' [145] These things the King wrote, as wisely as possible. For who could sufficiently describe how great a kindling and source of division, revolution, and ruin that translation of the New Testament was? That man of quarrels changed many things in it, contrary to the ancient and proven reading of the Church, and removed many things, and added many other things, and twisted the sense into another meaning – and bestowed great care on doing so. He added many erroneous and sarcastic glosses of his own in the margins throughout the book, and in his prefaces he omitted no kind of malice that might draw the reader into his own camp. Therefore, scholars were found among the Germans who would collect the errors – which he himself admitted – and the alterations from throughout that translation; some of them found over a thousand such, others fewer.

Among these critics, Jerome Emser certainly deserved the greatest praise, since he not only noted the errors Luther made in translation and published them for the people, but even published his own translation, which agreed with the Latin text that was approved and accepted by the Church.[146] He published this as an antidote to Luther's poison, and it was not a negligible comfort to the Catholic people. For from this labor the Catholics learned where Luther had been mistaken, and they were able to refute with confidence the Lutherans who were priding themselves in their Gospel. But before Emser's work appeared, Luther's New Testament had been reproduced by the printers to an amazing degree, so that even shoemakers and women and every kind of unlearned person, whoever of them were Lutherans and had somehow learned German letters, read it most eagerly as the font of all truth. And by reading and rereading it they committed it to memory and so carried the book around with them in their bosoms. Because of this, in a few months they attributed so much learning to themselves that they did not blush to dispute about the faith and the Gospel, not only with laypeople of the Catholic party, but also with priests and monks, and furthermore, even with Masters and Doctors of Sacred Theology. Nay, more – even mere women were found who of their own accord dared to challenge the proposed themes and published books of the Germans – and that indeed they did by most boldly insulting men, reproaching them with ignorance, and holding them in contempt. And not only laymen and private citizens; but even certain Doctors, and licensed members of the whole faculty of Theology, and even whole universities. This information was obtained from Argula, a certain noble woman.[147]

The Lutheran women, with all womanly shame set aside, proceeded to such a point of audacity that they even usurped for themselves the right and office of teaching publicly in the Church, despite the fact that Paul openly speaks against this and prohibits it. Nor were they lacking defenders among the Lutheran men, who said that Paul forbade the right of teaching to women only insofar as there were sufficient men who knew how to teach and were able to do so. But where men were lacking or neglectful, there it was most permissible for women to teach. And Luther himself had long before taught that women too were true Christian priests, and what is more, that whoever crept out of Baptism was truly Pope, Bishop, and Priest, according to this saying of Peter: 'Moreover, you are a chosen people, a royal priesthood, a holy nation, etc.'

Therefore, since the mob is everywhere more intent on and avid for spreading revolutionary ideas abroad than for preserving accustomed things in their normal state, it happened that the crowd of Lutherans devoted themselves much more to the work of teaching the translated sacred Scriptures than did the Catholic people, among whom the laity by and large entrusted that responsibility to the priests and monks. Thence it happened not infrequently that in discussions more passages of Scripture were quoted extemporaneously by the Lutheran laypeople than were quoted by the Catholic priests and monks. And for a long time already Luther had persuaded his throngs that no trust should be put in any words save those that are taken from the Holy Scriptures. For this reason, the Catholics were reputed among the Lutherans to be ignorant of the Scriptures, even if they were the most erudite of theologians. Indeed, some laypeople would sometimes even contradict the theologians openly before the crowd, as if the theologians spoke mere lies and human fictions in their arguments. And other misfortunes followed. For the venerable theologians had for many years past neglected skill in languages and in the more refined studies. Therefore, right from the beginning, working through Philip Melanchthon and through Zwingli, Oecolampadius, and Bucer (before they began to differ from him in not a few articles), Luther had drawn into his camp all the youths who were dedicated to the study of eloquence in letters and languages, and were most greatly improved in their intellects by the keen and polished works of Erasmus of Rotterdam. And the youths, keen in their intellects and enduring in their labors, soon were so proficient in the literal interpretation of the Sacred Scriptures (to which Luther attributed a single sense, and that only the literal one) that not even Theologians with thirty years' experience seemed so prompt in citing passages of Scripture as they were. And since the youths were proud of their skill in languages and their elegance of style, they soon began not only to show contempt for theologians of the old type, but even to challenge them – most especially while they were debating before the people.

And if anyone spoke against their novelties, they quickly produced as a pretext a Greek or Hebrew reading, or something else from the most ancient authors, and immediately with whole cartfuls of abusive statements inveighed against theologians who were ignorant of Greek and Hebrew literature, whom they hatefully called sophists, asses, pigs, creatures of the belly, and useless weights upon the earth. [148] To these comments they most immodestly added catcalls and loud laughs. And commending Luther alone to the people as a true theologian, they most hatefully denounced his adversaries as ignorant, nay, even as enemies of the truth, who hated Luther on account of their own abridged and diminished nourishment.

Furthermore, if God mercifully preserved for Himself any people who would not bend their knees to this Saxon Baal, but through pious zeal resisted him, and either wrote or preached publicly against him, such people soon found that the saying of Paul was only too true. For all who wish to live piously in Christ Jesus will suffer persecution. For the Lutherans said things that were pleasing to the people, against laziness and avarice and luxury. For instance, they cried out against the whorings and concubinage of the Clergy, and claimed a false Christian liberty, saying that we should be free from all precepts of Church, Pope, Bishops, and Councils. And they proved – by deceitful use of the Scriptures – that fasts, long prayers, vigils, and other deeds of penitence are nothing; Christ had made enough reparation for our sins; faith alone was sufficient; our good works are not merits, but sins, even if they are done in the best way possible. And they said many other sayings of this kind, and said them all promptly, keenly, and eloquently. But the Catholics, following what was owed to their office, rebuked the people for their sins, and rebuked the new teachings of Luther. They bade the people obey the precepts and rites of the Church; they taught that one should fast, and pray, and that other good works should be pursued, so that we may make a worthy return of penitence for our sins. For this reason it surely happened, that the Lutherans were more persuasive to the people, while the Catholic orators were hateful to them – to such an extent that in many cities frivolous youths, novices, and recently converted Lutherans, even those whose life had been contaminated by lusts, Apostasy, and other sins, not only were easily accepted for preaching to the people, but were even preferred to serious and mature men, pastors and priors, who had always conducted themselves honestly and had taught the people most faithfully by word and example.

And it was not a rare occurrence that true and legitimate pastors (however dear and venerable they had been previously) were either driven away by force by the rebellious people, or left of their own accord, worn out and broken by derisive gestures and daily injuries, or, when they were deprived of their assessed tithes and oblations, were reduced to extreme poverty and forced to seek a living for themselves elsewhere. Meanwhile, the new preachers were glorying in their triumph and even growing rich, as by the word of their new Gospel they led the eagerly following people wheresoever they wished. And they led the people into hatred of the Clergy especially, and into licentious freedom in every wickedness, so that they were straight away formidable foes, not only to the Clergy, who were anxiously fearing and every hour expecting an outbreak of the teeth-gnashing people, but also to the Senate, and to whatever citizens and magistrates were most honest. The common people, who were in debt, were planning a fraternal division of these men's goods and houses – fraternal, for they were brothers in Christ, although by no means in their moneychests.[149] For the time had come (concerning which the Apostle had prophesied), when they would not endure sound doctrine, but would heap teachers together for themselves, according to their own desires, with their ears itching.

And the activity and industry of the Lutherans in fighting for their sect was astonishing. For many, setting aside their domestic affairs, wrote hither and thither to their friends that they should pay the greatest attention to this business. Many, in imitation of the true Gospel, left their parents and friends, so that they might proclaim their new Gospel – according to which we have all heretofore been piteously deceived by the papists, and in truth all are equals and brothers in Christ. And – what was most harmful to all Germany – Luther and many others with him bandied about the notion that the Gospel had never been preached genuinely [150] and sincerely to the Germans up until that day; but he brought them the true Gospel, which for many centuries had been hidden under a throne. If anyone of the faithful muttered in opposition, soon the whole assembly of the common people was stirred up against him, as if he resisted the Gospel for the sake of his belly.

And the Lutherans freely insinuated themselves everywhere by a voluntary pilgrimage through the cities, clearly for no other reason than to inculcate their Gospel in those cities. And since this circumstance gave a great appearance of piety beyond that presented by the accustomed ministers of the Church (who had fixed and certain stipends), no doubt it turned away from the true Church many people, who were more carefully considering this saying of Christ: 'Accept freely, give freely,' than His other saying: 'The laborer is worthy of his hire;' and this saying of Paul: 'What soldier ever served at his own expense?', and again, 'If we have sown spiritual things, is it a great matter that we should reap your carnal things?'

Though truly the Lutheran orators, after they had put down roots, were no less intent and eager in their own business than the Catholics were, still in the first sowing, their industry and generosity were amazing. First, in order that they might never be reproached with this saying of the Apostle to the Romans: 'How shall they preach, if they are not sent?' or this one to the Hebrews: 'No one takes this honor upon himself, except he who is called by God, as Aaron was,' they procured secret letters or messages, so that they might be invited either by the people themselves or by someone of the magnates whom they knew to favor their faction; or, if they were not invited, in order to be more easily admitted into a city they either pretended that their exile was voluntary or that it was a necessary flight, forced upon them by the tyrannical persecution of the Gospel (even if they had fled because they were entangled in their own misdeeds). And when they had found some friends in a city in which they intended to announce their Gospel, they endeavored through those friends to be allowed, at least once or twice, to present the Word of God to the people of Christ, free of charge. And if they gained their wish, they soon inflamed the people with hatred of the Clergy; but if not, they acted secretly in hiding places, until they drew certain people over into their camp and then prevailed on them to solicit others who – either by prayers or by threats – might gain permission from the Magistrates and the Senate for them freely to preach the Word of God. Clearly, it seemed hateful to the magnates to deny the Word of God or to prohibit it from being announced free of charge to the people. And so, although it seemed dangerous to admit the Lutherans, nevertheless it seemed more dangerous to reject the Word of God, and to deprive the people of Gospel nourishment. And so it happened that, under this pretext, the Gospel of Luther crept into all the most populous imperial cities of Germany, with only a few exceptions. The most important exception was Cologne, which so many thousand Holy Martyrs, who either suffered there or lived there most religiously, had preserved by their merit from this plague up until this time.

Furthermore, the judgment, industry, financial outlay, and works of the printers and booksellers greatly promoted this new Gospel. For whatever was favorable to Luther was printed as carefully and faultlessly as possible; but whatever was favorable to the Catholics was printed as slothfully and with as many errors as possible. And the printers printed works that were by Luther or supported Luther at their own expense, and in the greatest number, so that these works might be disseminated very widely. For the number of apostate monks who had left their monasteries and returned to the world was already vast; and these monks, seeking to make a living from Lutheran books, were wandering far and wide throughout the provinces of Germany in the guise of booksellers. But the printers scorned the books of the Catholics, as if they were the unlearned and trivial writings of an ancient barbarism, and would print none of these books of their own accord.

Some printers, driven by the lack of congenial material, or mostly led on by their hope of profit, and helped by the money and resources of others, accepted some of the Catholics' books for printing. However, they printed them so negligently, hastily, and badly, that they brought more gratification from this work to the Lutherans than to the Catholics. If any of them produced a more correct work for the Catholics, they were tormented and ridiculed by the others in the public marketplaces of Frankfurt and elsewhere, as being papists and servants of the priests. And although the Emperor and other Princes and Catholic Kings had prohibited by the most severe edicts that Lutheran works should be either printed or sold, nevertheless they accomplished nothing by these edicts except that even more profit accrued to the Lutheran booksellers; especially since the Magistrates and Senators to whom the task had been entrusted of inquiring about and censuring these things either conspired together evilly, or dealt with the matter lazily and negligently, as if it were an odious thing and full of slander in the people's eyes. The booksellers, not unaware of these things and frequently warned by the inquisitors themselves, hid away in secret those books which had to do with Luther, and in public certain secular books having to do with other business were offered for sale. For this reason it happened that the buyers who were seeking Lutheran materials were forced to buy them more dearly and at a higher price in secret than they would have bought them in public, because the bookseller would allege that he was afraid and in danger.

At this time the Emperor Charles V was far away from Germany, involved in a serious and long-lasting war which had been declared against him by the King of France while the Emperor was residing in Worms. His brother Ferdinand, the Archduke of Austria, etc., was then the Imperial Vicar or place-holder. Ferdinand and the other Catholic princes, seeing that the people were greatly lured and enticed into the Lutheran sect by Luther's new translation, decreed through published mandates that any subject who had Luther's New Testament, or any other of his books at all, in his house should publicly hand the books over to those on whom the task was laid of receiving them. And in very many places, the Princes' subjects, whose consciences instructed them not to keep prohibited books in their houses in defiance of the edicts and prohibitions of the Pope, the Emperor, and other Princes, obediently handed over books of this sort, which were gathered together in each place into one pile and were publicly burned.

For Luther seemed to the best people to have proceeded too maliciously against the Sacred Scripture of the New Testament; since he had, with an audacious censorship, rejected the Letter to the Hebrews, the Letter of James, the Letter of Jude, and the Apocalypse of John from the canon of the New Testament. He defamed these books openly, with savage falsehoods, in his prefaces.[151] And in his general preface, he even set his hand most audaciously against the most Holy Gospels. For he wished particularly that this most ancient opinion and verdict of the Church, which is known and received by all Christians, should be rejected: namely, that there are only four Gospels, and the same number of Evangelists.[152] By saying this, he rejected as well the most sacred figures, and visions, and mysteries of the Scriptures, which predict that number, Four, in Genesis, in Ezekiel, in the Apocalypse, and so on. Moreover, he rejected the common, accustomed division of the books of the New Testament into legal, historical, prophetic, and wisdom books.[153] Furthermore, he instructed the reader to take care not to make a book of law or of doctrine out of the Gospel, 'as has been done until now' (he said) 'and as even *Prefaces* taught.' For he asserted that the Gospel did not require works, or prescribe rules, but taught only faith in Christ, and sweetly consoled believers.

And he himself took great pains to translate many passages of Scripture differently, and force them into another meaning, than the Church held. He did this especially in those passages which were best known to everyone in common. Among these were the Lord's Prayer, the Angel's Salutation, the Song of Mary, and the Song of Zachariah. He did this so that the people would more easily believe that the Church had not, up until that time, had the true Gospel text. Therefore, in the Lord's Prayer, which is recorded by Matthew in his sixth chapter, he quickly changed the beginning, saying: 'Our Father in Heaven, let your name be blessed' [*Noster pater in coelo, tuum nomen sit sanctum*]. But the universal Church and all Germany had, until that time, said it thus: 'Our Father who art in Heaven, hallowed be thy name' [*Pater noster, qui es in coelis, sanctificetur nomen tuum*]. Nor do the Greeks have a different version. And in the middle of this prayer, he substituted 'daily' [*quotidianum*], which Luke says, for 'necessary' [*supersubstantialem*]. At the end of the prayer he added a whole clause, which the Churches' earliest copies, written earlier than the years 700 or 800, nowhere have. For the Church says: 'But deliver us from evil. Amen.' But Luther says it as follows: 'But deliver us from evil. For thine is the kingdom, and the power, and the glory, throughout the ages. Amen.'

The other three passages are in Luke 1. For in the Angelic Salutation, where the Church says, 'Hail, Full of Grace' [*Ave gratia plena*], Luther says, 'Hail, gracious one' [*gratiosa*] or 'lovely/lovable one' [*amabilis*]. In German, this is 'du holdselige,' which means, 'worthy to be loved.' In the Song of Mary, which is commonly called the Magnificat, where the Church reads or sings, 'All generations shall call me blessed' [*Beatam me dicent omnes generationes*], Luther says, 'All the sons of sons shall glorify me as blessed' [*Beatam me glorificabunt omnes filii filiorum*]. Finally, in the Song of Zachariah, which is read in every morning service and is called the 'Benedictus,' where the Church sings, 'In holiness and righteousness before him, all our days' [*in sanctitate et iustitia coram ipso, omnibus diebus nostris*], Luther translates thus: 'Until we live in holiness and righteousness, which is pleasing to him' [*quo ad vivimus in sanctitate et iustitia, quae ipsi placita est*]. These things have been mentioned as examples, from which it is clearly understood that Luther at that time translated the New Testament into the German language with the most evil intention, namely that he might convince, or at least persuade, the people that the Church had often erred in the Sacred Text, and (as he later dared to boast publicly) that the Germans had, up until the time of his own preaching, had never before heard the true and genuine Gospel.[154]

Nevertheless, after a few years he himself altered his first edition in many places; to such an extent, in fact, that some people noted thirty-three passages in the Gospel of Matthew alone, in which his second edition has a different reading from the first edition, which preceded the later one by five years. Nor was he content with these versions; he also published a Latin edition, which differed from his own German version in many places. He did this, clearly, so that he might confuse not only German readers, but also any Latin readers of the Holy Gospel. And so that there would be no end to his wickedness, in the same year he published other seditious pamphlets in German. Two of these were especially destined for confusion – one, concerning the monastic life, and the other, concerning married life. The first of these had the title: *About Avoiding the Doctrines of Men*;[155] the second, *About Married Life*.[156] The first, under a great show of Scriptures, condemns all precepts and institutes of the Church that are not expressed in the Holy Scriptures. Among these were: that we should not eat eggs or meat during Lent; that on Ember days and the Vigils of the Apostles, we should fast; that Benedictines and Carthusians should abstain from meat; that it is not lawful for a monk to discard the monastic habit and return freely to the world; and so on. The second book speaks most shamelessly, and in defiance of natural modesty, about the commingling of male and female. It claims, from this saying of God 'Be fruitful, and multiply,' that this type of commingling is no less necessary than food, drink, sleep, and the other works of nature. And it adds that, as a man cannot change his sex, so he cannot be without a woman, nor can a woman be without a man; since this is not a matter of free choice, or mere advice, but is a necessary and natural thing, that every man should have a woman, and every woman should have a man. And this is more necessary than to eat, to drink, to cough, to sleep, to wake, etc. Therefore, priests, monks, and nuns are obliged to renounce their vows and to give their attention to marriage. And there was nothing concerning the impediments to marriage, the degrees of affinity and consanguinity, which this book does not confuse and taunt, whatever the holy fathers had determined about this subject beyond what is expressed in the Scripture. Nor on these matters was his German book any better, which he wrote about the abuse of the Mass. It was translated from the Latin, *About the Abolition of the Mass.*[157] Indeed, in that book he vomited out on to the people so much pestilence against the holy rites of the Church, that if his wickedness had not been inexhaustible, he would have seemed to have discharged all the pus of his whole poison there.

1523

But when Luther learned that the Catholic Princes forbade his New Testament to be sold, and that in public edicts they ordered any copies that had already been bought to be handed over to chosen commissaries and magistrates, truly he burned with such anger and raved with so abusive a pen against the secular Princes that he would seem to have held back all his powers of cursing and all the weapons of his slanders for them alone, and not to have vomited anything out against the Pope and the Bishops previously. Therefore, soon after the beginning of the following New Year, he published a German book, *On Temporal Authority*, addressed to his Prince Johannes, Duke of Saxony, who was not yet Elector since his elder brother was still alive. In this book Luther attacked Princes with as much ferocity as if the man to whom he was writing either had not been born a Prince or had, as an enemy or a degenerate apostate, defected from the other Princes to the common crowd. For who would not be amazed that a famous Prince, descended from a long line of exceedingly renowned and noble ancestors, was able to accept with calm ears these words in that book of an ignoble Apostate, sprung from the dregs of the common people?

'In Meissen,' Luther wrote, 'in Bavaria, in Marchia, and in other places the tyrants have published an edict, that New Testaments should be handed over, on this side and on that, to the government offices. In this circumstance, let the subjects act as follows. Let them not hand over a page, not a single letter, on peril of their salvation. For whoever does this hands Christ over into the hands of Herod. For the tyrants act like Christ-killers, like Herods. However, if it is so commanded, subjects ought to endure invasions into their homes, and the seizure by force of either books or goods. One ought not to resist this audacity, but it must be borne; however, it must not be justified, nor should it be shown submission, or deference, or obedience, not even for a moment or to a single finger's breadth. For these tyrants are acting as Princes of the world ought to act. They are worldly Princes; and the world is an enemy to God. Therefore, it is fitting that they too do a thing that is opposed to God but in agreement with the world: so that, obviously, they may not lose repute but may remain worldly Princes. Therefore, you should not wonder if they rage against the Gospel, and busy themselves with this; it is proper for them to prove sufficiently their title and their name.[158] And you should know, that from the beginning of the world a wise Prince has been a very rare bird, and even rarer than that, a virtuous Prince; they are usually the greatest fools and the worst idlers on the face of the earth. For these reasons, the worst should always be expected from them, and very little good should be hoped for from them: especially in divine matters, which pertain to the salvation of souls. For these men are God's magistrates and executioners, whom the Divine Wrath uses for the punishment of evildoers, and to preserve external peace. Our God is a great lord, and therefore it is proper for him to have such executioners and magistrates – namely, noble, famous, and rich ones; and he wants them to receive riches, honor, and fear copiously and abundantly, from everyone. It pleases his divine will, that we should call his executioners merciful lords, that we should prostrate ourselves at their feet, and that we should be subjected to them in all humility – but only so long as they do not extend their skill too far, so that they should wish to become shepherds instead of executioners. If a Prince enjoys good fortune, so that he is wise, virtuous, and Christian, this is one miracle among the great ones, and a most precious sign of Divine Grace upon that province. For in the common course of events, it happens according to this saying in Isaiah 3: "I will give them children as their Princes, and effeminate men will dominate them." And this of Hosea 13: "I will give to you a king in my fury, and will take him away in my wrath." The world is too evil, nor is it worthy to have many wise and virtuous princes: it is proper for frogs to have storks.' [159] Luther wrote these things, in hatred and contempt for secular princes, to his own Prince and protector.

And shortly afterwards he wrote much more threateningly and seditiously, in these words: 'These' (he said) 'are our Christian princes, who defend the faith and devour the Turk: beautiful comrades indeed, about whom it can well be believed that they will, with their lovely wisdom, accomplish something of this sort: namely, that they will break their necks on a precipice, and lead their lands and their people into catastrophe and misery. However, I would exceedingly faithfully counsel these utterly blind men, that they should consider the application to themselves of this little, little saying which is contained in Psalm 106: "He pours out His contempt upon Princes." I swear to you by God that, if you disregard the fact that this little saying that is coming upon you with speed, you are lost, even if everyone of you is as powerful as the Turk is; and it will benefit you nothing to brag and rave. And already a great part of this saying has come into effect. For already there are few Princes who are not considered fools or idlers; and because of this, since the Princes show themselves to be such, the common people are becoming intelligent and the scourge of Princes, which God calls contempt, is advancing strongly among the populace and the common people. And I fear that it cannot be restrained, unless the Princes act as Princes should, and begin once again to govern with reason and modesty. The people will not bear, they neither can nor wish to bear your tyranny and impudence for long, good Princes and Lords; accordingly, think about your actions. God no longer wishes to be indulgent. The world now is no longer as it once was when you used to hunt and harass men like wild beasts, etc.' [160]

Meanwhile, while Luther was raving in this way, certain Germans began to uphold the pious and erudite declaration of the King of England (in which he gloriously and bravely defended the Seven Sacraments of the Church from Luther's *Babylonian Captivity*) and to turn Luther's lies back against his own mouth and pen. Dr Johannes Eck did this in Latin [161] and Dr Thomas Murner in German.[162] The former did this most amusingly, when he counted and condemned fifty lies of Luther from his one published book against the King. And Murner marked Luther's fiftieth and last lie with a distinguished crown in the margin, since that lie was the most distinguished and the king, as it were, of his other lies. For Luther had said at the end of his book exactly as follows, in Latin: 'I have refrained from mentioning the venom and lies with which the King's book is fully packed.' But in the German version he said as follows: 'I have also fought on every side, so that no one yet can charge me with any lie at all.' This noble lie of his seemed worthy of the crown to Murner, since it is well known that all his adversaries, however many wrote against him, always charged him with as many lies as possible. For one Dr Johannes Dietenberger, a pious and distinguished theologian, charged and convicted Luther of 873 lies, in merely two refutations which he wrote against him, one concerning vows and the other concerning confession – not to mention the innumerable other lies which Dietenberger imputed to Luther, neither falsely nor unjustly, in his other responses.[163]

Furthermore, two Englishmen also defended their King, in published books, from Luther's accusations and slanders; the first of these was Dr John Fisher, Bishop of Rochester, a man of the greatest, all-encompassing erudition, and also of the purest life, reputation, and piety. Since Fisher was the greatest Theologian and the most knowledgeable in the three principal languages, [164] he most seriously and thoroughly indeed refuted the two principals and leaders among the heretics of this time, Luther and Oecolampadius. The latter he refuted in five books *Concerning the Venerable Sacrament of the Eucharist*;[165] the former he refuted first in a large volume, *Against the Assertion of the Forty-One Articles*,[166] which Pope Leo X had condemned in his Bull. He refuted him for a second time in another book, *In Defense of the King's Declaration*,[167] and again in another book, *In Defense of the Sacred Priesthood*.[168] In all of these books, certainly, he used a wondrous moderation against the most immoderate of men, and a profound erudition in refuting errors and lies, citing now Scriptures, now the testimonies of ancient authors. Indeed, because of the outstanding malice of his adversary, the beginning of Fisher's work in defense of the King's book is somewhat more bitter, due to his just sorrow, than the utmost kindness and gentleness of the man had been accustomed to speak. For he says: 'This is the word of Christ in the Canticles: "Capture for us the little foxes, which destroy the vines." In this He plainly warns us that heretics must be captured before they mature. For such men are eager to destroy the vines, that is, the Church of Christ, by their vulpine deceits. Therefore I would wish that those men, on whom the duty is laid that they seize heretics while they are still small, would hear this saying. For there would not today be so serious a storm and a disturbance of all matters in the Church, if Luther had been subdued while he was still a little fox. But now he has turned into an enormous fox, aged and cunning, trained in such wiles, crafts, and arts that the means by which he might be restrained is very difficult [to find]. But what have I said, a fox? It would be insufficient, if I had said a rabid dog, or an utterly voracious wolf, or the cruelest she-bear, who is driven by a kind of fury when her cubs are stolen: or better, all of these at once. For this monster nourishes many beasts within himself. But he even glories exceedingly in names of this kind: for he himself calls himself a she-bear and a lioness. For he promises that he will be both of these to the Catholics: he says, "You will have Luther as a she-bear in your road, and a lioness in your footpath." Into a monster of this sort Luther has already grown, from a little fox cub.'

The other Englishman who admirably defended his King is William Ross, clearly a man of the keenest intellect and noted both for his learning and for his eloquence.[169] With a wonderful dexterity, both lightly joking and seriously reproving, he so convicted Luther by the most certain proofs, and thrust his lies back into his shameless mouth, that Luther did not even dare to open his mouth in response; just as neither Luther nor any of the Lutherans ever attempted to answer the Bishop of Rochester. And since Ross's book was published in London and is not generally known among the Germans, it will be worth the trouble to quote one or two passages from it, from which the Germans may clearly learn that Luther has no good reputation among foreigners to whom faith and honesty are dear. Therefore, Ross says:

'Reader, have you ever seen a blind man, who has been angered and wishes to avenge himself by fighting? And so that he may know in which direction he should aim his blow, he provokes a word from his adversary. When he hears this word spoken, he immediately proceeds to strike, so that the other may not change his position too quickly, before he can be struck by the blind man. Luther seems to me to imitate this blind man – but in such a fashion that no one ever acted more ridiculously. For when the King, called by him, replies to him on the right, Luther in return flings out a blow on the left. And so watch, I beg you, how amusingly Luther plays this game. Think that you now see him, intent (because of his blinded eyes) on standing to deliver a box on the ear. "Where are you," he asks, "Lord Henry?" "Here, close to you." Still he invites him to come closer, obviously so that he may strike more surely.

"Produce," he says, "your outstanding book against Luther." "I produce it." Still closer. "What does your Lordship assert? is it the Seven Sacraments?" "It is." Still a very little closer. "By what doctrines? Those of God, or those of men?" "By those of God." Now, obviously certain of hitting him, behold how straight he hurls his blow: "Let your Lordship hear," he says: "In vain they honor Me with the doctrines of men."

"'Friends, if you were admitted to view this, could you refrain from laughing,'" [170] when you see how this ignorant blind man has wandered far aside into another place, and how he rejoices beyond all joy so that he is scarcely in control of himself, as if he had struck his adversary an admirable box on the ear.' [171] And below he says, 'But who can endure such an idler, who demonstrates that he has a thousand vices, and that he is driven by a legion of demons, and yet boasts so stupidly about himself? "All the Holy Fathers have been mistaken; the whole Church has often been mistaken; my doctrine cannot be mistaken, because I am most certain, that my doctrine is not mine, but Christ's." Clearly here he is playing with these words of Christ: "My words are not mine, but are my Father's, who sent me." And this: "The Pope will fall, but my doctrines will stand." Does he not seem here compete with this saying of Christ: "Heaven and earth will pass away, but not one jot of my words will perish"? And when he says, "The Lord dragged me, unaware, into the midst of these crowds," this is more than "The Devil picked him up, and stood him on the top of the Temple." And if someone should respond, "Your evidence is not sound, because you assert evidence about your own self," he will immediately run back to his new scripture: "I am certain that I have my doctrines from Heaven."

'And there he will take his stand, on this principle of his, as if on the firmest foundation, which not all the Popes, Kings, Doctors, men, or Angels will be able to overturn. Therefore he is certain, nay, most certain, that he has his doctrines from Heaven – just as those who sleep are certain and most certain that all the things which they dream are true. Nay indeed, he is certain and most certain, and vigilant to deceive himself that his doctrines are from Heaven – which his conscience within him murmurs were sent to him by the trickeries of demons. He curses men and angels, whoever contradicts his doctrines, and cries out that they are exalting their own brazenness to Heaven; that whoever does not hesitate to censure his own most filthy blasphemies is besmirching holy things and blaspheming God. He cries out only, "All are accursed, who attack my doctrines, since I am certain that I have my doctrines from Heaven." Therefore, when the revered father had demanded this one thing from the beginning but no one had granted it, then this reverend brother, father, drunkard Luther – a fugitive from the Order of St Augustine, one of the insipid teachers of Wittenberg, a misshapen Bachelor and Master of Bacchanalian studies, [172] and an unlearned Doctor of Sacred Theology – further clarifies, "I am certain, that I have my doctrines from Heaven; therefore, my doctrines are heavenly." And then he argues still further, as follows: "My doctrines are heavenly; therefore, whoever contradicts my doctrines, exalts his own brazenness to Heaven, and blasphemes God. Now therefore it is my right, through the majesty of my God, to anathematize anyone – Pope, Emperor, Kings, Bishops, priests, laypeople, and all in the highest estate – who contradicts my doctrines. It is my right to anathematize them, to attack them with curses and reproaches, and to spew out from my mouth mud, filth, dung, shit over the crowns and heads of them all." ' [173]

And later, in the end of his second book, Ross says, 'Now how ridiculous this is, that he excuses himself, lest he seem to bite at the Prince too unmercifully. I certainly do not doubt that the King will easily forgive him all those bitings, since he clearly sees how true this saying of Seneca's is: "A dog who barks rarely bites." Indeed, in his barking Luther equals Cerberus, but in his biting he scarcely equals a gnat. But why should he not bark bravely, this man who is obviously the best and most humble, when as he says he is among irrational monsters, who do not perceive that all his writings are the best and most humble proclamations of this one man – proclamations, that is to say, more puffed up with heresies and blasphemies than anyone ever puffed up a skin with wind. And these monsters were even hardened by the most humble submission, with which this little brother submitted himself to the Vicar of Christ – in just the same way as the Jews submitted themselves to Christ, when after they had slapped Him they bent their knees and cried out as a joke, "Hail, King of the Jews!" Truly now this man swears that he has thus far abstained from lies and poisonous statements, this man who has nothing else in his pen but slanders, lies, and deceits; who has nothing else in his soul but poison, pride, and envy; who conceives nothing in his head other than stupidities, rages, and insanities; who has nothing in his mouth other than sewers, shit, and dung – with which he plays the buffoon more filthily and obscenely than any actual buffoon ever did. No buffoon was ever found who exceeded him, so stolid a bearer of blows that he will thrust filth into his own mouth which he spits out into another's bosom. Therefore, since he is of this sort, I wonder not at all if he is now considered unworthy for anyone to dispute with him.

'Certainly, since indeed he has pledged himself entirely to Hell, and remains obdurate in schism, he has declared that he will never recant his heresies; nevertheless, he ought to resolve in himself that at least he will obtain some rational argument of civil honesty, by which he might claim the authority of a specialist in dogma rather than of a vile buffoon deep in heresy. If he will desire at some time to do this, if he will decide it in earnest, if he will recant his lies and deceits, if he will set aside his stupidities, rages, and furies (which up until now have been all too familiar), if he will reswallow his effusions of excrement, and will relinquish the dung with which he has so foully spotted his tongue and his pen – then there will not be lacking those who will debate about this serious matter seriously, as is fitting. But if he continues to act the buffoon in the same manner as he has begun, and if he continues to rage, to cast insults about, to talk nonsense in his stupidity, to rave in his insanity, to play in his buffoonery, to carry nothing in his mouth other than cesspools, sewers, latrines, shit, and dung – then let others do what they will, we will take counsel at that time to consider whether we should treat him as he raves thus according to his own strengths, and paint him in his own colors, or whether we should leave this raving little brother and this idler in the latrines, with his furies and ravings, befouling and himself befouled with his shit and his dung.' [174]

And in the peroration of this work he also added: 'For he deals with the subject in this way: he openly declares that he is meditating in his mind on a most absurd kind of immortality for himself, and that he has already begun to enjoy it fully, and entirely to exist, to act, and to live in the sensation and titillation of this kind of tiny glory, which he presumes is going to last several thousand years after this present time – that men will remember and will recount that once, in some previous age, there lived a certain rascal whose name was Luther, who because he had outstripped the very devils themselves in impiety, surpassed magpies in his garrulousness, pimps in his dishonesty, prostitutes in his obscenity, and all buffoons in his buffoonery, so that he might adorn his sect with worthy emblems. Since he was eager for this immortality, he paid attention to it, and brought it about, just as the sects of Philosophy have their names taken from their founders; and he thought about Gnathos, and how parasites are called Gnathonicans.[175]Thus this most absurd race of heretics, this offscouring of impiety, of sins, and of filth, is called "Lutherans."' [176] These things Ross said.

But when the King himself had seen Luther's raving – for such it is, rather than a book – against his majesty, although he was angry, he did not write lightly or contentiously in response to Luther. But seriously, with both the greatest piety and the greatest prudence, he wrote letters warning the Dukes of Saxony, Frederick the Elector Prince as the elder and his brother Johannes and cousin George, of the danger. Duke George was a Catholic, but Duke Johannes, following his brother's example, was a Lutheran. The King wrote in the same way to the Dukes of Saxony, the Landgraves of Thuringia, and the Margraves of Meissen. These letters were written in Latin, and the Nuncio of the King brought them to the Princes. He was honorably received and generously entertained by them, and then, when he had been given letters and gifts, he was dismissed and returned to his King. But in his letters, which were truly most serious both in their wording and in their subject-matter, the King first requested their good will because of the relationship between them and then warned the Princes of many dangers which he wisely foresaw and which Germany later disastrously experienced. Duke George honestly exculpated himself from these matters, and reverently thanked the King for his exhortation. But what the other two Princes wrote in reply has not been made publicly known.

Among other things, the King's words included the following: 'What' (he said) 'is more appropriate for you, two Princes so powerful and so devoted to the service of Christ, to attend to, or what ought to move you more vehemently, than the zeal of repressing this Lutheran faction? The Evil Genius has never attacked the earth with a more harmful sect than this, which very soon will bring even greater destruction, unless all good and faithful people resist it, and especially those who before all others both can and should resist, namely the Princes.' [177] And later he said, 'Although I do not think it wholly fitting that I should ready myself publicly to be opposed to and to dispute with such a man; nevertheless, since David, a King and a Prophet, did not consider it unfitting to dance naked before the Ark of the Covenant with any and all comers, thus I myself surely shall consider no one unworthy with whom I may dispute concerning the grace of religion, for the truth of the faith. However, since this man answers nothing to the purpose, but in the place of arguments offers pure ravings, I will neither encourage nor forbid others to engage with him. Certainly I myself will not act so that I rave back at a raving lunatic. For any impartial and wise reader who carefully reads my book side by side with his book will surely easily conclude that mine has already answered Luther's babblings sufficiently and more than sufficiently. But if anyone favors Luther so excessively that he cannot bear to examine my words, or is so markedly stupid, that when he has compared passages from both books he cannot perceive that the subject no longer requires an answer, then I could not ever satisfy such a person by any answer at all.' [178]

And later he said, 'But now the enemy has brought it about that one of two things should become known to the whole world: namely, either that he is wholly an imbecile, or that my arguments were absolutely valid, since he was able to devise nothing against them except crude taunts and wholly insane slanders. If he thinks that I will be moved by these, he is certainly exceedingly mistaken. And indeed let him call me insane as often as he pleases (I believe he so calls me more than a thousand times), nevertheless I will never be so insane that I will be distressed at being called insane by a lunatic. Thus, either my opinion deceives me, or, most Noble Gentlemen, the insulting filth of this man, hurled against me and my royal name, will scarcely move you more than it does me. For well-born minds are accustomed to be bound by a certain reverence for those of noble birth, so that even in an enemy, when they hate and attack the man, nevertheless they honor the rank and reverence the office. Nor was any well-born person ever found who was so uncivil and barbarous that he could be brought by any hostility whatsoever to besmirch a nobleman, in a scurrilous fashion, by the heedlessness of his tongue.' [179]And below: 'Now if Luther mixed in with his curses something concerning whose truth someone who did not know the subject might perhaps have some doubt, then this will suggest itself to the readers' minds: that nothing should be trusted in that stream of abuse, since it produces a permanent condition of lying, certainly about all the Princes, and even about the Emperor himself.

'For this was not new for Luther, to devise and feign all sorts of things through which he might wickedly stir up hatred for Princes and might excite the people. In order to promote this business, he had for a long time gathered together and joined to himself a band of wicked men. And so no faction which schemed to destroy all religion, break all laws, and corrupt all good customs was ever so seditious, deadly, and nefarious, as this Lutheran conspiracy now is — this conspiracy which both profanes all sacred things and corrupts all profane ones; which so preaches Christ, that it tramples on His Sacraments; so trumpets God's grace, that it demolishes free will; so extols faith, that it pulls down good works, and brings on license for sinning; so exalts mercy, that it buries justice, and refers the inevitable cause of all evils, not to some evil in God — as the Manichaeans at least claimed — but rather, truly, to His unique good. A man who, when he has treated divine things impiously in this way, as though he were a serpent thrown down from Heaven, pours out his venom over the land, causes dissension in the Church, repeals all laws, weakens all magistrates, stirs up the laity against the priests, both laity and priests against the Pope, and the people against the Princes — that man clearly is intending nothing else than (may the Heavenly Powers avert this omen!) that the people of Germany be the first to undertake a war, as though for liberty, against the nobles. Finally, he intends that Christians fight against Christians, for the faith and religion of Christ, while the enemies of Christ look on and laugh. And if someone perhaps should not believe that such a great degree of peril could ever arise from one worthless man, I would wish him to bear in mind that Turkish madness, which, although it now spreads itself over so many lands and seas and occupies the greatest and most beautiful part of the entire world, once took its beginning from two ne'er-do-wells. And if I meanwhile say nothing about the Bohemian faction, still who does not know how it quickly grew from so tiny a worm into such an immense dragon, and that scarcely without great harm to Germany? Indeed, it is easy for a bad seed to grow, if no one cuts it down. Nor did anyone ever lack a companion for doing harm, nor was anyone ever so weak that he could not safely, and as though in sport, inflict a lethal wound on a spectator.' [180] So the King of England wrote, no less lovingly and faithfully than wisely and truly. And the pious and Catholic Prince, George, the Duke of Saxony, wrote back to him, saying (among other things which he recounted seriously and at length) as follows:

'No responsibility ever burdened my mind more than that of both prohibiting this faction, when it first came under suspicion, and of repressing and restraining it later, when it was working its mischief everywhere. For it is now the fourth year since I gave a place for debating certain points of the Lutheran doctrine to Johannes Eck, Luther, and Karlstadt (such ill-boding leaders of the first battle) in our city of Leipzig and its Academy. I gave them this place with no other intention than that the truth might appear clearly when both sides had diligently expounded their arguments, and that every seedbed of controversy might be destroyed once matters had been referred to the judicial authority of the Academies of Paris and Erfurt. But since Luther (as the course of events has clearly indicated) placed little hope in the sentence of the Judges, and burned with desire to throw everything into confusion, he anticipated the Judges' decisions, and celebrated his triumph in published books of various sorts, before the actual victory. And certainly, if it were in my hands, I would by no means hereafter permit any edition of any of his books to be published by the printers without punishment.

'For I knew at once what this seditious man intended, and to what point he would at length progress, if he were not resisted. For when he saw that one thing only was in the prayers of all good people, namely that certain ecclesiastical abuses should be corrected according to the severity of ancient religion, then covered with this as if with a mask he gave a starting point to his tragedy, to great applause of the spectators, in the theatre of almost the entire world. But when, not long after this, he attempted to overthrow those things which cannot in safety be moved at all, if our religion is to remain safe, then wise men easily understood that under this sheep's clothing there lurked a wolf. For indeed, the unheard of audacity of this man afterwards reached such an extent that he not only assailed men of middle estate – although famous equally for their learning and their integrity – with his impudent pen; he even dared – a thing which no one would easily have imagined – to let go the reins of his malice against the King of England, who is most excellent in the merit of all human distinctions. By so doing, he gave the clearest possible testimony about himself, both his shameless character and his malicious mind, to all people. Truly I am unable to express in any words how angrily I bore the writing of his impudent pamphlet. However, when I found out about these things, I immediately took care through edicts that his book should be neither sold nor read in my domain, and I punished the bookseller who first offered it for sale with the many bitter sufferings of prison.' [181]

And below Duke George wrote: 'Furthermore, it relieves my mind in no small measure that I am attacked, more than the other German nobles, in Luther's writings and sermons, sometimes openly, sometimes covertly; for this falls to my lot in common with certain most praiseworthy heroes: with the Emperor Charles, Fifth of that name, whose oaths I consider it glorious to have sworn; and with Henry the Eighth, the most powerful King of the English. I would prefer to be slandered equally with these two men than to be praised along with the Lutheran dregs. Nor will Luther through his threats and slanders ever cause me to do less than the duty of an honest Christian Prince.' [182]

And a little later he wrote: 'And so, I prohibit the writings of this man, whatever argument may be given in them, both from my cities and from my borders, just as though they were the most vicious of our enemies. And I have pursued this policy so diligently that just now, when against my expectation there appeared that German translation of the New Testament (which your letter also mentions), with my own money I bought back all the copies of it, however many of them had been brought in and sold, from those who had bought them. No wonder, since my mind was already telling me – and a very careful examination gave sufficient confirmation – that this labor of translating had been undertaken by Luther for this cause: so that once the universal scripture had been translated to his advantage, he might by this skill twist it for the purpose of confirming his own doctrines. For since he saw that it could not happen that he should prove those absurd paradoxes of his to the learned men among the old theologians (from whose learning and way of life he was equally distant), he began to abuse the simplicity of the Scripture, which many times is able to be twisted into another sense, and even into an incompatible one, in this way. For what more cunning and clever plan could he have found for capturing the minds of the more simple people, than this – that he present to the crowd the universal Scripture of the New Testament, altered according to his judgment into a new form both of interpretation and annotation, like a fishhook adorned with bait? Otherwise he would never have persuaded anyone, or none except the most stupid, that the fate of the good, just as of the evil, depends on God. Since Pagan peoples did not tolerate this dogma in their philosophies, should we Christians, on whom the doctrine of the faith has shown with the clearer light of truth, embrace it in Luther? For if once we accept, with Luther, that everything happens by necessity, then clearly at once every force of human reason, every counsel, finally every law by which either the reward of the good or the punishment of the evil should be determined – all of these are proved to be in vain.' [183]

These things, and many other things of this sort, Duke George wrote seriously and from his heart (which was sincere and without deceit) to the King of England. After he saw Luther's German pamphlet addressed to a certain noble, Hartmann of Croneburg, in which Luther had publicly attacked Duke George with many injuries and slanders, the same Prince began to question Luther in letters as to whether he would confess that the pamphlet was truly his. But he, a fierce scorner of Princes, soon answered him most ferociously, almost inflicting more injuries through his letters than he had done earlier in his pamphlet – although in the Leipzig debate he had held a very different opinion about this Prince and had even publicly written that opinion earlier.

He began his letter in German with these words: 'Cease raging and fulminating against God and his Christ: this is in the first place, instead of my obedience, Ungracious Prince and Lord. I have accepted a letter from your Illustrious Disgrace, along with the pamphlet or rather the epistle which I wrote to Lord Hartmann of Croneburg. And I had that passage read to me, about which your Illustrious Disgrace was complaining, as though about atrocious injuries which had to do with your soul, your oath, and your reputation. This pamphlet has been previously explained, both here and elsewhere. Therefore, since your Illustrious Disgrace wishes to know on which of the words in it I would wish to take my stand, my response is brief: it is worth just the same to me if my pamphlet should be accepted in your Illustrious Disgrace's eyes in any way whatsoever: standing, lying down, sitting, or running.' And a bit later he said: 'For if your Illustrious Disgrace were not uncivilly lying by saying that I slandered your soul, honor, and good name, you would not so wickedly accuse and persecute the Christian truth. However, this is not the first time that I have been slandered and evilly accused by your Illustrious Disgrace.' And at the end of the book he wrote: 'At Wittenberg, on the 8th day of John; [15]23;' with this subscription: 'Martin Luther, by the Grace of God Evangelist to Wittenberg.' [184]

A little bit before this Dr Johannes Faber, who was then the representative of the Bishop of Constance in church matters, had published a notable book against Luther at Rome. Since this book very thoroughly supported the power of the Pope, the sacraments of the Church, and its sacred rites, and supported its arguments from the scriptures and from the most ancient writers, both Greek and Latin, it was reprinted in Germany too, not only in Leipzig under the command of the abovementioned Prince, but also in Cologne, where it was given this title, according to its worth: *The Hammer of the Lutheran Heresy.*[185] And indeed, Luther wrote nothing else in response to this book except, in German, a certain most violent misrepresentation in the preface which he affixed to his *Exposition of Chapter Seven of the First Letter of St Paul to the Corinthians.* For he says:

'Wise generations fill the world with their stupid and wicked writings and clamors against the state of matrimony, and dissuade everyone from it; when nevertheless all the while they themselves know very well, and also sufficiently demonstrate through their action, that they cannot be without women – so that they, who were created for nothing if not for matrimony, hunt, harass, and deal with whores day and night. Now of such a type, too, is that archfool Johannes Faber of Constance, indeed that famous fornicator, who has written a huge book, recently published at Leipzig, against the state of matrimony, in order to dissuade everyone from it. However, he says nothing further than that there are many troubles and hardships in matrimony, just as if the whole world did not already know this long since, and this ass's head himself were teaching us for the first time this very thing which no rustic or villager does not know. If I were Chastity herself, I would not know of a greater or more unbearable injury and shame than that rascals of this sort, hunters of whores and enemies of chastity, should praise me. They are rascals, not only on the surface, but down to the very depths of their hearts; and they do not deserve a response.' And a bit later he says, 'Therefore, since God created woman in such a way that she must be, and is driven to be, near to man, it will be enough for us that God is with us: and therefore let us honor matrimony as a divine contract with us. And if these filth-spreaders do not wish to enter into it, let us leave them in their blindness to fornicate and go whoring for so long as God will permit them. We have the word of God on our side, which will endure, and will not be awe-struck clumsy smiths [186]of this sort, even if there were more of them than there are grains of sand in the sea.' [187]

By this shameless slander Luther labored to make Faber's whole book suspect and hateful to the people. But that most learned man had not written against matrimony in that book, but rather in support of it, namely, that it is properly numbered by the Church among the Seven Sacraments (which Luther had denied); and indeed, he had written that section as a digression, since his primary intention was to refute Luther's pamphlet about the power of the Pope. And truly, against this pamphlet he composed 126 responses, in a long series – for he was of the richest intellect. Johannes Eck too, a most learned man, wrote three righteous books, and published them in Paris. Neither Luther nor any of the Lutherans ever responded to these books.

Nevertheless, in truth Paul commends virginity by many arguments in that chapter which Luther perverted by the most vicious of expositions, and even prefers it to matrimony, as, for instance, when he says: 'I wish that all you men were as I am,' and again, 'I say to the unmarried and to the widows, it is good for them to remain as they are, even as I do.' And again, 'But about virgins, I have no order from the Lord; however, I will give advice.' And again, 'Since it is good for a man to be thus.' And again, 'You have been freed from a wife; do not seek a wife.' And much more openly than hitherto: 'I want you,' he says, 'to be without care. He who is without a wife, cares for the things of the Lord, and for how he may please God; but he who has a wife, cares for the things of the world, and for how he may please his wife, and he is divided. And an unmarried woman, a virgin, thinks about the things that are the Lord's, so that she is holy in body and in spirit. But she who is married, thinks about the things that are of the world, and about how she may please her husband.' And again: 'Therefore, he who gives a virgin in marriage, does well; and he who does not give her, does better.'

Luther most shamelessly and also most impiously perverted all these sayings of Paul, and distorted them into a defense of wicked lust, by which monks and nuns could feign sacrilegious marriages, in his German exposition which he called *Epithalamion*. Therefore, where the Apostle says, 'I wish that all men were as I myself am, but each one has his own gift from God: one thus, another thus,' there Luther, by his extraordinary exposition thus infers: 'From this it follows,' he says, 'how immensely they err, who praise nuns by saying that their state is superior or better in the eyes of God than marriage, and feign special haloes for them, and I don't know how many prerogatives and honors, and call them Brides of Christ, who are rather Brides of the Devil, since they do not use Chastity as it ought to be used: namely, not that it is better in the eyes of God than marriage, but that it makes people more free and more fit, on earth, to apply themselves to the Word of God, than marriage does.' [188] And a bit later, he says: 'But since we are in this place, where Paul extols marriage so highly, and calls it a divine gift, we also will more fully consider and prove that marriage is the most spiritual state of all, and that certain Orders have falsely and wickedly been called spiritual, while marriage has been called a worldly state. But on the contrary, matrimony ought truly to be called a spiritual state, as it is, and the Orders ought to be called truly worldly states, as they are. Therefore, they have plainly imposed a perverse abuse of words upon the world, and have inflicted it on everyone, misleading people so that what is spiritual is called worldly, and what is, in the truth of the matter, worldly is called spiritual.' [189] And below he says, 'When Paul says, "Virginity is not commanded by God, any more than is matrimony; that is to say, it should be unrestricted for everyone;" by this saying he removes from virginity every honor which had up until that time been given to it by ancient preachers. For where there is no command, there in the eyes of God is neither merit nor reward, but rather a certain freedom according to personal choice. For in the eyes of God it is worth just the same, whether you are or are not a virgin. And just as he says above, that "Whoever is called a slave, is a free man in the eyes of God," so here also it can be said, "Whoever is called a virgin, is a wife [190] in God's eyes; and whoever is called a wife, is a virgin in God's eyes." For in the eyes of God, all things are equal, nor is there any distinction of persons nor merit in works; but only equal faith in all and for the sake of all things.' [191]

When this book was translated into Latin, the excellent Theologian Dr Conrad Kollin, Ordinary Professor of Theology at Cologne in the Dominican Monastery, refuted it.[192] He answered it so extensively that the first part of his Refutation extended over six not at all short books; so minutely did he respond to Luther's individual points. But in summation, he said that in his indecent *Epithalamion* Luther had perverted the true sense of the Pauline text: he had denied Paul's virginity (for he asserted that Paul was a widower) and had annulled the ancestral laws of Germany; he had denigrated the reputation of Religion, and had taken away the fruit and the halo of continence before God; he had besmirched the celibacy of the priest with shameful and forbidden marriages, and had admitted the marriage of priests; he had profaned our holy things and had deformed the beauty of the Church; he had turned the modesty of nuns into the shamelessness of the brothel, and had trampled upon the holy vows of the Monastics. In brief, he had thrown Christ out of the people's hearts, together with all piety and religion, he had brought the doctrine of the Turk to the Germans, and had by this book prepared a road for that doctrine, by which it could take Germany – which he had filled with faithless apostates – by force.

Johannes Cochlaeus had already published, in Strasbourg, one book about the grace of the Sacraments and another about the baptism of infants.[193] As soon as Luther saw the first of these, he quickly prepared a response; one so ludicrous and abusive, indeed, that he himself said very imperiously to his friend Nesen (whom he later, in the hope of a miracle, tried to recall to life by vain incantations, when Nesen was pitifully drowned in the Elbe) that if he seemed to play the fool in the book's wild ravings, Nesen himself was the author of that foolishness in him. And in order that his contempt might appear the greater, he prefaced the book with seven joking lines of verse. These had the following beginning:

> *I sing of arms and a man, who recently from the shores of Mainz*
> *came to Wittenberg and the Saxon coasts, a man whose fate made him stupid.*
> *He was greatly troubled by rages and frenzy through the power of sins,*
> *because of the remembering wrath of the barbers' destruction.* [194]

Cochlaeus, induced by the suitability of the occasion into a type of joking that was not very dissimilar to Luther's, immediately responded to this pamphlet. For not long before, in the regions around Wittenberg, a cow had given birth to a monstrosity, which appeared to have a monk's cowl around its bald head, so that it clearly portended to us that monstrous apostate who not long before had thrown off his cowl – although he himself tried, in vain, to interpret it differently. Therefore, Cochlaeus's book had this title: *Against the Cowled*

Minotaur of Wittenberg; Johannes Cochlaeus Concerning the Grace of the Sacraments, Again. And the beginning of the book answered verses with verses, in this way:

> *I sing of monsters and a bull, who first from the northern shores*
> *having fled to German lands contaminates them,*
> *and under the guise of a monk violates all peace and all faith.*
> *Through the power of Satan, driven on by cruel rages and frenzy*
> *of savage Tisiphone [one of the Furies], with avenging Anathema seeking penalties,*
> *he rages, a shapeless monster, with his inane mooing*
> *under the mangled cowl of a half-man, half-bull.* [195]

Furthermore, a certain printer in Cologne printed the book without Cochlaeus' knowledge, and in his edition put these words on the frontispiece. He said, 'We have intentionally arranged Luther's accusations, to which answers are given in turn in this work, side by side with the individual responses, so that a fair-minded judge may see, when the subject is weighed in an equal scale, that every Minotaur has his Theseus.' At the end of his book, Cochlaeus says the following: 'But why is it surprising, if in this pamphlet, however short it may be, you have three times changed your opinion about every single subject, when you already did this same thing previously, and three times changed your opinion about the same subject in a single page of your declaration? Who would not therefore become disgusted with debating you, when you are so inconsistent, changeable, and shameless?' [196] But neither Luther nor any accomplice of his answered these things at all.

But Luther published another pamphlet, about the Mass and Communion; and he wrote so imperiously that he claimed for himself the right of establishing the ritual, a right which he had previously, due to his immense pride, refused to allow either to the highest Pontiff or to the General Council. This is the beginning of that book: 'Up until now,' he said, 'I have dealt with the people by pamphlets and sermons, so that I might first draw their hearts away from impious beliefs about ceremonies. I thought that I was doing a Christian and serviceable thing, if I could be the cause by which that abomination, which Satan had set up in the sacred place through a man of sin, could be worn away, without the use of force. Therefore I have attempted nothing either through force or power, nor have I exchanged old things for new ones.' [197] And a little later he says, 'Therefore we will deal with a certain pious formula for celebrating Mass (as they call it) and communion. And we will deal with it in such a way that we shall no longer rule hearts only by the word of our teaching, but we will also put our hand to it and by public administration will put it into action. However, we are in no way prejudging that no other form may be embraced or followed,' etc. [198]

An extremely illustrious theologian, Dr Josse Clichtove of Paris, a man of blameless life and one renowned for the richness of his learning, wrote a certain *Defense of the Church* in response to this pamphlet of Luther's. [199] He had earlier written *Antilutherus*, a work comprising three volumes, which were notable for their facility of style as well as for their abundance and variety of multifaceted learning.[200] But the German Evangelist remained silent about these works, since they were in Latin, cautiously concealing them in the hope that the German people, among whom he claimed apostolic authority for himself, would find out nothing about these books. But here, for the sake of brevity, it will suffice to quote a few words from them, which Clichtove wrote in response to Luther's introduction. 'It is worthy of severe censure,' he says, 'that Luther labels "impious" beliefs about those ceremonies which are accustomed to be performed in the Church's rite. For no one of a sound mind could call "impious" those rites of the Old Law, which were accustomed to be observed by the oblations and sacrifices of their own time, since the Lord very frequently commanded, in Exodus, Leviticus, Numbers, and Deuteronomy, that those rites be observed diligently and strictly, during the tenure of that Law. Who therefore – unless he were clearly dishonest and scarcely of sound mind – could call the ceremonies of the New Law "impious" or "sacrilegious": ceremonies which were instituted by the authority of the Holy Spirit, which represent the Holy Mysteries, and which move the people to a greater reverence for the divine service?' [201]

And later Clichtove writes, 'I ask you, what more deadly plague could be brought into the Church of God, or what more dreadful confusion, than that there should at length be no fixed form for celebrating the divine mystery of the Mass which is the most excellent and the highest of all the things that are done in the usage of the Church? Since there was a uniform rite among the Hebrews for sacrificing and eating that figurative paschal lamb for as long as this ceremony was performed in the old Synagogue, would it not be a matter for shame and abomination, that the true lamb, Christ, should be sacrificed on the altar in a diverse and variable rite, and one that can be changed according to anyone's inclination?' [202] And later he says, 'But now I would wish to ask Luther this one thing: By what authority does he do these things, and who gave him that authority, that he should change the ancient form of celebrating the divine mystery, and create a new form? For if he claims that he has been sent from Heaven, or by the Spirit of God, to undertake this work, then it behooves him to give signs of his status as an Apostle, by which he can demonstrate that this thing he is attempting is from God. But signs of this sort have not yet been seen or known by anyone at all.' [203]

These things Clichtove wrote. But Luther took it very badly that at Wittenberg, under his very eyes, the ancient ceremonies of the Church still endured in the Collegiate Church dedicated to All Saints. For Duke Frederick the Elector, although he had already permitted Luther to do too many things against the Church, nevertheless did not permit him to commit at random any act of impiety he might desire, as the Duke's brother later permitted. For while Duke Frederick lived, Luther was not yet permitted to undertake his sacrilegious wedding; he could not yet empty the monasteries of their people and despoil them of their goods; he could not yet drive the Catholic pastors together by force or banish them, and so on. And so Luther writes at the end of that pamphlet of his which he published about the Order of the Mass, 'Nor let it deter you, or anyone else, that here in Wittenberg that sacrilegious Topheth [204] persists, which is an ungodly and damned source of money for the princes of Saxony: I mean the Church of All Saints. For since God is merciful, there is so great an antidote among us through the abundant Word of God that this plague languishes in its own little corner and is harmful to no one except to itself. Indeed, there are scarcely three or four swine and bellies left to care for that money in that house of perdition. To all others and to the whole populace, it is a great source of loathing and an abomination.' [205]

In that year a thing occurred that had been unheard of in Germany up until that day, and was indeed the most brazen of crimes, contrary to all civil laws and church canons, and exceptionally wicked and sacrilegious: namely, a citizen of the town of Torgau (where the Duke Elector of Saxony was accustomed to reside for the most part) dared secretly to abduct nine holy virgins at once from one convent at Nimbschen, and that, indeed, in the most holy of times, when all the populace is accustomed to be occupied with the service of God and the zeal of devotion, in recalling the memory of Christ's passion, in confessing their sins, and in the communion of the most holy Eucharist. But Luther was so utterly undisturbed by this crime that he soon had made it known to all of Germany in a published book, following this saying of Solomon: 'They have left the straight road, and walk in shadowy roads; they rejoice when they do evil, and exult in the worst deeds.' [206] And also following this saying of Isaiah: 'They declare their sin as Sodom, nor do they hide it.' [207] Therefore Luther, praising this unholy kidnapper (whom he named as Leonard Koppe), said in German in that book he published: 'You have done a new deed, about which countries and people will sing and speak, and which many will proclaim as a enormous injury. But those who understand according to God will glorify it as a great favor, so that you may be sure that God ordered it thus, and that it was not a work or a plan of your own; and you should count as a trifle the clamoring of those who will consider this the worst of all works and one neither ordered nor allowed by God. "Ah, ah," they will say, "that stupid Leonard Koppe, led astray by a damned and heretical Monk, dares to abduct nine nuns at once from their convent and to help them so that they may deny and desert their vows and their monastic life." And here you will have said, "This certainly is a lovely way to keep and to hide a secret, namely, to publish it and sell it, so that the whole convent of Nimbschen may be incited against me, when they now hear that I was that kidnapper." I answer you' (said Luther) 'that indeed you are a fortunate kidnapper, just as Christ was a kidnapper in the world when through His death He stole away from the Prince of this world his arms and military equipment, and led him captive. Thus you too have led these miserable souls out of the prison of human tyranny, and indeed have done so in that most appropriate season of Easter, in which Christ also led captive the captivity of His own.' [208]

And so that there should be no reason or shame left in this bestial crime, at the end of his pamphlet Luther listed the nine nuns by name, each one by her given and family name – they were all of noble families – to the perpetual dishonor and shame of those very renowned families, which he defamed by such a notable crime. And so that this iniquity might be made still more complete, after two years in the world, which time she spent in aimless conversation among the scholars of the Academy in Wittenberg, the seventh of those most wretched female apostates, Katharine von Bora, was – so please the Heavenly powers! – made the wife of Luther, just as soon as the Elector Duke Frederick died. A nun married to a monk; a damned woman to a damned man; an infamous woman to an infamous man; clearly so that this might be a work worth the trouble of performing, [209] and equal might be easily joined to equal, and St Paul might lie when he said 'They have damnation, because they have made their first faith void.' [210]

And Luther's hatred was so great, not only toward the Pope, but also toward the universal Catholic Church, that he preferred to be united with those who were manifestly excommunicates, such as the Pighards and the Hussites, than to return to the Catholics, with whom he had earlier received communion for so many years. And so he wrote two books to those whom he considered enemies of the Pope; one was to the Waldensians, whom we call Pighards, who were dispersed throughout Bohemia and Moravia; and the second, in Latin, was to the Senate at Prague, since they were pre-eminent Hussites. However, a few years previously he had actually attacked both these groups, as heretics and schismatics, in published writings. And indeed he had castigated the Pighards bitterly, both in his *Ten Precepts* and in his *Resolutions*. In the latter of those works he wrote these words, 'And even if there were no Purgatory in the time of the Apostles, as this disgusting Pighard boasts, is that any reason for trusting this heretic, born scarcely fifty years ago, and for scorning as false the belief of so many centuries? Especially since he does nothing more than say, "I do not believe it." And this is how he proves all his beliefs, and disproves all of ours – as though the very sticks and stones would not disbelieve him.' [211] And in his *Ten Precepts* he said: 'But let those accursed heretics, the Pighards, not trust that their cause will be helped by me. Due to their excessive rusticity, they accuse us Germans (in great indignation, and with the proudest disdain) of worshiping God's Saints and of practicing idolatry. And for this reason they heap up a great pile of Scripture verses against us, in which verses it is forbidden to worship any other than the One God. They are at one and the same time impious perverters of Scripture and cunning slanderers of our piety. For thus these country bumpkins teach us at long last that God alone must be adored; and they pride themselves on this, as if we would ever deny this same thing!' [212]

Later, however, this wretched Apostate began to conduct himself as an open enemy of the Roman Church, and these enemies, whom he had earlier condemned, fawned on him in a womanly fashion with shameful flatteries, so that he was rewarded by being made their ally. And so he wrote in German to the Waldensians (in a book which was later translated by Jonas, the idolizer and interpreter of Luther): 'A pamphlet is being circulated which your fellow priests published first in German and now in Bohemian as well, about instructing children in the highest Christianity. Among other articles, the pamphlet contains the following: that the body of Christ is not naturally contained in the Sacrament of the Eucharist, nor should it be adored there. This teaching of yours has moved us Germans not a little. For you certainly know that I have asked you, through your messengers, to shed more light on this article, over and beyond this righteous pamphlet which you have published, since you have seemed to discourse rather obscurely on this topic.' [213]

And below, in friendship to them, he slanders and tramples on all our sacred things: 'And yet' (he said) 'all the temples, monasteries, in a word all the street corners are full of these ceremonies and this type of adoration, and the whole service of the Papistic reign was nothing else than an incessant mockery in these words: "Hail, King of the Jews!" For although there are so many Cathedrals, Collegiate churches, and more sects of monks than types of birds; so many monasteries, so many altars, so many chapels; nevertheless in all of these you will find scarcely one person among a thousand who honors God with spiritual adoration; but all in the same way laugh at Him and mock Him through this outward hypocrisy. And Christ and God are laughed at most especially in all the Masses (as they call them) on the feast days of Easter and Corpus Christi, when in pomp and procession, in gold and silver, the Eucharist is carried around. There a great deal of outward honor is shown to God, which nevertheless is nothing other than mockery of God, since faith and the Holy Spirit are absent.' [214]

And below: 'We are certain' (he said) 'that through the indescribable gift of God, the pure doctrine and the great light of the Word has touched you, even if there has perhaps still been weakness and a sufficient amount of sin in your habits and lives.' [215] And a bit later: 'Nevertheless, among us all the matters that concern the outward distribution of the Sacrament have not yet been arranged in such good order as I hear is the case concerning you. But pray you also for us, that there may be among us the most unceasing exercise both of the Word and of charity, and of a good life; especially since we have only recently struggled out of that mud of the Papistic reign.' [216] And at the end of the pamphlet: 'I beseech you by the love of Christ' (he said) 'that you will not take my writing in such a way, as though I had entertained myself by writing about your errors. However, as you know, up until now you have been proclaimed throughout the whole world as the most pestilential heretics; I wanted here to bring forward this testimony concerning you, that you approach the purity of the Gospel more closely than all others whom I have known.' [217]

However, Luther clearly declared in his *Commentary on Galatians* what he once felt concerning the Bohemian Hussites. But since a little later he regretted his opinions, those words were at that point left out by his printers. However, they still remain in the first edition. And so, when the Apostle says, 'Bear one another's burdens,' there Luther most excellently declares that separation from the Church because of evildoers is not permissible. 'These people' (he says) 'pervert this teaching, who want their own burdens to be borne, but desire only to enjoy and be carried by others' advantages. They are the sort who consider it unworthy to have unlearned, useless, wrathful, clumsy, or foolish people as associates in their lives, but rather look for gentle, sophisticated, kind, quiet, and holy people. That is, they want to live not on earth, but in paradise; not among sinners, but among angels; not in the world, but in Heaven. And they should fear lest they are also receiving their reward here, and are possessing their kingdom of heaven in this life. For they do not want, with the bride, to be a lily among thorns, nor, with Jerusalem, to be placed in the midst of the nations, nor, with Christ, to be condemned in the midst of His enemies. For they make void the cross of Christ in themselves, and have an inactive, snoring charity which is carried on the shoulders of others. And therefore, those who flee the society of such men, in order to be made good, accomplish nothing else than to be made as bad as possible. And yet they do not believe this: since for the sake of charity they flee the genuine business of charity, and for the sake of salvation they flee the true straight path to salvation. For the Church was always best, when it had its dealings among the worst people.'[218]

And a little later he said: 'The consequence is that the separation of the Bohemians from the Roman Church can be defended by no excuse whatsoever: for it was impious and contrary to all of Christ's laws, since it stands firm in opposition to charity, in which all the laws are summed up. For this thing, which alone they claim, that they separated from the Church due to the fear of God and to their conscience, lest they should live among evil priests and popes – this most of all accuses them.'[219]

But afterwards he wrote very differently, both in his *Babylonian Captivity* and in the assertion of his *Forty-One Articles*, and long afterwards in his book to the Senate of Prague about the installation of ministers. In that book, indeed, he began to write in this fashion: 'When Satan grew very strong, the Kingdom of Bohemia was left empty and bereft of Bishops and High Priests (as they call them) by the authority of the Roman Pontiffs; you were driven to the wretched and harsh necessity of sending your clerics into Italy every year to buy Papistic Orders. For the neighboring Bishops would not condescend to ordain your priests, since they regarded you as obstinate heretics. And how many inconveniences and dangers did that necessity bring upon you, drawing them in its wake?'[220] And below he says, 'For this reason, a most cruel band of every sort of idlers, apostates, and those whom in general no other land would tolerate was finally created to provide ministry for you, so that this pitiable necessity of yours would turn out as in a story: namely, that a priest was fit for the Bohemians who among the Germans would merit nooses and irons. Thus it was notably fitting that Bohemia should be filled, at one and the same time, with crimes and with unlearned priests, or rather, with rapacious wolves. From this source flows that chaos and that utterly confused Babylon in your most famous realm, partly from the necessity of having ministers and partly from the impossibility of correcting it, since anyone at all may teach whatever he wishes; different doctrines are preached in different places; a considerable number to trick the people with the fictitious name of priest; some sell parishes, others force their way in by violence; the successor enacts rulings contrary to those of his predecessor.' [221] And below: 'Now' (he said) 'after we have warned you Bohemians about your own evils, so that you will bid farewell to Papistic Orders, let me also add one general argument, by which we may excite disgust and apostasy, both in you and in the whole world, against those accursed and abominable orders.' [222] And below: 'And clearly, the principle of our salvation drives us by necessity to abstain from those accursed and damnable orders. For woe to those who, although they were already knowledgeable and wise, became devotees of that adversary of God, worse than Baal. But this argument ought to move you Bohemians most of all, beyond all other nations. Since for you it is a shameful thing not only in the eyes of God, as it is for others, but also in the eyes of men, that you should either ask or accept Orders from your enemy, who burned Jan Hus and Jerome of Prague and many others, on the worst pretext; who has always wished your destruction; who defiles you throughout the world with the opprobrium of the name "heretic", without end, without moderation; and for whose pestilential undertakings you have paid with so much blood. However, that bloody Tyrant does not yet repent of his evil deeds, nor does he revoke the example of blood innocently condemned, nor has he made restitution for his sacrilegious plunder of the Christian name.' [223]

Luther wrote these things and many others of this sort, which were extremely harsh against the Pope and extremely impious against the sacred Orders; but he blabbered completely uselessly and in vain to the Bohemians, for they had a much greater hatred for the Lutherans than for the Catholics. Indeed, even today the Catholic Church at Prague holds fast to the ancient rites of its fathers, and throughout all Bohemia it is possible to find priests and Catholic monks everywhere, so that there is no doubt that, if Luther had been discovered in Prague, he would have paid a great penalty for that book, so impious, false, and infamous. For his writings were put under a general ban there by a public edict of the Senate.

And he had no greater luck when he wrote in German to the Jews that Jesus, our God and Savior, was truly born a Jew. Even though in that pamphlet he piled the heaviest possible slanders upon the Catholics and praised the Jews with many flattering words, nevertheless he did not convert a single Jew to Christ, but rather made them more bitter toward Christians; and by encouraging them to feel contempt for the Christian faith, he hardened their hearts in their Jewish blindness. And finally, in another pamphlet, using the most shameful flatteries and the crudest pretexts of Scripture, he set up the German common people as the judges of doctrines and decrees – not only decrees of the Pope and the Bishops, but also of the General Council. For, among other things, he said as follows:

'In business of this sort, namely in judging doctrines and in appointing and removing teachers, or caretakers of souls, it is by no means appropriate to pay attention to human laws, rights, habits, usage, or custom, etc.; whether a matter has been so ordained by the Pope, or by the Emperor, by Princes or Bishops; whether the whole world, or half the world, has held to it; whether it has lasted one year or a thousand years. For the soul of a human being is an eternal thing, and above all that is temporal; therefore, it ought to be ruled only by the eternal Word.'[224] And again, 'The words and doctrines of men' (he said) 'have decided and ordained that judgment about doctrine should be entrusted to Bishops, Teachers, and Councils; and that all the world should accept whatever these people have decided as a law and as an article of faith. But see how shamelessly and foolishly this vainglory of theirs, through which they have placed the entire world under a yoke, fights against God's Law and Word. For Christ decreed precisely the opposite, and took the right and the power of judging doctrines away from any Bishops, Teachers, or councils at all, giving both of these universally to each and every Christian. For he says, in John 10, "My sheep know my voice," and again, "My sheep do not follow strangers, but flee from them, for they do not know the strangers' voice," and again, "However many came, they are thieves and robbers: my sheep do not hear them." Here you see entirely clearly whose the right of judging doctrines is. A Bishop, the Pope, the learned, and anyone else at all have the power of teaching; but the sheep must judge, whether these men teach the voice of Christ, or that of strangers. I ask, how can Bulls about waters[225] contradict this, Bulls which clamor, "Councils, Councils − Bishops, teachers, and everyone must listen to the councils"? Do you think that the Word of God should yield to your usage, your custom, your bishops? Never. For who does not here see that all bishops, colleges, monasteries, universities, with their whole community, rage against this plain word of Christ; who does not see how shamelessly they take the judgment of doctrines away from the sheep, so that they may hand it over to themselves, through their own decrees and acts of boldness? Therefore, they most certainly must be considered as robbers and thieves, as wolves and Apostate Christians, as people who − as has here manifestly been proven against them − not only deny the Word of God but even decree and act in opposition to it, as befits the Antichrist. They create the Antichrist's Kingdom, according to St Paul's prophecy in 2 Thessalonians 2.'[226] And below: 'Owing to their seditious delusion, Paul concludes, as one certain of victory, that for this reason alone those who lord it over us, and teach us contrary to God's word and will more than deserve to be driven out of Christendom and to be avoided as wolves, thieves, and robbers.'[227]

But Luther in his excessive pride claimed for himself and usurped the right, which he wished to be taken away from all Bishops and councils, of passing laws − and not only in Church matters, but even in civil ones. For in the same year he published several German pamphlets about his own laws. One was about the order of baptism; another about the order of divine worship; and a third about the common chest. In this last book he first reckoned up the funds and all the goods of the rural monasteries of the Benedictine, Cistercian, Celestine, and other orders. And concerning these, he said that it would be better if none of them had ever existed upon the earth; however, since they exist, it would be best if they were allowed to go to ruin, or – if it could conveniently be done – that they be destroyed utterly, from their foundations. Then he similarly made over to the public treasury all the funds and goods, and even the towns, of the Episcopal Colleges and Chapters; unless perhaps it would be better to make secular principates out of them. And all the income, property, and goods of the ecclesiastical benefices he assigned in their totality to the same public chest. Furthermore, he judged that in the cities the monasteries of the mendicant brothers should be turned into schools for boys and girls, or into some other public uses of the city. But in the distribution of the wealth, he said that the first part should go to pastors and lecturers, and for the administrators of the chest and the church sacristans. The second should go to the director of the school for each sex. The third, for the aged and infirm. The fourth for orphans, the fifth for debtors, the sixth for foreign newcomers, the seventh for buildings, the eighth for buying up flour in a fertile time. Furthermore, it was decreed that henceforward no begging concession should be allowed to any monk, stationer, foreign student, or mendicant.[228]

Since the Emperor Charles was far away in Spain, the Imperial Assemblies at Nuremberg were celebrated by the Deputy of the Empire, the Emperor's brother Ferdinand, Archduke of Austria, etc. In these assemblies, there was a great deal of varied discussion concerning the business of the Faith. For Hadrian the Sixth, the Roman Pontiff, had sent there a certain Archbishop, Francis Chiregatto, a learned man. The Pope sent him, with the fullest instruction and a fatherly gift, to soften the spirits of the Germans, so that they would not be further estranged from the Apostolic See. For the Pope himself was German, and had so handled himself in the Imperial Court that he merited the greatest praise for his integrity. He had served the Emperor as a most faithful administrator of orders, not only among the Germans but also among the Spaniards, whom he had even ruled while the Emperor, the Catholic King of the Spaniards, was far off among the Germans. But the more kindly he bore himself as Pope, the more ferociously the Lutherans acted in response. Indeed, when Luther himself saw the Apostolic Brief of Hadrian (in which the Pope, who was a most learned man and an excellent theologian, dissuaded Christians from Lutheranism), he published a most slanderous book against the Pope. And the other Lutherans complained to the greatest extent about the abuses of the Roman Curia, although the Pope himself had of his own accord most kindly promised to devote all his attention to abolishing these abuses.

Certain Princes of the Empire had declared some grievances by which the German nation seemed to be unjustly burdened, not only by the Roman Curia, but also by the Bishops and Prelates of Germany. And they had declared these grievances not only in the Assemblies at Nuremberg, but also earlier at Worms, in the presence of the Emperor. But the Lutherans, who twisted and perverted everything to fit their own sinister and hostile intention, took their opportunity from this and published a book, both in Latin and in German, to which they gave the title *One Hundred Grievances of Germany*. In recounting these complaints, indeed, they not only maliciously exaggerated everything and interpreted everything as badly as possible, in order to increase the hatred for the Pope and the Clergy; they also impiously disparaged and wished to have repealed many of the most ancient ceremonies of the Church, which the Bishops and Clergy rightly used in their offices. And in order that hatred for the Pope might be increased still more among the people, they even included the amounts of all the annates which the Bishops of the whole world, in their role as primates, were accustomed to enumerate to the Highest Pontiff for his confirmation. They did this so that it would appear, from this most serious charge, that an utterly limitless amount of money was unjustly demanded by the Pope each year. And when the Princes of Nuremberg had published the Imperial Edict that speakers should use approved doctors of the Church and received expositions of the Gospels against the Lutheran novelties, Luther by a frivolous falsehood appropriated that edict as referring to him, and published a book *Against the Perverters and Falsifiers of the Imperial Mandate.*[229] He did this, clearly, for the following reason and pretext of deceit: that the people might believe that in the Edict the princes were on Luther's side.

1524

Pope Hadrian the Sixth had already died. He was a German of the most blameless private life, who, when he had heard of the exceedingly famous worthy deeds and miracles of the Blessed Benno (who was once Bishop of Meissen) and had by certain testimonies accepted them as proven, solemnly enlisted Benno in the number of the Saints by the unique authority of the Apostolic See. Johannes of Schleinitz, the Bishop of that same Church in Meissen, had been most concerned with this matter. He was a noble man, as well as a pious and learned one, and exceptionally able to endure journeys and labors. By the assistance and advice of the pious and most Orthodox Prince, George Duke of Saxony, Schleinitz reverently and in the midst of a great gathering of people took up the bones and relics of that Blessed Father Benno (who had just been canonized) from the earth and his ancient tomb, and by the Apostolic authority instituted an annual festival in his memory. This celebration and the fame of his ancient piety seemed likely to overshadow, for the most part, the barbaric novelties of Luther. For this reason it happened that Luther, driven by anger and jealousy, soon published a pamphlet that was both most slanderous and most impious. He gave it this title, in German: *Against the New Idol and the Old Devil Who Is Being Exalted in Meissen.*[230] Undoubtedly, he acted hastily in order to turn the people aside from that devotion by his pamphlet. But that impious and infamous Son of Earth fought in vain against the pious and glorious inhabitant of Heaven. For the crowd of people was so great then, and continued to be so great every year, on the day when the relics of St Benno were lifted up in a solemn apotheosis, that God Himself seemed in very fact, through the pious simplicity and devotion of the people, to be laughing at the stupid and impious strivings of that clever and wordy Apostate.

Now Meissen is scarcely ten miles distant from Wittenberg; each city is situated on the banks of the Elbe river, and each gains its fame from the most noble of Princes – the one from the Margraves of Meissen (since the greatest number of them lie buried in it) – and the other from the Dukes of Saxony, since it belongs to the Saxon Elector. And due to this work of God, Luther – had he not been completely blinded by his impious rebellion – would have done well to consider that he would kick against the pricks in vain, since he would always have so many adversaries nearby, drawn even from the rustic people. But the foolhardy man, full of empty trust, was hoping in vain that he would be able to turn the people away from that celebration by his pestilential pamphlet of slanders. Therefore, with a thousand lies and detractions – and not fearing to pervert the truth of history in every way – he reviled not only the life and miracles of Benno, but also the pious deed of Pope Adrian and the past piety of those most worthy holy men, Gregory VII and Thomas Aquinas. For he reproached St Benno for having fawned on Pope Gregory VII in opposition to Emperor Henry IV, and having unjustly stood by him against all human and divine law, and having helped him in every kind of crime. 'What, therefore' (he said) 'do the people of Meissen now exalt? A versatile and bloodthirsty robber, the cause of every calamity in Germany; an enemy of the Gospel, and a comrade of the Antichrist, to whom he clung, and in whose iniquity he was made a partner.'[231] And from the Wittenberger's page this opinion was offered about Pope Gregory VII, who receives much praise in any true history: that he acted in opposition to Emperor Henry IV as a traitor and a good-for-nothing; that he incited Henry's son against his father; that he condemned Henry to die as an excommunicate; and that he did all this for the sake of temporal riches, pomp, and powers. But it is sufficiently clear from the histories that this Gregory was unjustly harassed, beset, and driven into exile by the Emperor, and that he died in exile, long before the death of Henry IV; and that indeed even before the estrangement which later arose between father and son in the Empire.

For the rest, since the life of Hadrian VI was so honored and praised among the Germans that it could not be censured without offense to them, Luther tried with other sneers to diminish Hadrian's authority and reputation. For he says in that same pamphlet: 'First (let us begin at the beginning), it is very appropriate for that Satan of Meissen to be elevated through the agency of Pope Hadrian. For although I hear about that Hadrian that he was a man of splendid and praiseworthy life, nevertheless (as is common among hypocrites of this sort) he was the worst possible enemy of God and His Word. For the Word's sake, he committed two murders in Brussels and provided two martyrs for Christ, and unknowingly and unwillingly elevated them as true saints.' And a little later he says, 'Things are done thus Popishly, just as was the case in the Council of Constance also, when Jan Hus and Jerome of Prague were condemned and burned, men who were truly holy sons and martyrs of God. And on the other side, Thomas Aquinas was elevated – the font and sewer of all heresy, error, and destruction of the Gospel (as his books indicate). And now it is fitting for Master Hadrian to act in the same way. He burned true saints, Johannes and Henry, in Brussels; now, on the other side, he elevates Benno, truly a very Devil. The Roman pontificate is an extraordinary office, and it is fitting for them to act thus: to kill true saints and to elevate false ones; to condemn the Word of God and to confirm their own doctrine, and then to say, "All this is done for the honor of God and his Saints," etc.'

But Jerome Emser responded gravely and learnedly to Luther's calumnies of this sort.[232] Emser had long before described the life of the Blessed Benno most elegantly in a Latin book, before the name of Luther had been known to the world. And the words of all the Princes and Estates of the Empire had been able to vindicate Pope Hadrian from Luther's calumnies, since they had responded to the Papal Nuncio in the Diet in Nuremberg. To be exact, they responded that they knew Hadrian drew his descent and was born from the most noble German nation and that they considered evident his exceptional and outstanding gifts and virtues of mind and body, which had been famous throughout nearly all the world even while he was still in his youth, etc.

When Pope Hadrian died, after a long consultation in conclave, Giulio dei Medici was elected [pope]. He was a Florentine, related on his father's side to Leo X, and was given the name Clement VII. When he heard that the Imperial Diets were again being held in Nuremberg, he sent a man who was noteworthy among the Cardinals for his integrity, his wisdom, and his learning: the Most Reverend Lord Lorenzo di Campeggio of Bologna. After the death of his wife, he had succeeded his father, a most famous lawyer, in the public profession of Law at the Academy of Bologna. Called from there to Rome, he soon was made Auditor of the Rota, and after a short time he so shone among other Auditors of the Rota, because of his knowledge and honesty, that he seemed worthy to be sent into Germany, to the Emperor Maximilian, to handle the most delicate affairs of the Pope. And in the Imperial court he so conducted himself that by the Emperor's favor he was first made Bishop of Feltri and then a Cardinal of the Roman Church. Therefore, in the judgment not only of the Pope but also of the whole congregation of Cardinals – whose judgment is the most exacting in the whole world – he seemed the most appropriate person according to the unanimous vote of all, to be sent as Lateran Legate not just to Germany, but to Hungary and Bohemia as well. For apart from his learning and his great and lengthy experience of affairs, he also had a familiar acquaintance and friendship with many of the Princes of Germany.

Therefore, he left Rome on 1 February, making his journey through the cities of Italy, and being received with the greatest honor everywhere. He remained for a few days in his father's house in his native land of Bologna, where he was also Bishop, and solemnly celebrated Mass in the Cathedral Church there with a great multitude of people present. But when he reached the borders of Germany, he received letters from the Princes gathered in Nuremberg and made his way to them more quickly. And when he came there, he was met outside the gate by almost all the Princes of Germany (for one or two were kept inside by bad health) together with the Emperor's Deputy himself, the Archduke Ferdinand of Austria. And he was kindly warned by them not to enter the city in that attire which Cardinals who were Apostolic Legates were accustomed to wear, because of the numerous Lutheran populace who were incited into hatred and contempt for the Pope and all Clergy by the tireless haranguings of their preachers. Therefore, so that he should not, in place of the highest honor, suffer contempt and ridicule because of his solemn attire (which was unfamiliar to that people), he dressed in common clothing, such as he would wear to go through fields or forests, and was not accompanied by any clergy or by a cross carried before him. In this fashion and surrounded by the Princes who were accompanying him he proceeded to his inn, whose name was The Golden Cross.

And the clergy who were going to meet him and had convened in the chapel of St Sebaldus were kept there behind closed doors, so that no one at all could see him entering the city. And after the Senate and the assembly of Princes in the Curia of the city had been presented to him, two speeches were given there. The first was by Italo Potenziano, Bishop of Scarens of the Franciscan Order. He was a most eloquent man who was a member of the Legate's retinue and household. The second speech was given by the Legate himself. After his expression of good will, of the Pope's paternal affection for the German nation and his own manifold duty and service towards the German people, he entreated the Princes and the Orders of the Empire strongly to withstand and earnestly to oppose the growing Lutheran faction which was scheming for the ultimate destruction not only of religion and the Apostolic See, but also of the universal Republic which was well founded upon laws; and he entreated them to fulfill the Pope's and the Emperor's sentences thoroughly. Because of his long-standing good will toward them and his lasting familiarity with the Germans, he promised that he himself would prescribe whatever could honorably be done by the Apostolic See; he would especially pay attention to the grievances of the Nation, provided that they themselves see to it that, once the Lutheran heresy was extinct, he should be able to proceed with strength, in wars and incursions, against the most cruel attempts of the Turks.

Then after a few days, spokesmen also came from Louis, King of Hungary and Bohemia, who was married to the Emperor's sister Maria. These spokesmen gave a very learned but also tearful and supplicating speech in the public assembly of the Princes and the Apostolic Legate. In this speech they tearfully beseeched and entreated the Princes and the Orders of the Empire that they bring aid against the attacks of the Turks to the King and the Kingdom of Hungary, which was beset by extreme peril; since the Hungarians, worn out and exhausted by long-continued wars, could no longer rely on their own strength alone to resist so powerful an enemy. After these speeches had been heard, a great deal of deliberation by the Princes and various discussions used up the entire period of Lent. But at length it was decreed by the common opinion of the Princes and the Imperial Estates that through the intercession of the Cardinal Legate and with the Emperor's consent, the Highest Pontiff should as soon as possible declare that a free and general Council would be held in Germany, through which the Lutheran dissension would be quieted and would be destroyed from its roots up. But meanwhile, so that everyone might know what he should do and what he should believe, let other Diets be proclaimed, to be held soon after the festival of St Martin of Speyer. And so that it might more efficiently and wholesomely be determined what ought to be done and debated in these Diets, let each one among the Princes and Imperial Estates entrust to the learned men in his own territory the care and attention of this: that they distinguish the good from the evil in Luther's books and other new teachings, so that the good should not be suppressed equally with the evil. Furthermore, let them consider the grievances of the German nation, which were imposed upon it both by the Roman See and by the German Church, as carefully as possible, and let them reduce these grievances to a tolerable form.

The Emperor's instruction, which he had entrusted to Johannes Hannard (the best orator among his secretaries) to be relayed to the Princes and Estates, earnestly demanded that the Edict of Worms, which had been published by the common consent of all, should actively be put into performance and should be approved in their deeds, not just in their words. Therefore, it was added in the Decree of Nuremberg that all the Princes and Imperial Estates should carry out that Edict to the extent that it was possible for them, and should obey it and conform to it. Furthermore, concerning providing help for the King of Hungary against the Turks, since the greatest, unavoidable necessity demanded that the Turk's attempts be resisted in season, as soon as possible, and with a strong hand, it was decreed – with a notation of general contribution – that each individual Prince and Estate would consider that matter with the greatest attention, so that it could be fairly concluded and efficiently decided in future Diets, soon to be held at Speyer.

But while the Princes and Estates were meeting at Nuremberg, a serious and dangerous conspiracy of nobles was taking place in Germany, under the leadership of Franz von Sickingen, whom the Apostates had incited towards revolution by their seditious suggestions. He was especially influenced by the married, uncowled monks Oecolampadius and Bucer, who under the pretext of defending the Gospel persuaded him that he should seize the territories and goods of Church officials. And so Sickingen declared war against the Archbishop of Trier, in such a fashion that soon after he had sent hostile letters to the Archbishop, he followed them up with an armed host, and invaded one of the Archbishop's cities. Once this was captured, he immediately led his army directly to the walls of Trier, the Metropolitan city, and attacked it.

And if the Archbishop himself had not luckily been in that city at that time, and had not by his diligence (for he was a wise man, and one able to bear physical labor) shut off every entrance to it, the invasion would have been an accomplished fact – not only in that city, but indeed throughout that whole Archepiscopate; nay, indeed (as many feared) throughout all the episcopates and colleges and monasteries of Germany. For Sickingen's entire army could have been enriched through the plunder of that city, and soon an innumerable crowd of rebels would have joined itself to the army, attracted by the scent of its reputation – and not slowly, but in the way that crows and vultures are accustomed gather around a slaughtered body. But when the first impetus of the invasion was strongly repelled by the Archbishop, this imparted courage and an enthusiasm for defending themselves to the besieged citizens, so that thereafter the besiegers had no hope of getting possession of the city. And so, after a few days, during which he besieged the city in vain and became afraid of help from the neighboring princes, Franz lifted the siege and ingloriously dismissed his army.

But the Archbishop had made a treaty with Louis, the Duke of Bavaria, the Elector Prince and Palatine Count of the Rhine, and with Prince Philip, the Landgrave of Hesse. Each of these men had promised him forces and aid that were not to be sneered at, and other necessary matters for war. Therefore, he implored their help in avenging this injury. And so these three Princes, with their forces united into one, first set out for Frankfurt, an imperial city (which had an artfully constructed stone bridge over the Main river), against Hartmann of Croneburg. Hartmann's extremely well-fortified citadel, which was placed on a built-up hill and oversaw a town of the same name – i.e., Croneburg – was not more than one German mile distant from Frankfurt.

Now this Hartmann, a handsome, strong, and wealthy man, since he had been allured into Luther's sect by letters and pamphlets, and moreover was connected with Franz by blood and association, had openly been an aid to Franz against the Archbishop of Trier. Therefore, he seemed worthy to be the first to pay the penalty. But when he saw those Princes approaching with equipment of war, with chariots and cavalry and foot soldiers, and with great cannons, he secretly fled, leaving a sufficient guard behind in the citadel. Then, when the siege engines and cannons had been set in place, the Princes began to shoot out iron balls from the great, long cannons, with a horrible noise. The walls and the stones were shaken very strongly by these cannonballs – to such an extent, indeed, that the sound was even heard in the citizens' houses in Frankfurt. And the besieged people in the citadel, when they saw that they could not resist by their own strength, nor could they long withstand the force of the breaking and besieging, bargained for their lives by handing over their city; and once it was handed over, they were sent away unharmed. By this means, therefore, Hartmann was despoiled of the most precious possession of his ancestral goods, which the Landgrave of Hesse holds up until this present day.

For the rest, the same three Princes were going to direct the force of war against the Cardinal and Archbishop of Mainz; not because he had given any cause of war himself, but because several nobles who were his officials and salary-holders had helped Franz against Trier. Nevertheless, so that it would not seem that war was being waged against him without reason, it was decided by each of the Princes that the matter would first be discussed in a meeting at Frankfurt. And in the course of this meeting, the person of the Cardinal himself was excused, even by his enemies, so innocent was he of any fault. But several Nobles were accused: as, for instance, Froben von Hutten, Prefect of the Archepiscopal Curia; Caspar Lerchus the Marshal; and certain others. In fact, even several Canons of the Chapter of the Greater Church of Mainz were held under suspicion that they had assisted Franz with advice and aid. Therefore, if the Cardinal and Archbishop of Mainz would not give these men over as defendants to be punished according to the judgment of the three Princes, the Princes said that they would in fact wage war against him.

Moreover, while the Cardinal was considering this matter, Franz, who was not yet entirely ruined but was still powerful, promised him great assistance; as did other nobles too, including his full brother, Lord Joachim, Margrave of Brandenburg and Prince Elector, etc. These all were trying to persuade the Cardinal that war should rather be undertaken than that he should act according to the will of those three Princes. But the Cardinal himself greatly loved peace, and, in order to guard against the shedding of human blood, preferred – even though he was innocent – to be milked for monetary damages than to try his fortune in war. Therefore, it was agreed, after various discussions, that in compensation for the damages inflicted on the Archbishop of Trier by Franz and his helpers, the Cardinal should pay 25,000 gold pieces; and his nobles should both ask pardon for the help which they had already given, and should promise on good faith that they would in the future offer no advice or help to Franz against the Archbishop of Trier. When the nobles refused to do this, they were left under their own protection, since the Cardinal could not keep them in his household in defiance of the peace agreement, and other Princes regarded them as enemies. And so when the Landgrave of Hesse was returning home, on his journey he occupied by force the citadels and towns of Lord Froben von Hutten, a knight and the Master of the Curia of Mainz, a man who was in general most prudent, and had both great authority and great wealth. Later, during the peasants' uprising, he was noteworthy for his great courage, and recovered his goods.

Now it was already winter, and the season's harshness made it impossible either to pitch camp in the fields or to besiege citadels or towns. And so the three Princes who had joined together against Franz dismissed their army and returned home so that they could reconvene in arms in the early Spring. The Prince Elector and Palatine of the Rhine had graciously befriended Franz many years previously; and so he interposed himself, as a mediator and arbiter of peace, between the Archbishop of Trier and Franz. But when he saw that Franz refused equitable conditions of peace, and trusted more than was just in his own strength and the aid of the nobles, the Prince left him and began to aid the cause of the Archbishop. And so at this point Franz's luck began to diminish; up until that very day he had been considered famous for his many successes in war. For he had imposed the heaviest damages on the Landgrave of Hesse, while the Landgrave was still a boy, having already as an infant lost his father; and he besieged the city of Metz and forced it, most wealthy city that it was, to accept prejudicial conditions of peace; and he was famous for many other terrible deeds. And Luther had written secretly about Franz von Sickingen to his partisan Ulrich von Hutten, saying that he had felt more confidence in Sickingen, and had more hope in him, than he had in any Prince under Heaven.

Luther was grieved, therefore, by the misfortune of Franz and the other nobles, especially those who were considered Evangelicals. And so, taking his occasion for mockery from the Decree of Nuremberg, because of his lust for vengeance he raved against the Princes with the most furious reproaches. And indeed he published a pamphlet in German, to which he gave this title on its frontispiece: *Two Discordant and Contradictory Imperial Decrees Pertaining to Luther.*[233] But within, in the pamphlet, he first wrote an epistle to all the Christians of Germany, and it was so harsh that he seemed to grow enraged in the fashion of a rabid dog, and (if God had permitted it) to bite lethally. After which letter, as if it were a kind of preface, he added the Edict of Worms, and after it he added the Decree of Nuremberg, which had been written to the Counts from Mansfeld. And at the end of this decree again he spewed out against the Princes whatever of his ire was left over from his preface. For he says in this preface, 'I was very concerned that these two Imperial Decrees should be printed, because of my great compassion for us wretched Germans, in the hope that perhaps God would deign through this to touch certain Princes and others as well, so that they would be able to feel and to perceive (for this is not a question of seeing; pigs and asses can see) how blindly and obstinately they are acting. Indeed it is shameful, that the Emperor and the Princes openly depend on falsehoods; but it is more shameful, that at one and the same time they publish contradictory decrees, as you see here, where it is ordered, that I should be dealt with according to the Edict of Worms. But a contradictory decree is nevertheless put forward, that in the future Diet at Speyer it should first be inquired into, what is good and what bad in my teaching. Surely, these must be drunken and raving Princes!'[234] And below, 'Good Princes' (he said) 'and Lords, you hurry along too quickly with me – a poor, solitary man – toward my death; and when this has been accomplished, then you will have conquered. But if you had ears to hear, I would say to you something strange: What if the life of Luther is worth so much in God's estimation, that unless Luther is living, none of you may be certain of his own life or realm, and Luther's death would be a calamity for you all? For God is not to be trifled with. Go on eagerly, therefore; kill and burn; I will not yield, if God wills it so: here I am, and I ask you, in a very friendly fashion, when you have killed me, not to revive me again and then kill me anew. As I see it, God has given me my task, not with rational men; but German beasts must kill me, if I am worthy, just as if wolves or boars should tear me to pieces.'[235] And again, 'And if they kill me, they will commit such a murder that neither they nor their children will be able to survive it. I would prefer for them to be warned about this, and certainly I would not wish it for them; but it is of no use: God has blinded them and made them obstinate.'[236] And below, 'Truly, truly, a calamity is before your hands and the wrath of God grows stronger, from which you cannot flee if you continue in this course. What do you want, good Lords? God is too wise for you; in an instant He will make you stupid. Again, He is too powerful, in an instant He will destroy you. One part of His Speaking says: "He has put down the mighty from their seat." And this will now have been said to you, good Lords, if you will not pay attention.' [237]

These things Luther said in his preface. But in his conclusion, he raged against them still more vehemently and rebelliously. 'In closing' (he said) 'I beseech all pious Christians to think it proper to pray to God at the same time for pitiable and blinded Princes of this kind, with whom, beyond doubt, God afflicts us in His great wrath. Let us not follow them, in setting out against the Turks or in contributing to the expedition. Since the Turk is both ten times wiser and ten times more upright than our Princes, what that is done against him could turn out well when it is done by fools of this sort, who attack and blaspheme God so thoroughly? For here you see how a miserable mortal sack of worms or maggots, the Emperor, who is not certain of his life for one blink of an eye, shamelessly boasts that he is the true and supreme defender of the Catholic faith.' [238] And below: 'From my inmost heart I bewail these things to all upright Christians, that they may lament with me over dull, foolish, insane, frenzied, and mindless fools of this sort. One should rather die ten times over than hear such blasphemies and slanders against the Divine Majesty. Truly, their reward is very well deserved, because they have persecuted God's Word; on that account, they deserve to be punished in this way, and to arrive at this palpable blindness. May God free us from them, and through His Grace give us other rulers. Amen.' [239]

Such was the conclusion of the angry Luther. But the Decree of Nuremberg did not displease the Lutheran cities to the same extent. For since the cities had many eloquent debaters who were skilled in languages, they were hoping that, when the matter was put forward for examination, they would prevail concerning the Scriptures. And so in the month of July, speakers from the Imperial cities convened in Speyer; the greater part of them were of the Lutheran sect. After examining that Decree, they made the following declaration among themselves: that the free and Imperial cities, especially those which had among their citizens persons who were distinguished, learned, experienced, and intelligent with regard to the Sacred Scripture, should with the greatest diligence entrust it to those people that they should consider faithfully and with diligence those points and articles which touch upon our Christian faith, and particularly those which are unclear to a poor intelligence. They should be appropriately undaunted in this task, and should offer their conclusion in writing to the Senate, which would entrust it to those speakers who were going to attend the future Imperial Diet, where, when all the conclusions of all the cities had been collated, one final conclusion would be drawn from them all, and that conclusion would then be used. And so this laborious diligence of Apostates with a thirst for writing was burning the midnight oil throughout all the Apostates' cities – and through these methods the unlearned papists were going to be conquered.

But meanwhile, the Princes too, according to the tenor of the Decree, instructed their theologians to examine Luther's books. For this reason, Johannes

Cochlaeus excerpted and confuted 500 articles from thirty-six of Luther's sermons, so that he might indicate to the Princes in that brief little work how great would be the forest of damnable articles, if they were collected from all of Luther's writings by a rigid examination and published in one volume – since so great a number of them had been collected, and justly refuted, from a few brief, popular sermons.[240] And the Emperor Charles, who was at that time occupied in Spain, when he had received a copy of the Decree of Nuremberg and had considered all its points seasonably and diligently, soon wrote an answering letter to the Princes and Estates of the Empire according to his own wisest counsel. This letter was, indeed, quite long, but it was also very sagacious, and very full of seriousness and authority. In it, he not only reproached and rejected the form of the Decree; he also most severely forbade the convening of an assembly at Speyer and its method of proceeding. For among other things, he said the following:

'Although we commanded in the Diet that was recently held at Worms, in the general gathering of the Elector and other Princes and of all the Orders of the Holy Roman Empire, that by the unanimous advice, understanding, and consensus of those princes and orders, the Lutheran teaching and illusion should be publicly denounced and forbidden, under the most severe fines and penalties, as heretical, malignant, and poisonous; and furthermore, that all Lutheran writings and books, after they had been legitimately reproved and condemned by the Holy Apostolic law and by Christian order, should be destroyed and burned; nevertheless, in the Diet that was recently held at Nuremberg, you and the universal Estates proposed and gave out a regulation concerning only the injurious and slanderous pamphlets of Luther and the indecorous printings and pictures; and you enjoined each and every person to observe your ordinance to the extent that it was possible. You did this as if we, in our earlier decrees and edicts, had imposed and set out something strange, burdensome, or evil, and as if it would not be easier, and more just, to continue in the earlier, ancient, praiseworthy, and Catholic rites and regulations than thus to accept and maintain strange and unheard of abuses.' And below he said, 'Moreover, as if acting in your own right, you and the Estates together proposed and determined, on the next St Martin's Day, to hold a general and universal assembly of the German Nation in our Imperial city of Speyer; and in this assembly to consider and propose ways, means, and regulations, concerning how, in what manners and forms, the Divine Service and other ecclesiastical offices and orders, arrangements and customs should be performed and preserved, until the next general Diet; and also that in the meantime persons learned in the sacred Scriptures, and other erudite people, should discover whatever in Luther's writings seems inharmonious with the Faith and contrary to it, and should with all their powers determine the dubious passages and the other passages. Such things we neither can, nor do we wish to, admit or permit in any fashion whatsoever. But rather it is in the first place appropriate and fitting that we, as the defender and protector of the Apostolic See, should greatly be on our guard, lest through this matter we incite the wrath and indignation of God Almighty and the Apostolic Holiness against us. For what great injuries, insults, and dishonors would be imposed on the holy, divine, and Catholic Church, if the pious fear of God and obedience to Him were injured and diminished in such a way that the German nation alone (a nation which up until the present time has been judged to be most filled with devout fear of God, and which obediently and continuously has observed the decrees and regulations of the Catholic Church) should take up and set into motion a plan of this sort, which all the other Christian princes, and even the Pope himself, would not dare to begin or even to have in mind? A plan which would reject and abolish the holy and praiseworthy Catholic ordinances, customs, regulations, and rites, which for so many years, up until the present time, have been perfectly and without contradiction observed in all Christendom, and have been a solace to all the faithful, living and dead;[241] from which ordinances and rites, truly, no one has ever withdrawn, whom the just judgment of God did not heavily punish on this account. Nevertheless, the inhuman and impious Luther presumes, alone, to resist these rites and ordinances, and to infect them so far as he is able with his sweet poison, and to destroy mortals in soul and body, and to make himself great and conspicuous in the eyes of all people through his adroit malice.'[242]

And later he said, 'Since we, because of the abovementioned reasons and other well-founded ones, know about this intention and action – which we consider evil – of yours and of the universal Estates, and since we understand how much damage, how many abuses, uproars, and revolts, would result from it in all Christendom, but especially in the German nation, if we did not forestall it and attend to it in time; therefore we ask you, and we enjoin this upon you: by the oath which binds you to us and to the Holy Empire, and under peril of the crime of *lèse-majesté*, which must be avoided; by the command and recommand of us and of the Empire; under penalty of the loss and removal of all the favors and privileges which you have obtained from our predecessors, the Roman Emperors and Kings, and from us, and from the Holy Empire; and in addition to these, under those penalties which are contained in our Imperial Edict about this matter which was published at Worms – by all these things, we solemnly order you by our Imperial power, that you depart from our Decree and Edict in no way or form whatsoever, and that you do and undertake nothing against it, but that you obey it and follow it, wherever it possibly concerns you or applies to you, completely and simply. And we especially order that, in the aforementioned intention of the Estates about the Council and other disputations, declarations, and interpretations which concern the Catholic faith, you attempt, do, and proceed by no means whatsoever apart from the authority, ordinance, and approval of the Apostolic Holiness, of us, or of the General Council. We further order that you wholly defer to that which ought to be announced and will be announced, as was said above, by the authority and agreement of our most Holy Father the Pope, in the next General Council, and that you demonstrate that you are obedient in all these matters. For you are bound to act thus, according to your conscience and your duty to God

Almighty, to the Holy Catholic Church, to the Apostolic Holiness, and to us, as your superior and head predestined through Divine providence; and how precious a thing it is to you to avoid our grave wrath and the Empire's, and to avoid the aforementioned fines and penalties. We wish these things which we have said to be taken very seriously. Given in our city of Burg, in Castile, on the 15th day of July, in the year 24, the 6th year of our Roman rule.' [243] These things the Emperor wrote in German.

When the Imperial Diet at Nuremberg had been dissolved, the Apostolic Legate, for the sake of security, had gone from there to Stuttgart in the company of the Most Serene Prince Ferdinand, Infante of Spain, Archduke of Austria, etc., the brother and viceroy of the Emperor. In Stuttgart, when they had compared their suggestions, they appointed a particular assembly of certain Princes, to be held at Regensburg on a set day – namely, the day of the birth of John the Baptist.

And so they all convened there on that set day; indeed, Cardinal Campeggio, the Lateran Legate, was there in person, together with the aforementioned Archduke and Viceroy. Also present were Matthew, the Cardinal and Arch-bishop of Salzburg; and the two Dukes and most illustrious Princes of Bavaria, Wilhelm and Louis; Bernard, the Tridentine Bishop; Johannes, the Adminis-trator of the Church of Regensburg, by birthright the Palatinate of the Rhine, and the Duke of Bavaria. And the following Bishops appeared through their spokesmen and counselors, who had been instructed in the full Decree: Wiegand of Bamberg; Georg of Speyer; Wilhelm of Strasbourg; Christopher of Augsburg; Hugo of Constance; Christopher of Basel; Philip of Freising; Sebastian of Brixen; and Ernest the Administrator of Padua, the full brother of the aforementioned Dukes Wilhelm and Louis. Indeed, all of these, fired by a pious zeal for the Catholic faith, had made and had even confirmed a voluntary confederation among themselves, in order to resist the Lutheran faction more efficiently. Therefore, before the Emperor's stern answer had arrived in Germany, nay, even before it had been written, these Princes had of their own accord concluded and decreed, before all other things, that the Emperor's Edict of Worms be obeyed. Second, that the Gospel be interpreted according to the exposition of those fathers who were approved and received by the Church; that no one be allowed to preach in the Church except one who had previously been examined by the Ordinary of the place, or by his Vicar or Official; that in the most sacred mass and the administration of the Sacraments, and universally in the cere-monies, fasts, prayers, offerings, and other ancient rites of the Catholic Church, nothing be changed; that the illicit marriages of priests and monks be prohibited and punished; that the printers publish nothing, unless it had first been duly examined and approved. And among many other things, they resolved with outstanding foresight and severity, that their subjects' children who were devoting themselves to their studies in Wittenberg should be summoned home from there within three months, and should not return there for schooling, under penalty of the loss of all their goods and inheritance. Nor would they admit any student from Wittenberg into any ecclesiastical benefice in their territories, nor appoint such a student to any lectureship in their schools. Moreover, no Prince would receive into his lands a Lutheran whom another Prince had proscribed because of his transgressions and faults; but any Lutheran who was proscribed by one of them, would be considered proscribed by all. Finally, if anyone of them should suffer rebellion or sedition from his subjects because of these matters, the rest would provide him with help and advice.

Furthermore, when the Apostolic Legate learned that the minds of the laypeople were gravely offended by the shameful abuses and depraved habits of the Clergy, and that the Lutheran heresy gained not a small opportunity from this, he made an agreement with those Princes that they should choose and send experienced men from their counselors, who would note down, one by one, the excesses and lacks, the scandals and abuses, of the Clergy of Germany. And he himself appointed Johannes Cochlaeus to that chosen group, whom he used as an interpreter in those matters which were conducted in German. And so from the articles which were presented by that delegation, he drew up and published an excellent decree, which would remove the abuses and reform the lives of the Clergy. The other Princes approved and confirmed this decree.

Moreover, when George Duke of Saxony, a Prince in all ways Catholic, had accepted the Decree signed by the Emperor together with the Edict of Worms, he published both of these throughout all his realm, and most severely commanded all his subjects that they obey the Emperor's Edict and Decree in every point and article; and warned them even more severely that he would punish every transgression against these. For he is not only a pious and religious Prince, but also one most loving and at the same time most attentive toward the Emperor, following the example of the glorious memory of his father, Albert, Duke of Saxony. No other Prince was more useful or faithful to his Emperor, Maximilian (the grandfather of this Emperor) in the wars than was Albert; this was especially the case in his earliest youth, when Albert recovered by force of arms the hereditary provinces of Maximilian's only son, Prince Philip (the father of our Emperor), who was at that time still a child. The King of the Franks had unjustly occupied those provinces after the death of the most famous and bellicose Prince Charles, the Duke of Burgundy, Philip's maternal grandfather and the great-grandfather of our Emperor. Before that, Maximilian, son of Emperor Frederick III, had married Charles's only daughter Maria.

For the rest, when the assembly at Regensburg was dissolved, the Emperor's brother Prince Ferdinand and the Apostolic Legate traveled down from there into Austria, following the Danube river. They remained for some time at Vienna, where the Prince – mature and stern far beyond his young years, and also learned and intelligent – maintained his brother's Edict as eagerly as possible, especially against two heretics, Jacob Peregrinus, presbyter of the Diocese of Padua, and Caspar Tauber, a Viennese citizen. Each of them had been suspected and convicted of Lutheran heresy, had confessed to it, and had been condemned by the legitimate process of the law. The Prince mercifully induced them, through men learned both in Theology and in law, to recantation and penitence. But when Tauber returned to the heresy which he had publicly abjured, he was punished with the ultimate penalty. For he had concluded his recantation, written in German, with these words:

'Since I, Caspar Tauber, in defiance of the Imperial Edict and the decree of my most merciful Lord Frederick, kept certain books published by the damned heretic Martin Luther, and even myself wrote my own treatises, and in them embraced many injuries and scandals, and manifold heresies and damned errors, by which, under the guise of the Gospel, both I and others of Christ's faithful were seduced away from all obedience, both divine and other, to evils and rashness of every sort, against God and the salvation of our souls – therefore I vow and promise that henceforward, so long as I shall live, I shall never either read or keep damned books of this sort, whether large or small; nor will I preach, disseminate, defend, or assent to the abovementioned errors, which are all damned heresies. And if I shall transgress these promises, then, according to the form of the law, may I be punished by the secular power, as a convicted heretic. I confess all this in the sight of Church, by these letters, which I have written with my own hand.' [244]

Luther, however, wrote a book – *On Business and Usury* – in German, so that he might in some manner both reconcile the people to himself and render them hostile to the Princes. In it he recounted the very numerous grievances of Germany caused by the excessive greed of merchants, so that he might seem most loving toward the people and his country, and most zealous for the public good concerning the common people. But that eager seeker of popular favor, that most wicked schemer of sedition, was aiming at this: that because of the misdeeds of the merchants, he should incite the poor people more strongly against the Princes, as if they were allies of thieves and sharers in evil gains. Thus, among many other things he proclaims:

'Kings and Princes ought to direct their attention here, and to prohibit such things according to the strict law. But I hear that they have a major share and part in the matter. And so it has come about according to the saying of Isaiah 1: "Your Princes are made the allies of thieves." And meanwhile they hang thieves who have stolen a florin, or even half of one, although they themselves do business with those who despoil the entire world and steal more than all other thieves, so that this saying should remain true: "Great thieves hang small ones." And as the Roman Senator Cato said: "Private thieves languish in towers and prisons; but public thieves walk about in gold and silk." But what will God, at length, say about these things? He will do just as Ezekiel says: Princes and Merchants, he will melt one thief together with another, just as lead is melted with copper. And so a certain city is being destroyed, and there will no longer be either princes or merchants. Thus I fear, that this is already at our doors, etc.' [245]

Later, when another occasion was afforded him, however shameless, trivial, and dishonest it might be, he published another German pamphlet, which had the title: *The Way in Which God Rescued a Certain Honorable Nun*, with a letter of Martin Luther to the Counts of Mansfeld.[246] For it had happened in one of those Counts' towns, whose name was Eisleben, where there was a very famous convent of holy virgins, that a certain Florentina, infected with the Lutheran turmoil, looked again at the world, and said secretly to one of her relatives that she no longer wished to remain in the convent, since that mode of life was contrary to her nature and her condition. She referred the matter to the Abbess, and the Abbess, when she made no progress by instructing her with many admonitions, made her a prisoner. But another nun, who was taking care of the prisoner, once forgot to lock the doors, and Florentina secretly made her escape from the Convent and fled to Luther. However, when the Abbess complained, in words and letters, that she was guilty of perjury, flight, and vow-breaking, Luther published a pamphlet in which he demonstrated that it had been a great miracle of God which snatched her out of Hell. For these were his words, in his preliminary Epistle to the Counts (as whose subject he too had been born):

'I do not doubt' (he said) 'that people were incredulous when they heard that this Florentina had been miraculously snatched by God from the jaws of the Devil; nor do I doubt that some, who believe that the condition of nuns is a good thing, will say that the Devil helped her to leave; and that others, who take little regard of either God or the Devil, will say, "Look, why is it a miracle, that some nun should run away from a convent?" It is fitting for these things to happen. But if some rebellious spirit should institute a pilgrimage and should perform one of those miracles about which St Paul speaks in 2 Thessalonians 2, where he says: "The man of sin will appear with many signs and wonders," or if the Devil should allow himself to be tormented with holy water, and should pretend that he suffered great anguish in so doing (as occurred recently, in this very year, in a certain place): this would appropriately be considered a miracle of God. But we, who already know the Gospel, and through God's grace recognize the truth, neither should, nor dare to, dismiss miracles of this kind, which make for the confirmation of the Gospel, and promote it.' [247]

And below he said, 'What are you doing, you Princes and Lords, when you compel people to God against their will, although it is a matter neither of your duty nor your power to do this? You ought to compel people to external uprightness: allow vows to be vows, allow precepts to be precepts. But God does not desire these things, unless they are observed voluntarily and with joy. For He Himself says, "No one comes to Me, unless My Father has led him there." Good God, is this not sufficiently clear? It is fitting for the Father to lead, and man wants to compel. What God does not attempt, this miserable worm wants to attempt, and through someone else, who is unwilling, to do what God himself cannot do. You do not want to be forced to our Gospel; why therefore would you force us to yours?' [248]

Furthermore, when all the schools, both public and private (as they are called) were left vacant in Germany because of Luther's Gospel, and through their shameful diminution and emptiness caused great disgrace in cities everywhere, the Lutherans began to be in bad repute because of this, since some of them had lapsed into such madness that they wished to use only the Hebrew and German languages, and to eliminate Greek and Latin. For they held Greek and Latin in contempt, and claimed the inspiration of the Holy Spirit for themselves. Because of these things, and so that the blame might be transferred from him on to the Universities and the monks, Luther wrote a pamphlet in German to all the Senators of all the cities of Germany in common, about founding Christian schools. From the very beginning of that pamphlet, he bandied about many praises, attempting to strengthen and increase his followers and his doctrine, although the tyrants were unwilling for him to do so and were fighting against him in vain; but he wished all to know that the matter was God's work, not Luther's. For among many other words of vainglory, he said the following:

'Let me be whatever I am, but in the eyes of God I am able to boast with a clear conscience that in this matter I do not seek the things which are mine, which I would have been able to acquire much better by keeping silent; but from my heart and faithfully I intend both your good and the good of all Germany. God has destined me for this, whether anyone wants to believe it or not; and through charity toward you I say this freely and confidently. Anyone who obeys me, beyond doubt obeys not me but Christ; and anyone who does not obey me, shows contempt not for me, but for Christ. For I know very well, and I am certain, what and to what purpose I speak and teach. And moreover anyone at all will discern this well for himself, if he will desire to understand my teaching rightly.' [249]

And below he says, 'Is it not evident that any boy at all can now so be taught in three years, that at age fifteen or eighteen he will know more than all the universities and monasteries have known up until this time? Indeed, what have they been learning up until now in the public training-grounds and monasteries, except to be made into asses, blockheads, and numbskulls? Someone could study there twenty or forty years, and still he would not know how to speak either Latin or German – and let me keep silent about the sordid and sinful life in which noble youth was so pitiably corrupted. But indeed it is true that before I would wish universities and monasteries to continue as they have been up till now, so that no other method of teaching and living were available for youth, I would prefer that every boy be dumb, and never learn anything. For it is my earnest intention, prayer, and petition that these stables of asses and training-grounds of devils either be sunk into the pit, or be changed into Christian schools.' [250]

And a little later he says, 'Let us look at our earlier misery, and the shadows in which we were. I judge that Germany has never before heard so much of God's word as it is now hearing. Certainly, we find no trace of this in the histories. Therefore, if we let this slip away without gratitude or honor, then it must be feared that we will suffer still more dreadful shadows and misfortunes. Dear Germans, buy while the market is before your doors; reap, while the sky is clear and the wind favorable; use the grace and word of God, while it is there. For you must know this, that the word and grace of God are a passing shower of rain, which does not return to the place where it has once been.[251] Nor ought it to deter us' (he said) 'that some boast of the Spirit and make little of the Scriptures. Some, like the Waldensian Brothers, even deny that the languages are useful. But my good friend, the Spirit is here and the Spirit is there, and I also was in the Spirit, and I even saw more, perhaps, of the Spirit (if to be sure one may boast about one's own matters) than these men themselves will see in an entire year, however much they boast. And my spirit also shows itself in some places, while theirs is silent in its corner, and does not do much more than boast about its own glory.'[252]

He wrote about the same matter to the people of Riga also and to the Livonians, most bitterly complaining about the stupidity of the Germans, because they would not give just stipends to the preachers of his new doctrine, although they had earlier given such large and ample salaries to the papists for their pernicious doctrine. 'But now,' he said, 'when God sends to us good, trustworthy, and learned men, who by word and deed encourage discipline and chastity, and reduce fornication through holy marriage; and in addition, who serve us with all zeal both in body and in soul, and show us the true path to heaven, we abandon them; and those whom we should, by all expenses, bring in from the ends of the world, we treat in almost the same way as the rich man treated the pauper Lazarus.'[253]

But when he learned that Henry Sutphen (an Apostate from the Augustinian order who had previously been Prior in the monastery of his Order at Antwerp, and who had come to Bremen as a fugitive because of his lapse and faithlessness) had been burned by the neighboring peoples of Dania at Diedmar (or Theitmas, as some call it), he wrote a letter of mourning to the people of Bremen, who because they had been led astray by him had deserted their archbishop and every cleric of their city in matters of faith and religion. He began this history in these words:

'In the year of the Lord 1522 Henry Sutphen came to Bremen, not so that he might give public speeches there, but because he had it in his mind to travel to Wittenberg, since he had been expelled from Antwerp by the tyrants, because of the Gospel, etc.'[254] But Luther described his suffering as truly as if he were truly a blessed martyr: an apostate, and a useless, nay, a pernicious man, who always conducted himself with a twisted view and at all times sowed discord between the laity and the clergy: first at Antwerp, then at Bremen, most recently at Meldorp near Diedmar, where finally he paid the penalty demanded by God's just judgment for his broken vow, his treachery, and his perjury. For at Antwerp, when he had been arrested for the Lutheran heresy, he had publicly recanted and abjured Lutheranism; and when he relapsed shortly afterwards, he would have met with the ultimate penalty, had he not escaped from prison. For he had infected the remaining brothers of his monastery with the Lutheran turmoil to such an extent that there was no hope of remedy; and for this reason they say that whole monastery was torn down to the ground.

1525

Now the pretended amity between Luther and Karlstadt had broken out into open enmity. The latter of these two wanted to be of some account, the former to be everything; and each of them was equally desirous of vainglory. Luther was foremost in intellect, eloquence, and style; Karlstadt had cultivated his rough intellect, which was like a hard crag, by much study and labor, until he already seemed to Luther to be a great and learned theologian, before he had debated with him in any matters. And indeed the Wittenbergers had thought so much of Karlstadt, before he began to disagree with Luther, that they encouraged his forbidden and sacrilegious marriage with the highest zeal and marked it with the greatest celebration. Concerning this marriage, they put together a private Mass, which they did not hesitate to publish openly. The Introit of this mass was as follows:

'The Lord God said, it is not good for the man to be alone; let us make for him a helper like himself.'

Again,

'A man will cleave to his wife, and the two will be in one flesh.'

The prayer, or Collect, was as follows:

'God, who after the long and unholy blindness of your priests, have deigned to give to the Blessed Andreas Karlstadt that grace, that he should be the first who will have dared to marry a wife, though this is allowed by no argument of the Papistic law: Grant, we beg, that all priests, with their minds restored to health, following in his footsteps, may either put their concubines away or may marry them and so may be turned to the companionship of the legitimate marriage-bed. Through our Lord Jesus Christ, etc.'

And the Prose, or Sequence, was as follows:

'God, in your virtue Andreas Karlstadt rejoices and is glad, joined in the marriage-bed. That fishery of the Bishop is himself made the first fisherman of wives. At last, he has led the whoremaster priests back to the standard of marriage. He, as hardy victor, subdued the Roman rule to your laws, God; following the advice of Your servant Paul, and now showing himself to be a good husband. With the papists amazed and unwilling, he has just now taken his long-sought wife into his house. And with great honor, he, a priest, has signed the marriage certificate, Lord. We believe that he is truly Your priest, and the little brother of Christ Your Son. We therefore, burdened by our own concubinages, beg you, God, that we may rejoice eternally in the imitation of him, who pleases You by having followed our ancient fathers.'

And moreover, the Secret ran thus:

'Lord, we pray You to accept our sacrifice kindly, which we devoutly offer to You in these first marriage ceremonies of Andreas Karlstadt: that we may by its efficacy be defended from all whorish dangers. Through our Lord.'

Finally, the Compline was thus:

'May the mysteries of the Sacrament which we have taken be an aid to us, Lord, and may we rejoice, as does Andreas Karlstadt, in the marriage celebration; grant, we beseech You, that the marriages of priests throughout all the world may begin happily, continue happily, and finish as happily as possible. Through our Lord Jesus, etc.' [255]

But how vain this hope and how wicked this prayer of theirs, and how unhappy were the auspices of that marriage, can be plainly seen from the events that followed. For they say that Karlstadt had asked a certain local Prince for bread and meat for the nuptial feast, and that this Prince ordered that he be sent ass's meat in place of stag's meat, with the ass butchered and skinned by the handler and cut up into little parts, and the pieces closed up in a vessel. They ate these pieces, thinking that they were stag's meat, until the ears and hooves of the ass were found in the middle of the vessel.

For the rest, while Luther was absent in his feigned Patmos, Karlstadt endeavored to put into action whatever Luther had taught in words. And so he flew into rages against the images of the saints, and against the venerable rite of the Mass, from which he gained great fame and seemed almost equal to Luther himself. Indeed, Luther was touched by jealousy when he returned home from his Patmos. In order to obscure Karlstadt's fame, he publicly reproved his deeds in a speech, and refuted him openly in the sight of the people; on this pretext, not that his deeds were evil, but that they had not been undertaken on the authority of the Prince. Karlstadt, since his eloquence was unequal to Luther's, was confused before the people, and he stored that injury deep in his heart, nor did he ever again favor Luther from his soul. Moreover, when he was unable to communicate his opinions openly in Wittenberg, since Luther opposed him, he at length left there and went to Orlamünde, a town which is situated on the Saale river and belongs to the same Prince as does Wittenberg.[256] He found freedom to write there, due to the favor of the people, and he openly rebuked Luther, not only about the Mass and about images, but also about the sacrament of the Eucharist. Luther was very distressed by this, and made it his business, in his home and indeed through the whole community, and even in the court of the Prince (through George Spalatin the Prince's confidential secretary) to have Karlstadt recalled to Wittenberg, through the oath he had given to the University, so that he would preach, lecture, and debate, in accordance with his office, as he had done previously. But when Karlstadt kept on delaying and excusing himself in letters to the people, Luther himself was sent to his Prince's towns situated on the Saale river, so that by speaking there he might turn those people away from Karlstadt's opinions. But when he accomplished very little and many of the people resisted him to his face, and cited scriptures from the Old Testament in opposition to images, at length through the aid of the junior prince Johannes Frederick, who was the son of the brother of Frederick the Elector, Luther brought it about that Karlstadt should be prohibited from all the towns and borders of the Dukes of Saxony.

And so Karlstadt was made an outlaw, and wandered most miserably with his most unhappy and illegitimate wife among the crowds and rebellions of the peasants who were rising up in Franconia. Sometimes he lay hidden in

Rotenberg on the Tauber river, at others he fled to his maternal home of Karlstadt, which is a town of Franconia near to Mainz; he could never settle in safety. But finally, after the seditious peasants had everywhere been killed, the unhappy Karlstadt was held in the worst repute and was considered suspect as the author of the rebellion, the inciter of the uprisings, and the leader of the peasants. He was reduced to such a point of necessity and misery that he was driven to implore help from his most hostile enemy, Luther. And Luther seized this opportunity of increasing his own glory, since he would seem to be an Evangelist, not just in his words, but also to the greatest extent in his deeds. He heeded the prayers of his enemy, and he made Karlstadt's self-justification publicly known in German, through the printers, and himself added a preface to it.[257] In this preface Luther not only boasted that he had come to the aid of his greatest enemy, as Christ taught, but he even asked that both the Princes and the people should be persuaded by Karlstadt's justification – although he himself had earlier most vehemently accused him, as being suspected of sedition, in published books. Moreover, he saw to it that Karlstadt was permitted to return into Saxony – on this condition, however, that he would not publicly assert his opinions against Luther either in word or in writing.

Therefore, Karlstadt returned to Wittenberg, where because of his shame he was unable to bear being seen by those among whom he had earlier been outstanding for his wealth, his honors, and his dignity. Therefore, he retreated ingloriously into a nearby village and into the surrounding hamlets, where for some time he led the most miserable of lives. From being a Doctor of Theology and an Archdeacon in Wittenberg, he became a poor farmer and an untaught peasant, who, although he did not know how to plow, was driven to plow by poverty. He had unruly horses; one of them would go in one direction before the plow, the other in another direction, or one would go forward but the other would walk backwards, so that the plowman was an object of both laughter and pity to all his neighbors. And his wife seemed deservedly pitiable to their neighbors, since she had been born into a noble family and educated nobly, but had married a priest, as the worst of examples and under the worst possible auspices, against all human and divine law. And not only a priest, but an ignoble and alien man, who then became infamous for so many reasons, an outlaw, poor and abject, at whose house one could not even eat one's fill of coarse peasant bread; and whom, as a false husband, the Wittenbergers had falsely hailed as blessed at his marriage; and, before all, whom Luther had most gravely accused of sedition, not only privately in letters but also publicly in two very lengthy books. In the first of these he said,

'Now even if it were true, and it were fitting for me to believe, that Dr Karlstadt intends neither murder nor seditions, nevertheless so long as he continues with the violent breaking of images, and draws the unruly mob to himself, it would be incumbent upon me to say that he has a seditious spirit, and one eager for murder, like the one at Allstedt.'[258] And a little later he said, 'But you will say, "He will not be so obstinate; he will allow himself to be taught, and will desist from such things." Who? Dr Karlstadt? Indeed, he knows how to say words prettily, and to make it known in his writings that he wants to be taught and to defer to his superiors. If he means this sincerely, I am made of gold. When has he listened or yielded to anyone? How often did Philip warn him at Wittenberg that he should not make such a turmoil about Moses, about images, about the Mass and about confession? And when I returned and preached against his image-breaking and his Mass, why did he not desist, or listen? Also, when Dr Justus Jonas and Lord Theoderic of Bila mediated between us, how prettily was he yielding then, or allowing himself to be admonished when he even called down the Last Judgment against me because of that Mass of the revolutionaries.' [259]

And below he said, 'This also is not a trivial reason why he associates with the heavenly prophets, from whom – as is well known – the spirit of Allstedt comes. He learns from them, he is allied with them. These men secretly creep about, wandering through the land, and they congregate in one place on the Saale, where they intend to build their nest. The powerless Devil does not wish to go anywhere except to our places, where we have earlier, through the Gospel, prepared a respite and security; and he wishes only to defile and destroy our nest, just as the cuckoo plays with the sparrow, etc.' [260]

And in his German letter to the people of Strasbourg, he said:

'I could bear that the matter should be thus, that Dr Karlstadt denounces me, because I expelled him; I would even wish, God willing, to excuse him. However, I rejoice that he has left our land; I wish also that he were not among you, and that he had resolved to abstain from complaints of this sort. For I fear my defense of myself will accuse him extremely harshly. I advise this: whoever is able to do so, let him beware of that deceitful spirit; there is nothing good in him. When I met him at Jena he very nearly convinced even me, through a certain Scripture, that I should not confuse his spirit with that seditious and murder-craving spirit of Allstedt. But when I came to Orlamünde and its Christians, at the command of the Princes, I found out very well what sort of seed he had sown there – so well that I rejoiced at not having been driven out with stones and dung. There not of few of them were giving me a benediction of this kind: "Get out in the name of a thousand Devils, and may you break your neck before you have left the city," etc.' [261]

But the most turbulent firebrand of war and sedition was the priest Thomas Müntzer, who with a greater madness than Karlstadt's prepared to put Luther's words into action. For indeed, he tried to destroy not only the images of the Saints, but even the churches and monasteries themselves, and to abolish the Sacraments utterly, and to kill bishops, priests, and monks, and even to snatch all power of governing away from the Princes. Truly, he was a most restless and most audacious man, who could be tired out by no labor, frightened by no danger; traveling far and wide, he sowed the tares of discord, everywhere inciting the people, first against the clergy, then against the Princes. He first made his plans known to Luther himself at Wittenberg. But when Luther (as he himself confirmed) did not approve, Müntzer turned elsewhere and tried every possible means by which he might draw the more unsophisticated people of Thuringia into all sorts of disaster. Moreover, he had earlier traveled long distances through many provinces and had stirred up the people wherever he had been permitted to speak.

But in many regions, as soon as his most malicious intention was discovered, he was thrown out, before the hidden spark of revolt and scheming broke out into a blazing fire. Thus he had been thrown out of Prague, in Bohemia; of Gutterbach, a town of Marchia; of Zwickau, a town of the Elector of Saxony; of Hall in the Alps, a town of the Count of Tyrol; of Allstedt, where the pretended Patmos of Luther had been. For there, when Müntzer usurped the pastoral role for himself, Luther vehemently denounced his attempt, in a German letter written to the two brothers, the Dukes of Saxony; and he at length gained his purpose, so that Müntzer was driven thence. But when he had been driven out of Allstedt, he came to Mühlhausen, an imperial town of Thuringia; and there, in the outlying villages and castles, by speaking he enticed both the citizens and the peasants to the most abominable acts of impiety: namely, that they should abolish every divine service, banish clergy and monks, despoil churches and monasteries, break into pieces images, altar canopies, and baptismal fonts; trample on the Divine Sacraments, and do many other such things that are wicked even to say and abominable to pious ears. And, not content with these crimes and sacrileges, they proceeded further, to overthrowing secular powers and taking other people's goods; to subjugating the counts of Stolberg, Schwartzburg, Honsteyn, Mansfeld, etc., to themselves, oppressing the nobles, demolishing the citadels.

It would be worth the trouble to quote the thundering, sesquipedalian words of the instigator himself. Therefore, this is how he wrote from Mühlhausen to the peasants of Thuringia: 'To begin with, pure fear of God! Dear brothers, how long will you sleep? how long will you disagree with the will of God, because it seems to you that He has deserted you? Ah, how often have I said to you, how things must be. God cannot show Himself any further; it is necessary that you stand firm.' And a little later: 'Beware, therefore, lest you be timid and negligent: do not any longer adore perverse fools, and impious rascals; begin, and fight the war of the Lord, for it is most definitely time. Instruct all your brothers not to mock the testimony of God, otherwise you will all perish. All Germany, Gaul, and Italy are in motion; the master is about to begin the game, and it is necessary that the rascals perish. In Fulda, during Easter week, four colleges of monks were destroyed; the peasants in Klegau, Hegau, and the Black Forest are in arms, 300,000 of them, and the crowd grows greater and greater daily. This one thing I fear, that stupid men will agree to some false concord.' And below he said, 'Beyond all measure it is most, most necessary: Go on, go on, go on! Do not feel pity, if Esau speaks good words to you in Genesis 33: "Do not regard the calamity of the unbelievers." For they will supplicate you kindly, and will weep, and beg for mercy, like children; do not pity them, as God commanded through Moses in Deuteronomy 7, and he has made the same thing manifest to us as well. Seek out in hamlets and towns, miners above all, but other good companions as well, who will be strong enough for these things. For it is necessary that we sleep no longer, etc.' [262]

Moreover, he wrote most imperiously and harmfully to certain counts of Mansfeld, and boasted that he was the servant of God, bearing the sword of Gideon against the unbelievers.[263] These things happened in the fourth week after Easter, at the time when Duke Frederick of Saxony, the Elector, met his last day. But his brother Duke Johannes, either disregarding such great crimes or despairing, kept on delaying. And his paternal uncle, Duke George, as soon as he was made more certain about such great evils, immediately was going to set out against the criminal mob, and he gathered an army of knights and foot soldiers, and a great force of engines of war. Moreover, he called on several Princes for aid: his son-in-law Philip the Landgrave of Hesse; Henry Duke of Brunswick; and the two Elector Dukes of Mainz and Brandenburg, his full brothers. Immediate destruction threatened all of these men, unless they joined together their forces and moved quickly against the rebellious mobs. For their peasants too were in revolt and astir.

Müntzer came from Mühlhausen into Frankenhausen, where the rebels were gathered whom he strengthened so boastfully in their crime, that he said that he would receive any and all cannonballs without harm in his sleeve. But it turned out very differently. For the Princes so terrified the rebels, the moment they came into their sight, that they were soon receiving deprecatory letters from the rebels, in these words:

'We confess Jesus Christ. We are not here to hurt anyone, but in order to preserve divine justice. Nor are we here to shed blood. If you also want the same thing, we will do no harm to you. According to these things, let each one consider what he should do.' The Princes replied to them as follows:

'Since due to deliberate iniquity and the seductive teaching of your false Evangelist against our Redeemer Jesus Christ, in manifold ways you contaminate yourselves with murders, arson, various impious acts against God, especially against the venerable Sacrament, and with other blasphemies: therefore we, as those to whom the sword has been entrusted by God, have gathered here in order to punish you, as blasphemers of God. But nevertheless, since we judge that many pitiable men have been evilly seduced to these actions, out of Christian charity we have decreed that, if you will hand your false prophet Thomas Müntzer over to us, alive and before your gates, together with his accomplices, and will yield yourselves to our mercy and our indignation, we will receive you in such a way, and will so deal with you, that in accordance with the nature of the case, you will learn of our mercy. We ask from you a speedy reply concerning these things.'

But the peasants did not wish to hand Müntzer over. They had occupied a hill outside the town, and when they were driven from it by the blows of the war engines, they fled into the town. And the Princes followed and immediately broke in and seized the town, where they slaughtered over six thousand peasants and other rebels in the ensuing battle. But the unhappy Müntzer, who was found after the battle in bed, simulating illness, came into the hands of the Princes. After he was sent into the nearby, very well-fortified citadel of Helderung, he was handed over into the custody of Lord Ernest, the Count of Mansfeld, a pious and Catholic man, against whom the miserable Müntzer had written most threateningly just shortly beforehand, within a space of three days. But the Princes, who were going to pursue the remnants of the war, led their troops to Mühlhausen; after the battle Duke Johannes of Saxony, the Elector, whose brother was now dead, joined them there also. However, the citizens, seeing that they were greatly unequal to the Princes in strength, sent out speakers, who ceded the city to the Princes after imploring pardon. But the Princes did not immediately promise them pardon or safety, but wished to have the citizens indebted to their mercy and their indignation, due to the nature of the details of the case.

When a comrade of Müntzer, an apostate monk whose name was Fistulator, heard this, he fled secretly by night with 400 comrades. But he was captured around Eisenach and brought back to the place from which he had fled. However, Müntzer ended his life in a far better fashion than did Fistulator. For the latter, stubborn in his apostasy, without confession or contrition, as though he were a beast, took his death from the blow of a sword. But Müntzer is said to have been led into great penitence, and with the highest devotion both to have recanted his errors and to have accepted the venerable sacrament under one form, after having made his confession according to Catholic rite, before he fell by the blow of the sword. This was the death of Müntzer, and these the rewards of the rebellions in Thuringia.

When Luther heard these things at Wittenberg, he quickly published a German pamphlet, with this title: *The Terrible Act and Judgment of God against Thomas Müntzer, in which God clearly proves that his was a lying spirit, and damns him.* And in the preface he said as follows:

'Here you see how that spirit of slaughter boasts about himself and says that God speaks and acts through him, and that it is God's will; and how he acts, just as if everything concerning him was a victory. And before he looked around, he is lying with some thousands of others in the mud. But if God had spoken through him, this would not have happened; for God does not lie, but firmly maintains His Word. Therefore, since Thomas Müntzer is mistaken, it is clear that, under the name of God, he spoke and acted for the Devil.'[264]

These are, indeed, true opinions, but they apply to Luther no less than to Müntzer. For Luther too prophesied many false things, and deceived himself and many others. And so that we not be led far afield, in this very business of the upheavals and rebellions, he was very often found to be a false seer and a pseudo-prophet. For in that German letter which he called *A Sincere Admonition to All Christians, to Guard against Sedition and Rebellion* he writes as follows:

'Although I am not unwilling to hear that all the ecclesiastics are in such a state of fear and anxiety, nevertheless, I find myself to be quite certain, and I have no fear at all that there will be any insurrection or rebellion, at least not one that would penetrate and invade the whole crowd.'[265] And below he says,

'Look at my deeds. Have I not, with my mouth alone, without a single stroke of the sword, taken more away from the Pope, bishops, priests, and monks than all the emperors, kings, and princes with all their power ever did up to the present time? Why? Because Daniel 8 says, "This king must be broken by no human hand," and Paul says, "He will be destroyed by the mouth of Christ." I am utterly certain that my words are not mine, but are the words of Christ. Therefore, it is necessary that my mouth also is His, Whose words it speaks. And for this reason there is no need to seek a bodily rebellion; Christ himself has already begun a certain rebellion with His mouth, which will be too heavy for the Pope. See to it, therefore, that you work at and promote the Holy Gospel: teach, speak, write, and preach that human laws are nothing. Forbid and dissuade that anyone should be made a priest, monk, or nun, and persuade whoever is in such a state to leave it; give no more funds for bulls, candles, bells, tablets, and churches, but say that that Christian life consists in faith and charity, and let us do this for two years; then you will see where the Pope, bishops, cardinals, priests, monks, nuns, bells, towers, mass, vigils, cowl, cap, tonsure, rules, statutes, and all that swarm and crowd of the Papal regime will remain. It will vanish like smoke.' [266]

These things he said there; but he is a false seer. For the two years have long since passed since he wrote those things, and through the grace and mercy of God all these things are still standing, so that from Luther's own judgment we may learn that his mouth is not (as he boasts) the mouth of Christ, which speaks true things and is the Truth itself; but rather, his mouth is the mouth of the Devil, which is a liar and the father of lies, John 8. Moreover, his own words – which he used at the funeral of his Elector Prince Frederick – declare that he lied about corporeal revolution as well. For he said thus:

'Ours is the common lament of all, that we have lost a good Prince. For this is the worst of all things, that this head should fall; but especially now in these heavy and astonishing times, when all Germany is in rebellion; since it must be feared that, unless God intercedes all of Germany will be devastated, etc.' [267] But in his first pamphlet about the rebellion of the peasants in Swabia, as a calumny against the Princes, he said as follows: 'First, we can refer this disaster and this rebellion to no one on earth except to you Princes and lords, and especially to you blind bishops and dull-witted priests and monks.' [268] And just as he had falsely prophesied his own victory over Müntzer, so Luther also falsely prophesied victory for the peasants, and the slaughter of princes and extermination of bishops and clergy. For in the abovementioned pamphlet, which he falsely titled *Exhortation to Peace, on the Twelve Articles of the Peasants of Swabia* – although in reality it was rather an exhortation from peace to war, and a comfort for the rebels in their criminal intention – he says, 'A sword now hangs over the necks of you Princes, but nevertheless you still think that you sit so firmly in your seats that no one can throw you down. This security and stubborn presumption will break your necks; you will see this. I have very frequently before now warned you to beware of that saying in Psalm 104: "He pours his contempt upon princes." You struggle for this, and you want to be hit over the head, and no admonition or exhortation does any good against this stubbornness. Therefore, since you are the cause of this wrath of God, without doubt it will be poured out upon you, unless you reform yourselves in time. The signs in heaven and the prodigies in the earth are designed for you, good Lords; they portend no good to you; no good will come to you from them.' [269]

And a little later he said, 'For you should know, good Lords, that God is attending to this matter in this way, since people neither can, nor wish to, nor ought to, endure your tyranny any longer. It is necessary for you to become other men than you are, and to yield to the Word of God. If you will not do this in a friendly and voluntary manner, you will have to do it through violence and ruinous disorder. If these peasants do not manage it, it will be necessary for others to do so. And if you kill all of them, nevertheless they would still not be destroyed – God will raise up others. For He wishes to slay you, and He will slay you. It is not the peasants, good Lords, who oppose you, but it is God Himself, Who has set Himself in opposition to you, to visit your tyranny upon you, etc.' [270]

These things were neither more trivial nor more empty than the things which Müntzer bandied about. But Müntzer never said anything about the signs of Heaven and prodigies of the earth against the Princes, nor did he ever say 'It is not the peasants, good lords, who oppose you; it is God Himself, Who has set Himself in opposition to you, to visit your tyranny upon you.' And who, therefore, would trust Luther, boasting that he was certain that his words were the words of Christ, and his mouth the mouth of Christ? But he acted even more shamelessly than this a little later, when he heard that the peasants were everywhere surrendering. For immediately he published a pamphlet against them to which he gave this title in German: *Against the Robbing, Rebelling, and Murdering Peasants who, under the pretext of the holy Gospel, falsely resist and rebel against all superiors.* And in this pamphlet, among many other things, he said the following:

'Therefore everyone who is able should here strike, kill, and stab, either secretly or openly; and should think that there is nothing more poisonous, hurtful, or more diabolical than a rebellious person. Therefore, just as if he were a rabid dog, he must be killed. If you do not strike him, he will strike you and your whole province with you.' [271] And below, he said, 'I think that there is no longer any Devil in Hell, but they have all come up among the peasants. For this madness exceeds both every mode and every measure.' [272] And later, 'The peasants are now no longer fighting for the Gospel, but have openly become faithless, perjured, rebellious, seditious highwaymen, robbers, and blasphemers.' [273] And again, 'These times are now so much to be wondered at that a prince can merit heaven by pouring out blood better than others can by prayers, etc.' [274] Johannes Cochlaeus immediately answered this book, and turned everything Luther imputed to the peasants (who had learned whatever they unjustly attempted from Luther's books) back against him, drawing on Luther's own writings.[275]

But since Luther was ill spoken of by many because of his bitterness and because of that pamphlet which was so savage and bloodthirsty, he published a third pamphlet about the peasants. In it he quickly laid out his threats and said that those who should say that his earlier book was too harsh should themselves be considered rebels, as should those who felt any pity for the slain peasants, whom God Himself did not wish to pity. Therefore, he ordered everyone to beware against muttering something to the contrary, and against soon harboring rebellion somewhere in his own heart, for which he would pay with his life. He said, 'I fight in such a way, the babblers must respond, that blood runs from my nostrils. On this point I wish neither to hear nor to know anything about pity, but to consider what the word of God desires. And for this reason it is necessary that my book should be just, and should remain so, even if the whole world is scandalized by it. What does it matter to me if it displeases you, when it pleases God? For He desires anger and not pity. Therefore, what are you doing with pity? Did not Saul sin through his pity toward Amelec, because he did not accomplish the wrath of God as he had been commanded?' [276] And in the end of the pamphlet he said, 'I would wish to be left in peace; no one will gain anything from me, and it is necessary that whatever I teach and write should remain true, even if the whole world should be broken into pieces on its account. But if at all costs they want marvels, I too will be marvelous, and will appear so, to whoever at length considers things rightly.' [277]

Indeed the appearance of upper Germany was then wondrous and marvelous: unheard of and irreparable calamity, terror and great trembling, when at one and the same time the subjects of almost all the Princes (who had opposed the Lutheran ferment with too little caution and too much leniency and negligence) either planned open violence or fomented rebellion secretly in their hearts. Many thousands of peasants rebelled in Swabia, many others in Alsace, in Franconia, on the banks of the Rhine, in Thuringia; when one crowd of them was subdued, another would soon spring up. And before the Princes drew up their just armies, the most grievous damages had been caused everywhere and in all areas by the rioting crowds, as they demolished and destroyed monasteries, churches, and citadels. And during the single month of May upper Germany suffered more massacres, slaughters, and devastations than Italy suffered in its ten-year-long war against the French and the Spanish. For the serious and learned man Dr Conrad Wimpina, who was an elderly Frenchman, writes that in Franconia alone 293 monasteries and citadels were laid waste. And Antony, Duke of Lorraine, writes that in Alsace alone over 26,000 peasants were killed. How many, then, did the Swabian League kill, in the many battles and conflicts in Swabia and Franconia? How many did the Elector Palatinate kill? How many did the Margrave Casimir kill? How many did others? For this was a very different type of fighting than is accustomed to occur in just wars, when king against king or prince against prince fights with disciplined battle ranks and lines. For here, the peasant crowd, ignorant of military science, rushing forward unarmed and without any order, or else huddling together in a mass because of fear, met not with battle, but rather with slaughter, from the trained armies of the Princes. This was the reason that almost all of the peasants were killed, but on the Princes' side, only a very few men fell, since the peasants did not know how to fight or how to stand in battle.

And many rebellions arose in that time not only in the country, but also in the cities, when the common people rose up against the clergy and also against the Senate. But these rebellions were carried on in such a way that the common people did not run amok with murders, arms, and devastations, as the peasants did, but rather they expressed their temerity and insanity in impious and false laws, thanks to their New Gospel. For example, at Frankfurt-am-Main or at Mainz, the common people rose up with great ardor during the festival of Easter. Two leaders of the rebels particularly encouraged this sedition; one of these leaders was a tailor and the other a shoemaker. When the common people heard that the bands of peasants who were rebelling against the Archbishop of Mainz were not far away, they rushed to arms, so that they might inspire both the Clergy and the Senate with more fear and terror. And so the first gathering and attack of these rebels was against the Dominican monastery, but without any plundering or destruction at all; they merely asked imperiously for wine to drink. Two deacons, Frederick Martorff of St Bartholomew's Church and Johannes Cochlaeus of the Church of the Blessed Virgin, well aware of how angry the common people were at them (at the latter, because he had written several books against Luther, and at the former, because he would not permit Lutheran rites in the parish church), fled the city before the gates were locked. When the common people progressed to open rebellion, the gates were quickly locked, and everything was done at the people's pleasure; the Senate feared violence and the plundering of goods no less than did the clergy. Therefore, the two deacons would have been in the greatest danger, had they remained in town. When their houses were broken into, and the rebels did not find them at home, the rebels' wrath directed itself toward wine alone; and indeed, Cochlaeus suffered less damage, because his infirm mother, left alone at home with only her daughter's daughter, moved the people to pity by her old woman's lamenting.

Then the common people, claiming the rule for themselves and setting aside the Senate's power, established a new Curia, in the House and Curia of St Anthony. In this Curia twenty-four men chosen from among the common people usurped the highest power and every legislative right of the whole community for themselves. And they wrote forty-seven Articles, which they intended to be considered as laws; nor did they desist from their threats and acts of terror until they extorted complete assent from the Clergy and the Senate. They even wrote menacingly to the absent deacons, saying that if they did not agree and return within the next month, they would lose their priestly offices, which would be conferred upon others who did assent. And by these threats, at length consent was wrung from Martorff, whose full brother was in the Senate – and indeed, Martorff was an excellent man. But Cochlaeus answered that he could not assent without the advice and desire of his superiors.

Therefore, he requested a longer period of armistice – not, indeed, because he intended ever to assent, but so that he might deflect the minds of the enraged populace from violence and plunder, until God would provide otherwise. And this happened shortly afterwards.

For when the peasants in Franconia had been slaughtered and disbanded, the common people of Frankfurt were returned to their previous state by the two Elector Princes, the Archbishop of Trier, and the Palatinate Count of the Rhine. All their bold, rash acts were recalled and brought to naught, which they had vainly attempted; moreover, their letters and seals, which they had evilly extorted from the Clergy by threats, were destroyed. However, from that time Cochlaeus never again resided at Frankfurt, but lived for some time as an exile in Cologne. After another year, by the kindness of the Pope, he obtained a priestship at the Church of St Victor in Mainz, where he lived peacefully, until at the death of Emser he was called into Meissen by the pious and Catholic Prince George, Duke of Saxony, to take Emser's place.

But the rebellious members of the common people of Frankfurt copied down their articles and sent them, not only to the neighboring people of Mainz, but also to the far-distant people of Cologne (who were in general pious and religious). They did this in order to move other peoples by their own example. In Cologne, the printers published those outstanding articles in many copies, so that they could be disseminated more widely. And among those articles these were considered the most important: namely, that thenceforward the Senate and the people would have the power of selecting and putting into office pastors and lay-ministers, who would teach the pure word of God and the Gospel without human additions. Also, that all clergy should carry all civic burdens, in tolls, watches, wards, taxes, and so on. Also, that no monk should be permitted any longer to beg, preach, or hear confessions. Also, that thenceforward neither monk nor nun should be admitted or received into the monasteries there, and that those who were already inside, should be able to leave whenever they wished. Also, that every rent for which there did not exist certain letters and seals should be abolished, and that no one should any longer be obligated by any possessor's claim. Also, that hereafter the benefices of the church should be conferred only on the children of citizens, not on any strangers or courtiers; and whatever money from the benefices was not needed should be handed over from the benefices into the public chest, as rent and largess, for the support of the poor citizens, so that no one would beg. Also, that all bequests from wills, and other acts of charity, should be transferred into the public chest, and all anniversary dues, fraternal organizations, and church obsequies for the dead should be abolished, etc.

And so articles of this sort, which the rebels had learned from the Wittenbergers, soon incited the common people of Mainz also against the clergy; and on St Mark's Day, while a solemn procession was being held, in a similar uprising they locked the gates of the city, and threatened the clergy with every sort of extremity, and by violence snatched three Lutheran pastors out of prison. And for three entire days there was tumult and disorder behind the locked gates, and the common people, standing in arms, terrified the clergy with the thunder of their cannons, and began menacing treatment of the Major Canons of the church. At length the Canons' Deacon, Lord Laurence Truchses, accepted in the name of all the clergy a peace which had been offered by the common people on the most unjust terms. But shortly thereafter, when the peasants had been killed, those letters and promises were overthrown and recalled, and the heads of the rebellion were expelled and proscribed forever. For the peasants of Rincavia were then rioting in the nearby countryside as well, and were plaguing the very rich monastery at Erbach with all sorts of depredations. In that monastery there is an extremely large and noteworthy vessel, which can hold 84 plaustra of wine. Therefore, when the peasants approached that vessel, they drank from it to such an extent that only 30 plaustra were left in it. They were deterred from drinking these by the arrival of Froben von Hutten, the Captain of the Swabian League, who punished that uprising by very harsh penalties, both in the city and in the country. (For the rest, that vessel today remains empty, not without great loss to the monastery.)

Not long after, the artisans of Cologne also mounted an insurrection, during the festival of Pentecost, and by means of wicked acts of terror and threats compelled both the Senate and the clergy to agree to conditions of peace. They were in arms for around fourteen days. The Archbishop of Cologne, the Elector Prince, through his advisers soothed and allayed that disorder, but not without heavy cost to all the clergy, who through that peace lost many of their privileges and freedoms for six years. For the rest, three of the rebellion's leaders were shortly thereafter arrested by the Senate, and executed; they paid the penalty as an example to others. The Lutherans could never manage, by any means, to be allowed to speak there publicly. Moreover, in very many cities of the Empire, in order that the Senate not be oppressed by similar boldness of the common people, the Senate had – at great expense – to bring soldiers in for assistance in repressing the effect of the new Gospel on the people. Cochlaeus was then an exile, since he had left first Frankfurt and then Mainz because of the rebellions. He was at that time a guest in Cologne. Dr Johannes Eck visited him there on his way to England, and told him a great deal of news about the defeats of the peasants, which Cochlaeus then published there in certain of his books, which seemed to keep silent about the point at issue, due to the nature of the time. He published four books: *Concerning Peter and Rome, against Velenus*; *Brief Refutations, against 500 Articles of Luther's, excerpted from Thirty-Six of his Sermons*; *A Brief Commentary on Luther's Pamphlet, in which he himself, by whom the unhappy farmers were most misled, destined and betrayed them to the sword and to Hell*; and a *Catalog of the Rebellions which have risen up in various German provinces, and have filled the earth with the blood of the wretched*.[278] But although truly Luther was the cause of all evils, miseries, and calamities of this sort, or at the very least of their origin and opportunity, nevertheless he was so far from grieving over them that he showed no indication of compassion, not even externally, and was so driven by some Fury that he seemed to exult over the evils of his country and to triumph over the slain peasants, and to rejoice in the death of his Prince. For shortly after the Prince died and the peasants were slain, and all Germany was pitiably consumed with grief, confusion, and mourning, Luther disregarded all these things and married a nun, and publicly celebrated his joyous wedding, which was a sacrilegious form of incest and vow-breaking, and was polluted by the deaths of so many thousands.

Jerome Emser published a very elegant poem (for he was a man of polished intellect) about this wedding. He embellished the poem with a harmony for four voices. Among other verses, taking the character of the Lutherans, he says:

Our masters are permitted every sacrilege,
　　and to shout down all honest people.
With a song of joy!
They can trample rights and laws;
　　they can slander Kings, the Pope, and the Emperor:
With a song of joy!
And we too will laugh at Christ's saints, and will destroy their images.
　　With a song of joy!
And we will worship Priapus of Lampsacum,
　　and Silenus, Bacchus, and Venus.
With a song of joy!
These are our ancient colonists, the patrons of our order,
　　for whom our order fights.
With a song of joy!
We will destroy the enclosures of the cloister,
　　we will plunder the sacred vessels, which will supply our expenses.
With a song of joy!
Go, cowl, farewell, cap, farewell, Prior, Custodian,
　　Abbot, together with obedience.
With a song of joy!
Go, vows, prayers, hours, goodbye, reverence –
　　together with shame, goodbye, conscience.
With a song of joy!
Hip hip hooray![279] *Let us rejoice with a song of joy, Sweet Lutherans.*
With a song of joy!

And in another poem he said:

You too, buffoons, gluttons, and parasites,
who alone among the people take evil delight in the fasts of Christ,
and you pimps, perjurers, sacrilegious people,
who consider virginity, and vows, and rites, as trifles,
finally, you braggarts, babblers, busybodies,
who have long weakened Christ and who deny the faith,
you impure people, whose treacherous tongue deprives them of comrades,
and you of false understanding, who are led by crimes,

and you, dregs of the mob, on whom now rest the harsh reins
of the highest power, who now unbind your raving yoke;
all of you lawbreakers together, celebrate your Master's wedding,
whose teachings make you the masters of vows.
And you, new bride, put off your veil for your husband,
tear the sash of your modesty, and with it your vow and your faith.
How excellent a thing – since each of you was consecrated to Christ!
Defile the marriage bed, and your minds, and your bodies
with sacrilegious incest: from you will be born
that ruin of the world, the most certain Antichrist.[280]

These things the pious Emser wrote, at whom many young Wittenberg poets had aimed for a long time, in vain. For up until his death that most constant man defended the holy religion of his fathers against them.

And at that time in Cologne a famous and excellent citizen was circulating many books. This was Peter Quentell a printer of Cologne, who printed the books which two theologians who were most celebrated for their learning as well as for their integrity – John Fisher, the Bishop of Rochester in England, and Josse Clichthove, a Doctor of Paris, in France – had written and published against Luther, both of them writing equally seriously and substantially. But Luther ignored all their writings, and never responded to either of them in a single word, because their doctrine was too solid to be shaken by his sophistic deceits; and furthermore, their lives were by far too virtuous and too well known and admired by all to be denigrated or reviled by any of his slanders or calumnies without offense to the reader. Nor indeed did he make any answer to the serious and learned, albeit short, speech given by Andreas Krzycki, the Bishop of Przemysl in Poland (who was later made Bishop of Plock and finally Archbishop of Gnesen), before Sigismund, King of Poland, and later published. The beginning of this speech was as follows:

'Those who have committed the affairs of the Church to memory, greatest and most wise King, mention innumerable heretics and apostates: who, driven astray by their own opinions and the spirit of pride, have been accustomed to split and confuse the Church of God by devious and obstinate teaching. Although the Roman Church has always shown herself the tamer (like the club of Hercules) of these monsters, nevertheless the tares of these demons have been sown especially against her; and here whirlwinds, there waves, have attempted to destroy that ship with her foremost men.' And below, he said, 'But among so many and so various heretics, who have lived up until now, there has been no one who did not set the foundation of his teaching in the Gospel, and who did not make of the Word of God a pretext and lure for his poison. Just so at the present time does that new oracle of his own hiding-place, Luther. For he acts so humbly, so chastely, so gently and peaceably, according to the doctrine of Christ and the Apostles, that nothing more arrogant, more shameless, more seditious or harmful, can be spoken of or imagined; since he not only calls Kings butchers, buffoons, and rascals; and Popes, Antichrists, pimps, and idols; but he even despises, and denigrates with his most execrable tongue, the Saints, and even the Virgin Mother of God Herself (as is obvious from many of his arguments).' And at the end of the speech he says, 'Meanwhile, Most Unconquerable King, since I know that it is a matter of concern to you that you should ward off from your realm and dominions this destruction that creeps like a snake in your region, for the present I have poured out these preliminary remarks in whatever way was possible. Accept them with a kindly mind, while other matters are being undertaken by our men and by others, and make it so that you guard Christendom not only from the Turks, Tartars, and other foreign races, but also from domestic enemies, apostates, and heretics.'[281]

When this oration was published, various songs of many Poles were added to it, and some of them were very ingenious and cutting. The first of these was In *Luther's Image*, which began as follows:

> *I am that Luther, famous throughout the world,*
> *whom the wickedness of the crowd has given so many titles.*
> *For whatever has been said or condemned before now,*
> *Now once again I boast that my spirit is of God.*
> *I write against councils, fathers, custom,*
> *and when I've done so, I seldom even agree with myself.*
> *I want my writings to be mystical, when my subject matter demands it;*
> *I want them to be unadorned, when the subject calls for that.*
> *Believing nothing, but serving myself, I take away Christ's laws,*
> *for which it's perfectly acceptable to seize any pretext at all.*

Then there was another song about the Lutherans' conditions:

> *Speak evilly of sacrifices, scorn your superiors, disparage*
> *honest customs, laugh at sacred fasts and prayers,*
> *resist councils, make jokes of the ancient rites*
> *of the Fathers, and as for pardons, anathemas, vows –*
> *don't count these as worth a penny, so long as confession of sin is absent.*
> *Let religion too be absent, and let churches give place to taverns.*
> *Persuade yourself to think more of yourself than is true or fitting;*
> *Consider Popes and Kings as filth, when compared to you.*
> *Understand the sacred scriptures as you wish, and negate*
> *the ancient Doctors, the laws, and the deeds of the saints.*
> *Be a good imposter; be learned in abuse.*
> *Ridicule church officials to the people; break all bonds*
> *of order and faith; stir up confusion everywhere.*
> *Do thus, if you wish to be an honest follower of Luther.*

And there was another, about the cowled monster born from a cow:

> *A Saxon cow produced a cowled fetus,*
> *signifying the monster which that land nourishes.*

Poor Saxon, be on your guard, and destroy that monster; always
show that it met its end in your lands.

And again, there was another against his slanders:

Since Luther considers everyone shit compared with him,
and in his filthy mouth has nothing but shit,
I ask you, wouldn't you say that he's a shitty prophet?
Such as a man's words are, so is the man himself.[282]

The silence of the Lutherans and the Wittenberg poets in response to these
and many other such songs of the Poles was remarkable. Before this, these
people, when irritated, had been accustomed not only to answer and pay back
in kind, but often of their own accord to attack and to provoke impudently;
but perhaps they were deterred by an unfortunate example. For the most
learned among them, Philip Melanchthon, had earlier responded to an accusation which Thomas Rhadinus from Piacenza, an eloquent man and a theologian,
had most seriously and learnedly written against Luther to the Princes of
Germany.[283] Melanchthon had falsely thought that this accusation had been
written by Emser, but he was so thoroughly refuted in another speech by
Rhadinus that he did not dare to murmur against him. For he had been
wretchedly deceived by his judgment about the author, and was very much
depressed by the state of the matter, so that he preferred to remain silent
rather than to refer disgracefully to his disgraceful mistakes in writing, or to
defend those mistakes. When Luther saw that he was being so strongly attacked
by outsiders and was being hemmed in by such learned books, and convicted
or ridiculed by so many true arguments, he ignored all these men's writings
with a serpentine cunning. He did not only close his ears to them, as a deaf
asp does to the songs of wise enchanters, lest by listening to their voices and
not knowing how to contradict them he might seem to have been conquered;
but he also restrained his forward tongue and his shameless pen, so that he
never dared to name one of his foreign opponents, however keen and strong
they were, to the people.

And since he was oppressed by a serious dislike among the Germans, due to
the numerous rebellions, slaughters, and calamities which had recently been born
from his Gospel, he decided to vindicate himself admirably in a new pamphlet
against the clergy, written in German. And so, rising up with an impulse of the
strongest fury and anger, he gave the pamphlet the title, *About the Abomination*
of the Secret Mass. Then, setting out a long prologue, he began as follows:

'I have already written and preached frequently and to great extent about
the wicked Papistic Masses and in what way an attempt might be made, that
we might be freed from that abomination. And now it is necessary that we
hear from our lords, the Papists, what fault they attribute to us: they complain
that we intend to incite rebellions. But let this, too, pass; let them tell that lie
too about us; surely they have told many more lies than this. For since they
dare shamelessly to blaspheme the divine majesty every hour, and to outrage

it with their abominable Masses and idolatries, what harm can it do if they censure us, a poor man, with a lie?' [284] and a little later, 'We have preached these things and have reiterated it so often that anyone at all can well know and conclude from them that all our works which are performed for the purpose of doing penitence for our sins and of escaping death are blasphemies, since they deny God and outrage Christ's sacrifice and His blood. For they try to do what only Christ's blood can do.' [285]

He wrote these things and many others of this sort, impiously and seditiously, in the prologue. But in the course of the pamphlet he recited the entire Canon of the Mass in German, and did not only impiously distort it, but also scurrilously accused the Mass itself of impiety and blasphemy, in many pretenses and false expositions, so that one might wonder how a human heart — and one which had been accustomed to these rites from childhood, and even instructed in their use and performance for twenty-five years, and had been practiced in them and gentled by them — could be depraved by such malignity that, knowingly and voluntarily, it would not shrink from so scurrilously attacking the most sacred matters, and mysteries which should be trembled at.

For example, he dared to say as follows: 'Should we offer a mouthful of bread and wine to God, so that he may accept it on behalf of Christendom? And furthermore, should we say that it is a holy and immaculate sacrifice? Is this not the same as saying that God should be pleased by bread and wine, which nevertheless is nothing more than any other bread which anyone and everyone eats?' [286] And again, 'Do you pray for good Christians, although you yourself are a rascal and a blasphemer of God? And you do nothing more than offer a mouthful of simple bread and wine? If anyone would rightly open his eyes, and understand the abominable blasphemy against God which takes place every day in the entire world, his heart would surely burst asunder. For it is just the same thing as if they said to God, "You lie through your teeth. It is necessary for us to help Christendom by bread and wine, and You say that only the blood of Your Son can do this." We have to bear these things' (he said) 'and daily to see and hear them, etc.' [287]

Jerome Emser, who was the one among Luther's adversaries closest to him in location, answered in German this unbelievable malice of his, and this heretofore unheard-of sophistry. Before this time Emser had strongly upheld the same sacred Canon, in Latin against Ulrich Zwingli of Zurich in Switzerland, and in German against the *Two Provosts* of Nuremberg.[288] Therefore he divided his answer into two parts. In the first of these, he proved that Luther was the instigator of the rebellions, from very many of Luther's books and various writings. And Emser proved and deduced this so clearly from Luther's own words that up to the present day no one has attempted to refute him. But in the second part of his pamphlet, Emser refuted in a few arguments all the calumnies which Luther had spewed out against the Canon; for he had already defended the Canon in longer arguments, against Luther's associates. For already most of them had progressed to such a degree of boldness and impiety

that there was nothing which they scorned and detested more than the Mass
and the heavenly mysteries of our religion.

And at Strasbourg a certain rascal Sapidus had dared to compose verses out
of unadulterated slanders and blasphemies as a monument against the Mass,
as though it were for his own burial and funeral. He was indeed an overly
insipid poet, and impious in his deadly contempt for sacred matters. His verses
had the following beginning:

> *The Mass is an evil; no century ever bore*
> *a greater evil than this shameful, dishonorable destruction.*
> *Gall, hatred, sacrilege, a monster, a sin, an ulcer,*
> *a prostitute, poison, destruction, a pit;*
> *Ghost, scandal, torment, sickness, ruin,*
> *refuse, shadows, butchery, fear,*
> *shipwreck, robbery, violence, plunder, tyranny,*
> *slaughter, pain, sorrow, death, madness, horror, burdens,*
> *treachery, ambushes, imposture, infamy, terror,*
> *inundation, hunger, shit, sewers, stench,*
> *specter, superstition, impiety, injury — by no hateful name*
> *whatsoever is the Mass sufficiently described.*
> *Not by the cross, nor by the sword, nor by plague, nor by fire, nor by wave —*
> *but only by the voice of Christ, will it be killed and lie conquered.*[289]

These criminal and impious verses of Sapidus were converted into praise and
victory for the Mass by Arnold Besalius of Cologne, a most learned man,
a Theologian who was fully expert in the three languages and a famous
philosopher. He changed the verses in this way:

> *The Mass is a good, whose better no century ever found.*
> *The Mass is the people's glory, life, cure, health.*
> *The man full of anger, the idler, the embezzler, the man full of hate,*
> *the whore — these are all accustomed to tear the Mass in pieces.*
> *The Mass drives away crimes, it repels ruin and torments,*
> *it dispels refuse, shadows, and fear.*
> *The robber reproaches the Mass, the looter and the tyrant flee it,*
> *slaughter, pain, sorrow, death, madness, horror are all absent.*
> *And absent are ambushes, imposture, infamy, terror:*
> *candor, cleanliness and comeliness are present.*
> *Religion, piety, guardianship of the true and the just —*
> *the Mass is sufficiently described by these triumphant names.*
> *The cross, the sword, plague, and fire, and wave*
> *look up towards Christ, through whom steadfastness flourishes.*[290]

Furthermore, a certain dialogue in German, about the sickness and death of
the Mass, was being passed around — than which the world has nothing more
absurd or more shameless. And so the impiety of the Lutherans against this
one awe-inspiring mystery of the Mass justly seems — and is — so execrable,

that if all Germany should perish completely by the vengeance of Heaven, the remaining nations would be able both to recognize and to praise the just judgment of God, according to Moses' saying in Deut. 29: 'And all peoples will say: Why did the Lord act thus towards this land? What is this immense anger of his rage? And they will answer: Because they abandoned the covenant of the Lord, which he had made with their fathers, etc.' And perhaps this would already long before now have happened, had there not remained, up to the present day, more than seven thousand in Germany who would not bend their knees to this Saxon Baal. Abraham, praying for them and standing in the presence of the Lord, says: 'You will not destroy the just man with the impious?' To whom the Lord will respond (as we may hope): 'If I find fifty just men in the midst of Germany, I will spare the entire region for their sakes; certainly, so that mercy may be exalted over justice.'

But the Lutherans, burning and eager to propagate their sect, wherever they knew that there were people who favored their faction, there they incited the people and busied themselves through letters and messengers, so that once a foundation had been laid, they could build themselves a nest there. They did this everywhere, but especially in the regions of Aquilo. Indeed, in Wittenberg, at one and the same time Martin Luther, Johannes Bugenhagen, and Melchior Hoffman wrote and published three letters, in German too, to be sent to Livonia; not only to strengthen the Lutherans there, but also to boast among the Germans about how widespread their sect was. Yet nevertheless the third one of these men later disputed against Pomeran in Flensborg, having embraced the sect of Karlstadt. Moreover, Bugenhagen wrote a Latin letter too, to the Saints (for so the title called them) who are among the English.[291] Johannes Cochlaeus responded to this letter from Cologne.[292]

And Luther also wrote in Latin to Charles, Duke of Savoy, who was truly a Catholic prince and much too learned in literature to be easily subverted or seduced by Luther. But the old fox wrote very cunningly, in the manner of the ancient serpent, to try to gain the good will of the Prince:

'In the first place, I beg your Grace's pardon, Most Illustrious Prince, that I, the dregs of humanity, who have been neither bidden nor summoned by you, dare to write first to your Highness. The glory of Christ's Gospel causes this, the Gospel in which I too glory and rejoice, wheresoever I see or hear it ring out or surge forth. Your Highness will therefore credit it to the cause of the Gospel, that on account of joy I first salute your Most Illustrious Lordship. For a report has come to us, and Annemundus Coctus (a French knight who is incredibly fervent in the glory of the Gospel) has confirmed it, namely, that the Duke of Savoy is extremely zealous for true piety, which is certainly, among Princes, a very rare gift of God, etc.' [293] But Luther achieved nothing at all by this adulatory cunning; in fact, nothing would have been more unfortunate for him than to come into the hands of this Prince, since he was most hostile to these new sects.

And with a similar astuteness Luther wrote a letter to the people of Antwerp, and another to the Christians who are in Holland, Brabant, and Flanders, so that at least the Saxons might believe that Luther had filled almost the entire world with his Gospel, covering more territory even than had St Paul, who says that he had propagated the Gospel from Jerusalem all the way into Illyria.

Moreover, it was well established that no opportunity would be given to Luther's Gospel in all the abovementioned provinces, except insofar as it was preached furtively and hurriedly by bold Apostates in hidden corners. But nevertheless Luther shrewdly ignored the fact that his Gospel was publicly forbidden and proscribed there, and he wrote at length and under a general heading, just as if all Holland, Brabant, and Flanders belonged to his adherents, although they by no means did.

The Emperor's brother Ferdinand, the Archduke of Austria, in his office of Imperial Viceroy, commanded that an Imperial Diet should be held in Augsburg on the Festival of St Martin. But he quickly dismissed this Diet when few of the Princes made an appearance there; and he arranged for another Diet at Speyer, on the 1st day of May.[294] And this hope was held out to the Princes, that the Emperor himself would attend at that time. But so far as religion was concerned, Ferdinand ordered that the Speakers should interpret the Gospel and Scripture in accordance with the sound opinion of approved Doctors of the Church. He further ordered that all Princes and Estates should be prepared with arms and guards, in case any new disorder should arise. Finally, he softened the rigor of the law concerning the rebels, lest those who had been restored to favor by their superiors should, on account of the previous rebellion, be considered as scoundrels during their trials.

1526

When Luther saw that he could not prevail against the Princes by threats or insults, nor even by stirred-up rebellions and seditions, to such an extent that they would accept his Gospel, or at least would tolerate it, he began with serpentine guile to deliberate on another way of deceiving them – namely, that he would in his writings offer prayers and appeals in the place of threats, praises and flattery in the place of insults, and sweet and calm admonitions in the place of seditious and virulent incitements. He would send these writings privately and secretly, especially to those Princes whom out of all of them he had most gravely offended and had publicly traduced. Now in the court of George, Duke of Saxony, there existed not a few men who secretly, against their Prince's opinion and against his decree, favored Luther's Gospel over the clergy. (Among them there was even one of the Duke's counselors, who had a considerable amount of authority in the management of affairs, and who afterwards, when he had been faithless to the best of Princes by the worst of crimes, proved himself most shameless.) Therefore, when Luther learned of these men and of others, he was lured into vain hope, and he wrote flattering words and appeals to that Prince, whom he had earlier called a Tyrant and a liar, to see if perhaps by womanly flatteries he could conquer and defeat the firm mind and manly heart of that strong constancy. For he had read that what could not be done by threats, calumnies, and insults, had been done by the whore Delilah to that strongest of men, Samson. Therefore, among other things he wrote as follows, in German:

'I come now, and with all my heart fall at Your Illustrious Grace's feet, and most humbly beg that Your Illustrious Grace will deign to desist from this ungracious design of persecuting my doctrine. Not that much harm can be done to me by Your Illustrious Grace's persecution; I have nothing to lose but this wretched sack of worms, which already hastens day by day to its grave. Besides, I have an enemy who is truly greater than you, namely, the Devil with all his angels. But God has until now given me (although I am a pitiable and weak sinner) the spirit to remain safe from the Devil. And if I sought my own advantage, nothing better could befall me than that I be grievously attacked by persecutions. How notably persecution has profited me up to the present time I am not able to relate, since I should have to thank my enemies on this account. But if the misfortune of Your Illustrious Grace were pleasant to me, I would irritate Your Illustrious Grace still further, and would wish you to choose always and continually to persecute me. But it was enough that Your Illustrious Grace revealed yourself well. Now is the time for acting in another manner. For although Your Illustrious Grace does not wish to believe it, my doctrine is the word of God (but then, it knows very well how to represent itself, and has no need of my exhortation). Moreover, I know and am certain that it is necessary for me, on pain of danger to my soul, to be concerned for Your Illustrious Grace's soul, and to pray, supplicate, and exhort, in the hope that I may accomplish something. Let not Your Illustrious Grace despise my humble person, for God once spoke through an ass. For he thunders in Psalm 13 at those who despise the advice of the powerless. However, neither Your Illustrious Grace nor any other person will extinguish or impede my doctrine: it is necessary for it to progress, just as it has done up until now. For it is not mine. I grieve over this one thing, that I must see in what manner and how dreadfully Your Illustrious Grace strikes at our Corner-Stone, Christ, since elsewhere God has given Your Illustrious Grace many good virtues and qualities, for other matters. May Almighty God grant that I shall have come in a good hour, and that my writing shall find a favorable place in Your Illustrious Grace's heart. For if (which God prevent!) Your Illustrious Grace does not accept my humble and heartfelt exhortation in this way, then it will be necessary that I commit myself to God. Moreover, I wish by these words to keep my conscience unclouded, both in God's eyes and in the eyes of Your Illustrious Grace, because I have done as much as is in me, and I am willing and ready to do or to abstain from doing anything that I know will well please Your Illustrious Grace — with my doctrine excepted. For it I cannot abandon, according to my conscience. But I pray, I prostrate myself, and I seek the favor of knowing how else and where I have offended Your Illustrious Grace, in writings or words. Besides, I forgive from my heart everything at all that Your Illustrious Grace has done against me, and furthermore I will ask, and will most certainly find, pardon from my Lord Jesus Christ for anything Your

Illustrious Grace is doing or has done against His Word. Only let Your Illustrious Grace soften yourself with regard to this one article, and all will be simple: That the word of Christ, which through me has come into the light, should be free. Without doubt, for this all the angels in Heaven will rejoice over Your Illustrious Grace.' [295]

So Luther wrote. The strong and pious Prince, who was always constant in his manly sobriety, answered him in these words:

'Your letter came to us on the Birthday of Christ — whose grace and peace we wish for you, just as you for us; and in addition, we wish for you the understanding of yourself. And first, indeed, we want this to be understood, and we know also that we are untroubled in our conscience before God our Redeemer: that although we are provoked by your recent writings, nevertheless we do not make our reply to you through an angry spirit, but rather through our will, which is inclined toward bringing you back into an understanding of yourself, and one separated from all flattery — since we are suspected by you of being surrounded by and abundantly provided with flattery. And we give this sign to you: if in this response we shall have flattered you, you may say freely that "our wine has gotten its scent from the vase." But if we have not flattered you, then seek your flatterers in those places, where they call you Prophet, Daniel, Apostle of the Germans, Evangelist. Here, certainly, you will find no flatterer.'

And a little later he said, 'Moreover, you give the name of "truth" to the attack on us which you have made so bitterly, against divine custom and Gospel law. For you know how God has told you what you should do, if you have anything against your neighbor. But you have falsely accused us, behind our back and by name, to Hartmann von Croneberg (and how praiseworthy his actions were at that time is well enough known), of being a tyrant and an enemy of the Gospel. You added abusive nicknames about our person, curses of both our body and our mind, and many abusive and wily words, which you have never found in either the Gospel or in Scripture, to which you compare your slanders of this kind. We wrote to you mercifully enough, according to the nature of the case, in order to understand either your guilt or your innocence; but we would have wished to discover your innocence much more than to discover the opposite. But you, because of your madness and your incivility, gave us so violent a response that you attacked us with yet more lies, and behaved toward us as though we were to you an unmerciful Lord; even though we had given you no reason for these actions in either our simple writing or in any other thing.' And below he wrote: 'And moreover, on what grounds is it appropriate for us to be a merciful Lord to you, since you so slanderously and wickedly attack our most merciful Lord, the Roman Emperor, to whom we are bound by faith and by our sworn oath, and since you so shamelessly despise his injunction? And in addition to these things, you have instituted a kind of asylum at Wittenberg, so that all the monks and nuns who with thievings and plunderings have despoiled our churches and monasteries may have a refuge and a reception-place with you; just as if Wittenberg were publicly named the common citadel of all the apostates of our province. Nor is there any doubt in our mind that our most Holy Father the Pope has never given any indulgences (about which you made such a commotion) greater than those indulgences which your Wittenbergers were promised for the abduction of nuns, who were brought to you from our convents. Truly, into what calamity and damnable misery you drove those women, and how they were treated, and for what purpose, is well known enough. We certainly do not believe that the Devil is your enemy on account of these matters. However, if he does you any injury because of these things (unless he is driven to do so by the permission and power of God), he can be accused in this way: that he gives you the same reward which an executioner is accustomed to give his assistant. And it is not the case that these things should procure our mercy for you. For if even a cow were led out of our lands by the least of our peasants, it would displease us; far less, since we are Christ's servant, can we bear that His own herd should be estranged both in body and in soul.'

And later he wrote, 'Moreover, we can affirm that your Gospel is of little interest to us, since it has been judged as harmful by the heads of Christianity. We have been concerned about this one thing: that we should be especially on our guard, to our utmost power, not to receive it. The evil fruits produced from it have given us reasons for this opinion. For neither you, nor anyone else, can truly say anything other than that blasphemy against the holy and venerable Sacrament, against the most holy Mother of God, and against all the saints, has its origin in your teaching. For from your teaching and your disciples' teaching, all the ancient, harmful heresies are being renewed; every honest worship of God is being abolished – a thing which certainly has never been so widespread, from the time of Sergius onward. When were more sacrileges committed against persons consecrated to God than happened after the production of your Gospel? When, I ask, were more rebellions held against superiors, than were caused by your Gospel? When were there more plunderings of sacred houses? When were there more robberies and thefts? When were there more uncowled Apostate monks and nuns at Wittenberg than there are now? When were wives abducted from their husbands and handed over to other men, as is now devised by your Gospel? When were there more cases of adultery than after you wrote that, if a woman does not wish to be impregnated by her husband, she should betake herself to another man, by whom she may be impregnated, and that her husband is bound to rear that offspring; and on the other side, that a man may do the same? Your Gospel, which you produced when it was hidden beneath a bench, has accomplished these things. And indeed you rightly give it that title, that you produced it "which was hidden beneath a bench." Indeed, it would have been a good thing had it continued to be hidden beneath a bench up until the present time. For if you should bring forth another such, we will keep not a single peasant. If Christ had wanted such a Gospel, he would not have said so often "Peace be with you." Peter and Paul would not have said, "One's superiors must be obeyed." Therefore, the very fruits themselves of your teaching and your Gospel produce both great nausea and great horror in us. For our part, God willing, we will defend Christ's Gospel with our body, soul, substance, and rank – may He, through His Grace, help us to do so.

'You warn us about death, of which we are certain. But what will be the result, if we should die after embracing your Gospel? Could not God say, "How does it happen, that your new Gospel brings so many evil fruits with it? Have I not told you, that you may know a tree by its fruits?" If we should respond, "But Luther told us that this was the Gospel, which had been hidden beneath a bench," then God would answer, "But the Catholic Church has told you differently. Therefore, why do you believe Luther, and not the Church? By no means believe Luther." Keep your Gospel, Luther, which you brought forth when it was hidden beneath a bench; we will persist in the Gospel of Christ, as the Catholic Church has received it and maintains it – and may God help us to do so, etc.' [296]

When Luther had received this rebuff, he entered into another and much more malignant path of attack, and wrote most flatteringly to the Cardinal and Archbishop of Mainz and Magdeburg, the Elector Prince Lord Albert, hereditary Margrave of Brandenburg. He tried by many arguments to persuade Albert to renounce celibacy and take a wife, and to transform his Archbishopric into a worldly principate, so that he might be an example to other Bishops and prelates that the ecclesiastical state should be removed from their midst from the roots up. Therefore, Luther began in German, as follows:

'The grace and peace of God the Father and our Lord Jesus Christ. Most illustrious and noble Prince, most merciful Lord, I have often enough before now troubled Your Illustrious Lordship with my writings on behalf of others; now I am driven to write on behalf of your Illustrious Lordship's self. And I very humbly ask that your Illustrious Lordship will deign to receive my words in good part, as I faithfully intend them. Among other cares and worries, since it perturbs me that this dreadful and dangerous sedition (which is kindled through Satan, though it appears as a stroke of God) should be settled, it came into my mind that I should exhort and implore your Illustrious Lordship, indeed with great hope and trust, that Your Illustrious Lordship both is able and knows how to be a many-sided aid, if only Your Lordship so wishes – together with a devout prayer to God that the matter should improve. And here, in brief, is my theme: that Your Illustrious Lordship should enter into the state of matrimony, and should convert your Episcopate into a secular Principate, and should renounce and reject the false name and pretense of the ecclesiastical state. And these are my reasons. First, that through this means the divine vengeance will be avoided, and the cause of rebellion will be taken away from Satan. For now it is clearer than day that the ecclesiastical State is manifestly contrary to God and to His honor. And for this reason it simply cannot be hoped, on any ground whatsoever, that God will cease from wrath and vengeance, so long as so manifest an abomination and slander to His holy name does not cease. Lord God! If you Bishops and Princes had supported this matter in time, and had given a place to the Gospel, and had begun to modify that which is a manifest abomination – how beautifully and tranquilly all this, which now the Devil throws into disorder and madness, could have been legitimately instituted and erected, through ordered power. But since they wished neither to see nor to hear, but tried with temerity to sustain a manifest abomination, God has nevertheless with indignation permitted it to fall utterly, so that He might demonstrate that His Word is more powerful than all other matters, and that it is necessary to follow His Word, even if the world were a thousand times greater than it is.

'Furthermore, the common people are now educated enough to understand already that the ecclesiastical Estate is worthless; a great number of songs, doggerels, and derisory jokes prove this more than sufficiently. On every wall, in all sorts of leaflets, most recently even in humorous papers, priests and monks are caricatured; and it is considered either a laughing matter or a portent, whenever an ecclesiastical person is seen or heard. Therefore, what is the point of fighting against the course of the torrent, and of holding on to something that neither ought to be nor can be held on to? This could surely be perceived even by a blind man: Since the ecclesiastical Estate has departed from people's hearts, and even excites contempt, it is not to be hoped that there will be any rest or pause, until it also departs from their sight. But the more it is maintained and thought highly of, the more it will be laughed at and considered worthless. And so what good does it do further to urge men toward the ecclesiastical Estate with such stubbornness and to provoke them against oneself: especially, since God himself, eager to destroy the Ecclesiastics, is pushing forward His sentence and vengeance. So says Psalm X: "You destroy the impious, so that even their name eternally perishes." This has come about; the ecclesiastical state cannot survive, much less return to honor. God has touched it, it must perish. It is so, and not otherwise.

'Your Illustrious Lordship can be in the vanguard of these matters and can be an aid, in your own person, in the ecclesiastical Estate's actual abolition. And there is hope that God will be participate and the business be carried on through Grace, and that He will not be driven in His indignation to use the Devil for this matter. And your Illustrious Lordship has a great motive for this, beyond others: because you yourself have transgressed against God in maintaining the ecclesiastical Estate, and have undergone great expenses to strengthen it. Therefore, if the people should now see you acting differently, their hearts would easily be converted. But if your Illustrious Lordship will still resist, and delay this matter, then it must be feared that you will not be able to last for long. For the people's hearts will not desist, and neither does God's wrath desist. And your Illustrious Lordship has an excellent example in the Grand Master of Prussia. How beautifully and graciously God managed so great a change, which ten years previously could neither be hoped for nor believed – not even if Isaiah or Paul had announced it! But when the Grand Master offered the Gospel a place and honor, it rendered back to him much more glory and honor than he would have dared to hope for. But your Illustrious Lordship would be a much greater example. If in the midst of Germany your

Lordship should stand forth as one man among so many leading men, you would calm many people and would convert them, and also would subsequently encourage other Bishops. And then God would exhibit Himself in glory, if your Illustrious Lordship would humble yourself before Him, and would yield to His Gospel and His name, and give place to Him: for so He promised in John 5: "Whoever will honor Me, him also will I honor. But whoever dishonors Me, he shall be dishonored as well." May your Illustrious Lordship quickly give heed to so powerful and comforting a promise of this sort, and remove yourself from that wicked and impious condition, and enter into the blessed and holy condition of matrimony, where God will make Himself well disposed toward you. But if so great a public benefit to Germany (which I consider very important, and certainly it is a pious work) does not sway your Illustrious Lordship, then let this single thing suffice, which your Illustrious Lordship knows and are forced confess: that you were created a male person by God. Now truly, it is certainly God's work and will that a man should have a woman. Genesis 1: "It is not good (said God) for the man to be alone; I will make a helper for him, who will be with him." Therefore, since God has not performed a miracle by making an angel out of a man, I cannot see how a man can, without incurring God's wrath and indignation, remain alone and without a woman, etc.' [297] These things the ancient serpent said through Luther.

But for the rest, that Prince scorned the shameless levity and the boldness and vanity of that man, and wisely held his peace by ignoring this letter, although Luther had openly published it. And certainly Johannes Cochlaeus, who was then in Mainz, would have responded to this letter if it had not come too late into his hands, when its reputation was already quiet and worn out, since the Prince had rendered it beneath contempt by his seriousness and constancy. For he had by this time heard a great many Sirens of this sort, many of which were even conspicuous for their nobility. A good many of these suggestions were made in secret, by Counts and Barons as well as Princes, who were encouraged by the Bishop's leniency and gentleness and did not hesitate to suggest matrimonial matters secretly to so great a Pontiff, in familiar admonitions. And by these acts of rashness it was brought about, that the crowd, mislead by the vain hope of the Lutherans, often put about the lying story that the Prince had thrown aside his ecclesiastical office and had married.

But Luther attacked Henry VIII, King of England, with audacity more shameless by far.[298] He had earlier held this King up publicly to ridicule by peoples and nations with all sorts of open insults, jokes, and calumnies. And he even said that he had been chosen by Christian, King of Denmark, to write to the King of England himself. (Christian was then a fugitive from his realm and an exile, wandering through Germany.) But two English Apostates, who were for some time at Wittenberg, not only strove to corrupt those merchants who had cared for and fed them secretly in their exile; they also hoped that all the people of England would in a short time become Lutherans, whether the King wished it or not, through Luther's Testament, which they had translated into the English tongue. They had already arrived in Cologne, so that they could secretly, through other merchants, smuggle the translated Testament from there into England, once many thousand copies of it had been made by the printers. They had such great faith in matters turning out well that in their first approach to the printers they asked them to print six thousand copies. But the printers, fearing the great damage which they would suffer if anything adverse should occur, brought out only three thousand. If these sold well, the same number could easily be printed anew. Pomeranus had already sent letters to the 'Saints' who were in England, and Luther himself had also written to the King. And since it was believed that the New Testament would soon follow these letters, such great joy came upon the Lutherans due to that hope, and filled them with the wind of empty faith that – puffed up with delight – they revealed the secret in vain boastings before the appointed day.

At that time, Johannes Cochlaeus, Deacon of the Church of the Blessed Virgin in Frankfurt, was living in exile in Cologne. He was introduced and made friendly with the Abbot of Deutz by his host George Lauer, Canon at the Church of the Apostles. When Cochlaeus heard from the Abbot that certain works of Rupert, formerly abbot of Deutz, were being sent to Nuremberg so that they might be published by the Lutherans, he began with the greatest zeal both to argue against this and to impede it. For up until that day, although the Lutherans had most diligently poured over and looked into all ancient libraries, nevertheless, out of so many Doctors of the Church who had lived in so many centuries, they had been able to find no author at all who would confirm the dogmas of Luther. When at length, a book by this Rupert (who had lived 400 years ago) was found, with the title *Concerning the Victory of God's Word*, it was speedily made known at Nuremberg by the Lutherans.[299] This book soon pleased all the Lutherans, because of its title, to such a degree that nothing seemed more desirable to them than that author. Meanwhile, they learned from Trithmius that Rupert had written a great many works, but they had acquired only two small ones. The subject-matter of one of these concerned God's power, and the other His Will. In publishing these books Osiander (a married priest and preacher) added many Lutheran-like things, by which he tried to present the pious author as a member of the impious sect of his own patrons.

And the Lutherans had already arranged with the Abbot of Deutz himself that the other works of Rupert should be sent to Nuremberg to be printed. But he heard from Cochlaeus how much peril there would be in that under-taking, if he betrayed a pious author into the hands of the impious, who would not only foully contaminate him with impious prefaces and annotations, but would also distort his honest and healthy opinions, and from an ancient Catholic would make a new heretic, who would appear to have confirmed Luther's dogmas 400 years previously. Therefore, that Abbot, who was a good man, changed his opinion, and kept with him those volumes which had already been packed into a large bundle for conveyance to Nuremberg. And in that bundle there were fourteen volumes about John's Gospel, twelve about his Apocalypse, and twelve about Divine Offices.[300]

But since the monks would not rest unless these books were published, Cochlaeus diligently persuaded Peter Quentell and Arnold Birckmann to undertake publishing these works, between the two of them, at their common expense and profit. However, he could not so persuade them until he had promised them that he would direct all his own attention to that edition. And when that edition appeared sufficiently profitable to them, they no longer needed Cochlaeus's urging, but they themselves of their own accord wanted more works by Rupert, asking now the Abbot, now Cochlaeus, to collect more of these works from any and everywhere. And so the Abbot sought out thirty-two volumes on the twelve minor prophets and seven volumes on the Song of Songs, from the ancient Monasteries of St Benedict. And in Cologne, in the Library of the Great Church, Cochlaeus found nine volumes about the glorification of the Trinity and the procession of the Holy Spirit. And in the School of Arts he found a great work, which was titled *About the Works of the Trinity* and comprised forty-two volumes.[301] Nine of these were about Genesis; four about Exodus; and so on. And when Cochlaeus learned that Rupert had once been a monk at Liège, in the Monastery of St Laurence, he wrote to Dietrich Heeze, Canon at Liège, whom he had known well at Rome after the death of Adrian VI (whose private secretary Heeze had been). Cochlaeus asked Heeze to search out any book of Rupert's that might exist in his monastery. And he discovered the work that was most desired of all, thirteen volumes on Matthew, about the glory and honor of the Son of Man. But Heeze could not send the manuscript to Cologne, unless Cochlaeus himself and two other Canons would hand over all their goods to the monks' care, as a pledge that they would return the manuscript. And so Cochlaeus was summoned from Mainz; he took all those other volumes with him, and settling in there at the monastery, prepared editions which he sent to Cologne for publication.

In this way Cochlaeus became more known and familiar to the printers in Cologne, and on a certain occasion he heard them boast faithfully, while in their cups, that whether the King and Cardinal of England liked it or not, all England would soon be Lutheran. He also heard that there were two Englishmen hiding there, both of them educated men who were skilled and fluent in languages, but he was never able to see or speak to them. And so he invited certain printers to his inn, and after they had warmed up from the good wine, one of them in a secret conversation revealed to Cochlaeus the secret plan by which England was to be brought over to the Lutheran side. This was the plan: to print 3,000 copies of the Lutheran New Testament, translated into the English language. The undertaking had already reached the letter K in the order of the quires. The expenses had been abundantly supplied by English merchants who, when the work was printed, would secretly carry it into England and intended to disperse it widely before the King or Cardinal could find out about or prohibit the plan.

Cochlaeus, internally torn between fear and wonder, and openly amazed, concealed his grief. But on another day, sadly pondering in his own mind the magnitude of the danger, he was considering how he might most effectively obstruct these evil attempts. Therefore, he secretly went to Hermann Rinck, a patrician of Cologne and a knight, who was a familiar friend and an advisor of both the Emperor and the King of England, and he disclosed to him the whole affair as he had learned it, through the agency of wine. Rinck, in order that everything might be more certainly known, sent another man to look into things in that house where, according to Cochlaeus's information, the work was being printed. And when he learned from this man that the matter was indeed under way, and that a great supply of paper was in that house, he went to the Senate, and brought it about that the printers were forbidden to proceed any further in that work. The two English apostates fled, taking with them the quires that had been printed, traveling up the Rhine by ship to Worms, where the people were in the full frenzy of Lutheranism; there, they thought, they could finish the work they had begun by using another printer. But Rinck and Cochlaeus soon warned the King, Cardinal, and Bishop of Rochester about these things in letters, and advised them to keep watch over all English ports as diligently as possible, lest that most pernicious merchandise be brought into England.

They say that Lord Cuthbert Tunstall, a most learned man and the Bishop first of London, then of Durham, bought one of these copies and in a great speech to the people of London publicly announced that he had found, in that one book, over two thousand distortions and perversities. While these things were going on, Luther's letter (which he had written at Wittenberg on the first day of September in the previous year) finally arrived in the hands of the King of England. After the salutation, he began the letter as follows:

'Although, most serene King and most illustrious Prince I ought deservedly to shrink from approaching Your Majesty through a letter, since I am fully aware that your Majesty was gravely offended by my pamphlet, which I published foolishly and precipitately, not through my own inclination but at the prompting of certain men who favor Your Majesty very little; nevertheless I am given hope and daring to believe that one who knows that he himself must die will not believe that hatreds should be kept deathless. Not only does that kingly clemency of yours, which is daily hymned to me in letters and words by very many people indeed, give me this hope and daring, but also, I have learned from trustworthy witnesses that the book which was published against me in Your Majesty's name was not the King of England's book, as those subtle sophists wished it to seem to be, who when they abused Your Majesty's title did not perceive how great a danger they prepared for themselves in these dishonorings of their King. This was especially true of that monster and public object of hatred to God and men, the Cardinal of York, that plague of your realm. So that I am now terribly ashamed, and I fear to lift my eyes in Your Majesty's presence, since I suffered this triviality, which was done by those malignant intriguers, to move me against such and so great a King; especially since I am rubbish and a worm, one who should be either restrained or ignored with mere contempt. But in addition to all this, something has happened that earnestly compels me, however abject I am, to write: Your

Majesty has begun to favor the Gospel and, what is no less, to tire of that race of ruinous men. This news was indeed a true gospel – that is, joyful tidings – to my heart. Therefore, in this letter I prostrate myself at Your Majesty's feet, as humbly as I can, and by the cross and glory of Christ I pray and beseech you, that Your Majesty will deign to lower yourself and to grant pardon for any things in which I have injured your Majesty, just as Christ prayed, and as he ordered us also to forgive trespasses in turn. Next, if it would not seem contemptible to Your Serene Majesty that I should publicly declare my recantation in another pamphlet, and should honor Your Majesty's name anew, then may Your Majesty give me some gracious sign. Then there will be no delay in me, I will most gladly do that, etc.'

Later, near the end of the letter, he wrote: 'But what wonder is it, if the Emperor and some Princes rave at me? Does not the second Psalm say that "the nations rage against the Lord and his Christ; the people plot, the kings of the earth conspire, and the Princes gather together"? It would rather be a matter for wonder if any Prince or King should favor the Gospel. How greatly I hope, from the very marrow of my bones, someday to congratulate Your Majesty on this miracle! And may the Lord Himself (in whose presence and by whose will I write these things) bring my words to fulfillment, so that the King of England may in a short time be made a perfect disciple of Christ, and one who professes the Gospel, and also Luther's most merciful Lord. Amen. I await a merciful and kind response, if it will seem good to Your Majesty. Wittenberg, 1 September 1525.'[302]

To this letter the King immediately responded, when he had sufficiently scented out where Luther's subtle oration was tending. And since his very eloquent response was filled with learning and with seriousness, it was distributed in many ways and in many places by the printers, and was even translated into German by Emser and Cochlaeus. Here it will be sufficient to call to mind a few of the King's words. And so, the King thus responded first:

'I do not know if you say this truthfully, that you are ashamed of your book. But I do know this one thing, that there is sufficient reason why you should be ashamed, not just of that book alone but indeed of nearly all your books – for they contain almost nothing other than the most shameful errors and the most insane heresies, supported by no rational argument nor resting on any learning. Rather, an obstinate impudence asserts and affirms them, while you, the author, demand to be considered in such a way as no one today is, nor anyone hitherto ever has been. I do not sufficiently see how it might be true that you were urged to publish your pamphlet against me by men who favored me little; since the matter itself demonstrates that you were rather urged by those who favored you little. For your pamphlet is of such a sort that it can bring nothing but shame to its author, while it confers honor on my book. Your book declares that you have not discovered even a single word of a sane mind, that you could ever oppose to my book. This thing sufficiently indicates, I think, which of us two has the better case. Now pretend, as much as you like, that you believe the book I published was not mine, but was adorned with my name by subtle sophists; nevertheless, that it is in fact mine many witnesses know, who much more worthy of trust than those "trustworthy witnesses" of yours. And for my part, the less it pleases you, the more happily I acknowledge it. For when you write that my book brings me dishonor, certainly (however much you dissemble) there is no one who does not understand how badly your spirit takes it that my book has been praised by so great a consensus of all good and learned men. And then there is the honorable evaluation of the See; when it condemned your heresies, so great was its authority in the eyes of that most holy man Jerome that he considered it enough, if he could make his faith acceptable to the See.'³⁰³

And a little later the King wrote: 'Now, as for the fact that you rail, with that pestilent tongue of yours, against the most reverend Father in Christ, the Cardinal of York, our Prime Minister and Chancellor of England: I have a better acquaintance with his matchless wisdom than to believe that he would be at all moved by the taunting slanders of that tongue which taunts the whole Church, which reviles the most holy Fathers, which does not refrain from blaspheming any saints and scorns the Apostles of Christ, which dishonors the most holy mother of Christ, which blasphemes God Himself as the fount, author, and instigator of sins. That detestable offscouring of your blasphemies never fails to be openly obvious, both from every part of the noxious works which you have written to such great harm of Christian people, and from the things which the peasants, driven mad by your heresies, are accomplishing so insanely throughout Germany. Therefore, that most reverend Father, although he has already been most dear to us for a long time, due to his exceptional virtues, now is yet dearer to us and will daily become still more so, the more we see that he is hated by you and those like you. As for the fact that you call him the plague of my realm, there is no reason to give an account to a mere friar of how many benefits we and our kingdom have received from that man's matchless wisdom, faith, labor, zeal, and salutary diligence. But even if I omit the other things, this alone is a sufficient indication of how beneficial he is for our entire land: that according to the judgment of our mind, when it was demanded of him that he thoroughly purge our realm of the pestilent contagion of your heresies, he accomplished this task extremely diligently. For from time to time certain people enter England who are suffering grievously from these things – namely, from those venomous plagues which the noxious breath of your unhealthful mouth disseminates. However, when such men are convicted through persistent questioning, which is carried out by the beneficial diligence of a most reverend father of his type, we not only prevent any of that leprosy from creeping on to our people, but we also return the people themselves to the purity of the faith, by handling them kindly, and taking care of them with great charity.'³⁰⁴

And below he wrote: 'Luther, you write that you are grievously ashamed to lift your eyes to us, because you suffered yourself to be moved so easily against us by intriguers of iniquity, as you call them. But I truly am much more amazed that you are not completely ashamed to open your eyelids and lift your eyes either to God or to any honest person, since you have permitted yourself, with the Devil driving you on, to fall into such inconstancy of intellect that, because of fleshly lusts that are inappropriate and obscene (since you are an Augustinian brother), you have with your sinful embrace violated a nun who was consecrated to God. Moreover, you did not limit yourself to that alone. If you had committed such an outrage of old among the Roman pagans, the woman would have been buried alive and you yourself would have been punished by being beaten to death. But – what is beyond measure execrable – you even received her as your wife, publicly, through the most polluted wedding ceremony. And now, openly, to amazement of everyone, to your own greatest reproach throughout the whole world, with the greatest contempt for holy matrimony, with the greatest insult to most sacred vows, through your unspeakable sin you abuse her in daily prostitution. Finally, what should be most detested of all: when shame and sorrow for so execrable a sin ought to overwhelm you, in the place of penitence, you wretched man, you exhibit a shameless pride, so far fleeing from begging pardon, that you even, in letters and books, cite the example of your sin everywhere among the other false religionists.' [305]

And after many more things, he wrote: 'Now as for that very great honor, namely the one which you offer us so politely, that, if you thought it would please me, it would not trouble you to publish another book, in which you would abundantly proclaim my unmixed praises, at the same time recanting and annulling everything which you formerly wrote to the contrary: Luther, I free you from any such labor, completely and gladly. For I am not so aflame for empty glory that I would entreat you to write books of my praises. Rather, I wish for what is more your business; namely, that you might admit your errors and recant your heresies, and might at long last recover your senses and return to the faith, and that you might then proclaim the faith in good writings and good works, from which you could give praise and glory to God. Otherwise, if you persist in this manner in which you have begun, in your impious heresies and your dishonest life, then certainly you could not praise me more weightily than by vituperating me; nor, on the contrary, could you slander me more hatefully than if you extolled me to the very utmost of your ability – if what we read in Seneca is true (as it certainly is): "Let it be just as base a thing for you to be praised by the base, as to be praised for your own base acts."

'And on this account you write that you are grievously ashamed of the book you published against me, and you transfer the blame to others – who they are I do not know – to whose urging you yielded, and having thrown yourself at my feet you beg for pardon: in the hope that, since I remember that I myself am mortal, I will not want to cherish immortal enmities. Indeed, Luther, you think so magnificently and highly of your own self, and you have always considered yourself as such a great man, that you were not ashamed even to acknowledge in your writings that you not only are, but will always be, not only while living but also when dead, indeed even when your ashes have been burnt and scattered over a thousand seas, an eternal foe and enemy to the

Pope (to whose rank even kings are unequal by I do know not how great a
gap). However, for my part I have never ranked your worth so high that I
would ever deign to be an enemy of yours: even though I consider your heresies
detestable, just like any other heresy. But none of those slanders with which
you tauntingly raved at me moved me so strongly that you could not have
given us full satisfaction with a much lesser prayer than the one which you
now used – if only the matter were treated sufficiently sincerely by you, and
from your heart, etc.' [306]

In the prologue to these two letters, some Englishman wrote as follows:
'The books the King published demonstrate his intellect and wisdom, books
in which he so thoroughly refuted Martin Luther's insane and impious dogmas,
and so stripped Luther himself of any method of arguing to the contrary, that,
with every chance for reasoned argument taken away from him, Luther resorted
to whorish quarrels and buffoon-like slanders. When the most wise and also
most learned King became aware of this, he did not deign to descend to the
level of this jeering, impure rascal; but from the greatness of his soul, he
disregarded all those babbling trivialities, and the jeers of this frigid friar, as
though they were the uncouth gesturings of a cackling fool. But now, when
Luther has dared so stupidly to entreat the King's favor so that he may misuse
the King's name to commend his own faction, the King has thought that this
is scarcely to be allowed, and would rather make it plain to all that he is not
so fickle as to wish to be lured or caught by the fickle praises of a foolish friar,
nor so inconstant that he could in any way at all be led away from that which
he knows is true and right.' [307]

And Johannes Cochlaeus wrote: 'If you are a Catholic, reader, the King's
response can certainly displease you not at all, since throughout it displays
such great integrity, learning, and piety. But if you are a Lutheran, perhaps it
will displease you to see Luther depicted for you in such a manner. However,
consider for just a moment, while you read the first letter, whether it is fitting
for one who wants to be considered an Evangelist, Prophet, Preacher, Man of
God, Apostle of Germany, and so on, to engage in such fickleness that he even
convicts himself of fickleness toward his adversary. What he earlier wrote with
the utmost seriousness, and asserted with such great certainty (if you can
believe him) that he boasted that he had received all his doctrine from heaven,
he now (currying favor – with a womanish wheedling – from his adversary,
whom he had attacked so ferociously and proudly, against decent custom, and
even against Gospel charity and gentleness) wants to recall and to recant in
a published pamphlet, as soon as he may learn by even the smallest hint that
this would be pleasing to his adversary. He does not care that Princes and
politicians, and those most learned men, about whose adherence to his faction
he has boasted, will say that he has wickedly deceived them; to their utmost
shame he now wishes to recant, so that he may at length give them that reward
which he earlier gave to those peasants who were most wickedly misled and
then pitiably slain, if only he may find some foreign supporter, etc.' [308] Furthermore, Cochlaeus wrote a response to a letter to the English written by

Bugenhagen Pomeranus, a citizen of Wittenberg. Pomeranus said that he himself marveled why anyone would shrink from accepting the Holy Gospel of Christ, and moreover, as for the fact that evil things were said about the Lutherans, those who said them did not know that the Son of Man must be scorned by the world, and that the preaching of the Cross must be considered as foolishness. To these things Cochlaeus responded as follows:

'If the King of England were not gentle and merciful, due to his truly Christian spirit, and more inclined toward forgiving injuries for the sake of Christ than toward punishing them with an avenging sword, then certainly long before now he would have overturned your nest, together with all its crows and cuckoos, from its very foundations. And it would scarcely have been difficult for him to do this, when he has control of so much strength and wealth, and of so many friends. And if that race which is no less fierce and warlike than famous and wealthy had not been so far divided from your cave by the limits of nature, it can hardly be doubted that it would have admirably vindicated both its own injuries and those of its King, which you spewed out from that cave, you most hideous sons of Vulcan.[309] Or is it indeed not injurious to write that there are certain ones among that most religious and truly Christian people, who shrink from accepting the Holy Gospel of Christ? Which Gospel of Christ, I ask – Matthew's? Mark's? Luke's? John's? But the English accept these four, and have always religiously maintained those Gospels among themselves for nine hundred years (as is said by Gregory), while your nest was, until just now, a shapeless wood. Nor do the See of Peter or the Church of Christ accept more Gospels than these. Why therefore do you slander a religious people by saying that the Gospel of Christ is not accepted? Who might grant to you that your books, foul with so many heresies, be rightly called a Holy Gospel of Christ? Finally, who could receive with friendly ears that whatever is said against you heretics is immediately said against the Son of Man? That people certainly acknowledge the Son of Man, and revere Him most religiously; but all the English, along with the Pope, and the English King, and the whole Church of Christ, rightly shun, shudder at, and detest you, as new Hussites and Wycliffites, and as most filthy blemishes and blots on our faith and religion. For the sheep of Christ do not hear the voice of strangers, but flee from them.'[310]

But when Erasmus of Rotterdam, a man of the greatest eloquence and learning, and of the greatest authority in Germany, published a pamphlet about Free Will, which he modestly titled a *Rhetoric-Piece* or *Comparison*, in it he rendered suspect many of Luther's teachings which earlier had seemed in accordance with the Gospel. For he says in his preface:

'I will say nothing else in this preface than what is the fact of the matter: that I have never sworn allegiance to Luther's words. Therefore, it should not appear unseemly to anyone if here and there I openly differ from him in opinion – to be sure, in no other way than one man differs from another. Thus it is very far from being an abomination to disagree over some dogma of his; and this is all the more the case if someone should confront him with moderate argument due to zeal for discovering the truth. Certainly I do not judge that Luther himself will take it badly if somebody disagrees with him here and there, when he permits himself to dissent from the decrees, not only of all the doctors of the church, but also of all schools, councils, and Popes. Since he proclaims this openly and frankly, it should not count against me with his friends if I follow his example. Furthermore, lest anyone interpret this battle as the kind that usually happens between two gladiators engaged with one another, I will contend with one of his teachings alone, for no other reason than that, if it can happen, by this clash of scriptures and of arguments, the truth may be made more plain; the investigation of truth has always been most respectable among scholars. The matter will be carried on without slanders, whether since this is most fitting for Christians, or since truth is more certainly found in this way, but is very frequently lost through too much quarreling.'[311]

And below he says: 'Now since Luther does not recognize the authority of any writer, however approved, but only hears the canonical books, certainly I very gladly accept this reduction of my labor. For since among both the Greeks and the Latins there are countless writers who treat of free will, either directly or in passing, it would not have been a inconsiderable task to extract from all of them what each one had said for and against free will; nor to undertake the lengthy and tedious labor of explaining the meanings of individual sayings, or of refuting or confirming them through arguments – which would have been pointless, so far as Luther and his friends are concerned, especially since they not only disagree with each other, but many times do not even agree sufficiently with their very own opinions. However, I wish the reader meanwhile to be warned that, if we appear merely to do the same thing as Luther with testimonies from Holy Scripture and from sound reasoning, then let the reader keep before his eyes that very long list of extremely erudite men, whom the consensus of many centuries, all the way up to the present day, has approved. The piety of life of most of them, in addition to their admirable knowledge of the sacred writings, commends them. Some even added the testimony of their blood to Christ's doctrine, which they had defended in their writings.'[312]

And below: 'Therefore, if the reader shall perceive that the battle equipment of my disputation fights in equal balance with the opposite side, then let him ponder in his own mind which of these two things he judges should be granted more authority: the previous judgments of so many scholars, so many orthodox believers, so many saints, martyrs, theologians both ancient and modern; of so many academies, councils, bishops, and highest Pontiffs; or the private opinions of some individual or other. Not that I would pass sentence from the number of voters or the rank of the speakers, as happens in human assemblies. I know that it frequently occurs in practice that the larger party conquers the better one; I know that those things are not always best, which are approved by the greatest number; I know that in the investigation of truth, there is never a lack of something which should be added to the diligence of one's precursors. I admit that it is proper for the sole authority of Holy Scripture to conquer all the votes of all mortals. However, the controversy here is not about Scripture;

each side embraces and venerates the same Scripture. The fight is over the meaning of Scripture. And in the interpretation of Scripture, if anything may be ascribed to intellect and erudition, what is more acute or more sagacious than the intellects of the Greeks? Who is more widely versed in the Scriptures? Nor has intellect or experience in the Holy Scriptures been lacking among the Latins, who, if they yielded to the Greeks in the fecundity of their nature, still were surely able to equal them in industry, with the assistance of the Greeks' writings. But if in this judgment holiness of life should be looked to, more than erudition, then you see what sort of men the side which supports free will has. Let us set aside the odious (as the lawyers say) comparison; for I would not want to compare certain heralds of this new Gospel with those older ones.' [313]

And again Erasmus wrote, 'And so, how shall we examine the Spirit? According to erudition? There are scribes on both sides. According to manner of life? There are sinners on both sides. On one side stands the whole chorus of saints who maintained free will. They spoke the truth, but they were human. However, I compare men to men, not men to God. I am asked, "What can a great multitude of people do for the sense of the Spirit?" I answer, "What can a small number of people do?" I hear, "What can a bishop's miter contribute to understanding Holy Scripture?" I answer, "What can a hood and a cowl contribute?" I hear, "What can philosophical knowledge contribute to knowledge of Holy Scripture?" I answer, "What can ignorance contribute?" I hear, "What can a congregated Synod do for an understanding of Scripture, when it may perhaps happen that no one there has the Spirit?" I answer, "What can a little private gathering of a few do, when it is most probable that no one is there who has the Spirit?" Paul exclaims, "Do you seek a proof of the Christ who dwells in me?" The Apostles were not believed unless they added miracles to faith in their doctrine. But now anyone at all demands that he should be believed, because he affirms that he has the spirit of the Gospel.[314] The apostles were at length believed, because they cast out vipers, healed the sick, raised the dead, gave the gift of tongues through the laying on of hands – and still they were scarcely believed, since they taught paradoxes. Now, although according to the common opinion, certain people present even greater paradoxes, still none of them has appeared who could heal even a lame horse.' [315]

Luther was silent for a long time concerning this book, since Erasmus had written it in Latin and not to the unlearned common people of Germany, over whom Luther especially brooded. However, driven on by the complaints of many, especially when Erasmus's book was translated into the German language by Emser and Cochlaeus, finally with the aid of his comrades he published a book, *On the Bondage of the Will.* In this book Luther loaded Erasmus down with slanders, in order to deprive him of his reputation for learning and his authority. Erasmus soon vindicated himself in his *Hyperaspites.* However, among the slanders and calumnies, Luther occasionally mixed in various praises and flatteries, contrary to his custom; perhaps because his helpers and advisers, Jonas and Melanchthon, wished him to do so, or perhaps he acted out of fear of the orthodox Princes and Kings, whom he knew were gracious and kindly disposed toward Erasmus; hoping by flatteries to render Erasmus more suspect, as a secret friend of Luther, in the eyes of the Princes and Theologians. Therefore, in these words, he began his book *On the Bondage of the Will.*

'It has happened contrary to everyone's expectation and contrary to my own custom that I answer your *Diatribe Concerning Free Will* rather tardily, venerable Erasmus – for up till now I have appeared not only to have gladly accepted opportunities for this kind for writing, but even to have sought them out of my own accord. Perhaps some people will marvel at this new and unaccustomed patience or fortitude in Luther, who has not been aroused even by such a great number of speeches and letters of his adversaries, which they have spread around, congratulating Erasmus on his victory and singing their paean of victory: "And so that Maccabee, that most obstinate Champion, at long last has met a worthy antagonist, against whom he does not dare to open his gaping mouth." However, not only do I not blame them, but I myself yield you a palm such as I have never before yielded to anyone; not only that you greatly surpass me in powers of eloquence and in intellect (which we must all rightly concede, all the more since I am a barbarian who has always lived in a barbarous state), but also that you have inhibited my spirit and vehemence, and left me exhausted before the fight; and this for two reasons. First, by your skill, because you treat the matter with such amazing and persistent moderation that you make it impossible for me to be angry with you; and second, by your luck, whether it is by chance or by fate, because on so great a subject you say nothing that has not been said before. Indeed, you say so much less, and you attribute so much more to free will than the sophists have hitherto said and attributed (about which I shall say more below) that it even might seem superfluous to answer these arguments of yours, which have already been refuted by me on many occasions; and have also been trampled down and crushed in Philip Melanchthon's unconquered pamphlet *On Passages of Theology*, which in my judgment is worthy not only of immortality but also of the Church's Canon. When your pamphlet was compared with this, yours seemed so mean and trivial to me that I strongly sympathized with you, because you polluted your most beautiful and ingenious diction with these bits of filth, and I felt indignation at this most unworthy material which was being conveyed in such precious adornments of eloquence, as if refuse or manure should be transported in gold or silver vessels.' [316]

And below he wrote, 'In sum, these words of yours declare the following, that it makes no difference to you whatever is believed by anyone anywhere, so long as the peace of the world remains firm, and that on account of danger to life, reputation, possessions, and good will, it is permissible to act like that person who said, "If they say it, I say it; if they deny it, I deny it"; and to consider Christian dogmas as in no way better than the opinions of philosophers and common people, about which it is most stupid to quarrel, fight, or assert, since nothing comes from these actions but discord and the disturbance of external peace; things which are above us are nothing to us. And so, for the sake of ending our conflicts, you come as a mediator, so that you may stop both sides and persuade us not to fight for our lives over stupid and useless matters. Thus, I say, your words sound; and what I am here suggesting, I believe you to understand, my Erasmus. But, as I said, let the words go; in the meantime I absolve your heart, so long as you do not make a further exhibition of it; but fear the spirit of God, Who scrutinizes our vitals and hearts, nor is it deceived by carefully arranged words. And I have said these things for this reason: so that from now on you may desist from accusing our cause of stubbornness and willfulness. For by this plan you do nothing other than demonstrate that you nourish a Lucian in your heart, or some other pig from Epicurus's herd, who, because he himself believes that there is no God, secretly laughs at all those who believe and confess their belief.' [317]

And later he says, 'But this is still more intolerable: that you rank this subject of free will among those things that are useless and unnecessary, and in its place you recount for us those things which you judge are enough for Christian piety. Any Jew or pagan, who was utterly ignorant of Christ, could easily write out such a list. For you make not even a single iota of a mention of Christ, as if you imagine that Christian piety can exist without Christ, so long as God is worshiped with all one's powers, as most merciful by nature. What may I say here, Erasmus? Your whole being exhales an odor of Lucian, and you breathe out Epicurus's vast drunkenness upon me. If you consider that this subject is not necessary for Christians, then leave the arena, I beg you; there is nothing between you and us, since we consider it essential. If, as you say, it is irreligious, if it is inquisitive, if it is superfluous, to know whether God has contingent foreknowledge of anything; whether our will accomplishes anything in those matters which pertain to eternal salvation, or merely passively undergoes whatever is done by active grace; if whatever good or evil we do, we do or rather passively undergo by mere necessity; then what, I ask you, is there that it is religious or serious or useful to know? This certainly is worth nothing at all. Erasmus, this is too much.[318] It is difficult to ascribe this to your ignorance; since you are a man who is already aged, and has lived among Christians, and has long contemplated the Holy Scriptures, you leave us no room to excuse you or to think well of you. Nevertheless, the papists pardon you for these enormities, for this reason – because you are writing against Luther; if there were no Luther and you wrote such things in other circumstances, they would rip you apart with their teeth.' [319]

When Erasmus saw this book of Luther's, with a remarkable quickness he wrote his *Hyperaspites*, that is, the 'Defender' of his Diatribe, as his own words to the reader indicate. He writes, '*The Bondage of the Will* has appeared, which is nominally by Martin Luther, but has been worked on by many, over a long time. For the book had begun to be printed a year ago, as those who assert that they saw some pages of it say, and with the greatest care; as the event itself shows, the book was returned to me late, and that by chance. For they themselves concealed it, so that they might celebrate their triumph for a few months at least; and this was done not only by devotees of Luther, but also by those who are enemies to both of us – to me, because of my good writings, and to him, because of his unapproved teachings. The amount of time which it was possible to devote to rereading the *Diatribe*, and then to reading Luther's book (which was not lengthy so much as wordy), and then to my response, was not longer than ten days.'[320] Then, turning to Luther himself, he says, 'How many utter irrelevancies there are in that book of yours! How many superfluities, what lengthy delays in commonplaces, how many slanders, how much obvious vanity, how many tricks, how many elaborate attacks, how many things twisted and distorted in a shameless manner, how many tragic conclusions follow from these depravities, and then from these tragic conclusions, how many outcries against one who doesn't deserve them! Since it seemed good to you to waste your precious time in these things, I myself am forced to use a considerable portion of my own time in refuting them.'[321]

'First, therefore, I wonder why – when my *Diatribe* contains nothing except a moderate discussion of the subject, and when Jerome Emser rails at you nearby, while Johannes Cochlaeus attacks you from afar; when from England, apart from Ross and the others, John the Bishop of Rochester wounds you with his righteous volumes, and from Gaul Josse Clichthove fights Luther with Anti-Luther; when from Italy Christopher Longolius turns his carefully worked oratory against you; and finally, when you have here, out of the chorus of your own fellowship, those who will assiduously take up this business with you, and among them Ulrich Zwingli, who in a published book (which is by no means toothless, as they say) fights both against you and against the Church concerning your doctrine about the Eucharist; when Capito does the same, and Johannes Oecolampadius too, not with slanders, indeed, but with very abundant and acute stratagems; when all these things are so, I say, I wonder on what account you remain silent about all of these men but think that my *Diatribe* must be answered.'[322]

And a bit later he says, 'But here you have followed those brothers, among whom I know that there are a great many whose morals are very far distant from the Gospel under whose name they hawk themselves. Luther, you make it clear that you are excessively submissive to the desires of such men, and you do this not without grave damage to the cause which you support. For it is no secret to me who you were trying to please when you wrote in this fashion against Cochlaeus and against the King of England.[323] He it was, undoubtedly, in whom you could recognize two comic characters: the most stupid and most vainglorious Thraso and the most servile Gnatho.[324] Certainly he did not merit that you should, at his prompting, write even a letter, in so difficult and dangerous a business. No, rather you should have considered what sort of a character you had assumed: namely, as someone who claimed that he was going to call back into the light the Gospel, which for more than fifteen hundred years now had lain buried and hidden, and, setting aside the authority of Popes, Councils, Bishops, and scholars, and someone who promised to the world the certain and true path of salvation, of which the world had remained ignorant up until now. How out of harmony it was, then, that someone who took upon himself so serious a business, like Atlas taking the Heavens upon his shoulders (for now I so deal with you, as though everything were true which you claim for yourself), should then gambol with jokes, buffooneries, sarcasms, and guffaws, in whatever manner he chose, as though in a matter of sport; and at the fancy of some Willy should control or moderate his pen against anyone – I will not even say, against a King.' [325]

And below he said, 'Besides, that you compare your own knowledge with Paul's – would that you could truly claim this, and at the same time would show the Evangelical Spirit, which perfumes Paul's writings, although another spirit clamors in your books. But finally, what kind of insult is it, if you deride my knowledge, when you have long since in the same way disparaged the Universal Councils, and the Popes, and all Bishops, and the ancient and the modern Doctors of the Church alike, and then all schools? Whoever knew anything at all, who differed from your teachings by even a finger's breadth, as they say? Everyone at all who before now was learned, as soon as they begin to contradict you, suffers this metamorphosis – they are transformed from lynxes to moles, from men to mushrooms.' [326]

And below: 'For the rest, who could without laughing read this thing that you write, that you returned to battle more slowly due to respect for me, when that boldness of yours had already struck the entire world with fatal disagreements, and I called you back in vain? Was it necessary to apply spurs to a horse who was already galloping? We have the fruit of your spirit, the matter has already progressed to the point of bloody slaughter, and we would have feared even worse things if God in his mercy had not averted them. You will say that this is the nature of the Word. But I judge that it makes something of a difference, how the Word of God is preached, since what you teach is already the Word of God. You do not acknowledge those rebels, I think, but they acknowledge you. And it is already widely known that many who hawked themselves about in the name of the Gospel were the instigators of the cruelest rebellion. If their attempt had succeeded, perhaps there might be some who would approve it, who now curse it – since the thing turned out badly. You, indeed, deflected suspicion away from yourself by your most harsh pamphlet against the farmers; however, you did not manage to make people believe any less that the opportunity for these rebellions had been provided by your books, especially those written in German, against all anointed or shorn men, against monks, against bishops, in support of Evangelical liberty, and against human tyranny.' [327]

And later, 'Finally, when you several times make me out to be like one who says in my heart "There is no God", like Lucian the godless; you make me out to be a pig from Epicurus's flock, as if I believed that there is no God, or that, if there is, human affairs are none of his concern; when, I say, you fasten these things upon me (than which no one could ever feign anything more savage), you even add this embellishment: that I know what you mean here. This was the place for raving against you, if I wanted to imitate the petulance of your pen. But there was no need for such impudent comments; I was able to discover from the opinions of others what monster you hide in your heart, and what spirit your writings breathe out upon us. And indeed, if it was just for you to hurl against me whatever weapons you wished, either from the accusations of your esquires, from the writings of your brothers, or from the divination of your own spirit, then how much more justly could I do the same to you, from the diplomatic writings of the Emperor and the Pontiffs, and from the books produced against you by serious men?' [328]

And at the end of the book Erasmus wrote, 'In the business of salvation, I ask for no other protection than from the mercy of the Lord; nor, next to God, do I have more hope or more solace in anything than in the Holy Scriptures. And although it may have occurred – I do not deny it – that in my night-time labors I have, here and there, not touched the genuine sense of the Scripture, still I can most reverently and solemnly swear that I know that I have never, either to please any man or in fear of any man, taught otherwise than I have believed, merely for a good reputation. Those who have shared my household can be witnesses, if not of my sanctity, which I desire rather than have, then certainly that I have this character: I have never babbled out a word, either in jest or in earnest, that savored of Lucian, Epicurus, or Porphyry. It would be tasteless to testify to these things in writing, if Luther, the champion of the Gospel, had not wished, in his carefully prepared book, to play such jokes upon his friend Erasmus. Now, if anyone prefers to have faith in the most shameless accusation of that man, who does not know me, than in my own testimony, let him do so at his own risk; this declaration of my mind will absolve me.' [329] These things Erasmus wrote.

In that year, at the Emperor's command, the Princes and Imperial Estates were summoned to Speyer to hold assemblies and to confer with one another both about peace and the business of religion, and about the aid that should be given to Hungary against the Turks. Since the Emperor was involved in wars, he could not be present in his own person. But he provided his brother, who was acting as his regent in the Empire, with the aid of four Commissaries, men of great authority, so that everything could be carried out with greater energy. The Lutheran Princes were summoned as well: Johannes, Duke of Saxony, the Elector Prince, who had recently succeeded into the electoral rank when his brother Duke Frederick died; and the Landgrave of Hesse, Philip, who had finally been won over by the Lutherans after the peasants were killed, and had gone over to the Lutherans' sect, although both his father-in-law Duke George of Saxony and his most pious mother (who remained a Catholic until her death) tried in vain to call him back. These Lutheran Princes brought with them their own preachers and the priests of their new rite, and asked that some church be assigned to them, in which they might freely enjoy both their rites and their speeches. But George, Bishop of Speyer, who was by birthright the Duke of Bavaria and the Palatine Count of the Rhine, strongly forbade them to perform any new rites or any of their speeches in any church whatsoever. Therefore, since they cared little about rites or sacrifices, they ordered their preachers to address the people daily from the forecourts of their own houses.

And thus there was an enormous number of the common folk and the peasants gathered at these sermons (not so much for the sake of learning as because of the novelty of the location and the unusual manner of speech) to hear slanders against the clergy and the Pope. And in order to entice more people to their sect, when the business was finished cooked meats were openly carried around in dishes, on Fridays and other fast days, in the sight of all the listeners, through the forecourt to the table of the Princes and the courtiers, though this was done in open defiance of the Church and the Catholic public. And many other such things of this sort were done there, in a fashion that was scarcely Evangelical, by those Evangelical men. Their ministers, horsemen, stable boys, and fools impudently bandied the word of the Lord about, and on the right sleeve of their garments they wore these letters: V.D.M.I.AE. These stood for 'The Word of the Lord Remains For Ever.'[330] The other Princes and Bishops, together with the Emperor's brother, attended public service on feast days in the great church (which was a famous work of the Emperor Henry, whose monuments can be seen there). But the Lutherans heard preachers in their own homes at that time, and through those preachers they turned the people away from the holy rites.

The Catholics were forced to overlook indiscretions and boldness of this type, not only due to the safe conduct and public trust that had been promised to them, but also because of the wickedness and trouble of that worst of times. For the German people, enticed by the Lutheran turmoil and gazing longingly at the goods of priests and monks, were inclined to disorder and rebellion; and there were very serious upheavals in foreign countries as well. For the Emperor and the King of France were engaged in a long-lasting war over Italy; and the Turkish Emperor in his own person threatened Hungary with the most dangerous of armies and the most abundant troops.

Moreover, Lutheran books were being carried about and sold throughout the whole city, and two pamphlets especially, which although they were small in size were exceptionally large in venom. One of these was Luther's sermon *On the Destruction of Jerusalem*, in German;[331] the other was the most bitter letter of a certain buffoon who called himself by the false name Argyrophylax, or, in German, Treasurer. By this word he brought Prince Ferdinand's Treasurer under suspicion of being a Lutheran, and in his name made the letter more acceptable to the Princes and the Imperial Estates. Since the letter was brief and easy to read, and was printed not only in Latin but also in German, an exceedingly great number of copies were sold. And this widespread publication was an extremely harmful stratagem, trick, and act of malice against the Churchmen, not only because the language was artfully adorned with well-chosen words to commend Luther's doctrine, but also because it appeared to concern the well-being of the Republic, and to recommend the removal of the privileges with which the Churchmen were endowed. For it says,

'I am often accustomed to wonder, most Illustrious and Powerful Princes of the Germans, why several of you rage so bitterly against those whom you call heretics, so that you do not hesitate, for the sake of questions and opinions about religion, to punish men – who are in other respects innocent and useful to the republic – with exile, confiscation of their goods, the sword, water, and fire. However, if they have transgressed against you or against the Republic, then let them be punished according to a more just accusation. But since they assert and teach things of a sort which would incline toward the greatest benefit for your authority and for the republic (and for this reason they should even have received a reward from you), it is a cause for wonder, nay, rather for astonishment and pity that such punishments are meted out to them without any reason or moderation. Are you perhaps lacking money necessary for the management of the republic? Behold – I show the greatest of treasuries to you. Allow the monks and nuns (if any so wish) freely to leave their monasteries, and to seek a living by working. Provide only a meager living for those who wish to linger in their houses of ill repute, and be on your guard lest anyone hereafter choose the idle state of such a life. Then, whatever wealth remains in their hands, turn to the needs of the poor and of the republic, and to your own use. Within a few months (I have no doubt) you will discover how many hundreds of thousands of gold pieces monks and people of that sort possessed, in your one territory alone. Let no one judge that this advice of mine is either seditious or impious. For I could prove how pious it is (if there were need), since clearly those impious Princes must be censured, who do not heed this advice but prefer to extort tribute from farmers, vine-growers, artisans, citizens, and others of their subjects, than to take their own goods, and the goods of the Republic, away from those who possess them in such bad faith, etc.' [332]

In this way also Luther's sermon commending his own Gospel threatened all kinds of evil and even the destruction of all of Germany, unless his Gospel were listened to, just as befell those Jews who would not hear Christ. 'For now would be the time', (he said) 'for us to acknowledge our own good, and to accept the Gospel with joy. For now grace is offered to us, through which we can be brought into peace. But we do not accept it in our hearts; we believe that we are safe, and we do not see the great disaster which already has occurred; we do not see how heavily God punishes us through pseudo-prophets and sects, which He everywhere sends out against us, and who preach as confidently as though they had entirely fed on the Holy Spirit. Those whom we consider the best of men direct the people into such errors that they scarcely know what they should do or what they should leave undone. Therefore, it is now the time for open and obvious grace, but we despise it and cast it back upon the wind. God neither wills this, nor can he pardon us for it. Therefore, the fact that we so scorn His word is worthy of vengeance, and will be avenged, even if the vengeance should be delayed by one hundred years – but it will not be delayed so long. And the more clear the Word is, the more heavy will be the vengeance; I dread lest all Germany perish. God cannot leave this wickedness unavenged, nor will He long shut His eyes to it. For the Gospel has been so abundantly preached that it was not so clear even in the time of the Apostles. Therefore, all Germany will perish, as I fear; it is necessary that it be destroyed from its very roots. The Princes want to accomplish matters with the sword alone; they pluck too fiercely at God's beard. Therefore, He Himself will strike them in their faces.' [333]

And below he said, 'The Jews put forward the same excuse, as now our people do: "Indeed we would gladly accept the Gospel, if it did not bring danger to our persons and our property, if our wives and children would not be destroyed by it." And they did not consider the great and rich promise made by God, when he said, "I will repay you one hundredfold in this world, and in the next I will give you eternal life. Leave wife and child, I will nourish them well, I will give them back to you; only dare boldly for My sake. Do you think that I do not know how to build another house for you? How trivial you think Me. I will give you Heaven; will you not therefore be daring for My sake? If your goods are taken away from you, that is well for you; Heaven and earth are Mine, and I will surely repay you," etc.' [334]

And so many, not only of the common people and the throng of country folk, but also of the upper class and nobles, were drawn by books of this sort to favor the new Gospel and to hate the ancient religion and clergy. Therefore, since this novelty could not be prohibited or abolished without rebellion and turmoil, the Princes and Imperial Estates tentatively decreed that each one of them would conduct himself in matters of religion, and in his own lands would act in the manner that he believed he could justify and answer for before God and before the Emperor's Majesty. And for this reason, when all their minds were hesitating in this fashion and when there was no certain peace or security, it came about that no German prince brought aid to Louis the King of Hungary and Bohemia. The Emperor of the Turks had already invaded Louis's borders with a very great number of troops. For at home, nothing was safe from the rebellious spirits of the Princes' subjects, and Luther had already rendered every soldier unwilling to proceed against the Turks. For he had written that to do battle against the Turks was to fight against God, Who was visiting our iniquities on us through them. He had written, that up until this time we had never had any success against the Turk, and that the Turk's strength and dominion had been immensely increased by our wars. He had written, that it is not lawful for Christians to fight in wars, but that they must endure violence and injury. Finally, he had written that the Turk was ten times more virtuous and wise than our Princes; therefore, we could expect no prosperity from fighting him, nor should anyone contribute anything against the Turks, etc.

And so the pious, innocent, and famous King Louis, brother-in-law of our Emperor, was utterly forsaken by all the German Princes. When he received most threatening letters sent by the Turk from Belgrade, and heard that he treated most cruelly not only the conquered but even those who had surrendered, and that he did not keep any sworn faith, Louis raised as great an army as he could from his own subjects. He called on the Bohemians for aid, and on Johannes Waiwoda, the Count of Cilia, and from the Kingdom of Hungary he gathered together an army that would have been proper enough, if he had been dealt with in good faith. For it is said that he had around 30,000 cavalrymen. Therefore, when he had learned how savagely and barbarously the

Turk had run wild through City of Five Churches, Louis marched out of Buda with his army to meet the enemy. But the Bohemians and Waiwoda had not arrived in time, and he also had many traitors in his own army. Louis's engines of war were badly forged, while the Turk's were of the best quality; therefore, when the weapons of both sides were directed at the enemy and gave out their great destruction, the Hungarians were soon routed at the beginning of the battle. The King received many wounds and fled with a few comrades; during his flight, he drowned in a certain lake.

This disaster was not only fatal to the very wealthy kingdom of Hungary, which had most bravely resisted the tyranny of the Turks for over 200 years; it also laid open to the enemies of Christ a means of access to Germany. For they say that the Turk had threatened the pious king in letters, saying that he was not only going to attack and shortly to overthrow Louis's kingdom and nobles, but that he wished utterly to wipe out their religion and their Crucifix, and to reduce those things to silence. Therefore, after the king had fled, the Turk gained the greatest plunder, especially of cannons, chariots, and ships. For it is said that he carried off 80 great cannons, 5,000 smaller ones, and 10,000 of the smallest cannons; 4,000 chariots; and 5,000 ships. He came to Buda and pillaged everything. The Queen, the Lady Maria, sister of the Emperor, despoiled of all her belongings and even deprived of her womanly garb, scarcely managed to flee and arrived in Vienna in a pitiable condition.

Prince Ferdinand was at first elected by the Bohemians to take the place of the dead king; the Hungarians also elected him, since they knew that the rightful authority of the kingdom devolved on him according to ancient usage and treaty. But as soon as the Turk left, Johannes, Count of Cilia, was elected as the King's successor by certain people, and he caused a great deal of effort and trouble to the legitimate King Ferdinand. For he intended to dispute with the king over the realm not only by division, but also by arms; nor did he desist, until he had once again involved that country, which had already been afflicted, in the most serious evils.

In that same year there was a very famous debate between Catholics and Lutherans in Baden, a town possessed by the Swiss. For Master Ulrich Zwingli and Dr Johannes Oecolampadius, learned men who were very skilled in the Greek and Hebrew languages, had already in part misled the religious and Catholic people of Switzerland, and had incited a considerable split in religion by means of the new Lutheran doctrine. Therefore, so that this disagreement and turmoil might be removed, this debate was instituted by the common consent of the twelve Cantons (for so they call the twelve independent regions of the confederated people). And to this debate were summoned, from the Catholics, the most celebrated men, Dr Johannes Faber (an advisor of the Most Serene Prince Ferdinand), who had already published a large volume arguing against Luther's errors; Dr Johannes Eck, who seven years previously had disputed with Luther himself at Leipzig, to the public praise of all; and Dr Thomas Murner. These three men were especially prepared to dispute with Zwingli and Oecolampadius. The four local Bishops, to whose dioceses the

Swiss people belonged, also sent speakers of their own to this Debate. For Hugo, the Bishop of Constance, sent well-known men: his own Suffragan, Dr Melchior, a most excellent theologian; Dr Othmar Luscinius, a very fluent speaker; Father Antonius Pyrata, the most eloquent speaker of the Great Church; and certain other prelates and churchmen, who were not without fame. And the Bishop of Basel, Christopher, sent Dr Augustinus Marius, the Suffragan of Frisingen; Dr Jacob Lemp, the Ordinary of Theology in the Academy of Tübingen, and some other learned men. Sebastian, the Bishop of Lausanne, sent Dr Conrad Tregarius, the Provincial of the Augustinian brothers, and Louis Loblius, the Deacon of Bern. Finally, the Bishop of Curia sent Dr Peter Speifer, with some other Canons of Curia. Moreover, a great crowd of learned men was in attendance. For the rest, Zwingli rejected every public faith and safe conduct which were offered to him in many places, and refused to attend the debate under any circumstances whatsoever. But Dr Eck disputed for many days, under the restrictions set out by the Notaries, now with Oecolampadius, now with Jacob Imel, now with Berchtold Haller, and even with Ulrich Studer. They debated concerning other points of our religion, but chiefly concerning the Venerable Sacrament of the Eucharist. And by how much Dr Eck was superior and more firmly grounded than them all was declared in a public decree of the Swiss. And in this decree the observances of the Catholics and the propositions of Eck were confirmed with an acknowledged and full strictness. This was the tenor of those propositions: [335]

1 The true Body of Christ, and His Blood, are present in the Sacrament on the altar.

2 These are truly offered in the office of the Mass, for the sake of the living and of the dead.

3 The Virgin Mary and the other holy inhabitants of Heaven are to be invoked as intercessors.

4 The images of our Lord Jesus Christ and of His saints are not to be destroyed.

5 After this life, there is the fire of Purgatory.

6 Even the children of Christians are born in original sin.

7 The Baptism of Christ, not that of John, takes away original sin.

The content of the public decree was made to conform with these propositions. And, in that decree Luther's doctrine was prohibited to the people of Switzerland, as a perverse doctrine that had been solemnly condemned in many judicial decisions by Pope Leo X, by Charles V, by the most famous universities of Paris, Louvain, Cologne, etc. The ancient observation of the Catholic faith was approved in this decree, and it was ordered that nothing should be rashly altered in the sacred mass, in the administration of the Sacraments, or in the sacred rites of ceremonies, fasts, prayers, confession, feasts, oblations, invocations, and funeral processions for the dead. And therefore, so that all these

things might be more firmly maintained, a statement was added at the end of
the decree, saying that certain watchmen should be appointed, who together
with the magistrates and public officials would diligently investigate this matter,
and would denounce transgressors, of whatever rank they might be, so that
they would be punished according to their faults. And, in addition, it was
decreed that someone accused in one Canton would be considered as an accused
man and an exile in all the Cantons alike, so that it would never be possible
for fugitives to avoid punishment.

Dr Johannes Faber, because of Zwingli's absence and stubbornness, could
not debate with him orally; he therefore produced many arguments in writing,
which he would have set up against Zwingli, if Zwingli had made an appearance.
For he collected into one volume a great number of Zwingli's *Counterarguments*,
in which Zwingli spoke most shamefully and in contradiction to himself, and
demolished his own and Luther's doctrine. But it would take too long to recount
everything which that most learned man, by his varied reading and inexhaustible labor, corrected and confuted from Zwingli's books. Some of these
things were contradictory among themselves, some were in opposition to the
Catholic faith and in themselves impious, absurd, and hostile to the truth.
Moreover, he reviewed over 150 lies in the writings of Oecolampadius, by
which that man artfully deceived the people, when he asserted that the ancient
Doctors of the Church held the same opinions about the Holy Eucharist as he
himself held. The most pious and learned man John Fisher, Bishop of Rochester
in England, also wrote five books against Oecolampadius, refuting his errors
and lies in detail. But Dr Thomas Murner, who at this time was preaching the
word of God in the Catholic manner at Lucerne, railed against Zwingli by far
the most harshly. In his *Forty Conclusions*, he proved that Zwingli was infamous
in many ways, because of the sins and sacrileges he had committed. It will be
sufficient here, for the sake of an example, to cite one of these, which was
seventh in Murner's list; and, for the sake of brevity, it is permissible to abridge
even that one. Murner, therefore, says,

'Anyone who dares to divert property and income that is designated, for
pious reasons, for the divine worship into profane uses is infamous; as is anyone
who dares to make one man rich by the loss and injury of another; as is anyone
who dares try to transfer more power on to another than he himself has.' He
proves this conclusion by citing many laws, both of Constantine the Great and
of the Emperor Justinian. And he adds, 'When the yearly income from immo-
veable goods is computed, we count one hundred from the most holy churches
as fifty; but these goods ought neither to be removed nor taken away. Therefore,
whoever does this, should be punished, not only the one who actually does it,
but also the churchwarden and the scribe, who writes a contract of this kind,
and the judge who approves it, and the churchwarden [who approves] that
[count of] fifty. Do you hear these things, you thieves of the churches?
Therefore, nothing remains for you to expect, except that you will proceed
barefoot to the gibbet.'

And below he writes: 'From this it follows, first, that anyone is a scoundrel, who by force deprives churches and religious people of their pledges, and despoils them of these things by force and injury. On this topic, the magistrate says, "Anything accomplished by force or by force or arms should be punished according to the Julian Law concerning public trials." It follows, secondly, that anyone is doubly a scoundrel, and a double thief, who withholds capital goods along with the pledges that he has taken. And it follows, thirdly, that this man is a triple scoundrel, who in addition to pledges and capital goods, steals even the documents and seals of these things. The Julian Law does not concern itself with private violence. It follows, fourthly, that he is a fourfold scoundrel, who in addition to these three things also compels people by force to give him their property and income, when they do not owe him even a halfpenny; see the Julian Law on embezzlement. O you who are so infamous in so many ways, you wicked Evangelists, crime-ridden and scandalous robbers of churches, against whom things of this sort are truly said! Oh what scandals, what infamy have you brought to our pious native soil, and to your parents buried in that earth. I pray that these laments may reach the Throne of the Divine Majesty, so that your misdeeds may finally meet with vengeance.' [336]

Murner wrote these things and many others of this sort, which it would take a long time to recount. Moreover, when the Zwinglians falsely claimed that even Erasmus of Rotterdam (who at that time was residing in Basel) agreed with them about the Eucharist, Erasmus refuted that calumny most resolutely in letters written to the Swiss people. However, the disagreement was not settled by this Debate; for the error had driven its roots too deeply into the hearts of many to be able to be removed by any logical arguments whatsoever. And very Lutherans, Zwingli and Oecolampadius, now even began to write against Luther himself. Their disagreement has continued up until the present day.

1527

Luther would have remained silent for ever about the serious and learned letter of the King of England, had it not been translated into German by his neighbor Jerome Emser, and openly published. [337] Therefore, so that the German people (whom he claimed for his personal property and inheritance, as God once claimed Israel) should not be recalled to the ancient faith by that strong and lucid refutation, Luther wrote a short pamphlet in German. In it he insisted on the permanence of his doctrine and most bitterly incited against himself not only the papists (as he called the Catholics) and the Princes, but also the Fanatics, [338] who had just a short time before been his comrades and dear friends. Very near the beginning of this pamphlet about doctrine, he boasted in these words against the King of England: 'He has even attacked with his slanders' (he said) 'my pamphlet written against free will. But Erasmus of Rotterdam, one of that King's best friends, was forced to release my pamphlet untouched, and he leaves it untouched up to the present day – although he has more intelligence in one of his fingers than the King of England has with all his smatterings. And I say *"Trotz!"* [339] not only to the King and Erasmus, but even to their God, and to all the Devils, since they did not refute my pamphlet rightly and justly,' etc.[340]

Then he railed against the Princes as follows: 'Good God,' (he said) 'how diligently, and in what subtle ways, they examine me! Am I not then a precious and noble man? Indeed, certainly, in a thousand years there has scarcely been a man of nobler blood than Luther. Why is it so? Figure it out yourself: Already three Roman Popes, so many Cardinals, Kings, princes, Bishops, priests, monks, great Johans, learned men, and the whole world, all of these are – or at least eagerly wish to be – traitors, thieves, and hangmen, for the sake of Luther's blood. But let the Devil too be with his own. Bah! I myself hate my own blood, when I think about these things, that I should have so many magnificent and outstanding hangmen and thieves. Such honor ought to be shown to the Emperor of the Turks, not to a poor beggar such as I am.' [341]

And below he said, 'In the eyes of the world, I both wish to be virtuous and am so; to such an extent that my detractors are not worthy to untie the laces on my shoe, nor can they with truth prove me guilty of ever, in the eyes of the world, living or acting scandalously toward any person – as I can well prove them guilty of. In short, I am neither too humble nor too proud toward anyone; just as Paul says, "I know how to be proud, and I know how to be humble; I know how to go without, and how to enjoy abundance." So far as regards my doctrine, I am – to the Devils, to the Emperor, to the Kings, to the Princes, and to all the world – much much much much too forward, steadfast, and proud. But so far as regards my life, I am as humble and submissive as any boy. Let anyone who has not previously known these things, listen now.' [342] And later he said, 'Concerning my office and my doctrine, and the way in which my life is consistent with this, let no one look for any patience or any humility from me; especially not tyrants and persecutors of the Gospel. For in this regard they ought to consider me as a living saint, and treat me in no other way; if they do not want to, they ought to, for as long as I hold fast to my doctrine. Because God helps me, even to the very end; otherwise this matter would be lost. If my doctrine had no enemies other than the King of England, Duke George, the Pope, and their allies – wretched bubbles [343] of water! – then before now I would before now have resolved the matter with one particle of the Lord's Prayer. However, since there are others in their camp as well, I consider them such enemies as just-laid nits, who before lice are born from them are empty and barren membranes. However, I greatly applaud nits of the sort that from time to time boast and chant: "Here we sit, we nits, on the head of the most noble animal on the earth, in his hair. We are not members of a worthless family; our parents are lice, those great giants, who killed even the Roman Emperor Sulla and many others. What does it matter to us, if Luther is a mendicant?" It is true, you are all nits, but you have not yet become lice. Ah, but what is the world to God, and to God's Word? It is a little dust, Isaiah says; this is still less than nits.' [344]

And below he said, 'But why should I any longer be angry at the papists, who are publicly and by declaration my enemies, and do whatever they perpetrate against me according to the law of hostility, as is fitting? But these others are, in the first place, truly noxious to me: my tender little children, my little brothers, my beloved friends, those seditious spirits and Fanatics, who, as it seems to me, would have known nothing clearly about either Christ or about the Gospel, if Luther had not first written it; and certainly would have had great difficulty in bringing themselves out of the tyranny of the Pope into such freedom and light through their own knowledge. Or, if they had been able to do it, nevertheless they would not have dared to begin or to attempt the business.' [345]

And again, 'Up until this time' (he said) 'I had experienced and had suffered adversity on almost every side. But my Absalom, my beloved boy, had not yet fled from David his father, nor had he yet committed shameful deeds. My Judas, who terrified the disciples of Christ and betrayed his Master, had not yet done against me what was his to do. But now this thing is in motion.' [346]

Johannes Cochlaeus translated this pamphlet of Luther's into Latin, so that the English and Erasmus might know how this wretched man responded to their serious and painstaking books;[347] for in the same pamphlet Luther added these words, too, to his other vanities. 'What do I, a smoke-covered ash-worker, seek in the courts of Princes and Kings? where, I know, the Devil sits in the highest place, and there is his greatest throne. I am setting out to make the Devil righteous against his own will, and to find Christ in the Devil's house; deservedly, therefore, he gives me this reward: "Come back, good Luther, and seek John the Baptist one more time in the courts of Kings, where they are dressed in the softest clothes; I believe you will find him there." I am a sheep, and I remain a sheep, to believe this so easily and allow myself thus to be led and directed toward joking or flattering of this sort with household servants, and not much rather to follow my own sense. In this way, if I had given one blow to some tyrant or sublimely learned man, and they were angry on this account, I would then add thirty more blows to it, as an apology and penance. Let them understand from this in what way I will retract my doctrine.' [348]

To these things, Cochlaeus responded as follows: 'When Luther was inveighing against the Bishops, then the courts of Princes were to him as the most sacred monasteries, where Christ sat in the highest place. But now, when he is angry at the King of England, and at Duke George, the courts of Princes are to him the Devil's thrones, where the Devil sits in the highest place. In the same way, Erasmus too was to him the most learned and greatest theologian, so long as he hoped that Erasmus might join his faction. But as soon as he saw that Erasmus held a different opinion, straight away the good Erasmus became more unlearned even than all the Sophists. And so Karlstadt too was full of the Spirit of God, so long as he agreed with Luther; but soon, when he disagreed with Luther in even one particular, he turned into a Devil, entirely filled with the spirits of sedition. Finally, I would be very glad to learn whether Luther intends at length to discover the same thing about Christ. Certainly he has already snatched Christ away from the Pope, the Cardinals, the Bishops, priests, and monks, and has made Him flee from all Bishop's courts and monasteries. Nor, indeed, was he able to leave Him with the peasants; for he wrote that they were full of the Devil. If this, and things that he wrote about merchants, are true, then he will surely be unable to find the true Christ anywhere at all. He believed for some time that he would be able to find Him among poets and his beloved Greek-speakers, while they were his intimates and his bosom friends. But, since now they do not agree with him in every respect, they have become Fanatics, and seditious spirits, and they destroy Christ more than the papists do. So, where will he finally find or leave the good Christ? Nowhere at all, indeed, so far as one may conjecture, but among decowled nuns, whom he has received as fugitives and maintained in his house as though in a monastery. These women are completely submissive to his will, nor do they oppose him in anything. Therefore, Luther's Christ dwells in them, and performs His miracles in them; just as Luther himself pretended and published in an elegant pamphlet about one of these women, which tells how his Christ so miraculously offered aid to that woman in her escape from her convent.'349

But Erasmus learned that Luther was vainly boasting in this pamphlet of his that even Erasmus had been unable to answer anything to him concerning free will. Furthermore, Erasmus's friends were beseeching him, in frequent letters, at last to prepare and publish that fuller response which he had promised in his *Hyperaspistes*. And so he published a noteworthy and very thorough book. Indeed, in this book he so energetically and lucidly dissolved all of Luther's arguments about free will that neither Luther nor anyone else from the other sects has yet attempted to answer him. In that book, among many other things, Erasmus gave this general opinion about Luther's books:

'It seems to me' (he said) 'that I have noticed the following in Luther's writings. He is not always intent on the things he writes; it could not happen that a human mind should be eternally fixed on any business, but nevertheless his pen always runs on. And so, as the book grows, many things come into it, which do nothing other than fill up pages. Now he repeats, more than ten times, things he has already said, only varying the words; now he preaches, dealing with commonplaces; now he fills up pages with assertions; now he wastes time in crude witticisms and humorless jokes; now whatever offers itself or comes into his mind, he turns in some manner to his cause. And in addition to slanders, with which his nature overflows, he considers certain words as though they were some sort of magic, which influence the reader's mind not by reason, but by a certain vehemence – if the reader's mind is weak or little learned. For in these minds, imagination is extremely strong, according to the physicians, so much so that they frequently produce serious illnesses and even death. This happens when they are breathed on by any spirit at all – would it were the Holy Spirit. Irenaeus tells us that Valentinus and Marcion imposed on many by a similar art; and not just on weak women, but even on their judges. They used certain barbarous, unknown, vehement, and peremptory words: and by pronouncing these with an wondrous assurance, they terrified

their judges and led the weak astray into their own opinion. They even granted
the spirit of prophecy to women, again and again ordering, instructing, and
commanding them that they should at least open their mouths – asserting that
whatever the women said was prophecy. What would you? Weak minds take
heat from magic words, and are puffed up by them, no differently than those
who have pledged themselves to false voices become swollen up and rave, just
as if they were being harassed by the true words of the Exorcism. All of
Luther's books, and especially this latest one, abound in these sorts of voices.
Add to this the loquacity of the air of Dodona,[350] or anything that is more
loquacious than that, and at length the reader, however healthy and sane, will
be worn down by this tedium.'[351]

And below he said, 'Moreover, what could be more foolish, than to argue with
one who admits nothing except the words of Scripture, but reserves the interpretation of those words to himself alone? Nay, one who even permits himself
to invent whatever is useful, which can no more be gotten from the Scriptures
than milk from a stone? And yet he considers himself a wonderful debater; and
when the matter has been completed, he sings his own encomium.'[352]

And much later he said: 'What evidence he exhibits to the world, everyone
knows. If I had been persuaded that Luther was advancing the cause of God,
there is no monarch in the world so powerful that he could prevail upon me
to write even three words against Luther; I would sooner go into the fire. And
it is possible that I, either because of a lack of learning, or because of sluggish-
ness of intellect, may judge with insufficient subtlety about dogma. But certainly
common sense teaches me this, that it is not possible that someone advances
the cause of God with a sincere heart, who has incited so many turmoils in
the world, and who sports and takes delight in sarcasms and witticisms, and
is never satisfied. Nor can such arrogance, such as we have never seen in any
other before now, be free from folly. Nor is such jeering impudence congruent
with the Apostolic spirit; rather, annoying Princes and learned men with crude
witticisms and the indecorous word *Trotz* amounts in itself to handling God's
cause negligently. This diligence was the highest negligence. If Luther truly
desired to be diligent in God's work, he should have imitated Paul, who although
he was free among all people, made himself the slave of all; who became all
things for all people; who tried to please everyone in everything; who did not
seek the things that were his, but rather the things that were Christ's; who
did not pursue what was permissible, but rather what was serviceable; who
commanded us to refrain from every evil appearance, so that Christians'
propriety of conduct would be known to all people.'[353]

And a little later he said, 'What is this Gospel, which receives such people
(of whom we know there are too many), which acknowledges the bankrupt,
the whore, the gambler, the man ruined by banquets, leisure, and luxury, and
the one who refuses himself nothing, so long as he can write "Knight" after
his name, and thinks that this title gives him the right to defraud his creditor;
and if he receives the same treatment in return, takes it as a cause of enmity;
and as often as his poverty urges him, undertakes war on this side and that,

wherever there is hope of plunder, and decks out open robbery with the name of war. The right to declare war does not belong to a Prince, without the approval of the council; yet this man, who does not have a place to set his foot, declares war against whomsoever he pleases. And there is a place for such people in the New Gospel, although there was no place for them in a well-run city of the pagans. This is enough; it proves my teachings. What do deeds matter, so long as faith is present? I admit that of old the Gospel also received such people; but only when they had recovered their senses, only when they had been transformed. Now, indeed, they are so far from being corrected by the Gospel, that they rather seem to become worse; nor does it transpire that they cease from sinning, but rather that they sin with greater impunity. Now, if there was anything that needed to be corrected in our customs, or altered in our rites, this ought to have been carried out by the authority of great men, or at least at the consensus of the majority; and finally, it ought to have been done gradually; nor should anything have been taken away, unless something better were first prepared, which could assume its place. But now, certain men attack the business as if they could suddenly found a new world, all at once. There is nothing that does not displease them: constitutions, Orders of the Church, oil, the tonsure, the Mass, chants, churches, images, vestments, schools, ceremonies, studies, literature. Yet what excellent advantage have we seen result?

'Things have never been so well managed in human affairs, nor in this world will they ever be so well managed, that there were not many things worthy of correction. But the better course is to overlook many such matters, and many others ought to be condoned because of the feelings of the simple folk. Concerning those which cannot be borne, nor ought to be tolerated, if the cure which is suggested seems to involve more danger than the illness itself, then they should be corrected with care and by degrees, in such a way that they do not seem to be flung away, but to defer to the succession of things that are better than they. If Luther had exhibited this moderation, he would have found that the Princes and Electors, and those of the monks and theologians whom he now considers his most bitter enemies, were each of them most favorable to him.

'I say these things because I think that the way Luther wishes to be perceived is the cause of everything. For he presented himself as one who would restore the fallen customs of the Church, and not a few teachings that were accomplishing more for the people's convenience than for the glory of Christ, to their ancient purity. Now, all the best people had long since been sighing for this business. But since they perceived that, unless God inspired the Princes' minds, such a thing could not be tried without great damage to the public tranquility, they were wishing for it rather than hoping for it. Luther undertook this matter, to the greatest applause of the whole world; but he conducted himself in such a way that he seemed to seek for that rebellion, which he should first and foremost have avoided. Now it is not pleasing to me to detail what sort of disciples he has for the most part. It is sufficient to say that they are the sort that they are, because they approve his dogma. But Paul would not even break bread with a brother who was called covetous, or a whore-master, or accursed; but certainly many of Luther's followers are so harmful to the public tranquility, that even the Turk is said to despise the name of the Lutherans, through a hatred of sedition, although he tolerates Christians who are strangers to his dogma. Why should I mention here how much dissension there is among the Evangelists (for so they call themselves), how fierce the hatred, how bitter the disagreement, indeed, how great the inconstancy, when Luther himself has so often changed his likings? And from this point, new paradoxes spring up. Luther promises himself a wonderful memory among posterity. But I predict, rather, that it shall happen that no name under the sun will ever be more execrable than the name of Luther, among both Papists and Antipapists. He has provoked the Princes of this world, who are dedicated to this world, under the pretext of emending Church discipline, which all the best people favored; he has so enraged them, that he has both increased the strength of the adversaries on both sides, and has rendered the evil incurable. And, unless God comes to our aid by playing the part of a *deus ex machina*, this evil will never be assuaged without the greatest shedding of Christian blood. We have already seen the beginnings of this among the peasants. And in this state of affairs, he plays with his witticisms, and finds enjoyment in them.' [354]

These things, and many others of this sort, Erasmus wrote. And Luther was so completely silent in response to all these things that he never afterwards dared to annoy Erasmus further by any word at all, no matter how boldly he inveighed against others. Moreover, when the New Testament, translated into the German language by Luther and distorted in many places and embellished with completely false annotations that would confirm his heresies, was brought out and made public by the printers, in many thousand copies, and was publicly offered everywhere, the famous and most Catholic Prince, George, Duke of Saxony, not only rejected it with the utmost constancy in private, but also forbade it to his subjects in public Edicts, throughout his entire realm in Thuringia, Meissen, and Saxony; and because of this, he was met with great envy, hatred, and disparagement by the Lutherans, as though he were one who tyrannically suppressed the Word of God and persecuted the Gospel of Christ. For this reason it happened that the Chaplain Jerome Emser, who was most faithful and devoted to the Prince and who had already published *Annotations* to Luther's New Testament and had openly convicted him of many errors, now most faithfully translated the New Testament into German from the Latin version which is received and approved by the whole church. He made this translation at the order and request of the aforementioned Prince, who also made that work most commendable to all good and pious people by his own Preface. And for this reason it came about that Luther's Testament lost the largest part of its reputation and authority among the Germans, due to the popularity of Emser's edition.

For among other things the Prince says the following in his German preface: 'On account of these things we, after mature and deliberate consideration, and also on the mandate and commission of His Roman Imperial Majesty, Charles V, Most Merciful Lord of us all, forbade the aforesaid interpretation and New Testament of Luther to our beloved and faithful subjects, and by exertion that was wholly appropriate, good, and fatherly even ripped it from their hands, so that they might avoid pains and damnation both of body and of spirit. And wickedly attacking us on this ground, Luther and several of his accomplices accused us of being a tyrant and a persecutor and enemy of the Holy Scripture and the Word of God, who would not let it be freely read and preached in our lands. And in this, truly, they were most evilly troublesome to us. For we hope in the Lord, and all those who know us truly have never perceived otherwise than that we freely have heard the Gospel and Word of God, as it is received by the Catholic Church. Would that we followed it in our action also; which however we have striven to do, so far as God has bestowed grace upon us, and will continue to strive for hereafter, to the best of our power. Therefore we intended to suppress in our lands neither the true Gospel, nor the true word of God, but only the false doctrines, sermons, and writings of Luther and other pseudo-evangelical preachers. And in that purpose, God willing, we will persevere resolutely, through divine grace, until the end.

'Furthermore, we hope and are confident that those who will come after us, and to whom we are unknown, will easily consider us absolved from blame in this, from the following account of the fruits which have arisen from the doctrines of Luther and the other Fanatics. For although at first Luther undertook this matter under the pretext of a certain Reformation and emendation of abuses, which arose from both ecclesiastical and secular roots, nevertheless he soon proved, in words and deeds, that he did not intend to amend the situation, but entirely to overturn it. So, for instance, often he boasted that he would bring the business to such a point (nor did he ever cease from this labor, and he acted fiercely and mainly for its sake) that within a few years no temple, college, chapel, or monastery; no priest, monk, or nun; and in addition no Bishop, or Prince, should remain under Heaven. Nor was he content with these, but he even [intended] utterly to extinguish the whole Catholic Church, and our holy faith, partly through his own efforts, and partly through those of his fanatic followers and pseudo-Evangelists. And he tried to throw down not only the Saints, but even Christ Himself, from Heaven. For instance, Luther's followers in fact attacked, one after the other, first the Scholastic Doctors, then also the ancient, holy Doctors who are called "ecclesiastical," whose writings, canons, and decrees (which had been bestowed on them by the Holy Spirit for the edification of the Church) the Lutherans publicly burned in fires; they destroyed and cut into pieces the images of the saints and the statues of the Crucifix, which were set up not as idols, but merely for the sake of memory and to excite devotion among the people; and they did this not only in public streets, but even in the temples. All good works, such as virginal chastity, poverty, prayers, feast days, visitations of churches, processions, litanies, Matins, Vespers, and other canonical hours, and in addition vigils, masses for the dead, funeral processions, offerings of thirty masses, anniversaries, and whatever is done by the church with the approbation of pious souls, together with all the rites and ceremonies which have been observed since antiquity, they not only wickedly hold as trifles, but completely annul and omit. Furthermore, they have become so carnal and bestial, that even on holy Fridays, and on other set fast days, they eat and glut themselves on meat, not from necessity, but from sheer impudence and in disrespect of the Church. Moreover, they ask and desire that after their death, they may be buried not in consecrated, but in profane ground, just like any other irrational animal; and they ask that no other good thing be done for them, nor that they even be prayed for. And so that they might remain unpunished in all these matters, they have overthrown every power of the Councils and the Church, and have transferred power to the common people, not only over writings and councils, but even over both kinds of authority, Ecclesiastic or secular, for imposing judgment and punishment. And in addition they shamelessly attempted not only to do away with ceremonies and sacraments (such as the benediction of water, salt, herbs, candles, and other things of that sort, which − as Paul says − are sanctified in the temple through prayer and the word of God), but they even arrogantly attack the Sacraments themselves. These they so utterly reject, somehow, that they abide by no Sacrament, such as Confirmation, Extreme Unction, Holy Orders, Confession with penance and absolution, and the others; but they change and pervert the Sacraments in many various manners and forms, etc.' [355]

In that same year Luther published the *German Consolation*, to the people of Halle in Saxony, for the death of their preacher George, who, called to Asciburg by his Prince, was suddenly killed on his return by certain Knights, while he made his way through a vast forest. Nor is it completely clear why, unless it was as the rather widespread rumor said: that he had secretly contracted a marriage with a certain rich, noble, old lady, whose relatives, both because of the illicit marriage and for the woman's goods, which that priest laid hold of on the pretext of marriage, watched his journey and killed him − not in order to rob him, but for vengeance or through the desire to avoid scandal. For as soon as they had killed him, they fled through trackless places, seizing no booty or money for themselves. But Luther imputed that death to the Chief Lords of the Metropolitan Church of Mainz, as if by their scheming the traps had been laid for that George (who nevertheless had nothing to do with them). For among other things, he said as follows:

'The first part of our consolation, therefore, is that we know who the highwayman who killed our beloved brother George was: Namely, the Devil; although we cannot know who it was of his servants who ordered this, or which were the hands or arms that carried it out. For I hear that the Bishop of Mainz fervently defends himself as innocent − which from my heart I hope for, and I allow that it is so. But since I have known many Bishops, who certainly would have acted differently, if it was permitted to them by the tyrants of their Chapter; indeed, my mind is more inclined, if one of these two things must be believed, to believe that the tyrants of the Mainz Chapter incited a murder of this sort for lord George. For it is hardly a long time since they were intending a much greater slaughter, when in their murderous plan they were eager to stir up the German princes against each other and to drown Germany in an inundation of blood, through that noble blood, the Emperor Charles. They planned all this so that they might safely nurture their whores and their own libidinous bellies in peace and voluptuousness. Someone who schemes to plunge a whole province into murder and blood would consider it a trivial thing if he killed one single man. But God then forbade this evildoing to those murderous, blood-desiring dogs. So these are the ecclesiastical, holy people who sustain Christianity by masses and prayers, but who in addition to these things are intending and desiring to offer up the whole world, through treachery and murders, to that ancient murderer, their God, the Devil, etc.'

Johannes Cochlaeus, while he was at Mainz, responded without delay to these false statements of Luther's in a published book, which was also in German. And he reproached Luther with many impieties, by which Luther had schemed most maliciously against the Archbishop and his Chapter. Cochlaeus noted these and further said: 'However vehemently the lying monk rages, lies, and accuses, nevertheless there is certainly nothing dishonest or reprehensible in that consultation, about which he so furiously rails and shouts. For anyone at all is able to ask his superiors for counsel and help, for the maintenance of those things which are his, and for the conserving of his rights, without prejudice or damage to anyone. And the malicious monk has more enjoyment in exciting and conferring evils, one after another, and more greatly praises those who deny, to colleges, monasteries, and churches their owed property, income, and tithes, those who take these things away, transfer them, and seize them by force, contrary to God, contrary to appropriate behavior, to all law, and usurp them for themselves – he praises such people more than those who try to take away from no one that which is his, but who also desire to preserve their own goods. And although it is explicitly forbidden to churchmen, by both ecclesiastical and secular laws, to sell and transfer their goods, incomes and properties, Luther calls them murderers and traitors, when they do not wish to allow or permit ecclesiastical goods, which were donated to the service of God by pious people, to be seized by others, handed over, and transferred from the divine service to worldly pride, to whorings, and to revels.

'Therefore, since it is not permitted to them to sell or to give away goods of this type, how should they keep silent or connive at it, if others attempt, against the law, by force, to steal them, withhold them, or transfer them? O Luther, outstanding lawgiver on this point, the German Moses! For when he feared for his own skin, and therefore was praising the Princes, and was accusing the peasants, then he wrote as follows: "Our peasants want to make others' goods common property, and to retain their own property for themselves: indeed, fine Christians! I think" (he said) "that there is no Devil in Hell, but all have flown into the peasants: this madness is beyond all bound and measure, etc." Indeed, here Luther did not speak evilly, although he had earlier most wickedly taught such things to the peasants – just as I clearly demonstrated from his own writings when I responded to his book about the peasants. But I think that it is much more wicked that some men keep their own goods for themselves, and also steal the Church's goods and retain those as their own, in doing which they are most pleasing to Luther: when it would be much more tolerable, and further from the sin of avarice, if the Church's goods were turned not into private but into common use (as the peasants wanted), when once they had been transferred and stolen. But either one of these is against God, and against every law. For in the true Gospel Christ says, "Give to God those things which are God's, and to Caesar those things which are Caesar's." But He does not say, "Seize those things which are God's and give them to Caesar and the Princes of the world." Therefore, he who wishes to be a true Christian ought not to seize or to steal that which is his from any man, much less from God, but ought rather to give than to take away.'

And below Cochlaeus said: 'The false and lying accuser says, "Therefore it is certain, that Satan did this; I am not certain about accusing the Mainz Chapter, etc." From this sort of accusation, what judge would pass sentence against the good Lords of the Venerable Chapter of Mainz, in so great a capital charge, which bears on their body and life, their honor and substance; since common law dictates that in cases of this sort the proofs must be clearer than noonday light? Therefore, if Luther is uncertain about accusing the said Chapter, how then does he dare to call them tyrants and assassins? Or is it proof enough, that he says, "Thus I hear, I do not know for certain, thus I am informed? Certainly" (he says) "they called him from one Diocese, namely Magdeburg, into another, namely Mainz, to whose jurisdiction he did not belong. In addition, they killed him secretly and treacherously on the road. For thus I am informed, etc." But how may Luther know, or be able to prove, that the Mainz Chapter called that George from Asciburg? What business does the Mainz Chapter have with Magdeburg or Halle, and with the preachers of those cities? But Luther is, so he says, informed that George had been summoned by a letter from the Bishop. Oh most shameful mouth of slanderers, which dares so quickly to call princes and lords assassins and secret thieves, when it is not able to prove so savage an accusation, neither in its greatest nor its least point, nor in its first nor its last article! Etc.' [356]

That year was troublesome and destructive not only to Germany, but even to Italy, to the City of Rome, Mistress in important matters of worldly affairs, and Head of the Empire. For when the Pope, leaving the Emperor to one side, undertook a compact with the King of France and with the Venetians and the Florentines, then the Emperor's Captain, the Duke of Bourbon, who was in charge of the Italian army, began to harass the Pope's castles, and even his towns and cities. But when he saw that he was unequal to the conjoined forces of his enemies, and that his troops were lacking both supplies and money, he decided to try his utmost fortune. Therefore, he suddenly led his army out of the field of Bologna, against Rome herself, and he came there more quickly than was expected; and soon, when he arrived at the walls on 5 May, which was the third Sunday of Easter, he sent an envoy into the city, to seek safe passage and supplies. When this was denied, he sent the envoy back again to ask that the city be yielded to the Emperor. But the envoy, rejected and scorned by the Pope's Captain, returned to the Duke, who soon decided, after taking counsel with his men, to besiege Vatican City at first light.[357]

Nor did Fortune desert the daring; for immediately the Spanish troops scaled the walls, and the Germans broke down the gate, which is the closer to the Hospital of the Holy Spirit. However, the Duke himself, author of the victory, was not able to taste of that victory for long. For he was struck by a cannonball during the attack on the walls, and soon died, in that very hour in which he was the victor. But the soldiers, who knew that there would be no safety for them unless they followed through on their just-begun victory to their utmost strength (for outside the walls the Duke of Urbino was leading a great army against them, and inside there were no few men, both knights and foot soldiers, who were standing on the side of the Pope and the Romans). Accordingly, they gathered together into a mass and, breaking through by force, prepared an entry-way for themselves by using the sword against everything, slaughtering whomsoever they met. There was barely time for the Pope and those who were with him in the Palace to flee into Hadrian's Mound (which they call the Castle of Sant' Angelo). And so the German and Spanish soldiers, having no respect for sacred things in this fight, killed very many, not only in the atrium and portico of the Basilica of St Peter, but even in the shrine itself; and what is more, they poured out a great deal of blood both around the most holy altars, and around the memorials and monuments of the Apostles and of other Saints. And when the Vatican had been devastated in this way, they soon poured into that part of Rome which is called Trastevere, seizing everything as booty and forcing any and everyone to pay ransom for their lives. And since everyone they encountered was stunned by this sudden and unexpected terror, they invaded greater Rome on this same day, carried on by the very rush of their victory. They entered the city by the Sistine bridge, where there was much less slaughter than in the Vatican, but much more seizing of booty and of money. For since the Pope had been driven into the Castle Sant' Angelo, no one dared to oppose arms to the victorious troops: and so it was more a capitulation than a battle. Therefore, when Rome had been taken, captured, and invaded in this way, the fierce and unbridled soldier, in the absence of any leader, confiscated everything as booty, the sacred together with the profane. Capitulation saved no one from the soldier's plundering; sacredness of place saved no one; the name or favor of the Emperor or the Nation saved no one. All the inhabitants, whether they were Romans or Spaniards or Germans, when they had lost all their goods, were forced to ransom even their very bodies and lives, according to the estimation of their worth, as appraised by their furious and scoffing conqueror. A part of them fell to torment and the most savage torture, losing their lives along with their money; another part, once they had been ransomed, went away spontaneously, leaving everything behind, lest they be appraised again. For it was scarcely a rare occurrence for the same person, whether citizen or resident or member of the Curia, to be captured now by the Spaniards, now by the Germans, and to be tortured, 'appraised,' and ransomed by the exchange of money.

The Lutheran plague had crept into that army through certain Germans; and certainly the soldiers who were infected by it held all sacred matters in contempt. They laid hands on and despoiled sacred chalices no differently than profane ones; tossing aside the Venerable Sacrament, they seized for themselves the pyxes and silver monstrances; as a mockery of our religion, they clothed common camp-followers and grooms in holy vestments. They threw away the venerable relics of the Saints, as though they were the bones of dogs, when once the silver had been wrenched off of them; and they even raped holy virgins, just as though they were whores. A certain Lutheran, writing a history of this affair in German, affirms that a certain German soldier proclaimed that he had taken a vow, that he would devour a piece of the Pope's body, so that he might announce it to Luther, because the Pope had so far impeded the word of God. This author adds that the soldiers made a stable for their horses in the ancient Chapel of the Pope, in which his Choirs were accustomed daily to sing the Mass and the Canonical Hours, and that they spread about the Papal Bulls and Letters as bedding for the horses. He adds that, as a mockery, the soldiers put on the vestments and tokens of the Pope and the Cardinals, and that they made a mock-Pope from a peasant,[358] who said, in a mock counsel and creation of his Cardinals, that he would give the Papacy to Luther. And a certain soldier approved of this, and raised his hand on high; and then all the soldiers lifted their hands, and exclaimed, 'Luther for Pope! Luther for Pope!' All these things were done without the knowledge of the Emperor, nor did he ever approve of or ratify any of those things which the soldiers extorted from the Pope and the Cardinals by force or by fear.

But although that booty was the most sumptuous of any that ever came from any siege or battle, as much, indeed, as a German soldier could gain in two or three hundred years, nevertheless only a very few of the German soldiers were enriched from such great treasure: the best part of them lost all their goods in gaming, a great part died either from plague or heat; part lost their life, together with their booty, at the cannonballs' blow. And the greatest damage, which is especially deplored by the learned, was inflicted by the barbarian soldiers on the Vatican Library at St Peter's, where there was a most precious treasury of books, which, for the most part, the soldiers' barbarous fury ruined, destroyed, and most villainously tore apart. Moreover, the Pope, who had been besieged in the castle for a long time, at length bought peace with these soldiers, on the heaviest conditions. But the Emperor considered nothing that they had done either valid or pleasing;[359] rather, as soon as he was able, he reinstated the Pope in his previous liberty. The Lutherans sorrowed and grumbled greatly over this, because they would no longer be able to rejoice in or make use of this fruit of their Gospel.

There was then at Rome a certain Italian, who dressed in sackcloth had often foretold, before the capture of the city, that a great disaster was hanging over the city, unless the people would correct their evil life and by doing penance avert the wrath of God. And when he had often done this publicly with great outcries,[360] he was arrested and thrown into prison, where he had been detained until God gave proof, by the event itself, of what he had foretold. And when he was released from prison by the soldiers, he foretold to them as well, that their joy in that booty would be brief. Therefore, when these things which he had foretold came about, he was believed to have the spirit of prophecy – which the austerity of his life also demonstrated, since he had the name of John the Baptist and followed his manner of life.

But meanwhile, Germany was foully confounded with harmful dissensions among sects. And indeed, not only the Catholic Princes and Doctors, but even many Lutherans as well, earnestly strove to stamp these out. For the Duke Elector of Saxony publicly punished the Sacramentarians and the Anabaptists with prison, fines, and torture. And Luther himself published a very eloquent German book against Zwingli and Oecolampadius and other new Wycliffites, to which he gave the name *That These Words of Christ: This Is My Body, etc., Still Stand Firm, against the Fanatic Spirits.* And therefore he makes many complaints against the fanatics in that book, although very little forgetting or disguising his own boasting. For thus he says: 'Now in our times, when we saw that the Scripture was completely ignored [361] and the Devil was holding us captive and making fun of us with the mere straw and hay of human laws, we wished, through God's grace, to attend to this matter. And indeed, through immense and difficult labor, we brought the Scripture into the light, and we have bidden farewell to human precepts, and have made ourselves free, and have fled the Devil, although he strenuously resisted and still resists even now. Nevertheless, he has not forgotten his art, and among us too he has secretly sown some of his seed. But he does not halt at this point, but starts with the details, namely the Sacraments. Although in this matter he has already torn at least ten gaping holes and escape-routes in the Scripture, so that I never read a more shameful heresy, which at its very beginning had so many heads and so many sects for itself, even if they appear unanimous in the principal point, that is, in persecuting Christ. But he proceeds further, and attacks more articles: now, for instance, his eyes flash – Baptism, Original Sin, and Christ are nothing. Here once again there will be commotion over the Scripture, and such much discord, so many sects, that we will well be able to say, with Paul, "The mystery of lawlessness is already at work," because after him many sects were going to come into being.' [362] And a little later he says, 'I see nothing else in this matter than the wrath of God, who gives the Devil free rein to produce crude and clumsy errors of this sort, and palpable shadows; so that He may punish our filthy ingratitude, since we have considered the Holy Gospel so despicable and contemptible; and so that we may believe iniquity, as Paul says, because we did not receive the love of truth. Nor is anything lacking to this Fanaticism except some novelty. For we Germans are fellows of the sort who seize upon anything new and cling to it like fools. If anyone restrains us, he simply makes us even wilder for it; but if no one restrains us, we ourselves quickly grow tired and bored, and then go gaping after some other novelty.

And so the Devil has this advantage, that no doctrine and no dream can possibly arise that is so silly he cannot find disciples for it – the sillier, the quicker. But the Word of God alone remains into eternity; errors always spring up around it, and then die.' [363]

And below, after many other things, he says, 'Due to this talk I shall perhaps attract other Fanatics who may seize upon me and say, "If the Body of Christ is everywhere, therefore I shall eat it, and shall drink it in all the taverns, from every bowl, glass, and mug. And so there will be no difference between my table and the Lord's. Oh, how admirably we will eat Him!" For we unlucky and lost Germans are such disgusting pigs, for the most part, that we have neither discipline nor reason, and when we hear something about God we reckon it as if it were the stories of actors. Such words and deeds against that Sacrament are now being found, among the common people who have been seduced by the Fanatics' teaching, that one ought rather to die than to write even one sermon for them. For they immediately throw it down, when they hear that it is nothing, and they want to shit on it, and to wipe their buttocks with it. The secular power ought to punish blasphemers of this sort; it is impudence and reckless temerity. For they know nothing whatsoever about it, and nevertheless they blaspheme in this way. And God knows that I write unwillingly about high matters of this sort, when it is necessary that my writings be thrown before such dogs and pigs. But what should I do? The Fanatics, who drive me to these things, must give an answer for it. Do you now hear, you pig, you Fanatic, or whatever kind of irrational ass you are: Even if Christ's body is everywhere, nevertheless you will not immediately eat it, or drink it, or feel it on that accord. But I do speak to you about these things; get to your sty, pig, or into your filth, etc.' [364]

Such, therefore, was Luther's judgment at that time about the Germans, when he saw that very many people crossed over from his own sect to the new Fanatics. However, a few years previously, when they were in agreement with him, of his own accord he handed over to the Germans the power of judging every doctrine, and every matter, even the decrees of the Pope and the General Councils. But against that book of his to his Princes, the Elector of Saxony and the Landgrave of Hesse, Ulrich Zwingli and Johannes Oecolampadius quickly wrote other German books, which were safeguarding the opinion of Karlstadt about the Venerable Sacrament. And these two men always, for so long as they lived, were opposed to him. [365] And they had not a few confederates, especially at Strasbourg, Basel, Constance, Ulm, Augsburg, Zurich, and Bern. But the Revered Father John Fisher, Bishop of Rochester in England, most clearly refuted and convicted all of these men in five books; and Josse Clichthove, an outstanding theologian in France, did the same in two books, to which none of them has responded as of yet. Moreover, Johannes Cochlaeus translated Fisher's five prologues into German: but so great is the perversity and stubbornness of the demented common people that they will deign neither to hear nor to read anything in opposition, nor, once they have formed an opinion, will they ever appear to vacillate from it or to doubt it.

In addition, a new pseudo-prophet arose at Worms, Jacob Kautz, whose German name comes from Owl, about which Ovid says: 'The lazy owl, a dire omen for mortals.' This man, because he was a fluent preacher in German, led the populace, pursuing the desire of its ears, into every sort of error, wherever he desired. For this reason it happened, that in a short time he became so strong there, not only against the Lutherans but even against the Senate, that he did not even respect the neighboring Prince Duke Louis, although he was exceptionally powerful, being Palatine Count of the Rhine and Elector of the Empire. For Kautz inveighed against the Duke in these words in a public speech: 'You shall not drive me out,' he said, 'nor will I permit myself to be driven out by you. This is reason, since you did not receive me: indeed, if you want to expel me, whom you did not receive, I will not permit it, even if a thousand heads must perish because of this. But you say that I preach and teach nothing except that which tends toward sedition and the overthrow of the powerful. On that account, it is no wonder that I say to you, your reign and your power are against the Word of God, and are not from God, but are from the living Devil. Therefore, you shall not drive me out of here, unless first this whole region, and some other realms besides, are devastated on account of these things. I speak to you, since I have been sent here by God to teach you.' [366]

These things wrote Kautz, who two years previously is said to have been both an accomplice and an instigator for the rebelling peasants. But when two Lutherans strongly responded to him from a public stage, Kautz openly hung up seven articles, which he promised he would debate with them in the presence of the people; and they too publicly offered the same number of articles in response, so that this contention seemed little distant from sedition. But the Palatine Elector brought it about that shortly afterwards both adversaries were driven out of that city.

Among Kautz's articles two were pre-eminent, the Third and the Fourth, since they were notable beyond the others for their impiety. For the Third Article holds thus: 'Baptism of infants is definitely not from God, but directly contrary to God, and contrary to God's doctrine, which was given to us by Jesus Christ His Son.' [367] And the Fourth Article says thus: 'In the Sacrament or Supper of the Lord, there is neither the substantial body or blood of Christ, nor has its use ever been correctly celebrated here.' [368] Therefore, when Cochlaeus saw these articles at Mainz, he quickly published a German book addressed to the Senate of Worms, as a neighboring official body, briefly reproving the articles on both counts, and repeating the elegant letter of Cyprian to the Bishop of the Faithful, written in German; so that they might know that the baptism of infants has always existed in the Church of Christ. And he responded briefly to the articles in this manner: 'In the Third Article' (he said) 'Kautz is altogether a Pagan; for it has never been forbidden to baptize infants, and the baptism of infants has always existed in the Church. This is what the distinguished martyr Cyprian demonstrated both by many Scriptures and by many arguments in the eighth letter of his third book, *To the Faithful.*

But to forbid the baptism of infants is openly opposed both to Christ Himself and to His most holy doctrine. For Christ gave the command to baptize all peoples, excepting no one, neither old nor young. And He says, "Unless one be reborn through water and the Holy Spirit, he cannot enter into the Kingdom of God." John 3. Nay, indeed, he specifically mentioned infants, saying at Matthew 19, "Suffer the little children, and forbid them not to come unto me: for of such is the kingdom of Heaven." But Kautz does here as Luther has secretly done elsewhere, who in the first place attributed sin to children after baptism, and then claimed that unless the children have their own faith, they ought not to be baptized. However, we baptize infants in the Faith of the Holy Mother Church, and thus all sin is taken from them through baptism.

'But in the Fourth Article, Kautz is an unbelieving Jew. It would be fitting, therefore, that it should turn out for him as it has often turned out for the Jews, both in Germany and elsewhere, who punctured the Venerable Sacrament with needles, to find out if blood was contained in it. And 400 years ago, Berengarius the heretic, against whom many very famous books were written, recanted this article. But even in these times of ours, the King of England, and also the Bishop of Rochester, and many others, have argued seriously and powerfully from the Scriptures against Luther, who denies the holy conversion, or Transubstantiation, in this Sacrament. For it follows from that denial, that the body and blood of Christ are not there in substance, as they are not there before the words of consecration are offered. Therefore either part of these articles is long since worthy to be proscribed, to the utmost limits of the world, in honor of the Venerable Sacrament.' [369]

These things Cochlaeus wrote there. But in a letter to the Senate he added the following things also: 'Christ prayed to His Father for His people, on the Mount of Olives, that they might be one, just as He and the Father are One, John 17. Therefore, since so many sects arise from Luther's doctrine, you will very easily understand, that that doctrine is not from God, as is the doctrine and practice of the Holy Fathers of the Catholic Church; but rather, it is from the Father of Lies and Discords, just as all other heresies and schisms were from him. Therefore, since doctrine of this sort, which the Lutherans profess, has been condemned, not only by the Universal Council of Constance one hundred years ago and in many other Councils, but also in our own times by three Highest Pontiffs, and by all the Universities of the whole of Christendom; and even by His Imperial Majesty, and in addition by the entire Roman Empire, before you in your city six years ago; and now, after so many calamities and after the outpouring of so much blood, condemns itself through its own discords and its contradictory articles; no better advice at all could be given to you, that would be more useful or more healthful for you both in soul and in body, than that once and for all you banish all this conflict of theirs from yourselves, and drive out their error, one together with the other, from your city, and thus return again to ancient tranquility and Catholic unity. But if you permit them to write one book after another against each other by turns, and by turns to attack one another in daily speeches, you will certainly never arrive at peace. For there is no end to writing and speaking of this sort, Ecclesiastes 12. Nor is it your business to give any judgment in matters of this sort, which bear on all Christendom, or to appropriate for yourselves a final inquiry, without the counsel and knowledge of your superiors, both ecclesiastical and secular.'[370]

And he translated all those articles into Latin, and used these words in his preface to Robert Ridley, the distinguished theologian of England: 'Lest I seem entirely uncivil and ungrateful to you, I send to you certain articles of the new Evangelists of Worms, which, in the German version, they recently and with great pride affixed publicly to doors, and bandied about in stentorian speeches from the stage. Therefore, I send them to you, translated into Latin. Not, indeed, as a gift (for who indeed would consider so absurd, not to mention so barbarously impious a thing, worthy to serve as a gift?), but as a novelty, which perhaps you have never seen nor heard before. For you will see that in these articles the baptism of infants is openly prohibited, which (as I know) no Lutheran has prohibited before now. Luther has certainly proved harmful to baptism through various impieties, but he has never ordered rebaptism, and he has never forbidden (at least not openly) baptism to be applied to infants; although for various reasons I have written a book (sufficiently long, I think) against him concerning the baptism of infants. Therefore, so that the rest of his comrades in impiety might seem to be doing something, they invent something new, day and night, from which they themselves may acquire a name. For they know that Luther would not have gained a great name for himself, except by impieties; since earlier he was of such an unknown name, that he was not familiar even to his neighbors at Dresden or Leipzig. In fact, that name 'Luther' was not previously known, even to his parents. For he was called not Luther, but Luder by his parents, and he himself, at the beginning of this Tragedy, was called by himself now Luder, now Luter; but at length the name LUTHERUS seemed more august, so that for the glorifying of the Majesty of both the Prophet and the German Evangelist, that holy name was written everywhere in very large letters. No wonder Kautz has now burst forth with a similar sign and an equivalent omen: since his German name is owed to the bird that is most hateful to the other birds. I pray to God that He avert the omen! Certainly to me the name of Kautz seems far more abominable than that of Luther, since he offers more impiety in seven articles alone than Luther once offered in his 95 theses, at the beginning. Therefore, what should we think will happen, if Kautz spews forth as many books after these articles, as Luther did after those theses? How much more tolerable to us would be those Harpies of poetry, who befouled the table of Aeneas with their filthy flight, than is this Kautz, who with his all too ill-omened and abominable shriek defiles not the common table and human feasts, but the table of the Lord and the heavenly, divine bread, etc.'[371]

Other new articles of certain people were also being spread about, eight from Saxony and the same number from Moravia. The Anabaptists in Nicolsburg promised to argue for the latter, and a certain Apostate Premonstratensian Canon of Magdeburg promised to argue for the former. And truly, on either side they were raving with such impiety against Christ Himself, that even the Emperor Julian, who turned as an Apostate from Christianity to Paganism, was scarcely guilty of such shameful and absurd errors. For that Premonstratensian said as follows: 'There is no Hell. Christ did not descend into Hell; the Holy Patriarchs and prophets were not in Hell; when Christ said this phrase, "Eli eli lama sabachthani," he was damned, because he despaired; etc.' And those Moravians were saying, 'Christ was not the true God, but a prophet. His Gospel ought not to be preached publicly in Churches, but only privately in houses and to individuals.[372] Among Christians there should be no power and no magistrate; all things should be held in common among Christians. The Day of the Last Judgment will happen in two years. Etc.'[373]

There were other people as well, three hundred in number, who in Appenzell in Switzerland ascended a fortified mountain, as if they would be assumed thence into Heaven, body and soul together. For evil spirits had deprived them of all intelligence to such an extent that they cast aside all human modesty and gathered together in the manner of brute beasts, and they believed it to be necessary that they should be united with one another; to such an extent that not even virgins thought that they should abstain from this sort of intercourse. And such things were said to have been both preached and practiced, from Luther's doctrine, in the region of Saxony around Bremen. For Luther had written, 'A man is less able to go without a woman, and a woman a man, than to go without food, drink, and sleep, unless there be granted a high, rare, and even miraculous Grace.'

And a certain priest who was arrested in Swabia had said that the end of the Christian faith was at hand, and that another Law must be given. For just as the Law of Moses endured for fifteen hundred years, so also the Law of Christ had now endured for the same number of years; thus it was now the time for another Law to be given to men, and another Faith. Along with these sayings, other impious and absurd things of this sort were heard and done everywhere; and many Princes, moved by the shamefulness of these matters, not only threw men of this sort into chains, but in some places even condemned them to the extreme penalty. For in Rottenburg, at the Neckar River, many of the Anabaptists had been arrested, both men and women; and whichever ones of them refused to recant and to abjure their errors were punished with the ultimate penalty. Indeed, nine men were burned in the fire, and ten women were drowned in the water. But their teacher and leader Michael Sattler, an Apostate monk, who had sinned far more gravely, accepted this sentence in public judgment, that first his blasphemous tongue should be cut out by the executioner; then he should be tied upon a cart, and two pieces of his flesh should be torn out by red-hot pincers, in the marketplace; then in addition he should be mangled in the same way five times, in the street; and finally he should be burnt into ashes.[374] And this was done, on the 17th day of May. For he had seriously misled the people, teaching that the body and blood of Christ are not present in the Sacrament; that infants must not be baptized; that loyalty oaths must not be sworn to superiors; that the Turks must not be resisted;

that Saints must not be prayed to; etc. And thus in the citadel of the Elector
Palatine, which is called Alcea, many men of this sect were detained for a long
time, and brought before many judges, until at length they either recanted
their errors, or underwent punishment according to the laws. Thus also in
Bavaria, at Salzburg and Munich; thus it was in Austria at Vienna; thus in
Thuringia at Eisenach; thus at Augsburg and Worms, and in many other cities
of the Empire, many were detained in prisons and were corrected either by
punishments or by recantations and public penances.

When Cochlaeus saw the articles of the Moravians, in order to make it plain
to the Princes that nothing can be imagined so impious or absurd that it cannot
be given some disguise and color of probity from the great forest of the
Scriptures, if it is thus permitted that anyone at all may interpret the Scriptures
in a new way at will, he wrote for and against the question 'Whether Christ
is truly God,' from the Scriptures alone, giving not only arguments but also
answers on either side. And he added these words, among many others: 'Now
if, although my faith struggled against it, my conscience trembled, and my hair
stood on end as my mind shuddered, I could in a few hours of a single day
collect so many passages of Holy Scripture and twist them into an impious
sense, against my God and Savior; what, I pray, do you think that those Fanatics
could do, who at the just judgment of God have delivered themselves to false
understanding through heresy, and are going to write what they feel, what
they believe, what their mistaken faith and conscience declare to them? And
they will do this earnestly, and not at all unwillingly but with every effort and
to the utmost of their strength, not only on this day or that, but at all times:
for as long as they live, they will strive to establish and defend this article of
theirs by some deceit. They will even add rhetorical flourishes, they will bring
forward tropes, they will likewise counterfeit and conceal [375] many things.
Finally, they will use violence against the Scriptures, so that, all unwilling, the
Scriptures may be dragged forward and serve their intention; which all the
Lutherans whom I have known are especially accustomed to do, and Luther
himself above all. For thus he alleged against the Holy Sacrament in the first
article of his declaration: "The Scripture says" (he wrote) "at Romans 1,
Habakkuk 2, Hebrews 10, that 'The just man lives by his faith,' it does not say,
'The just man lives by the Sacraments.' The last chapter of Mark: 'Who will
have believed and will have been baptized.' And Romans 10: 'From the heart
one believes, towards justice.' And Romans 4, from Genesis 15: 'Abraham
believed in God, and it was credited to him as justice,'" Behold, how many
passages of Scripture are here, dragged forward by deceit and smoke,[376] which
actually speak about Faith, but the article is discussing the Sacraments. As
though, indeed, Faith and the Sacraments were opposed to one another, just
like white and black, which is not at all the case. And in his five hundred
articles, the seventh holds as follows: "So, just as Christ is not at all Christ,
thus a Monk or a Priest cannot be a Christian: since the Lord said, 'I came to
bring not peace, but a sword.'" Now, if I wished to cite Scriptures in a sense
so strange, so false and violent, for the purpose of arguing that Christ is not

God; indeed, I do not think that it would be difficult for me, even in one day, to bring forward more than six hundred passages of the Scriptures that would be able to have a better appearance of probity than the passages now cited by Luther have. But whether I (and may this not be!) or some Fanatic adduces, against the Divinity of Christ, ten times one hundred thousand passages in the Scriptures, nevertheless, the truth of the matter is that Christ remains truly God, and will so remain into eternity. And for us to believe this, against all the deceits and subtleties of the heretics, one saying of the Evangelist, albeit a brief one, is sufficient: "And the Word was God."'

And below he said, 'What would it profit, to kill those fanatics and the Lutheran peasants, when Luther remains alive, scattering his books abroad? For he is the root, which (as Moses says) sprouts gall and bitterness. He is the root of bitterness, as the Apostle calls him, which is growing tall, by which many are defiled. He is the Serpent's root, from which come forth many vipers, by whose blasphemous hissing we are now too greatly terrified. In vain, therefore, Princes, you cut down the branches and shoots of this evil, if you allow the root itself always to bear aloft some new fruit of evil. But once the root is cut out, the branches and shoots will soon wither of their own accord. For indeed, so he himself confesses and bruits about. For he says, "The papists think something which I myself almost believe: that, if there were no Luther, the Fanatics would become weak as quickly as possible, and would hurry away into hiding." Therefore, however vehemently he now struggles, with words, against those Fanatics of his, in very fact he does no less damage – nay, rather, much more – than the Fanatics. For their articles rise out of his doctrine in a swarm.[377] And if in Kautz's articles we most detest and execrate (as is right and pious) those which forbid that infants be baptized, and which deny that the body and blood of Christ are present in the Eucharist, still Luther provided the opportunity for those impieties long ago now, when he taught that sin remains in children after baptism, and that bread and wine remain in the Eucharist after consecration. For this is the root of that bitter fruit which we now at length condemn in Kautz, and which the Apostolic See, and you with it, condemned six years ago in Luther. Moreover, in those articles which were just recently made public in Moravia, I find nothing which is not most greatly to be detested and execrated; but nevertheless, these too, for the most part, take their seed from the Lutheran root.'

And again he said, 'Oh most admirable Gospel of the Lutherans! Which, according to Luther, is not a book of the law and of Christ's doctrine, nor requires our good works, but indeed condemns them. Indeed, according to Otto of Brunfels, the Gospel does not contain commands or precepts of Christ, but only recommendations; nor ought one to judge by the Scriptures, since they are merely a Cabalistic report, and an unheeding story, without the Holy Spirit. Moreover, following Kautz, he forbids infants to be baptized, and he rebaptizes adults, and teaches that every power and realm of Princes is from the living Devil, not from God. And according to other Fanatics, either the Gospel is nothing at all, or it should be preached only to individuals and in private homes. Behold, then, you Princes, the Four Gospels of the Lutherans, which indeed are so diverse and fractious that they neither wish to nor can agree either among themselves or with our Gospels. And these Fanatic Gospels are now forced upon the simple people, in the place of our Gospels, through a zeal that is no less malicious than it is seditious and destructive; so that all faith, peace, and ecclesiastical discipline may be destroyed, and may at last utterly perish – with, no doubt, a much greater slaughter and destruction than we suffered two years ago.' And below, 'But because these things happened some time ago they do not greatly move your spirits, certainly the things which are now happening every day will move you. For how many books, letters, and sermons, in these recent years, has Luther written about the Venerable Sacrament of the Eucharist, against the ancient faith of the Church? And how many have men of the Church written against him? And how many, today, both against him and against the Church, have Zwingli and Oecolampadius written – and how many others? (For Luther says, that the heresy has already been divided into more than ten sects.) And again, how many books have Catholic men written against Oecolampadius and Zwingli? How many have Luther and his cronies written? And what good do so many books do? What is the result of these harangues? Is it not that the faith, reverence, and devotion of the people toward that Sacrament are much less certain and less steadfast today than was the case ten years ago? Therefore, it would have been much safer and more steadfast, and also better and healthier, simply to have remained in the ancient faith of the Church, than thus to have allowed Luther a new disputation against the Church's faith. For we now see how many errors, how much doubt, have evilly grown from that disputation.

'But the Scriptures contain much less about the Sacrament of the Eucharist, than about Christ. For Christ is the Measure and the Theme of all Scripture, both of the Old and the New Testament. For thus He Himself said to the Apostles: "For it is necessary that all should be fulfilled, which is written in the law of Moses, and in the Prophets, and in the Psalms, concerning Me." Therefore, as many more books could be written, both by heretics and by Catholics, disagreeing about Christ, since more is contained in the Scriptures about Christ than about the Sacrament of the Eucharist. But what could be more disgraceful or more irreligious in us, than now at long last to call Him into doubt and dispute, on Whom all our salvation depends? "For there is" (says St Peter) "no salvation in any other at all" (Acts 4). Nor is there any other name under Heaven, which has been given to men, by which we may be saved. What more disgraceful news of us could reach the Turks and the Jews, than that now, at length, in the final days, we are in doubt because of our disputes and are disputing because of our doubt – about our Christ, Whom we hold to be not a Prophet, but the true God, and our only Savior, and from Whose Name we have been called Christians, throughout the whole world, for fifteen hundred years? When, I ask you, are the Turks permitted to dispute thus about their Mohammed? Or the Jews about Moses? And yet, the Jews do not regard Moses as God, nor do they take their name from him. But although their swords nowhere have power, but everywhere they humbly live as subjects, pay tribute, and are under the authority of another religion; nevertheless, they observe the law and the traditions of their elders with reverence and diligence, so that their restless or evil people, or their proud legal scholars, are never permitted to deviate either from Moses or from their elders' traditions, by so much as a finger's breadth, etc.' [378]

1528

But when Luther saw that such troublesome sects were growing strong, and when he heard bad things about them, although he himself was the first root and wellspring for all of these truly barbarous sects, he himself wrote a German book against the Anabaptists. [379] In that book he first complains that the leader of the Anabaptists, Dr Balthazar Hubmaier, unjustly made mention of Luther in his pamphlet, as though Luther agreed with his foolish opinion. Second, he complained against the Devil, because he had opened ten mouths, when Luther had closed one. Third, he imputes this evil to the Catholics, whom he calls papists, because they do not receive the Gospel, since under the authority of his own Prince there were no rebaptizers; but the shameless slanderer lies, since at Eisenach many were arrested and punished, under that Prince. Fourth, he rebukes the Princes, who condemn rebaptizers to death. For he says that everyone should be free to believe as he wishes. For if someone believes evilly, there will be enough punishment for him, eternally, in Hell; therefore no one should be punished by secular law. But Luther either does not know, or ignores, that there have been strictures against rebaptizers in public law since ancient times. Fifth, he recounts the good things which we receive from the Papacy, so that all of them should not be rejected due to hatred of the Pope. 'We admit' (he says) 'that there are many Christian goods under the Papacy, indeed all Christian goods, and even that they have flowed down to us from that source; indeed, we admit that true Holy Scripture exists in the Papacy, true Baptism, the true Sacrament of the altar, true powers for remission of sins, true office of preaching, true Catechism, concerning the Lord's prayer, and the Ten Commandments, and the articles of the Faith.' [380] Although he himself says the opposite, according to us (even though he condemns us as heretics) and according to all heretics the Sacred Scripture, Baptism, keys, catechism, etc., do exist. Sixth, finally, he argues against the Rebaptizers to the very end of the book, holding that one should trust not so much to the faith of the baptizer, or of the baptized, or of the sponsers, as in the promises of Christ and the undertaking of baptism: for faith is uncertain, but the Sacrament certain. And when the Rebaptizers say that it is never ordered in the Scriptures that infants have their own faith or that they should be baptized, he himself answers as follows: 'That infants should believe, we cannot prove by any passage of Scripture that clearly pronounces, in these or similar words: "Baptize infants, for they too believe." If anyone urges us to point out a verse of this sort, we must yield to him, and give him the victory, for we will never find it written.

But good Christians, and those endowed with reason, do not require such a thing of us; but argumentative and stiff-necked leaders of sects do require it. But on the other hand, neither do they themselves produce any verse that says "Baptize adults, and no infants." ' [381]

So Luther wrote then. But indeed, he had written a very different opinion about the same matter some years previously. For when he wrote to the Waldensians or Pighards of Bohemia, among those things which he reproved in them he included this article, that they baptize infants for their future faith, which they will follow as adults. For he said that it is preferable entirely to omit the baptism of infants than to baptize without faith; for the Sacraments neither should be nor can be received without faith. But if you receive the Sacrament without faith, you receive it to your own great evil. 'To this doctrine of yours' (he said) 'we oppose the word of Christ: Whoever shall believe and shall be baptized, he shall be saved, etc.' [382]

And so also he said, writing against Cochlaeus: 'We do not deny that infants should be baptized; nor do we affirm that they receive baptism without faith; but we say that they believe at baptism through the power of the Word by which they are exorcised, and through the Faith of the Church which offers them and by its prayers obtains Faith for them. Otherwise, it would pure and intolerable lying, when the baptizer asks of the infant whether he believes, and he will not be baptized unless it is answered by his proxy, "I believe." But why ask whether he believes, if it is certain, as Cochlaeus claims, that infants do not believe? Let it be, that Augustine says so at some point; but though it may be enough for Cochlaeus, that this has been said by a man, we want this saying to be proved by divine testimonies. Indeed, we assert that infants should not be baptized, if it is true that they do not believe through baptism, lest the Sacrament and Word of Majesty be mocked.' [383]

These things Luther wrote against Cochlaeus. But in that book against the Rebaptizers he wrote as follows: 'I both give thanks to God and rejoice, that I was baptized as an infant. For then I did what God commanded. Therefore whether I believed, or not, nevertheless I was baptized according to God's command. Baptism is true and certain; whether my faith up to the present day is certain or uncertain, I am able to tend it until I again believe and am made certain. In baptism nothing is lacking; in faith there is always a lack. We have enough labor to learn the Faith throughout the entire span of our life.' [384] Thus Luther wrote in contradiction of himself, as Cochlaeus later showed at length in his book *Seven-Headed Luther*, by various arguments supported by Luther's own words.

But when the Duke of Saxony, the Elector Prince, heard that many excessively barbaric things were being done in his lands against religion, he appointed four Visitors. Two of them were nobles, Lord Johannes from Plaunitz and Erasmus from Haubitz, and two were learned men, Jerome Schurff, Doctor of Law, and Philip Melanchthon, Master of Arts. And they, going around from town to town, everywhere were examining pastors and speakers, and were handing over to them a new rule of pastoring and teaching, midway between the Catholic and the Lutheran; for they were drawing something from each side. They pressed Catholics into this rule, or drove away those who resisted it; and they were restraining and regulating the overly ferocious Lutherans by the moderation of their Rule. The communities to which they traveled were driven to supply them at lavish expense. And they, indeed, acted rather moderately. But after them other appointed Visitors behaved themselves so imperiously and extravagantly that a Visitation of this kind seemed very serious and intolerable to all later Synods of Bishops and Communities of Archdeacons.

Philip Melanchthon first described that Visitation in Latin, and Luther afterwards described it in German. The latter was more wordy and imperious, the former more succinct and moderate. For Philip wrote twenty articles on the subject, with regard to the examination of priests by visitors, in which he used this beginning: 'Pastors' (he said) 'ought to follow the example of Christ: Since He taught penitence and the remission of sins, the pastors ought also to convey these things to the Churches. Now it is common to make a lot of talk about Faith, and yet it is not possible to understand what Faith is, unless there are set penances. Clearly, those who preach a faith without penitence pour new wine into old skins, and one without a doctrine of the fear of God, without a doctrine of the Law; and they lull the common people into a kind of fleshly security; that security is worse than were all the previous errors under the Pope.' [385] And below he wrote, 'If they are generous in alms, God will increase our private good, He will publicly give a richer crop, peace, and similar goods; not because of what we have done, but since He Himself promised such things to those who do so. And in the first place, they should be generous concerning priests, since it is written: "They are worthy of double honor."' [386] In addition, he wrote: 'I also wish to write something about free will as well and how it should be taught – about which many speak extremely unsuitably. And since they assert that we can do nothing at all, they teach nothing other than distrust, which provides many sins in the common people. For the human will is a free power, and can accomplish justice of the flesh, or civil justice, when it is so urged by law and force: as in "Thou shalt not steal, thou shalt not kill, thou shalt not commit adultery." For when Paul speaks of the justice of the flesh, he teaches that there is a certain part of justice, which the flesh, when compelled, accomplishes by its own powers. Romans 2: For the Gentiles do by nature those things which are of the Law. And what do they do, if not the justice of the flesh? But God establishes that justice. 1 Timothy 1: The Law was laid down for the unjust. For God wishes to correct the unlearned and those who are ignorant of the doctrine of the Law. Therefore let them teach that it is in our own hand, if driven by force, to restrain the flesh and to fulfill civil justice, and let them diligently urge the people toward living correctly. For God also established that justice, and gravely will punish those who live so neglectfully, and dream that this justice is not in our hands, if it is compelled. And just as we ought to use the other gifts of God well, so also we should use well those powers which God has entrusted to nature.' [387]

These things that Philip wrote on that occasion, and with a cunning moderation he was dictating many other things of this sort, which might render Luther's doctrine less absurd than earlier writings, both Luther's and his own, had done. And Luther himself agreed to these things in his *German Rule for Visitation.*[388] Here an opportunity was given to the Catholics for collecting many contradictions and disagreements from Luther's writings, by which they taught that according to the sentence of the Apostle Paul Luther was condemned by his own judgment, and was judged by his own mouth to have been as a worthless slave in the Gospel. Hence came that monstrous offspring of Germany, the *Seven-Headed Luther*, whom Cochlaeus published both in Latin and in German;[389] where seven heads, hideous in aspect and of diverse clothing and appearance, protrude from one cowl and yammer at one another, with the most shameful quarreling of words, over many things.

In that same year an amazing and horrible tragedy occurred at Basel, which the most learned Doctor Erasmus of Rotterdam wrote about privately to Johannes Cochlaeus, in these words: 'A few days ago, on 4 August, which was a Sunday, something happened at Basel that was truly a tragedy, and was almost worthy to be compared to Thyestes' feast.[390] A certain honest, rich citizen, Christopher Bomgartner, suspected that his wife Elizabeth (the daughter of a very rich businessman, Henry David by name) was having a secret association with a serving-man, whose name was Angelo. This was all a matter of jealousy, and was supported by no certain evidence. But, as it happened, his jealousy grew more bitter. When the serving-man was away, having been ordered by his lord to collect money from certain debtors, the husband entered his chamber, seeking – so I suppose – evidence by which he might prove his suspicion. And he found among the servant's clothing certain silken straps.

'He quickly summoned his wife and asked her if she recognized these straps. "Where did he get them?" he said; "for they are mine." She admitted that they had been given to the servant by her. Then the husband, hoping to extort the truth by means of fear, held the point of his dagger against his wife's stomach, promising that she would suffer no harm, if she would confess the truth, but threatening her with instant death if she did not confess. And in order to encourage her more toward confession, he first admitted that he himself had committed adultery, and that he suspected the same of his wife, but it was no more than suspicion. And she too confessed, for the first time, that she had been corrupted, after her husband pressed her for a long time.[391] And immediately her husband dismissed her. Terrified, she fled to her sister in a village named Prattelen. But a reconciliation was effected by her relatives and neighbors, for the husband presented himself as being appeasable. The woman returned on Saturday, 3 August, with several relatives and neighbors escorting her, whom the husband received with a merry drinking-party. They all left after congratulating him, and, so they say, on that night the husband and wife shared a bed, so that no trace of any ill-feeling seemed to remain. On the next day, which was Sunday, they breakfasted together in similar intimacy. Rumor reports that several relatives were also present at that meal, and that when it was done, the husband thanked them and asked them to come to dinner, saying that he would entertain them a little more sumptuously then. But this report is of uncertain credibility; this is certain, that shortly after breakfast, he sent away the serving-maid to hear a sermon, and his children from his previous marriage to buy pears. Having thus gained his solitude, he bolted the door, stabbed his pregnant wife, and shortly thereafter his little daughter, scarcely four years old. After these things were done, he himself wrote a letter to the Senate. Then, without delay, he climbed to the highest part of the house, called out the name of Jesus three times, and threw himself down headlong, so forcefully that he splattered the street with his brains, as the proverb for the Comrade says – but too tragically.[392] He tied the letter, which I mentioned above, with one of the laces of his shoes. In this letter was contained what he had done, for what reason, and what he was about to do. He killed the confessed adulteress – she had deserved that penalty; he killed his daughter, lest someone in after time should taunt her with her mother's and her father's crime. He was his own executioner, so that he would not die by a lengthy torture. He was condemned by the judges' sentences, and when his bones had been broken, he was displayed on a high wheel. Then, closed in a wooden casket, he was thrown into the Rhine. What will have happened to his soul, God knows. So savage and unheard-of a crime was such a blow to his father-in-law, his wife's father, that he was completely thunderstruck. The husband's brother, Jacob Bomgartner, went mad through grief[393] and now is in chains. However impious the example, it will not have been useless as a deterrent to adultery, which already had begun to be a joke among the Evangelicals.' [394]

Another tragedy of excessive malice, too, happened in that same year, due to the new inventions of the Lutheran faction. It happened as follows. Otto Pack, a Doctor of Laws, a noble man, and a secret follower of Luther, although he was a sworn Counselor of the pious and Catholic Prince George, Duke of Saxony, through evil deliberation boldly and openly undertook a crime that was worthy of his teacher, that is, one that was completely Luther-like.[395] For he invented the rule of a certain league, under the names of certain Catholic Princes, undertaken against the Elector of Saxony and the Landgrave of Hesse, through which he strove secretly to incite the Lutherans to arms – which he accomplished. For while he was performing the duties of a Counselor, through that opportunity he gained the secret Seal of the Prince, and pressed it on the 'Rule' of the supposed League, and then handed that over to the Landgrave of Hesse as though it were a great gift. And the Landgrave, when he saw the Seal of the Prince, immediately believed that the state of affairs was really thus. And after he had consulted with the Elector of Saxony, both of them prepared a strong army, with great zeal. When they led their army in public, none of the other princes knew who on earth they were going to attack with so great a preparation for war; the Landgrave sent a copy of the League to his father-in-law, George Duke of Saxony, with the earnest prayer, that either he would renounce such a League, or would promise that he would not bear arms either against the Landgrave or against the Elector of Saxony. But Duke George immediately responded in a German letter, on the very same day that he received the Landgrave's writings (that is, on the 6th day of the Ascension of the Lord). He wrote these words:

'Excellent Prince, Kind and Beloved Kinsman and Son, today I received a written from Your Grace, in which Your Grace indicates that a certain League has been formed against my cousin, the Elector of Saxony, and also against yourself, in which I too am implicated, which grieves Your Grace in your soul, and you would prefer to have lost a limb from your body than to have learned such a thing about me. A most kindly and humble prayer in God's name is added, that I should give an answer to Your Grace, in which I should repudiate this League, and do nothing against my Cousin and you, according to the wider tenor of the letter which I read. On this subject, I make it known to Your Grace, that however simple and unfit I may be, nevertheless may Your Lordship believe that I have enough fortitude of soul that, if anything had truly been done or achieved by me in this cause, I would not wish to deny it before Your Grace or before a Greater, Whom I rightly fear more than I fear you. But since this feigned copy, which Your Grace sent to me, contains so many lies in itself and can never be checked or proved by the original, I feel not a little astonishment that Your Grace accords belief to it and accuses me through it. I condole with Your Grace much more because you are my kinsman and my son, that Your Grace should permit yourself to be led astray by unfounded, false, and lying trifles of this type, and to be incited to rebellion; from which there could arise ruin and calamity for Your Grace, your wife and children, and your lands and subjects. I therefore say and also write that whoever has said to Your Grace that he has seen the original letter on which was bestowed my signature and my seal, or has said that he read or heard that Original, is a desperate, infamous, and perjured rascal. I will affirm this constantly, before anyone at all.

'Moreover, as a friend, and (just as Your Grace did) in God's name, I wish Your Grace to accept this request: that Your Grace might wish to undertake your business with greater deliberation than was done here; and that Your Grace will not wish to be urged to that chase, where another may rightly be hunted. Moreover, may Your Grace wish to show me that lying man, so that both I and anyone else may know to be on our guard against him. For if this is not done by Your Lordship, I could be moved to suspect that Your Lordship yourself forged that document, and thus wished to gain an opportunity for beginning your hostile will against me, a wretched old man. Furthermore, I shall not neglect to write to those who are included in the copy of this "League," which was made at Wroclaw, and to pass it on to them: in no way doubting that they will sufficiently absolve both themselves and me. For I well know that most of them neither were present there nor sent their spokesmen there. Therefore, I am conscious of no League, nor can it ever be shown that I know anything about it. For those things which are recounted against others in a copy of this sort are most certainly manifest lies. Moreover, whatever touches me in it is absolutely false. Therefore I now judge that if Your Grace had lost some member of your body on this account, you would now repent that fact, since it would have been done wholly in vain and for nothing. Nor is there any need for me to desist from or renounce something which by its own nature is nothing at all. I will conduct myself, God granting toward Your Grace and toward anyone at all in such a way that I may know I can answer for it honorably before God and my superiors, and before all the world. So I did not wish to conceal this response from Your Grace, whom I am prepared to serve. Given in haste at Dresden on the Day of Christ's Ascension, in the Year of the Lord 1528. Neither will I omit to write to my relative, so that I may tell him of these things. And His Grace will consider me thoroughly excused from them. George, Duke of Saxony, etc.' [396]

Moreover, names of other Princes are known from the text of the feigned League. For it had this opening: 'We, Ferdinand, by the Grace of God King of Bohemia, Regent for his Imperial Roman Majesty, Archduke of Austria, Duke of Burgundy and Wittenberg, Count of Tyrol, Etc.; and we, Albert, S. R. E.[397] of the Title of St Peter's Ad Vincula, Priest, Cardinal, Archbishop of Mainz and Magdeburg, Arch-Chancellor of the Holy Roman Empire for Germany; Elector Prince and Primate, Administrator of Halberstadt; and we, Joachim, Arch-Chamberlain of the Holy Roman Empire and Elector Prince; both Marquises of Brandenburg, Dukes of Stettin, Pomerania, Cassabia, and Wenden; Burgraves of Nuremberg, and Princes of Rugia; and we, Matthaeus S. R. E. of the Title of St Angelo, Priest, Cardinal, Archbishop of Salzburg, born Legate of the Apostolic Holiness and the Roman See, Etc.; and we, Wigand, Bishop of Bamberg; and we, Conrad, Bishop of Würtzburg and Duke of Franconia; and by the same Grace we, George, Duke of Saxony, Landgrave of Thuringia, and Marquis of Meissen; and we, the brothers Wilhelm and Louis, Dukes of Upper and Lower Bavaria, and Palatines of the Rhine – do acknowledge and make note, openly, by the virtue of this writing, that after many blasphemies and injuries, and offenses toward neighbors, arose in that dangerous and hostile state of affairs, which Almighty God let loose upon the human race because of its iniquities and sins.[398] Thus God is attacked with injuries and slanders not only against His Sacraments, which He instituted on the earth both for our bettering and for the strengthening of our weak conscience, but also against His own omnipotence and Godhead. Indeed, in this time temples and monasteries are robbed and laid waste, persons consecrated to God are expelled from His service, are driven into unseemly places, and are by force despoiled and deprived of their incomes and goods. And what is most horrifying of all, the office of the Sacred Mass is not only abolished, but is even ascribed to idolatry and sin. For us as Catholics – King, Elector Princes, Archbishops, Bishops, and Princes – because of the vow and the promise which we made to God our Creator (to Whom we, as His creatures, ought to submit ourselves without any intermediary, and at Whose feet we should throw ourselves), and similarly because of the oaths and sworn fidelity which part of us owe to His Apostolic Holiness, and all of us to His Imperial Roman Majesty, Our Lord, Most Merciful of all (to both of whom, as our superiors, we ought and are bound to show due obedience), nothing else is appropriate than to hasten to meet the abovementioned blasphemies of this kind, to put them to flight, and to change them for the better, etc.' [399]

But although all these Princes and Bishops denied, under guarantee of their own seals and signatures, that they had formed such a League, nevertheless the neighboring three Bishops could not have avoided the danger of war, if they had not paid out one hundred thousand gold coins. For a great army, prepared for invasion, was threatening them, unprepared and undefended as they were, from nearby. Therefore, although they were not involved in that league, they preferred nevertheless to buy peace than to undergo an unjust war. And so the Archbishop of Mainz contributed 40,000 gold coins, the Bishop of Würtzburg the same amount, and the Bishop of Bamberg 20,000. What else could they do? The Emperor was far away in Spain, and the Swiss Confederation could not bring help so suddenly. Moreover, the hearts of their subjects were for the most part infected with the Lutheran turmoil. The Bishops preferred, therefore, to suffer loss in money rather than in damages to their subjects, their fields, and their populations, or in the storming of their towns. For there was a fear that the specious pretext of the Word of God and the claim of defending the Gospel (which the Lutherans were babbling on about everywhere) might stir up all of Germany into confusion. Moreover, so that the Landgrave of Hesse might not seem to have forged that League of his own accord, he named the author, the abovementioned Otto Pack, and held him in custody, so that he might answer to his adversaries for this crime. Therefore, the Landgrave wrote to King Ferdinand, the Elector of Brandenburg, and George, Duke of Saxony, and named a certain day, for bringing a legal action against the aforesaid Pack, if they had anything to accuse him of. And they ordered the Speakers whom they sent to accuse him as a defendant on the charge of *lèse-majesté*. Therefore, on the second day of the week after the festival of St Margaret, the Speakers convened in the town of Cassel, where the Landgrave held a public audience. But before Pack was accused by those Speakers, the Landgrave ordered him to be questioned on three points by his own Chancellor, in their presence. First, whether he had spoken to the Landgrave about that League, which was made in Wroclaw. Secondly, whether he had given a copy of it, sealed with Duke George's ring, to the Landgrave at Dresden. Third, whether he had promised, in many writings, to turn over the original text of that League as well. Pack confessed all these things openly.

Next an opportunity of accusing him was given to the Speakers. And so Duke George's Chancellor, Dr Simon Pistor, a most famous and learned legal scholar, began to accuse the man of many crimes; and he convicted him of them by most certain documentary evidence, both in his own hand and in others'. And indeed Pack, because he was proud and extravagant, had spent a great deal more than he had in all his possessions. Therefore, by various fictions he cleverly cheated many people, so that they would give him loans. Indeed, he forged several letters which he sealed with Duke George's seal, while he was doing the duties of the Chancellor, so that he might acquire money from all parts through these letters. He pretended, and wrote, that he had given

8,000 gold pieces to Duke George, for the Prefecture of the town of Weissensee, for his lifetime. He forged credentials for himself, addressed to many, and sealed with the Duke's ring. He forged letters in which the Duke admitted that he owed 5,000 florins to him. And when he had been sent by the Duke as a Counselor to the Landgrave of Hesse, he secretly set out on a side journey to Johannes Waiwoda of Hungary, an enemy of King Ferdinand. And at Wroclaw he invented another League of many princes against King Ferdinand. In it he listed by name not only the kings of France, England, Denmark, and Scotland, and the Venetians; but also certain Princes of Germany, such as the Dukes of Gelders, Pomerania; the Elector of Saxony; the Landgrave of Hesse; and the Archbishop of Trier. Finally, under the deceit and pretext of that feigned League, which he asserted had been begun against the Elector of Saxony and the Landgrave of Hesse, he received four thousand gold coins from the Landgrave as a gift, so that he might satisfy his creditors; nevertheless, he was not able to satisfy all of them.

Therefore, when so many crimes had been imputed to Pack, and he could not and dared not respond to the inquiry, all the Speakers rose together and said to his face that he was an infamous, treacherous, perjured, and wicked fool, and sprung from a worthless stock, since he had slandered their Princes and Lords with the most wicked calumnies; he was convicted of the crime of falsity and of *lèse-majesté*. So they declared, and they asked the Landgrave and all the others assembled there to consider him as such, until he should prove that the League had been made by their Lords. But Pack, miserably confounded and dishonored, nevertheless escaped the punishment of death, due to the grace and kindness of the Landgrave. However, he became a fugitive and an exile, and could never again safely set foot in the lands of the Landgrave and the Elector of Saxony or of the other Princes whom he had defamed. Therefore, turned into a wanderer and a fugitive over the earth, like a second Cain, he betook himself, by a series of hiding-places, to the coastal cities. And in this way peace was restored to Germany.

But how much this matter grieved Luther can be seen from that letter which he wrote shortly afterwards to his comrade, the apostate Augustinian, in these words. 'To the man equally good and pious, Wenceslaus Linck, the servant of Christ in the Gospel at Nuremberg, his brother: Grace and peace. You know more news than I can write. You see what great movements have been set in motion by that League of the impious Princes, which they themselves deny. But I interpret Duke George's extremely cold excuse almost as a confession. But let them deny, let them excuse themselves, and let them pretend; I am in the know, and I know [400] that this League is not a mere nothing or a Chimera, although it is a monstrous enough monster. And the world knows that in spirit, deed, edict, and most obstinate zeal they hitherto tried and did such things, and that they are still doing them. For they want the Gospel to be wiped out, which no one can deny. But why do I write these things to you, who without any doubt are certain of them all? Simply so that you may know, that we too do not believe those impious people, even though we may offer, and wish for, and grant, peace. God will confound this most foolish of fools,[401] who like Moab will dare more than he can do, and will be proud beyond his powers, just as he has always done. We will pray against these murderers, and let them be indulged up to the present time. But if they shall undertake anything anew, we will pray to God, and then we will urge the Princes, that without any mercy they may be destroyed, since these people who are insatiable for bloodshed do not wish to rest, until they perceive that Germany is dripping with blood. Farewell, and pray for us. Sunday after Barnaby 1538 [sic]. Martin Luther.' [402]

At the beginning of that same year, a famous and scandalous Disputation was held among the Swiss in the town of Berne, which was initiated by Zwingli and Oecolampadius and their accomplices Wolfgang Capito and Martin Bucer, who were pre-eminent in the Zwinglian sect in Strasbourg, and two wicked Apostates, Berchtold Haller and Franz Kolb, who led the powerful and warlike populace of Berne astray in their faith. Therefore, since the Order of Disputation that was approved and published by the Bernese senate was openly prejudicial and unjust to the Catholics, but acceptable and overly favorable to the Zwing-lians, it happened that no Doctor of Theology from among the Catholics would dispute there, nor even attend, except for the Provincial Augustinian, Dr Conrad Tregarius; nor would any Bishop send his Speakers to this disputation, as they had sent them two years previously to the Disputation at Baden. For the ten Articles which they proposed for dispute there were openly impious and erroneous, against the Church, against the truth of the Eucharist and the Mass, and the other Sacraments; against the merits and the veneration of the Saints, against services for the dead; in brief, against almost all the received and approved rites and ceremonies of the Church. And the Order itself was so imperious, and so swelled-up with pride, that it summoned four Bishops personally to appear there; and, should they not appear together with learned men who were skilled in holy letters, then they would lose all Episcopal jurisdiction in the Bernese lands.

However, when this Order was made public, there were numerous counter arguments and urgings against it made to the Bernese through the writings of others. In the first of these, out of Speyer, the Bernese were earnestly forbidden by Imperial Law, in the name of His Imperial Majesty, to attend that Disputation. Then it was abundantly proven by the four Bishops, in many arguments, that it was not profitable for that Disputation to be held. And eight Catholic Cantons of Switzerland, among which the Lucernians held the foremost place, argued against it still more eloquently. Indeed, their admonition was so pious and faithful that their words seemed to proceed from their inmost vitals and the deepest places of their hearts, without any deceit. They reminded the Bernese of the Disputation of Baden, which the Bernese themselves, among the twelve Cantons, had chiefly both sought and approved. They reminded them of the confederations, promises, public decisions (as they called them), oaths, and many other remembrances, which were all going to be violated by this impious Disputation. They declared that a Disputation of this sort would be not only contrary to the Disputation of Baden, which was held two years previously by their common consensus and approval, but would also be contrary to the oath which both the city of Berne and their territories had offered, and contrary to their sealed decisions. Moreover, it would be contrary to their confederations, and to the regulations of the Catholic Church. And from such a Disputation, a great many evils would arise for them, and great detriments, scandals, damages, seditions, upheavals; in short, what evil would not arise?

But even Johannes Cochlaeus, who was then staying at Mainz, when at length he had seen that Order for Disputing that was enjoined in the Public Edict of the Bernese, immediately gathered together as many arguments against it as possible, which he sent to Berne by his own private messenger, through the vast distances of lands that separated Mainz and Berne. He did this at just the time when the Disputation had already begun. He reminded them of the Divine Law, of the authority of the Church, of the Apostolic See, of the Imperial Laws; let them not call the articles of our Faith, proven and received through so many centuries, back into doubt through this ill-omened Disputation! And he most especially reproved them for their method of judging disputed matters, according to which, with every explanation by the Doctors of the Church cast aside, Biblical Scripture alone ought to decide and judge between the sides — although the Scripture itself, in and of itself, is an inanimate object which cannot speak, nor can it judge which side understands and explains it more correctly. Nor can it cry out 'Hey!' or 'Woe!' [403] against those who treat it with violence, or who drag it, pulled along as it were by the hair, into an incorrect interpretation. But these Bernese were boldly claiming for themselves the authority to judge and to pronounce which side understands the Scripture more correctly, the Catholics, or the heretics. And beyond any doubt at all, they would award the victory to the heretics, at whose instigation both the Order for Disputing and the impious articles had been published. However, the Divine Law laid down no such method for investigating; but it ordered, if anything were ambiguous, that it should be laid before the High Priest, who was in office at that time, and that his judgment should stand, and that anyone who did not wish to acquiesce in his judgment should be put to death, Deut. 17.

Finally, lest they trust too much in the naked Scripture, and reject the exposition of the Doctors of the Church, he set before them three Propositions which were in themselves most false and even absurd. The first of these was, that Christ is not truly God. The second, that God ought to obey the Devil. The third, that Mary the Mother of God did not remain perpetually a virgin. The first of these was the error of certain Anabaptists, and of the ancient Ebionites; the second of John Wycliffe; the third of Helvidius. He proved these three propositions on both sides, from various passages in the Scriptures, now arguing for them, now against them; so that by these examples he might make clear that it is not at all difficult to excerpt different passages from so great a forest of Scripture, by which, according to the appearance [404] and the outermost surface of the letter, any proposition at all can be both proven and disproven. Therefore, unless one takes one's stand on the authority of the

Church, of the General Councils, and on the explanation of the holy Fathers
(who spoke by the Holy Spirit) as upon a certain teacher of the truth – then,
according to the surface of the letter, everything can be called into doubt and
perverted by heretics.

But the Bernese contemptuously disregarded all these things and held their
Disputation; they disputed for seven days, until 26 January. Finally, they judged
that the ten articles were rightly proven, and were founded in the Scriptures.
Therefore, they soon instituted a new Reformation, in which they first ordered
that the ten articles be approved by all their subjects. Then that their subjects
should no longer be obedient to any of the four Bishops in ecclesiastical matters:
not in cases of matrimony; not in excommunications and absolutions; not in
the perception of the chrism; not in the offerings of tithes and first fruits, etc.
Then they absolved Deacons, Chamberlains, Pastors, Preachers, and all sorts
of ministers of the Church from the oaths which they had taken to the Bishop.
Furthermore, since the altars and images in their city had already been
demolished everywhere in their churches, they utterly abolished the Mass, and
ordered their subjects to do the same throughout all their territory. Then they
took away all masses, funeral rites, anniversary celebrations, and commemora-
tions of the dead from the fraternity of the living; they took away dedications
of temples, the habits of monks and nuns, the usage of sacred vestments, the
days of fasting, the feasts of the saints, and what not? Moreover, they permitted
priests to take wives, monks new brides, and nuns sacrilegious husbands. In
the end, moreover, so that they might prolong the uncertainty of their faith
and the trembling and fear of their conscience, they added that whenever they
might learn better things, they would freely embrace them, and would either
add to or diminish that Reformation.

But since in the Disputation of Berne, just as in the one at Baden, both the
spoken and the written proceedings had taken place in German before the laity,
Dr Johannes Eck refuted the Disputation in German, and Dr Johannes Cochlaeus did the same for the Bernese debate. Eck wrote at length and with great
subtlety; Cochlaeus, briefly and very simply, as was fitted to the understanding
of the laity. In addition to the ten articles of the Disputation, Eck recounted
also another twenty-five erroneous articles which they allowed into that Disputation. Moreover, ten of these articles were self-contradictory, and fifteen
were contradictory to the passages of Scripture, which they falsified during
their Disputing.

Cochlaeus, before he refuted the Reformation article by article, reproved the
Bernese for contempt and negligence toward the learned men whom they
should have summoned to their Disputation, most especially Dr Eck. Then he
reproved them for the incivility with which Dr Conrad Tregarius, the Provincial
Augustinian and a native Swiss, had been mistreated during that Disputation.
Then he responded point by point to the Chapters of the Reformation. From
these, it would be worth the trouble to quote a few about the Thirtieth Chapter,
as an example. 'In the Thirtieth Chapter,' (he said) 'You permit cloistered
persons to desert their monasteries and enter into matrimony; and, to encourage

them to do this, you wish to restore to them those goods which they brought into the monastery with them. If these goods were very small, you want to add more to them, whenever these people leave, whether they enter into matrimony or not. O my good lords, how great an enemy the author of a Reformation of this sort is both to your honor and to the salvation of your souls! How, I pray you, can you be so forgetful of all Scripture, of all law and statute, of all discipline and decency? How could you be permitted, you who are sworn by your oath, so shamefully and wickedly to undo oaths and vows that were offered to God, and to grant that which is not by any means under your authority? Decent regard for the law was established even among the Gentiles and the ancient Romans, so that they kept oaths and pacts, even those made to an enemy; but you do not want even those made to God to be kept! How, I ask, could you be greater or more vehement enemies of God and the Church than you are by doing this? You yourselves, consider. Now, how can a greater sorrow, or a greater wrong, be done to anyone, than if his bride or his wife should be abducted or snatched away? Or than if his son or daughter, with all honor lost, should be reduced to dishonor, publicly, before the whole world? Now nuns are the brides and wives of Christ, our God and Lord: Canticles 4, John 3, 2 Corinth. 11, Ephe. 5, Revelation 21. And they are the daughters of the Holy Mother Church, Galatians 4, 1 Corinth. 4, Psalms 44 and 47, Canticles 3, 1 Peter 3. Therefore, how do you presume, against all statute, against all Scripture and decency, to rescind their vows? Order your Apostates, I beg you, to scrutinize both every passage of Scripture and every history, to see if they can find that ever, in any province in the entire world, any concession was given to monks and nuns to enter into matrimony or to return from their monasteries into the world. For it is manifestly against God, thus to invalidate vows: Numbers 30, Deut. 23, Psalms 65, Eccle. 5. And it is against Christ: Matthew 8 and 19, Luke 9 and 14. And it is against Paul: 1 Tim. 5, where those who make their first faith (that is, their vow) invalid are condemned. Moreover, it would take too long to recount here what holy Councils, and Holy Pontiffs and Catholic Doctors, have written and decreed against this sin, and it would also be invalid and useless to do so among you, who despise all such things. However, I will recite to you the Imperial Law from the Codex, so that you may learn from it what you here deserve to learn, etc.' [405]

When Luther saw that Zwingli and Oecolampadius were growing stronger day by day, he again wrote a very long book against them in German. Its title is *Luther's Confession concerning Christ's Supper*. In the first part of it he censures and refutes Zwingli; in the second, Oecolampadius. Finally, in the third part he offers the confession of his faith, which he orders to be taken for the certain and final opinion of his mind, both in his life and after his death. In the first part, he brings many reproaches against Zwingli and his accomplices, which the Catholics had earlier, much more justly, brought against Luther himself. For instance, that disagreement and division of this sort among them come not from the Holy Spirit, but from Satan; that their Spirit of Confusion contradicts itself; that it should easily be concluded, that the Devil, Father of all dissension, is their teacher; that dissension in intellect and in speech comes from the Devil, etc. In the second part he contradicts himself, when he denies that there was wine at Christ's supper, since Christ had said 'I shall not drink from the fruit of the vine,' etc. But he had often previously confirmed it, both in his *Babylonian Captivity* and elsewhere, when he derided transubstantiation and the doctrine of accidents without substance. He also affirms there that Christ did not only give the cup to His Disciples, but drank from it Himself as well: which he had earlier denied in his book *On Revoking the Mass*, where he taught that the priests ought to give the Sacrament to others, but ought not to partake of it themselves, since Christ too had done so.

Moreover, in the third part, he lists among the articles of his faith that Free Will must not be believed in. 'I here simultaneously reject and condemn' (he says) 'as pure errors, every doctrine which boasts of our Free Will.[406] Moreover, I affirm that vigils, masses, and anniversary days for the dead are useless, and annual fairs of the Devil. And also, that the Saints must not be invoked. And also, that Extreme Unction, matrimony, and the Ordination of Priests are not Sacraments. But above all other abominations I hold the Mass, when it is preached or sold as a sacrifice or a good work, on which basis all colleges or monasteries of the Churches now are established; but, God granting it, they will soon lie fallen. For however great, weighty, and shameful a sinner I have been, who wasted and lost my youth in a damnable manner, nevertheless these were my greatest sins, that I was so holy a monk, and for more than fifteen years so horribly offended my beloved Lord with so many Masses, and inflicted martyrdom and tortures on Him.' [407]

These things Luther said in that book. And in the same year he published another book in German against the papists (as he calls the Catholics) about Communion in both kinds. In that book he sports, plays the buffoon, and snaps with amazing jests, while he boasts how much progress his doctrine has made even among the papists, who truth to tell are more Lutheran than Luther himself. For the canons and other priests and monks have learned very well to omit the Canonical hours or to treat them with neglect, and they are so strong in their own consciences that they no longer seek for a Papal dispensation. Moreover, the Bishops now know how to disregard an interdict and excommunication, when the Emperor was holding the Pope captive, which before Luther's doctrine they would scarcely have borne. Finally, the Princes who constantly pursue Luther with hatred are more Lutheran than those who foster Luther, since they take money, precious jewels, and ornaments from churches and monasteries, and seize them for themselves, and plot no less against their immovable goods by imposing many taxes upon them. Indeed, the Princes seek out treacherous writs and leagues against the Lutherans, which they themselves later blush over, etc.

From this book Johannes Cochlaeus excerpted 144 slanders and fifty distortions, which he refuted in Latin in brief little responses. He did this especially for the benefit of the Bishop of Rochester, whom he asked once again to publish something against Luther for the sakes of the Germans, who among all the adversaries of Luther granted most to him (justly, indeed). 'I wished' (he said in the preface) 'to collect for your Reverend Honor into one fascicule the calumnies, distortions, vanities, boasts, perversities, impieties, and blasphemies of that man against us, from one little German book of his. And I had already marked them all for myself in the margin by certain notations, when I skimmed through the booklet. But while answering I was overcome by such weariness that my soul was scarcely able to sustain such great nausea and worry until I could append brief responses to his calumnies and distortions. There was a twofold cause of such labor for me on your behalf, Reverend Father. The first cause was so that you might know how great his dishonesty is in his native tongue; and the second, that you might immediately write on the subject, not indeed to him, but to the Princes of the Empire, and to the Nobility of Germany, so that they might learn, although late, to what end all attempts at new sects tend, etc.' [408]

1529

However, when a transcript of the letter Luther wrote to Linck (the tenor of which was given above) had come from Nuremberg to Dresden, the Most Illustrious Duke George of Saxony sent a copy of it to Luther, inquiring through a letter if he would admit that this letter had been written and sent by him. But Luther answered impudently and ambiguously, and asked that the Duke not try his patience with such scraps of paper and transcripts of letters.[409] When the Duke could not learn the truth from Luther's response (since Luther neither denied nor acknowledged that letter), he sent a certain one of his secretaries from Nuremberg to the Senate, asking that Wenceslaus Linck be questioned about the letter, if it really had been sent to him by Luther. And when Linck was questioned, he openly confessed to the Senate that the letter was Luther's. However, he had passed the letter on to certain friends, in simplicity of mind and without any evil deceit, nor with any desire of accusing or offending either Duke George or anyone else. But that it had been copied and more widely published had been done without his knowledge or will. There the Secretary saw, through a certain friend, the original letter, of which he received a copy. When the copy was brought from Dresden, it agreed with the original. Therefore, since the Duke was now certain that the letter had been written by Luther, and because he knew that Luther had made public mention in a manner overly hateful and distrustful of that League of Princes (which he called seditious and treacherous) – nay, rather, that he had openly asserted it in that book which he had published against the Bishop of Meissen, concerning the sacrament in both kinds – the good Prince once again, in public letters, cleared and absolved himself of that fictitious League, which Dr Otto Pack had first suggested to the Landgrave of Hesse. And the Duke did this much more clearly and by more arguments than he had previously done in his writing to the Landgrave, both concerning the unjust suspicions which the writings of Luther produced and concerning Dr Pack, who had already been amply convicted of false crime in Cassel. And so it would be worth the trouble to quote here certain words of the Prince, translated from German into Latin. 'We' (he said), 'are certain about this – glory be to God! – that all this with which we are accused is most false, and neither Luther nor any of his partisans could bring forward even the lightest argument, from which it could be plausibly conjectured, considered, or proven that we ever deliberated on, incited, or even thought about these things which that feigned League contains. Nevertheless, this man of the Gospel [410] is so bold and impudent that he does not hesitate to preach this brilliant lie, not just as something that he had heard, but as though it were proven truth, despite the fact that all those whom that falsehood accuses clear themselves by denying it with one voice; nor does he hesitate to scatter it among the common people, and to write about us by name in the following words: "I interpret the extremely cold excuse of Duke George almost as a confession." How "cold" our defense was, the words themselves reveal. Nor do we yet see, by what more vehement or ardent a denial we could have repelled that accusation. But if this was as cold, and similar to a confession, as Luther claims, it certainly never displayed the name of an informer. And for that reason my response had much more fervor than the accusation of Luther, Pack, and all those others, etc.'

Then he produced, along with other arguments about that false and fictive League, eight proofs from the style itself and the tenor of the words, by which he showed that the author of the falsehood had erred, both in the titles of Princes and in various other matters. Moreover, Luther had written that he himself knew well that the League was neither nothing at all nor a Chimera. The Prince cleverly turned this back around on him: 'Indeed, he knows it so well, because he himself, perhaps, took part in preparing it, or gave advice about preparing this falsehood.' And the Prince did not want Luther to be free from that suspicion, until he should produce plausible proofs of his certain knowledge. Therefore, he wrote to his cousin Duke Johannes, the Prince Elector of Saxony, under whose shadow and protection Luther was lurking, and requested that Duke Johannes at least ask Luther whether he knew that the League was not feigned. But he was unable to find anything out by this method, either.

But Luther, like an enraged hornet, published a German book, to which he gave the title *Concerning Private Letters that have been snatched away by theft.* Indeed, in it he raved against the most honest Prince so coarsely and petulantly that such indecent crudity was even displeasing to not a few Lutherans. And so Johannes Cochlaeus, moved by indignation over this matter, wrote a book in German against Luther. In it, in addition to Luther's lies, he noted several of Luther's lapses both in the exposition of a Psalm and concerning the Hebrew language (of which he had once a modest study, at Rome, under the instruction of the Jew Elias). Cochlaeus dedicated this book to the Noble and Illustrious Princes and Lords, Johannes and Frederick, sons of Duke George. In its preface he said, among other things, 'And indeed, it is deservedly both heavy and troublesome to hear that this extremely malicious, and already long since condemned, bewailed-for, and disreputable Apostate, has dared so much against the most powerful and most praised house of Saxony, as though against any good man living in the Saxon realm. I say nothing about the fact that he dares to accuse and harass so blameless a Prince, and one praised in every fashion, and to do so with such lies, taunts, slanders, and injuries of every kind, openly before the whole world, and that along the way he scatters seditious lies and curses on many other Princes too, and even on the business of the Public Assemblies of the Empire. For instance, he wrote that the Edict of Worms (in which he was condemned as an obstinate heretic) had been promulgated without the agreement of all the best and highest Orders of the Empire; although His Imperial Majesty openly bears witness, in that Edict itself, that it was done according to the opinion and agreement not only of himself but of all the Elector Princes of the Holy Empire and the other orders then gathered together. And indeed he testifies to this three times in that Edict, and thus three times convicts Luther of lying. Therefore, since there is no one who does not know how shamelessly this monk habitually gathers together in his writing lies of every sort, and with them many most empty trifles and most petulant jeers, no differently than if he were some exceedingly annoyed buffoon or a bawd burning with anger, there is no cause for Your Highnesses to be greatly disturbed by his insults, just as your father is not disturbed. Your father is accustomed to say that he is no more disturbed, if Luther hurls an insult at him, than he used to be when his jester, who was named Pastor, had insulted him, etc.'

At this same time this same Cochlaeus published a rather long book in Latin, which was entitled *The Seven-Headed Luther*. He compiled this book from several short works of Luther, both in Latin and in German, for two reasons especially: first, for the sake of Catholic preachers,[411] so that they would be able easily to refute and disprove the Lutherans on any proposed theme, from Luther's own writings, without the work and tedium of a lengthy investigation; and secondly for the sake of foreign nations, so that learned men who were not fluent in the German language might in any future Counsel have a brief compendium from which they could read what Luther had written in German, and so might more easily judge him from his own mouth to be a worthless slave. Moreover, in the preface of this book, after he had advised the reader on how he might read the book with some benefit, Cochlaeus appended the following: 'Think, reader, I beg you, how dangerous it is to cling firmly to, and to be on the side of, a man who is so unstable everywhere in himself; or to believe more in him than in the whole Church, when he so frequently contradicts and does not believe himself, and condemns himself by his own judgment, and renders himself a liar. Indeed, he triumphantly casts as a reproach at the Fanatics (now his adversaries, but just a little while ago his most beloved little brothers, his little children and his golden friends) that "Where so much diversity about one thing is found, there are mere lies and works of the devil" – as for instance, concerning the Sacrament of the Eucharist. But how much more justly, I pray you, could we cast this same reproach at him, who, although he is one individual in substance, divides himself, through contrary assertions, into seven heads? Indeed, Africa once upon a time bore many monsters, but now Germany bears a monster still more wondrous. For what could be more monstrous than that so many heads, so contrary and dissimilar to one another, should reside in one cowl? What is Two-Faced Janus to this? What is Triple-Bodied Geryon? What is Triple-Jawed Cerberus? They are the stories and the humorous inventions of poets. But the Seven-Headed Cowl, indeed this cowled dragon of ours, all too truly and seriously confounds Germany with his seven heads, and lethally exhales the most evil poisons on it, and corrupts it. Who ever before saw such a portent, I ask you? Indeed, it is a marvelous mystery, one sublime and venerable beyond all sense or understanding, and full of Majesty, that in one Deity there are Three, and these Three are One: One in substance, Three in Persons. But in one cowl of one Luther there are seven, and these seven are not just one in substance, but one also in person. Indeed, a marvelous Theology, unheard before now not just by Jews and Gentiles, but also by Christians! In the ancient Christendom, there was one heart and one spirit of the host of the faithful: but in the new Gospel of Luther, the heart and the body are divided into many hearts and many heads; so that not only do the different ones perceive different things, but also the one claims senses and many heads for himself. Indeed, we have briefly searched out seven of them, as we unwillingly and with great tedium and nausea read Luther's books. But if anyone wishes for more monsters or more heads in these books, let him merely search about and inspect a little more diligently, and he will without question find very many, more marvelous still; and indeed, they will be so absurd, impious, blasphemous, that a pious and reverent man would not dare to say them with his tongue, nor to think about them or contemplate them in his mind.'[412]

In that same year, there was again at Speyer a famous Assembly of Princes and the other Orders and Estates of the Holy Roman Empire, for very much the same reasons as those for which the assembly had been held at the same place three years previously – except that greater necessity and greater dangers seemed to threaten. For the Tyrant of the Turks was now more powerful than before, since Hungary had been subdued and Buda conquered, and it was said that he was heading for Germany with a greater army; and in the Christian religion dissension was increasing day by day, while the sects were growing so strong that they were formidable not only to the Catholics but among themselves to one another. For the Zwinglian faction was now prevalent over the Lutheran sect among the Swiss and in many Imperial cities, such as Strasbourg, Constance, Ulm, Augsburg, etc., and both of these sects, no less than the Catholics themselves, suspected the Anabaptists of violent outbreaks and terrible savagery because of their secret conspiracies in several places. But just as much was accomplished in this Assembly as in the previous one. King Ferdinand, who both grieved over the occupation of Hungary and anxiously feared that he might lose his ancestral provinces Austria, Styria, Carinthia, etc., could obtain no aid from the sects, unless he permitted them to continue in their opinions peacefully and securely. Therefore, since necessity was driving him, he agreed in a public decree that, so far as faith and religion were concerned, each individual should be permitted to act and to believe in such a way that he would be prepared to render account both to God and to the Emperor about his deeds. And so it was left when the Assembly was dissolved.

Philip Melanchthon, whom the Illustrious Prince Elector Johannes Duke of Saxony had brought with him to Speyer, wrote two Letters to Speyer, which he made public. One was to King Ferdinand, and he gave it this title, *Preface to Daniel*; however, it was a preface without a book. But once he had captured the King's good will by praise both of the King himself and of his grandfather the Emperor Maximilian, he began to commend his Luther, and to incite hatred for the Catholic writers. 'There are many at this time' (he said) 'who are regarded by the multitude with great hatred, because they treat the Holy Writings purely. Since certain Sycophant Princes agitate against them, there is now no greater crime than to embrace the true teaching of religion, etc.' [413] The second book was to Johannes Oecolampadius, who together with Zwingli was still contending against Luther in many books. Melanchthon dissuaded him, as an old friend, from that struggle. 'I ask you' (he said) 'to consider how great a matter, and how dangerous also, you are undertaking. It is the case, that truth can be lost through too much quarreling; and the risk is much greater in these very violent disputes. I see that your cause rests upon the support of clever men, and that you have schools of theatre, not so much openly as in secret; but I scarcely know whether they do you more good that way than they would openly, etc.' [414]

Moreover, there was such bitter and vicious disagreement among the Swiss, about faith and religion, stirred up especially by Zwingli and Oecolampadius, that matters had proceeded from words to weapons. For the people of Zurich and the Bernese, who were most greatly won over to the Zwinglian sect, with the people of Basel and not a few other Swiss peoples joining to help them, had taken up arms and marched out into the field against the Five Catholic Cantons – Lucerne, Schwyz, Unterwalden, Uri, and Zug. And a great slaughter would certainly have occurred, had not other Cantons, namely Glarus, Solothurn, Freiburg, Schaffhausen, and Appenzell, interposed themselves in turn in order to gain concord. The forces of Zurich and Berne were greater, and so they were more bloodthirsty, and were panting for battle. But the mediators persuaded both sides to accept assured conditions of peace, so that thereafter no one from either side would be attacked because of religion. There were very many articles of peace and concord, less just to the Catholics than to the Zwinglians. For the Catholics were bidden, before they left the field, immediately to give over into the hands of the Mediators the sealed letters of the League, into which they had entered with King Ferdinand, so that, once the seals had been broken and the envelopes torn away, that League might be utterly defunct and useless. Moreover, it was decreed that no Swiss people should ever thereafter receive any funds or stipends from the Kings or the Princes – so that the pacts which had begun among themselves by the Bernese and the people of Zurich and their accomplices might remain strong. Nor was anyone who had demolished images or altars, or had seized holy vestments and other ornaments of the Churches, etc., ordered to make restitution or called into court.

The most illustrious Prince, Lord Philip Landgrave of Hesse, took hard this inimical disagreement and discord among Luther, Zwingli, and Oecolampadius, and summoned them into his town of Marburg, so that their disagreement might be concluded there by an amicable discussion. And so they convened, and many of their adherents as well; and so that it would seem that something had been accomplished, they wrote and published several articles, in which they agreed among themselves against the Catholic Church, like Herod and Pilate against Christ. But on the principal article, concerning the Venerable Sacrament of the Eucharist, about which they had always especially quarreled, discord remained and continued among them. The Zwinglians circulated 300 arguments, which they said had been brought up against Luther by Zwingli. And so that assembly disbanded, with its purpose unaccomplished.

Moreover, Luther's associate and friend Johannes Agricola of Eisleben (who was a poetic theologian and a priest, although neither anointed – as he himself boasted – nor consecrated), in order to stir up a greater hatred towards the Catholics among the German people, published certain Acts of the Counsel of Constance concerning Johannes Hus of Bohemia, who had been there condemned and burned as a heretic. He claimed that this 'history' (as he called it) had been written in Latin by some unknown author, who was present and saw, heard, and experienced everything. And in imitation of the Holy Apostle John the Evangelist, he added 'And we know that his testimony is true.' He wrote in the preface as follows: 'I have acquired' (he said) 'a book written in Latin, concerning the manner in which that virtuous friend of God, Johannes Hus, was burned at Constance in the Synagogue of the Antichrist, for the sake of the teaching of the Gospel. This book was found in the library of a certain Doctor of Medicine, Paul, a citizen of Rockenbach, and was translated into German by my good friend Nicolaus Krompach. In it you will clearly discover how Johannes Hus, without any human aid or consolation, stood alone against the two greatest powers on earth, namely the Emperor and the Pope, against the Holy Ecclesiastics and Doctors – and conquered.' Thus wrote Agricola. But that history is scarcely favorable to the Lutherans. For in that history Johannes Hus is said to have denied publicly, before everyone, those articles which the Lutherans most affirm, both in the Church of Constance before his degradation, and in public in the field around the place of his punishment. Therefore, there is no reason for the Lutherans to boast about that history.

At the same time, since the Tyrant of the Turks was threatening Germany, Luther published a German book, to which he gave the title *On War against the Turks*. In it he argued that war must be undertaken against the Turks, in such a manner that he seemed more to terrify Christians away from that war than to urge them to it. For there in many words and many pages he complains that Pope Leo X unjustly condemned that article of his, 'To join battle with the Turks, is to fight against God, Who is visiting our iniquities on us through them.'[415] Among very many other things, he said as follows:

'Let it be inquired from the experience of these matters, how profitable it has been to us so far to wage war with the Turks, when although we have fought as Christians and in Christ's name, still at length we have lost Rhodes, and nearly all of Hungary, and a large part of Germany as well. And so that we may perceive and feel that God is not with us in our fight against the Turks, never yet has He given to our Princes enough heart or spirit in their minds that they could even once seriously deal with a war on the Turks, although many – or, rather, nearly all – Imperial Assemblies were called together and held on that account. But the matter never consented to be put in order or decided upon, so that an Assembly of this kind seemed to mock God, and to allow the Devil to hinder it and guide it, until the Turk crept near at a favorable time and destroyed Germany without effort or resistance. Why was this so? Without doubt, for this reason: so that my article, which Leo the Pope condemned, might remain blameless and efficient.'[416]

In many other points in that book he attacked and blamed and slandered the Pope, the Emperor, Kings, Princes, Bishops, and especially the Roman Curia. Johannes Cochlaeus extracted 136 of these points, but it would take too long to recount them; therefore, it will be sufficient, as an example, to mention one or two of them.

'The Emperor' (he said) 'is not the head of Christendom, nor the Defender of the Gospel or the Faith. Indeed, it is necessary that the Church and the Faith have some other defender than the Emperor and Kings. For these are in general the worst enemies of Christendom and the faith, as the second Psalm says, and the church laments on every side. Moreover, if you will say, "The Pope is as bad as the Turk, as you yourself call him the Antichrist, along with his Ecclesiastics and adherents, and on the other hand, the Turk is as good as the Pope, for he acknowledges the Four Evangelists, and Moses, and the Prophets; if, therefore, one must fight against the Turk, then one must also fight against the Pope" – then I will answer, I cannot deny that the Turk admits the Four Evangelists as holy and true, just as he considers the Prophets. In addition, he frequently speaks of both Christ and His Mother. Nevertheless, he believes his Mohammed to be greater than Christ. But God will strike both the Turk and the Pope with the same blindness, until what Paul says concerning sins against nature (Rom. 1) is done to them. For both are so blind and so maddened that they both commit silent sins, without any shame, as though they were doing a decent and praiseworthy thing.'[417] In these words and many others like them, Luther there most hatefully reproached every State of his superiors, through the most shameful slanders.

Therefore, Johannes Cochlaeus published a certain Dialogue against him. In it he presents a two-headed Luther, because he published so many statements that contradicted one another about the Turk in several books. And there three characters were gathered, the Speaker of King Ferdinand, Luther, and Palinodus,[418] in fifty chapters. The eleventh of these went as follows:

'Speaker: Your Luther says that up until now we have gained no advantage against the Turk. By this saying, he wishes to turn our minds away and to terrify us, so that we will not resist the Turk. For he says, "Whoever has ears to hear, let him hear, and refrain from the Turkish war, while the name of Pope still has strength under heaven." But what else is this, than to betray his native land to the Turks, and to persuade us to open our doors to the approaching enemy and give ourselves up voluntarily?

'Palinodus: The thing which especially moved him to this (as he told me) was that war should be proposed against the Turk under the name "Christian," as if our people should be called the army of Christians, whether against the Turks or against enemies of Christ; a thing which is directly contrary to the teaching and the name of Christ. It is clearly contrary to His teaching, which says, Christians ought not to resist evil, nor to fight, nor to quarrel, nor to seek vengeance, nor to sue. And it is against His name, since in an army of this sort there are, perhaps, scarcely five Christians, and certainly men who are worse in the eyes of God than the Turks are; and yet all of them want to bear the name of Christ. This, certainly, is the worst of all sins, such as no Turk commits.

'Speaker: Thus you recant, do you, Palinodus? But it would be much better for you openly to say what you think, than to snare the people with such tricks and riddles. Certainly, you yourself earlier proclaimed a seditious and intolerable sermon of this sort, and you proved, from Paul, that our magistrates ought to keep the Turk at a distance by the sword and by war, and by force to drive him away from their subjects. Nor did Christ ever forbid us to repel barbarity and Turkish tyranny. But that the Turks are the enemies of Christ, you also admitted earlier, from their own Koran. And in very fact, this is so evident that it would be both completely insane and utterly pointless to deny it.' [419]

For the rest, that year was most notable and memorable for the Turkish war in Austria, and the siege of Vienna, and the first departure of our Emperor Charles V, Augustus, into Italy, and his coronation at Bologna by the Roman Pontiff, Clement VII. For the tyrant of the Turks, Suleiman, after Hungary had been devastated, came to Vienna, the capital of Austria, on the 21st day of September. He had 400,000 soldiers in his army and surrounded the city with sixteen camps in a circle, which extended three or four miles. In addition, he occupied the bridge over the Danube and the outlying areas. Nothing was left to the citizens and the military guard except the city itself. Women, children, priests, monks, and the whole crowd of noncombatants had been ordered to leave the city. The greatest part of them fell into the hands of the enemy soldiers, among whom there was the greatest cruelty and no mercy at all. They hacked babies in two; women and old people whom they did not want to take into slavery they impaled on stakes, or transfixed with javelins, or hacked to bits with swords. Moreover, they made long forays of ten or twelve German miles, and devastated everything they met, showing mercy to no rank, sex, or age.

King Ferdinand had fortified the city with the strongest defense. In it there were chosen soldiers whose supreme commander was the most illustrious Duke of Bavaria, and the Palatine of the Rhine, Philip. And he had brought in as well all the greatest and best engines of war, whose price (as many said) could scarcely be equaled by two kingdoms. The enemy, who had not brought great cannons with them (for they intended to occupy the city quickly by coming against the inhabitants when they were unprepared), caused the greatest danger to the city and its defense by subterranean tunnels and caves, over which they made the city suspended, as it were. When they put gunpowder into these and ignited it, they demolished the walls by the most terrible crashings and ruptures. When the city had been for the most part denuded of its walls, they made very frequent attacks, but the unconquered strength of the defense always repulsed them, with losses; to such an extent that at length the Turks, although they were urged on to the attack by their Tyrant with swords and clubs, nevertheless completely withdrew. Meanwhile King Ferdinand, who was lingering on the Danube in the town of Linz, as if in a watch-tower, summoned great assistance from all parts to take aid to the besieged. A great part of this assistance was now ready for action. When the Turk learned this, he lifted the siege and, when his camps had been burned, on the 16th day of October, he ingloriously retreated towards Constantinople. On the way there, because of the lack of food and the cold, he suffered great misfortunes by land and sea, not only to his equipment and war-engines, but also to his men, camels, and horses.

But our most pious Emperor Charles, far more longed for, happy, and glorious, sailed into Italy from Spain. He did not violently exact money from his subjects, as the Turk had exacted it from his, throughout all his provinces; but so great was the Spaniards' love for the Emperor, that of their own volition they offered far more soldiers and far more money than another could have extorted from them by violence and threats. Indeed, 1,500 individual men of their own accord each offered His Majesty one thousand [420] golden ducats in four years, without any interest (as they call it) or profit. Many from the Princes offered cavalry and infantry; one offered 100 cavalry and 300 infantry, another more, another less, whom they ordered to serve the Emperor as soldiers for a year and a day, at the Princes' expense and cost. And before the Emperor left Spain, the King of France obtained peace and concord from him through women, that is through his own mother and the Emperor's aunt; he renounced all claim to Italy [421] and paid out twenty times 100,000 gold pieces for the liberation of his children, who had been held captive as hostages in his place in Spain.

But when the Emperor came into Italy, he restored peace everywhere by his approach, except for one city, Florence, which, ignoring the Emperor's desire, was unwilling to receive the famous de Medici family, whom it had violently expelled, back into the city at the Pope's instigation. Therefore, because of this obstinacy, the Imperial soldiers besieged that city, and after heavy misfortunes forced it to surrender. Moreover, after Francesco Sforza, Duke of Milan, had been returned to favor through the intercession of the Roman pontiff and had been restored to his Dukedom, the Emperor received the double crown, the first of iron and the second of gold, from the Highest Pontiff, with the customary ceremonies at Bologna, with great praise, glory, and triumph, and to the favor and happiness of all.

But for the Germans, that year was heavy and troublesome, not only because of the fear and danger of the Turkish war and because of the distressing quarrels of the sects, but also because of two fatal evils. One of these was famine, and a lack of all goods, such as had never been within human memory; and the other was a certain plague, which was called the 'English sweat.' This malady was so violent and deadly, that it would snatch the life away from a healthy man within twenty-four hours, unless the greatest care thoroughly conquered that sweat by the use of certain poultices. This plague had not been previously known in Germany, and thus many died before the doctors could discover the method of curing it. And the wine in that year was so bitter that it could not easily be drunk because of its acidity; and with time it became so vile and bad-tasting that not even vinegar could be made from it, but since it was entirely unusable, it was poured away in vain.

1530

Although Luther, as if he were some kind of lawgiver and a new Moses, had written many things to his accomplices about the way in which they ought to teach and to preach, both in his *Commentary* and in his *Saxon Visitation*, nevertheless there remained such variety and discord among the preachers of his sect that it appeared necessary to him again to prescribe another rule for teaching, which he called the *Catechism*.[422] And in that book, in various passages, he explained the Ten Commandments of God and the Lord's Prayer and the Sign of the Apostles, very differently than he had done ten years previously. For instance, he prescribed both belief in and use of two sacraments, namely Baptism and the Eucharist, in a new manner; but he did not recognize any other Sacraments. For although he there urged the people to confession, still he made confession something very different from what the Holy Mother Church instituted. For he permitted the penitent to mention, not every sin which he knew he had committed, but only those which he wanted to mention, so that he might receive counsel, consolation, and absolution from the priest.

Afterwards, many people who had a high opinion of their own worth followed Luther's example and published many Catechisms; but in such a way that none of them agreed with any other in every detail. And in this way they attempted to instill their dogma in boys and girls and young adolescents, through bedtime stories, as if with the milk that they had drunk, so that strong roots, once planted in those tender breasts, would remain there through every stage of life and could not be eradicated through any force or any argument. And so, they wrote their Catechisms most especially for children.

The Emperor, while he was still in Italy, announced by public edict to the Princes and the other Estates of the Holy Roman Empire that an Imperial Diet would be held in Augsburg, on the 8th day of April, for two causes in particular: Namely, so that discord in religion might be abolished, and that a sure method of fighting against the Turks, which would last, could be found by common discussion. Therefore, in that Edict he most kindly enjoined all the Orders of the Empire that in the matter of religion any party whatsoever should be allowed to express its opinion, and when all disagreements had been driven out, one faith of them all and pure religion should thereafter be preserved by lasting concord. And so that all fear and suspicion of deceit or danger might be absent, he awarded to everyone security and public faith, that is, safe conduct. It was for this reason that this Diet of the Imperial Orders was the best attended and most famous. In it not only the Lutherans but even the Zwinglians were permitted freely and securely to recite, to the letter, their confession of faith, publicly before His Imperial Majesty and all the Estates of the Empire. For the arrival of the Emperor, and his well-known clemency and love of his people, enticed everyone. Therefore, among the first who convened at Augsburg was the Most Illustrious Elector Prince Johannes, Duke of Saxony. In his train were several other Princes, namely his son, Duke Johannes Frederick; the two brothers Ernst and Franz, the Dukes of Luneberg; and Prince Wolfgang of Anhalt. There were other splendid nobles as well, and with them were leaders of the Lutheran doctrine, among whom Philip Melanchthon was eminent. He had conducted Luther himself as well along a good part of the journey, but he did not lead him all the way to Augsburg, because Luther had been condemned and proscribed by the Emperor as a notorious heretic in the Edict of Worms. Melanchthon wanted Luther to be kept in a certain nearby Imperial city under safe conduct, but he received the response from its Senate that it was not permitted to protect anyone in opposition to the Emperor. And so he left Luther in his very well-fortified city of Coburg.

However, the Emperor's arrival was somewhat slower, due to the great honors and display of pomp with which he was most honorably received everywhere in the Venetian lands, as he made his way through his ancestral Tyrolian lands. In these his brother King Ferdinand met him and entertained him with the greatest joy and splendor; and his people of Swabia, who had very famous silver mines, gave him one silver coin that was equal in worth to 1,700 gold coins, and showed all the family trees of the Emperor most beautifully. And he traveled through the lands of the Dukes of Bavaria, who together with King Ferdinand and Cardinal Campeggio, Legate of the Apostolic See, retained him for four days in their very beautiful city which is called Munich, where no form of honor was not shown to him. However, when the Emperor had drawn near to the city of Augsburg on the 15th day of June, the eve of Corpus Christi, all the Princes and Imperial Estates ran out to meet him on his way. In the name of them all, the most Reverend and Illustrious Lord Albert Cardinal and Archbishop of Mainz and Magdeburg and Prince Elector, in his role of Archchancellor of the Empire for Germany, greeted him most fittingly with a speech. Before they approached, however, they all dismounted from their horses about fifty or sixty paces before meeting them. But the Emperor himself, together with his brother, immediately also dismounted from their own horses when they saw this, as a token of respect. And when they drew closer to the city, they were received with humble devotion by the Senate and the people of Augsburg, who came out on foot, although they had with them several knights as well, most carefully adorned, and four cohorts, amounting to 2,000 foot soldiers.

In the city itself, the most Reverend Lord Christopher of Stadion, Bishop of Augsburg, was awaiting the Emperor's arrival. With the Bishop were all his clergy, who led the Emperor into the Cathedral Church under their escort, and there when the ceremonies of blessing had been performed by the Bishop, and the hymn *Te Deum laudamus* had been sung, the Emperor withdrew to the Bishop's Curia, which is called his Palace, as though into his own chamber, and all the others returned to their different lodgings, since the evening was now drawing toward twilight. Later on that evening, and early the next day, the Emperor requested through his messengers that the Elector of Saxony and the other Princes who adhered to the Lutheran faction might go together with His Majesty in the ancient manner in a public procession, in which the Venerable Sacrament of the Body of Christ would be carried. But they declined and offered many excuses, claiming them as obstacles to their faith in regard to this matter; at length he asked that if they would not accompany the procession out of respect for God, at least they might do so out of respect for the Emperor himself, since they were Vassals and Princes of the Empire. But they could not be persuaded even by that argument. And for this reason it happened that the time of the procession was delayed all the way to the noon hour. Nonetheless, the Emperor, together with the other Princes and Imperial Estates, and his Spanish and Burgundian nobles, made that procession both most devotedly and most splendidly. The Primate of Germany, Cardinal and Archbishop of Mainz, carried the Venerable Sacrament; King Ferdinand escorted him on the right and Joachim, the Marquis of Brandenburg and Elector of the Empire, full brother to the Lord of Mainz, on the left. Before the Sacrament itself the secular Princes walked in procession, and before them the Masters of the Curia, the flag-bearers, the heralds, the trumpeters (both the Emperor's and the King's); and before them walked the nobles of either Curia and the whole Clergy. And behind the Sacrament followed the Emperor himself, bareheaded for the whole time (although he was walking in extremely hot sunshine) and carrying a lighted four-pronged candlestick in his hand.[423] Behind him walked the Archbishops and Bishops. Furthermore, by the Emperor's command and foresight, all the Princes and Nobles carried lighted four-pronged candlesticks, with candles of white wax.[424] In this very long procession, musicians of different sorts were singing in praise of God, and the elder secular Princes, continually alternating one with another, bore the canopy under which the Sacrament was carried.

But the Emperor, being most distressed by the stubbornness of the Lutherans, desired them to depart under safe conduct immediately on the following day. However, other Princes, who longed for peace and concord, begged His Majesty to soothe his anger and give them an audience, in accordance with the tenor of the Edict by which they had been summoned. The Emperor granted their request, and on the 20th day of June, as he was about to begin his public proceedings, he ordered all the Princes and Imperial Estates to be present in the Cathedral Church. There the abovementioned Primate of Germany celebrated the Mass. But the Reverend Dr Vicenzo Pimpinella, Archbishop of Rossa and Apostolic Nuncio, most learnedly preached a sermon to the Princes. For Cardinal Campeggio, the Lateran legate of the Highest Pontiff, was hindered by podagra and disease of the joints, and could seldom take part in public proceedings. The Lutheran Princes as well were present, both at the Mass and the Sermon. When these things had taken place, a procession was held in solemn fashion from the Church to the public audience in the council chamber. The Elector of Saxony, according to custom, rode before the Emperor, carrying an unsheathed sword.

In the public audience, a general proposal was made for carrying out the proceedings. So that no quarrel should arise in so great a multitude of people, through difference either of languages or of religions, the Emperor employed 1,000 foot soldiers who would maintain guard over the doors and keep the nightly vigils. Moreover he forbade by public Edict under the most severe penalty, and posted placards to that effect in all the streets,[425] that there should be no public sermons to the people, except in the Cathedral Church by the man who was the ordinary Preacher there. This mandate seemed necessary, since before the Emperor's arrival, several sermons were being preached in various places in a kind of contest, as each one tried to draw a crowd to himself; here Lutherans, there Zwinglians, in yet another place Catholics, were preaching. But the greatest gathering of the people was at the Monastery of the Franciscan Friars, in whose house a certain Zwinglian Apostate – a fluent man and one apt and clever for stirring up the people – was preaching most copiously. This man was then reciting the book of Joshua to the people, for the following reason: that he might menacingly twist all the troubles which are there recounted to have afflicted the kings of the land of Canaan, against the Emperor and our Princes, comparing the men of his sect to the sons of Israel, the people of God; so that he might by that commentary strengthen them in their heresy, lest through fear of the Emperor they should return to the Catholic Church.

But the Emperor, following the ancient example of the Romans and the praiseworthy and religious custom of his ancestors, set the cause of religion before all other causes and necessities. In the next public audience he gave a hearing to the Lutheran Princes, who caused a confession of their faith to be recited in German, by Dr Christian Beyer, from a written text, which they exhibited in Latin as well; its principal Architect had been Philip Melanchthon. In this Confession, following the exordium, twenty-one Articles concerning their faith are recounted.[426] Then other articles are added, in which they survey the Abuses (as they call them) which have been altered. The titles of these articles are: About Both Kinds; About the Marriage of Priests; About the Mass; About Confession; About the Distinction of Foods; About Monastic Vows; and About Ecclesiastical Power.

In the articles about the faith they passed over many things which they had earlier taught differently. In the articles about abuses that astute Architect could be accused of open lying. For he says, 'They falsely charge our Church with abolishing the Mass. For the Mass is retained among us, and is celebrated with the highest reverence; almost all the accustomed ceremonies are also maintained, except that here and there German songs are mixed with the Latin ones.' [427] But it was plain to everyone, that many years previously Luther had both written a book *On the Abrogation of the Private Mass*, and had driven out the sacred Canon, both major and minor; and had removed and denied the very Sacrifice itself, both in Latin in his book *On the Babylonian Captivity*, and in German in his sermon on the New Testament. And afterwards as well he again wrote very many things against the Mass, which should be most detested by pious ears, not only in that German book which he wrote about the secret Mass and the consecration of priests, but also in a certain letter, when he wishes that among all peoples there would be as much difference between the Mass and the Sacrament as there is between shadows and light, nay even as there is between the Devil and God. In addition, he wishes that the heart in all Christians would be of such a sort that, when they hear this word 'Mass' they would be terrified and would defend themselves with a blessing, as against an abomination of the Devil. And in his lying Confession, Philip says as follows about confession: 'Confession in the churches has not been abolished among us. For we are not accustomed to offer the Body of the Lord except to those who have previously been examined and absolved.' [428] But it was clearly the case that none of the Lutherans had confessed his sins properly for ten years.

The Emperor, due to his inborn clemency and goodness, patiently heard all these things out to their end, and when he had accepted a copy of the Confession, dismissed the company; for it was already late evening. But he demanded the care and attention of the Catholic Princes' theologians for the examination and refutation of this Confession. When these theologians had within a few days composed a pointed and lengthy response (in which they not only refuted by Scriptures and arguments those things that were erroneous, but also pointed out that Luther and his accomplices had long before taught and written differently about those things that were correct in the Confession), they presented it to the Emperor, and he in turn presented it to the Catholic Princes. [429] But since all were eager for peace and concord, it seemed best to them to respond more gently and to omit whatever the Lutherans' preachers had earlier taught or written differently than their Confession now stated. Therefore, while the mode of the refutation was being altered, several days passed. Finally, when the shorter version was exhibited, again there was disagreement in the Princes' deliberation concerning who ought to recite that refutation. Due to that disagreement of the Princes, the different transcription of the refutation dragged the matter on for three weeks. Meanwhile the Lutherans were boasting, not just in conversations with anyone at all in Augsburg, but also in letters to various cities, that the papists were silent concerning their Confession. But when in the public assembly of the Emperor and all the Princes the refutation was recited in German by a certain Alexander, a private secretary of the Emperor, many of the Lutherans laughed inappropriately, and others noted down in writing the passages of Scripture that were cited, so that they might later refute them. But when it had been read through to the end, the Emperor and all the Catholic Princes with him approved of it, and they asked the Lutheran Princes to accept and approve it themselves as well. But these requested that a copy of the refutation be given to them. The Emperor did not wish to give this to them, for just reasons, except on certain conditions: namely, that they would keep it among themselves, and would not communicate it to others before the Emperor so ordered. They would not accept it on those terms. And so they departed from the Audience. The Emperor was distressed at their obstinacy, but they, safe under public protection, did not fear very greatly.

The Princes and other Imperial States, fearing that the Emperor would be more seriously displeased by those men's stubbornness and would contemplate heavier penalties, interposed their representatives and begged the Emperor that he would allow them to make a further attempt toward agreement concerning religion with those others. When the Emperor consented to this, they formed a delegation of certain persons, seventeen in number, from every rank and Imperial Estate, so that they might more easily put the matter in order, when there was no necessity to examine the votes given under seal by every member of the whole Imperial Diet. Therefore, the Two Elector Princes of Mainz and Brandenburg were selected; to them were added three Speakers of the other Three Electors of Cologne, Trier, and the Counts of the Rhineland Palatinate; and George Truchsess, Baron of Waldburg, called the 'House of Austria.' In addition, there were three Bishops, namely of Salzburg, Speyer, and Strasbourg; and three Dukes, George of Saxony, Henry of Braunschweig, and Albert of Mecklenburg; and in addition the Abbot of Weingarter, Count Martin of Ottingen, the Chancellor of Baden, the Speaker of Regensburg, and the Speaker of Jülich. This delegation, therefore, asked the Lutherans to come to a discussion with them in the Chapter House of the Greater Church of Augsburg, on Sunday, which was 7 August, the Feast of Blessed Afra; and the Lutherans came, not unwillingly. When they were all assembled, the Prince Elector Marquis of Brandenburg, a most eloquent man, began in the name of the Delegation to exhort them in a long and kindly speech, that they might acquiesce to the will of the Emperor, and re-establish agreement in faith and religion with him and with the other Princes and Estates of the Empire. For it was to be feared, if they did not do so, that great evils would arise from their refusal: wars, uprisings, and devastations of the provinces. This was the chief point of his speech.

After two days of deliberation, they responded through Dr Gregory Bruck, an exceedingly learned man, who in almost all their discussions was their common mouth and instrument. First of all, they resented the fact that threats had been joined to the admonition. Then they lengthened their response into four articles. In the first of these they complained that they had not been sufficiently heard by the Emperor, according to the tenor of the edict that summoned them. In the second, they complained that a copy of the Confutation had not been freely given to them, without any oppressive conditions. In the third, that they could not, without a burden on their consciences, approve a Confutation which they had not fully seen. In the fourth, that in the immediately preceding Imperial Diet, which was held at Speyer, a promise and a resolve had been made about holding a Council, but nothing had been done. And after this response was recited orally, they handed it over in writing.

But the Delegation of Princes and Imperial Estates answered once again through the Elector Marquis of Brandenburg, protesting first that they themselves did everything with a friendly and faithful intention, as toward relatives, neighbors, and friends of theirs, and that they had said and would say nothing with the intention of offending or threatening. What they said about the evils that would come upon them, should be referred to this cause: that they were afraid, if this Diet should be disbanded without agreement and decision, that a great number of the common folk would again be incited to rebellions and disturbances, and that from this cause the most heavy damages could arise for themselves and for the whole German nation. Then they responded to the four articles.

To the first article the Delegation said that, since the Emperor had with the greatest clemency heard their Confession, put forward both orally and in writing; and had ordered that if they had more things in addition to propose, they should propose them, in order that there might be a consultation over and response to all their points at once; and, after the response had been given by His Imperial Majesty, had allowed a friendly discussion about agreement to take place with them through the agency of the Princes and the Imperial Estates, therefore there was no reason for them to complain about the Emperor, as not having satisfied his Edict. To the second article they responded that the conditions under which the Emperor wished to hand over a copy of the Confutation did not seem to be unjust, since the Lutherans themselves knew and could remember how the Edict of Worms had been publicly and openly derided, despised, and perverted by their preachers, actions which showed dishonor, contempt, and mockery both toward His Imperial Majesty and toward all the other Princes and Estates of the Empire. Therefore His Imperial Majesty wished that this response of his should not be communicated to others before the proper time, lest something similar occur; although they were not ignorant of the fact that it was also prohibited by law, under penalty of death, to dispute openly with assembled crowds about the faith. To the third they responded, with a preface asking indulgence, that the Lutherans seemed to consider their conscience when there was no need, but where there was the greatest need, they consider it not at all. For they should most greatly fear in their consciences to withdraw from the unity of the Church; to trust more in Apostates than in the Roman Church, the Holy Fathers, and the General Councils; to permit many things, against the laws and Canons, which contribute to the destruction of many. This at least they should consider, how greatly they were in disagreement and contrary to one another among themselves, how many sects they were divided into, and what evil fruits their new doctrine had borne. Therefore, it would be much safer for their consciences to agree with the Emperor and the entire Church, than to entrust their souls to such Apostates.

Finally, in answering the fourth article they excused the Emperor, on the grounds that he had not been able to hold a Council because he was waging two very serious wars, one of them against the King of France and his confederates, the other against the Turks who were besieging Vienna; besides, they themselves were not unaware that Luther had considered the Councils at Worms of no account, and that the Princes and Imperial Estates had not been able to persuade him there that he should submit his cause to the decision of a future Council; and in the meantime he had written many things against the Councils, by which he made their authority contemptible in the eyes of the common people. Therefore, the Delegation asked the Lutherans to weigh all these things carefully and to choose rather to return into agreement with His Imperial Majesty and with the whole Church than to remain in schism, to the peril of their souls. And if they themselves knew of another way to agreement, let them put it forward, so that news of it could be carried back to His Imperial Majesty.

However, since the Lutherans took this response very badly, for it seemed to touch on their souls, their honor, their conscience, and the obedience they owed to the Emperor, they asked for time to deliberate, so that they would be able to respond more precisely. This was easily granted to them; however, the Marquis publicly asked all those who were in the Delegation whether everything which he said or answered had been decreed by the common consent of them all. And they all agreed that it was so.

In their response, therefore, the Lutherans absolved themselves from these objections by the great disguise of carefully chosen words. They especially denied that they had separated themselves from the general Church; or that they ascribed any guilt to the Emperor, or that they mocked his Edict, or that they did not pay due honor to the Councils. But whatever others wrote or did should not be imputed to them. And they gave the following advice about another way to agreement: that from either side certain persons should be appointed in equal number (so long as it was a small one), who both understood the matter and were inclined to peace and agreement; so that they might deal with the contentious articles among themselves, by turns, in kindly and friendly fashion, to see if somehow they might be able to come to agreement. And for this reason it happened that a smaller Delegation was drawn up with members from either side. The Catholics appointed only seven people, namely two Princes, two legal scholars, and three theologians: they were Christopher Bishop of Augsburg, Henry Duke of Braunschweig (and after his removal by order of the Emperor, George Duke of Saxony); the Chancellor of the Archbishop of Cologne; the Chancellor of the Marquis of Baden; Dr Johannes Eck; Dr Conrad Wimpina, and Dr Johannes Cochlaeus. The Lutherans too appointed the same number of persons, and in the same division: namely, two Princes, Johannes

Frederick son of the Elector of Saxony and George the Marquis of Brandenburg; two legal scholars, Dr Gregory Bruck and Dr Heller; and three theologians, although they did not have doctorates of theology, Philip Melanchthon, Johannes Brenz, and Johannes Schnepp.

Therefore, these men who had been appointed came into a certain anteroom of the council chamber on the 15th day of August, after lunch. After several preliminary remarks and consultations had been gone through and the assembly had been gathered, the Lutherans' Confession was put forward to be examined article by article. And in this first session, in which they sat until very late evening, they agreed on both sides, and with kindly interpretations of the words, on eleven articles. On the next day, they took their seats again both before and after lunch. For in this session it happened that out of twenty-one articles of that Confession which pertain to the Faith, they agreed on fifteen. There was still disagreement about parts of three of them, and three were sent to the end of the Confession. But concerning seven articles which the Lutherans had written about the 'Abuses' they carried on their labor more strenuously and for a longer time; but full agreement could not be arrived at on any of these, although it was vigorously sought for by each side.

And so on the 22nd day of August, the Catholics reported to all the Princes and Estates of the Empire concerning these accomplishments, in a public assembly. When the Princes and Estates heard that the matter tended toward concord in most points and that disagreement remained in a few (which might be brought into agreement at any rate, if they could remove the delegates' stubbornness), they appointed a still smaller delegation so that the business might be settled more quickly. Indeed, they appointed only three men, two legal scholars (the abovementioned Chancellors) and one theologian, Dr Johannes Eck. These were ordered to work on those things about which agreement still had not been reached, once the same number of people had been appointed from the other side. And these men indeed attempted the thing several times, in turns; but still they were able to accomplish nothing. And now the Elector of Saxony was in a hurry to leave, since he had been at Augsburg with his men for over four months. And when the Catholics learned that the Lutherans were displeased because no Prince had taken part in this latest discussion, they decided that they would meet again, those seven men from either side who had been previously appointed. But the Elector of Saxony would not endure a longer delay; he asked the Emperor for his discharge, and left with his men.

Meanwhile, while these things were going on at Augsburg, Luther published various books in German, in which he attempted to make the Emperor hateful to the Germans, and the Bishops to both the common folk and the nobility. And these books were not only distributed throughout several cities of Germany, but were also sent to Augsburg, and were even openly sold from time to time before the court of the Elector of Saxony. One of these was a certain letter to the Cardinal and Archbishop of Mainz.[430] In it Luther interpreted the Second Psalm, 'Why do the nations rage?,' as if the Princes had convened in

Augsburg in opposition to Christ and his Church. And in the end of that letter, as if he were a zealous defender of Germany, he railed most hatefully against the Pope, and also scolded the Emperor for receiving the Imperial Crown from the Pope, without the presence of the German Princes. And he added this irony, contrary to the tenor of the Bull, concluding in the following words: 'I am not able to be unconcerned for poor, wretched, forsaken, scorned, betrayed, and sold Germany – for whom I wish no evil, but all good, as I ought to wish for my fatherland. From the wilderness, on the fourth day after the Visitation, in the year 1530.' [431]

And Luther wrote another book to all the Prelates of the Church in general, which he called *Admonition to the Churchmen at Augsburg, Assembled in the Imperial Diet*. In this book, indeed, so great is his commendation of his own doctrine and the new ecclesiastical arrangement, and so great his censure of the Bishops and of all ceremonies and observations of the Church, that he could have written nothing that would more powerfully incite the laity's hatred toward the clergy; and yet he decked out all this bitterness of his with the ornament of good intention and advice for peace. There he rehearsed at length the benefits of his teaching, by which he purged the Church of its errors and abuses, and liberated the Bishops from the Pope's tyranny and from the demands of monks. And he so praised these things, and boasted over them in his malice, that no King or Emperor could have done more. Moreover, he repeated those abuses article by article: About Indulgences, About the Confessionals, About Confession, About Penitence. Concerning this last matter, he says that it is the refuse of Hell itself, so much so that, if every other abomination were to be forgiven the Bishops and condoned, nevertheless this one could never be forgiven, which both filled Hell and devastated the kingdom of Christ more cruelly than ever the Turk or the whole world could have done. 'For you have taught us' (he said) 'that we must through our works give satisfaction for our sins, even toward God, and this means to do penance for our sins. Now to say "you must make satisfaction for your sins," what else is that than to say "you must deny Christ, revoke your baptism, blaspheme the Gospel, convict God of lying, not believe in the remission of sins, trample the blood and death of Christ underfoot, violate the Holy Spirit, ascend into Heaven through your own merits, by virtues of this sort?" Ah, what tongues or voices could say enough about this matter? Indeed, what else is this Faith but the faith of the Turks, the Gentiles, and the Jews? For all of them want to give satisfaction through their own works. From this abomination' (he said) 'all others have come, and they must by necessity come from it; namely, the private sanctity of so many monasteries and collegiate churches, with their holy cults, sacrifices of Masses, Purgatory, Vigils, Fraternities, Pilgrimages, Indulgences, Fasts, Cults of the Saints, Relics, Confusions of Spirits, and the whole infernal procession of the cross.' [432] He laid these charges and many others like them in that book.

But in the discussion of that Assembly, which was held between seven men from either side, concerning the twelve articles of the Lutheran confession about which there was still disagreement, on the question of giving satisfaction (which we say is one-third part of penitence) it was decided by Cochlaeus and Melanchthon on the first evening that early the next day they would offer something for the sake of agreement on that point. And so from his *Seven-headed Luther* Cochlaeus brought forward one passage, which Luther had written against indulgences in the fifth article of his assertion of those forty-one articles which Pope Leo X had condemned publicly in a Bull. Luther had written these words: 'The Mother Church, through pious affection forestalling the Hand of God, chastises her children through certain satisfactions, lest they meet with the whips of God: Just as the Ninevites, by their own voluntary works, forestalled God's judgment. This punishment is not entirely a matter of the Church's own opinion' (he said), 'as some people want it to be, but it is nevertheless necessary. For either we, or men, or God punish sins, which these people take away entirely through indulgences; although if they were pious shepherds, they would rather impose punishments, and by the example of the Church forestall God, just as Moses forestalled him by killing the Sons of Israel for the sin of the golden calf. Moreover, it would be best if we should inflict punishment upon them.' [433]

Luther said these things there. When they were read out in the assembly by Dr Johannes Eck from a paper, the seven Lutherans, looking at one another, were silent for a little while. Melanchthon, who was sitting nearest, said (with a blush covering his face), 'I know that Luther wrote these things.' And when he added nothing more, Duke Johannes Frederick said, 'When did he write them? Perhaps ten years ago.' The Catholics responded 'What does that matter? It is enough for us that this is the opinion of the very man himself.' Then Brenz and Schnepp, moved by anger, said that they were not there to defend Luther's writings, but to argue for their own Confession. Therefore those writings of Luther's should be set aside. Here, so that they could proceed further, Melanchthon wrote their opinion with his own hand: 'We do not refuse to maintain three parts of penitence, that is, Contrition, which signifies the terrors that strike against the conscience when sin is acknowledged; Confession, but in this one must look to absolution, and believe in it; for sin is not remitted, unless it be believed that it is remitted through the merit of Christ's passion. The third part is Satisfaction, that is, the fruit of worthy penitence; but we agree with one mind that sins are not remitted through satisfactions so far as guilt is concerned. But it is not yet decided, whether satisfactions are necessary for the remission of sins so far as guilt is concerned.' When these things had been written by Melanchthon, they proceeded to the next points.

And since in their discussion of the Fourth article the Catholics did not want to admit that 'We are justified by faith alone,' since the Apostle James also does not admit it, it was agreed that the article should indeed say 'We are justified by faith,' but not 'by faith alone' — since no scripture has it so, but rather the opposite. And Dr Johannes Eck added a joke, that this word 'sola' should be sent to the shoemakers, who well know what 'sola' means in German [434] and know how to use 'sola' properly. Therefore, when that word 'sola' was omitted, it was agreed that Justification or Remission of sins is accomplished formally through grace, accepting favor, and faith, and instrumentally through the word and the Sacraments.

But when Luther was asked, in that same year, by a certain friend, why he said in his German translation in Paul's words at Romans 3 'Man is justified by faith alone,' when Paul did not say so, and through this gave the papists an opportunity for censuring his German translation, he answered him most proudly, with great scorn for the papists: 'First, that he would say to the papists as follows. If Luther had been able to know for certain that all the papists joined together into one would be skillful enough to know how to translate a single Chapter of the Scripture into German, correctly and well, then he would have wished to be humble enough to beg them for help and advice in translating the New Testament. Second, that he would say to them, Luther translated the New Testament into German, in accordance with his greatest diligence and skill, but no one is forced by him to read it. And so it is his Testament and his interpretation, and if he made mistakes there, he does not wish on that account to endure Papist judges, since they still have ears that are too long for this, and their "Hee haw, hee haw" [435] is too feeble to pass judgment on his translation from Latin into German. Indeed, he himself knows well that they truly know less than a builder's animal, what art, diligence, reason, and intelligence are required for a good translation, since they have not tried it. If they should translate the first two words of Matthew 1, the book of generations, none of them would know how to say *"Gack"* [436] to it, and yet they judge my whole work. Clever comrades, indeed! Therefore, if' (he said) 'your Papist wants to chatter a great deal about that word "Sola," then by all means let it be said to him as follows: Dr Martin Luther wants it to be thus, and says that a Papist and an ass are the same thing; thus I wish it, thus I judge it, let my will take the place of reason. [437] For we do not want to be the students or disciples of the papists, but their teachers and judges.' [438] There Luther said these things and many others of this sort, contemptuously and proudly.

But the Speakers of four Imperial Cities which followed the Zwinglian sect – Strasburg, Constance, Memmingen, and Lindau – exhibited another Confession of Faith to the Emperor, after the Lutherans had done so at Augsburg. [439] And although this sect was odious to the Catholics, especially because they denied the true presence of the body and blood of Christ in the Eucharist, and they utterly abolished the Mass, and they demolished altars, ciboria, holy images, and other ornaments of the churches, nevertheless in accordance with the tenor of the Edict of Summons, a public audience was granted them. And their Confession was recited in this audience, before all the Imperial Estates. It was so cleverly adorned with neatly arranged words that it could easily impose on the more simple folk, as seeming probable in all its parts; it had such a cleverly feigned appearance of piety. The Emperor ordered it to be confuted by the same Theologians who had confuted the Lutheran Confession, and their Confutation was publicly recited. And the Emperor then earnestly entreated those Speakers to set aside their errors and agree in faith and religion with His Imperial Majesty and with the other Princes and Estates of the Empire. But they answered, that they had no mandate or commission from their cities to do so. Moreover, they requested a copy of the Confutation, so that they might show it to their people. The Emperor denied this request, for just reasons, although he did permit that the Confutation be recited to them two or three or more times, if they wanted to hear it. But they remained obstinate in their opinion.

When the Lutherans were about to leave, the Emperor proposed certain articles in their public dismissal: namely, that before the 15th day of the coming April they should give a sealed response to the question whether in all matters they wished to agree in faith with His Imperial Majesty and the other Princes and Estates of the Empire, or not. Moreover, that in the meantime they should allow nothing new on the question of faith to be published or sold in their lands. Moreover, that they should not lure others' subjects to their faith (as had up to now been done), nor lead them away from the ancient faith. And if anyone still remained in their lands who held the Catholic faith, they should not drive them into their own sect, nor hinder them from the ancient rites. Moreover, that they should meet with the Catholics against the Zwinglians and the Anabaptists, to debate what should be done against those sects. But the Lutherans did not wish to accept articles of this sort, and they left without agreement. However, the Emperor nonetheless afterwards firmly concluded with all the other Imperial Electors and the other Princes, in a general Recess (as they call it) that they should all most constantly remain in the ancient religion and faith of their ancestors.

These things were done at Augsburg and were signed and sealed by all on the 19th day of November. Then all departed; the Emperor and the King his brother, and many princes with them, went down to Cologne, while others returned to their homes. But the Confession of the Lutherans was released to the printers, and was set in type and came to Augsburg before the assembly of Princes had been dissolved. The Emperor also had commissioned certain theologians to give his Confutation to some printer at Augsburg for publication. And when Johannes Cochlaeus had just begun negotiations about that matter with the printer Alexander Weissenhorn, who had previously printed several of his works, Cochlaeus's most merciful Lord and Patron the most Illustrious Prince George Duke of Saxony left Augsburg, and it was necessary for Cochlaeus to go with him, because of the dangers of the roads. Others, occupied with other business, neglected the printing of the Confutation. And for this reason it happened that to this very day that Confutation, though certainly not unworthy of the light, has not been published.

1531

When the Emperor and the other Princes and Estates of the Empire had firmly concluded in their general Recess that they must remain in the ancient faith and religion of their fathers, and that there should be no innovations or changes before the agreement of the General Council, Luther (who knew well how strongly some of the Princes and Cities who were confederates of the Elector of Saxony held to his own sect) began to rage most ferociously, publishing two books in German. One of them he titled *Commentary on the Alleged Imperial Edict*;[440] the other, *A Warning to His Dear Germans*.[441] In each of these he protested most wickedly that he was not urging either war or sedition, when meanwhile he did nothing more zealously and energetically, by defaming and accusing not only the Pope and all the ecclesiastical Prelates, but also the Emperor and all the Catholic Princes, whom he called traitors and worthless evildoers, and liars, buffoons, and so on.

In the *Commentary* he wants everyone to be persuaded that the Recess of Augsburg, which he calls the Edict, was forged under the Emperor's name. Cochlaeus answered him thus in German: 'Who are you, you disgraceful, infamous, and damned heretic, that you dare to say that the Recess which was publicly and legitimately agreed upon and unanimously concluded by the entire Roman Empire, which is, in fact, a General Imperial Decree, is an "alleged" or "putative" Imperial Edict? When it is obvious, and cannot be denied that not only did the Emperor himself, and also several Electors and other Princes and Prelates, and many Counts and Barons, who were personally present, subscribe to that Recess and Decree in their own hands; but also not a few other Princes, Prelates, Counts and Barons, and in addition cities both free and imperial, also subscribed to it in absentia, as though they were present, through their legitimate Procurators and the Speakers they had sent, who had their full mandate. (And indeed, five Electors, thirty Princes of the Church, twenty-three Secular Princes, twenty-two Abbots, thirty-two Counts and Barons, and finally thirty-nine cities, both free and imperial, are remembered to have signed the foot of that Recess, either in their own hands or through their legitimate Procurers or Speakers.) And they even added full strength by appending the seals both of His Imperial Majesty himself and of certain Electors and other Princes and Lords, in the place of all the others. Therefore, no faith or trust should hereafter be given to a desperate Apostate in books of this sort, since he does not blush to cast away, slander, and reject the signatures, the seals and the letters of so many Princes and Imperial Estates and of the Emperor himself; when his falsehood, already obvious enough, can through letters and seals be turned back around in his face visibly and even palpably, so that he would be easily suffocated, if all those seals were crammed into his jaws.'[442] Cochlaeus wrote these things in response to Luther's title and preface.[443]

But the book itself was no better and no more true than its title or its preface. For near the beginning Luther vehemently denounces the fact that it was written in the Recess that the Lutherans' Confession had been refuted through Holy Scripture and just arguments. Moreover, he calls the Confutation itself (because it had not been given over into the Lutherans' hands, nor published) a night-owl and a bat, which flees the light, since the Catholics do not dare to expose it to light. And treating of communion in both kinds, he presupposes that everyone has been persuaded that Christ commanded in the

Scriptures that both kinds be given to the laity; and on the basis of this custom, he attacks certain words of the Edict with amazing slanders, mockeries, and accusations: namely, that the Church, according to the prompting of the Holy Spirit and on the grounds of good arguments, has wholesomely established that outside of the Mass only one kind of communion shall be offered. Here he calls the Church the Pope's whore, here he affirms that the Church both sins and is mistaken; here he complains that Christ is made a liar by the papists, here he deplores the violence and injury brought to the Church by the papists; here he teaches that the Church must not be believed nor obeyed, if it speaks or institutes anything beyond or apart from the word of Christ; here the papists sin against the Holy Spirit and descend, impenitent, into Hell. But at length, after many pages of the book, he concludes by threatening thus: 'Blaspheme confidently,' (he says), 'Papist Asses, while you have time. Soon matters will be different; in the meantime, let no one pay heed to an Edict of this sort, except for the sons of the Devil.' [444]

Writing about the Mass there, first he derided with many ironical comments the saying of Cardinal Campeggio, the Lateran Legate, who was said to have told the Emperor that he would rather be torn into pieces than to allow the Mass to be abolished or changed. Then Luther derided the words of the Edict, which ordered both Canons to serve in the Mass, and ordered other customary ceremonies. For he said, ironically, 'Since our Confession has been refuted by the prompting of the Holy Spirit and according to the Gospels, it is necessary that both Canons be found in the Gospels, along with chasubles and chalices, tonsures and headgear; to sell Masses for six coins, on behalf of the souls in Purgatory, sailors on the sea, merchants on the earth, sick people in the house, and everyone in every circumstance whatsoever – in short, making market days and business-dealings out of the Mass. So, my brother, how does it seem to you about these teachers? It is often said, that eagles and lynxes see very well; but they are downright blind compared to these teachers, who can see in the Gospels both canons, vestments, and all sorts of business transactions of the Mass. These indeed can be called sharp Doctors, who everywhere have taken their seat higher up than among the hens.' [445]

After many other things, he returned to his bitter remarks and his slanders, and said: 'But why should I discuss many matters with these shameless blasphemers and impenitent asses of the Pope? It is as the Bishop of Salzburg said: "Ah, why do you want to reform us priests, when we have never been good?" Do not be good, then, and remain not good in the name of your God, the Devil. But how do you then endeavor to reform us, whom you admit to be good and to have a just cause? Is it not enough that you are rascals and betrayers of God, just as you shamelessly boast among your very selves? Etc.' [446]

Since in the Edict Luther's error concerning Free Will is pronounced to be not human, but rather bestial and a blasphemy to God, therefore, after a long accusation, he makes a ignominious comparison to pigs, saying: 'It is just as if that learned and illustrious herd, the Pigs, concluded in their Imperial Diet, "We pigs decree that no one shall hold nutmeg to be a precious and fragrant spice. But what it is, we do not know. However, some of us judge that it is husks; some, that it is bran; others, that it is cabbage leaves; others, that it is the precious jam of the peasants, under the hedges." [447] Thus also our learned and renowned Pigs at Augsburg act just as wisely, and meanwhile blaspheme God's truth, as though it were a bestial and blasphemous thing.' [448]

Concerning Faith alone, since it was prescribed in the Edict that it should not thereafter be taught that naked faith alone justifies, without charity and good works, Luther said with great contempt: 'How could good piggish doctors of this sort understand this sublime and sacred article, when they cannot bear even humble articles? As for instance, that a man may have a wife, and a woman a husband; that a person may eat and drink whatever God has given and provided to him; that a Christian may take both kinds of the Sacrament, and many other things of this kind. It would be a disgrace if so dull a herd and these filthy pigs should smell this nutmeg; I say nothing of their eating it and feeding on it. Let them teach and believe that he sins mortally who breaks wind while wearing a surplice, and that he is damned, who emits wind at the altar. But since I see' (he said) 'that the Devil continuously blasphemes this primary article through his piggish doctors, and can neither be quiet nor cease, I say, I, Dr Martin Luther, the unworthy Evangelist of our Lord Jesus Christ, that the Roman Emperor, the Turkish Emperor, the Emperor of Tartary, the Persian Emperor, the Pope, all Cardinals, Bishops, Priests, Monks, Nuns, Kings, Princes, Lords, all the world together with all the demons, must let this article stand, firm and unshaken: Faith alone, without any work, justifies before God – and in addition, they must have the fire of Hell on their heads, and no recompense of thanks. Let this be my, Dr Luther's, incitement by the Holy Spirit, and let it be my true and holy Gospel.' [449]

Luther bandied about these things and many others of this sort shamelessly, now by threatening and terrifying, now by boasting and vaunting, and most frequently by slandering, concerning the celibacy of Priests, his own Gospel, the property of Ecclesiastics, and other things. At length, at the end of the book, he sings a glorious encomium and victory song about himself. 'I, Dr Martin' (he says), 'have been called and driven to this, that I should be made a Doctor, without my own volition but through pure obedience. Then I had to accept the office of doctor and swear and vow to my most beloved Holy Scripture that I would faithfully and purely preach and teach it. And so, while I was teaching, the Papacy fell into my path, and wished to hinder me. What has happened to it, is before everyone's eyes; and still worse will happen. I, in the name and call of God, will walk on the lion and the serpent, and will tread down the cub of the lion and the dragon; this which has been begun in my life must be perfected after my death. The Blessed Jan Hus prophesied about me, when from his prison at Constance in Bohemia he wrote a letter saying, "Now they roast a certain goose (for they call Hus a goose), but after one hundred years, they will hear a certain Swan sing, whom they will have to endure."' [450]

Luther wrote these things there. But in the other little book, which he called a *Warning*, he is yet much more ostentatious in his lying, more prideful in his boasting, more terrible in his threatening, and more malicious in his slandering. Indeed, Cochlaeus quickly excerpted and refuted fifteen threats and lies from the first two signatures of that book. The last two of these excerpted passages ran as follows: 'For the rest' (he said) 'I do not want this Papist or that, but rather the entire Papacy piled up on top of me, until the Judge in Heaven shall give a sign. And I do not wish to, nor can I, be afraid of such enemies of God. Their impudence is my wrath: their anger, my laughter. And in addition, I do not want to cause people's consciences to be weighed down by this danger or fear, that their rebellion is seditious. For in such a cause, that name is both too evil and too serious. It should have another name, which the laws may well discover. Not everything which bloodthirsty dogs accuse of being seditious must really be so.'[451]

To these statements Cochlaeus responded in German, as follows: 'Certainly Luther does not lack for splendid words, but the fact of the matter is that these words contain nothing apart from sin, wickedness, misery, slaughter, and damnation both temporal and eternal of the wretched common folk whom he, through wicked plundering, calls his own men and his own people. For what has that unhappy head of the Devil accomplished up to now, except one calamity after another? Indeed, the Judge in Heaven has already given enough signs, if we would only believe them. Many members of the nobility have gone to their ruin through these machinations of Luther's. Furthermore, many learned men and still more farmers, nor indeed few town dwellers, have either been slain in battles or have been condemned to death in public trials. And it is greatly to be feared that they have been received still more badly in the other world. For the greatest part of them departed this world as heretics, faithless ones, rebels, and Apostate Christians, whom Christ the Judge cannot there recognize as his own, since they have defected from Him and from His Catholic Church to a certain Apostate Monk – one who, like another Nimrod, the violent and strong hunter, dares to say "I and my people," calling people "his" whom he has attained without any legal right. And this vicious Judas treacherously betrays "his people" not just to the Devil (as he betrayed the farmers) through defection, through schism, through ancient heresies; but also to the Emperor and the Pope, when of his own free will, as the most wicked and most vicious traitor, he gives "his people" over into their hands for execution. How so? Because he says "It is not sedition, when someone acts against the law"; although any transgression of the law is called sedition. And that man is called seditious, who does not wish to obey the magistracy and the law, but attacks and fights against them, and wants to overthrow them and to rule in his own person, to constitute laws, etc. Therefore from this it follows, that the rebellion of the Lutherans is clearly seditious. Why so? Because they do not wish to obey the magistracy and the law.

'And if any of the Lutherans should deny this or should make accusations against me, I now publicly by these writings wish to make my offer of the law and the magistracy, to discuss the doctrines and deeds of Luther with that man, at the risk of body and of life; to stand trial with him before the Magistracy until the case is decided; to stand foot-to-foot with him, and even to lie in prison or captivity, until the definitive sentence of the Judges. Which one of the Lutherans is courageous enough? Here I will clearly see, whether Luther spoke such bombastic and ferocious words in earnest. My wrath and my challenge are not new; I issued it to Luther himself, to his very face, at Worms, and I have very often repeated the same challenge in public writings, and I will always persist firmly in it – the longer it takes, the more constant I will be. Nor do I flee the light; I do not creep into a corner when matters become serious, as Luther did, treacherously after the Diet of Worms in the past, and just now fearfully during the Diet of Augsburg. I appeared openly and obviously at the Imperial Diets of Worms, Nuremberg, Speyer, and Augsburg, when these matters were being discussed. And I waited in vain for any Lutheran there to dispute with me about words of this sort, or to undergo judgment with me. And up to this very day none of them has come to make trial of me. However, I by no means wish for this to redound to my praise, as if I were so very learned. For I acknowledge that I have very little of all those things that pertain to learning and genius; but I want this honor to be paid both to Christ the Lord, on Whose promises made to His Church I continually take my stand and depend; and to His Spouse, the Holy Mother Church, which the Blessed Paul calls a pillar and a mainstay of Truth (1 Timothy 3).'[452]

These things Cochlaeus wrote there. But it would take too long to recount all Luther's lies and pompous boastings of vainglory from that one book of his, where he boasts about his peaceful and faithful published admonitions to the Ecclesiastics, and about his tranquil doctrine, and about his and his followers' valid prayers to God for the papists; and about his acts of patronage, by which alone the papists were saved from the violence of the seditious. And what is most impudent, vain, and wicked of all, he frequently boasts that the papists well know and confess of their own accord that Luther's doctrine is the true and pure Gospel, although they do not desist from persecuting it, against their own consciences. And although in that whole book he seeks for nothing rather than to make the Emperor's and the other Catholic Princes' subjects rebellious and hostile toward them, nevertheless with a shameless face he protests that he never persuaded their subjects to resist their orders or their acts of force. And among the most atrocious injuries, accusations, and slanders which he hurls thick and fast at the Emperor and the other pious princes, from time to time he seeks favor for his party by praising the Emperor. These are his very words: 'This is my faithful judgment. If the Emperor called his subjects to arms and wished to wage war against our party, either on account of the Pope's cause or on account of our doctrine – as the papists now horribly boast and brag that he did (although I still do not believe this of the Emperor); if he did this, it is my judgment that in such a case no man should offer his service to the Emperor for this cause, nor should he obey the Emperor; let everyone be certain that it is strongly forbidden to him by God to obey the Emperor in such a case. But whoever does obey the Emperor, let him know that he is disobedient to God, and he shall eternally lose his body and his soul in that war. For then the Emperor acts not only against God and the divine law, but also against his own Imperial law, against his sworn oath, and his obligation, and against his own seals and writings.'[453]

Against slanders of this sort Cochlaeus wrote a book in German, addressed to Dr Gregory Bruck, who had been the Lutherans' foremost mouth at Augsburg. Among many other things he said as follows: 'You know that at Augsburg there was long and serious discussion concerning the cause of the Faith, but by your party no mention was ever made of this accusation against the Emperor; rather, both sides brought forward the Gospel and the Holy Scriptures, but still there was disagreement about the understanding and interpretation of the Scriptures. But although you yourself were present at all the transactions, and did a great deal for your side both by speaking and by writing, still I never understood that you accused his Imperial Majesty of so impious and tyrannical an intention, namely of wishing to persecute the Gospel through war. For if the Emperor were such a tyrant and apostate that he would either intend or attempt to attack the Gospel (which is the strength of God for the health of all believers, Romans 1) in a war certainly he would be entirely unworthy of the Imperial crown, office, and dignity, and would on this account forfeit all authority and jurisdiction in the Empire, together with all subjection and homage of the Princes and other Lords, who derive their feudal and royal authority from him; and he would in our opinion be viler and worse than any Pagan, Jew, or Turk: just as the Holy Scriptures and both laws, namely Ecclesiastic and Civil, prescribe and decide. Now among all the past Emperors, from that great first Emperor Constantine all the way down to this Charles the Fifth, none was ever charged with such impiety – although many of them at times committed great sins, persecutions, and acts of tyranny – except for one Apostate, the Emperor Julian, who defected from Christ to Idols, and persecuted the Gospel. However, he did not persecute it by war and the outpouring of blood (as Luther does not blush to ascribe to our pious, Catholic, and religious Emperor), but only by edicts and bans which ordered that the Gospel could not be publicly preached. About him Eutropius, who took part in his war against the Parthians and the Persians, writes thus: "He was an excessive persecutor of the Christian religion, however in such a way that he abstained from bloodshed."'[454] Cochlaeus wrote these things and many others of this sort there.

However, Luther listed three reasons in particular in his *Warning*, according to which no subject should obey the Emperor in waging war against the Lutherans, and he enlarged these reasons with great exaggerations and hateful and violent accusations. 'The first reason' (he said) 'why you should not obey the Emperor or serve as his soldier in this sort of cause, is this: because you (in the same way as the Emperor himself) have sworn in Baptism to preserve the Gospel of Christ, not to persecute or attack it. But now you well know that in this case the Emperor has been incited and deceived by the Pope to wage war against Christ's Gospel, since our doctrine was openly found at Augsburg to be the true Gospel and the Holy Scripture. Therefore, if the

Emperor or your Prince calls you to such a war, you shall say to him as follows, "Good Emperor, Good Prince, when you keep your oath and your promise, which you swore in Baptism, you are my Dear Lord, and I will be obedient to you for going to war whenever you wish; but otherwise, seek out someone else for yourself, who may obey you. For my part, I refuse to blaspheme my God for your sake, or to attack His Word, or to rush so furiously with you and to leap down into the pit of Hell." This first reason' (he said) 'contains many other reasons – and great and terrible ones at that – within it. For whoever fights against the Gospel, must to the same extent fight against God, against Jesus Christ, against the Holy Spirit, against Christ's precious blood, against His death, against the Word of God, against all the articles of the faith, against all Sacraments, etc. Indeed, the Turk is not so insane as to fight or rage against his Mohammed or against his Koran, as our Devils, the papists, rage and rave against their own Gospel, which they admit to be true; and by so doing they make the Turk a pure Saint, but themselves complete and true Devils.[455]

'The second reason' (he said) 'is that even if our doctrine were not true (although nevertheless they themselves know otherwise), still this should most greatly frighten you away, that in such a war you would, in the eyes of God, burden yourself with and would make yourself a partner in all the abominations which came to pass previously in the whole Papacy and which will come to pass hereafter. This cause of the Emperor's contains in itself innumerable abominations and every malice, every sin and offense, in brief, it is, its very self, the pit of Hell with all sins; and you must be a partner of all these, if you obey the Emperor in this cause.'[456] Here, with terrible accusations, Luther lists the sins, offenses, and crimes of all ecclesiastical ranks, most especially of the Pope and the Cardinals, to whom he imputes all the most abominable acts, as if battle were to be joined by the mandate of the Emperor for the purpose of maintaining their sins. And in addition to the crimes of their life, he recounts abuses concerning indulgences, Purgatory, Masses, veneration of the Saints, auricular confessions, excommunications, etc. 'The sum of all this is' (he says) 'that everything which they teach or do tends toward this: that they should lead us away from Christ to their own and our own works. And there is no letter in their doctrine, however small, and no work however minor, that does not deny and blaspheme Christ, and do violence to the faith in Him, and lead unfortunate hearts first to impossibilities, then to despair; just as the true Antichrist ought to do.[457]

'The third reason' (he says) 'is that if you obey the Emperor in such a war, not only do you undertake and defend all the papists' evils, but you must also abolish and exterminate every good thing that has been recovered and instituted through the Gospel. This reason too contains many things in itself. For our Gospel has accomplished many great things. No one previously knew what the Gospel was, what Christ was, what Baptism was, what Confession was, what the Sacrament was, etc. In sum, we knew absolutely nothing which a Christian ought to know. Everything was obscured and crushed by the Pope's asses;

they are indeed asses, and great ones at that, unskilled and unlearned asses, in Christian matters. For I too was one of them, and I know that I am speaking the truth here.' [458] And below he said, 'It will be necessary for you to cooperate, in order for all the German books, the New Testament, the Psalter, the prayer books, the hymnals, and whatever we have written about many good things (as they themselves admit), to be completely destroyed. It will be necessary for you to cooperate, in order for no one to learn anything at all about Baptism, about the Sacrament, about Faith, about powers, about the state of matrimony, or about the Gospel.' [459]

This German rhetorician listed these things and many others of this sort there, with a pretended heat and fine-sounding exaggerations, in order to stir up the emotions of the misled common people. But in some places he cried out ominously against the Imperial Diet itself, saying: 'Oh how unhappy all of you are, who were at Augsburg on the Pope's behalf! You will be causes of shame to all your successors and descendants, who will not be able happily to hear your names, because they had such unlucky ancestors. Oh infamous Imperial Diet, such as never was celebrated or heard of, nor ever will be celebrated nor heard of, for so infamous a purpose; which must be an everlasting stain on all the Princes and the whole Empire, which overwhelms all us Germans with shame, both before God and before the whole world. What will the Turk say to these things, and his whole Empire, when he hears of so unheard-of a treatment of this Empire of ours? What will the Tartars and the Muscovites say? Who, out of the rest of the world, under the whole heaven, will fear for himself at the hands of us Germans, or will have any good opinion of us at all, when they hear that we allow the cursed Pope with his minions thus to make fools, idiots, children out of us, trunk and branches; that for the sake of their sinful, Sodomitical, and filthy doctrine and way of life, we deal so filthily, so much worse than filthily, in open Imperial Diets, contrary to justice and truth? Every German shall justly rue that he was born a German, and that he is called a German.' [460]

Moreover, from time to time he offered amazing threats. 'I have lived long enough' (he said); 'I have deserved death well, and I have begun honorably to rescue my Lord Christ from the Papacy. After my death, they will know Luther rightly for the first time; although even now, if I should be killed in a Popish or priestly uprising, I will take with me a certain troop of Bishops, Elders, and Monks, so that everyone will say, "Dr Martin was accompanied to his burial by a great procession. For he is a great Doctor, beyond all Bishops, Elders, and Monks; therefore, it will be proper for them to go on one another's heels [461] to burial with him, so that songs and stories may be made about this man." And thus we will make a certain pilgrimage together, for the last time: Those papists, indeed, downward into the Pit of Hell, to their God of falsehood and murder, whom they have served by lying and killing; but I to my Lord Jesus Christ, Whom I have served in truth and peace.' [462]

Against this book of Luther's, which was so malicious and abusive, a little book came out of Dresden, written in German by a certain layman, of which the beginning ran as follows: 'Luther just now published a certain booklet, which he calls a *Warning to his Dear Germans*. But it could more correctly be called a Seduction, and an Incitement to rebellion and sedition, since in point of fact he seeks nothing else in it but to make us Germans defect from the Emperor and rebel against all legitimate powers. With what deceitful tricks, lies, clamors, and deceptions he does this, and how often he uses the name of the Devil for this purpose, let those men see and answer, who always say that he is a holy man and that the Spirit of God is with him. For first he writes that the accusation of those who are not Lutherans depends on force, and that they found their cause on the strength of their right hands. For this reason, either sedition or war must come from their cause; whichever one occurs, the Lutherans will be innocent of it, since they gave neither advice nor cause to it. But how true this is, those men well know and can testify, who daily see and hear what conspiracies, what equipment of war, what assemblings of soldiers, what gatherings of cavalry, what leagues, have been attempted and instituted among the Lutherans during this entire time. And they know, on the other hand, that none of these things have been done by the Emperor or his followers; nay, rather, the Emperor himself, like a most kindly and gentle lord, is and always has been much more concerned to settle this matter and to bring it back to peace.' [463]

That layman wrote these things and many things of this sort. Luther wrote a most abusive little book in response to him, which had the title *Against the Assassin at Dresden*. In it, after his excuse for himself, he wrote as follows: 'See here, good reader, whether Luther lied in his two pamphlets, when he accused the papists, traitors, murders, rascals – and, alas!, did not accuse them enough. This Arch-rascal wants to teach us the virtues of the papists – namely, that subjects are by no means disobedient to their superiors when, contrary to God and justice, they wish to pour out innocent blood.' [464] And below he said, 'Since the papists now make it known through this Assassin that they think the Lutherans are engaged in preparing for war and in gathering soldiers – I hear this gladly, from my heart, and it pleases me that the papists should remain in this opinion and this anxiety, and should believe that this view of the Lutherans is true. If I could, I would happily wish to strengthen their opinion of this sort and their anxiety, until they died of fear. And I would want to sing a song of this sort about them: "Little master Cain, you know you killed your brother Abel; therefore, take your reward too, that you must tremble and fear lest whoever meets you on the road may kill you; and that you will never be secure, and even the rustling of a leaf will terrify you." The Lords Annas and Caiphas know that they persecuted Christ; they too have their reward, that they fear for their own treatment by the people, and they say, "Oh, oh, may there not be sedition among the people." Thus these murderers of ours too, who have poured out so much innocent blood, ought to endure this blow, that they must worry and fear lest there be sedition. And even if the Lutherans are making no preparation for war, nevertheless these men ought to fear that Germany will be full of armed Lutherans; nor ought they to think otherwise than that in this year no tree will produce leaves, but instead of leaves will bear Lutherans, armored men, and arquebus-shooters. They ought to think this; so I have prayed and will continue to pray, as it is written: "The impious man flees when no one pursues." ' [465]

And below he wrote: 'Therefore, since it is clearer than daylight that the papists themselves confess both in their words and their deeds that they are our enemies and opposed to us, let this be the truthful judgment of Dr Martin, both founded on the Scriptures and demonstrated from their own fruits, that the papists have most certainly planned in their own minds, and think day and night, and scheme and connive, in what way they may destroy and exterminate us. Each one of us can expect this and nothing better from them, nor is there any doubt. Furthermore, whatever they pretend in either a friendly or a peaceful manner, this must all be treachery, and a kiss of Judas; or else it is fitting for them to act from dread and fear, since they cannot yet do what they willingly would do. I want this judgment to be established among our people and in the entire world, so that according to it whoever wishes may know how to provide for himself: I know that I am not lying, unless the Scripture is false. Therefore, that two-faced Assassin is a rascal, since he knows all this very well in his heart, and nevertheless sends his bloody dogs against us as though they were good and peaceful, among whom there are more "fruits of the faith" than there are among us.' [466]

And below he says, 'I do not care at all about the complaint that is made, that for the most part pure curses and Devils are named in my book; this ought to be my glory and my honor. And thus I wish to have it, so that hereafter it may be said about me that I am full of cursing, accusations, and execrations against papists. And for the rest, I wish to exert myself against these rascals with execrations and curses, all the way to my grave, nor shall they hear any good word from me again; thus I will drive them to their graves with my thunderclaps and lightning-bolts.' [467]

While these things were happening in Saxony, and a great alliance was being made for the defense of the Lutheran sect by the mutual oaths of certain Princes, Counts, and Cities, the Emperor was busy in lower Germany, where he had many hereditary provinces. Among the Swiss the Catholics were being troubled by many injuries and tribulations, especially at the hands of the Bernese and the people of Zurich, who were more powerful than the others and better supplied with money and arms. For this reason it happened that the Five Catholic Cantons, namely, Lucerne, Uri, Schwyz, Unterwalden, and Zug, by a common decree undertook war against Zurich. They recounted the causes of the war at length in denunciatory letters. 'Since for a long time' (they said) 'we have all, together and singly, more than sufficiently offered ourselves to stand before law and equity; but you, against sworn alliances, against the public peace, against Christian discipline and concord, against the faith, charity, and friendship of your confederates, against even all natural law, and against all equity, draw our subjects away from us and make them rebels, so that they have now become forsworn and perjured toward us and reject our jurisdiction in the Captaincy of St Gall and in the prefects of the Rhine valley, and in not a few other places; but you defend them, and you attempt to sow discord among us ourselves through many deceits and wiles, so that by this danger you may drive us away from our ancient and undoubted Catholic faith; and you say that we refuse to hear the word of God or to allow the New and the Old Testament to be read; and on this account you have accused us of being impious and malicious traitors and treacherous rascals; therefore, since we do not adhere to your new and feigned faith, you deny us sustenance and the public marketplace, so that you may by this means drive us to famine, to the destruction not just of ourselves but even of our innocent infants who are still growing in their mothers' wombs; and moreover, every law is denied us, nor can anyone bring us any aid for obtaining justice; and we have borne restriction, violence, pride, and wickedness of this sort for a long time, nor is there any end to our injuries; we therefore are driven to denounce all these things to God and his Mother, to the most famous and universal heavenly Curia, and to all good people, to whom law and equity are pleasing. And if God will grant us the grace, virtue, and fortitude, we wish to avenge these things on you powerfully, by our hands and our deeds, as we clearly declare to you and all your helpers and your adherents by these letters, and we want our honor to be asserted before you through this, on behalf of ourselves and those who aid us. In the faith and testimony of these letters, we append the seal of our faithful confederation [468] at Zug, in the name of us all. Given on Wednesday the 4th day of October, in the year 1531 from the birth of Christ.' [469]

Therefore, when this declaration had been made, they soon prepared themselves for war on either side. And so on 11 October, the people of Zurich sent out in advance their Captain with one cohort and six wheeled cannons. They themselves followed with all the best soldiers and twenty large cannons, and when they had crossed Mt Albus, they attacked three Catholic canons, namely Schwyz, Zug, and Unterwalden, near the monastery that is called Kappel. But the Catholics had laid traps; immediately after the enemy's advance, they retreated, feigning flight. But they soon burst out again with a strong battle line, and put the people of Zurich to flight. And so they were all slain, however large a troop they had presented, and all their cannons and munitions were taken from them. The number of the slain was 1,500. Zwingli, the author of all the treachery and discord among the Swiss, was discovered by two Catholics in that massacre. He was lying prone on his face and still breathing. Since they did not recognize him, they asked him if he wished to confess, but he kept silent as though he were dead. But another Catholic, who recognized him, arrived on the scene and dealt him a mortal wound, and then immediately pointed him out to the Captains. They ordered him to stand public trial, in which he was clearly judged to be a traitor, and was burned as a heretic. But they say that certain people of Zurich carried his ashes away from there and bore them back home.

Other famous Apostates were also killed, namely the Abbot and Prior of Kappel, and Commander of Risnach, Antonius Waldner; the Cantor and Canon

of Zurich, Henry Utinger; the Custodian and Canon of the same place; and all
the strongest men from the citizens. Moreover, two famous men were captured,
namely the Prefect and the Underwriter of Zurich. Afterwards, another battle
took place on the 17th day of October, and again the outcome was favorable
to the Catholics and unfavorable to the heretics. For after the disaster which
they had suffered, the people of Zurich called the Bernese to help them, and
when they had gathered an army of nearly 300,000 foot soldiers, they marched
out on to the field. The army was divided into two bands: the men of Zurich
marched against Zug, and the Bernese against Lucerne. But the Five Catholic
Cantons by joining their forces had around 18,000 foot soldiers, and when they
met with the Bernese near a certain river, they put them to flight. Five hundred
men died in the river, and 700 were slain in the battle. On the next day certain
men of Zurich crawled out of the bramble-bushes. The Catholics treated
mercifully and kindly any of them who would receive the Sacrament. Battle
was joined once more on the 24th day of October. For the people of Zurich
and Bern, longing for revenge, called the men of Basel and Schaffhausen to
their aid, and were planning to rush against the unprepared enemy by night.
The Catholics were not all in the same place; for the people of Lucerne were
keeping their army in a separate sector, facing the Bernese. But the other four
Cantons, when they learned the plan of the heretics, put white tunics over
their weapons, so that they might have a token by which to recognize one
another at night. When the battle began, the first fighting was so bitter and
bloody that the Catholics in the front ranks were slaughtered all the way to
the fifth division or rank. But with God as their helper, at length they were
victorious and put the heretics to flight, after killing 6,000 of them.

But not yet did the enemies' anger cease. For on the last day of October,
on the Eve of All Saints' Day, once again the men of Zurich attacked the Five
Catholic Cantons – but with no greater success than previously. For in the
second hour of the night the Catholics attacked their camps with 6,000 soldiers,
and after they had killed 5,000 of the enemy, they captured whichever remaining
ones had not fled; for there were 8,000 soldiers in these camps. For the rest,
there is among the Swiss an utterly holy and venerable shrine, famous for
miracles, sacred to the Virgin Mary, Mother of God. It is called 'The Hermitage.' At it, the Five Catholic Cantons decreed that a public procession would
be undertaken by old men, children, women, virgins, and the whole crowd of
non-combatants. The people of Zurich, imbued with the perverse doctrine of
Zwingli, bore this very badly. And so they decreed that they would undertake
an expedition to destroy that shrine, and to break the Image of the Holy Virgin
Mary into small pieces and then burn it. When the Five Cantons learned of
this, they set out for that place with haste, and with their weapons once again
covered with white cloths they dealt severely with the heretics on the plain in
front of the mountain, killing 5,000 of them, more or less, and seizing four of
their standards. One of these is said to have belonged to Zurich, the second
to Basel, the third to Schaffhausen, and the fourth to Muhlhausen.

Indeed, the heretics were much stronger in provisions and resources, in the number of soldiers and in the equipment of arms and cannons, than were the Catholics. But the Catholics fortunately were always victorious, honorably armed with their faith, piety, religion, and good conscience, and with their upright trust in God and His Saints. For during the whole time of this expedition, they religiously observed their ancient devotion, and they had their priests with them, so that they might take part in their sacrifices in daily Masses, praying earnestly and religiously to God on bended knee, both before battle and when the battle was accomplished. In addition, they appointed eighteen widows in the territory of Schwyz, who taking turns with one another in groups of six would continually, in the shrine of the Blessed Virgin of the Hermitage, pray day and night to God for the army. Therefore, they deservedly conquered men who held the heavenly powers in contempt and trusted in humans, and who put their hands to worldly matters.[470] For this reason the Five Cantons can without harm be compared to the famous Maccabees, who said, 'It is easy for many to be enclosed by the hands of a few. And there is no difference in God's sight, to liberate with many and with a few; since victory in war lies not in the numbers of the army, but strength comes from heaven.'

Therefore, when the heretics had been conquered and routed so many times, they sought and at length entered into agreement with the Five Catholic Cantons, by the intercessions of the Speakers of many Imperial cities. The people of Zurich did so on the 16th day of November, and the Bernese on the 23rd day of the same month. Therefore it would be worth the trouble to recount the words of the first article, from the German formula of concord, which was undertaken by the arbitrators concerning faith (since the discord and the occasion of war were primarily about faith):

'First, therefore, we people of Zurich both wish to and must leave undisturbed our faithful confederates from the Five Cantons, together with their beloved fellow citizens and their provincials of Wallis, and all their adherents whether ecclesiastical or secular, with reference to their true, undoubted, Catholic faith, both now and hereafter, in their own cities, territories, prefectures, and dominions, without any contradiction or argument, and with all pretexts, exceptions, circumventions, and tricks forbidden and removed. And in return, we Five Cantons must leave our confederates the people of Zurich and their own adherents undisturbed with reference to their faith.' And this same form of words in regard to the first article of concord was employed with the Bernese as well.

They deservedly rejoiced about this, and all Catholics throughout the entire world congratulated those Five Cantons because, for the purpose of courageously freeing the Catholic faith, they had not hesitated to expose their bodies, their wives, their children, and their entire fatherland to the ultimate test. And for this reason, in return for their piety, God granted them glorious triumphs over the heretics, who were driven to admit, themselves, that the ancient faith of the Five Cantons was true and undoubted. And these Five Cantons deserve another form of praise, because by their promptness and their work two most bitter and despicable enemies of the Church, Ulrich Zwingli and Johannes Oecolampadius, were removed from our midst. The first of these two men was quickly killed and burnt in the first battle; but the second not long after at Basel was afflicted with such grief in his mind, that his whore (whom that Apostate Monk considered as a wife) found him one morning dead in his bed. About these men's death, that most famous man Thomas More, High Chancellor of the King, wrote from England to Johannes Cochlaeus as follows: 'After George returned to England, I received many letters from you at different times. The last was the one you wrote about Zwingli and Oecolampadius. The news of their deaths brought me happiness. For although they have left us causes of sorrow, and alas! very heavy ones, for many reasons which I cannot describe without horror and of which no one is ignorant, nor should pious people hear them without a heavy groan; nevertheless, we may rightly rejoice that two such monstrous foes of the Christian faith, so girded for the destruction of the Church, so intent always on every chance of destroying piety, have been removed from our midst.'

1532

The Emperor, in order to repress and restrain by councils without bloodshed movements and conspiracies of this sort and discord among the sects in Germany, declared an Imperial Diet (as they call it) to be held at Speyer. But when he learned that the largest possible mustering and army of the Turks was approaching for the purpose of invading Hungary and Germany, he transferred that Diet from Speyer to Regensburg, so that the Emperor himself might thus be nearer to the enemy of the Christian name, and might more quickly be able to resist him. Therefore, he summoned all the Princes and Estates of the Holy Roman Empire into the aforementioned Imperial city, Regensburg, by which the Danube flows, in Bavaria. And among the Elector Princes the following personally attended, after the Emperor Charles and Ferdinand, King of the Romans, of Hungary, and of Bohemia: Albert, the Cardinal and Archbishop of Mainz; Ludwig, Palatine Count of the Rhine, Duke of Bavaria; and Joachim, Marquis of Brandenburg, Duke of Stettin, Etc. From the Bishops, the Cardinals of Salzburg and Trent; also the Bishops of Bamberg, Würtzburg, Speyer, Augsburg, Holland, Batavia, Regensburg, Minden, Vienna. From the other Princes, the Dukes of Bavaria and the Counts of the Palatine Rhine, Frederick, Wilhelm, Louis, Otto Henry, and Philip; and also Duke George of Saxony, Duke Henry of Braunschweig, Landgrave George of Leuchtenberg; in addition, not a few Counts and Barons, together with Abbots and other Prelates. Moreover, many attended through their Speakers, just as did the cities, free and Imperial.

But the Lutheran Princes, with their confederates, met separately at Schweinfurt in Franconia. By the Emperor's agreement, two Electors, of Mainz and the Rhineland Palatinate, set out to join them there, so that they might confer with them about hastening their aid against the Turks (who already had arrived into Hungary with the greatest strength), as had been promised in the Diet of Augsburg. But when they arrived before the Lutherans, they were not recognized by the crowd; and so they returned to the Emperor at Regensburg. There the Speakers of other Kings and Lords also were, attending the Emperor's court. Among them was Thomas Cranmer, Speaker of the King of England, who had brought with him a book from England, in which both the divorce and the new marriage of the King of England were most precisely inspected. When he had handed this over to Johannes Cochlaeus for his perusal, he responded very briefly to all the rhetorical amplifications of cleverness, privately to Cranmer. And although that Englishman was a keen and learned Theologian and Priest, nevertheless he did not respond to Cochlaeus's writing, although he often spoke informally with him there.

In addition, there were present at that same Diet the Reverend Dr Cardinal Campeggio, Lateran Legate, and Dr Jerome Aleander, Archbishop of Brindisi, the Apostolic Nuncio. To them was handed over a certain book by a learned man, who strove to reconcile the Lutherans with the Catholics in doctrine. But although he abolished many things that had long been observed by the Catholics, he was found to Judaize in many respects. And so his book, by the order of both the Cardinal Legate and Aleander the Apostolic Nuncio, was examined by certain Spanish theologians (to whom Cochlaeus was added), and by their judgment was rejected on the grounds of Judaizing, since in addition its author had been converted from Judaism to Christ's religion. But Cochlaeus there found a much worse book openly for sale, with this title: *On the Errors of the Trinity; Seven Books by Michael Serveto, a Spaniard.* When Cochlaeus brought this book to Dr Juan de Quintana, a distinguished theologian, His Imperial Majesty's Confessor, and a Spaniard, he took the shame of this matter very badly, both because the author (whom he said he even knew by sight) was Spanish, and because in that book there were the most impious and unheard of heresies. And so he soon saw to it that the book was suppressed, so that it could not be sold any longer.

But at this time there arose against the Church a certain German, from Jülich, who had been a disciple of Luther's at Wittenberg for two years. He asserted more or less the same errors concerning the Trinity; and even the Lutherans and Luther himself resisted this man, so that heresy could not gain any strength. But the German Georg Witzel, who came from the town of Wach (which belonged to the Landgrave of Hesse), who had lamentably been a Lutheran for ten years, began then to recover his senses from reading ancient theologians and the Holy Fathers, so that he no longer approved of everything which Luther taught.[471] When Luther, together with his followers, perceived this, he caused Witzel to be brought by force from Niemegk (which town was three miles away from Wittenberg) to Wittenberg, as a captive, where he was shut up in a tower and held for a fairly long time in prison, just as though he were an evildoer and a heretic. And Luther quickly ordered that all of Witzel's books, papers, and letters be examined and picked apart, in case he might by chance be able to find anything there on the grounds of which Witzel might be justly accused. He most especially desired to find some judgment about that

Campanus, who had stayed with Witzel for a month at Niemegk.[472] But when all the corners had been examined and nothing further had been found that was worthy of accusation, Witzel was sent away free. And when he returned home, distressed by the disgrace of his captivity, he received letters from his father at Wach, which summoned him back to his native land. But so that he would not appear to have fled secretly, he asked for a document of release from the Elector Prince of Saxony. When this was granted him, he returned to his country.

But Luther and his partisans, fearing for their doctrine because of him, began to attack Witzel both with secret and with open accusations, both elsewhere and especially at Erfurt, where he had once labored at philosophy in the public Academy, and where he now intended to publish good letters. Therefore, three Lutherans took earnest care that he should not obtain any position there either for preaching to the people or for teaching in the schools. These three were Jodocus Koch, who calls himself Justus Jonas, a married priest; and two apostate monks, Langus and Aegidius. And he yielded to them and returned to his father. But since he did not feel that it was safe for him in that place either to do or to write anything against the Lutherans, he sought a Patron from elsewhere; and he found the best of patrons, a pious, religious, and powerful man, Lord Hoyer, a noble Count from Mansfeld, who honorably kept him safe at Eisleben, even though he was in the midst of Lutherans. There that man, since he was talented, sharp, learned, extremely skilled in the Greek and Hebrew languages, and moreover young in years and most tolerant of labor, wrote and published many works against the Lutheran sect and doctrine, in which he struggled to frighten the Germans away from that most pernicious sect and to recall them to the path; and he did this with no small profit to many people. Indeed, he fought against many of Luther's dogmas, but none more vehemently, fully, or frequently, than that one which extols faith alone and rejects the exertions and merits of good works. Against the Lutherans' accusations, he published a certain Apology in German, and a Confutation in Latin against that accursed slanderer Justus Jonas, whom he more rightly calls Jodocus Koch or Cocus. Later he wrote another book, in German, against the same man, which he titled *On the Catholic Church*.[473] I will quote a few lines (for it is quite long) from it, which pertain to that [anti]Trinitarian heretic, Johannes Campanus or Campensis, here. He says, 'On this point you lie, Cocus, that Campanus spread his sect among us at Niemegk. God is my witness, that that Campanus spoke not a single word about his notion to anyone at Niemegk; but did this one thing (for which purpose he had come there). He scrutinized the books of the Orthodox fathers, for what reason we do not know. Indeed, he only rarely either kept company with me or spoke to me. Nor could I ever find out from all his speech that he wanted to become an [anti]Trinitarian. But this I quickly perceived: that he was no longer a Lutheran. Concerning that, you lie on this point too, that he lay secretly hidden among us. Nothing was done there in secret or suspicion, nor was anything done impiously or dishonestly. About this I call to witness all the inhabitants of that town. But let it be; let Campanus be the Arch-blasphemer of Christ. Where, I ask you, and from whom did he learn this? He was with us for four weeks, but with you for two years. And you, not we, taught him. But you did not teach him this; well, let it be so. But who opened the door for him, the door to that error, so abominable, so horrible? Did I, or did you? Here it will clearly appear who should be brought to trial for the Campanian heresy, since he remained at Wittenberg and made his nest there for so long. In that same nest there still broods the Ostrich, that man who maintains very little about that word *Homousion*, and openly wrote that this noun, Trinity, does not please him in German. And could not even a Campanus hatch firstly from such an egg?'

These things Witzel wrote there. But that Spaniard, Michael Serveto, otherwise known as Reves from Aragon, in the same year published two *Dialogues* in addition to the *Seven Books* mentioned above. In these he slyly and craftily taught a new Theology about the flesh of Christ, basing it on several passages of the Scriptures; namely, that Christ has an eternal substance, both in regard to His flesh and in regard to His spirit, and that in the same substance in which He now is, both in flesh and spirit, He was previously as the Creator in Heaven. And in the preface he speaks as follows to the reader: 'All the things which I previously wrote in seven books against the received opinion about the Trinity, I now retract, honest reader; not because they were false, but because they were unfinished, and written as though by a child for children. However, I beg you to take from them whatever can help you toward understanding the things which must be said.' [474] These things he wrote, a man who was certainly keen and active in his intelligence, who seemed skilled in both the Greek and the Hebrew language.

But this is the common disease of almost all new theologians, that, puffed up with their skill in languages and depending on the literal sense of the Scripture, which they derive not from proven doctors, but from their own heads, and holding both the wholesome expositions of the Fathers and the well-founded representations of the scholastic Theologians in contempt, they trust in their own wisdom; but they are unstable because of the mobility of their wit, so that, with an easy impulse, through the agency of some new discovery they change, vary, increase, or diminish their earlier opinion, which they had praised in the first heat of discovery; just as in that saying of the Apostle James: 'A man of double mind is inconstant in all his ways.' [475] So also Luther, too eager in arguments for the most part, in the manner of a torrent and with flying pen set many things in motion, when had he considered them at greater length, he would not have offered so great an opportunity and origin for others' dreadful errors. For Cochlaeus too had made those same retorts to Philip Melanchthon which were quoted above out of Witzel. For these were Luther's words, published long ago against Dr Jacob Latomus: 'There is no cause for you to cast up this word *Homousion* at me, which was accepted contrary to the Arrians; it was not accepted by many, and among them very famous men. Jerome too wished it to be abolished, and they have not yet expelled the danger from this invented word, so that Jerome complained that he had not known what poison lurked in syllables and letters. Therefore, if my soul detests this word *Homousion* and I do not wish to use it, I will not therefore be a heretic. Who forces me to use it?' [476] Etc.

But Cochlaeus keenly defended Jerome from this slander in a certain book, and convicted Luther of falsehood. For Jerome was not in doubt about *Homousion*, but about *Hypostasis*, in his *Letter to Pope Damasus* in which he asked the Pope, through the word *Homousion*, to respond about the Trinity. Moreover, Luther could attack the word 'Trinity' for the same reason that he attacked *Homousion*, since it too is not mentioned in the Sacred Scriptures; just as these words, 'Three Persons,' are not mentioned. Therefore a certain one of these poetic Theologians said – both most stupidly and most impiously – 'Three Persons, Three Chimeras,' and so imitated Luther's audacity concerning *Homousion*. For Luther had dared to justify the Arrians in this, that they refused to accept *Homousion* (which he calls a profane word).

Meanwhile, while the Emperor takes counsel at Regensburg with his brother the King, and other Princes and Estates of the Empire, about the overall state of affairs and the well-being of Germany, with the greatest number of troops the Tyrant of the Turks struggles throughout Hungary against Austria, so that he may again besiege Vienna. And the Emperor, after a strong garrison had been sent there, demanded that the Princes and Imperial Estates hastily furnish the help that they had long since promised at Augsburg, and he also raised an outstanding Cavalry from Burgundy and Lower Germany. And so many soldiers from throughout Germany hastened against Vienna. The Emperor wanted to be the Leader and Commander of all of them himself, since he had already announced to the Tyrant of the Turks his approach, for the purpose of joining battle with him. But the Turk had for many days besieged a small town – Gynsa by name – near the borders of Austria, to the utmost of his powers and with all his troops. When he could not defeat it, he was amazed by the valor [*virtus*] of the defense, and summoned the Prefect of the town to a conversation with him. The Turk considered this Prefect, a most vigorous man and most faithful to King Ferdinand, who was weakened by wounds, labors, and keeping watch, both a source of admiration and a sight worth seeing on account of the constancy [*virtus*] of his mind. [477] But when the Turk learned that the Emperor himself (who had departed rather late from Regensburg because his shin was injured in a fall from a horse, and was being treated by warm poultices) had arrived at Vienna, from which the town of Gynsa was nine miles distant, heedless of the battle that was under way he lifted the siege and retreated back again in shameful flight, although in general he was most eager for the glory of war. However, so that he should not flee unpunished, the Emperor overtook 17,000 Turks who had stayed back to get plunder, and gave them to slaughter. Then, when the army had been disbanded, which indeed was so beautiful and so strong that in many centuries Germany had not seen a greater or better equipped one, the Emperor left Germany behind and returned to Italy.

In the same year Johannes Bugenhagen Pomeranus, an Apostate whom the

Wittenbergers call their pastor and Bishop, wrote in German a book that was full of abuses, lies, and hateful slanders, to which he gave the title *Against the Thieves of the Chalice*.[478] In it he most bitterly condemned both the giving of communion to the laity in only one kind, and the sacrifice of the Mass which is offered for the living and the dead. Moreover, in order to stir up in the laity good will toward him and hatred toward every cleric, he absolves the laity since they acted through ignorance and suffered injury at the hands of the Thieves of the Chalice (that is, the Bishops and Clerics). But he quickly accuses the Bishops more seriously, saying, 'But the Bishops, who wish neither to see nor to hear Christ's commandment, and do not care what the Apostles taught about communion in both kinds,' etc. These things that most pestilential Apostate wrote, who like a stallion and a neighing horse often went in season from Wittenberg to the great and rich maritime cities (which are commonly called the Stagnales), now to Lubeck, now to Hamburg, now to Flensburg, now elsewhere, to sow Lutheranism there, not without seditious uproars, until, enriched by the various donations of these cities, he now safely enjoys their riches in Wittenberg.

But a certain distinguished Theologian of the Dominican Order, Dr Michael Vehe, responded seriously and learnedly in German to his book. Because of Vehe's honesty and erudition, the Reverend and Most Illustrious Lord, the Cardinal and Archbishop of Mainz and Magdeburg, had made him Prior of the Church of Halle in Saxony, and had enlisted him as his own counselor. But since that book is very long, here we will quote only a few sentences from its beginning, to offer just a taste. He says, 'There is a familiar proverb: whoever has a bad cause, is more vehement in his curses; and whoever is lacking the truth, depends on lies. This author acts according to this proverb in his whole book, since in its beginning, middle and end he everywhere sings the same song; that is, it is everywhere crammed full of vehement accusations, slanders, curses, and lies. But if everything that is not true were removed from the book, it would be a slender pamphlet indeed. If it was written for the sake of slandering, it has a well enough crafted beginning; but if it was written for the purpose of declaring and inquiring about the truth, then the author certainly should have approached the topic differently. For in every case truth is the best foundation, but he omitted truth and began his book from lies. Therefore, let us return his slanders to his own house, until he proves his lies. But if he does not know what he must prove, we will willingly teach this to him. First, surely, he must prove that the Chalice, in Christ's commandment, is necessary for salvation for all Christians. This he has not sufficiently done in his writings, nor will he ever be able to do so. For these words of Christ's, "Drink from it, all of you," do not apply to all Christians; just as we and others have clearly proven from the Gospels, both of Mark and of Luke. But let it be so; let these words of Christ be spoken with reference to everyone; nevertheless he must prove that they are a necessary precept. But if he consults with his own people, he will find that distinguished members of his sect deny that, and say that Christ did not command the taking of communion either in one or in both kinds, because he said "However often you shall do this." Next, let this too be granted, that these words are a necessary precept; he will have to prove that they were said to individuals in particular, and not to everybody in general, as for instance the following was said; "Be fruitful and multiply." But again, let even this be granted, that the words were said to individuals in particular; he will further have to prove that all the words of this command apply to individuals. For there are many words here: consecrate, offer, eat, drink, do this in His memory. And he will never prove this, unless he wants to impose the duty of consecration on each and every peasant. Finally, let that too be granted; nevertheless he will have to prove still further that Christ our God and Lord, in the case of necessity and danger, did not leave us this free mandate, and that the Church in such a case does not have the power of making an ordination by which such danger might be avoided. And indeed, he will not be able to prove this; we, moreover, will hereafter prove the opposite from the Holy Scriptures.' [479] These things Vehe wrote in the beginning of his book against Pomeranus.

But while the Emperor was endeavoring to battle against the Turks, the famous Duke of Saxony, Johannes, Elector Prince, died not far from Wittenberg on the hunting field. At his funeral Luther made two speeches to the people, which he wrote down and openly published in German. In the first of them he takes his theme from the first letter of Paul to the Thessalonians and explains it; in the second, from the first letter to the Corinthians. And Cochlaeus wrote in German a brief Postilla (as they call it) against each one of these to the Illustrious Prince Lord Johannes of Anhalt, who was then involved in no small danger, since Luther was attempting (through Nicolaus Haussman, whom he had sent to him in Dessau as a preacher) to subvert him from the Catholic faith and to entice him into his own sect, as though into a snare. Therefore Cochlaeus showed briefly both how wandering and fanatical Luther was in his first speech, and how slippery and inconstant in the second – to such an extent, that no one could safely either cleave to him, or trust him in anything. For example; Luther says, 'Why do we grieve at other people's deaths, or even at our own? For man dies only so much, not however the whole man, but only one part, namely the body. However, in Christ's death is the very Son of God, and the Lord of all creatures dies.' [480] Cochlaeus responds, 'What does Luther want to argue here? Was more dead in Christ than dies in us humans? In us only the body dies, Luther says; I admit it. But what more was dead in Christ than His body? Was His Soul, immortal and sinless, also dead? Or was His Divinity, which is exempt from suffering and omnipotent, dead? Just as the whole man does not die, so neither was the whole Christ dead.' [481] Again, Luther says, 'God intends to bring to Himself both you and all others, whoever has been baptized and sleeps in Christ; since He included them in the death of Christ, and embraced them in His resurrection, He will not send them below the ground.' [482] Cochlaeus responds, 'I say here, as I said above; since Luther cannot know the thoughts of God, nor was he ever His counselor, as Isaiah says. This indeed is true, that God will not send below the earth either

Christians or Pagans, Turks or Jews. For all must arise, and stand before the Judgment Seat of Christ, on the last day, so that each may receive according to his works. But that Christ will lead to Himself all the baptized, this has never been written. For many fall away from that innocence, and are not mindful of whence they fell; and while they do not keep what they have, even that which they have shall be taken from them and given to another. Indeed, Christ died for the whole world. But since many sin, and make themselves unworthy of the death of Christ, they are not included in the death of Christ, as Luther babbles and dreams; but, not having a bridal garment, they shall be cast into the outer shadows. Indeed, Christ included us all in His death, through Baptism. But whichever ones remove themselves again through subsequent sins, and do not do penance, they shall for ever remain outside, and shall be punished more heavily than those who did not taste of this Grace, as Paul says. It is not necessary to conjecture this from one's own head; for God judges each one according to his works.'

Luther further says, 'For you all know how our Head, the Elector Prince, following Christ, two years ago died at Augsburg and suffered true death, not merely for himself but for us all.'[483] Cochlaeus responds, 'The poisonous Apostate often repeats these words very hatefully, against the Emperor and all the other Catholic Princes; however, the stupid babbler does not know where these words tend. For the Elector certainly did not die in the body at Augsburg. But the death of the spirit is far more serious than the death of the body, as Luther himself admits. Therefore, if the Elector died there in his spirit, what praise or glory does he get from that? Did he not, by such a death, fall away from God? For He is not the God of the dead, but of the living; I mean of those who live in the spirit, even if they are dead in the body, so that He is the God of Abraham, Isaac, and Jacob. Therefore, if the Elector Prince there suffered true death, as Luther says, not in his body, but in his spirit, then Luther does not rightly compare him to Christ, who certainly died in the body, not in the spirit. And he says, much more inappropriately, that this Elector suffered death at Augsburg not merely for himself but for us all – as though he were another Christ. But Paul says, on the contrary, "There is one God, and one Mediator between God and men, the Man Christ Jesus, who gave Himself as redemption for all."' Luther further raves, when he says 'There it was necessary that he devour all evil morsels and poison plants or hemlocks, which the Devil delivered to him. But that is a true and horrible death, by which the Devil destroys someone.'[484] Cochlaeus answers, 'Behold how terribly God has blinded the proud Apostate, so that he has become an open traitor and soul-murderer to his own patron and his Prince, who he says devoured all bad morsels and poison plants, etc. Oh, how powerful and accurate is that saying of the Apostle concerning the heretical man: By your own judgment you are condemned. What morsels and hemlocks does he mean there? Bodily ones? But that Prince did not die there bodily. Therefore, he means spiritual ones, which are false doctrines, heresies, schisms, pride, disobedience, etc., through which diseases the Devil destroys wretched souls. But I would that the Prince had dissembled there, as he did before, and had not openly subscribed to the Lutheran Confession (which is certainly full of evil morsels and poisons), and had not, finally, persevered in it against every power and his own high rank.'

Again, Luther says, 'There our Beloved Elector Prince confessed the death of Christ and His resurrection, publicly before all the world, and persisted in that confession, and for its sake placed his provinces and subjects in danger, and indeed his own body and life. Truly, that confession transcends and absorbs a multitude of sins, just as the great sea does a spark of fire.' [485] Cochlaeus answers, 'Oh empty fairytales and stinking fish! Who at Augsburg, I beg you, attacked Christ's death and resurrection? Who wanted to deter or prevent the Elector Prince from confessing those things? Let the response of the Emperor and the other Princes and Imperial Estates concerning the Third Article of the Lutheran Confession be inspected, I pray, and also the Treatise that was produced by the discussion there between seven members from each side. And surely it will be most clearly discovered that in no word was there ever any dissension there concerning the death and resurrection of Christ. How can any people be so stupid and insane, that it can either hear or believe such open and incredible lies of a babbling idiot? Indeed, we confess every day in the Apostles' Creed that Christ died and was resurrected; and Luther, for this reason, wants to so extol his Patron that he makes a Martyr of him, because he confessed Christ's death and resurrection before a Christian Emperor, and other Christian princes – just as if he had stood before Nero, Decius, or Diocletian.'

These things have been quoted incidentally from Luther's first funeral speech. In the second speech Luther is more keenly charged with inconstancy, concerning the veneration of saints. For when he first began to write and openly to publish his books, he bitterly inveighed against the Thaborites and the Bohemian Waldensians, on behalf of the cult and veneration of the Saints. For in his book *On the Ten Commandments* he says as follows: 'But let not the Pighards, unhappy heretics, hope that their party has been helped by me; since due to excessive boorishness (and they take offense, with the most prideful hatred) they charge us Germans with worshiping the Saints of God, and with making Idols, and on that account they heap up against us a whole pile of verses of Scripture, in which it is prohibited that anyone should worship any except the one God. And so that they might appear among their own people to kindle a most just ill-will against us, they most hatefully omit that it is written that King David, and Solomon, and many others were adored; they are at the same time impious perverters of Scripture and subtle slanderers of our piety. For in this way these rustics at length teach us that only God must be adored, and they boast about it as if we had ever denied that very thing.' Again, in the same book he says, 'All the Saints can accomplish everything, and the more is given to you by God through them, the more you believe that you will receive. For what else are the Saints, but as the drops of dew, or moisture of the night, on the curls and head of the Bridegroom?' [486] Thus also in his sermon *Concerning Preparation for Death* he teaches the sick person to invoke all the Holy Angels, especially his own Angel, the Mother of God;[487] and all the Apostles and other Saints, especially those to whom God has granted him a special devotion. But after pride and disobedience had driven him into madness, he wrote and preached very differently about the Saints, so that scarcely any *Schwermer* or Fanatic was his equal. For then, MARIA the Mother of God was in no way any better nor any greater than Luther; then, his neighbor could help him as well as She; then Her prayer was only as good as the prayer of that man; then the *Ave Maria* ought to be ejected from children's prayer-lists; then the songs *Salve Regina* and *Regina Coeli* were impious. Moreover, the Holy Apostles Peter and Paul could do no more than Luther could. And whoever gave a florin to a beggar did a better deed and deserved more than if he built a golden shrine to Blessed Peter. And again, the Saints, while they were still living in the earth, were as gems; but when dead (as he calls those whom we believe to be alive with God in Heaven) they were as stone; nay, indeed, they were mere Idols, and whoever revered them an Idolater.

From this argument there arose seditious Prophets, who threw all the Images of the Saints, even of the Savior Himself, out of the shrines, no less tumultuously than impiously and in such a way that whoever knew how to treat the Images with the most and the greatest outrages was considered the best and most pious man. Nor were they gentler toward the bones and other such relics and traces of the Beatified, or toward Chalices and gilded Monstrances; until at length raging peasants came on the scene, who devastated both shrines and monasteries with such great madness and impiety that Luther himself judged them worthy of both the temporal sword and eternal damnation. But in this funeral speech he began once again to commend the Saints, no doubt as a favor to his Patron, whom he was endeavoring to make both a Martyr and a Holy Sleeper. Therefore, he began to argue concerning the Saints that their death is worthy and precious in the sight of God, by as much as He more esteems the dead Saints than the ones still living in the flesh; it is worthy and precious by as much as He cares less for the Saints on earth, whom He leaves sick and miserable, just as if He did not see them, than for those who, having been removed by Death from the sight of men and lying under the earth, then first begin to become precious in the eyes of God. He asserts all these things for this reason, so that he may persuade the people that the Elector Prince, whom he calls his Head, and who was removed from the sight of men, is precious in the sight of God and has been received into rest, where he is safe from all Devils and enemies, and so that his memory may remain into eternity without loss or oblivion.

Cochlaeus declared his opinions about this matter to the Anhaltine Prince, in order to demonstrate to him how windy and unstable Luther's doctrine is, which like a reed is turned and changed by every wind, a thing which both Christ in the Gospel and Paul in his Letter to the Ephesians ordered us to beware of.

1533

Meanwhile, there arises a new cause for disagreement at Leipzig (which city is renowned both for its famous Academy and for its excellent Market, and is subject to Duke George of Saxony, a Prince who remained Catholic through everything): because on Sundays many of the common folk were rushing into a neighboring town, Holtzhaus by name, which faces the territory of the Elector of Saxony. There a Lutheran man was preaching and was distributing Communion in both kinds to the people. Some said he was a Deacon, but others that he was a complete layman and a weaver of linen. When Duke George found out about this, he forbade the people of Leipzig to go there any longer. But since many had already been infected by that man and were secretly becoming Lutherans, the pious Prince, in order to tell the sick flocks from the healthy sheep, ordered that a certain symbol be made, in the form of a coin. The priests would give this coin to those who made their confession and took communion at Easter time, and they would give it in turn to the Senate, each person with the mention of his own name. Certain of the citizens, who had become Lutherans, were distressed by this order and feared the anger of their Prince; they wrote to Luther for advice on whether they could with a clear conscience take communion in one kind only out of fear of their Prince. He immediately responded (for Wittenberg lies only seven miles from Leipzig) to them in German in these words:

Luther's *Letter to the People of Leipzig.* 'To my honorable and cautious good friends at Leipzig, whom the Duke George, an enemy of the Gospel, now outlaws: Grace and Peace in Christ, Who must suffer and die among you, and Who will most certainly rise again and rule you. Dear friends, I have understood that certain ones among you undertook to inquire whether with a good conscience they may receive the Sacrament in one kind only, under the appearance as though they received both kinds, so that in this way they might pacify your Superior. Truly, since I know none of you, nor do I know in what condition are your heart and conscience, this seems to me to be the best judgment: Anyone who has been instructed on this matter and holds in his conscience according to the Word and regulation of God that both kinds are rightly given, on peril of his body and his soul, let him not act against his conscience in this way, that is, against God Himself. But now, since Duke George is striving to examine even the secrets of conscience, he is by all means worthy to be deceived, as an Apostle of Satan, by whatever method that may be done. For he has neither any law nor any appropriate occasion for demanding such a thing, and he sins against God and the Holy Spirit. But since we ought to consider not what others do, who are evil men, whether murderers or robbers; but only what is appropriate for us to endure and do: in this instance it would be best to say to the face of that murderer and robber, "I refuse to do this; if on this account you seize from me either my body or my possessions, you will have seized them from Another, to Whom you will have to render precise account, as Peter says: 'Jesus Christ is prepared to judge the living and the dead.' Therefore, good robber, go on your way; what you wish, I will not do. But what I wish, that God too will very soon wish." You will find this out through experience: for it is necessary to thrust the Cross into the Devil's face and neither to applaud nor to boast much; so that thus he may know, with whom he is engaged in this business. Christ Our Lord strengthen you and be with you. Amen. Dated at Wittenberg, on Good Friday, 1533. Dr Martin Luther, by his own hand.' [488]

When this letter arrived at Leipzig during the most Holy Days of Easter, when the people ought to be most devout and single-minded, it kindled torches of hatred and discord in the minds of the citizens as it was carried about hither and thither among the citizens and copied many times. When the Senate learned about this, in order to be on their guard against sedition they immediately sent a messenger to Dresden (which is thirteen miles distant from Leipzig, and where the Prince's Court is), with this letter in German: 'Most Illustrious and Most Noble Prince: First, our obedience (which is devout, ready for all circumstances, and dutiful) is zealously at Your Royal Clemency's disposal at all times. Merciful Lord, only a few days ago we discovered that a copy of a certain troublesome writing (which some say Dr Martin Luther wrote to this city) was being circulated hither and thither through the city; for instance, two copies of it even came into our own hands. Concerning this, indeed, we made both a very diligent inquiry and an examination, for the sake of obtaining that Letter, and also of finding out who acquired it, to whom it was written, and who now had it in his keeping. And at length after much zealously done work, today we have discovered the matter for certain, in this way. There is here a well-known and ingenious gem-cutter and goldsmith, called Stephen Steinber, who retreated here from Nuremberg. The story going about was that this matter was known to him. And when we desired by all means to learn from the aforesaid Master Stephen where that letter was, he promised that he would devote himself to the task of bringing it into our hands; as in fact at length he did, and handed it over to our Consul. We now send it to Your Most Illustrious Clemency, included in this letter. Furthermore, we saw to it that the aforementioned gem-cutter or goldsmith promised, through summoned guarantors of faith, that he would not leave here for four weeks, until this matter should reach an end. We were unable, due to our devoted attention, not to report these things to Your Most Illustrious Clemency, whom indeed we are most ready always to serve with all submission and obedience. Given under the Seal of our City, Saturday the Fourth after the birth of Quasimodo, in the Year of the Lord 1533.' [489]

When he had read these things, Duke George wrote to the Elector Prince of Saxony, who had followed his father in rule and in dignity, and complained about this harmful letter of Luther's, in which that man not only seriously injured the Duke's name and the reputation of his person, but even attempted to make his subjects rebels. And by so doing he had violated the sworn agreements which the Elector's father had undertaken with Duke George through their respective Counselors in the year of the Lord 1527. Therefore, he was requesting the son, the new Elector, to conduct himself with reference to Luther, due to this evil attack, in such a way that it would be clearly obvious that Luther displeased him; and to attend to putting an end, at long last, to injuries at that man's hands. Moreover, the section about concord, which Duke George here cites, runs thus in German, word for word:

'As for what pertains to Luther, our Most Clement Lord the Elector Prince of Saxony ought to announce to Luther (since Luther tarries in his lands and principalities) through his representatives that it has been made known to His Clemency that Luther is planning threatening writings; from which it may be presumed that he has it in mind to excite sedition and rebellion against His Most Illustrious Clemency's kinsman, Duke George of Saxony, and his lands and subjects; and even to use infamous and vicious books for this purpose. And although His Illustrious Clemency does not wish to suspect that it is Luther's intention to agitate for rebellion, either against His Clemency's kinsman or against anyone else, a thing which would be no less intolerable to His Illustrious Clemency than to his kinsman; nevertheless His Illustrious Clemency wishes earnestly to order Luther – since he himself knows that sedition and the imposition of injuries are contrary to Divine Scripture and to the Gospel – to admonish himself in this matter, and to refrain from all such things.' And a little later it says, 'Moreover, our Most Clement Lord ought sternly to order Luther that nothing should be attempted, practiced, proposed, or done either by him or by any adherent of his in Duke George's lands, in any manner whatsoever or on whatsoever pretext.'[490] These things are written there.

Meanwhile, because of various suspicions among the people about that letter, the Consul of Leipzig, Wolfgang Wideman, wrote to Luther himself, and sent a copy of the letter, kindly asking that Luther give a clear answer as to whether that letter was sent out in this form by him, and to whom it was written, or in what way the matter was otherwise; since many people at Leipzig were suspected on its account. Therefore, he wished to see to it that those people who had had nothing to do with that letter but were nevertheless held in suspicion because of it should be freed and released from that imagined suspicion. But Luther responded to him thus:

'Honorable, prudent, and beloved Lord and friend, I have received your writings, and I have understood their meaning sufficiently well. And in response to your entreaty and request, here in return is an entreaty and request of mine – that you may deign to indicate to me who ordered you or incited you to write letters of this sort to me. Either Plebanus in Kollen did this, or Sicarius in Dresden, or indeed your Lordling, Duke George. Then, indeed, you will receive a response, in full measure, crammed in, filled to the brim, and over-flowing – God willing. For I am ready to serve you. Given at Wittenberg on Sunday after St George's Day, 1533. Martin Luther, Doctor, etc.'[491]

When the Consul of Leipzig had sent this impudent response of Luther's to Duke George at Dresden, the Duke wrote again to the Elector Duke, his paternal kinsman, attaching copies of both letters, the Consul's and Luther's, and adding Luther's threats that had been made to the Consul about what would happen if he should come to him in the future with another such letter. Therefore the Duke kindly asked that the Elector should act in this matter just as he would wish to be done for himself. In this Luther found a new chance for accusing and published a book, to which he gave the title *Refutation of the Sedition Imputed to Him by Duke George, and Consolatory Letters to the Christians Who Were Expelled by Him from Leipzig without Cause.* In the opening passage of this book he quotes certain words of the Elector which were written to him, in German, with the following sense:

'But if this was your intention, to incite our kinsman's people, or any others, to any sedition through your writings, this we must not tolerate from you on any account at all. And you can easily guess that we will not neglect to exact a fitting penalty from you; but we wish to think that your mind was not set on this. For which reason it will be up to you, according to your need, to defend yourself by your own writings from such a charge and imputation, so that your innocence may be known, lest we also, should such a defense not be made, be compelled to view you as guilty of these things.' [492] These things the young Elector wrote, who seemed fervently to love and esteem Luther.

Therefore, depending on his power, protection, and command, Luther inveighed against Duke George with an attack full of slandering and wounding. First he set forth his shameless contempt toward the pious Prince, saying in German, 'Now since Duke George is an enemy of me and my Gospel, I do not wish to treat him with either such honor or such obedience that I would admit that this letter is mine, even if my hand and my seal are on it, since the letter is secret, and it is not fitting for him to have it, much less to act against it or to rage at it. Nevertheless, since he grows angry about and rages at that letter, and wishes to accuse me before my most clement Lord and Prince, I shall acknowledge [493] the letter as mine; and it ought both to be mine and to be called mine, so that we may find out if I can defend a letter of this sort against the very high and keen skill of Duke George. I joyfully hope that God will grant me grace for this.' [494]

Then he vainly protests that he would never say anything against Duke George's person or rank, just as he had never before said or written any such thing. And boasting about his own prudence, he added, 'I have always so arranged my words' (he said) 'and weighed them beforehand, because I very much wish my words to challenge Duke George and all his papists together to court, and to rage against them all in such a way that they cannot with truth make any sedition, or heresy, or slanders, or infamous libels,[495]out of my words.' [496] And so he boldly challenges Duke George, if he is a good and true Christian, to come forward and to prove the things he has written, in which he accused Luther, before the Elector, of making Duke George's subjects rebellious and disobedient, etc.

When Cochlaeus saw this book, he was inflamed with a great zeal and wrote a Defense of his most pious Patron, Duke George.[497] In that he freely recounted many things which later distressed the Elector of Saxony, to whom he sent his book by his own courier, as soon as it was printed, just as he had openly promised to do in that Defense. For there he recounts the sequence of events and all the abovementioned letters. Then he expresses astonishment that the Elector, with all his new counselors, was not able to perceive that such a letter of Luther's was both contrary to the former agreements and openly seditious; since it is written there, in plain words, that the best thing would be to say fiercely to the murderer's and robber's face, 'I refuse to do this.' For who can maintain or conceive a good intention toward a murderer and a robber? or towards an enemy of the Gospel and an apostle of the Devil? But especially seditious is what Luther adds in the same place, that Duke George deserves to be deceived by whatever means that can be accomplished. For what else does that contriver of sedition intend than to deceive his Prince and Magistrate by whatever art or means possible? Cochlaeus also castigates that impudence by which Luther wants freedom for himself, now to admit, now to deny, that the letter is his; when elsewhere his inconstancy and contradictoriness have been most detestably confounded and refuted very often, even at Augsburg before the Elector himself. And against Luther's plea, by which he attempted to excuse his inconsistencies, Cochlaeus asserts six arguments, by which he closes off every path of excuse. Moreover, when Luther again reproached Duke George with the feigned League of certain Princes, Cochlaeus pointedly refuted that slander by five arguments, and turned it back against Luther himself, that he was no less worthy of proscription than Dr Pack because of that seditious fiction. He also refuted another slander that had recently been thought up, about a certain formula of swearing, according to which Duke George forced his subjects (so Luther said) to abjure the Lutheran heresy. Therefore, Luther said, 'If there is an art of venomously interpreting and maliciously perverting someone's words against him, then I myself would wish carefully to interpret for Duke George the oath which he imposes on his subjects at Leipzig, by which he forces them to swear that they want to help condemn and persecute the Lutheran doctrine. Therefore, I would wish to say, "Duke George shakes his sword with these words, and sets out on to the battlefield against the Elector, the Landgrave, and their confederates."' And a little later he adds, 'Nevertheless, since the matter itself teaches that Duke George is not his own master, and the Devil is in the world, wicked everywhere; I would wish that His Nobility and the people of his province would attend this sport, and the neighboring Princes as well. I do not understand this oath, but I know well that the Devil intends nothing good, and that a great conflagration can arise from a contemptible spark. I would not take all the goods of the world to have my epistle sound so seditious as the oath imposed by Duke George sounds: in that case it would be necessary for me to die of shame in the twinkling of an eye.'

Against this slander Cochlaeus produced the public testimony of the Leipzig Senate, which in its letter to Duke George answered as follows: 'According to your Illustrious Clemency's letter, in which Your Clemency indicates that Luther writes about a certain oath imposed here by certain men for the condemnation and persecution of the Lutheran sect, we convened the Three Orders of the Senate, to whom we read the letter, and we thoroughly questioned them. They all unanimously said that they knew nothing either about this proposal or about the oath itself; just as we also do not know by whom this had been proposed here, nor had it been commanded us by Your Illustrious Clemency. Therefore, we cannot know at all what Luther may mean by it.' These things the Senate wrote. However, later Duke George obtained two copies of the feigned oath, which had been publicly displayed here and there in the Lutheran lands by certain rascals, for the purpose of exciting and increasing dislike of the Duke. And it had been devised quite cleverly enough that it could easily be believed to be true. For the words were arranged in accordance with the common form of the law for abjuring any heresy. However, those hateful words about condemning and persecuting the Lutheran doctrine were not contained in that formula; but Luther added them so that he might incite greater hatred toward the good Prince in this way. For he seemed to take this most badly of all, that Duke George said he had written seditiously. Therefore, Luther said, 'If any grace can be deserved from a cursed and sinful world, and if I Dr Martin had taught or done no other good thing than thus to have brought to light and decked out the secular government and power, for that one deed at least they should both thank me and favor me. For I have such glory and honor, through the Grace of God, concerning this matter (whether it pleases or pains the Devil with all his fish-scales) that from the time of the Apostles no Doctor or writer, no theologian or legal scholar, has so notably and clearly strengthened, instructed, and consoled the consciences of the secular estates as I have done – through the extraordinary Grace of God, this I know for certain. For neither Augustine nor Ambrose (who nevertheless were excellent in this business) were my equals in this, etc.' [498]

Against this boast of his Cochlaeus answered as follows: 'The Wise Man says, "Let another praise you, and not your own mouth; a stranger, and not your own lips." I certainly have never so far heard that this praise was given to Luther by learned men who read his writings. Indeed, he bandies about many other things too concerning himself and his doctrine, which are pure lies: for he boasts, that his Gospel is more lucid and more clear than it was in the times of the Apostles, and that before his doctrine the Germans never had the true Gospel. But boasts of this sort, so stupid and so monstrous, are never found among ancient, serious authors. Perhaps this book of his (whose title is *On Secular Power*) continuously boasts thus proudly about all Doctors. However, anyone who reads through this book will beyond doubt discover that no other book is either more seditious or more serious for the consciences of the secular powers.' [499]

Finally, the same Cochlaeus recounts twenty articles from that book, for the sake of example. Among them these words too are contained: 'The Secular Lords should govern their provinces and people from without; they overlook this, knowing no more than to scalp and to flay, than to impose one tax upon another, one tribute upon another; to let loose a bear here and a wolf there; in addition, they preserve no faith or truth among themselves. And so they do worse than robbers and rascals do. And their secular government lies as low as lies the government of the ecclesiastical Tyrants. For this reason God has handed them over into false understanding, so that they act perversely and want to rule spiritually over souls: just as they want to rule in the secular sphere so that they may confidently load themselves down with others' sins and with the hatred of God and all people, until they go to ruin with the Bishops, priests, and monks, one rascal with another.' These things Luther published there, and others much worse still and more seditious, a little before the uprising of the peasants.

However, when Duke George had arrested some seventy men who, following Luther's tenets, would not take the Sacrament of the Eucharist in one kind only, he set a time limit for them, from Easter to Pentecost, in the hope that by chance they might decide to follow and embrace the usage of the Church rather than Luther's new rules. If they refused to do so, then let them sell their houses and emigrate. These men, through a shrewd German rhetorician (for all these things had been both said and written in German), devised a very eloquent entreaty. In it, indeed, with a feigned devotion, they presented themselves as ready for every obedience which they could offer with a clear conscience, and they cunningly recounted many demonstrations of their point, so that by this supplication they could move the common people of Leipzig to hatred toward the Prince and sympathy toward themselves. Moreover, since among other things they had written that they would willingly obey if anyone could teach them otherwise, that they could properly take communion in one kind only, the pious Prince asked the Bishop of Merseburg, as an Ordinary of the place, to recall them from their erroneous conceptions by healthful admonitions. He did this most faithfully, having taken with him several Prelates and Doctors. But the recent division was still raging, and an empty vainglory was titillating people's minds, that they would seem both to themselves and to other Lutherans to have suffered persecution for the Word of God, and the greater part of those people had already hired houses to live in elsewhere with the Lutherans in the nearby towns, and the part of them who were independent youths and artisans could easily change location. For these reasons it happened that out of their whole number scarcely two could be recalled by healthful admonitions, although it was said to them by some people individually and by some in groups that if they prided themselves on the Word of God, they should hold this word of God as certain and clear, in which Christ expressly commands us to listen to the Church; but they have no word of God in which Christ expressly orders that both kinds of the Sacrament be given to the laity. But to them it seemed a shame and a disgrace to shrink from what they had begun, and to give up the reputation of persecution (which titillated untrained minds as if they were martyrs). And so they preferred to go rather than to remain. Certainly, the Prince could have dealt with them more severely according to the law, but he did not wish to; he sought this one thing only, to separate the sick sheep from the healthy ones. Therefore he decreed nothing else against them than that they not live personally in Leipzig; however, he permitted them to maintain not only their houses and their goods there, but even their wives and children, together with their households. Indeed, it was permitted to them to revisit Leipzig themselves three times a year at market times, just like other merchants. For the rest, he did not punish any of them in the slightest degree.

But Luther, while he wrote them a consolatory letter, extolled their rebellion and division in the greatest praises, through many arguments disguised with a rhetorician's persuasive wording. The third of these arguments runs as follows. 'The third consolation' (he said) 'is strong and powerful, if you consider the cause for which you suffer and are exiled. Indeed, the Devil and Duke George, together with their fellow tyrants, clearly pretend that you are expelled on account of one article, concerning both kinds of the Sacrament. But under the guise of article it is their intention (which they demonstrate in their deeds as well) that you should deny the whole doctrine of our Gospel, and adore all the abominations of the Pope. This should deservedly gladden your heart, that you have departed from that city and that province, in which it is commanded that the Word of grace and the remission of sins be denied and attacked, and how we are justified and saved through Christ alone, apart from our merits. For this is the principal article from which all our doctrine flows, and it has come forward so clearly into the light that even at Augsburg, before the Emperor, the way in which it is founded in Scripture was confessed and recognized; and the adversaries themselves were forced to admit that it could not be refuted through the Holy Scripture. Therefore, who would not feel nausea? Whose hair would not stand on end? Whose heart would not tremble in his entrails (if he wants to be a Christian) to think that he lived in that city in which the Gospel, St Paul, and all the Holy Scripture are prohibited and condemned, and where it is commanded and ordered by law that they be denied and attacked? Indeed, one ought rather to run naked out of that city, and not to remain in it even for one blink of an eye.' [500]

These things and many others of that sort Luther wrote there, both most abusively and most slanderously, by which he tried to incite the people to hatred of the pious Prince. Cochlaeus published a book specifically against these things, in which he refuted many of Luther's lies and defended his patron the pious Prince. There, among other things, he said as follows: 'Indeed, Luther takes it badly that Duke George so strenuously protects the cause of the Faith, and he says that Bishops and Preachers should renounce the rule of Confession, etc. But this most wicked monk knows well that the Lutherans grant nothing at all to ecclesiastical power, but remove all obedience from it, without any fear or shame. He knows as well that Duke George does not set his hand against Confession or against the secrets of individual consciences, but merely inquires outwardly (where it was needed), either through a sign or through some other means, which of his subjects confesses and takes communion, as the Church ordains and commands. Certainly, he does this not from any tyranny or thoughtlessness, but from a proper obedience, which has been enjoined on his conscience as a Christian prince, on pain of his soul's salvation, both by God and by either law, as has been demonstrated before. And woe to him, if he had not done this, but because of human fear had neglected or passed over such serious commands of God and of both laws. For he would have had to fear lest it happen to him as it once happened to the warlike and victorious King Saul, whom God chastened and made destitute and cast out of his kingdom, for no other reason than that he had not completely destroyed the people of Amalech, as God had commanded him through the prophet Samuel, but had taken and preserved the King Agag, and granted the best of the sheep and the flocks to the people, for sacrificing to the Lord. So also Duke George would have sinned against God, if he had not resisted all heresies in his lands to the utmost of his abilities (as the Imperial Law enjoined on him, under sworn oath). Moreover, although all heretics in general who fight against the Church are designated by Amalech, who fought against the Children of Israel, nevertheless the Lutherans especially can be understood through Amalech. For Amalech is translated as a brutish race, or a gobbling [501] people, who live according to the flesh and animal sensation, as now the Lutherans live: and in their forefront is their Idol, that monk with his nun. Therefore every Christian prince, subject to the Roman Empire, is bound by his sworn oath to tolerate no heresy in his lands and to support the ecclesiastical power (which in this time is most greatly scorned by heretics), so that Christian rites, ordinances, and ceremonies may be preserved in his lands.'

Moreover, Cochlaeus sent his book to the Elector Prince of Saxony himself (as he had publicly promised in it), with a certain letter written by his own hand. In it he humbly begged the Prince, in accordance with Luther's own challenge to take the matter to law, to compel Luther to stand trial and to contend in judgment with Cochlaeus himself, who would offer himself of his own free will, at the peril of his body and his life, to prove sufficiently that Luther is a heretic and seditious; which Luther had written could never be proven. The Elector, when he had received and read Cochlaeus's book and letter, gave no answer. But his Chancellor gave a written statement to the messenger which testified that both the book and the letter had been given to the Elector Prince by the messenger, with the addition of a threatening expression of displeasure that the Elector and his father had been treated injuriously by that book, and those injuries would be stored up in their unforgetting minds.

And while Cochlaeus's book was being printed at Dresden, a certain legal scholar from Wittenberg, whose name was Benedict Paulus, deceitfully obtained six quires of that book from the printer through a middleman, having given his pledged faith that he would return them before he left Dresden. But this Evangelical man, who always has 'faith' in his mouth, gave his counterfeit faith and left without returning the quires.

And so Luther soon wrote another book, to which he gave the title *Luther's Brief Answer to the Latest Book of Duke George*, so that an answer to Cochlaeus's book, which at that time had just been published, might be ready for the same markets in Leipzig. But how malicious Luther was in that book toward Duke George, how haughty toward Cochlaeus, and how impious concerning the vows and lives of Monastics, cannot easily be described. And he even ascribed

Cochlaeus's book to Duke George, as the author, because the Printer had impressed the Duke's arms on the frontispiece of the book, to give it a pleasing appearance. On this account, Luther said, 'Indeed, I considered Duke George to be a proud and wrathful man; but I did not think him so uncultured and thoughtless that he would foolishly smear his paternal arms, the noble and precious Rue-crown, which is his greatest glory on earth, with the excrement and filth of his nostrils, and allow it to be carried about the world in that condition.[502] A worse disgrace to the noble Rue-crown never occurred, a crown which so many memorable Emperors, Princes, and Lords have borne for so long a time up to this day, and still bear, in the highest honor, and under its standard have accomplished such outstanding deeds and virtues, both in war and in peace, etc.'[503]

To these words Cochlaeus responded as follows: 'The Rue-crown was placed on the frontispiece by the printer, voluntarily; he was not ordered to do this either by Duke George or by me myself; just as he himself admits, and wants to admit, whenever he has been asked for an explanation of this matter, since he has for more than twenty years previously printed it in many of the books he has published. Nor does that praiseworthy ancestral crown stand undeservedly alongside the truth which, by the grace of God, was in my book asserted, confirmed, and brought openly into the light, in contrast to the empty trifles and presumptuous lies of Luther. But Luther also says, in a bitter exclamation, "Oh if only Duke Albert, that noble hero, were alive, and saw that his son had sunk so low: Ah, how much more happily he died, etc." This is a rhetorical trick, by which Luther makes an elephant out of a mouse. Certainly, if that most praiseworthy and most brave Prince had lived until the present day, he would by no means have permitted that an apostate monk (whom the Pope, the Emperor, and all Estates of the Holy Roman Empire, and many universities in addition, and other nations of Christendom, have publicly condemned as a heretic) should, under the protection of the most famous House of Saxony, incite and nurture so great a schism, so much confusion in universal Christendom, so much harm, calamity, slaughter, and bloodshed in Germany by his lies and his heretical and seditious writings; and that he should besmirch the very emblem of the Dukes of Saxony, the Rue-crown, with so heavy and indelible a blot. Nor, if the glorious Elector Prince Duke Ernest with his Catholic progenitors should arise from the dead, and should see what Luther within twelve years has instituted in their Catholic provinces, do I doubt that they would cause him to be torn apart by red-hot pincers and burned into ashes, and that they would hail their grandson and descendent Duke George with the highest praises, because not only did he actively conserve their provinces in the Catholic faith and the ancient ceremonies (just as they had left them to posterity), but also elevated and enriched them by increases of secular holdings and by many very noble buildings, through his prudent and careful skill in ruling, so that they had never before been better.'[504] These things Cochlaeus wrote there.

Furthermore, the same Cochlaeus declared throughout his entire book how

many slanders and impieties of Luther's there were in that book of his, against
every monastic state. But a recitation of them all would take too long. In sum,
Luther there calls all monks faithless, denying, apostate Christians, and even
blasphemers and new crucifiers of his redeemer Jesus Christ, and slanderers of
His passion and blood. And in this regard he advised the people that they
should become accustomed to understand nothing else by the word 'monk'
than a Christian who had denied the faith, an apostate from belief in Christ, a
confederate of the Devil and of magicians, etc.

And so there was a great dissension between the related princes, the Duke
Elector and Duke George, not just in the cause of faith and religion, but also
in certain other matters which pertained to their secular rule. But since the
division of lands between the Elector Duke Ernest (the grandfather of this
Elector) and Duke Albert (the father of Duke George), who had been full
brothers, was done in so mixed a fashion that one could not wage war against
the other without lasting damage to his own lands, a delegation of counselors
and distinguished men was drawn from either side. When they came together
in one spot, as arbiters by whose decision each Prince had agreed to abide,
they so favorably settled all the causes of disagreements that it was henceforward forbidden both to Luther and to Cochlaeus and others to embroil in
their disagreements about religion the names and interests of those Princes or
their cities.

Meanwhile the works of Georg Witzel began to be read, not without the
praise of many. Witzel had for ten years been a Lutheran; but he recovered his
senses, and was learnedly and fiercely attacking Luther's teachings. But Luther
was much too proud to deign to answer him; however, Jonas and Cordatus and
a certain Raidenus sent out their wagons full of accusations and slanders against
him, partly in Latin and partly in German. He answered these things undauntedly. Indeed, among many other words, he answered Jonas as follows: 'And
what is more' (he said) 'you yourself, Jonas, admitted to Balthassar Fach, an
upright man, four years before I left there, that I had been very harshly treated.
Where now is the strangling snare, which I abandoned not long ago? Nay,
rather, where is your countenance, Jonas? O holy man, who grieves from his
very heart that I was not long ago condemned to the cross, and that I do not
feed the crows there! It was not enough, that I had been made a Cethegus, unless
he also made me a Verres, and afterwards an oath-breaker, an enemy of all virtue,
born with a vicious mind, a raging butcher, etc. Oh tongue rightly Evangelical,
truly making for salvation! But I could wish, Jonas, that you had had some
consideration for your name and your sect in this disturbance of yours, which
however great you are drove you, completely absorbed and even maddened, over
so many precipices of slanders and lies, etc.' [505]

But the Lutherans were particularly distressed that Witzel imputed all the
blame and every origin of the insurrections and calamities to Luther; for in
the same book he wrote as follows: 'The one who stands out as the cause and
origin of the whole calamity, prettily gains control of matters; truly he is a
Lion (for so they wish him to be proclaimed) lying in his den, who has caught

enough for himself and his cubs. Therefore he terrifies the poor lowly animals with his roar, so that they will not dare even to mutter against him, and he draws the poor man to himself, so that once there he may devour him. Tell me, to whom did the Secretary of Baden address these words in the Diet of Worms: "your books are going to incite great insurrections?" Did his opinion deceive him? Who first wrote, "The Word of Christ heralds insurrection for Tyrants?" Who persuaded anyone who could and who so desired to tear apart and abolish Bulls, nay rather to turn to ash the doors on which they are displayed? Who argued that Monasteries should be leveled to the ground, as though they were the Devil's brothels, and said that there was reason enough why the ecclesiastical Colleges, together with the Monasteries and Chapels, should be eradicated? Who sang this Dorian song, that the Bishops deserved to be driven out of Christendom, just like wolves, thieves, and robbers? Who wrote about the washing in blood of the Roman Church's clergy's hands? O Thracians, O Scordisci,[506] who delight so greatly in human blood! It is a wonder that they do not prefer to drink from skulls rather than from golden chalices. I say nothing here about the Bohemian example with which that blood-drinker threatens. To whom does his Epistle to Linz refer, in which the papists are damned without any pity?'

Witzel exposed these seditious writings and not a few others of this sort from the Lutheran books of Luther. And Luther did not answer at all, except that he wrote a German preface for Raidenus's book. In this he says with great disdain and contempt, 'Manifest lies are not worthy of an answer; moreover, Witzel is so shameless in both mouth and heart, in opposition to his own conscience, and lies so openly that even his papists can realize it, even if they are blind. Therefore, this trifling fool does not deserve that his writings be answered.'[507] By this slander, Luther refuted all Witzel's arguments, in his own judgment and that of his blind mob. But among more intelligent people, Luther's doctrine became daily more suspect, when they saw that certain learned and eloquent men, who were skilled in both their pen and their natural talent, were deserting it. Among these men, Luther and his followers especially denounced and hated Dr Johannes Crotus and the aforementioned Witzel.

In that same year two orators had been sent into Germany, one by Pope Clement VII, the other by the Holy Roman Emperor Charles V. They announced to the Princes and Estates of the Holy Roman Empire that there would be a celebration of a General Council. How this was to be conducted was declared in eight articles. When these articles had been announced to the Elector of Saxony, he requested to delay his response until he might consult about this matter with the other princes who agreed with him, in the Schmalkald League, which was going to meet at the end of the month of June. Therefore, after a deliberation had been held there, they wrote a response, throughout which they preferred the Roman Emperor (whom they acknowledged as their Lord) to the Highest Pontiff (as if they owed him no obedience). Therefore, although they saw that both in proposing and in assenting, the foremost portions of the articles had throughout been given to the Apostolic Nuncio, the Reverend Lord Hugo de Rangoni, a Count and royal Bishop, who had signed himself as Prince, and after whom the Emperor's Speaker, without any addition, had simply signed 'Lambert of Briaerde,' nevertheless in their response they used this opening: 'Warmest greetings and our duties. Magnificent and Reverend in the Lord, matchless friend of the Lord Who is worthy of reverence: When recently you were with us on the second day of June, in our town of Weimar in Thuringia, after you revealed to us certain matters that had been decided by the most unconquerable Emperor Charles V, Caesar Augustus, our most merciful Lord, and by the Roman Pontiff Clement, about the Council, and the Pontifical Nuncio showed us certain articles that had been written about the Council, we replied to you that we would discuss this matter with other Princes, Counts, and Cities who agree with us concerning religion, etc.'

The first article ran thus: 'That this Universal Council, which is put forward for proclamation and celebration, shall be free, and shall be celebrated according to the accustomed fashion of the Church, which has been observed through many centuries past, from the beginning of Universal Councils up to these times.' And the second, thus: 'That they who shall take part in the Council shall publicly declare and promise that they will abide by and inviolably comply with these Decrees.' And the sixth article established a location for the Council in Italy, in one of these three cities: Mantua, Bologna, or Piacenza, since each one of them is safe, capacious, fertile, and healthy; furthermore, this location was in an area that was more convenient for Germany than for all the other Transalpine nations.

The Lutherans complained most greatly about these articles in their response, on the grounds that the articles absolutely disagreed with the deliberations of the Princes, which had been held and concluded in the Imperial Assemblies. 'For even if in the first Article' (they said) 'the Elector calls the Council free, nevertheless the matter itself will turn out differently, since in the first place he wishes to put all the potentates under obligation to himself. For if he wished to have a free Synod, he would not require this obligation; which would be of no use to him, if any point from the Word and Scriptures of God should be adjudged against him in a free Synod. Now since he places the Princes under obligation, under the appearance and name of a Council certainly, he does so for the sake of stabilizing his own power, and he wants everyone's will to be submissive, etc.'

Cochlaeus wrote a preface against these points in a certain pamphlet addressed to the Primate of Scotland, the Archbishop of St Andrews, as follows: 'That the Lutherans refuse to consent to these eight articles about holding a Council appears to be pure subterfuge. For what is there in the articles, I ask, either harsh or unjust, which can honestly be objected to with any fairness or reason? For in the first article it is requested that the Council be free – a place where, obviously, the Fathers may safely and securely determine whatever shall seem good to the Holy Spirit. But the Lutherans demand that the Council be celebrated in Germany, where the Fathers would be captive to such an extent that unless they determine those things that please the Lutherans, they will soon be met by the arms of the Nobles and the Lutheran common folk's rage for killing. It is requested in the same article that the Council be celebrated according to the customary fashion of the Church, preserved from the beginning through so many previous centuries. But they ask for a new fashion, according to which the Roman Emperor is given precedence over the Highest Pontiff and Princes and Secular Lords over Cardinals and Bishops; which is to say, sheep are given precedence over shepherds, the laity over priests, and sons over fathers. And Bishops and Theologians shall not resolve questions of the Faith, but noisy rhetoricians and quibbling laymen, who, carrying in their hands the new interpretation of the Bible which Luther published, shall insult and contradict the Doctors of Sacred Theology, and shall prevail in contentious outcries, so that the text of whatsoever Scripture shall not be understood differently than they themselves, with their Luther, understand it.

'In the second article it is requested, moreover, that the Decrees of the Council be obeyed. This seems utterly foreign to the Lutherans, as though it were against Christian liberty to obey a Council. They would wish, rather, that the Council be conducted in the same way as many Imperial Councils have heretofore been conducted among us Germans, in which the Lutherans were permitted, under safe conduct, to contradict with impunity anyone at all of the other Princes and Orders, and what is more even the decrees of the Emperor himself. Many thousands and even tens of thousands of golden coins were thus consumed in vain, while with feigned words they put before us the hope of agreement, etc.'

The Lutherans said in that same response of theirs that it pertains to His Imperial Majesty's duty that the Emperor should undertake to understand and judge the matter according to the Word of God, whenever the Roman Pontiff fights against the truth; lest the Pope, since he is a party to the case, should also at the same time be the judge. To these remarks Cochlaeus responded as follows: 'How will the Scripture be the principal and only Judge in the Council (as the Lutherans want it to be), since by itself the Scripture neither forms an opinion, nor understands it, nor is able to express it? In saying this I would by no means detract from the Sacred Scripture, which I venerate as the work of the Holy Spirit and hold as sacrosanct, and on which I depend, and from which, as a knowledgeable and prudent man, I would not depart by even a finger's breadth. But in controversies I do not demand Scripture's true meaning from Scripture itself, since it does not know how to speak; but rather from the Holy Fathers, who spoke after they were inspired by the living Spirit of God; or from the Roman Pontiff, whom Christ Himself questioned concerning his faith; or from a General Council, in whose midst Christ Himself is and the Spirit of Truth emerges, really present, and truly dictates Its opinion through the mouths of the Fathers (who represent the Church). For that Spirit lives, not in the dead letters, but in the living Body of Christ, which is the Church, which It directs, as the soul does the body – not in written words or syllables, but in the hearts of the faithful, which are the living Epistles (as the Apostle says) for they truly live by Faith. For just as the body lives by the soul, so also the soul lives by faith. Therefore, when the Lutherans declare (for the sake of example, concerning the words "This is My Body") that their interpretation is true; but against them other heretics, such as Zwingli, declare that theirs is truer; and both contradict the Catholic Church – in this case who, I ask, shall pronounce judgment? Certainly no one more rightly than the Highest Pontiff, or a General Council. For the Divine Scripture orders that in controversies we should go, not to the mute Scripture, but to the Highest Priest, so that the judgment of truth may be sought from him, Deut. 17. Thus too Malachi says, "The lips of the Priest guard knowledge, and they shall demand the Law from his mouth, since he is the Messenger of the Lord of Hosts." Thus Christ orders us to hear not silent letters, but the Living Church. Finally also, Paul and Barnabas, in the controversy about circumcision, appealed not to the Scripture, which cannot make determination, but to the Apostles and the Elders in Jerusalem. And in deciding this controversy, they appointed as judges not the Scripture but the Holy Spirit and themselves, saying, "It seemed good to the Holy Spirit and to us, etc." Now, if Paul's adversaries had been as obstinate and rebellious against the Church as the Lutherans are today, they would by no means have acquiesced to this judgment, but would have said, "Which Scripture decrees that the Gentiles should not be circumcised?" And so that controversy would have endured to the present day, since it was not the Scripture that decided it, but the Holy Spirit, through the Apostles and Elders.' [508]

Cochlaeus wrote these things and many others of this sort to the Primate of Scotland against the objections and subterfuges of the Lutherans. At about the same time he wrote another Apology, for the Bishops of Scotland, against the Scot Alexander Alesius, who had fled from the kingdom of Scotland to Wittenberg because of his perfidious apostasy, and there had published a hateful complaint and accusation against the Bishops of that realm, addressed to the Most Serene King of Scotland, James V, concerning a certain Decree which forbade the books of the New Testament to be read in the vernacular tongue. Alesius said, 'What could the Turks do, or other peoples who are enemies of the name of Christian, that is different from what these men do – that the people shall not touch the Holy Books, nor know the benefits and most holy precepts of Christ, etc.' Cochlaeus answered, 'In this edict the Bishops do not at all act like Turks or other peoples who are enemies to the name of Christian. For the Turks, whenever they can, take the Holy Books away from all Christians, priests as well as laity, without any discrimination or respect. But the Bishops, through the best intention, not in hatred of Christ or of the Christian people, decree thus, that the people shall devoutly hear the Word of God and the benefits, precepts, and promises of Christ in Church, from priests who are properly called and ordained, and shall thus learn with profit. For it is written: "The lips of the priest guard knowledge, and they shall demand the Law from his mouth." For this is far better, and far more congruent with divine ordinance, than is the Lutheran novelty, by which the untrained people are drawn away from the public sermon, and are seduced into a private sermon or interpretation by laymen, whom no one established as Doctors in the Church. And so they derive no good profit. The Lord says about these men, speaking through the Prophet, "I expected them to produce grapes, and they brought forth wild vines." And Christ says in the Gospel, "Can they harvest grapes from thorns, or figs from thistles?" About these men Erasmus of Rotterdam, by far the most learned man of our age, also wrote as follows to Vulturius: "I never entered their churches, but from time to time I saw people coming back from a sermon, as though they were filled with evil spirits, all wrath in their faces and bearing a wondrous ferocity before them. But who ever saw anyone in their sermons pouring out tears for his sins, beating his breast, or groaning aloud?" These things Erasmus wrote. Therefore the Bishops should be praised, not contradicted, since they prohibit such disorders and perversities.' [509] In this manner Cochlaeus answered fifty objections of this sort by Alesius, which it would take too long to quote.

But he also wrote against Sebastian Franck in German, that is to say against a Zwinglian man who wrote a large book in German, which he entitled *Chronicles* and which was divided into three parts.[510] In the first of these, he recounts history from Adam up to Christ; in the second, from Christ up to the coronation of our Emperor Charles V, Augustus, which was held at Bologna. But in the third (which is longer than the others and likewise more pestilential by far), with all the strength of his talent he fights against the Roman Pontifical authority and its deeds and constitutions. He divided that part into eight books, each one quite long. In the first of these he seeks to prove, out of Velenus and other heretics, that St Peter never came to Rome; and he describes the lives of the Pontiffs so maliciously, that there are far more accusations and slanders there than histories of deeds they accomplished. In the second book he writes about Councils; in the third, about heretics; in the fourth, about the orders of Monks; in the fifth, about the cult of the saints and the Mass; in the sixth, about the vices and wicked arts of the Roman Pontiffs; in the seventh, about the court occupations of Ecclesiastics; in the eighth, about signs concerning the Pope and the Antichrist, and about the Last Judgment.

Indeed, the whole volume was so packed with impious errors and with hateful lies and seditious slanders against the Pope and every Cleric, and even against the tributes and taxes of the secular Princes, that the Magistrate in Strasbourg forbade the sale of books to the publisher, and the city to the author. Nevertheless, many copies were sold furtively in secret through deceit. Therefore Cochlaeus published two pamphlets, so that he might briefly demonstrate to his Germans how pitiably and evilly they were deceived by rascals of this sort. One of these books, *Against the False Reformation*, was dedicated to the pious Prince, Sigismund the August Ruler of Poland;[511] the other was against only one chapter of the fifth book of the third part of the *Chronicles* of the abovementioned Franck, to which that Franck had given this heading: 'When, how, and from whom the Church of Western Europe accepted the Mass and the transubstantiation of the bread and wine into the body and blood of Christ.' To this, indeed, Cochlaeus sorrowfully responded thus: 'Most certainly, we accepted them both from Christ our Lord; for each of them comes not from human strengths or words, but from the mandate, virtue, and word of Christ, the Omnipotent Son of God, Who said, "This is My body; do this in remembrance of Me." But that Franck, as an enemy both of the Mass and of the Church, wants to make each of these things something new and recently introduced, and invented by the Devil. However, neither he, nor Luther, nor the spirit of any rebellion, together with all the demons, will ever be able to demonstrate this, etc.'

He then responded point by point to eighty-eight articles excerpted from one chapter. Concerning the last of them he says as follows: 'For my part I would far rather pursue a contemplative life from the Holy Scriptures and the religious writings of the Holy Fathers, and console and delight my heart in the wondrous praises of God, than to strive thus against the empty and impious triflings of heretics of this sort; but it befits me, however insignificant a member of the Church I am, to do what is in my power, to the extent that God shall grant, against these enormous, virulent, and savage enemies of the Church. For this reason am I forced to endure and to witness such great annoyances, boastings, poisonous deceptions, odious lies, accusations, abuses, and slanders from these unwashed, demon-obsessed babblers. I derive nothing pleasant, witty, or edifying from them, but the bitterest gall and every sort of filth, and with nausea I behold the heresy and refuse of these most uncultured oxen and asses of ancient wickedness and impiety, namely the Leonists, the Albigensians, the Pighardians, the Thaborites, the Hussites, etc. – filth which these novice heretics belch out in full spate, in public, and, taking turn after turn in defilement, vomit out on to the people of God.' [512]

In that year there was among the Lutherans so great a rumor of the Final Day and the Last Judgment, and even a belief that it would occur on a certain day of that very year, that many of the common people were unwilling to build, many farmers would not plant or plow; not a few nobles received the Eucharist, as if they were going to die on a specific day (which would be the Last Day of the world). But when that day, which had been named by the pseudo-prophets, passed by without any transition of the world, those miserably deceived and deluded Evangelical men both blushed before others and mocked one another in turn, in Wittenberg and in many other towns. In the same way, the Anabaptists terrified many of the simpler folk by this warning; but if they truly were or had ever been Evangelists, they would have known that Christ said, in Matthew 24, 'But of that day and hour, no one knows, not even the angels of the heavens, except the Father alone.' And in Acts 1, 'It is not yours to know the times or the moments, which the Father in His power has set.'

1534

Meanwhile, Luther published a much more savage and virulent book in German, which he entitled *About the Corner Mass and the Consecration of Priests*. He prefaced it with these words: 'We have always, up to the present, conducted ourselves humbly toward the Pope and Bishops, and especially in the Imperial Diet at

Augsburg. For we did not want to overthrow their Law and ecclesiastical power, but if they would not force us to accept impious articles, we were willing, with pleasure, to be both consecrated and governed by them; moreover, we were willing to assist them in maintaining such Law and power. However, we were not able to get this or obtain it from them; rather, they wish either to compel us to their lies and abominations, or to put us to death. Therefore, if eventually it shall turn out for them (since they are such hardened Pharaohs) concerning power and consecration as it turned out concerning indulgences, then whose fault, I ask, will it be? For when I offered to remain silent about indulgences, if only others would remain silent about me, then neither the Pope, nor the Cardinals, nor the Bishops were willing to hear me, but continued to desire simply that I should recant and allow others to shout aloud. And what have they gained from this? Here indulgences lie prostrate, and the letters together with their seals have vanished, nor is there anything in the world more contemptible than indulgences.' [513] And below he wrote, 'What if very soon it shall turn out for them, with regard to ecclesiastical power and the consecration of Holy Orders, that just as indulgences together with their letters have disappeared and vanished, so in the same way the chrism and the shaven crowns shall be overthrown, so that it shall not be known where a Bishop or a Priest remains? God is wonderful, He abolished indulgences, He extinguished the fire of Purgatory, He suppressed pilgrimages, and through His Word He laid low many other cults of the God Mammon and idolatries of the papists; does He still have enough strength in His hands that He can waft away the rancid chrism, which was introduced through mere human fabrication, against His Will?' [514]

These things Luther wrote in that preface. Then he added the disputation that the Devil held with him. In that discussion, indeed, the Devil proved by five arguments that for fifteen years, during which he was celebrating Mass almost daily, Luther had committed pure idolatry, because he did not there produce the body and blood of Christ, but adored mere bread and wine, and offered them to others to be adored. Then Luther pretended that he answered the Devil that he had been a consecrated Priest, and had accepted from the Bishop the chrism and Holy Orders, and had done everything by command and through obedience, and had uttered the words of consecration in earnest, and had celebrated Masses with great devotion. Therefore, how could the Devil say, that he had not consecrated the elements? Then the Devil responded, that indeed these things were true; but the Turks too, and the Pagans, do everything in their Temples by command and through obedience. And the priests of Jeroboam (he said 'Jerabeam') in Dan and Beersheba had done everything with greater devotion, perhaps, than the true priests in Jerusalem. And so, what if your order, your chrism, and your consecration were impious and false, just like those of the Turks and Samaritans? Here, Luther says, a sweat broke out upon his body, and his heart began to tremble and palpitate, as though he had been conquered by the Devil. Afterwards he took over the Devil's arguments, which he accepted as unconquerable.

Against these impieties, Cochlaeus immediately published six books by the most learned and praiseworthy Pope Innocent III, titled *About the Sacred Mystery of the Altar*,[515] and he dedicated them to the most noble Prince, Lord Ferdinand, King of the Romans, Hungary, and Bohemia. Among other things, Cochlaeus said as follows: 'I do not judge that it would be either proper or necessary for me, in writing to Your Majesty, to declare in elaborate arguments how much more justly and safely so pious and erudite a Pope should be believed than a desperate Apostate, given over to heresy, whose bitterness, rage, inconstancy, pride of soul, and diseases of a blinded mind are already well known to Your Majesty through wide experience of his actions and discussions. Nor do I consider it worthy or reasonable that so insane, infamous and impious an accomplice of the Devil should in any part either of his doctrine or his ability [*virtus*] be set beside such a Pontiff, or be admitted into any comparison; since in him not even a grain of any excellence [*virtus*] or doctrine any longer remains.' These things Cochlaeus wrote there; he then published another three pamphlets by the same Pope, titled *About the Contempt of the World or About the Misery of the Human Condition*,[516] and also two short little books by Isidore about ecclesiastical Offices,[517] which were written by him 900 years previously; which deservedly command more trust than the ravings of Luther. And so that he would not seem to neglect the German people, he also responded in German to that very impious and clearly diabolical book of Luther. There, Cochlaeus began his preface as follows: 'That restless enemy of the Church Luther has once again published a new book, with this title: *About the Corner Mass and the Consecration of Priests*. In it, indeed, he insultingly calls our most Holy Father the Pope the "King of the Dormice" (as if the Emperor, the Kings, Princes, Cardinals, Bishops, and other Lords who acknowledge him as the supreme Vicar of Christ and the supreme Prelate of all Christendom should be considered dormice). And our Bishops and Pastors he calls thieves of God, sacrilegious, corner-priests, damned, fools, etc. He calls the Mass an abomination; the immaculate sacrifice of the Altar he calls dung, mud, filth, dregs; Holy Orders, he calls the rancid and putrid chrism. Certainly these slanders, horrifying beyond measure, deservedly should be intolerable to all Christians, and should be most greatly abominated, like the fiery weapons of the serpent, and should be cast down into eternal shadows, just like diabolical blasphemies, etc.'[518]

And in response to the threats of the Lutheran preface Cochlaeus thus consoles the Catholics: 'Moreover, what he now threatens, that he will put an end to Holy Orders and the ecclesiastical power, just as, he boasts, he did to indulgences, should not discourage us Catholic priests (who originally hold this power and this Holy Order, not from any man or angel, but from God Himself). For Luther already published new Bulls and indulgences, fully twelve years ago, in his seditious book against every ecclesiastical estate; as if those who attempt both by council and action to destroy the Bishopric, the College of Priests, and all monasteries were true Christians and children of God. Moreover, when that diabolical attempt evilly succeeded among the pitifully deceived farmers, this new Pope published new indulgences against them, saying that whoever killed those peasants by whatsoever means, openly or secretly, offered the best obedience to God. And if he himself were killed in this work, his soul would on the spot immediately fly into Heaven. For then the time was of such a sort that any Prince could better deserve Heaven by slaughter and the outpouring of blood than other people could by prayers. But if due to the Wrath of God, in his hiding-place he now renders indulgences, Masses, and sacerdotal ordinations contemptible (and has already done so) by his wicked slanders and sophistical triflings, nevertheless he is forced, on the other hand, to hear and to learn by experience that Masses are still daily celebrated (to God be praise and thanksgiving!) by consecrated priests not just in the richest kingdoms and faraway provinces of Spain, Gaul, Italy, Scotland, etc., but also in the nearest principalities of the Catholic Princes of Saxony, the Marches, Meissen, and Thuringia, which are under his very eyes; and that on the appointed days indulgences are announced. Moreover, the name of Luther in many places is so hated and accursed that one is not permitted to mention it, either for good or for evil purpose. Certainly this is an extraordinary injury and insult, and one unheard of before now, that Luther's name should be more odious than that of Judas the betrayer or the Devil himself, whose names can be spoken far more safely and securely in those regions than can the name of Luther.'

These things Cochlaeus wrote there, against Luther's threats. But to the five arguments of the Devil, by which Luther says he was conquered, Cochlaeus responded both in general and in specific. For the general response, after Cochlaeus refuted Luther about Transubstantiation out of the man's own words, he added the following: 'It should not be necessary to answer the arguments of Luther, which he says the Devil proposed to him; since we all well know that the Devil is subtle, the enemy of truth, and an evil spirit, who in evil both is and remains obstinate for ever, so that he can have nothing good in his mind or his will, just as Christ says about him: "That one was a murderer from the beginning, and has not stood in the truth, since the truth is not in him." Thus also Peter, Paul, John the Apostle, and all the Saints complain about him, that he is a cheat, a liar, a slanderer, and a seducer. Therefore no Christian ought to expect any good from his arguments; but rather will say to himself, "Even if these arguments appear valid due to their Sophistic tricks, which I cannot refute, nevertheless they should not move me at all; for I have the certain truth of Christ, Who says, 'The truth is not in him'; and of Paul, who says, 'For Satan himself can transform himself into an angel of light.' I will remain, therefore, in the Faith of the Church, which Paul says is a pillar and pedestal of truth." '

In his specific response, Cochlaeus addressed Luther's individual fallacies and lies. For example, 'In his first argument he manifestly lies, when he says that we do not believe in Christ as our Savior, and that the Turk and the Devil believe in Christ in the same way that we do. Even if Luther admits that he himself was such a one, certainly he will never be able to prove it about us. Moreover, when he asserts that we have fled from Christ to Mary and the other Saints, he clearly lies. For Christ, Mary, and the Saints are not at odds with one another; therefore it does not follow that someone who takes refuge with Christ's mother has deserted Christ. And Luther deceives the people's ears with this fallacious tickling, that Christ is not to be feared as a judge, but rather to be looked to as a mediator and redeemer; when, however, Christ Himself says in the Gospel "For neither does the Father judge anyone, but He has given all judgment to the Son," and we say this about Him daily in the Apostles' Creed: "From whence He shall come to judge the living and the dead," and Peter, in the Acts of the Apostles, says about Him, "And He commanded us to preach to the people and to testify that it is He Who has been appointed by God as Judge of the living and the dead." Therefore, we rightly implore Mary and the other Saints that they may intercede for us before Christ our Lord and Judge. For the Psalmist also says, "All you Saints of the Lord, fear Him." And so due to these points, the first argument lies in the mud, like a rotten and empty piece of rubbish, stitched together from lies and not invented by the clever Devil.' These things Cochlaeus wrote there; it would take too long to quote the others.

Moreover, Witzel made clear, through forty-four Chapters written in German, just what sort of thing Luther's Gospel was. In each of these, he briefly recited many errors and wickednesses of Luther; for example, in the first chapter, about free will, he begins thus: 'This prophet and Evangelist Martin Luther teaches that all things which come about, whether good or evil, do so from necessity. Moreover, that God works in each one, both good and evil. And that no one knows how to intend either good or evil, but everyone intends as he is forced to. But if this were so, who would be able to beware of vice? And so it would follow, that anyone who commits murder, robbery, or adultery, does so forced by necessity, nor could he not do so; especially since he says that even Judas was forced by necessity when he betrayed Christ.' This is the Fourth part of the first chapter, quoted as an example.

In addition, the same Witzel published not a few other books in German in this same year; one, for instance, *On Penitence, Confession, and Excommunication;*[519] another *On the Holy Eucharist, or Mass.*[520] In them he seriously refutes many of Luther's errors, making reference to the Scriptures and the ancient Fathers. And shortly thereafter he published another book, *About Prayer, Fasting, and Alms.*[521] In it indeed he cleverly holds the vices of the Lutherans up to ridicule, and their neglect of good works. Concerning prayer, among many other things he says as follows: 'There is no nation of people living upon the earth which does not pray, and does not admit that the practice of prayer is effectual, whether they are Christians, or heretics, or Jews, Pagans, Turks, Islanders, etc. The Lutheran sect alone for many years now has everywhere fought against this work in public sermons, saying "Why pray? Why pray? By praying you achieve very little in the eyes of God." In support of this, they have cited Christ's words in Matthew 6 and 23, where the Lord reproved the prayers of the Pharisees; and in John 4, where he censured the prayer of the Samaritans. And they cite as support this verse from the Psalm: "Their prayers are turned into sin." In one sermon they condemned the seven hours of the Priests, saying that the braying of an ass or the babbling of an infant would be more pleasing to God; in another they rejected the accustomed prayers of the laity; here, they said that there is no good in any prayer books, whether in Latin or in German; here, that no prayer should be allowed, except the "Our Father," although even that prayer, along with the others, was passing into disuse; here, that prayer should be brief, if one should pray at all, since God does not attend to the prayers of the mouth; here, widows who kneel on bended knee and pray were mocked as devourers of the Saints; here, those prayers which had been enjoined in Confession were hissed from the stage. And so, what sermon did they ever give, in which prayer and fasting were not jeered at? Besides, this is known to be true from their own people, who by unremitting harangues have been led so far away from this practice that there are very few of them who either pray or intend to pray once a week. How great a crowd of them is there which from one whole month to another does not even once repeat one "Our Father" all the way through? Therefore, this practice has become as rare among them (not to say actually opposed by them) as if they had ceased to be Christians.'

Concerning Fasting, moreover, Witzel rebuked them as follows: 'If our people could, by this hateful practice, be turned away from prayer, how much more easily from fasting? For we shrank back from fasting earlier as well; therefore, it was easily abolished. For it is much more difficult for the body of worldly folk to fast than to eat and drink. From this was born that proverb: "Who fasts willingly?", which confers little honor on Christendom. Therefore it would have been better had you haters of these practices considered the matter more thoroughly, and had not brought such evil against Christendom, which indeed neither wishes to nor can do without fasting, any more than without prayer. Therefore, why do you fight against so good a practice? By so doing, to whom are you showing contempt? Is it an evil practice to fast? Was it a human invention? Did priests either think it up or institute it? Does it not have foundation in the scriptures? So where now is that boast of yours, "We repealed nothing that was not evil in the Church; what was good, we preserved"? This boast of yours has been believed for too long, although anyone at all may see and perceive that it is an utter lie, which stinks to high Heaven.'

Concerning Alms he reproaches them with still more points, because they have abolished many pious usages of alms, such as the funds, baths, and meals that are usually offered to the poor on behalf of the dead, and in addition, the priesthood's rents and incomes, the goods of monasteries, the revenue of hostelries, etc., which indeed against charity and against the last wills of the testators were taken away from the poor and turned to the use of the rich and of gluttons. For example, about the abolition of monasteries he argues as follows: 'Where do the goods of the great monasteries now go? Who devours these alms? The monks should not have them; should you therefore have them? Allow a judgment: which party has the more just claim to their possession? They were founded on behalf of God; on whose behalf do you take them? The monks were beggars; what are you? You say that they did not act at all piously toward these things; what do you do that is so pious toward them? They sinned through these things, although not all of them did so, I believe; but you – for what other purpose do you usurp the goods of rich abbots and provosts, than for worldly pomp and pleasure? Were not they much more merciful and much kinder toward their subjects, toward wanderers, toward the poor of every sort, than you new monks now are? Oh this is every bit as true, as you are the true Harpies! Did not the people gain more benefit from the monasteries previously than they do now? Did not many farmers there have solace and refuge in their times of trouble? What do they have now?' Witzel wrote these things and many other things of this sort in German, and since he had lived among them for ten years, he knew all these things well.

Meanwhile two famous epistles appeared in public against Erasmus of Rotterdam, one by Nicholas Amsdorf, who preached Lutheranism at Magdeburg, and the other by Luther. Amsdorf pronounced briefly that the sum of Erasmus's doctrine was this: 'Luther's doctrine is heresy, since it was condemned by the Emperor and the Popes, but his own is orthodoxy, since bishops and cardinals, princes and kings send and give golden goblets to him; if there is anything else in his books, may I die.' [522] But Luther's epistle, since it was much longer, so also was far more savage. Erasmus, responding immediately to him, and forbearing from slanders, gave this title to his book: *The Defense of Erasmus of Rotterdam, against Martin Luther's immoderate letter.*[523] And in this defense, among many other things he says the following: 'What Luther charges me with is so inhuman as to be more than demonic. For he tries by this to persuade the world that Erasmus not only believes nothing concerning divine matters, but also that for a long time now he has with deceits, tricks, and all his powers, been undertaking this, that he may at length give a headlong fall to the universal Christian religion, which is already tottering, and may recall Paganism into the world in its place. I do not fear' (Erasmus said) 'that so savage and impotent a slander (for it is nothing else) will adhere to my reputation among those who either have read my musings or through domestic familiarity have looked rather closely into my conduct and character; but it must give sufficient proof in the minds of those who, although they neither know me nor have ever opened my books, are so devoted to Luther that they consider whatever he says to be an oracle. Would that in my life I had so restrained myself in accordance with the divine commands, as I have in regards to those that concern the Faith; about those I have a free and quiet conscience before God. In what concerns conduct, I daily beseech the Lord's mercy, with sighs and sorrow of heart. However, I would not want Him ever to become gracious to me, if ever even the slightest thought of this diabolical sin pierced my mind – I do not mean that I might obscure the universal glory of Christ, but that I myself might shrink from the Catholic Faith. And if only I might, by the laying down of this trivial body, lull to sleep this division of the Church, how gladly and joyfully I would undertake that death! Meanwhile, I do indeed beg for mercy from the Lord, night and day, for the sins I have committed, and moreover I pray for faith – not that He may give it to me, but rather that He may confirm and increase the faith which He has already given. I say these things before God, from my soul; and may He immediately exact punishment from me, if I lie in any way.' [524]

And below he wrote, 'See' (he said) 'how inconsistent the judgments of men are. Martin declares that I know nothing, that I by no means understand those subtleties which he writes against the papists, that I scarcely understand his most obvious points, and that I do not teach anything at all. But others charge against me that Luther took these very subtleties, for the most part, from my books. I confess that I have drawn many of the things I write from the books of ancient Orthodox Christians. For the rest, if you take from this man's books the hyperboles, slanders, trivialities, tautologies, overblown statements, earnest affirmations, and in addition to these, the things which agree with Johannes Hus, John Wycliffe and not a few others, perhaps not much will remain of which he can boast as his own. I would rather delight my leisure time with these obvious things, than with those subtle points to disturb the tranquility of the entire Church, and to set cities against cities, common folk against Princes and Bishops, and the Princes themselves against one another. Nevertheless, I am not so leaden-witted that I cannot understand Martin's paradoxes, which seamstresses and shoemakers squawked out at us from memory; I speak about those which he produced in Latin. Now even if there is nothing false or erroneous in his books, nevertheless such unrestrained reviling against everyone infects the readers' minds, especially those of ignorant people, and produces nothing else but schism.' [525] These things and many like them Erasmus wrote in his *Defense*.

Moreover, a plague of Anabaptists was then prowling about in lower Germany; but it was especially strong in Münster, the famous fortified city of Westphalia, in which there is a Cathedral Church and many clergy. For this reason it happened that Luther's doctrine had lately been preached publicly in that city, and once it was admitted, soon from every side Lutheran and Anabaptist exiles poured into that place from Lower Germany. At first these people were modest, and appeared worthy of hospitality and Christian mercy, as people who had been driven from their own dwellings for the sake of Christ's Gospel. But the pestilent Doctors, joining these vagabonds to themselves, infected many cities with their plague, and step by step, by their art, enticed the entranced people into their lost and damned sect. At length, when their conspiracy seemed to have gathered enough strength, they suddenly erupted into the marketplace, prepared to try the issue with arms. But the rest of the citizens did not want to fight, even though they were superior in numbers, either because they desired to spare the citizens' blood, or because they feared lest their Bishop, who had both cavalry and foot soldiers nearby outside the city, might in that battle fall into the city's hands. And so the Anabaptists prevailed, and soon did away with every administration of the Magistrates; and after delays of a few days, at first they permitted those people who wished to export their goods to leave, unless the goods were something edible or drinkable. Of these sorts of goods they would allow nothing at all to be carried out of the city, to such an extent that they took jars full of ale from certain women, some of whom were carrying their infants in their arms while others were leading them by the hand. The women were planning to refresh the children, when they were tired by the journey, with the ale. And they snatched from the hands of the children themselves the wheaten bread which the sad mothers had given them, either as a comfort or even as a relief for hunger.

After a few days, they at one time drove out all those who were not of their sect, first despoiling them as an enemy would, leaving them nothing of their own property, not even if they happened to be clothed in a garment that was not sufficiently good. They did this to such an extent that they even took toys [526] away from the infants, nor did they refrain from insulting the people as they were going along, calling them impious and Pagans. For they considered anyone who did not belong to their sect to be Gentiles and infidels. And so when all the priests, the monks, all the Catholic people, and even the Lutheran party had been expelled, the Anabaptists obtained the city and constituted a new body and rule for the city from the people of the worst sort and the wandering refuse of vagabonds, and distributed the most beautiful houses of the Canons, the Patricians, and the Senators among themselves. Moreover, outside the city walls the Bishop besieged all the gates, to prevent both new assistance and free passage. But to him the neighboring Princes and Bishops, the Archbishop of Cologne, the Duke of Cleves and Jülich, and the Bishops of Westphalia, sent troops and instruments of war. However, 300 mercenary soldiers made their way into the city, without the Bishop preventing them — indeed, some of his soldiers had been killed in the conflict, and others taken in the city, whose heads the Anabaptists quickly cut off and mounted on the walls as a spectacle.

Now this city was excellently fortified both by nature and by art. For it is situated in level ground, and it has water which no one can easily divert from it; nor does it have any nearby hills, which an enemy could occupy. Moreover, it had been abundantly provided with provisions and money, from the spoils of the rich citizens and the Churches. But the siege was drawn out for much longer than either side had expected. Certainly, the Bishop lost not a few soldiers during the process of besieging the town. For a large part of them died in the attack, and part, hit by poisoned arrows, breathed out their souls in dire torment. But the Anabaptists, a people wasteful of life and equally disposed to kill and to die, were not dreading death, but were hoping for great assistance, since they were expecting many troops both from other nearby cities that were infected with that plague, and especially from Frisia and Holland. Therefore, after the Bishop had vainly attempted the siege, the Anabaptists' foremost prophet, Johannes [Beukelsz] of Leyden (a town in Holland), who was a tailor by trade, persuaded his people that God had ordered him through the Spirit that he be crowned King of Israel and of Righteousness, just as David had been, and that he should rule over all the world, and destroy every power, both secular and ecclesiastical; and that he should spare no one, except those who accepted his faith and were made subjects of Righteousness.

Therefore, since no one dared to contradict an oracle of the Spirit, he was made King by his followers' general consent. Once he had obtained the rule, he quickly with great ceremony instituted a Royal Court, with diverse offices and magistracies, and with notable pomp adorned himself and his ministers in silken, gold, and silver vestments, which he had taken out of the chapels. Moreover, he himself wore a triple crown, made principally from gold, and a golden chain adorned with gems; and he had a golden orb, on which a little golden cross was mounted, with this inscription: 'The King of Righteousness upon the earth.' In addition, he had a golden sword, with a silver hilt. And he caused his queen and her maidens to be adorned thus, in the most costly splendor. And so, three times a week, adorned in this way, he processed into the marketplace, and there took his seat on a high throne, surrounded by a throng of attendants. And whoever was going to plead his cause before this King would, in his approach, twice bend his knees and then move forward prone upon the ground, before mentioning his business.

Moreover, the King, who was dreadful in his Majesty in everyone's eyes, passed new laws. He permitted each man to have four, five, six or seven wives; he himself had four, and added a fifth. He ordered all girls twelve years of age to marry; moreover, he ordered the men to sleep with one of their wives until she should become pregnant, and then to sleep with another. Shortly afterwards he instituted the Lord's Supper around the porch of the larger Church. Four thousand two hundred people are said to have attended this, and the King and Queen, with their ministers, served them at table. Moreover, at first they served three courses of boiled and roasted meats. The King and Queen took up wheaten cakes, which they broke and held out to the others, saying, 'Take and eat, and proclaim the death of the Lord.' In the same way, they offered a tankard of wine, with these words, 'Take and drink from it, all of you, and proclaim the death of the Lord.' Thus those sitting behind them, one to another, offered these things, with these words: 'Take, brother or sister, and eat of it; just as Christ delivered Himself over for my sake, so I will deliver myself for your sake.' Afterwards the King and Queen and their ministers, and with them those who had come from keeping watch to the dinner, celebrated in the same way, sitting at the table.

When the meal was finished, the King asked the entire company in general, 'Are you all prepared to do or to endure the Will of the Father?' When they all said that they were, he said, 'This is the Father's Will and this is His command, that I should send some of you out to announce His miracles, which He has done among us.' Then his prophet, Johannes of Warendorf, read out by name from a list the six who would travel to Osnabrück, the six who would go to Cassel, the five to Warendorf, and the eight (among whom that prophet himself was) who would travel to Soest. The King gave each one of them a golden coin worth nine florins, and money for the journey as well. When everyone else had left, these men soon went out of the city, with evening already falling. When they arrived in the abovenamed nearby cities, they cried out with a horrible noise, saying, 'Convert, and do penance; for the time is short, during which the Father will be merciful to you. The hatchet is already set to the root of the tree. If you will not accept peace, your city will quickly be thrown down.'

Then they marched forward and approached the council chamber of whichever city, and in front of the city they laid their cloaks on the earth, and throwing those precious gold coins on to them, they said, 'We have been sent hither by the Father, to announce peace to you. If you accept it, deliver your goods in common; if you refuse, we proclaim before God, by this gold coin, that you do not accept His peace, but hold it in contempt.' And they added, 'Now is that time, about which all the Prophets prophesied, when God wants to have nothing else upon the earth but justice. Therefore, after the King has fulfilled his office and has subjugated the entire world to justice, then Christ will hand His kingdom over to His Father.' And even though these miserable fanatical men were at first graciously heard and received by the citizens, especially at Warendorf and Cassel, which towns were under the rule of the Bishop of Münster, nevertheless their joy was brief. For the Bishop summoned his army and quickly compelled those citizens to hand over their raving prophets into his hands. At Osnabrück, they were captured as soon as they had arrived, so that they could be handed over to the Bishop; for that city too obeyed the Bishop. But the eight others, who had come to Soest, were captured and condemned to the ultimate punishment when it was discovered that they intended to arouse sedition. For that city is large and populous, and even if it ought to obey the Archbishop of Cologne, nevertheless it does not accept him, but enjoys liberty and its own law.

And those who had been handed over to the Bishop were questioned, both freely and under torture, and they undauntedly admitted everything, and were prepared for death; to such an extent that not a single one of them, even when free pardon was offered to him, wished to recant or to admit his error, so powerfully were they puffed up by the savage and bloodthirsty spirit. And so when they were asked many things about the condition of the city of Münster, they are said to have answered similarly about how much abundance there still was in gold, silver, and other precious things, and also in white flour, barley, in bacon, and in gunpowder. For the rest, there was still a moderate amount of salt, cheeses, and butter; and there remained yet in the city 2,200 men, strong in arms and for war, each of whom had six wives, and 500 kept watch every night. Moreover, their King was expecting new troops out of Frisia and Holland, and when he had received them, he would leave the city and subdue the whole world to himself.

These things happened in the month of October. And since winter had already begun, and the siege of so great a city required the greatest expense, the Bishop undertook a plan, by which he could keep the wicked men besieged with less expense. He constructed several fortifications before the gates of the city, and several soldiers were stationed on them to prohibit any free passage or access to the city. Moreover, since his resources were already exhausted, he begged assistance from the Princes and Estates of the Holy Roman Empire, since he himself was also a Prince of the Empire. These, indeed, convened at Worms through their Speakers, where according to established proportions they decreed the common contribution of everyone toward the expenses of the soldiers, so that through the unrelenting siege of hunger, at least, that city might be forced to surrender.[527] Therefore, in this way the siege was extended through the Feast of the Nativity of John the Baptist in the next year. But then a certain deserter showed the soldiers a way of getting into one gate (which was rather carelessly defended) by water; the soldiers entered the city through this gate at night, killed the guards, gathered themselves together there, and at dawn's first light burst into the city in their battle lines and killed anyone they met in the road. Then battle was begun around the greater Church, where the Anabaptists had their fortifications; whoever carried arms was captured and slain. But the King, with two of his foremost counselors, was lurking in a certain tower, from which he was dragged by the soldiers. He was kept in prison for many months with the other two, and at length he was made a spectacle of horrifying punishment and a terrible example of sedition, together with those two foremost counselors of his, in that same city in which he had arrogantly set up his reign.

Moreover, at that same time, while the Anabaptists of Münster were besieged, twenty-one of their articles were being circulated, as repulsively barbaric as they were monstrously impious. Cochlaeus, indeed, published a short pamphlet against these, both in German for the Germans and in Latin for the Poles. There he showed that these articles had their origin and root in Luther's doctrine. For example, the first article runs as follows: 'To avoid the Greater Church, and all those things which are called "divine service."' On this point, Cochlaeus responds as follows: 'This is without question a diabolical doctrine, through which the divine service in public churches is abolished and heresies of every sort are disseminated in private corners. On this topic Christ says, "Whoever does evil hates the light." But the unhappy Anabaptists took this doctrine from Luther, who for more than twelve years now has taught that churches and monasteries, together with everything that happens or is done in them, are pure devils and faces of the Antichrist. And he published Bulls and indulgences for all those who make an attempt, and in so doing endanger their body, their faculties, and their honor, to lay Bishoprics waste and destroy the rule of Bishops. And even recently, not six months ago, he wrote that monasteries, which he calls nests of dormice, deserve to be constructed and conserved in such a way that not one stone remains upon another; nor, he said, was there any injury done to them by the uprising of the peasants, except for this one thing – that some stones and certain remnants still remain. Therefore, if the Anabaptists ought to be corrected on this account, namely that they avoid churches and monasteries, Luther ought to be punished much more, who orders that these things should not only be avoided, but should be destroyed and wiped out – which his followers have often done.'[528]

And at the end of the pamphlet Cochlaeus added the following: 'From these things everyone may easily know that the Anabaptists and other fanatics and leaders of sects can neither be abolished nor extirpated, so long as Luther's heretical books shall not have been abolished and extirpated. For those are the trunk and the root, from which such sprouts grow every year. Indeed, however often they are cut back, it is useless to prune them, so long as the root from which others can grow remains untouched.' [529] These things Cochlaeus wrote there.

But for the rest, since many people, even Lutherans, suspected from Luther's book on the Corner Mass that he now agreed with the Zwinglians and the Waldensians, who deny that the body and blood of Christ are present in substance in the Eucharist, certain members of the nobility admonished Luther about this matter, due to that suspicion. For this reason it happened that Luther published a new epistle in German. In it, indeed, he vehemently denies that he agrees with the Zwinglians. But he rages even more savagely against the Mass in it than he had done in his earlier book. For among other things, he says as follows: 'Truly, I hope and I would very gladly see and hear that these two words, "Mass" and "Sacrament", should be understood by everyone to differ from one another just as greatly as "Shadows" and "Light" differ; nay, indeed, as much as "Devil" and "God" differ. For the Mass is nothing other than a perverse distortion and trafficking of the Holy Sacrament, even if it is celebrated most devoutly.' [530] And below, 'May God give such a heart to all good Christians, that when they hear this term "Mass" they shall be terrified, and shall defend themselves with the sign of the cross, as they would against an abomination of the Devil. But in contrast, when they hear the term "Sacrament" or "Lord's Supper," may they leap up for joy and even weep sweetly.' [531] And below, 'The Mass must fall, nor is there any remedy. For Daniel stood forth in his own place to bring this about, just as the angel Gabriel declared to him. For that Prophet writes that he will stand forth at the end of the age, which he now does, and says, "The Antichrist takes his stand upon two things, namely, upon an Idol and upon Celibacy." The Idol he calls "Maosis," using letters which this word "Mass" [*missa*] also gives. He would gladly have said "Mass" clearly, if it had not been necessary for him, according to the angel's command, to use disguised [532] words.' [533] Luther wrote these things and many more of this sort there.

Cochlaeus published a brief pamphlet in German against these things, addressed not to Luther, whom he did not consider worthy of his answer, but to Justas Jonas, who was one of the Four Evangelists of Wittenberg, whose arms occupied the four corners of the page in the frontispiece of Luther's book. Therefore, Cochlaeus put ten questions to him, taken from Luther's epistle, so that Jonas might respond to them and refute the arguments that were offered against them. In addition, Cochlaeus cited twenty-eight lies from the same epistle, so that Jonas, that Provost of Wittenberg, might prove them to be true. But neither Jonas nor anyone at all of his associates answered these points, but rather disregarded them contemptuously, even though they were openly warned against doing so in Cochlaeus's preface, in these exact words: 'Since I saw you and spoke with you in the public Imperial Diets of both Worms and

Augsburg, I decided to write several questions especially to you, simply and from my heart, without any trick or deceit, in honor of the truth, and in submission to and edification of my neighbor; asking you, friend, that you respond to these questions in the same manner and with the same intention, and that you not hold me (who am your senior as Master and Doctor, and am also the Provost of an older Church than are you) in such contempt as does the infamous Apostate Monk, who can bring neither Holy Scripture nor public Law against me, however often I present myself publicly and privately for the purpose of demonstrating clearly to him that he is a seditious heretic, and that according to the nature of a heretical man and an evil servant, he condemns himself through his own mouth and his own judgment. If you people truly intend, in earnest and from your hearts, to defend the Gospel and the truth, surely you should not all remain silent in this way to all my appeals and my offers; one at least of you should come forward with a similar offer, to defend your master. But since all of you, for more than thirteen years now, have kept completely silent about that point, on which the sum of the matter and the head of the business depend, but nonetheless babble out many things and write books thick and fast, with great scandal to the people, with waste of time, with the loss of money on useless trifles and noxious merchandise – you should deservedly fear lest the secular authority shall at length take badly and disdainfully your cowardly heart and timid conscience, since you do not dare, on so serious a matter, to submit to any law or to undergo any danger in earnest, etc.'

Among his questions, moreover, Cochlaeus asks in the following way: 'If the Mass were abolished, as Luther hopes, how could we either have or receive the venerable Sacrament of the Eucharist? For this cannot be accomplished apart from the Mass, since to accomplish it is to celebrate Mass, about which Christ said to His apostles, "Do this in remembrance of me." If you deny this, then tell me, I beg, how the body and blood of Christ may be made from bread and wine without consecration? And when and to whom did Christ give the commandment to make his flesh and blood out of bread and wine?' And again, 'In which verse of Scripture, I ask you, was this word "Mass" prohibited? Or which Scripture orders that the flesh and blood of Christ be called only "Sacrament" and not also "sacrifice"? In addition, which Scripture orders us to take the Lord's Supper in the morning rather than in the evening?' And again, 'In what way does this Epistle of Luther's not contradict either his book *About the Saxon Visitation*, where he commends Masses, in both Latin and German, which he calls especially useful to the living, or else the *Confession and Apologies of the Lutherans*, where it is said, "Our Churches are falsely charged with abolishing the Mass; for the Mass is retained in them and is celebrated with the highest reverence," etc.'

The first of the twenty-eight lies that Cochlaeus quoted runs as follows: 'My pamphlet *About the Corner Mass* very often admits that even among the papists (if they guard Christ's ordinance), even if it is given in one kind only, still the body of Christ is there and is received.' Against this lie, Cochlaeus cites these words of Luther's, from that same pamphlet *About the Corner Mass*: 'Since it is uncertain, whether the body and blood of Christ are present in the Corner Mass or not, and since it most certainly is a human invention; see to it, at peril of your body and your life, that you do not believe that Christ's body and blood are there present.'

After he had listed the ten questions, Cochlaeus addressed Jonas as follows: 'Friend, I do not only ask you, as Evangelist and Provost of Wittenberg, for a response; but also, trusting in the spirit of truth, I challenge you to defend these things justly. And I here publicly proclaim, before everyone, that I am going to call you a timid deserter from the field of battle, and a vain word-sower and fighter in words, if you do not respond to these questions, Aeolus, since for more than thirteen or fourteen years now you always assisted in consulting, writing, preaching, and making war against the Mass, and now you have even translated that wicked book of Luther's *About the Corner Mass* into Latin, so that you may wholly become a participant in all Luther's iniquities, scandals, and sins.'[534]

However, although neither Jonas nor anyone else at all responded to these things, nevertheless Jonas undertook vengeance against Cochlaeus by another method. For Cochlaeus had privately written a consolatory letter to Witzel, against whom the Lutheran poets had shamefully produced a slanderous play, and a Dialogue full of derision. Witzel received it, certainly, at Eisleben, but kept it very carelessly and lost it by dropping it out a window. And so the Lutherans, his neighbors, found it and when they had read it through they straight away sent it to Wittenberg, where Jonas immediately gave it, befouled with bitter annotations and a wordy preface, to the printers for publication with this subscription: 'We have in our possession the manuscript of this letter, in Cochlaeus's own hand.' Certainly, Jonas did not sign his own name to it; however, he did not lose the opportunity to boast of his own malice, since he subjoined to it a feigned letter to Witzel, under the name of a certain Papist. At the end of this letter he wrote, 'There are those who say that Cochlaeus's letter came into the hands of Justus Jonas, who is going to publish it with a preface; but Jonas is said to scorn you nobly and to laugh at you, and – having spit upon you all from on high – to attend to more serious business. Farewell, and call all the winds to justice before Aeolus,[535] even though he is an unjust judge and one suspected by you. Given on 1 October 1534.'

Certainly, in his letter to Witzel, who was his friend, Cochlaeus wrote many things that he had by no means wished to be revealed by the Lutherans, who were his enemies. However, he had included nothing that was worthy of accusation, or about which he would blush before good and wise men. But Jonas seized upon everything and interpreted it in the worst way. For example, Cochlaeus had written, 'These are perilous times, in which our greatest labor is patience. But do not doubt, "God will grant an end to these things as well."[536] Indeed we are forsaken for a long time, few consider our labors; but so much the more will God Himself consider them, if our eye is single, as it ought to be. Certainly, if at any time Fortune looks more kindly upon me, I shall not forget Witzel. And there is hope that it will very soon happen that I shall be able to remember you effectively; not, indeed, that I am seeking any rank, but because I expect the bounty of Fortune. For no one knows under what a weight of labors and expenses (let me disregard all other burdens) I groan and sigh in secret.' Jonas not only made fun of these words of Cochlaeus through mocking annotations, but he also denounced them with perverse interpretations in his preface. For he says, 'Truly, lest anyone doubt that these people are at the same time evil and untaught, I give you a copy, dear reader, of the letter which Cochlaeus, the Defender of the Church – so please the gods! – wrote to the Defender Witzel. You will find there what kind of plans these hypocrites consider among themselves, and will clearly learn whether they seek the glory of God, or, in truth, prebends and offices, and (as Cochlaeus says with a laughable modesty), the bounty of Fortune.' Nonetheless, this slanderer had read these words of Cochlaeus in the same letter: 'Certainly, I knowingly and prudently intend never to write against the truth, although the Lutherans call me a slanderer. Now they complain that in the Dialogue with Corvinus I published a deceitful, seditious, and bloody book in defense of Duke George; but where the reputation and innocence of the Prince demanded it, I could not have kept silent about such serious and seditious insults by Luther, which he had published earlier. And so they throw all the fault back on us; but let us see to it that we prove our heart and our intention to God, and let us care very little how the human epoch shall judge us, etc.'

For the rest, Witzel's successor in the parish of Niemegk, Conrad Cordatus, a bold and impudent man whom the Wittenbergers themselves forbade to preach in public among them due to his unbridled rashness and his uncontrolled tongue, wrote in German against Witzel and Cochlaeus, to whom he slanderously imputed heresy and several errors, which made them odious to the papists as well. And he babbled many things in succession against Cochlaeus, among which these words were contained: 'I am' (he said) 'a Licentiate of Theology even under the Papacy, as I myself somewhat frequently repeat; but certainly, we Theologians do very evilly, when we dishonor the Holy Scripture as Cochlaeus does. For he wants to be a Doctor of Holy Scripture, and nonetheless he teaches, clearly with the utmost diligence, that certain things must be believed, which are not written in the Holy Scripture. On this point, a Christian person certainly ought to respond to him as follows: "Whatever is not written in the Holy Scripture, the Word of God, let the Devil entrust to you and your comrades, and let him give you thanks, as indeed he does." On this account, Cochlaeus is not a Doctor of the Holy Scripture, but a Doctor of Non-Scripture, a Doctor of Theology in the negative; about which it is written, "The fool has said in his heart, there is no God." He teaches us the Turkish faith. For the Turks too believe and teach that things which are not written; moreover, the things which are written, they do not accept.'[537] These things Cordatus wrote there.

Against this new adversary, Cochlaeus responded in German, more bitterly than usual due to these terrible accusations. He divided his book into six

Chapters, on six articles, namely, about the Trinity of Persons, about the words of the consecration, about the Mass, about indulgences, about communion in both kinds, and about the Holy Orders of priests. Indeed, Cordatus had added this slander concerning the Trinity, that Cochlaeus had denied that the Scripture ever bore witness about the Trinity of Persons in one essence. But he had not written in that fashion, but as follows: 'The highest article of our Faith, namely, that there are Three Divine Persons in one essence, is not expressly stated in the Scriptures.' But Cordatus cleverly omitted and kept silent about this adverb 'expressly', which Cochlaeus had included; giving this judgment, just as if in these words: 'Three Persons and one Essence, even if it is not expressly stated in the Scriptures, nevertheless must not be denied or rejected. So also these, Mass, chrism, Canon, and other things of that sort, must not be denied or rejected, although they are not expressly stated in the Scriptures.'

Moreover, Cochlaeus cast this impiety about the Trinity back against Luther, who twelve years earlier had written against the doctrine of *Homousion*, with a serious accusation against St Jerome. After quoting Luther's words on this topic, Cochlaeus says, 'Do you hear these words of Luther, Cordatus, you lying flatterer? You cannot deny them; for they remain there in his book which he published against Dr Jacob Latomus. If you are honest, then tell me which Catholic Doctors – not which Arian ones – ever rejected this sacred term *Homousion*, or Consubstantial; and show me where St Jerome wrote that poison hides in the letters and syllables of this word. Therefore, for as long as you Lutheran preachers will not show me this, I will consider you to be infamous and faithless Arians, and will accuse you as such, unless you shall urge and drive your Luther, because of this impious lie, to public recantation. Go now, Cordatus, curse me and slander me more; to be sure, you will pursue great honor in slandering me. However, when you write that I collected these absurd and Turkish remarks out of the Bishop of Rochester's book, this strikes me as much worse than all those accusations and slanders which you have thrown against me personally, even though I never knowingly offended your person. But if there are Turkish sayings in Rochester's book (as you say, you Turkish Mamaluke!), it would have well befitted you Evangelical (as you call yourselves) Doctors to refute a book of this sort as a warning to Christians, so that they might beware of Turkish sayings, and not to have kept silent about that book for so long – more than ten years now! But what could you repulsive stage actors reprehend or refute in that honest and holy man (who is the glory and crown of all the Bishops and Doctors of this age), who has more of Scripture and erudition in his little toe than all of you have in your whole Behemoth of a body?' [538]

About the Words of the Consecration, Cochlaeus responded as follows, among many other things: 'Moreover, when Luther mocks us for fleeing to the Faith and the mind of the Church, he acts like an Apostate. I would gladly hear, in return, from which Scripture Luther or his Devil (who, he says, disputed with him over the Mass) can demonstrate that, when a Lutheran priest (who although he is baptized, still has not been legitimately initiated into Sacred Orders) in his new Evangelical Mass chants or speaks these words of Christ, "This is My Body," in a very loud voice, through this the Flesh and Blood come into the bread and wine. Where is this written? Luther and Cordatus are the biggest babblers you please, yet they keep silent and are mute on this question. Therefore, the Lutherans could have seen to what place the Devil was leading them through Luther, as long as he wished to admit nothing except that which was expressly stated in the Scriptures — namely, he was leading them into the sect of the Zwinglians or the Pighardians, who deny Transubstantiation; just as Luther too denies it, saying "The substance of the bread and wine remain the same after consecration as before it." Therefore, if there is not Transubstantiation there, which is a transmutation of the substances, nothing is achieved by the words of consecration; since the bread remains bread, and the wine, wine, after just as before. Moreover, Cordatus inanely poured out as many words as you please, this man who wishes in the cause of the Faith to admit or receive nothing beyond the Scripture; nevertheless, he does not indicate any Scripture which says that the flesh and blood of Christ are made by the words of Consecration, when they are pronounced at the altar; but not when they are said or chanted at another time, in the Passion or the Gospel reading or elsewhere; or, if the words are said over bread and wine, but not if they were said over stone and water or ale. Be bold here, Cordatus, you mighty boaster about Scripture, and clearly pass judgment on these things for me from the Scriptures, I charge you by the eternal Truth. But for as long as you Lutherans will not pass judgment on these matters, I will consider you pure Zwinglians and Pighardians, bread-eaters and wine-bibbers, since you will receive nothing outside of clear Scripture. But we believe most firmly, with undoubted faith, that Transubstantiation is achieved by the words of Consecration, that is, that from the substance of the bread and wine are created the body and blood of Christ. For even if we do not have a Scripture about this, nevertheless we have the belief and approbation of the Church, which has taught and accepted this from Christ and His Apostles up to the present time. For these sublime mysteries are not set out in public Scriptures, lest they be mocked by infidel Pagans, Turks, and Jews; just as Christ ordered in Matthew 7, when he said "Do not give a holy thing to the dogs," etc.' [539] He added sayings of Paul, Dionysius, and Augustine in support of the same opinion, which it would take to long to quote.

But then the pious and learned man Lord Paul, the Abbot of Altzella, of the Order of St Bernard, also wrote, in German, about the Mass. In his prologue he argues in general for the Mass, as follows: 'If the Mass were an abomination (as Luther blasphemously says that it is) or an impious and damnable work, the Devil would not argue against it, and would not make it a matter of concern that the Mass should be abolished, but much more, rather, would promote it so that it might be and might remain in the fullest use, in contempt of and insult to God. For this reason, Luther's book about the Corner Mass, the faithful, and those called by God does more for the strengthening and augmentation of devotion to the Mass than it does for its diminution and abolition.

Open, I beg you, your understanding, consider in earnest and diligently, and examine all Luther's writings; truly, you will never find in them a place where Luther boasts about any divine vision, or revelation of the Spirit of God; but all his communication, every conversation, every boast and vision of his, is with the Devil. Indeed, he often made mention of him in his other writings; but here he openly confesses that the Devil is his teacher, who by disputing with him taught him that the Mass is nothing good. Truly, I have very often marveled that Luther was proud to such a degree that he absolutely would not accept instruction or any admonition, nor would he bear anyone's judgment, not of the Universities, or the Councils, or the Church, or even the Angels; although the Apostle Paul, who was snatched up into the third Heaven and could not doubt at all about his Gospel, because it had been revealed to him by the Lord, nevertheless did not disdain to confer with the other Apostles about the Gospel, and humbly to submit himself, together with Barnabas (who was full of the Holy Spirit), to their judgment. But Luther, who learned his Gospel from the Devil (as he here openly admits) absolutely will not submit his doctrine to anyone's examination, for the purpose of judging it. In this he is, to be sure, like his teacher, who is king over all the sons of Pride, as the Book of Job says. Therefore, my amazement at his elevation now ceases, since the Lord says in the Gospel: "It suffices the pupil to be like his master."' [540] These things that venerable Abbot said in his prologue. The other things he wrote were too lengthy to be repeated conveniently here.

Moreover, Cochlaeus had sent his servant far away into Scotland, to warn the Bishops of Scotland and even the King himself about the Lutherans' tricks, which they were plotting by the agency of the Scot Alesius (a fugitive and exile who had thrown aside his cowl and had fled from Scotland to Wittenberg) against the famous King of Scotland, who remained Catholic through all circumstances. They had plotted in the same way against the King of England by the agency of William Tyndale and other Apostates. Meanwhile, Alesius published a bitter book against Cochlaeus at Wittenberg, with Philip Melanchthon dictating and assisting. Cochlaeus immediately responded to this, censuring Philip more severely than Alesius, since from the style and other indications he clearly recognized the architect of these lies. Therefore, among other things he wrote as follows to the King of Scotland, in another book: 'It would take a long time to recount how many lies and slanders have been invented there in respect to the exile Alesius, and perhaps it would be unbecoming before Your Majesty, Most Serene Prince. For his vanity and virulence are so great that he is not unfittingly called Melanchthon, that is, 'Black Land,' whose sport and custom it is to blacken the reputation of good and Catholic men. For how many did he blacken in his *Didymus*? How many in his *Commonplaces*? How many in the *Apology for His Confession*?' [541]

Moreover, he lists specifically the injuries that have been caused to the realm of Scotland by Melanchthon; namely, first, that previously in his *Didymus* he openly ridiculed the renowned theologian Scotus, who is called 'the Subtle Doctor' – affirming that subtlety is not rightly attributed to him, since he left his doctrines so unexplained that he earned his name Scotus, which is derived from Shadows, because there is nothing more obscure than his doctrine. For it is clearer than noontime light that he has twice sixteen times been beaten in the race[542] by Luther, if the argument turns on the energy of native talent, on eloquence, on humanistic and historical studies.[543] Second, just recently, under the person of Alesius, Melanchthon babbled out many inappropriate things against the Scots. Therefore, among other things, Cochlaeus said, 'In truth, is this a trivial injury to a people and infamy to a realm, to say that Patrick, a Scottish nobleman, was most cruelly killed, not because he was a heretic or a criminal, but because he followed the judgment of the Scripture and the Fathers and threw away or reproved any manifest abuse or error?'[544] And below: 'What more barbaric, wicked, or monstrous thing could be said, than what that man says: that in your reign savagery holds sway against the best men of the best ranks? For what more could either the most monstrous Phalarism or Cyclopian barbarity do?[545] And in addition, what could be more irreligious, or more impious and less Christian, than to put forward a most savage Edict, which prohibits the books of the New Testament from being brought into your island? For it is the work of Turks or Jews, not of Christians, to prohibit the New Testament, in which are the Four Evangelists of Christ, and the teachings and deeds of Paul and the other Apostles.

'But I understand, King, the clever subtlety of this most wicked Rhetorician, in which he signifies to his own people, by the term "the best men", those who approve of Luther's doctrine; by "New Testament," Luther's new translation, which was just now spread abroad in German for the Germans and in Latin for foreigners, for the purpose of attracting them to Lutheranism.'[546] And below he wrote, 'He does not only impiously lie about the invocation of the Saints when he says that it did not exist among the ancients before Gregory, but he also wickedly blasphemes and mocks God in His Saints, and most especially in those Saints who are most famous among the Scots, namely Ninian and Bodulf, whom Melanchthon even compares ignominiously to the Lupercine Gods of the Gentiles.'[547] Cochlaeus wrote these things and others of this sort to the King of Scotland, James V, against the man who impersonated Alesius.

Moreover, many Poles were then living in Wittenberg; noble youths, who while they were pursuing good studies[548] there, were at the same time drinking in the Lutheran poison, so that there was fear lest, when they returned home, they might infect all the realm of Poland (which was outstandingly Catholic) with Lutheranism. Also, the parents and relatives of many of them did not know that they were spending time in Wittenberg, but thought that they were attending to their studies in Leipzig, where there is a Catholic Academy and an honest citizenry. Therefore, Cochlaeus published various pamphlets in Latin, in order to warn the Poles about this danger while there was still time. He inscribed these books to the Bishops and Nobles of that realm, so that on that account at least they would understand that they and their people should beware of the Wittenbergish ferment. Moreover, since the name of Philip Melanchthon was in favor with many Poles because of his great learning,

Cochlaeus published four 'Philippics' and other works against Philip, so that they might more closely and more clearly perceive that man's poisons. These books dispersed throughout the booksellers in Poland. Therefore, at Cochlaeus's entreaty, Lord Mathias, Archbishop of Gnesin, and several other Bishops and Nobles of the realm brought it about that the Most Serene King of Poland, Sigismund, promulgated anew a stern Edict, in which he both recalled those Poles who were studying in Wittenberg, and forbade the others to send anyone there any longer. The Edict begins thus:

'We hear that there are very many factious people in our realm, who desire to overthrow the government. They follow sects which have been condemned by the orthodox fathers in universal Councils, and they do so not only in secret, but they also publicly proclaim and disseminate them, not without contempt for the pious sanctions that have been instituted and received by the Catholic Church and by our Edicts. In addition, there are not a few who send their children, neighbors, and associates to Wittenberg, so that there — from the beginning of their adulthood, before they know how to discern bad from good — they may quickly imbibe pestiferous dogmas from Luther himself (who is the head of these evil people), and afterwards spread and propagate these dogmas through our realm. How fortunately this business has turned out, in the neighboring regions round about us, is obscure to no one. For we see more clearly than noonday light how many seditions, how much slaughter, plundering of goods, and disorder in all matters, how much ruin of piety, and finally how much destruction of honesty, has been produced from these beginnings. And we see how up until now it has been impossible to extirpate this plague, once it has taken root in people's souls, however many may exert themselves against it. We have several times taken care, through our Edicts which have established severe punishments against transgressors, that it should never occur among us and our subjects.' And below it says, 'As for those who pass their lives with Luther or any other Princes of these factions, for the future we preclude them from every avenue to any offices or magistracies at all, etc.' [549]

After this Edict, certain Poles who were recalled from Wittenberg into their own country threw all the blame on to Cochlaeus. One of them, a layman who was associated with the Canonry of the Metropolitan Church of Gnesin, wrote a bitter letter against Cochlaeus to his own Archbishop. In it, indeed, he honored Philip Melanchthon with many praises, as his own teacher; moreover, he most savagely charged that Cochlaeus contended against Philip more from hatred of Philip and of good studies than from love of religion and the commonwealth. But God, Who sees into one's heart and thoughts, will finally judge, and will know what should be given to each one according to his works. Certainly, Cochlaeus had very often openly confessed, both elsewhere and in these very books which he then published against Philip, that he had written against Philip not out of hatred for him, but out of zeal for the Faith and the Catholic religion. For he kept the *Philippics* and the *Skirmishing* against his *Apology* at home with him for three full years, and the *Confutation* of his *Didymus* for more than twelve years, before he published them, because he hoped that at some time Philip would return to the Church, after setting Lutheranism aside.[550] But when he saw that Philip daily made more progress in that sect, he preferred, at the risk of his life, to offend a few Poles by publishing the books than, against charity and at the risk of his soul, to neglect many of them by concealing the books and keeping silent, and by wickedly forbearing and shutting his eyes to make his conscience a defendant before God, against which this verse of Isaiah might be cast up: 'They are mute dogs, without the strength to bark.' [551]

These chapters about the deeds and writings of Luther had been written at Meissen in the year 1534. Those which were later added to them as a supplement, up to Luther's death, were written at Regensburg.

1535

A lamentable disturbance of the faith and of religion happened in this year in the most flourishing realm of England, due to the exertion and instigation of evil men, who seized their chance through the unlucky divorce of the King (although Pope Clement VII had refused to permit that divorce). Cochlaeus, too, published a book against it, entitled *Concerning the Marriage of the Most Serene King of England, Henry VIII*.[552] In it he proves at length the sanctity of matrimony, contrary to which many had recommended divorce to the King. However, since the best and most learned men John Fisher, Bishop of Rochester, and Thomas More, Lord Chancellor of the Realm, had argued against that divorce, they were captured and held in prison for quite a long time, and at length – since they would not approve either the divorce or the King's defection, in which he forsook his obedience to the Roman Pontiff and the Unity of the Church, and appointed himself as Supreme Head of the Church in England – in that year they were both beheaded, and suffered the ultimate penalty publicly. About their Passion, someone wrote in these words: 'On 2 July, Thomas More was beheaded in Britain, showing no less constancy in his judgment and punishment than did Socrates when he was condemned by the most wicked decree of the Athenian assembly. A few days before him, the Bishop of Rochester was killed, against whom the King's furor burned more vehemently for no other cause than that he had been inducted into the order of Cardinals by the Pontiff. But hear something which surpasses all savagery. Rochester's head had been placed on a stake and exposed for many days to the eyes of everyone; but not only did it not decay, it was even said to have become much more venerable. When this rumor grew, it was moved from the place. And so that nothing which might stir up the people in their religion would happen concerning More's head, hear now the most monstrous evil deed. The story of Thyestes was renewed, and More's head was softened by nothing else than a long boiling so that it might decompose more quickly, and then was set upon a pole.' These things that man wrote there.

Other public executions also followed, which were more than tragic and

monstrous enough, carried out against many monks. Serious movements and
rebellions against the King also arose, which were suppressed by military force
and arms. The teachings of sects were also admitted and in time even preached
in sermons to the people. Moreover, speakers were sent to Wittenberg, among
whom was Thomas Fuchs, an English bishop. Also, openly Lutheran books were
published among the English; and the monasteries were demolished and utterly
devastated, and their richest properties were added to the King's treasury.

And when Pope Clement VII died, by the unanimous vote and consent of
all the Cardinals Alexander Farnese was elected and thereafter called Paul III.
He had complained of the King of England's defection and cruelty in many
letters to Kings and Princes. But even Erasmus of Rotterdam, although he had
often been very liberally honored by that King, nevertheless freely bore public
witness to his grief over the death of Rochester and More in his *Ecclesiastes*
(which he wrote about the method of preaching). 'Merchandise lost in shipwreck'
(he said) 'is wept for. But what merchandise is so precious that it could be
compared with a genuine friend? Therefore, what could be more cruel than
this storm, which has deprived me of such proven friends? William Warham,
Archbishop of Canterbury, long since; just recently, William Montjoy, the
Bishop of Rochester, and Thomas More, who was the chief judge of his realm,
and whose breast was whiter than any snow, and his intellect [553] such as England
never had before nor will ever have again, even though she is by no means a
mother of ill-favored intellects in general.' [554] These things Erasmus wrote.

Luther was made fiercer and prouder by his doctrine's unhoped-for successes
of this sort among the English. Again, he inveighed in German against the
Cardinal of Mainz with many slanders; and not just against the Cardinal, but
also against any and all other Catholic Princes and Estates of the Empire.
'Christ' (he said) 'is in His Word, and in the manifestly acknowledged Truth
of the Gospel. And yet through pure violence and obstinate malice they
condemn and persecute His Christians.' [555] And again, 'They are seditious and
rebels against the Emperor, and thieves of God, who do not deign to obey
either God, or the True Church of Christ, or the Emperor, or any power.' [556]
And again, 'They are not only disobedient, but they also steal from and rage
against innocent Christians, since they kill them and by robbery take away
whatever they can, just as if they would gladly destroy the whole Kingdom of
God at once.' [557] And from this point, he concluded thus: 'Therefore, they can,
according to the Pontifical Law, be either driven out or killed; since we are
not bound to suffer violence, but it is lawful to repel violence with violence.' [558] And against that Cardinal, specifically and by name, he said as
follows: 'If the citizens of Halle and the provincial towns subject to the
Archepiscopate of Magdeburg drove out or killed their tyrant the Cardinal of
Mainz, they would act justly against him, according to Pontifical Laws. For
he himself best knows' (he said) 'that he does them notorious injury, and
persecutes the acknowledged Truth.' [559]

Responding to these remarks, among other things Cochlaeus said as follows:
'That cardinal imposed an entirely light and moderate penalty upon those

subjects of his who, against the will of their own ruler, through disobedience defected from allegiance to the Catholic Church, to Luther's heresy. Naturally he ordered that they sell their goods and betake themselves elsewhere, lest like contagious sheep they should infect other good Christians and obedient subjects by living with them. Indeed, the Cardinal was bound to do this, under peril of his soul's salvation, not just as a Catholic Prince, on whom this was enjoined and commanded both in civil justice and in the Imperial laws, but also as a legitimate Shepherd and as an Ordinary Bishop, who was called and stationed by the Holy Spirit, as the highest watchman to whom the care of souls has been entrusted by God – just as the Apostle Paul teaches him in Acts 20, and Christ the Lord in John 10, that the Good Shepherd, when he sees the wolf (that is, heresy) approaching, neither flees nor overlooks him, nor allows the wolf to scatter, kill, and destroy the sheep; but he lays down his own life for his sheep, to defend them from the wolf's bite. So also the Prophet Ezekiel announces, from the Mouth of God, in chapters 3 and 33. Therefore, since heresy must be regarded as a rapacious wolf, as Christ teaches in Matthew 7 and Paul in Titus 3, certainly the Cardinal could, with the greatest right, have punished his Lutheran subjects who would not desist from their Lutheranism not only in their goods, but in their bodies; and he could have taken from them not just all their property and substance, but even their bodies and their lives, according to the dictate of the Imperial Laws in the Codex concerning heresy. For Luther has been publicly condemned as a notorious heretic, and has been so declared, by both authorities, the Pope and the Emperor. Therefore, the Cardinal ought much more to fear that he has been too mild and merciful toward obstinate heretics of this sort, than that he has acted too harshly or tyrannically toward them, as Luther lyingly imputes to him. For it must be feared that heretics of this sort, once they have been driven out, will elsewhere too, like rapacious wolves, infect Christ's simpler sheep, and urge them to rebellion, and snatch them away into eternal death; or else that through poison-laden letters and books, which they will secretly send from other places to the Cardinal's subjects, they will by their example incite subjects who are up until now good and obedient to similar rebellion and disobedience.' [560]

For the rest, a certain layman, Casper Querhamer by name, who was a citizen of Halle and subject of the aforementioned Cardinal, with an astounding zeal collected out of several of Luther's books thirty-six contradictory statements on one article alone – namely, about the communion of the Eucharist, in one or both kinds. He published these contradictions in German, drawn up in a long chart, so that they might be affixed to the walls of houses and might openly display to everyone's sight Luther's infamy and inconstancy. Cochlaeus translated them into Latin and in a preface addressed to Giovanni Matteo, Bishop of Verona, he said as follows: 'And just recently the Lord aroused against Luther the spirit of a certain layman, at Halle in Saxony, who laid this horned bull so low that he cut Luther's throat with Luther's own sword – Goliath the Philistine was not laid more low by David, nor could the lust and slander of the two elders against Susannah seem more surely or openly convicted by Daniel. Therefore, how should learned Theologians fear Luther, when a simple layman thus plucks his beard, makes faces at him, and confounds him?' And the title which that layman gave his work, was *A Table, which is useful and necessary to all those who do not wish to be misled by Luther.*[561]

1536

Since the preachers on either side were ill spoken of up to this time, because of the continual disagreement which existed between the Lutherans and the Zwinglians, they began once more to negotiate with one another about concord, just as they had done previously at Marburg, when Zwingli was yet living. And so emissaries were sent from the Zwinglian cities of the Empire to the Lutherans in Wittenberg, so that they could come to an agreement with them. Capito and Bucer were sent from Strasbourg, Boniface and Musculus from Augsburg, Frecht from Ulm, etc. And they dealt there particularly with Baptism, the Eucharist, and Penitence; and after many reproaches and complaints had been made on both sides, they drew up a Formula of Concord, but an ineffective one. For because of the absence of others and without the consent of their Magistrates, they did not dare to establish it conclusively. Therefore, when they returned they wrote the *Acts* of that conference, while they were halted at Frankfurt; but they were afraid to publish it openly. However, Cochlaeus published three books by St Julian, who was once Archbishop of Toledo. He had found them in a monastery of Altzella, which was most famous in Meissen. And he published them for this reason above all – that many things were contained in them by which many errors of the new sects could be refuted, especially those errors concerning the burial and funeral services of the dead, and the state of the soul after death, and the fire of Purgatory, which the new sects scatter among the simple people by means of barbarous slanders and denials. And he also published an ancient and famous epistle of Pope Nicholas I, which was written of old to Michael, the Emperor of Constantinople, many fragments of which were quoted by Gratian in his volume of Decrees. Cochlaeus found this in Cologne, in the Monastery of Deutz. He also attached many other decrees and rescripts of the same Nicholas I, which can be discerned here and there where they were interposed by Gratian in other writings, and he divided them under twenty headings. He added too a History of King Lotharius (briefly excerpted from Reginus and Sigebert), who had been excommunicated by Nicholas I because he had rejected his wife and taken another through the agency of false witnesses and judges. Cochlaeus did this so that the King of England might know how evilly he was separated from his most holy wife, the most excellent sister of our Emperor's mother. Therefore, in the preface Cochlaeus said as follows to him: 'Deceived by rumor (for a lying report had reached me that your most holy wife had been reunited with you), I wished to confirm Your Highness in your good intention through writings and arguments, in that little book addressed to the Pontiff Paul III concerning your marriage. Indeed, I was mistaken, insofar as it touched upon your action; but insofar as the book regards the justice under the laws and the position and main point of the case, I neither repent that labor nor blush for it – although I understand that because of it you are scarcely of a merciful mind regarding me. But whatever may happen to me, I cannot through fear of death desert the truth, which is besieged throughout Gaul and Italy by your flatterers who have been allured by gold, and in England is oppressed by violence, savagery, and the barbarity of slaughter; nor can I betray it by dissembling, etc.' [562]

In addition, he included a defense on behalf of Rochester and More, against the Englishman Richard Samson, who impudently praised the King's deeds and impiously reviled the piety and constancy of those best of men. In this defense, among other things, Cochlaeus said, 'It is certain that there were never any more harmful enemies of your King than you are, you who seek riches and offices for yourselves out of his most serious faults, and convert every part of his glory into everlasting shame, so that now that saying of Isaiah's may truly be said to him, "Your silver has been turned into dross." For what does the King himself assert in his edicts, the new sons of that Bishop in their injunctions, or you yourselves in your defensive books which you have published against the Roman Pope, which cannot be most clearly disproved, refuted, and contradicted from your King's own words, which he once produced against Luther (before he had been bewitched and blinded by your flatteries) in his book *About the Sacraments of the Church*, and in two letters (one of which he wrote to the Dukes of Saxony and the other to Luther himself)? Here I, for the sake of brevity, will quote a few things from only one book of yours, which you call *An Oration*. From these quotes you may understand your very great confusion, etc.' [563]

1537

In that year the Roman Pontiff Paul III announced a General Council, to be held at Mantua, to which he summoned the Lutheran Princes too. When Luther and his associates learned of this, they began by various devices and writings to assail the authority of the Council. For at Wittenberg they published thirty propositions to publicly argue against the Council. The twelfth of these runs as follows: 'Therefore a Council, or Bishops gathered together, can be mistaken, just as well as other people can.' And the one following this said, 'Moreover, if they are not mistaken, this is by chance, or from the merit of some holy and good man, who is among them, or even from the merit of the general Church, etc.' And in opposition to these thirty Propositions Cochlaeus set out thirty Testimonies to the Council's authority, taken from the Scriptures, the laws, the canons, and the Holy Fathers. And he added seventy Propositions to these testimonies, which confirmed the same thing. He also wrote against their *Excuse*, which was produced at Schmalkald and issued in four forms, partly in Latin and partly in German.[564] For by bringing many vain complaints and taunts against the Bull of Indictment, they sought to disguise their cause; although the words of the Bull could not justly displease any good man. For in it the

Pontiff said as follows, 'We hope and – with God's help to us – we promise through this remedy [i.e., the Council], so holy and healthful, not only to extirpate all heresies and errors from the field of the Lord, and to correct the habits of the Christian people; but also to gain universal peace among the faithful, and, by undertaking a general expedition under the banner of the salvation-bringing Cross against the infidels, to recover our realms and lands that have been occupied by them, and to liberate innumerable captives, and – the Lord willing – to convert the infidels themselves to our holy religion; so that in this way the entire world, coming together in one and the same sheepfold of the Lord, may live soberly, justly, and piously in true Faith, Hope and Charity, and thereafter may look for a crown of justice from Almighty God, etc.'

But the Lutherans, paying attention to none of these things, preoccupied the people's ears, eyes, and souls with laughable figments, lest the laypeople should perceive the usefulness of what the Bull proposed. And so they forged new lampoons,[565] new letters of Beelzebub, fabulous legends about John Chrysostom, which they attributed to the Council.[566] Four letters of Johannes Hus and a little book about the Donation of Constantine the Great, against trifles and figments of this sort, had also been published in German.[567] In like manner Cochlaeus published brief refutations in German,[568] so that the people might see from them the Lutherans' malicious zeal for slandering and for deceiving through lies. In addition, they drew into their sect the Most Illustrious Duke Henry of Saxony, the brother of Duke George; that is to say, the brother of the man whom Luther had harassed with so many injuries, annoyances and slanders, through various machinations of his malice. Even those who, although they were laymen, undertook the pastoral care of souls under the new rite published new Orders of Ceremonies, and new Catechisms from this viewpoint and that. And that Prince also instituted new articles through new Visitors, which he imposed and promulgated on the clerics as well as the laypeople of his dominion. Some of them were addressed generally to all his subjects; but some were addressed in particular to the Holy Virgins who lived in the town of Freiberg.

And Cochlaeus published a small book in German against these articles, which he entitled *A Brief Gloss on the New Articles of the Visitors*.[569] In this book he includes the following introduction: 'First, the Title is a false and impudent lie. For it says that these articles are in conformity with Holy Scripture and with the Confession and Apology of Augsburg; when neither Holy Scripture nor that Confession and Apology forbid or repeal either the Mass or the canonical Hours. For the Scripture says, "My Name is great among the nations from the rising to the setting of the sun; and in every place a pure oblation is sacrificed and offered to My Name." And again, "Seven times in the day I gave praise to You." And again, "I arose in the middle of the night to acknowledge You." And that Confession holds as follows: "Our Churches are falsely accused of abolishing the Mass, etc." And in addition, the Apology says, "Again it must be said in advance that we do not abolish the Mass, but we preserve it and claim it religiously; for Masses are performed among us on every Sunday and Feast day." However, these articles ordain, contrary to these things, that from henceforth the nobles shall not permit their rectors and pastors to celebrate Mass any longer. Moreover, they prohibit the ringing to the *Ave Maria*; they forbid them to sing the *Salve Regina* and *Regina Coeli*; they forbid the blessing of water, salt, cakes, herbs, palms, etc. Certainly neither the Confession nor the Apology do so; therefore, the Title is false and lying. But since those Articles were drawn up by these men – who have neither Papal nor Episcopal authority, but are rapacious wolves rather than legitimate and ecclesiastical shepherds – the articles cannot bind or circumscribe any person's conscience. And they are also refuted in this way by that new Wittenbergian Idol of theirs himself. For Luther, in his pamphlet on Secular Power, denounces as insane and perverse those Princes who presume, in matters of the Faith and the Church, to give, prescribe, or prohibit laws to their subjects.' These things and many more of this sort Cochlaeus wrote there, against the latest rash indiscretions of those articles.

And there were two pastors of this sort in Wroclaw, in the famous and foremost city of Silesia. One of them was a layman, and the other was a married priest and a bigamist. Therefore, Cochlaeus wrote a short pamphlet in German, *Against the Catechism of the Laity*, in answer to their errors concerning Baptism and the Eucharist.[570] There he put forward this question in the preface, whether it was written anywhere at all, either in the Holy Scriptures or in the writings and histories of the Fathers, that a layman should be permitted to perform a pastoral office, to administer the sacraments to the people, to consecrate, and so on; or that a priest should be permitted, after he has taken his Holy Orders, to wed a wife, and even, when one wife has died, to take another. But neither of them gave an answer either to that question or to the refutation of the errors which they were teaching about Baptism and the Eucharist – meanwhile, they were freely enjoying riches and the applause of the crowd.

1538

So that our Germans, and foreign nations as well, might more clearly understand how much less evil and impious Johannes Hus had been (who by his heresy had led the most flourishing realm of Bohemia into every sort of evil and misfortune) than Luther is, who so seditiously and impiously disturbs the Roman Empire and the realms of Germany, Cochlaeus excerpted seventy articles from several of Johannes Hus's sermons,[571] and set against them from just one of Luther's sermons the same number articles – but Luther's were much more repulsive than Hus's were. For example, Hus said, 'Just as Moses found favor in the sight of the Lord, so also does the Priest in the presence of the Lord, that is, in the divine office.' But Luther said as follows:

'Let that Consecration worthy of Saturnalias and Bacchanalias hinder no one here. For these Orders and Consecrations are considered as a laughable trifle before the Lord.' Moreover, when someone said, 'Every holy man is a priest, but not every priest is a holy man,' and another objected to this, 'Consequently, he will sacrifice ancient things on the altar,' Hus responded, 'That does not follow, for the altar was not consecrated for that purpose.'[572] Moreover, Hus said, 'If you honor the Father, to Whom we daily say "Our Father, Who art in Heaven," then you also honor our Mother, His lawful Spouse, Who is on high in Jerusalem; that is, the Holy Church, triumphant in Heaven, preserving [us] here by Her body and in Heaven by Her mind; and in Purgatory sleeping because of Her own merits – Who, collected together as one from these three parts, is called our Mother.' However, Luther said that the whole Church had erred, right from the very beginning, in the first Council, which even the Apostles and their pupils attended, because they had been of the opinion that 'The Law and work are necessary for the purpose of Justice and Salvation.' Therefore, so that it might clearly be shown that Johannes Hus had been less impious than Luther, that pamphlet was entitled *Concerning the Immense Mercy of God towards the Germans* – namely, that we have not yet been consumed, who for so many years now have been gnawing at one another, and have been contending fiercely in hurtful disputations and dissensions concerning the Faith, against the pious admonition of the Apostle Paul, who says, 'But if you bite and gnaw at one another, take care lest you be consumed by one another.'

Furthermore, there was a great dispute at Wittenberg between Luther and certain Lutherans, who were rejecting the Law of Works, just as Luther himself had earlier taught. Therefore, he fought against them – whom he abusively called Antinomians – in many disputations. However, in order to show that Luther was more reprehensible than those other men were, Cochlaeus published 153 Propositions against Luther's fifth disputation, which contained seventy propositions. The beginning of Cochlaeus's book is as follows: 'Consider, I beg you, Lutherans, whichever ones of you are learned and clever, what sort of man this Architect of the New Gospel, your Duke and Prince Luther, is – who due to his ceaseless zeal for refutation and dispute and his perpetual hatred of peace and unity thinks it of no account that he should be in disagreement with himself, so long as he can contradict others at every opportunity, etc.'[573]

Moreover, in that same year a book by Richard Morison, an Englishman, was sent to Cochlaeus from England. It was a lengthy and acrimonious book against Cochlaeus, which had been published in London. In it, after the slanders of a most longwinded preface, finally in the fifth section he sets out the sum of his book, saying as follows: 'But so that I may join with the foe at close quarters, unless I am mistaken the entire accusation set out by Cochlaeus against the King contains the following as the primary heading of its slanders. The wife was repudiated, the Pope ejected from England, the defenders of the Pope killed; the wife should have been kept, the Pope should have been recalled, and the defenders could never have been killed without sin.' Moreover, among many other bitter slanders, he notes this one too: that Cochlaeus was given the Canonical Prebend in the Cathedral Church of Merseburg on the stipulation that he not write against Luther thereafter. Therefore, that Englishman wrote as follows, attacking him: 'Then did you write those things for the sake of defending the truth – or wasn't it rather for the sake of earning favor for yourself with the Emperor and the Pope? You who give the promise that you will no longer exert yourself against Luther. What could a great sum of money not procure from you, when the Prebend can drive you to such disgrace?' [574] To these remarks Cochlaeus said briefly (since they were pure lies) that not only his friends, but even his enemies, his neighbors at Wittenberg, knew very well that none of these things was true. For the rest, he said that he had produced many strong arguments in support of the Roman Pontiff's authority and the ecclesiastical power in his book *Concerning the King's Marriage*, not drawing them from his own intelligence, indeed, but from the Holy Fathers and great Doctors; namely, he took nine of them from St Bernard, twenty-four from St Thomas, twenty-six from the ancient Decrees of the Fathers, and fifteen from the Abbot Panormitanus. That Englishman responded to none of them. Moreover, responding on behalf of Rochester and More, among many other things Cochlaeus said, 'Those men did not resemble you, Morison, so that they should exercise the art of Gnatho the parasite on the belly's behalf, and should praise impious and dishonest things, against their own soul and conscience, while condemning those things which no good man, even if he were a Turk or a Heathen, could condemn. For who among the Turks has done what you do not blush to do? For you say that Queen Katherine, than whom England has not had a Queen more noble or holy, was all along the King's whore. And you affirm that Anne was the King's legitimate spouse, while the Queen his wife was yet living – that Anne, indeed, whom the King himself shortly thereafter ordered to be executed, for whose sake he had most cruelly held those holy men captive in prison for fifteen months, and at length had killed them. But even you yourself, you worst of Gnathos, occasionally rashly praise and excuse those same men, whom you have dared, in an impious slander, to call traitors to their country. For you say about both of them that they were not the first who preferred to suffer death than to be involved in the first rank of inconstancy and the brand of infamy; it would be a lesser evil to die with the hope of immortality than for so many of their own volumes to give everlasting testimony against them. And here you openly insinuate, although you did not dare to say it, that the King is involved in the first rank of inconstancy and the brand of infamy. For you cannot deny that in many of his writings the King asserted the authority of the Roman Pontiff, and that these writings give everlasting testimony against him, etc.' [575]

And since a General Council had been ordered, to be held in Vicenza, Luther published articles in German, which he wanted his followers to propose at the Council in his name. In response to these articles, Cochlaeus answered on behalf of the honor and health of the German nation, and asked that articles which were so exceedingly absurd and impious should not be proposed to the Council, because they would be a matter of shame and ridicule in the eyes of the other Nations. For most of these articles were contrary to the *Confession* of the Lutherans, which had been displayed to the Emperor and the whole Empire in Augsburg. For example: in the *Confession* they say, 'Our Churches are falsely accused of abolishing the Mass; for the Mass is retained among us, and is celebrated with the utmost reverence.' [576] But Luther's second article, which he wished to be proposed to the Council, runs as follows: 'It is necessary that the Mass be the greatest and most horrible abomination in the Papacy, because it directly and violently fights against this foremost article: Only faith in Christ justifies us.' [577] Cochlaeus says besides that the shame of those proposing these things to the Council would be the stronger, since the second [claim] is founded on the first, which has many times been convicted of falsity and was founded on no Scripture.

1539

There had been published, without the Pontiff's knowledge, the excellent advice about reforming the Church and amending the abuses of the Roman Curia, which had been given to the Pope himself in secret by seven most learned and virtuous men, namely, by Cardinal Contarini, Cardinal La Thiene, Cardinal Sadoleto, Cardinal Pole, the Englishman, the Archbishops of Salerno and Brundisi, the Bishop of Verona, the Abbot of San Giorgio in Venice, and Brother Thomas, the Master of the Holy Palace.[578] These, therefore, near the end of their advice, added the following: 'These are the things, Most Blessed Father, which at present, due to the slightness of our abilities, we considered should be collected, and which seemed to us to need correction. But you, through your goodness and wisdom, will moderate all things; certainly we have satisfied our own consciences, at least, even if we have not fulfilled the magnitude of the matter, which was far beyond our powers. We have acted not without the greatest hope that under you as our Prince we may see the Church of God cleansed, beautiful as a dove; agreeing with itself and concordant, in one body; with eternal remembrance of your name. You took to yourself the name of Paul; you will imitate, we hope, the charity of Paul. He was chosen, as a vessel that would carry the Name of Christ throughout the Nations; and we hope that you were chosen, so that you might reinstate the Name of Christ, which has been forgotten by the Nations and by us Clerics, in our hearts and in our works; and that you might heal the sick, lead the Sheep of Christ back into one sheepfold, and remove from us the Wrath of God and that punishment which we merit, which has already been prepared, which is even now hanging over our necks.' [579]

Against this pious and healthful advice of these best of men, two pamphlets appeared. One was by Luther, which translated the advice into German and soiled it and twisted it by the worst sort of marginal annotations.[580] The other was by Johannes Sturm, a Rhetorician at Strasbourg. Cochlaeus wrote a brief pamphlet to him, which was entitled, *An Investigation of Justice concerning the Advice of the Chosen Cardinals, etc.*[581] In it, among other things, he said as follows to Sturm: 'Nevertheless I do not at all doubt that your letter is read with a much calmer mind by learned and serious men than is Luther's German interpretation, done against those men. For you occasionally restrain yourself from slanders; but Luther does not hesitate to call such men (whose learning and blamelessness of life – as even you admit – all Italy knows and praises) lost and bewailed Fools. You write in Latin, so that they may understand what you approve and what you disapprove of, and what more you would wish from them; but Luther translates them evilly into German for the unschooled common people of Germany, just as the dishonest Rapsaces once did against the King Ezekiel. You praise them and commend them in certain matters; Luther, without discrimination, refutes everything, even if the things which they say are so manifestly good that they cannot be censured by anyone except impious and insane people who lack common sense. He himself, through slander, twists every meaning into its contrary, as though these things had been said by them deceptively or trickily, or through irony and perversity of mind. You urge the Cardinals to complete things which have been begun; but he calls down dreadful things upon them, because of their advice of such a kind about peace and reform. You do not entirely reject or spit out of your mouth the General Synod; he slanders and rejects the whole Ecumenical Synod in very many pamphlets and with various inventions and portrayals, in Germanic verses. You leave us some hope for concord; he long since threatened us with perpetual war, and that, living or dead, he would not allow us any peace or quiet, etc.' [582]

But Cardinal Sadoleto, writing to the same Sturm, and doing so very humanely and modestly, censured him for his slanders. For he said as follows: 'I would not have wished, my Sturm, and it struck me as a very grievous thing indeed, that I saw so great an excellence in oratory as is in you be defiled with almost endless slanders and the rudeness of insults. And I thought that this befitted Luther alone, to rush against all men, of course with haste and noise; but this is very far from fitting for men who are learned in the liberal arts. Therefore, how did this downfall occur in your ability,[583] which is so great? And what passages in your book are not full of curses and bitter scolding, when you everywhere drag in and repeat our infamies, villainous desires, evil cruelty, shameful acts, and sins; obviously bringing all of us who disagree with you into blame, under one name; although nevertheless, if judgment were made according to individual merits, there would be a greater number of good men even in the city of Rome – I mean, of those men who preside over priests – than of evil ones, etc.' [584]

And Cardinal Contareni wrote to Cochlaeus as follows, among other things: 'But you, Cochlaeus, because of your prudence and your experience of German matters, and because of your Christian piety, see to it that this schism be repaired, so that we may, in our time, see the Church one in the bond of charity and peace, and so that your Germany, a most noble and powerful part of the Christian Commonwealth, may at last become quiet, and attend to itself, and take care lest – if these seditions should last – it destroy itself by its own strength.' To these remarks Cochlaeus responded as follows: 'Oh how pointedly and deeply these words of this best and most learned man strike and penetrate my sense, my mind, and my heart – especially the last of these words. For I fear nothing more anxiously than this one thing especially, that Germany may destroy itself by its own strength, and, piteously consumed with civil wars, may at last become booty of the Turks. How much better it would be if learned men would humbly refer their disagreements about faith and religion not to the laity and the ignorant crowd, but rather to public academies, and especially to the General Council, so that they would trust in and depend on the Church rather than on their own judgment. For it is not this or that man, however learned and eloquent, but the Church, that Paul calls the pillar and foundation of the Truth. So far as I am concerned, surely there is nothing in this life so dear or so precious to me, which – in order to regain concord among us concerning faith and religion – I would not spend or give up as willingly as possible, if anything could be done through me for the peace and unity of the Church, etc.'[585]

Moreover, the Catholic religion sustained a most grave injury and misfortune in this year, through the death of the most Illustrious Duke George of Saxony and his truly guileless and innocent son, Duke Frederick of Saxony. For his successor and heir, his brother Duke Henry, who had already been led astray by the Lutherans, introduced Luther's sect by public mandates into all the lands of Meissen, Thuringia, and Saxony, which had been under Duke George's control. And in the Cathedral Church of Meissen (where previously God had been praised by Divine Offices and various alternations of singing and chanting, day and night alike, every hour, without any cessation) he abolished divine service for the most part, and utterly changed the ancient face of religion. And so Cochlaeus was expelled from there, and shortly thereafter, due to the sympathy of the venerable chapter of Wroclaw, he was entered as a member of the Chapter of that Cathedral Church. And while he lived for a time as an exile in Bautzen in Lausitz, he wrote a pamphlet on this question: 'Whether he who has not been legitimately ordained and consecrated as a priest by some Bishop, may perform the Eucharist through the words of Consecration.'[586] There, he proved the negative viewpoint by every kind of Holy Scriptures and by the histories of the Fathers, and also refuted the arguments of the opposing side.

1540

In this year the Emperor happily returned to Lower Germany from Spain, after being conducted through France with the most magnificent hospitality, and decreed that an Imperial Diet should be held at Speyer. But because of the plague that was then at Speyer, the Diet was moved to Hagenau. In this Diet, in place of the Emperor (who could not attend) his brother, the King of the Romans, conducted the Empire's business. He ordered Cochlaeus, too, to travel there from Wroclaw. And he asked Cochlaeus to collect a brief compendium from the Acts of the Diet of Augsburg (which Dr Jerome Vehus, the Chancellor of Baden, had written and had handed over to His Majesty), and from the twenty-eight Articles of the Augsburg Confession to explain the

opinion of his mind concerning whatever, with good conscience and the preservation of the Faith, could or ought to be admitted for the sake of peace.
Cochlaeus therefore went through all the articles individually, noting what
should be conceded, and what censured or denied, as briefly as he could; and
affirmed that he had done this religiously, with the greatest faith, as he intends
to acknowledge before God, both in the extreme hour of his own death and
on the Last Day. At the end he also added that there were many other articles
by Luther and his accomplices that were in opposition to the Catholic faith,
which were left out of that Confession but were published in other writings
of theirs; and that lasting peace and concord could not be established without
the discussion of these articles and a decree about them.

But the Lutherans did not want, in public discussions there, to deliver a
ratified decree of those articles which had been agreed upon in Augsburg by
the Colloquium of the Seven. And now they made public two writings which
they had given to the Emperor, one in Latin and the other in German. In
these, indeed, they put forward six articles in particular, as being necessary,
and asked that these be conceded to them. But Cochlaeus indicated in a brief
writing what could be admitted in these articles, while preserving the Catholic
faith. These men asked for another Colloquium, and obtained their wish that
it should be held at Worms a few months later in the same year. Moreover,
Melanchthon and Bucer made known, in published books, what should be done
and disputed in it. After a very long discussion was held with the presiding
lords, two members of the Colloquium, Dr Johannes Eck and Master Philip
Melanchthon, disagreed concerning Original Sin. Indeed, they would not have
made an end of their dispute about that article had not the Emperor's Commissary, the Illustrious Lord of Granvella, who would soon depart, made a
selection, and established two men from either side, who somehow reached
agreement about that article, after breaking it down into four points. But
nothing could be accomplished there concerning the rest of the articles. However, lest nothing at all should have been achieved there, Cochlaeus published
his *Colloquium,* which he had held privately with Luther himself in Worms,
nineteen years previously.

And there was a great deal of talk in that year about a certain Prince, who
in addition to his legitimate wife had married another as well, and was said to
have done so by the advice and with the approval of Luther and some of his
accomplices. Cochlaeus therefore wrote a short pamphlet against this new
scandal.[587] In it he demonstrated, by six arguments from the Old Testament
and the same number from the New, that it is not permitted for any Christian
to have two or more wives together and at the same time. And since another
Diet had been ordered by the Emperor, to be held at Regensburg, in which
there would be discussion about religion, in another Colloquium, Cochlaeus
published a short pamphlet in Mainz, both in Latin and in German, on the
seventh article of the Augsburg Confession, *Concerning the True Church.*[588] In
that pamphlet he showed that the True Church exists not among the Lutherans,
but among the Catholics: for the whole controversy about religion seems to

depend on this point. And at the same time, before he left for Regensburg, he published that pamphlet which he had entitled *Concerning the Ordination of Bishops and Priests, and Concerning the Consecration of the Eucharist.* And he had already published, at Ingolstadt, his *Fifth Philippic*, which he showed at Worms to Philip himself, who desired to see it.[589]

In the same year a great change in religion, so far as concerns the disputed points, came about in the realm of England. For the dissension (which the King had against the Roman Pontiff because of the judgment the latter had given concerning the former's marriage) had provided an opportunity, and freedom as well, to the Lutherans for creeping into that country and dispersing their heresy widely and sowing it among the people, by sermons and published books. From that matter arose many commotions, many scandals, many seditions and rebellions (certainly, innovation usually brings such troubles with it, but Luther's new Gospel especially does so – that Gospel to which he himself ascribes and applies, in a depraved sense, this saying of Christ: 'I came to bring not Peace, but a sword', Mt. 10: 34). Therefore the King, on the advice of the Bishops and magnates, ordered a public assembly of all the Nobles and Estates, which they call a Parliament. In this Parliament, for the sake of establishing concord of religion, he proposed six questions, concerning which it was reported as follows, in the public Acts:

'At length, after long deliberation over these articles, after very many consultations, finally after endless arguments, linked this way and that, by the full common consent of all, His Royal Majesty as well as both orders Senatorial and common convened in this Council, it was and is resolved, decided, and decreed, in this manner and form, as follows. First, In the most Blessed Sacrament of the Altar, through the virtue and efficacy of the most powerful Word of Christ, as soon as the Priest shall have spoken that word with his mouth, under the form of bread and wine, the natural body and blood of the Lord, conceived by the Virgin Mary, are in reality present; and after the Consecration, no substance remains of either bread or wine, or of anything else than Christ, God and Man. Secondly, it must be believed and not doubted that to take communion in both kinds is not, under Divine Law, necessary for salvation for all people, since in the Body, under the kind of the bread, is the True Blood, and with the Blood, under the kind of the Wine, is the True Body, as well when they are separated as when they are joined. Thirdly, after they have been initiated into holy orders, priests may not, under Divine Law, take wives. Fourthly, vows of chastity or of widowhood that have been made to God, not rashly, by either man or woman, under Divine Law must be kept, and Christian peoples deprive them of a certain liberty which, if they had not so vowed, they would have been able to use and to enjoy. Fifthly, it is both good and necessary that Private Masses be admitted and celebrated in this Anglican Church of the King and its Congregation, through which Masses good Christians, whose livelihoods make appropriate return,[590] receive good and divine comforts and benefits therefrom; and it accords with Divine Law that Masses be celebrated. Sixthly, it is advantageous and necessary that auricular Confession be retained in God's Church. Therefore, by His Royal Majesty's authority, and according to the full common consent of both orders, Senatorial and common, convened in this Council, in this manner as follows the Decree of the Council is passed: Those who in this Kingdom of England, or in any other dominion of His Royal Majesty, after the twelfth day of July next following, in word, writing, printing press, artificial characters, or any other means whatsoever, publicly preach, teach, say, affirm, declare, explain or argue that in the Blessed Sacrament of the altar, under the kinds of bread and wine, after their consecration, the natural body and blood of our Savior Jesus Christ, conceived by the Virgin Mary, are not in reality present; or that after their consecration some substance of bread and wine, or any other substance than that of Christ, God and Man, remains; those who, after the day noted above, publish, preach, teach, say, or affirm that in the Flesh under the kind of the bread the true Blood of Christ does not exist, or that with the Blood, under the kind of wine, the True Flesh of Christ does not exist, as well when they are separated as when they are joined; or who teach, preach, declare, or affirm that the aforesaid Sacrament is of another substance than has been demonstrated above; or in any other way despise or censure the Blessed Sacrament of the altar; all these people – the principal defendant as well as the other subsidiary ones, and those who aid him either by advice or action – after the form of law which follows below shall have been established concerning his and their evil, shall be considered heretics, and every offense of this sort shall be judged as heresy. Those condemned of this heresy shall undergo the loss of life by fire, all abjurations of a cleric or benefits of sanctuary having been removed; and the condemned people's goods, moveable and immovable alike, shall all be conferred into the Treasury, whatever they shall possess, either in their own right or through others, at the time of this crime having been committed or afterwards, as in the crime of *Lèse Majesté*, etc.' [591] These things the King of England decreed.

In the same year His Imperial Majesty promulgated an edict that was not greatly dissimilar, in his hereditary provinces of Lower Germany. There, among other things, he said as follows: 'Therefore, by mature and well-deliberated advice, and also by the advice and consent of our dear sister the Lady Mary, Dowager Queen of Hungary and Bohemia, etc., who rules and governs in our lands that lie in this direction, and likewise by our own highest consideration and opinion, we have ordained and resolved, and we do ordain and resolve, through an Edict and an everlasting law, as follows. First, that no one, of whatsoever state or condition he may be, should be able to have about himself, to sell, to carry, to give, to read, to preach, to teach, to tolerate, to defend, to bestow, or to argue, whether secretly or openly, concerning the doctrine, writings, and teachings which **Martin Luther, John Wycliffe, Jan Hus, Marsilio** de Padua, Oecolampadius, Ulrich Zwingli, Philip Melanchthon, Francis Lambert, Johannes Apel, Otto Brunfels, Justas Jonas, Johannes Purpuri, and Gorcianus, or other authors of their sect, made or could have made; similarly with all other sects which are condemned by the Church. Nor even may anyone have doctrines by those who adhere to, favor, or join with them; nor even the New Testament which was printed by Adrian de Berg, Christopher de Remunda, and Johannes Zell; nor excerpts from Holy Scripture, a translation of the names of the Chaldees, the topographical Epitome of Vadianus, the *Chronicles of Memorable Events*, the *History of the Origin of the Germans*, the works of Eobanus Hess, the Sunday Prayers of Gryphius, the *Path into Noteworthy Passages of Holy Scripture*, the *Catechism* of Erasmus Sarcerius, etc. And if anyone should have books of this sort about him, let him burn them immediately, under penalties that shall be described and executed (if anyone shall be found to have acted against any point written above): namely, the men shall be slain by the sword, the women buried alive, if they do not wish to maintain or defend their errors. But if they wish to persevere in their errors and heresies, they must be put to death by fire. And all their property must be added to our Treasury.'[592] These things the Emperor decreed.

1541

The Emperor came in good time to Regensburg, and remained there in lengthy expectation, until the other Princes and Imperial Estates arrived. There also came from Rome the Cardinal and Lateran Legate Gaspar Contarini, an excellent and most learned man, on the twelfth day of March. The Lutheran Princes and Imperial Estates also arrived with their preachers, who were preaching to the people in profane houses, and were utterly averse to the sacraments, fasts, and rites of the Catholics, and were giving their attention to hunting still on the most sacred days of Holy Week, and even on Good Friday itself as well. Moreover, a book had been written by several people, among whom Bucer insinuated himself by deceitful pretense, and this book had been delivered to the Emperor, as a most serviceable mediator of peace and concord. And so once again new negotiators were appointed from either party, who would debate over that book in a friendly manner and would adjust everything toward the desired concord in faith and religion. From the Catholic party the Emperor appointed three men, Dr Julius Pflug, Dr Johannes Gropper, and Dr Johannes Eck, a most highly trained theologian. Three from the Lutheran party were also appointed, Philip Melanchthon, Martin Bucer, and Johannes Pistorius. Auditors from both sides were also added, and two chairmen, the Most Illustrious Duke of Bavaria and Count of the Palatine Rhine, Frederick, and the Illustrious Lord of Granvella. Therefore these men discussed the book by sitting in council for the space of a month, and meanwhile, with all the other affairs of the Empire postponed and left hanging, at length they reached agreement about certain articles of that book. Dr Eck, who had been seized by fever, was unable to attend the entire Colloquium; and so for some time only two of the Catholics discussed with the three others. But when the Colloquium had been completed, they returned the book to the Emperor, not in the same form in which they had received it, but in another form which they considered was nearer to concord. And now the Emperor gave the book for thorough consideration not only to the Apostolic Legate and to the Catholic Princes and Estates, but also to the Protestants.[593] But nothing was accomplished; for neither party approved that book in all its details. Certainly, the Catholics brought forward many points against it, according to which they could not approve or accept it; in addition, the Legate considered that the whole case should be committed to the Apostolic See, and that without the See's authority nothing could be decided. Moreover, the Lutheran Preachers added nine articles in writing, marked by the letters A, B, C, etc., in which by a versatile evasion rather than a declaration they rendered more ambiguous the articles of the book which had been agreed upon in the Colloquium. The Wittenbergers also, a little later, added still more declarations concerning these articles, declarations so intricate and so wound up in variable glosses and interpretations, that the reader could not see what they wished, in these declarations, to hold steadfast in all points. Moreover, the Lutheran Princes and Estates themselves, in their response to the Emperor about that book, approved neither the book nor the agreed upon articles in all points; but they bound their faith to their Augsburg Confession and its Apology.

'We understand' (they said) 'that certain articles in this book seem acceptable in the judgment of the Negotiators, and some seem reprehensible. We have diligently considered those which are said to be acceptable, which are the articles concerning the freedom of the human will, concerning original sin, concerning justification, concerning penance, and certain other ones; and yet some of them still need a longer explanation, lest their brevity and ambiguity produce new struggles. For we, at least, understand those articles in the same way as these same matters are taught in our Confession and Apology. Controversies that have not yet been brought to an end remain in the book' (they said), 'concerning which our people produced articles, which – since they are true, and written very moderately – we hope will be satisfactory to the other side as well.' [594] And below, 'Therefore we judge' (they said) 'the articles which were produced by the Negotiators chosen from our side to be both moderately written, and true, nor do we dissent from them; and we ask that Your Imperial Majesty may take this answer of ours in good part. For in the first place, since the point at stake is the glory of God and the light of the Gospel, depraved forms of worship or opinions which throw shadows over the Gospel must not be confirmed. How many abuses are confirmed, by the received opinion of the book about the Invocation of the Saints and other forms of worship that have been instituted without the Word of God.' [595] And again, 'What a fetter is imposed upon the Church, if we acknowledge that no lapse whatsoever of the General Synods may be censured!' [596] And again, 'And so that no one may have any doubt what kind of doctrine is everywhere taught in our churches, once again we testify that we have embraced the Augsburg Confession which was shown to Your Imperial Majesty, and the Apology which was added to it; nor do we doubt that this doctrine is truly the consensus of the Universal [Catholic] Church of Christ.' [597] These things the Lutheran Princes and Estates wrote.

Moreover, their Preachers attacked even Cardinal Contarini in a certain writing. 'We are injured' (they said) 'by this wicked prejudice, since certainly he sees that we believe nothing absurd, we profess nothing that does battle with the holy judgments of pious and learned men in Christ's Church, nay indeed many matters of Christian doctrine have been piously and usefully illustrated in our Churches; and yet he published a criticism in which he says that we dissent from the common consensus of the Catholic Church. He even orders, on another page, that the Bishops should devote their attention to destroying the form of doctrine which we profess.' [598] These things they wrote. But Cochlaeus, who was attending as a private citizen, in several private writings criticized the nine articles which they had appended to their book, including their article On justification, as well as two propositions which had been brought from Wittenberg and were being circulated in that place: namely proposition 18 'On original Sin,' and 21 'On justification by Faith.'

At length, when so much zeal, labor, and expense had been lost for the sake of concord, along with a great waste of time, the Emperor announced the Imperial Recess and left at the end of the month of July. He traveled through Italy, where a most beautiful fleet had been constructed, and made an expedition against Algiers, crossing to Africa in the month of October, when he suffered a serious shipwreck. For he had lost the more favorable times for sailing in that fruitless Colloquium at Regensburg, which he, indeed, decreed with the best of intentions and the most sincere mind, but his opponents took pains to pervert everything with their wiles.

1542

In this year two Imperial Diets were conducted by the Roman King, with the Emperor absent. One was held at Speyer, and the date of its Recess was 11 April; the other at Nuremberg, and the date of its recess was 26 August. However, in each of them the primary order of business concerned the expedition against the Turks, which was made in Austria in that year. For this expedition, indeed, the most Illustrious Elector Prince Joachim, Margrave of Brandenburg, was made Commander in Chief of the Christian army, by a general contribution imposed throughout the whole empire. For indeed neither in this year nor in the previous one, when the Diet was being held at Regensburg, had the expedition around Buda and Pest turned out favorably, although the equipment for war had been very great, especially in this year. For the rest, in the cause of religion, the most famous Theologian Dr Johannes Eck in this year published a book, which he titled *Apology for the Catholics, against the slanders of Bucer, concerning the Acts of the Assemblies at Regensburg.*[599] And in that book he first showed that there are many more, and greater, controversial articles which were not reconciled or agreed upon in that Colloquium, than are those which Bucer says were reconciled. Then in many various annotations he points out everything in the book that had been proposed to the Negotiators and that deserved censure, in whatsoever chapter of the book; and there are twenty-three chapters in the book. Next he condemns the many errors of the Lutherans, which are contained in their nine articles, which they designated by the letters A, B, C, etc. Also, he refuted at great length, through twenty-one points, the complaints and slanders which Bucer published against the Response of the Catholic Princes and Estates, given to the Emperor concerning the book of the Colloquium. Also, he defends the Response and Declarations of Cardinal Contarini, the Legate, as well, which Bucer slanderously insulted. And he censures the Response which was given to the Emperor by the Protestants, about the articles that had been reconciled and those that had not been reconciled. 'If I wished' (he said) 'to imitate Bucer's evil sayings, a place where I might affix an Annotation (for a juster and better cause than his) to this response would not be lacking. But since evil-speakers shall not possess the Kingdom of God, I do not wish to offend the Most Noble Princes and Estates of the Protestants, considering the gift given to them by God; since all power comes from God, and since the Princes do not produce these things of their own accord, but an inspiring breath – not of life, but of death – has suggested to them things which do not agree with the orthodox Faith. For deserters of the Church, apostates, the flock of Epicurus, heretical preachers, and schismatics by this lethal drink lure those most excellent Princes and Estates, with God permitting it, to another place. A most ample field for engagement would not be lacking, because they so anxiously ask that the Augsburg Recess be removed, as if our Blessed Augustus, Charles, who was crowned by God, together with so many Catholic Princes (who pledged their faith to His Majesty for the preservation of that Recess) were unstable and inconstant like young women, who say yes one moment and no the next;[600] but the Sentence stands, to remain steadfast both to the Apostolic faith and to His Imperial and Royal Majesty. Oh how admirably the Saxon Duke George, a Prince of blessed memory, said, "The Neo-Christians do not know today what they will believe next year."' These things, and many more of this sort, Eck wrote against Bucer.

And in the same year Dr Albert Pighius of Kempen in like manner wrote an *Apology* against the same Bucer;[601] in its Preface he said, among other things, as follows: 'Although Bucer recognizes and asserts that there are many gifts of God in me – for by this excellent doctrine, he both considers some other person methodical in investigating questions and skilled in discussing matters, and yet deplores such genius, so excellent by birth and so cultivated by studies – nevertheless, on the contrary, he scourges me with open, shameless, and intolerable slanders, calling me now a sophist and now a false accuser.' These things Pighius wrote in his preface. Moreover, in the same book, censuring Bucer and Luther for many things, he here and there added Erasmus in to the same points. For example, concerning the works of penitence which the Ninevites did in order to appease God toward themselves, he says as follows: 'Therefore, what are they going to say about these things? Certainly, following that axiom of Erasmus, that these works of theirs could not please God, because they were undertaken spontaneously beyond His command and did not pay attention to this, that their neighbor should be accommodated through them.

But according to the doctrine of our adversaries, which they publicly assert in the Confession of their faith and its Apology, they will be struck by even harsher blame. For not only were these works not pleasing to God and useless to those who did them, but they were also pernicious, impious, and introduced by the doctrines of Demons, since they were done for the purpose of placating God, of gaining His grace, and of earning His mercy. And what does the Holy Scripture say? God, it says, saw their works, since they were turned from their evil road, and He felt pity for the malice which He had said that He would do to them. And here do you not see the completely opposite opinion of God by Erasmus and the Lutherans?' Pighius wrote these things and many more like them.

1543

In this year, once again an Imperial Diet was held at Nuremberg by the Roman King, since the Emperor was still absent in Spain, from the month of January to April. Its Recess was made and published on the 23rd day of April. Three Commissaries were joined with His Royal Majesty by His Imperial Majesty, namely Christopher the Bishop of Augsburg, Frederick the Palatine Count of the Rhine and Duke of Bavaria, and Johannes of Navis; the first of these three fell asleep in the Lord during that assembly at Nuremberg. Moreover, the discussion there too was principally about the course of the war being waged against the Turks, and about providing garrisons and reinforcements and contributions in the proper time. But concerning the cause of religion, nothing else could be conveniently established, except that the public peace would be protected by either side, lest on the pretext of religion violence or injury should be occasioned against anyone.

In the same year a General Council was ordered by the Supreme Pontiff, to be held at the City of Trent, to which the Pontiff sent three Cardinals as Legates. But because of the wars which were being waged among the most powerful monarchs, very few Bishops made an appearance; the Legates were recalled to Rome and that Council was suspended for the time being. In addition, the Fates robbed the Catholics in Germany of two most famous and learned men, Dr Eck and Dr Pighius, the strongest defenders of the Church and the Faith against the heretics. Moreover, they both died within the space of a single month, indeed of the first month, not without the public grief and lamentation of very many people.

Cochlaeus was traveling from Wroclaw to Trent for the Council; but when he reached Kempten he learned that the Assembly of the proclaimed Synod had been dissolved. And he saw the Emperor in the same place on the 15th day of July, as the Emperor was making his way with his army from Italy into Lower Germany, against the Duke of Cleves, who had defected from him to the King of France, and had occupied the Duchy of Geldern and, in the Emperor's absence, had inflicted many injuries upon the people of Brabant. But when within a few months the Emperor had conquered and subjugated him, through his innate Clemency the Emperor received the Duke into his favor once more.

Moreover, Bucer, having ingratiated himself by impious deceit to the Archbishop of Cologne, Hermann (who was the hereditary Count of Wied), stirred up the most serious discord concerning religion between the Archbishop and his Clergy. For he led the Archbishop into Luther's heresy, although not only the Reverend and Illustrious Chapter of the Greater Church in Cologne, but also every cleric of the entire city, and the whole University of Cologne, cried out in vain against this. But Cochlaeus, who by the grace and kindness of the Most Reverend Bishop of Eichstätt had been made a Prebend in the Choir of St Wilibald, returned from Kempten to Eichstätt. And there he published a new preface to his *Fifth Philippic*,[602] which had been published earlier, and addressed it to the aforementioned Archbishop. There, among other things, after quoting the response of St Ambrose to the Emperor Valentinianus II, he added the following: 'It would have been proper for you, Most Reverend Prince and Lord, to respond to the most evil Lutheran and Zwinglian tempters and advisers in this way: "Far be it from me to betray the heir of the Holy Fathers, Severus, Cunebert, Bruno, Herebert, Peregrin, Anno, and all the faithful Bishops before them, my predecessors, who by so many colleges and monasteries (which they founded with their money and their labor) enriched the service and praise of God, and the memory and veneration of His Saints, into the hands of such rapacious wolves, and openly condemned heretics, who are the most abominable enemies of the Collegiate Churches and Monasteries. Which of my predecessors ever did such a thing?" By such a response, indeed, you would have kept a good conscience before God, good faith before Christ, the Prince of Shepherds (whose little sheep have been entrusted to you), the obedience and fidelity which you owe with respect to the Highest Pontiff and the Emperor of the Romans, your Lords and Superiors; praise in the eyes of foreign Christian nations; unblemished good will in the eyes of the clergy and people of Cologne (who for many years now have unanimously, with your agreement, loathed and detested these sects which are condemned to perdition); and you would have guarded against countless scandals among Christ's people, scandals which now, through your deed, are heard everywhere, not without the groans of many.'[603]

And below he said, 'But if that wolf Bucer has been let in by you, the Shepherd, you well understand how serious an account of such an evil deed you will have to render to the Prince of Shepherds on the Last Day, when there will stand up against you, in great constancy, not only all your Holy Predecessors (whose works and holy foundations you attempt, through these wolves, to abolish and to carry away from their sheepfold and their people, if you do not at the earliest time also remove and expel the people), but the numerous crowds of Holy Martyrs (whose sacred Relics have been held in great reverence by everyone in Cologne for so many centuries, and are still so held today) will also rise up against you before the eyes of the Judge. Nor, meanwhile, will God turn deaf ears to the groans, tears, and sighs of so many holy virgins, priests, and monks, who serve God within the walls of the holy city of Cologne, and whom you so monstrously disturb and torment through these wolves of yours.' [604] These things Cochlaeus wrote there.

He also in the same year published a pamphlet at Ingolstadt, against Henry Bullinger, the leader of the Zwinglians among the people of Zurich, which was entitled *Concerning Canonical Scripture, and the Authority of the Catholic Church.* In its preface he said as follows: 'Now, if you reproached only those abuses which (as the world declines into old age) burst out through the negligence of Prelates, and openly censured only the scandalous life and depraved habits of most of the Clergy, who do not correctly perform their office in the Church, and attacked them however bitterly you liked, I would not only approve of this in silence, but I would even feel no shame to praise you publicly. But since you attack and hostilely fight against the principal points of our whole religion, I may not (when urged by my conscience to the duty I owe) keep silent about all these things or lazily ignore them, as if I did not know what your condition is, what your status, your function, etc.' [605] Cochlaeus also published a pamphlet on the souls in the fire of Purgatory, against two sermons by Andrew Osiander.[606] For the rest, the subordinate clergy of the city of Cologne wrote and published an excellent opinion,[607] after long deliberation, against Bucer's recently published book. In it, the errors and impious teachings of Bucer and his accomplices are most learnedly revealed and refuted in Latin; the book was also translated into German.

1544

In this year a famous Imperial Diet was held, with the Emperor himself being present, in Speyer, at which all seven Elector Princes were personally present (which happens rarely). There, again, the discussion concerned the course of the defensive war against the Turks, and the expenses and contributions that were necessary for that war. There was also serious discussion there about the cause of religion, and due to their ruthless insistence not a little was conceded to the Lutherans which could not please the Supreme Pontiff in all points. And so the public Recess was given at Speyer on the 10th day of June. When the Roman Pontiff learned its tenor, he paternally admonished His Imperial Majesty, in a certain letter, that in the cause of faith and religion he should, according to the custom of his ancestors, decree or permit nothing that would be prejudicial to the Apostolic See without consulting the Roman Pontiff. 'The custom' (he said) 'of your ancestors is of this sort, that whenever there is discussion of those things which pertain to religion, every judgment should always be referred to the Apostolic See, and nothing should be decreed without consulting the See. But now you, my son, when you make mention either of a General Council, as if it would be the most opportune remedy of all for the damaged affairs of the Church (and you do so among the foremost men of Germany itself), or of a National Council, which you also remember; or of the Imperial Diet which is to be held next Autumn, in which you promise to deal with religion and other things which pertain to it; when you do these things, you act in such a way, and you decree in such a way, that you everywhere suppress the name of him to whom divine and human laws (with the approving consent of so many centuries) have given the authority both of ordering Councils and of passing decrees and ordinances about those things which tend toward the unity and utility of the Church, etc.' [608]

Against this letter of Pope Paul III the Lutherans wrote horrible slanders, some in Latin, some in German. Luther himself wrote a long book against it in German, which was so abusive and obscene that it cannot be quoted or read without shame. He also published another pamphlet in German, divided into four parts. The first of these parts has the title, 'Concerning the principal articles of the Christian Faith, against the Pope and the upholding of the Gates of Hell.' The second contains his Confession. The third is 'About the true and false Church, and how they may be discerned'; the fourth, 'Concerning the three symbols or the Confessions of the Catholic faith.' Cochlaeus too published not a few books in Latin in this year, some of them against the Lutherans and some against the Zwinglians. For example: *The Sixth Philippic*, against Melanchthon and Bucer,[609] and for the judgment of the people of Cologne; *A Defense of the Ceremonies of the Church*, against the three pamphlets of Ambrose Moibanus of Wroclaw;[610] *A Debate concerning New Translations of the Old and New Testaments*;[611] *A Fourfold Argument for Concord, against the Augsburg Confession.*[612] These things he wrote against the Lutherans. But against the Zwinglians he wrote *Concerning the Invocation of the Saints and their Intercession* and *Concerning the Relics and Images* of the same, against Bullinger;[613] *A Brief Reply*, in answer to the lengthy response of the same Bullinger;[614] *Concerning the Priesthood and the Sacrifice of the New Law*, against two sermons of Wolfgang Musculus.[615] And in addition, *A History of the Life of Theodoric, King of the Ostrogoths and of Italy.*[616] He also wrote one pamphlet in German, *Concerning the Ancient Manner and Custom of Praying.*[617]

But the Emperor, when the assemblies at Speyer had been concluded, undertook war against the King of France in Gaul itself, and when that had been advantageously accomplished, he returned among the Belgians in the same year; he had reached all the way to Paris with his army. Meanwhile the clergy at Cologne were fighting back manfully, with books and diverse actions, on behalf of the Catholic faith, against the attempts and attacks of their Lutheran Archbishop.

1545

In this year as well an Imperial Diet was decreed and celebrated at Worms, which had been promised in the Recess of Speyer, and established for the first day of October of the previous year. And so the Emperor ordered his Commissaries to appear there on that day. The others arrived rather late; the King of the Romans came there in the month of December, and the Emperor, hindered by bodily infirmity, arrived much later. Moreover, only one of the Elector Princes attended in person, Frederick, the Illustrious Count Palatine of the

Rhine and Duke of Bavaria. The others sent their Speakers. Therefore this Diet was less crowded and less famous than was the one at Speyer, although it was famous enough because of the personal presence of the Emperor and the King. There too the most Reverend Lord, Otto the Bishop of Augsburg, was elevated to the dignity and rank of Cardinal, and rendered that Diet more noteworthy by this honor. And this same Diet was continued all the way into the month of August, on the fourth day of which month the public Recess was given. In that Diet, due to the small number of Princes and Estates who were present in their own persons, the greater and more serious causes which were discussed were not determined, but were postponed and put off to another Diet, which the Emperor decreed would be held in Regensburg, and would soon be begun in the next year, on the feast day of the Epiphany or the Three Kings. All Princes and Estates had to attend it personally, except in the case of infirmity. Moreover, so that they might more easily reach concord in the cause of religion there, the Emperor again decreed, at the request of the Protestant Princes and Estates and with the Catholic Orders of the Empire not consenting, that a new Colloquium would be begun at Regensburg on the Feast of St Andrew, and would be undertaken by four Negotiators from either side and the same number of Auditors, under Presidents who would be appointed by His Imperial Majesty.

Bucer wrote three books in German addressed to this Diet.[618] In them he pleaded at length for a National rather than a General Council, and he added many things against the Pope and every ecclesiastical estate, many against the Edict of Worms and the Recess of Augsburg, and many against the Sacraments and ceremonies of the Church; and, as though he were blameless in all these matters, he dared to offer himself to stand trial against any adversary whatsoever. Cochlaeus took this very ill, and wrote a letter in Latin to the Princes and Estates of the party of the Catholics, and sent it by his own messenger from Eichstätt to Worms.[619] He humbly warned them to beware of Bucer's deceitful and lying remarks, and even bound himself to punishment in kind, if he did not convict Bucer, before judges, both of errors in faith and of crimes in life. Moreover, since that letter was read publicly in a mixed gathering of Catholics and Protestants, Bucer quickly acquired a copy of it, and wrote and published a lengthy book in Latin in response to it. Cochlaeus too acquired a copy of Bucer's book, and without delay answered it in Latin, having extracted eighteen articles from that book, concerning which he wished to stand trial before judges with Bucer.[620]

In addition, in this year there was a great report, or rather an ill report,[621] about the diversity of new sects that had arisen in Lower Germany. For a certain layman had risen up in Frisia, in the town of Westeremden, David Joris by name, from Delft, a town in Holland.[622] He put forward the most absurd articles. In them he even renewed the errors of the Saducees, denying the resurrection of the flesh, the Last Judgment, angels, devils, baptism, marriage, the Scriptures, Paul, and eternal life in Heaven. Moreover, he affirmed that he was the Third David, who should reign in the Kingdom of Christ upon the earth; he wanted wives to be held in common; he taught that it is not a sin to deny Christ before the people; that not the souls, but only the flesh sins; that the Apostles and Martyrs were fools, because they suffered torments and death because of their confession of Christ – since the souls of unbelievers will be just as well saved as the souls of believers; and the flesh of the Apostles will be just as well condemned, as the flesh of unbelievers. And so the Emperor, when he learned of these things, used great severity and punished heretics of this sort with sword and fire, and by the most searching inquisition stamped out so nefarious a sect. And so that his people might have undoubted articles of the faith and of Catholic doctrine, against all errors and blasphemies of new sects, he entrusted this task to his theologians at Louvain.

For this reason it came about that the Dean and all the faculty of Theology at the University of Louvain, gathered together by sworn oath in the College of Theologians, by unanimous consent signed and approved thirty-two articles, to be believed by all Catholics and Orthodox Christians.[623] The Emperor himself also approved these articles in a public Edict, both in Latin and in the language of Burgundy, and he ordered them to be distributed, taught, and accepted throughout all the peoples and provinces of Lower Germany.[624] Nor did he do this undeservedly; for, a sound and Catholic doctrine is asserted in them, with an elegant brevity, against all errors and ravings of the new sects.

However, the leaders of the sects took this piety of the Emperor's badly, but especially Luther and Bucer;[625] and they attacked the authors of those articles, the Theologians of Louvain, with various slanders and insults. Indeed, the people of Strasbourg published new commentaries against them in German, but Luther sent out seventy-five propositions against the same people, with the most haughty disapproval, in Latin and German. Among these propositions, for the sake of example, these also were contained, and among the very first, as if a foundation for the other articles: 'Whatever is taught' (he said) 'in the Church of God without the Word, is a lie and an impiety; if the same is established through the articles of faith, it is impiety and heresy. And if anyone believes it, he is an Idolater, who worships the Devil in the place of God. It is asserted without the Word, by the heretics and idolaters of Louvain, that there are seven sacraments. In addition, the doctrine of the Louvain Synagogue concerning baptism must be condemned as heresy. Also, the doctrine of our little Louvain friends [626] concerning the practice of the Eucharist must be driven off the stage and loathed, since it is most full of profanation, heresy, and idolatries. In addition, to offer Masses for the dead is heretical and a blasphemy, and the Louvain Hydra lies most notably in saying that it was instituted by Christ. Also, the bloody and inflammatory refutations of the Louvainites apply to parricides, not to learning, of which they certainly have none concerning the Holy Scriptures. What article of heresy, I ask, should these men refute, who are themselves filled and swollen with countless heresies, blasphemies, and idolatries? Finally, they spit, vomit, and shit nothing from the Scriptures, but everything from the teachings of men, in the Church, which is not their Church, but the Living God's. In addition, the rite of ordaining Mass-sacrificers, that is, crucifiers of Christ, is an ordinance of the Devil. Also, marriage is called a sacrament without the Word, and was seen in the mirror of Marcolfus by our little friends.[627] Also, the Church of the Pope and the little Masters is more truly the Church of Evil, the bloody adversary and destroyer of Christ's Church.'[628] Luther wrote these things there, and many more of this sort, with a more than heretical fury. He also attacked the Zwinglians most bitterly in a new pamphlet. The people of Zurich answered this, both in Latin and in German, and among other things said as follows: 'The prophets and Apostles were zealous for the Glory of God, not for private honor, not for their own stubbornness and pride; but they sought only the salvation of sinners. But Luther seeks his own advantage, is stubborn, is carried away by excessive insolence, and immediately hands over to Satan all those who do not wish to subscribe to his opinion on the spot; and in all his reproofs a great deal of the Evil Spirit is detected, but as little as possible of a friend and a paternal character.'[629] These things those people wrote.

Yet another new heresy broke out in many towns of Swabia, which they call the Schwenkfeldian heresy, whose author was Silesian, from a noble family. This man, accordingly, so that he might offer something new, through which he could become known, took an old dogma from the ancient heresy of the Manichees and renewed it, teaching that Christ had not been conceived in the Virgin Mary's womb, from her nature and blood by the work of the Holy Spirit; nor had He been born from her, but had appropriated for himself from elsewhere a man created by God. Among these various devices and impious attempts of the heretics who were raving and bursting out everywhere, Cochlaeus for his part employed himself in the interests of the Catholics, and published certain little works of his that were written in Latin, as a kind of antidote: namely, three books of Miscellanies, which contain thirty different treatises;[630] in addition, *A Consideration of the Treatise of Concord*, in response to two writings of the Lutherans;[631] *A Skirmish against the Four Conjectures of Andrew Osiander about the End of the World*;[632] in addition, *A Reply to the 'Anticochlaeus' of Musculus, about the Priesthood and Sacrifice of the New Law, and to Bullinger's 'Counterstroke,' and to Certain Writings of Bucer*;[633] in addition, *Against the Night-Owl of the New Gospel*, etc.[634]

The people of Cologne also both undertook public actions against the new and impious Reformation of their Archbishop, and in published books confirmed the sound doctrines of the Church through every type of proof. Among these, indeed, the *Defense of the Opinion of the University and Clergy of Cologne, against the Slanders of Melanchthon, Bucer, and Oldendorp*, published by the Reverend Father Everhard Billick, a Carmelite, a Doctor of Sacred Theology, and a Provincial of Lower Germany, was especially outstanding.[635] And in the same year the Supreme Pontiff once again ordered a General Council at Trent, to which he sent three Cardinals as Legates, who were most outstanding in virtue and learning. Their task was to advise the Church,[636] both against the heresies that were so impious and various, and against the corrupt habits and abuses of the Churchmen.

1546

The Colloquium on religion that had been decreed by the Emperor for the feast of St Andrew in the earlier Diet held at Worms, and which he had later postponed in letters, for various reasons, to the 13th day of December, could not begin at Regensburg until the 27th day of January, due to the rather late arrival of those who had been sent to the Colloquium. For those who were sent to the Colloquium by the Elector of Saxony, namely Dr Laurence Zoch, as an auditor, and Dr George Maior, as a Negotiator, arrived first on the 21st day of January, although the others on either side had already appeared, they had waited in vain for many days for Melanchthon (who had been indicated by name in the Emperor's letters as a Negotiator), since Dr Maior had been substituted for him by the aforesaid Elector. Therefore, on the 27th day of January, the Lords President, after Mass had been solemnly celebrated in accordance with the Catholic rite in the Cathedral Church, convened in the council chamber with the Negotiators and Auditors from either party, and when His Imperial Majesty had taken his seat, the Presidents exhibited the commissions which had been give to them, and caused them to be read aloud by either side. Moreover, they handed over to each side the method of procedure which had been prescribed by the Emperor. But since the Lutherans dragged the matter out with various suspicious objections and exceptions, and did not want to take part in the Colloquium unless they were permitted to have their own notaries, they brought it about that at length, on the 5th day of February, the material concerning the article of Justification could be proposed for the first time by the Catholic Negotiators, in accordance with the formula prescribed by the Emperor. Moreover, on the following day, before they would respond to the topic that had been proposed, the Lutherans spoke in advance and protested in an extended display, and wandered away from the subject in their complaints and excuses, and dragged the matter out with their writings, recitals, and dictates all the way to the 12th day of February, before they gave the Catholics a space or an opportunity for responding. Finally on the 17th day of February, when the chance to speak was again conceded to the Lutherans, the matter was once again prolonged, partly by dictates and writings and partly by friendly arguing back and forth and oral discussion, up to the 24th day of February, which was the feast of the Veneration of the Apostle Matthew. Meanwhile, the Emperor, who had consulted with the Lords President and had been informed about the method of proceeding (which had been somewhat changed from his prescription, due to the stubbornness and rudeness of the Lutherans), gave a new commission concerning certain doubtful areas to the Presidents, and Letters of Credentials to either side, so that of their own free will they might confide in the Mandate to the Presidents and might receive the Reverend Dr Julius Pflug, who was elected and confirmed at Nuremberg, as the Third President.

These things were made known to both sides on the 26th day of February. The Catholics, certainly, accepted them obediently, but they were refused by the Lutherans, by means of various evasions and excuses. Indeed, although this matter was debated for several days by the Presidents and the Lutherans, using various approaches, it could not be brought to an agreement, because the Presidents were not permitted either to go beyond or to retreat from the commission prescribed to them by the Emperor. But the Lutherans would not retreat from the conditions and limitations which they asserted in opposition to the Emperor's commission. Therefore, the Lords President were forced by the Lutherans' stubbornness to write about these matters once again and to refer them to His Imperial Majesty (who had already set out upon the journey from the Low Countries to Regensburg), so that they might know from him what they ought to permit or to concede to the Lutheran party, which was so obstinately taking exception to the commission.

But before an answer could arrive from the Emperor, on 20 and 21 March (which was the second Sunday in Lent), the Lutherans suddenly left, against anyone's expectation and against the Presidents' will. They did so with an unusual haste, although not secretly, and by their obstinacy obstructed any benefit of the Colloquium and cut short the hope of concord. This action displeased all the best people, who were held by a desire for peace and concord, and the Emperor himself took it very ill. For when he arrived at Regensburg on the 10th day of April, and found very few of the Princes and Estates at the Imperial Diet which he had commanded, he sent out a new mandate to individuals that they should all come there without further procrastination. This was given at Regensburg on the 22nd day of April. In it, among other things, he said as follows: 'For the rest, since those Auditors and Negotiators belonging to the party of those adhering in name to the Augsburg Confession, who had been called and ordered to the next Colloquium for the purpose of reconciling disparate articles of religion, turned tail with an unexpected haste immediately before our arrival, without our knowledge, neglecting (as we learn from others) even the deliberation (the reason for their departure) that was undertaken by our Presidents, who were our deputies for this matter; and they did so without any necessary or legitimate cause (because this would surely escape no one's notice). By the fault of their departure, the business of the entire Colloquium is now silent and lies idle; once again, in this matter, necessity requires your advice again. Therefore, since all your rightful service to us has thus been considered in advance and well prepared, do not by any means fail in it.'[637]

So much for the Colloquium. For the rest, while the Colloquium was still going on a most sad message reached the Lutherans, about the death of their Father (as they call him) Luther. He had gone from Wittenberg to Eisleben, so that he might take part in the secular discussion about the profane causes of discord, which was going on among the Counts at Mansfeld, because he was born under those Lords at Eisleben. On the 17th day of February, after he had taken his supper in public with others – a supper where they had eaten plentifully and which had been cheerfully lengthened with jokes – on that same night he died. Many people are writing many things about his death. The

Catholics in the neighboring areas tell the story and write in one way; the Lutherans speak and write of it in another. For they are producing, in hordes, many pamphlets in German, to persuade everyone of how holy a death that most holy (as they say) father of them all died. The writings of three of his colleagues in particular are being circulated, namely of Jonas Cocus, who falsely calls himself 'Justus,' of Philip Melanchthon, and of Johannes Apel, who in the frontispieces of Wittenberg books are accustomed, together with Luther, to occupy the four corners of the first page, as though they were four new Evangelists.

Jonas was present in person at the nocturnal, sudden, and unexpected death of that man; he immediately wrote a letter on that same night on which Luther died to the Elector of Saxony, and after the funeral procession he composed a history. The other two made speeches at the funeral. Apel spoke in German to the people, and Melanchthon in Latin to the scholars (a speech which was soon translated into German by Cruciger and published). Both were full of praise and lamentation. They would very much like to persuade everyone that he did not taste of death, but that like Enoch, or Elijah, or John the Evangelist had been translated without death. For they apply to him Christ's saying in the eighth chapter of John: 'If anyone shall pay heed to my words, he shall not taste of (or see) death, for ever.' [638] They say that Luther had written this with his own hand in a certain book of his host, a few days before his death, and had interpreted it in this sense: if anyone seriously meditates on the Word of God in his heart, believing in it, and during this meditation should fall asleep or die, he will depart from here before he sees or perceives death. But the dead man's body (and a most fetid one it was) stood in the way of this shamelessness of theirs, since the eyes of many plainly saw it buried in the earth, which they certainly cannot assert about the body of Enoch, Elijah, or John.

Therefore, if anyone will look carefully and closely into that history of Jonas, he will easily understand that everything there reverts to vain glory and secular pomp in his funeral, and to the joys of the flesh and honors of the world in his life. And all these things are far different from the practice of the true disciples of Christ. For what one of the Saints made his journey in this way, with pompous ostentation, as though he were being carried in a triumphal chariot, with three sons who were conceived and brought forth by the damned and incestuous intercourse of monk and nun – as this Luther did? Or what was his rank or nobility, that he should be met on his way by 113 knights, sent to the border by the most generous Counts of Mansfeld, for the sake of honoring him? Or by what example of our ancestors or the Apostles did that notorious heretic, who was condemned by the legitimate rule of law of both supreme powers and was never elected or ordained Bishop, ordain and consecrate two priests at Eisleben (as Jonas says in that history of his) using a new rite that was frivolously thought up by himself, when he neither celebrated Mass nor then took communion with others? What kind of sanctity or of a miracle is there in this, that every evening after a supper lavishly prepared and abundantly partaken of, with his belly distended by food and drink, he looked out of the window of his dwelling and prayed for a little while, occasionally so seriously and earnestly (as the history recounts) that those standing around, when they were silent, were overawed as they heard certain of his words – when nothing is said there either about the Canonical Hours (which he was obliged by law to say, both as a professed Monk and as a priest who had once been rightly ordained), or about other prayers said by him during the day (if in fact he did say them)? Oh miraculous sanctity, and such as has never before been heard of among Christians, that this new Apostle of Saxony, busy the whole day long with worldly business and burdened with a surfeit of lunch and dinner, after omitting the Canonical Hours through the entire day, should snatch a little moment to pray, within sight of a window, before he went to bed – by whose heresy and sin so many monasteries, collegiate churches, and even cathedrals throughout almost all Saxony, Pomerania, Denmark, Sweden, and Norway are forsaken, with their Masses and Canonical Hours not only omitted but even prohibited and forbidden by a violent public, and grow silent, no longer saying the praises of God by day and by night, and cease from every service and ancient solemnity. But what of the fact that he requested of the Counts themselves, that before lunch he might abstain and rest from profane discussions of causes, although in their lunches and dinners, he always lolled in his place (as if it were his own and quite excellent)? Certainly it befitted him to keep that saying of Christ's, 'They love those who recline first at their dinners.' Not only in dinners, however, but even in lunches, from which meal most of the holy Fathers and monks have always abstained, except on Sundays and feast days. Moreover, how outstanding (as Jonas boasts) is this apothegm of his, 'Is it necessary for us to live so long that we can look at the Devil's back and, by experiencing so many evils, treacheries, and miseries of the world, bear witness that the Devil was so evil a spirit?' And again, 'The human race is like a sheepfold for the slaughtering of sheep.' And also that remark which was omitted in the history, which was inserted in the letter of Jonas to the Elector of Saxony in capital letters: 'To be solitary does not bring joy.' As if it had not been said by Paul to monks, 'Rejoice in the Lord always, and again I say rejoice'; or as if the human race had been created by God, not for life and salvation, but for slaughter and perdition – or did the Apostle speak falsely when he said, 'God wants all people to be saved'? Or as if Moses had not been Luther's senior, when God said to him, 'You shall see My back, but you will not be able to see My face.' Therefore, old people should look rather at the back of God than at the back of the Devil.

Finally, what shall we say of Luther's last prayer, which the history recites to us, marked in capital letters: 'Oh my Heavenly Father' (he says) 'God and Father of our Lord Jesus Christ, God of all consolation, I give thanks to You, because You have revealed Your beloved Son Jesus Christ to me, in Whom I believe, Whom I have preached and have confessed, Whom I have loved and praised; Whom the abominable Pope and all impious people revile, persecute, and blaspheme, etc.' Here let Jonas inquire of all the Fathers, let him look as diligently as possible into all the Scriptures, laws, and Canons, and into the corners of the Councils, to see whether he shall be able to find in the writings of any Christian a dying man's prayer of this sort, in which anyone at all thus boasts of himself, thus in comparison to himself condemns and accuses all those who, under the Pope, have worshiped Christ, thus attacks and slanders the Shepherd of the Church, the Supreme Pontiff. Or is it not rather to be believed, that soon after these words of Luther's Christ the Judge said to Luther's soul, just now snatched from his body in death itself, 'From your own mouth I judge you, you wicked servant – since you yourself earlier both said and wrote that you heard Christ's voice in the Pope, Who was speaking and governing in him'? Moreover, let that man be anathema and cursed, who speaks against the truth of the Apostolic privileges. Moreover, I aver that there are more good Christians under the Pope – nay, rather, every good Christian; and that under the Pope is the true Christianity, and what is more, the true kernel of Christianity. Therefore, what hope of salvation can a man so hardened possibly have, and one who persists, to the very end, against charity, in his heresy, schism, and rebellion, and in his everlasting hatred against the Pope, and so breathes out his stubborn and obstinate soul? For not only does the judgment of Christ and of Paul, Cyprian, Augustine, and others like them, attested many times over, judge him, but also his own speech and the judgment of his own mouth. Therefore, Jonas stupidly and impiously praises him for this prayer.

In the same way, too, Apel stupidly boasted, in the end of his funeral oration to the people, of this filthy prophecy of Luther's, in this verse: 'I was a plague to you when I lived, Pope, but dying I will be your death.' For he was, when alive, a plague not so much to the Pope, as to Germany, and to innumerable souls; and dead, he is a plague and a destruction to none more than to those who believe him; and beyond doubt, he now knows and experiences how savage a plague he was to his very self, both living and dead. But if in his dying he is death to the Supreme Pontiff, as he vainly boasts, how is it, I ask, that the Elector of Saxony, in his Edict that was just now promulgated through all his lands on the 14th day of February, so vehemently fears (as he says) for himself and his confederates due to the practices of the Pope, and orders his people to remain at home, and to remain in continual preparation of arms? Is a dead Pope so greatly to be feared? There is a popular Italian proverb, 'A dead man doesn't make war.' And so the Pope remains, and will remain until the fulfillment of the ages; but the heretics slip away like water, one after another. Where now are the eloquent attackers of the Pope, Zwingli, Oecolampadius, Karlstadt, Capito, Grynaeus, Luther, and so many others? A second death now consumes them, for eternity; the Pope and the Apostolic See, firmly founded on the Rock, remain for ever.

And what profit to Luther's soul, caught up before the tribunal of Christ, was that most vain pomp of his funeral, when his body, enclosed in tin, carried around through several churches, and accompanied and lamented by a long procession of people who had been led astray by him, and borne back to Wittenberg by a splendid troop, both of horsemen and pedestrians, was laid in the tomb with vain lamentations? But they unwisely laid the body in a tin coffin, not an iron one, not paying attention to the example and wisdom of the Saracens, who made the sepulcher of their Mohammed out of iron, not tin, so that the point of a compass in the air is said to be turned toward the mosque of Mecca, a city in Arabia; for the physicists write, and the craftsmen know, that the magnet stone attracts not tin, but iron.

Furthermore, by whose example did the nun Catherine, Luther's wife, display herself and her three sons by Luther (John, Martin, and Paul, as the history lists them) to be gazed upon in a coach behind the funeral cart? In this way, of old, was the funeral of the Blessed Martin carried out, or that of St Ambrose, or that of the Holy Augustine? Oh miserable and blinded people, who were not ashamed to do such things, who have so blind a judgment both about human affairs and about the Christian religion! And woe to their dishonest and impious praise-givers, who say that evil is good and good evil, putting the shadows in the place of light and light in the place of the shadows! Let the pious consider what Luther accomplished through so many labors, troubles, and efforts of his depraved intention, by whose rebellious and seditious urging so many thousands of people have perished eternally, in both body and soul, and still continually will perish; and through whom all Germany was confused and disturbed, and let go all its ancient glory, to the great perturbation of the Empire, and now trembles, looking upon wars both external and internal, and shrinking away from the peaceful General Council and from the Pope, from whom it received Christ's faith, as if from the Antichrist, because of Luther's sinful teachings it fears for itself.

Now that stupid history of Jonas recounts this stupidity, as impious as it is ridiculous, of Luther as he was dying; that on the night that he died, he said to Jonas and to Caelius, and to others who were standing around, 'Pray for the Lord our God and for His Gospel, that things may turn out well for Him, since the Council of Trent and the abominable Pope are grievously opposed to Him.' Who ever heard that the Lord our God should be prayed for? There are very many other stupidities in this lying and futile history, which in the eyes of learned and intelligent men detract from Luther's fame rather than celebrate it; but here, for the sake of brevity, they are omitted. But Cochlaeus, for the sake of asserting and confirming the truth of the Catholic faith against any heretics whatsoever, in this same year also published several books in Latin. One of them was against the articles of Luther, which he had ordered to be proposed to the Council;[639] another was against the eighteen articles of Bucer.[640] A third was against Melanchthon's Prefaces and Annotations,[641] a fourth was an *Epitome of Charles Capellus on the Apostolic Constitutions*, etc.[642]

Finally, in order to celebrate an Imperial Diet here at Regensburg in the accustomed manner, after long expectation, with the Emperor's brother the Roman King present, and a large part of the Princes, both ecclesiastical and secular, attending, yesterday (that is the 5th day of June, Saturday after the feast of the Ascension of the Lord) after Mass was solemnly celebrated in the Cathedral Church, with His Imperial Majesty, the King, and the other Princes and Estates of the Empire present; and divine aid had been implored, the

Emperor exhibited in the Council Hall a public Proclamation concerning those things which were to be treated in this Diet, and by that announcement he happily (as we hope and pray to God) began that public Assembly.

This Compendium of Luther's Acts was written at Regensburg, after the dissolution of the most recent Colloquium, deserted due to the rapid departure of the Lutherans, by the urging and petition of the Reverend Dr Jerome Verall, Archbishop of Rochester and then Apostolic Nuncio to His Imperial Majesty; now, by the authority of Paul III, the Supreme Pontiff (with his merits demanding it) created and enrolled in the Company and College of the Cardinals of the Holy Roman Church, in the Year of the Lord 1549.

This work was printed at St Victor in Mainz, by Francis Behem the Printer, in the month of September, 1549.

Translator's note

It has become a commonplace to say that any translation is also a critical interpretation of the original work; as is often the case, this commonplace is no less true for being frequently repeated. The translator inevitably faces a whole host of interpretive decisions in every sentence of the original text. When that original is from another era, the task of translation becomes still more complicated. Faced with Cochlaeus's sixteenth-century Latin, should the translator try to update the voice of the original author, to make him speak rapid, colloquial modern English (and in this case, American English at that, since I am an American translator)? Or is the translator's job rather to try to preserve for the reader some sense of the distance between the original and this week's best-seller, in terms of style, tone, and presentation? Cogent arguments can be and have been made for both of these approaches, often called the 'foreignizing' and the 'domesticating' schools of translation, and this is not the place to rehearse those arguments. In practice, each translator must find his or her own path, which usually meanders somewhere between the two extremes, winding closer at some points to the foreignizing pole and at others to the domesticating. Probably no individual reader will ever be quite satisfied by or wholly in agreement with any translator's choices, but this is hardly surprising, since translators would be the first to agree that no translation ever gets it quite right.

In this rendering of Cochlaeus's *Commentaria*, I have tried to take a middle path, but one that runs closer to the strange and foreignizing than to the familiar and domestic. My intention has been to adhere as closely to Cochlaeus's own syntax, sentence structure, and verbal organization as I could without doing violence to English syntax. Obviously, there are many ways in which I have modernized Cochlaeus; to give one example, his Latin text often runs for several pages without paragraph breaks, and so I have inevitably imposed certain emphases on his text by my decision about where to end one paragraph and begin another. But I have resisted the impulse to rework his elegant, flowing Latin sentences into the short, simple form most familiar to readers of modern English. I learned to love and admire Cochlaeus's voice as I worked with his text, and my goal throughout has been to let as much of that voice sound through the English as I possibly could, in the hope that readers will be able to hear in my translation some echo of Cochlaeus's learned and elegant style, of his complex but lucid sentences, and of the fervor which clearly motivated his writing.

Appendix

Concluding materials in Policarius' book of Melanchthon's *Life of Luther*.

Some Distichs follow, About the Deeds of Luther, which comprise together the number of years, even a certain day in itself, as: Dr Martin was born in 1485. Which time is contained in this following Distich.

> You were born of Eisleben, O divine Prophet Luther,
> Religion shines, with you as Leader, the Pope lies dead.

MASTER'S YEAR. 1503.

> The Youth captures the ranks of Master in the city of Erfurt
> Dwelling there after completing four *lustra* of his life.

MONASTIC YEAR. 1504.

> The empty superstition the youthful body with a hood
> Adorns, this all was for a deceit to you − good! − O Pope.

THE YEAR in which he came to Wittenberg. 1508.

> With Christ aiding, Luther is sent to the Elbe,
> How great was the Seer? how much glory for the School?

THE DOCTORAL YEAR and in which he was in Rome. 1511.

> He obtained the Doctoral ranks by the order of Staupitz,
> When he came from the city of the fierce Italian Wolf.

YEAR OF RESTORING religion. 1517.

> You drag the work of religion out of the muck, with Christ
> As leader, O truthful Luther leaning on the right hand of God.

THE YEAR OF THE CONFESSION BEFORE Imperial Cajetan, which is extant in Volume 1, page 207.1518.

> Luther publicly declares Christ in the city of the Emperor
> Not caring about your looks, O severe leader.

THE YEAR OF THE DEBATE at Leipzig. 1519.

> Eck is defeated by the virtue of Just Luther,
> As he debates on the July day in the city of Leipzig.

YEAR OF THE CONFESSION IN the Senate of Worms. 1521.

Before the foot of the Emperor, he stands before the
Powerful nobles, the Neighbor who approaches the bank of the Rhine at
Worms.

YEAR OF PATMOS. 1522.

On account of the rages of Carlstad he runs back
To the Saxon homes, and he again snatches the sheep
From the cruel throats.

YEAR OF MARRIAGE AND of the Peasants' Revolt. 1525.

The Revolt of the Farmer is quelled by powerful iron,
Luther enters into the pure promises of marriage.

YEAR OF THE CONVENTION of Marburg. 1529.

At the Marburg Feast he harshly treats the enemies of Christ,
As all Vienna stands off from the cruel Danube-residents.

YEAR OF THE CONVENTION of Augsburg. 1530.

The confession of faith to all the States of the Empire
Is proposed, the joyous glory of Christ returns.

YEAR OF THE DEATH of Luther. 1546.

The light stood in an obscure origin for twice nine purifications,
So that, O bright Luther, you would die on your ancestral soil.

These Distichs we [i.e. Pollicarius] changed from some papers which my Friend
Johannes Stoltz of Wittenberg gave as a gift to M. Wolfgang Stein in 1547.

[Some poems of Johannes Pollicarius follow: a *Eulogy* of Luther; an *Epitaph* of
Luther; and 'On the Execrable and Abominable Papal Blindness, from which
God through Luther snatched us' (In Sapphic Stanzas).

Pollicarius, the self-styled *Cygnaeus*, Swan-like, wrote the Preface (*Praefatio*)
in which he says he collected some poems 'in praise of this our greatest
Theologian' and 'also added his Life, just as I found it written by our Dr
Philipp, along with the Proceedings of Worms' (*aliquid Carminis congessi, in
laudem huius maximi nostri Theologi. Adieci quoque Vitam eius, sicuti eam reperi
perscriptam a D. Philippo nostro, una cum Actis Vuormatiensibus*).

The Preface is dated 20 October 1547. Pollicarius signs it the 'Priest of the
Word of God at Weissenfels' (*M. Ioannes Pollicarius Cygnaeus apud Vueisenfelsenses
Verbi Dei Minister*).]

[Last is a 'Poem of Thanks, Because the light of truth long since extinct on earth, God again roused up in this age in Germany through Martin Luther,' by Georg Fabricius (1516–71), a poet, historian, and archaeologist, who was the rector of the Fürstenschule (Prince's School) at Meissen.]

Works cited

Works by Johannes Cochlaeus

Ad Paulum III. Pont. Max. Congratulatio Johannis Cochlaei Germani, super eius electione, recens facta nuperque promulgata (Leipzig, Michael Blum, 1535).

Adversus cucullatum Minotaurum Wittenbergensem. De gratia sacramentorum iterum (1523); J. Schweizer (ed.), (Münster, 1920).

Adversus latrocinantes et raptorias cohortes rusticorum Mar. Lutherus Responsio Johannis Cochlaei Wendelstini. Cathalogus tumultuum et praeliorum in superiori Germania nuper gestorum (Cologne, Peter Quentell, 1525).

Aequitatis discussio super consilio Delectorum Cardinalium ... ad tollendam per generale concilium inter Germanos in religione discordiam (Leipzig, Nicolaus Wolrab, 1538; Hilarius Walter (ed.), *Corpus Catholicorum*, vol. 17 [Münster, 1931]).

An die Herrenn, Schulteis vnnd Radt zu Bern, wider yhre vermainte Reformation (Dresden, Wolfgang Stöckel, 1528).

An expediat laicis, legere noui testamenti libros lingua vernacula? Ad serenissimum Scotiae Regem Iacobum V. Disputatio inder Alexandrum Alesium Scotum, & Iohannem Cochlaeum Germanum (Augsburg, Alexander Weissenhorn, 1533).

Annotationes et antitheses Joannis Cochlaei, in quaedam scripta et propositiones collocutorum Wittenbergensium (Ingolstadt, Alexander Weissenhorn, 1546).

Articuli orthodoxam religionem, sanctamque fidem nostram respicientes (Louvain, Reynier Valpen van Diest, 1545; rpt, n.p., 1787), translated as *Zwen vnd dreissig Artickel, die allgemeinen Religion vnd Glauben belangend* (Nuremberg, Johann Petreius, 1545).

Articuli CCCCC Martini Lutheri ex sermonibus eius sex et triginta (Cologne, Peter Quentell, 1525).

Articuli aliquot, a Jacopo Kautio Oecolampadiano, ad populum nuper Wormaciae aediti, partim a Lutheranis, partim a Johanne Cochlaeo doctore praestantissimo, reprobati (n.p., 1527).

Auff Martin Luthers Schandbüchlin, An die Christen von Halle geschriben, Antwort Jo. Cocleus Dr (n.p., 1528).

Auf Luthers brieff von dem Buch der winkelmess zehen Fragstucke Dr Johan Cocleus an er. Just Jonas Probst zu Wittenberg. Sampt ainem Auszug XXVIII Artickeln (Dresden, Wolfgang Stöckel, 1534).

Auff Luthers kleine Antwort ein kurtze widerrede Hertzog zu Sachssen betreffend (Dresden, Wolfgang Stöckel, 1533).

Auf Luthers newe lesterschrifft wider den Cardinal und Ertzbischoff von Mentz und Magdeburg ... Antwort Johann Cochlei (Leipzig, Michael Blum, 1535).

Bericht der warheit auff die unwaren Lügend S. Joannis Chrysostomi, welche M. Luther an das Concilium zu Mantua hat lassen aussgehen (Leipzig, Nicolaus Wolrab, 1537).

Canones Apostolorum ... (Mainz, 1525).

Catalogus brevis eorum quae contra novas sectas scripsit Ioannes Cochlaeus (Mainz, Franz Behem, 1549).

Colloquium Cochlaei cum Luthero Wormatiae olim habitum (1521, published 1540).

Commentaria Joannis Cochlaeis, De Actis et Scriptis Martini Lutheri Saxonis (Mainz, Franz Behem, 1549).

Cosmographia Pomponij Mele: Authoris nitidissimi Tribus Libris digesta (Nuremberg, Johann Weissenburger, 1511); *Meteorologia Aristotelis. Eleganti Jacobi Fabri De animarum purgatorio igne epitome, contra novas sectas quae Purgatorium negant* (Ingolstadt, Alexander Weissenhorn, 1543).

De baptismo parvulorum liber unus Joan. Cochlaei. Adversus assertionem Mart. Lutheri (Strasbourg, Johann Grieninger, 1523).

De Canonicae scripturae & Catholicae Ecclesiae autoritate, ad Henricum Bullingerum Iohannis Cochlaei libellus (Ingolstadt, Alexander Weissenhorn, 1543).

De Concilio et legitime iudicandis controversiis religionis ... (Strasbourg, Knoblouch, 1545).

Defensio ceremoniarum ecclesiae adversus errores et calumnias trium librorum (Ingolstadt, Alexander Weissenhorn, 1543).

'Defensio Joannis Episcopi Roffensis et Thome Mori, adversus Richardum samsonem Anglum,' in *Antiqua et insignis epistola Nicolae Papae I* ... (Leipzig, Melchior Lotter, 1536).

De futuro concilio rite celebrando ... *Epistola Johannis Cochlei ad Archiepiscopum S. Andree in Scotia* (Dresden, Wolfgang Stöckel, 1534).

De gratia sacramentorum liber unus Joan. Cochlaei adversus assertionem Marti. Lutheri (Strasbourg, Johann Grieninger, 1522).

De Immensa Dei misericordia erga Germanos: ex collatione sermonum Joannis Hus ad unum sermonem Martini Lutheri, quem in festo Epiphaniae habuit. X tituli et LXX propositiones tum Joannis Hus, tum Martini Lutheri (Leipzig, Nicolaus Wolrab, 1537).

De Interim brevis responsio Ioan. Cochlaei, ad prolixum & Calumniarum librum Ioannis Caluini (Mainz, Franz Behem, 1549).

De Matrimonio serenissimi Regis Angliae, Henrici octavi, congratulatio disputatoria Johannis Cochlei Germani, ad Paulum Tertium Pont. Max. (Leipzig, Michael Blum, 1535).

De novis ex Hebraeo translationibus sacrae scripturae, disceptatio Iohannis Cochlaei (Ingolstadt, Alexander Weissenhorn, 1544).

De ordinatione episcoporum atque presbyterorum et de eucharistiae consecratione, quaestio hoc tempore pernecessaria (Mainz, Franz Behem, 1541).

De Petro et Roman adversus Velenum Lutheranum, libri quatuor (Cologne, Peter Quentell, 1525; rpt in Cochlaeus, *Opuscula* [Farnborough, 1968]).

De Sanctorum invocatione et intercessione dequam imaginibus et reliquiis eorum pie riteque colendis. Liber unus (Ingolstadt, Alexander Weissenhorn, 1544).

De vera Christi ecclesia quaestio necessaria super septimo confessionis Augustanae articulo ad Caesarem Maiestatem ut Ratisponae in conventu imperiali discutiatur (Mainz, Franz Behem, 1541).

Ein nötig und christlich Bedencken, auff des Luthers Artickeln, die man Gemeynem Concilio fürtragen sol (Leipzig, Nicolaus Wolrab, 1538).

Ein getrewe wolmeinende earnung D. Jo. Cocleus, wider die untrewen auffrürischen warnung M. Luthers ad die lieben Teutschen (Leipzig, Michael Blum, 1531).

Epistolae antiquissimae ac sacris institutionibus plenae (Cologne, 1526).

Epistolae decretales veterum pontificum Romanorum (n.p., 1526).

Epitome Apostolicarum constitutionum, in Creta insula, per Carolum Capellium Venetum repertarum, et e Greco in Latinum translatarum (Ingolstadt, Alexander Weissenhorn, 1546).

'*Exhortatio ad principes sacri Ro. Imperij contra nefarios conatus Lutheri,*' in In Causa
  Religionis Miscellaneorum libri tres (Ingolstadt, Alexander Weissenhorn, 1545).
*Fasciculus calumniarum, sannarum et illusionum Martini Lutheri, in Episcopos & Clericos,
  ex vno eius libello Teuthonico, contra Episcopi Misnensis Mandatum aedito, collectarum*
  (Leipzig, Valentin Schumann, 1529).
*Fidelis et Pacifica Commonitio Joan. Cochlaei, contra Infidelem et seditiosam
  Commonitionem Mart. Lutheri ad Germanos* (Leipzig, Valentin Schumann, 1531).
Historia Hussitarum libri duodecim (Mainz, Franz Behem, 1549).
*Hertzog Georgens zu Sachssen Ehrlich und grundtliche entschuldigung, wider Martin
  Luthers Auffruerisch und verlogenne brieff und Verantwortung* (Leipzig, Michael Blum,
  1533).
Hystoria Alberti Krantz von den alten hussen zu Behemen in Keiser Sigmunds zeiten
  (Strasbourg, Grieninger, 1523).
*Illustrissimi ac maxime Orthodoxi piique Principis, Domini Georgii ... Edictalis Epistola
  adversus pravam interpretationem Novi Testamenti a Luthero heretico editam* (Dresden,
  Wolfgang Stöckel, 1534).
*In Cause religionis Miscellaneorum libri tres in diversos tractatus antea non aeditos, ac
  diversis temporibus, locisque scriptos digesti* (Ingolstadt, Alexander Weissenhorn, 1545).
*In Eyn Sendbrieff Martin Luthers, an den Konig zu Engelland Heynrichen dis namens den
  achten ...* (Zwickau, Gabriel Kantz, 1527).
*In Lutheri adversus Cardinalem et Episcopum Moguntinum et Magdeburgensem ...
  Responsum* (Dresden, Wolfgang Stöckel, 1535).
*In primum Musculi Anticochlaeum replica Johannis Cochlaei, pro sacerdotii et sacrificii novae
  legis assertione. In epilogo adiecta est brevis responsio in Antibolen Bullingeri. Addita est
  appendix gemina in librum Buceri, quem in Bart Latomum edidit* (Ingolstadt,
  Alexander Weissenhorn, 1545).
In quatuor Andreae Osiandri coniecturas de fine mundi, velitatio Johannis Cochlaei
  (Ingolstadt, Alexander Weissenhorn, 1545).
*In XVIII Articulos Mar. Buceri excerptos ex novissimo libro eius ad principes et status Sacri
  Ro. Imperii latine scripto* (Ingolstadt, Alexander Weissenhorn, 1546).
*Necessaria et Catholica Consyderatio super Lutheri Articulis, quos velit Concilio Generali
  proponi* (Ingolstadt, Alexander Weissenhorn, 1546).
Nycticorax Evangelii Novi in Germania (Ingolstadt, Alexander Weissenhorn, 1545).
Philippica quinta Joannis Cochlaei, in tres libros Philippi Melanchthonis (Ingolstadt,
  Alexander Weissenhorn, 1540; rpt 1543).
Philippicae I-VII, (ed.) R. Keen, (Nieuwkoop, 1995–6).
Philippica sexta (Ingolstadt, Alexander Weissenhorn, 1544).
*Prognosticon futuri seculi a sancto Juliano, Episcopo Toletano, ante annos DCC scriptum, in
  Hispaniis* (Leipzig, Michael Blum, 1536).
Pro Scotiae Regno Apologia Iohannis Cochlaei (Leipzig, Michael Blum, 1534).
Quadriuium Grammatices Johannis Coclaei Norici (Nuremberg, Johann Stuchs, 1511).
Ob Sant Peter zu Rom sey gewesen (Strasbourg, J. Grieninger, 1524).
*Quadruplex Concordiae ratio et consyderatio super confessione Augustana protestantium
  quorundam sacri Romani Imperii Principum ac statuum, Caes. Maiestati Augustae
  exhibita* (Ingolstadt, Alexander Weissenhorn, 1544).
*Quatuor Excusationum Lutheranorum Confutatio una, pro Concilio Generali ad Mantuam
  indicto* (Leipzig, Nicolaus Wolrab, 1537).
*Replica brevis Johannis Cochlaei adversus prolixam Responsionem Henrici Bullingeri De
  scripturae et ecclesiae autoritate* (Ingolstadt, Alexander Weissenhorn, 1544).

Responsio ad Johannem Bugenhagium Pomeranum, (ed.), Ralph Keen, (Nieuwkoop, 1988).

Sacerdotii ac sacrificii novae legis defensio, adversus Wolfgangi Musculi, Augustae concionantis arrosiones (Ingolstadt, Alexander Weissenhorn, 1544).

Scopa Ioannis Cochlaei Germani, in araneas Richardi Morysini Angli (Leipzig, Nicolaus Wolrab, 1538).

Septiceps Lutherus: vbique sibi, suis scriptis, contrarius, in Visitatione Saxonica (Leipzig, Valentin Schumann, 1529).

Sieben Köpffe Martini Lutheri Vom Hochwirdigen Sacrament des Altars (Leipzig, Valentin Schumann, 1529), translated as *Septiceps Lutherus* (Leipzig, Valentin Schumann, 1529).

Stapulensis Paraphrasi explanata. Commentarioque Joannis Coclaei Norici ... (Nuremberg, Frederick Peypus, 1512).

Tetrachordium musices Ioannis Coclei Norici (Nuremberg, Johann Meyssenburger, 1511; rpt Nuremberg, Frederick Peypus, 1520).

Vermanung zu frid vnd einikeit durch D. Johann Coclaeum, an den Achtbarn vnd hochgelarten Herrn Doctorn Gregorium Brück, de Churfürsten von Sachssen Rath +c. auff Martin Luthers Rathschlag, in Innhalt dieses Buchleins (Dresden, Wolfgang Stöckel, 1531).

Vita Theoderici Regis quondam Ostrogothorum et Italiae (Ingolstadt, Alexander Weissenhorn, 1544).

Von alten gebrauch des Bettens in Christlicher Kirchen zehen Unterschaid (Ingolstadt, Alexander Weissenhorn, 1544).

Von ankunfft der Mess unnd der wandlung brots unnd weins in hochwürdigen Sacrament des Altars. Ain disputation Sebastiani Francken, mit Antwort Johannis Coclei auf 88. artickeln auss der newen Chronica (Dresden, 1533).

Von der Donation des Keysers Constantini, und von Bepstlichem gewalt, Grundtlicher Bericht aus alten bewerten Lerern und Historien (n.p. 1537).

Von der heyligen Mess und Priesterweyhe Christlicher Bericht D. Jo. Cocleus (Leipzig, Michael Blum, 1534).

Von newen Schwermereyen sechs Capitel, den Christen und Ketzern beyden nötig zu lesen, und höchlich zu bedencken der Seelen seligkeit betreffende (Leipzig, Michael Blum, 1534).

Vom vermögen und Gewalt eines gemeinen Concilii. XXX bewerte und unverwerffliche Gezeucknüsse, in funferley unterschied. Widerlegung der XXX Artickeln, zu Wittenberg disputirt. LXX Sprüche zu disputiren, für ein gemeyn Concilio (Leipzig, Nicolaus Wolrab, 1537).

Wider die Reubischen und Mordischen rotten der Bawren die unter dem scheyn des heiligen Evangelions felschlichen wider alle Oberkeit sich setzen und empören Martinus Luther. Antwort Johannis Coclei von Wendelstein (Cologne, Peter Quentell, 1525).

Warhafftige Historia von Magister Johan Hussen, von anfang seiner newer Sect, biss zum Ende seines Lebens ym Concilio zu Costnitz, auss alten Original beschrieben (Leipzig, Nicolaus Wolrab, 1537).

Was von Kayser Sigmunds Reformation zu halten sei, ain disputation Johannis Coclei. Was auch von der newen Chroniken Sebastiani Franck zu halten sey? (Dresden, 1533).

Zwey kurtze Tractätlein vom Fegfewr der Seelen, wider die newen Secten, so dasselbe verneinen. Erstlich beschriben durch weylandt den Gottseligen und Hochgelehrten Johannem Cochleum der H. Schrifft Doctorn, und jetzo mit dolmetschung dess ersten auffs new widerumb in Truck gefertigt: durch Johann Christoff Hueber (Ingolstadt, David Sartorius, 1543).

Cited works by other authors

Allen, P. S. (ed.), *Opus Epistolarum Des. Erasmi Roterodami* (Oxford, 1941).

Anonymous, *Acta et res gestae D. Martini Lutheri, in Comitiis Principum Vuormaciae. Anno. MDXXI* (Strasbourg, Johann Schott, 1521).

—— *Brevis narratio exponens quo fine vitam in terris suam clauserit reverendus vir D. Philippus Melanchthon* (Wittenberg, Peter Seitz, 1560).

—— *Epistolarum Miscellaneorum ad Fridericum Nauseam Blandicampianum, Episcopum Viennensem, &c. singularium personarum, Libri x* (Basel, Johannes Oporinus, 1550).

—— *Hymns of the Reformation by Martin Luther* (London, 1845).

—— *Pasquilli de Concilio Mantuano iudicium: querimonia Papistarum ad legatum pontificium in comicijs Schmalcaldianis Mantuanae miseris nimium vicina Papistis* ('Rome,' no printer [possibly Wittenberg, Nickel Schirlentz], 1537).

Bachmann, Paul, *Lobgesang auff des Luthers Winckel Messe. Mit vnderricht von Christlicher Messe gemeyner Apostolischer Kirchen* (Leipzig, Michael Blum, 1534).

Bäumer, Remigius, *Johannes Cochlaeus (1479–1552): Leben und Werk im Dienst der katholischen Reform*, Katholisches Leben und Kirchenreform im Zeitalter der Glaubensspaltung, vol. 40 (Münster, 1980).

—— 'Johannes Cochlaeus und die Reform der Kirche,' in *Reformatio Ecclesiae: Beiträge zu kirchlichen Reformbemühungen von der alten Kirche bis zur Neuzeit*, (Paderborn, 1980).

Bennet, Henry, *A Famous and Godly History, etc.* (London, John Awdeley, 1561).

Bernard of Clairvaux. *Oeuvres complètes* (Paris 1993).

Bettenson, Henry (ed.), *Documents of the Christian Church* (Oxford UP, 1943).

Eberhard Billick, *Iudicium deputatorum vniuersitatis & secundarij cleri Coloniensis de doctrina & vocatione Martini Buceri ad Bonnam* (Cologne, Melchior Neuss, 1543).

—— *Iudicii vniuersitatis et cleri Coloniensis: aduersus calumnias Philippi Melanthonis, Martini Buceri, Oldendorpij, & eorum asseclarum, defensio: cum diligenti explicatione materiarum controuersarum* (Paris, Nicolas Boucher, 1545).

Brecht, Martin, *Martin Luther: His Road to Reformation 1483–1521*, tr. J. L. Schaaf (Philadelphia 1985).

Bretschneider, C. G. and Bindseil, H. E. (eds), Corpus Reformatorum, 28 vols (Halle, 1834–60).

Brieger, Theodor (ed.), *Kirchengeschichtliche Studien Hermann Reuter zum 70. Geburtstag Gewidmet*, (Leipzig, 1890).

Brunus, Conradus (Konrad Braun), *De Seditionibus libri sex* (Mainz, Franz Behem, 1550).

—— *De Ceremoniis libri sex* (Mainz, Franz Behem, 1548).

—— *De Imaginibus* (Mainz, Franz Behem, 1548).

—— *Libri Sex de haereticis in genere* (Mainz, Franz Behem, 1549).

—— *Opera Tria* (Mainz, Franz Behem, 1548).

Bucer, Martin, *Ein Christliche Erinnerung, an die Keis. vnd Kon. Maiestaten, sampt Churfursten, Fursten vnd Stende des H. Reichs Teutscher Nation, jetzund zu Wurms versamlet* (Strasbourg, Crato Mylius, 1545).

—— *Confessio Tetrapolitana und die Schriften des Jahres 1531*, (ed.) Robert Stupperich, (Gütersloh, 1969).

—— *Der newe glaub, von den Doctoren zu Louen, die sich Doctoren der Gottheit rhumen, in xxxij Articulen furgegeben: Mit Christlicher verwarnung dagegen, durch die Prediger zu Strasbourg* (Frankfurt, Hermann Gulfferich, 1545).

Bugenhagen, Johann, *Epistola ad Anglos* (n.p., 1525).
—— *Wider die kelch Diebe* (Wittenberg, Hans Lufft, 1532).
Bullinger, Heinrich, *Warhaffte Bekantnuss der Dieneren der kilchen zu Zyrich* (Zurich, Christoffel Froschauer, 1545).
Charles V, *Mandat Karls V. an die säumigen Reichsstände, sich umgehend auf dem Reichstag in Regensburg einzufinden* (n.p., 1545).
—— *Das kayserl. Edict wider den Nürnbergishen Reichs Abschied, aus der Stadt Burgos in Castilien an die Stände des Reichs. Karl von Gots gnaden Römischer Kayser zu allen Zeiten Merer des Reichs* (Burgos, 15 July 1524).
—— *Ordnung, Statuten vnd Edict, Keiser Carols des fünfften, publicirt in der namhafften Stat Brüssel, in beysein irer Mayestet Schwester vnd Königin, Gubernant vnd Regent seiner Niderland, den 4. Octobris, anno Christi 1540* (Nuremberg, Johann Petreius, 1540).
—— *Ordenung und Mandat Keiser Caroli V.: vernewert im April Anno 1550: zu ausrotten und zu vertilgen die Secten und spaltung: welche entstanden sind: widder unsern heiligen Christlichen glauben und wider die ordenung unser Mutter der heiligen Christlichen Kirchen: Item ein Register der verworffenen und verbottenen Buchern: auch von guten Buchern welche man inn der Schulen lesen mag: item eine vermanung des Rectors der Universitet zu Louen: item ein ander Keisers Mandat von des selbigen handel im 40. jar aus gangen* (n.p., 1550).
Caelius, Michael, *Newer Jrthumb vnd Schwermerey vom Sacrament* (Wittenberg, Georg Rhau, 1534).
Carolstadt, Andreas, *Missa de nuptiis Andreae Carolotadii, et sacerdotibus matrimonium contrahentibus* (Ausgsburg, Sigmund Grimm and Marx Wirsung, 1522).
Classen, Carl Joachim, *Rhetorical Criticism of the New Testament* (Tübingen, 2000).
Clemen, Otto (ed.), *Colloquium Cochlaei cum Luthero Wormatiae olim habitum*, in *Flugschriften aus den ersten Jahren der Reformation*, (rpt Nieuwkoop, 1967).
—— *Flugschriften aus den ersten Jahren der Reformation*, vol. 4 (Leipzig, 1911).
—— *Luthers Werke in Auswahl*, 8 vols (Berlin, 1930 and numerous reprints).
—— 'Der Prozess des Johannes Policarius,' *Archiv für Reformationsgeschichte*, 18 (1921).
Clichtove, Josse, *Propugnaculum Ecclesiae adversus Lutheranos* (Paris, S. de Colines, 1526).
—— *Antilutherus ... libri tres* (Paris, S. de Colines, 1524).
Deutz, Rupert of, *De Victoria verbi Dei*, ed. Hraban Haacke, (Weimar, 1970).
—— *Commentariorum, in Evangelium Iohannis libri XIIII* (Cologne, Franz Birckmann, 1526).
—— *Commentariorum in Ioannis Apocalypsin, libri XII* (Nuremberg, Johann Petreius, 1526).
—— *De divinis officiis libri XII* (Cologne, Franz Birckmann, 1526).
—— *De sancta Trinitate et operibus eius*, ed. Hraban Haacke, (Turnholt, 1971–2).
Duke George, *Das New Testament, so durch L. Emser saligen verteuscht, vnd des Durchlewchten Hochgebornen Furstenn herren Georgen hertzogen zu Sachssen* (Leipzig, 1528).
Eck, Johanne, *Asseritur hic Invictissimi Angliae Regis liber de sacramentis, a calumniis & impietatibus Luderi* (Rome, Marcellus Franck, 1523).
—— *Apologia pro reverendis. et illustris. principibus Catholicis: ac alijs ordinibus Imperij aduersus mucores & calumnias Buceri, super actis Comiciorum Ratisponae* (Cologne, Melchior Neuss, 1542).

Edwards, Mark U., '*Lutherschmähung?* Catholics on Luther's Responsibility for the Peasants' War,' *Catholic Historical Review*, 76 (1990).

Elton, G. R., *The New Cambridge Modern History* (Cambridge, 1990).

Emser, Hieronymus, *A venatione Luteriana Aegocerotis assertio* (Leipzig, M. Landsberg, 1520).

—— *Annotationes Hieronymi Emseri vber Luthers Naw Testament gebessert vnd emendirt* (Leipzig, Valentin Schumann, 1525).

—— *Das naw Testament* (Leipzig, W. Stöckel, 1529).

—— *Antwort auff das lesterliche buch wider Bischoff Benno* (Leipzig, Wolfgang Stöckel, 1524).

—— *Epithalamia Martini Lutheri Vuittenbergensis, Ioannis Hessi Vratislauiensis, ac id genus nuptiatorum* (n.p., 1525).

—— *Missae Christianorum contra Luteranan missandi formulam assertio* (Dresden, Emser, 1524).

—— *Canonis missae contra Huldricum Zuinglium defensio* (Strasbourg, Gruninger, 1524).

—— *Hieronymi Emseri Praesbyteri Apologeticon in Vldrici Zuinglij antibolon* (Dresden, Emser, 1525).

—— *Wyder der ztweier Pröbst zu Nirmberg Falschen grund und ursachen* (Dresden, Emser, 1525); (ed.) T. Freudenberger, Corpus Catholicorum, 28 (Münster, 1959).

Erasmus, *Hyperaspistes* II, in *Desiderii Erasmi Opera Omnia*, ed. Joannes Clericus, (Leiden, 1706; rpt Hildesheim, 1962).

—— *Purgatio adversus epistolam non sobriam Martini Lutheri* (1534), *Opera Omnia*, vol. 9/1 (Amsterdam, 1982).

Fisher, John (Saint), *De veritate corporis et sanguinis Christi in Eucharistia* (Cologne, 1527).

—— *Assertionis Lutheranae confutatio* (n.p., 1523).

—— *Defensio Regie assertionis contra Babylonicam captiuitatem* (Cologne, 1525).

—— *Sacri sacerdotii defensio contra Lutherum* (Cologne, Peter Quentell, 1525); ed. Hermann Klein Schmeink, Corpus Catholicorum, 9 (Münster, 1925).

Fraenkel, Peter and Greschat, Martin, *Zwanzig Jahre Melanchthonstudium* (Geneva 1967).

Friedensburg, Walter, *Der Reichstag zu Speier 1526* (Berlin, 1887, rpt Nieuwkoop, 1970).

—— 'Beiträge zum Briefwechsel der katholischen Gelehrten Deutschlands im Reformationszeitalter,' *Zeitschrift für Kirchengeschichte*, 18 (1898).

Gerson, Jean, *Opera cancellarii Parisiensis doctoris Christianissimi magistri Johannis de Gerson* (Strasbourg, Martin Flach, 1494).

Green, Lowell, *How Melanchthon Helped Luther Discover the Gospel* (Fallbrook CA, 1980).

Grossmann, Maria, *Humanism in Wittenberg* (Nieuwkoop 1975).

Hartfelder, Karl, *Philipp Melanchthon als Praeceptor Germaniae* (Berlin, 1898; reprint Nieuwkoop, 1972).

Henry VIII, *Assertio septem sacramentorum*, (ed.) Pierre Fraenkel, Corpus Catholicorum, 43 (Münster 1992).

—— Serenissimi ac potentissime regis Anglie, Christiane fidei defensoris inuictissimi, ad illustrissimos ac clarissimos Saxoniae principes, de coercenda abigendaque Lutherana factione, & Luthero ipso Epistola (Leipzig, 1523).

Henze, Barbara, *Aus Liebe der Kirche Reform: Die Bemühungen Georg Witzels*

(1501–1573) um die Kircheneinheit, Reformationsgeschichtliche Studien und Texte, vol. 133 (Münster, 1995).

Herte, Adolf, *Die Lutherkommentare des Johannes Cochläus: Kritische Studie zur Geschichtsschreibung im Zeitalter der Glaubensspaltung*, Reformationsgeschichtliche Studien und Texte, vol. 33 (Münster, Aschendorff, 1535).

—— *Das katholische Lutherbild im Bann der Lutherkommentare des Cochläus*, 3 vols (Münster, 1943).

Herte, Adolf, *Die Lutherkommentare des Johannes Cochlaeus Kritische Studie zur Geschichtschreibung im Zeitalter der Glaubensspaltung*. Reformationsgeschichtliche Studien und Texte, vol. 33 (Münster, 1935).

Hesse, Philip of, *Ein freuntlichs schreyben oder Sendtbrieff des hochgepornen Fürsten vnd Herren, herrn Philips Landgraffen zu Hessen +c. Vnd des hochgepornen Fursten Hertzog Georgen zu Sachssen antwort oder entschuldigung an den obgenanten Philips Landgraffen zu Hessen +c.* (Wittenberg, 1529).

Hillerbrand, Hans, *Landgrave Philipp of Hesse, 1504–1567: Religion and Politics in the Reformation*, (St Louis, Foundation for Reformation Research, 1967).

Honée, Eugène (ed.), *Der Libell des Hieronymus Vehus zum Augsburger Reichstag 1530* (Münster 1988).

Hus, Jan, *Etliche Brieue Johannis Huss des heiligen Merterers, aus dem gefengnis zu Costentz, an den Behemen geschrieben* (Wittenberg, Joseph Klug, 1537).

Immenkötter, Herbert, 'Von Engeln und Teufeln: Über Luther-Biographien des 16. Jahrhunderts,' in *Biographie und Autobiographie in der Renaissance*, August Buck (ed.), Wolfenbütteler Abhandlungen zur Renaissanceforschung, vol. 4 (Wiesbaden, 1983).

Innocent III (Pope), *Innocentij Papae, hoc nomine tertij, libri sex, de sacro altaris mysterio ex uetusto codice nuper exscripti & nunc per typographos excusi* (Leipzig, Nicolaus Faber, 1534).

—— *Liber de contemptu mundi, sive de miseria conditionis humanae* (Leipzig, Michael Blum, 1534).

Isidore, *Beati Isidori Hispaliensis quondam archiepiscopi De officiis ecclesiasticis libri duo, ante annos DCCCC. ab eo editi, et nunc ex vetusto codice in lucem restitui* (Leipzig, Michael Blum, 1534).

Kalkoff, Paul, 'Wie wurde Cochläus Dechant in Frankfurt?' *Theologische Studien und Kritiken* 71 (1898).

Kautz, Jacob, *Syben Artickel zu Wormbs von Jacob Kautzen angeschlagen vnnd gepredigt* (n.p., 1527).

Keen, Ralph, 'The Arguments and Audiences of Cochlaeus's *Philippica VII*,' *Catholic Historical Review* 78 (1992).

—— 'Political Authority and Ecclesiology in Melanchthon's *De Ecclesiae Autoritate*', *Church History*, 65 (1996).

Kittelson, James, *Wolfgang Capito: From Humanist to Reformer*, (Leiden, 1975).

Krzycki, Andreas (Critias), *Eucomia lutheri. Andree Cricij Episcopi Premislien. in Lutherum Oratio. In imaginem eiusdem Lutheri. Conditiones boni Lutherani. Ingressus Lutheri in Vuormatiam. Decij philomusi ac aliorum in Polonia varia de eodem Lutero Epigrammata* (Cracow, 1524).

Kusukawa, S. (ed.), Salazar, C. (tr.), *Melanchthon: Orations on Philosophy and Education* (Cambridge UP 1999).

Lehmann, Martin, *Justus Jonas: Loyal Reformer* (Minneapolis 1964).

Luther, Martin, *D. Martin Luthers Werke*, 89 vols, *including separate series of correspondence (Briefwechsel)* (Weimar, 1883–1986).

—— *Ein Sendbrieff Dr Martini Luthers, an Hertzog Georg zu Sachssen, Landgraff in Döringen, vnd Marggraffe zu Meichssen, darin er in freüntlich ermant, zu dem wort Gottes zu tretten. Ein Antwort Hertzog Georgen zu Sachssen, Landgraff in Döringen, Marggraff zu Meichssen, an Do. Marti* (Nuremberg, 1526).

—— *Von heimlichen und gestohlenen Briefen* in *Welcher Gestalt wir Georg von Gottes Gnaden Hertzog zu Sachssen Landtgraff in Duringen vnnd Marggraff zu Meyssen von Martino Luther der gedichten Bundtnus halben inn schriften vnerfindtlich angegeben: vnd darauff vnsere antwort* (Augsburg, Alexander Weissenhorn, 1528).

—— *Die Lugend von S. Johanne Chrysostomo, an die heiligen Veter inn dem vermeinten Concilio zu Mantua* (Wittenberg, Hans Lufft, 1537).

—— *Vier christliche briefe, so Johan Hus der heylig marterer aus dem gefengknus zu Costentz im Concilio, an die Behem geschriben hat, verteutscht, sampt einer vorrede D. Mart. Luthers, das zukunfftig Concilium betreffend* (Nuremberg, Johann Petreius, 1536).

—— *Einer aus den hohen Artikeln des Allerheiligsten Bepstlichen glaubens, genant, Donatio Constantini* (Wittenberg, Hans Lufft, 1537).

—— *Literarum, quibus invictissimus princeps Henricus VIII. Rex Angliae, & Franciae, dominus Hyberniae, ac fidei defensor respondit ad quandam epistolam Martini Lutheri ad se missam, & ipsius lutheranae quoque epistolae exemplum* (n.p., 1526).

—— *Epistola Martini Lutheri, Ad illustrisimum principem ac dominum Henricum … Admonitio Johannis Cochlaei in utranque epistolam* (Cologne, Peter Quentell, 1525).

—— *Contra XXXII. Articulos Lovaniensium Theologistarum* (Frankfurt, Hermann Gulfferich, 1546).

—— *Wider die XXXII. Artikel der Teologisten von Louen* (Wittenberg, Nickel Schirlentz, 1545).

Manschreck, Clyde L., 'The Role of Melanchthon in the Adiaphora Controversy', *Archiv für Reformationsgeschichte*, 48 (1957).

Matheson, Peter, *Argula von Grumbach: A Woman's Voice in the Reformation* (Edinburgh 1995).

Maurer, Wilhelm, *De junge Melanchthon zwischen Humanismus und Reformation*, 2 vols (Göttingen, 1967–69; 1-vol. reprint, 1996).

May, G. and R. Decot (eds), *Melanchton und die Reformation: Forschungbeiträge* (Mainz, 1996).

Melancthon, Philip, *Historia de vita et actis Lutheri*, (Heidelberg, 1548).

—— *Adversus furiosum Parisiensium Theologastrorum decretum Philippi Melanchthonis pro Luthero apologia, Melanchltous Werke in Auswahl*, ed. Robert Stupperich *et al.*, vols (Gütersloh, 1951–58), hereafter StA, vol. 1: 142–62; tr. C. L. Hill in *Melanchthon: Selected Writings* (Westport 1978).

—— *Corpus Doctrinae Christianae* (Leipzig, Ernst Voegelin, 1560).

—— *Didymi Faventini adversus Thomam Placentinum pro Martino Luthero theologo oratio* (1521).

Mellerstadt, Martin Polich von, *Defensio Leoniciana* (1498).

Miner, John N., 'Change and Continuity in the Schools of Late Medieval Nuremberg,' *Catholic Historical Review*, 73 (1987).

Mirbt, Karl (ed.), *Quellen zur Geschichte des Papsttums und des Römischen Katholizismus*, 4th edn (Tübingen, 1924).

More, Thomas (Saint), *Responsio ad Lutherum*, ed. J. H. Headley, (New Haven, 1969).

Morerod, Charles (ed.), *Cajetan et Luther en 1518* (Fribourg, Editions Universitaires, 1994).

Morison, Richard, *Apomaxis calumniarum, conuitiorumque, quibus Ioannes Cocleus, homo theologus exiguus artium professor, scurra procax, Henrici octavi, serenissimi regis Angliae famam impetere, nomen obscurare, rerum gestarum gloriam faedare nuper edita, non tam in regem, quam in regis inuidam, epistola studuit* (London, 1537).

Müntzer, Thomas, *Ein gloubvirdig, vnd warhafftig vnderricht wie die Dhoringischen Pawern von Franckenhawsen vmb yhr misshandlung gestrafft, vnd beyde Stett, Frankenhawsen vnd Mollhawsen erobert worden* (Dresden, 1525).

Murner, Thomas, *Ob der Künig us England ein Lügner sey oder der Luther* (Strasbourg, J. Grieninger, 1522; ed. W. Pfeffer-Belli, (Berlin, 1928).

Oberman, Heiko A., *The Harvest of Medieval Theology: Gabriel Biel and Late Medieval Nominalism* (Cambridge, MA, 1963).

Paul III (Pope), *Admonitio paterna Pauli III. Romani Pontificis ad inuictiss. Caesarem Carolum V.* (n.p., 1545).

Pelikan, J. and Lehmann, H. T. (eds), *Luther's Works, American edition, 55 vols. Philadelphia, 1955–86*.

Pflug, Julius, *Correspondance*, J. V. Pollet, ed. OP, (Leiden 1979).

Pighius, Albertus, *Apologia Alberti Pighii Campensis aduersus Martini Buceri calumnias, quas & solidis argumentis, & clarissimis rationibus confutat* (Mainz, Franz Behem, 1543).

Pochiecha, V. (ed.), *Acta Tomiciana* (Wroclaw, 1966).

Politus, Ambrosius Catharinus, *Excusatio disputationis contra Martinum Lutherum* (Florence, Philippus Junta, 1521).

Querhammer, Casper, *Tabula contradictionum Lutheri xxxvi. super vno articulo, de communione eucharistiae* (Dresden, Wolfgang Stöckel, 1535).

Radini, Tomasso, *In Martinum Lutherum ... Oratio* (Leipzig, Lotter, 1520).

—— *In Philippum Melanchthonem Lutheranae haereseos defensorem oratio* (Rome 1522; (ed.) Giuseppe Berti, *Orazione contro Filippo Melantone* (Brescia, Paideia, 1973).

Reicke, Emil (ed.), *Willibald Pirckheimers Briefwechsel*, (Munich, 1940-).

Richter, A. L. and E. Friedberg (eds), *Corpus iuris ecclesiastici*, 2nd edn (Leipzig 1879–81).

Rössner, Maria Barbara, *Konrad Braun (ca. 1495–1563): ein katholischer Jurist, Politiker, Kontroverstheologe und Kirchenreformer im konfessionellen Zeitalter*, Reformationsgeschichtliche Studien und Texte, vol. 130 (Münster, 1991).

Samuel-Scheyder, Monique, *Johannes Cochlaeus: Humaniste et adversaire de Luther* (Nancy, 1993).

Schatzmeister, G., *Getrwew Ermanung, So etlich christlich personen, auff yetz gehalten Reychstag zu Speyer den Fursten Teutschs Landts zugeschriben haben* (n.p., 1526).

Scheible, Heinz, *Melanchthon: Eine Biographie* (Munich, 1997).

Servetus, Michael, *Dialogorum de Trinitate libri duo* (Hagenau, Johann Setzer, 1532; rpt Frankfurt, 1965); tr. Earl Morse Wilbur in *The Two Treatises of Servetus on the Trinity*, Harvard Theological Studies, 16 (Cambridge, MA; rpt New York, 1969).

Sider, Ronald, *Andreas Bodenstein von Karlstadt: The Development of his Thought, 1517–1525* (Leiden 1974).

Siggins, Ian, *Luther and His Mother* (Philadelphia, 1981).

Skinner, Quentin, *The Foundations of Modern Political Thought* (Cambridge 1978).

Spahn, Martin, *Johannes Cochläus: Ein Lebensbild aus der Zeit der Kirchenspaltung* (Berlin 1898; rpt Nieuwkoop, 1964).

Steinmetz, David, *Luther and Staupitz* (Durham, NC 1980).

Stupperich, Robert (ed.), *Melanchthons Werke in Auswahl* (Gütersloh, 1978).

Sturm, Johann, *Consilium delectorum cardinalium et aliorum prelatorum, de emendanda ecclesia, epistola* (Strasbourg, Crato Mylius, 1538).

Tappert, Theodore G. (tr.), *The Book of Concord,* (Philadelphia, 1959).

Tauber, Caspar, in *Sententia lata contra Casparum Thauber ciuem Viennen. olim Lutheranae sectae imitatorem. Widerrueff etlicher verdambter yertung mit vrtayl vnd recht auffgelegt vnd erkant zu Wien in Oesterreych* (Vienna, 1524).

Vehe, Michael, *Erretung der beschuldigtem Kelchdyeb von newen Bugenhagischen galgen* (Leipzig, Michael Lotter, 1535).

Waite, Gary, *David Joris and Dutch Anabaptism 1524–1543* (Waterloo, Ont., 1990).

Wedewer, Hermann, *Johannes Dietenberger 1475–1537: Sein Leben und Wirken* (Freiburg 1888; rpt Nieuwkoop, 1967).

Wengert, T. J., 'The Day Philip Melanchthon Got Mad', *Lutheran Quarterly*, N. S. 5 (1991).

—— and Graham, M. P. , *Philip Melanchthon (1497–1560) and the Commentary* (Sheffield, 1997).

Wiedenhofer, Siegfried, *Formalstrukturen humanistischer und reformaorischer Theologtie bei Philipp Melanchthon*, 2 vols (Frankfurt and Munich, 1976).

Witzel, Georg, *Apologia: das ist, ein vertedigs rede Georgij Wicelij widder seine affterreder die Luteristen, mit sampt kurtzer abconterseyung Lutherischer secten, vnd preis alter Romischen Kirchen nutzlick zu lesen* (Leipzig, Nickel Schmidt, 1533).

—— *Von der Pusse, Beichte vnd Bann* (Leipzig, Valentin Schumann, 1534).

—— *Von der heiligen Eucharisty odder Mess, nach anweisunge der Schrifft, vnd der Eltisten schrifftuerstendigen heiligen Lerern* (Leipzig, Valentin Schumann, 1534).

—— *Vom Beten, Fastenn, vnnd Almosen, Schrifftlich zeugknusz* (Leipzig, Melchior Lotter, 1535; expanded edn, Leipzig, Nicolaus Wolrab, 1538).

—— *Confutatio calumniosissimae Responsionis Justi Jonae, id est, Jodoci Koch, una cum assertione bonorum operum* (Leipzig, Nicolaus Faber, 1533).

—— *Von der Christlichen Kyrchen: wider Jodocum Koch/der sich nennet/Justum Jonam* (Leipzig, Nickel Schmidt, 1534).

Wiedermann, Gotthelf, 'Cochlaeus as Polemicist,' in *Seven-Headed Luther*, P. N. Brooks (ed.), (Oxford, 1984).

Williams, George H. , *The Radical Reformation*, 3rd edn (Kirksville, 1992).

Wrede Adolf, *Deutsche Reichstagsakten unter Kaiser Karl V* (Göttingen 1962).

Yoder, John H. (ed. and tr.), *The Legacy of Michael Sattler*, Classics of the Radical Reformation, 1 (Scottdale, PA, 1973).

Notes

Notes to Introduction

1 Philip Melancthon, *Historia de vita et actis Lutheri* (Heidelberg, 1548). Luther's pupil, Johannes Matthesius, published a brief sentimental memoir of his teacher at Nuremberg (1566).
2 Henry Bennet, *A Famous and Godly History, etc.* (London John Awdeley 1561), fo. C. iir.
3 A prior edition appears in the anonymous *Hymns of the Reformation by Martin Luther* (London, 1845).
4 *Luther at Worms, LW,* vol. 32: 123.
5 1 Tim. 5: 12.

Notes to Chapter 1, Philip Melanchthon and the historical Luther

1 Melanchthon, 'Eulogy for Luther' (1546), at *Corpus Reformatorum* (hereafter CR), ed. H. Bindseil and C. G. Bretschneider, 28 vols (Halle, 1836–60), vol. 11, col. 728.
2 CR, vol. 11, 73.
3 The most thorough introduction to Melanchthon's early development is Wilhelm Maurer, *Der junge Melanchthon zwischen Humanismus und Reformation,* 2 vols (Göttingen, 1967–69; 1-vol. reprint, 1996).
4 See Maurer, *Der junge Melanchthon,* vol. 2, 9–67, and Lowell Green, *How Melanchthon Helped Luther Discover the Gospel* (Fallbrook, CA, 1980).
5 See Timothy J. Wengert, 'The Biblical Commentaries of Philip Melanchthon', *in Philip Melanchthon (1497–1560) and the Commentary,* ed. T. J. Wengert and M. P. Graham (Sheffield, 1997), 106–48; Carl Joachim Classen, *Rhetorical Criticism of the New Testament* (Tübingen, 2000), 99–177.
6 The 1521 texts is available in *Melanchthons Werke in Auswahl,* ed. Robert Stupperich (hereafter cited as 'StA, vol.'), vol. 2/1 (Gütersloh, 1978); it was translated by Wilhelm Pauck in the Library of Christian Classics series (Philadelphia, 1969). See Wilhelm Maurer, 'Melanchthons Loci communes von 1521 als wissenschaftliche Programmschrift: Ein Beitrag zur Hermeneutik der Reformationszeit', *Luther-Jahrbuch,* 27 (1960), 1–50.
7 Melanchthon, 'Unterricht der Visitatorn an die Pfarhern ym Kurfurstenthum zu Sachsen', StA, vol. 1, 215–71.
8 The title would become enshrined in the classic study of Melanchthon's work as an educational reformer, Karl Hartfelder, *Philipp Melanchthon als Praeceptor Germaniae* (Berlin, 1898; rpt Nieuwkoop, 1972).
9 Siegfried Wiedenhofer, *Formalstrukturen humanistischer und reformatorischer Theologie bei Philipp Melanchthon,* 2 vols (Frankfurt and Munich, 1976).
10 For examples see Melanchthon's 'Encomion eloquentiae' (1523) and 'De philosophia oratio' (1536), in StA, vol. 3, 44–62, 88–95.
11 For context and interpretation see R. W. Scribner, 'Politics and the Institutionali-

sation of Reform in Germany', in *The New Cambridge Modern History*, vol. 2, ed. G. R. Elton (Cambridge, 1990), 172–97. The Augsburg Confession is available in English in *The Book of Concord*, ed. T. G. Tappert *et al.* (Philadelphia, 1959), 24–96; a new version is in preparation.

12 He was not always amiable, and seldom flexible when articles of faith were at stake, as Timothy J. Wengert points out in 'The Day Philip Melanchthon Got Mad', *Lutheran Quarterly*, N. S. 5 (1991), 419–33.

13 Heinz Scheible, *Melanchthon: Eine Biographie* (Munich, 1997), with a wealth of detail at his disposal, makes this point forcefully.

14 For a review of viewpoints see Peter Fraenkel and Martin Greschat, *Zwanzig Jahre Melanchthoustudium* (Geneva, 1967), esp. 125–37.

15 A number of Heinz Scheible's papers in *Melanchthon und die Reformation: Forschungsbeiträge*, ed. G. May and R. Decot (Mainz, 1996) set this aspect of Melanchthon's career beyond question.

16 For example, in his 1539 *De Ecclesiae autoritate et de veterum scriptis*, CR, vol. 23, 585–642, on which see Ralph Keen, 'Political Authority and Ecclesiology in Melanchthon's *De Ecclesiae Autoritate*', *Church History*, 65 (1996), 1–14.

17 See his declaration of reasons for not participating in the Council of Trent, the 1546 'Ursache, Warumb die Stende, so der Augspurgischen Confession anhagen, Christliche Leer erstlich angenommen und endtlich auch darbey zuverharren gedencken', StA, vol. 1, 412–48.

18 See Quentin Skinner, *The Foundations of Modern Political Thought*, vol. 2 (Cambridge, 1978), 81–9.

19 For analysis of Melanchthon's position, see Clyde L. Manschreck, 'The Role of Melanchthon in the Adiaphora Controversy', *Archiv für Reformationsgeschichte*, 48 (1957), 165–81.

20 The Formula is translated in *The Book of Concord*, ed. Tappert, 464–636.

21 Melanchthon, *Corpus Doctrinae Christianae* (Leipzig, Ernst Voegelin, 1560); see the preface at StA, vol. 6, 5–11.

22 The death and funeral events are recorded in *Brevis narratio exponens quo fine vitam in terris suam clauserit reverendus vir D. Philippus Melanhthon* (Wittenberg, Peter Seitz, 1560).

23 CR, vol. 11, 726–34; there have been several translations into English.

24 CR, vol. 11, 727.

25 CR, vol. 11, 785.

26 The humanists' call to return to the sources is sounded in his inaugural lecture at Wittenberg, 'De corrigendis adolescentiae studiis', StA, vol. 3, 30–42. His classic statement is the 1539 'De ecclesiae autoritate', StA, vol. 1, 324–86. A number of other pronouncements of the value of historical study are found in Philip Melanchthon, *Orations on Philosophy and Education*, ed. S. Kusukawa, tr. C. Salazar (Cambridge, 1999).

Notes to Chapter 2, Philip Melanchthon's *History of the Life and Acts of Dr Martin Luther*

1 Johannes Policarius (originally Daum, probably; *c.*1524–*c.*1588), pastor and superintendent in Weissenfels, was an elegant composer of dedications in Latin and Greek verse. Policarius studied in Leipzig (1542) and Wittenberg (MA, 1545), and became deacon in Weissenfels in early 1546; and by 1552 was superintendent

there. In the 1560s he engaged in polemics against Julius von Pflug and other Romanist theologians. See Otto Clemen, 'Der Prozess des Johannes Policarius', *Archiv für Reformationsgeschichte*, 18 (1921), 63–74; Julius Pflug, *Correspondance*, ed. J. V. Pollet, OP, vol. 4 (Leiden, 1979), 514. Policannius's indroductory epistle and concluding distichs appear in the Appendix, pp. 353.

2   St Martin of Tours (d. 397) was a soldier who converted from paganism to Christianity and from the military to the ascetic life, becoming a promoter of monasticism and in 371 bishop of Tours. He is one of the patron saints of France.

3   Little is known of this teacher; according to Martin Brecht *(Martin Luther: His Road to Reformation, 1483–1521*, tr. J. L. Schaaf [Philadelphia, 1985], 12), we cannot be sure of the name of Luther's first teacher.

4   Hans Reinecke, like Luther the son of a master smelter, returned to Mansfeld after his schooling and took up his father's profession.

5   Luther matriculated at Erfurt in 1501 and devoted himself to logic as one of the first courses in the arts curriculum. The course would have included the *Prior* and *Posterior Analytics* of Aristotle and the *Summulae logicales* (*c.*1230) of Peter of Spain (later Pope John XXI).

6   Luther remained at Erfurt for this program; some have suggested that he left it so quickly because of scruples about the integrity of the profession (see Brecht, *Road to Reformation*, 44–6).

7   An order of the mid-thirteenth century pledged to the Rule of St Augustine; Luther belonged to the Saxon congregation of this order, a reform movement dating from 1419.

8   The commentators on the *Sentences* of Peter Lombard (1100–60), the standard theological textbook throughout the Middle Ages.

9   See Bernard of Clairvaux, In Laudibus virginis matris, Sermon 3.11, in Bernard de Clairvaux, *Oeuvres complètes*, vol. 20 (Paris, 1993), 194.

10 Luther's familiarity with Augustine had begun by 1509 (see *Luthers Werke in Auswahl*, ed. Otto Clemen, vol. 5 [Berlin, De Gruyter, 1955], 1–4) and continued throughout his career; the influence of Augustine's Psalms commentary is evident in Luther's 1513–16 Psalms commentary; and *The Spirit and the Letter* stands behind the 1519 Commentary on Romans.

11 Gabriel Biel (1420–95), German nominalist thinker. Biel was one of the founders of the University of Tübingen and a provost in the Brethren of the Common Life; his thought typified theology at the end of the fifteenth century. See Heiko A. Oberman, *The Harvest of Medieval Theology: Gabriel Biel and Late Medieval Nominalism* (Cambridge: MA, 1963).

12 Pierre D'Ailly (*c.*1350–1420), trained in nominalism at Paris, became chancellor of the University of Paris in 1389 and soon afterwards a royal counsellor, but takes his Latin name from Cambrai (Cameracensis), where he became bishop in 1397. In this role he participated in a number of the Councils that followed the fourteenth-century Schism, and wrote a number of reform documents that remained influential in Luther's time.

13 William of Occam (1285–1347), the Franciscan theologian most closely associated with nominalism, rejected the idea of universals and argued that only singular beings exist. Much of his work is in explanation of Aristotle's logical and metaphysical works.

14 Jean Gerson (1363–1429), a student of Pierre D'Ailly and his successor as chancellor at Paris, was the author of a number of reform treatises aimed at

bringing an end to the Schism; his chief influence lay in his advocacy of conciliarism, though he wrote a number of mystical manuals as well. There were editions of his complete works, e.g. *Opera cancellarii Parisiensis doctoris Christianissimi magistri Johannis de Gerson* (Strasbourg, Martin Flach, 1494).

15 Johann von Staupitz (1468–1524), vicar general of the German Augustinians, teacher and long-time mentor of Martin Luther. For Luther's relation to Staupitz, see David C. Steinmetz, *Luther and Staupitz: An Essay in the Intellectual Origins of the Protestant Reformation* (Durham, NC, 1980).

16 Martin Polich von Mellerstadt (d. 1513), first rector of Wittenberg University, moved there from Leipzig where he had been the center of a humanistic sodality, the Sodalitas Polychiana (the name is from Polich). He was a prolific author in his own right, known for the *Defensio Leoniciana* (1498) and two works against Simon Pistoris on the origins of syphilis.

17 Luther's lectures on Romans began in 1515 and continued through 1516, but a commentary did not appear in his lifetime. Rather, it was discovered in the late nineteenth century and first published in 1908. For a translation, see *LW*, vol. 25.

18 Luther's 1513–15 interpretation of the Psalms is usually considered the starting point of his Reformation theology; see *LW*, vols 10–12.

19 The Dutch humanist's direct influence on Luther's theology was limited; much more valuable for Luther were Erasmus's editions of the Fathers (including Irenaeus, Origen, Jerome, and Augustine) and the 1516 edition of the New Testament.

20 Johann Tetzel, OP (ca. 1465–1519), inquisitor in Poland and Saxony, achieved fame as a preacher of indulgences for the Archbishop of Mainz, Albert of Brandenburg.

21 The 95 Theses of 1517, which according to Melanchthon's narrative Luther posted on the door of the Wittenberg Castle Church. See *WA*, vol. 1, 223–28; *LW*, vol. 31, 25–33.

22 Luther was called to Heidelberg in May 1518 to defend his theses, having already prepared a written explanation of many of them. This explanation was not finished, however, until August of that year, and appeared as Explanations of the Disputation concerning the Value of Indulgences (*WA*, vol. 1, 525–628; *LW*, vol. 31, 83–252).

23 Tomasso de Vio, OP, known as Cajetanus (1469–1534), was the most influential Thomist of his day and one of the most trenchant critics of the early Luther. A cardinal, he attended the 1518 Diet of Augsburg and challenged Luther; for a record and analysis of the proceedings see *Cajetan et Luther en 1518*, ed. Charles Morerod, 2 vols (Fribourg, 1994).

24 Johann Eck (1486–1543), logician and theologian at the University of Ingolstadt, was one of the most prolific and influential opponents of Luther, whose *Enchiridion* (1525) became a standard manual of Catholic controversial theology. They first locked horns at the Leipzig Debate in 1519; and the study of papal authority proposed here would materialize in Eck's 1520 treatise *De primatu Petri*, in three books.

25 Andreas Bodenstein von Karlstadt (1486–1541), trained in the arts and theology, and with a doctorate in civil and canon law as well, was an early supporter of Luther but broke with the Wittenberg movement when he felt it was not sufficiently radical.

26 Andreas Bodenstein von Karlstadt (1486–1541), early supporter of Luther.

Differences over the pace of reform and the doctrine of the Eucharist led to their later separation.

27 Perhaps alluding to the followers of the radical German religious Reformer Thomas Müntzer (c.1490–1525), who advocated a classless society and led the Peasants' Revolt in Thuringia in 1524–5.

28 The Greek Father (c.185–254) credited with developing (from Jewish origins in Philo) the allegorical method of biblical interpretation, according to which scripture has a literal, moral, and spiritual sense. Admired by Erasmus, Origen was severely attacked by most Reformers.

29 The greatest of the Latin Fathers, Augustine (354–430) wrote works against the Pelagians which were used by the early Protestants in their attacks against Catholic emphasis on works, and treatises against Donatists and others that the Catholics used against the Reformers.

30 The record of the proceedings at Worms is a reprint *of Acta et res gestae D. Martini Lutheri, in Comitijs Principum Vuormaciae, Anno. MDXXI* (Strasbourg, Johann Schott, 1521), reprinted numerous times by various printers. It has been critically edited by Adolf Wrede in *Deutsche Reichstagsakten unter Kaiser Karl V.*, vol. 2 (Göttingen, 1962), 545–69.

31 The imperial marshal, Pappenheim, was part of Luther's escort to the hearing at Worms, but not much else is known about him.

32 The imperial herald, Sturm, issued Luther his summons to appear at Worms, and with Pappenheim formed Luther's escort during the trial.

33 Hieronymus Schurff (1481–1554), Swiss patrician and jurist, was one of the first faculty at Wittenberg and an early supporter of Luther.

34 Mt. 10: 32.

35 *Corpus iuris ecclesiastici*, 2nd edn, ed. A. L. Richter and E. Friedberg (Leipzig, 1879–81), vol. 1, 16, 1007.

36 Mt. 10: 34–5.

37 Hieronymus Vehus, chancellor in Baden, is best known for his participation at the 1530 Diet of Augsburg; see Eugène Honée, ed., *Der Libell des Hieronymus Vehus zum Augsburger Reichstag 1530* (Münster, 1988).

38 It was at the Council of Constance (1414–18) that the Hussite movement, one of the forerunner events of the Reformation, was condemned, and its leader, Jan Hus (1372–1415) put to death. He would be seen as a martyr to the gospel by Luther and other Reformers.

39 1 Thess. 5: 21.

40 Gal. 1: 8–9.

41 On Johannes Cochlaeus, see the biographical introduction in this volume, pp. 40

42 Nicholas von Amsdorff (1483–1565), a Wittenberg colleague of Luther's, went on in 1524 to become pastor in Magdeburg and Bishop of Naumburg-Zeitz in 1542 in a highly contested appointment.

43 Mt. 1: 25.

44 Conrad Peutinger (1465–1547) was a patrician of Augsburg and close to the Emperor Maximilian, and a humanist influential in promoting studies of German antiquity and related subjects. An Erasmian by temperament, he tried to be a mediator at Worms.

45 Ps. 146: 3.

46 Jer. 17: 5.

47 Acts 5: 38–39.

48 Justus Jonas, born Jodocus Koch (1493–1555), Reformer and German translator of the Latin works of Luther and Melanchthon. He assisted the latter in drafting the Augsburg Confession.

49 In the published text a series of chronological distichs on the principle events in the life of Luther follow, accompanied by occasional poems. See Appendix, pp. 353

Notes to Chapter 3, Johannes Cochlaeus: an introduction to his life and work

1 The best general treatment remains Martin Spahn, *Johannes Cochläus: Ein Lebensbild aus der Zeit der Kirchenspaltung* (Berlin 1898; rpt Nieuwkoop, 1964); more current but also more admiring is Remigius Bäumer, *Johannes Cochlaeus (1479–1552): Leben und Werk im Dienst der katholischen Reform*, Katholisches Leben und Kirchenreform im Zeitalter der Glaubensspaltung, vol. 40 (Münster, 1980). The very thorough biography by Monique Samuel-Scheyder, *Johannes Cochlaeus: Humaniste et adversaire de Luther* (Nancy, 1993) is stronger on the humanistic early Cochlaeus than the later polemicist.

2 *Quadriuium Grammatices Johannis Coclaei Norici* (Nuremberg, Johann Stuchs, 1511); *Tetrachordium musices Ioannis Coclei Norici* (Nuremberg, Johann Meyssenburger, 1511; rpt Nuremberg: Frederick Peypus, 1520); *Cosmographia Pomponij Mele: Authoris nitidissimi Tribus Libris digesta* (Nuremberg, Johann Weissenburger, 1511); *Meteorologia Aristotelis. Eleganti Jacobi Fabri Stapulensis Paraphrasi explanata. Commentarioque Joannis Coclaei Norici ...* (Nuremberg, Frederick Peypus, 1512). On the Pirckheimer circle and its educational activity see John N. Miner, 'Change and Continuity in the Schools of Late Medieval Nuremberg', *Catholic Historical Review*, 73 (1987), 1–22.

3 Cochlaeus to Pirckheimer, Bologna, 3 April 1517, in *Willibald Pirckheimers Briefwechsel*, ed. Emil Reicke *et al.* (Munich, 1940–), vol. 3, 94–6.

4 Hans and Sebald Geuder to Cochlaeus, Nuremberg, late 1517–early 1518, in *Willibald Pirckheimers Briefwechsel*, vol. 3, 266–8.

5 Theodor Kolde, 'Wie wurde Cochlaeus zum Gegner Luthers?' in *Kirchengeschichtliche Studien Hermann Reuter zum 70. Geburtstag Gewidmet*, ed. Theodor Brieger *et al.* (Leipzig, 1890), 197–201; Paul Kalkoff, 'Wie wurde Cochläus Dechant in Frankfurt?' *Theologische Studien und Kritiken, 71 (1898), 686–94.*

6 For background and later fate of this work see Joseph Greving's introduction to *Colloquium Cochlaei cum Luthero Wormatiae olim habitum*, in *Flugschriften aus den ersten Jahren der Reformation*, ed. Otto Clemen, vol. 4 (rpt Nieuwkoop, 1967), 179–83.

7 The view at Worms and shortly after was that Cochlaeus provoked Luther, a charge that Cochlaeus denies in his letter to Aleander, Frankfurt, 27 September 1521, in Walter Friedensburg, 'Beiträge zum Briefwechsel der katholischen Gelehrten Deutschlands im Reformationszeitalter', *Zeitschrift für Kirchengeschichte*, 18 (1898), 121; hereafter cited as 'Friedensburg'.

8 Greving, in *Colloquium Cochlaei cum Luthero*, 181–2.

9 Cochlaeus to Pirckheimer, Bologna, 28 May 1517, in *Willibald Pirckheimers Briefwechsel*, 3, 110–12.

10 Cochlaeus to Aleander, Frankfurt, 5 May 1521, in Friedensburg, 109–11.

11 Cochlaeus to Nausea, Frankfurt, 19 September 1524, in *Epistolarum Miscellaneorum*

ad Fridericum Nauseam Blandicampianum, Episcopum Viennensem, &c. singularium personarum, Libri x (Basel, Johannes Oporinus, 1550), cited hereafter as *Epist. Misc.*, sig. D2.

12 As early as late 1536 Cochlaeus begins to hint that he hopes to be useful in the coming council; see his letter to Nausea, iii cal. January 1537, in *Epist. Misc.*, sigs Z4ᵛ–AA1.

13 *Ob Sant Peter zu Rom sey gewesen* (Strasbourg, J. Grieninger, 1524); *De Petro et Roma adversus Velenum Lutheranum, libri quatuor* (Cologne, Peter Quentell, 1525; rpt in Cochlaeus, *Opuscula* [Farnborough, 1968]).

14 *Canones Apostolorum* ... (Mainz, 1525); *Epistolae decretales veterum pontificum Romanorum* (n.p., 1526); *Epistolae antiquissimae ac sacris institutionibus plenae* (Cologne, 1526).

15 Aleander to Cochlaeus, circa. October 1521, in Friedensburg, 126–31.

16 Cochlaeus to Nausea, Regensburg, 11 May 1532, in *Epist. Misc.*, sig. Q4; and Cochlaeus to Nausea, Regensburg, vi nonas Maij, 1541, in *Epist. Misc.*, sig. Qq3ᵛ. Such comments cast doubt on the sincerity of Cochlaeus's assurance to Aleander (Friedensburg, 123) that he would reconcile with the Lutherans immediately if asked.

17 See Cochlaeus to Nausea, Dresden, November 1528, in *Epist. Misc.*, sig. H2 (about the publication of a work by Fabri) and again on 27 August 1529 (about the publication of Nausea's 'Centuries', an otherwise unknown work), sig. K3.

18 *Fasciculus calumniarum, sannarum et illusionum Martini Lutheri in Episcopos et Clericos* (Leipzig: Valentin Schumann, 1529).

19 *Sieben Köpffe Martini Lutheri Vom Hochwirdigen Sacrament des Altars* (Leipzig, Valentin Schumann, 1529), translated as *Septiceps Lutherus* (Leipzig, Valentin Schumann, 1529).

20 See Gotthelf Wiedermann, 'Cochlaeus as Polemicist', in *Seven-Headed Luther*, ed. P. N. Brooks (Oxford, 1984).

21 It is perhaps worth noting, moreover, that Cochlaeus is scrupulously accurate in these early compilations and in his copying from them in the *Commentary*. Only rarely did he conflate separate quotations from his earlier patchwork books and present them as coherent passages.

22 For background, and the remaining fragments of the Response, see Cochlaeus, *Philippicae I–VII*, ed. R. Keen (Nieuwkoop, 1995–6).

23 *Fidelis et Pacifica Commonitio Joan. Cochlaei, contra Infidelem et seditiosam Commonitionem Mart. Lutheri ad Germanos* (Leipzig, Valentin Schumann, 1531), a response to Luther's *Warning to His Dear German People* of 1530.

24 E.g., *Hertzog Georgens zu Sachssen Ehrlich und grundtliche entschuldigung* (Leipzig, Michael Blum, 1533); *Illustrissimi ac maxime Orthodoxi piique Principis, Domini Georgii ... Edictalis Epistola adversus pravam interpretationem Novi Testamenti a Luthero heretico editam* (Dresden, Wolfgang Stöckel, 1534).

25 See Cochlaeus to Cardinal Contarini, Wroclaw, 9 March 1540, in Friedensburg, 424–5.

26 See Remigius Bäumer, 'Johannes Cochlaeus und die Reform der Kirche', in *Reformatio Ecclesiae: Beiträge zu kirchlichen Reformbemühungen von der alten Kirche bis zur Neuzeit*, ed. Remigius Bäumer (Paderborn, 1980), 333–54.

27 *Ad Paulum III. Pont. Max. Congratulatio Johannis Cochlaei Germani, super eius electione, recens facta nuperque promulgata* (Leipzig, Michael Blum, 1535).

28 *Aequitatis discussio super consilio Delectorum Cardinalium ... ad tollendam per generale*

concilium inter Germanos in religione discordiam (Leipzig: Nicolaus Wolrab, 1538; ed. Hilarius Walter, Corpus Catholicorum, vol. 17 [Münster, 1931]) – a work placed on the Index of Forbidden Books in 1559. See also, from this period, his *Quatuor Excusationum Lutheranorum Confutatio una, Pro Concilio Generali ad Mantuam indicto* (Leipzig, Nicolaus Wolrab, 1538) and *Ein nötig und christlich Bedencken, auff des Luthers Artickeln, die man Gemeynem Concilio fürtragen sol* (Leipzig, Nicolaus Wolrab, 1538).

29 See, e.g. Cochlaeus to Morone, Meissen, 19 March 1538, Friedensburg 283.

30 See Cochlaeus to Nausea, Meissen, December 1536, *Epist. Misc.*, sigs Z4ᵛ-Aa1.

31 See, for example, *De Canonicae scripturae & Catholicae Ecclesiae autoritate, ad Henricum Bullingerum Iohannis Cochlaei libellus* (Ingolstadt, Alexander Weissenhorn, 1543); *De Concilio et legitime iudicandis controversiis religionis ...* (Strasbourg, Knoblouch, 1545), with a letter by Cochlaeus to Bucer.

32 Mark U. Edwards, '*Lutherschmähung?* Catholics on Luther's Responsibility for the Peasants' War', *Catholic Historical Review* 76 (1990) 461–80.

33 Cochlaeus gives a wildly exaggerated 100,000 as the casualty figure in his preface to the *Commentary* (sig. c♣2ᵛ) and elsewhere.

34 For background to the work of Cochlaeus in the late 1540s see Ralph Keen, 'The Arguments and Audiences of Cochlaeus's *Philippica VII*', *Catholic Historical Review*, 78 (1992), 371–94.

35 'Exhortatio ad principes sacri Ro. Imperij contra nefarios conatus Lutheri', *in In Causa Religionis Miscellaneorum libri tres* (Ingolstadt, Alexander Weissenhorn, 1545), sig. h3ᵛ.

36 In *Catalogus brevis eorum quae contra novas sectas scripsit Ioannes Cochlaeus* (Mainz: Franz Behem, 1549), sig. B7ᵛ.

37 See in particular *Philippica VII*, in *Philippicae I–VII*, ed. Keen, vol. 1, 329–75.

38 The appendices to the *Historia Hussitarum* (Mainz, Franz Behem, 1549) and to the edition of Conradus Brunus (Konrad Braun), *De Seditionibus libri sex* (Mainz: Franz Behem, 1550) consist of responses to Melanchthon's, Osiander's, and Calvin's objections to the Interim.

39 *De Interim brevis responsio Ioan. Cochlaei, ad prolixum & Calumniarum librum Ioannis Caluini* (Mainz: Franz Behem, 1549).

40 In *Causa religionis Miscellaneorum libri tres* (Ingolstadt, Alexander Weissenhorn, 1545); *Historia Hussitarum libri duodecim* (Mainz, Franz Behem, 1549); *Commentaria Joannis Cochlaeus, De Actis et Scriptis Martini Lutheri Saxonis* (Mainz: Franz Behem, 1549).

41 *Catalogus brevis eorum quae contra novas sectas scripsit Ioannes Cochlaeus* (Mainz, Franz Behem, 1549); the missing works are listed at sigs B5–5ᵛ.

42 For the stages of composition see Adolf Herte, *Die Lutherkommentare des Johannes Cochläus: Kritische Studie zur Geschichtsschreibung im Zeitalter der Glaubensspaltung*, Reformationsgeschichtliche Studien und Texte, vol. 33 (Münster, Aschendorff, 1535) 3–14.

43 Cochlaeus to Cervini, Regensburg, 4 July 1546, Friedensburg, 614.

44 Cochlaeus to Farnese, Wroclaw, 27 April 1550, Friedensburg, 632.

45 See Adolf Herte, *Das katholische Lutherbild im Bann der Lutherkommentare des Cochläus*, 3 vols (Münster, 1943).

46 Functionally and formally, heresiography is the antithesis of hagiography.

47 *Hystoria Alberti Krantz von den alten hussen zu Behemen in Keiser Sigmunds zeiten* (Strasbourg, Grieninger, 1523); *Historia Hussitarum libri duodecim* (Mainz, Franz

Behem, 1549), with numerous Patristic hagiographies in between. One notices also his unpublished work *'Excerptum Historiae de sex primis annis Lutheri'* (mentioned in *Catalogus brevis*, sig. B5ᵛ): is this material about Luther's childhood that was not included in the *Commentary* or merely a duplication of biographical matter already included here? We will never know.

48 The elevation of Luther's stature is not unique to Cochlaeus; Melanchthon does the same when praising Luther in his funeral oration for him. On these and other treatments of the Reformer, see Herbert Immenkötter, 'Von Engeln und Teufeln: Über Luther-Biographien des 16. Jahrhunderts', in *Biographie und Autobiographie in der Renaissance*, ed. August Buck, Wolfenbütteler Abhandlungen zur Renaissanceforschung, vol. 4 (Wiesbaden, 1983), 91–102.

49 *'De ratione scribendi historians'* is the running title given to *'Ad universos pios et catholicos, sacrarum historiarum studiosos'*, *Commentary*, sigs b*3ᵛ-c♣1ᵛ.

50 Braun's major works are *De Ceremoniis libri sex* (Mainz, Franz Behem, 1548), *De Imaginibus* (Mainz, Franz Behem, 1548), *Libri Sex de haereticis in genere* (Mainz: Franz Behem, 1549), and *De seditionibus libri sex* (Mainz, Franz Behem, 1550); excerpts from these were published separately, and three shorter works appeared as *Opera Tria* (Mainz, Franz Behem, 1548). Cochlaeus's role in the publication of these is indicated by prefatory letters and other front- and back-matter. For Braun's career in general, see Maria Barbara Rössner, *Konrad Braun (ca. 1495–1563): ein katholischer Jurist, Politiker, Kontroverstheologe und Kirchenreformer im konfessionellen Zeitalter*, Reformationsgeschichtliche Studien und Texte, 130 (Münster, 1991).

51 Braun, in *Commentary*, sig. b*4.

52 Braun, in *Commentary*, sigs b*4ᵛ–5.

53 Braun, in *Commentary*, sig. c♣1.

54 Cochlaeus's *Historiae Hussitarum libri duodecim* (Mainz Franz Behem, 1549) was in fact the largest of the massive works by Cochlaeus and Braun issued by Behem's press in these years.

55 To see this strategy articulated in one work of this period, published as an appendix to the *History of the Hussites*, see Ralph Keen, 'The Arguments and Audiences of Cochlaeus's *Philippica VII*, *Catholic Historical Review*, 78 (1992), 371–94.

56 Cochlaeus to Ercole d'Este, in *Commentary*, sigs a♣2–2ᵛ. The Ferarra doctorate is reproduced on the following page, sig. a♣3.

57 The Edict appears at *Commentary*, sigs, Ee2–8.

58 That Cochlaeus still felt the Edict needed to be implemented is reflected in hortatory remarks he makes about Catholic princes' duties to their faith, in *Commentary*, sigs ♣3–4, the last of the prefatory documents.

59 Moreover, as an appendix to the *Commentary* Cochlaeus reproduces Luther's own listing of his works through 1528 (sigs Dd5–Ee1ᵛ). The resemblance to his own 1548 *Catalogus brevis* is striking.

Notes to Chapter 4, The deeds and writings of Dr Martin Luther

1 On Luther's family background see Ian Siggins, *Luther and His Mother* (Philadelphia 1981); Martin Brecht, *Martin Luther: His Road to Reformation 1483–1521*, tr. J. L. Schaaf (Philadelphia 1985), 1–21. For background and details of the entire course of Luther's life, Brecht's three-volume biography is the most useful supplement, and sometimes a necessary corrective, to Cochlaeus's depiction of the Reformer's work.

2 St Martin of Tours (*c*.316–97).

3 Translator's note: literally, 'I am not, I am not'.

4 Translator's note: *Missa Angularis*, a direct translation of the German *Winckelmesse*.

5 For the founding and early history of the University of Wittenberg see Maria Grossmann, *Humanism in Wittenberg* (Nieuwkoop, 1975).

6 Translator's note: *Ordinaria Lectio.*

7 For the Heidelberg Disputation see *LW*, vol. 31, 39–70.

8 Translator's note: *Magnus* and *Maximus*, respectively.

9 Albert of Brandenburg (1490–1545) became Archbishop of Magdeburg in 1513 and a cardinal five years later. He was a leading agent for the sale of indulgences in Germany.

10 Johann von Staupitz (1460–1525) was vicar general of Luther's order and dean of the Wittenberg theology faculty. He was Luther's most influential counselor, both pastorally and theologically. See David Steinmetz, *Luther and Staupitz* (Durham, NC, 1980).

11 Justus Jonas (1493–1555) was dean of the theological faculty at Wittenberg 1523–33; he lectured on a number of biblical books and translated numerous treatises by Luther and Melanchthon. See Martin Lehmann, *Justus Jonas: Loyal Reformer* (Minneapolis, 1964)

12 Andreas Bodenstein von Karlstadt (1486–1541) was trained in both theology and law and served as theological dean at Wittenberg; after 1523 he took up a pastoral position and moved toward a more radical social theology than his student Luther. See Ronald Sider, *Andreas Bodenstein von Karlstadt: The Development of his Thought, 1517–1525* (Leiden, 1974).

13 From a letter that Luther added to the 95 Theses; see *LW*, vol. 48, 46–7.

14 From a letter that Luther added to the 95 Theses; see *LW*, vol. 48, 46–7.

15 Johann Tetzel (1465–1519) was a Leipzig BA with a Frankfurt (Oder) doctorate, and a member of the Dominican order, who preached indulgences from 1504 onward; his 1517 campaign, in the service of Albert of Brandenburg, Archbishop of Mainz, aroused Luther's ire and precipitated the attack, in the 95 Theses, on the medieval system of works.

16 Found at *LW*, vol. 31, 83–252.

17 This passage from Luther's letter to Pope Leo X is found at *WA*, vol. 1, 529 (Clemen vol. 1, 21).

18 Translator's note: or perhaps, 'he desired to keep the judgment of his superiors safe'; the phrase '*superiorum suorum iudicium in omnibus volebat habere salvum*' is ambiguous.

19 Luther, *Proceedings at Augsburg*, *LW*, vol. 31, 263.

20 *Proceedings at Augsburg*, *LW*, vol. 31, 263–4.

21 Luther's letter to Cardinal Cajetan is found at *LW*, vol. 48, 87–9.

22 The 'bride' is the Roman Church and the 'groom' Christ.

23 Luther, *Proceedings at Augsburg*, *LW*, vol. 31, 259–60.

24 See the dedication of Luther's *1519 Lectures on Galatians*, *LW*, vol. 27, 157.

25 Luther, *Letter to Pope Leo X* (1520), *WA*, vol. 7, 7–8 (German); 46 (Latin); *LW*, vol. 31: 339; the letter appears as an introduction to Luther's *Freedom of a Christian*.

26 Luther, *Proceedings at Augsburg*, *LW*, vol. 31, 276.

27 Luther, *Proceedings at Augsburg*, *LW*, vol. 31, 277.

28 Luther's letter to Cardinal Cajetan, dated Augsburg, 17 October 1518, is found at *WA*, Briefwechsel, vol. 1, 220–1; the quotation is on p. 221.

29 Eck (1486–1543) was trained at Heidelberg, Tübingen, Freiburg (ThD, 1510), and Ingolstadt, where he taught from 1510 on. He was an accompished logician and the author of a number of influential textbooks; after the outbreak of the Reformation he became one of the most able adversaries of Luther, known for his *Enchiridion* (1525) and numerous other defenses of Romanist theology.

30 On the Leipzig Debate see Brecht, *Road*, 299–348.

31 See Luther's *Disputation and Defense against the Accusations of Dr Johann Eck* (1519), *LW*, vol. 31, 313.

32 Translator's note: 'Lion', *leo*, is a pun on the pope's name here. The phrase could also be translated 'would surely leave Eck dead and Leo prostrate'.

33 Luther, *Letter to Spalatin concerning the Leipzig Debate* (1519), *LW*, vol. 31, 316.

34 Luther, *Disputatio et excusatio, WA*, vol. 2, 160. Translator's note: the word translated 'old men' is *pappos*, 'dolls' is *puppas*. Both are puns on *Papa*, 'Pope'.

35 See Luther, *Letter concerning the Leipzig Debate* (1519), *LW*, vol. 31, 324. The sermon is found at *LW*, vol. 51, 54–60.

36 *Disputatio Iohannis Eccii et Martini Lutheri Lipsiae habita* (1519), *WA*, vol. 2, 275–6.

37 *Disputatio, WA*, vol. 2, 324.

38 This letter is found at *LW*, vol. 31, 319–25.

39 Luther, *Letter concerning the Leipzig Debate, LW*, vol. 31: 325.

40 Luther, *Resolutiones Lutherianae super propositionibus suis Lipsiae disputatis* (1519), *WA*, vol. 2: 392–3.

41 *A Certain ... Goat-Horned.* For background see *LW*, vol. 39, 107–10; the *Venatio* (hunt) has not been translated. Emser's original work is *A venatione Luteriana Aegocerotis assertio* (Leipzig, M. Landsberg, 1520).

42 Translator's note: or 'that mighty Capricorn'; it is possible that Cochlaeus intends *Capricornus*, which literally means 'goat-horned', to refer to the sign of the zodiac as well.

43 Translator's note: *Chirographum.*

44 Luther, *Letter to Pope Leo X* (1520), *WA*, vol. 7: 9 (German); 47 (Latin); *LW*, vol. 31, 340–1.

45 Luther's letter to Charles V is found at *LW*, vol. 48, 177–9.

46 Luther, *Erbieten (oblatio sive protestatio)* (1520), *WA*, vol. 6, 482–3.

47 The *Address to the Christian Nobility of the German Nation, LW*, vol. 44, 123–217.

48 Cf. *Address*, 158.

49 *Annatae*, annates.

50 Translator's note: the translation preserves the ungrammatical structure of the original sentence, which has no main verb.

51 Luther, *Why the Books of the Pope and His Disciples Were Burned* (1520), *LW*, vol. 31, 392.

52 Translator's note: *Summa summarum*, literally 'sum of sums'.

53 Luther, *Why the Books ... Were Burned, LW*, vol. 31, 392–3.

54 Translator's note: or perhaps 'their superiors'.

55 Ambrosius Catharinus Politus, *Excusatio disputationis contra Martinum Lutherum* (Florence: Philippus Junta, 1521).

56 Luther's letter to the reader at the end of *Prierias's Epitoma Responsionis ad Martinum Lutherum* (1520), *WA*, vol. 6, 347.

57 Luther, *Responsio Lutheriana ad Condemnationem Doctrinalem* (1520), *WA*, vol. 6, 181–3, abridged.

58 Luther, *Von den newen Eckischen Bullen und lugen* (1520), *WA*, vol. 6, 579.

59 Luther, *Von dem Bapstum zu Rome widder den hochberumpten Romanisten zu Leiptzick* (1520), *WA*, vol. 6, 285.

60 Translator's note: the text's *patentes* may be a misprint for *patientes*, meaning 'enduring' or 'patient', which would give better sense here.

61 Luther, *Babylonian Captivity of the Church* (1520), *LW*, vol. 36, 24.

62 Luther, *Babylonian Captivity*, *LW*, vol. 36, 125–6.

63 Luther, *Babylonian Captivity*, *LW*, vol. 36, 126.

64 Luther, *Adversus execrabilem antichristi bullam* (1520), *WA*, vol. 6: 598.

65 Luther, *Adversus … bullam*, *WA*, vol. 6, 603.

66 Luther, *Adversus … bullam*, *WA*, vol. 6, 603.

67 Luther, *Adversus … bullam*, *WA*, vol. 6, 606.

68 Luther, *Grund und Ursach aller Artickeln D. Martin Luthers, so durch römische Bulle unrechtlich verdammt sind* (1521), *WA*, vol. 7, 299–457.

69 Luther, *Grund und Ursach*, *WA*, vol. 7, 309.

70 Luther, *Grund und Ursach*, *WA*, vol. 7, 313.

71 Luther, *Assertio omnium articulorum M. Lutheri per bullam Leonis X. novissimam damnatorum* (1520), *WA*, vol. 7, 94–151.

72 Luther, *An dn christlichen Adel deutscher Nation von des Christlichen Standes Besserung* (1520), *WA*, vol. 6, 404–69; *LW*, vol. 44, 123–216.

73 This work by Aleandro does not appear to have been printed; Cochlaeus may have known about or had access to a manuscript copy.

74 Translator's note: *erroneus* normally means erroneous or wandering; it *can* mean heretical or sinful.

75 The cap may be a humble garment, and thus appropriate as a sign of humility or penitence, or a reference to the traditional headwear of those undertaking lengthy pilgrimages.

76 Translator's note: 'Da Da', nonsense syllables representing meaningless babble.

77 Translator's note: 'From the Vessel': this translation assumes the reading a sino (two words), rather than – as printed – asino (one word, meaning a fool or dolt), which is syntactically meaningless here.

78 Translator's note: or, 'Here I am'.

79 *Luther at the Diet of Worms* (1521), *LW*, vol. 32, 106.

80 *Luther at Worms*, *LW*, vol. 32, 106.

81 *Luther at Worms*, *LW*, vol. 32, 107.

82 *Luther at Worms*, *LW*, vol. 32, 107.

83 *Luther at Worms*, *LW*, vol. 32, 108.

84 *Luther at Worms*, *LW*, vol. 32, 108.

85 Translator's note: literally, 'horned'.

86 Translator's note: i.e., neither sophistical nor elaborate?

87 Printed in German in the original.

88 *Luther at Worms*, *LW*, vol. 32, 112–13.

89 *Luther at Worms*, *LW*, vol. 32, 113.

90 See *Luther at Worms*, *LW*, vol. 32, 114–15, n. 9.

91 Translator's note: i.e. a stumbling block or cause for scandal.

92 See *Luther at Worms*, *LW*, vol. 32, 117–18.

93 A very different description of Cochlaeus's visit to Luther is found in *Luther at Worms*, *LW*, vol. 32, 120.

94 Capito (1478–1541) was educated at Freiburg and Basel and was a promising humanist who shifted theological allegiance from Erasmus to Luther in 1522. He

later became a colleague of Martin Bucer and helped bring the Reformation to Strasbourg. See James Kittelson, *Wolfgang Capito: From Humanist to Reformer* (Leiden 1975).

95 Cochlaeus, *Colloquium Cochlaei cum Luthero Wormatiae olim habitum* (1521, not published until 1540); in Otto Clemen, ed., *Flugschriften aus den ersten Jahren der Reformation*, vol. 4 (Leipzig, 1911), 192–208.

96 *Luther at Worms, LW*, vol. 32, 120–1.

97 *Luther at Worms, LW*, vol. 32, 121.

98 *Luther at Worms, LW*, vol. 32, 121–2.

99 *Luther at Worms, LW*, vol. 32, 122.

100 *Luther at Worms, LW*, vol. 32, 120.

101 *Luther at Worms, LW*, vol. 32, 122.

102 *Luther at Worms, LW*, vol. 32, 123.

103 *Luther at Worms, LW*, vol. 32, 122.

104 Translator's note: correctly, '26 April'.

105 Luther, *Von der Beicht, ob die der Bapst macht habe zu gepieten* (1521), *WA*, vol. 8, 138–85.

106 Luther, *Von der beicht, WA*, vol. 8, 138–40.

107 Luther, *Against Latomus, LW*, vol. 32, 139.

108 Luther, *Against Latomus, LW*, vol. 32, 257–8.

109 Luther, *Against Latomus, LW*, vol. 32, 259.

110 Translator's note: *homoousion.*

111 Translator's note: *hypostasis.*

112 Luther, *De abroganda missa privata Martini Lutheri sententia* (1522), *WA*, vol. 8, 411–76.

113 Translator's note: again, the word is *leo*, the Pope's name.

114 The preface is not in *LW*, but can be found at *WA*, vol. 8, 573–6; the statement about his sixteen years as a monk is on 573.

115 Luther, terrified by a nearby lightning strike, had vowed to St Anne that he would become a monk if she interceded and preserved his life.

116 Preface to *De votis monasticis* (1521), *WA*, vol. 8, 576.

117 The Parisians' condemnation, with Luther's judgment of it and Melanchthon's defense of Luther, is found in *WA*, vol. 8, 267–312.

118 Melanchthon, *Adversus furiosum Parisiensium Theologastrorum decretum Philippi Melanchthonis pro Luthero apologia*, StA, vol. 1, 142–62; tr. C. L. Hill in *Melanchthon: Selected Writings* (Westport 1978), 69–87.

119 Luther, *Eyn Urtheyl der Theologen zu Pariss vber die Lehre Dr Luthers. Eyn Gegen Urtheyl Dr Luthers. Schuczrede Philippi Melanchthon wider das selbe Parisische Urtheyl für D.Luther* (Wittenberg: Johann Grunenberg, 1521), *WA*, vol. 8: 292.

120 OED: In early academic costume, the long tail of the graduate's hood.

121 From *Determinatio theologicae facultatis Parisien. super doctrina Lutheriana hactenus per eam visa* (Wittenberg, 1521); see *WA*, vol. 8, 261 for other editions.

122 Published as Henry VIII, *Assertio septem sacramentorum*, ed. Pierre Fraenkel, *Corpus Catholicorum*, 43 (Münster 1992).

123 Henry VIII, *Assertio*, 122.

124 Henry VIII, *Assertio*, 150.

125 Luther, sermon for 9 March 1522, *WA*, vol. 10/3, 9–10.

126 Luther, sermon for 13 March 1522, in *Eight Sermons at Wittenberg, LW*, vol. 51, 90.

127 Luther, *Bulla coenae domini* (1522), *WA*, vol. 8, 691. Translator's note: perhaps a vulgar usage of these two verbs – *crepo* and *frango* – since the first is cognate with *crepitibus* used later to mean 'winds from the belly'.

128 Luther, *Bulla*, *WA*, vol. 8: 704.

129 Luther, *Bulla*, *WA*, vol. 8: 708–9.

130 Luther, *Contra Henricum regem Angliae* (1522), *WA*, vol. 10/2: 214–15.

131 Cf. Luther, *Contra Henricum*, *WA*, vol. 10/2, 219.

132 Luther, *Contra Henricum*, *WA*, vol. 10/2, 220.

133 Luther, *Contra Henricum*, *WA*, vol. 10/2, 180.

134 Luther, *Contra Henricum*, *WA*, vol. 10/2, 188.

135 Luther, *Contra Henricum*, *WA*, vol. 10/2, 188.

136 Luther, *Antwort deutsch auf König Heinrichs Buch* (1522), *WA*, vol. 10/2, 232.

137 Luther, *Antwort deutsch auf König Heinrichs Buch* (1522), *WA*, vol. 10/2, 262.

138 Translator's note: Ecclesiastes.

139 Luther, *Against the Spiritual Estate of the Pope and the Bishops Falsely So Called*, *LW*, vol. 39, 248–9.

140 Translator's note: perhaps a play on insects: 'larvae et pupae'.

141 Luther, *Against the Spiritual Estate*, *LW*, vol. 39, 252–3.

142 Luther, *Against the Spiritual Estate*, *LW*, vol. 39, 278.

143 Of the New Testament in German, the so-called 'September Bible'. Henry's bishops and agents would aggressively suppress William Tyndale's English translation.

144 Translator's note: there's a non-translatable play on words here: *versio* (translation); *vertendo* (twisting); *pervertat* (pervert).

145 From Henry VIII, *Serenissimi ac potentissime regis Anglie, Christiane fidei defensoris inuictissimi, ad illustrissimos ac clarissimos Saxoniae principes, de coercenda abigendaque Lutherana factione, & Luthero ipso Epistola* (Leipzig, 1523).

146 Emser's translation, *Das naw Testament* (Leipzig, W. Stöckel, 1529 and numerous other editions), was in reality an adaptation of Luther's version. Emser's comments on the Reformer's translation are in *Annotationes Hieronymi Emseri vber Luthers Naw Testament gebessert vnd emendirt* (Leipzig: [Valentin Schumann], 1525, with numerous later editions).

147 Argula von Grumbach (*c.*1490–*c.*1564) was a vigorous defender of Reformation doctrines against attacks by theological faculties (Ingolstadt in particular) and dukes (William IV of Bavaria). See Peter Matheson, *Argula von Grumbach: A Woman's Voice in the Reformation* (Edinburgh, 1995).

148 Translator's note: there's a play on words here, since invehor, 'inveigh', can literally mean 'to ride out against'. Hence the 'cartfuls' of abuse.

149 Translator's note: there is a play on words here between brothers 'in Christ' (Christo) and 'in a moneychest' (cista).

150 Translator's note: this is a pun; 'genuinely' here translates *germane*, the adverb of *germanus*, German.

151 Luther's 'savage falsehoods' amounted to questioning the traditional attribution of these texts to their supposed apostolic authors, doubts that modern biblical scholars have corroborated. Only in the case of Revelation does Luther actually dismiss the book as unsuited to the NT canon.

152 Luther, *Prefaces to the New Testament*, *LW*, vol. 35, 357.

153 Luther, *Prefaces to the New Testament*, *LW*, vol. 35, 357.

154 Translator's note: again, 'genuine' translates *germanus*.

155 Luther, *Avoiding the Doctrines of Men* (1522), *LW*, vol. 35, 131–53.

156 Luther, *The Estate of Marriage* (1522), *LW*, vol. 45, 17–49.

157 Luther, *The Misuse of the Mass* (1521), *LW*, vol. 36, 133–230.

158 Translator's note: *titulo nominique* can mean 'pretext and pretence' as well as 'title and name;' both meanings are probably implied here.

159 Luther, *On Temporal Authority: To What Extent It Should Be Obeyed* (1523), *LW*, vol. 45, 112–14.

160 Luther, *On Temporal Authority*, *LW*, vol. 45, 116.

161 Johanne Eck, *Asseritur hic Invictissimi Angliae Regis liber de sacramentis, a calumniis & impietatibus Luderi* (Rome, Marcellus Franck, 1523).

162 Thomas Murner, *Ob der König us England ein Lügner sey oder der Luther* (Strasbourg: J. Grieninger, 1522); ed. W. Pfeffer-Belli (Berlin 1928).

163 Johann Dietenberger (*c.* 1475–1537) was a Dominican and defender of traditional practices against Luther. For life and bibliography see Hermann Wedewer, *Johannes Dietenberger 1475–1537: Sein Leben und Wirken* (Freiburg, 1888; rpt Nieuwkoop, 1967).

164 Translator's note: presumably Latin, Greek, and Hebrew.

165 John Fisher, *De veritate corporis et sanguinis Christi in Eucharistia* (Cologne, 1527).

166 John Fisher, *Assertionis Lutheranae confutatio* (n.p., 1523).

167 John Fisher, *Defensio Regie assertionis contra Babylonicam captiuitatem* (Cologne, 1525).

168 John Fisher, *Sacri sacerdotii defensio contra Lutherum* (Cologne, Peter Quentell, 15250; ed. Hermann Klein Schmeink, *Corpus Catholicorum*, vol. 9 (Münster, 1925).

169 The pseudonym used by Thomas More in his *Responsio ad Lutherum*.

170 Translator's note: Horace, *Ars Poetica*, 1.5.

171 More, *Responsio ad Lutherum*, ed. J. H. Headley (New Haven, 1969), 216–19.

172 Translator's note: *Bacchanalius*, follower of Bacchus, is a pun on *Baccalarius*, graduate; hence, 'Bachelor and Master of Bacchanalian studies'.

173 More, *Responsio*, 313–15.

174 More, *Responsio*, 681–3.

175 Translator's note: after a character in Terence's *Eunuch*, whose name became proverbial for a parasite.

176 More, *Responsio*, 685

177 Henry VIII, *Serenissimi ac potentissime regis Anglie, Christiane fidei defensoris inuictissimi, ad illustrissimos ac clarissimos Saxoniae principes, de coercenda abigendaque Lutherana factione, & Luthero ipso Epistola. Item illustrissimi Principis Ducus Georgii ad eundem Regem rescriptio* (Leipzig, 1523).

178 Henry VIII, *Epistola.*

179 Henry VIII, *Epistola.*

180 Henry VIII, *Epistola.*

181 Duke George's letter is included in the edition of Henry's letter; on Cochlaeus's copying of these documents see Herte, *Lutherkommentare*, 57–8, n. 22, and 61 n. 43.

182 Duke George, *Letter to Henry VIII*, in Henry, *Epistola.*

183 Duke George, *Letter to Henry VIII*, in Henry, *Epistola.*

184 Luther, Letter to Duke George of Saxony, Wittenberg, 3 January 1523; Cochlaeus seems to have been working from a manuscript, as it was not available in any printed book (Herte, *Lutherkommentare*, 35 n. 71); see also *WA*, vol. Briefwechsel 3: 4–5.

185 Johannes Faber (1487–1541) wrote the *Malleus in haeresim Lutheranam* in 1524; it was edited by Anton Naegele in 2 vols (Münster, 1941–52).

186 Translator's note: *fabris*, smiths, is a pun on Faber's name.
187 Luther, *Commentary on 1 Corinthians 7*, Preface, *LW*, vol. 28, 5–7.
188 Luther, *Commentary on 1 Corinthians 7*, *LW*, vol. 28, 16–17.
189 Luther, *Commentary*, *LW*, vol. 28, 17.
190 Translator's note: or 'a woman'.
191 Luther, *Commentary*, *LW*, vol. 28, 47–8.
192 *Eversio Lutherani Epithalmii* (Cologne, Peter Quentell, 1527).
193 Cochlaeus, *De gratia sacramentorum liber unus Joan. Cochlaei adversus assertionem Marti. Lutheri* (Strasbourg, Johann Grieninger, 1522); *De baptismo parvulorum liber unus Joan. Cochlaei. Adversus assertionem Mart. Lutheri* (Strasbourg: Johann Grieninger, 1523).
194 This poem may be found in Cochlaeus, *Adversus cucullatum Minotaurum Wittenbergensem. De gratia sacramentorum iterum* (1523), ed. J. Schweizer (Münster, 1920), 13. Translator's note: *Arma virumque cano, Mogoni qui nuper ab oris / Leucoteam, fato stolidus, Saxonaque venit / Littora, multum ille et furiis vexatus et oestro, / Vi scelerum, memorem rasorum cladis ob iram.* These lines are a very clever spoof of the opening of the *Aeneid*.
195 Cochlaeus, *Adversus Minotaurum*, 13. *Monstra bovemque cano, Boreae qui primus ab oris, / Teuthonicas terras profugus conspurcat, et omnem, / Sub specie monachi violat pacemque fidemque / Vi Sathanae, saevis furiis agitatus, et oestro / Dirae Thesiphones, ultrici Anathemate poenae / Exposcente, furit, mugitu vastus inani / Semiviri lacero sub semibovisque cucullo.* Tisiphone (Thesiphone) was one of the Furies.
196 Cochlaeus, *Adversus Minotaurum*, 50–51.
197 Luther, *Formula missae et communionis*, *WA*, vol. 12, 205; Clemen vol. 2, 427.
198 Luther, *Formula*, *WA*, vol. 12, 206; Clemen vol. 2, 428.
199 Josse Clichtove, *Propugnaculum Ecclesiae adversus Lutheranos* (Paris, S. de Colines, 1526).
200 Josse Clichtove, *Antilutherus ... libri tres* (Paris, S. de Colines, 1524).
201 Clichtove, *Propugnaculum Ecclesiae*, sigs a7–7ᵛ.
202 Clichtove, *Propugnaculum Ecclesiae*, sig. b1.
203 Clichtove, *Propugnaculum Ecclesiae*, sig. e3ᵛ.
204 Where the Israelites performed human sacrifice to idols (Jer. 19: 4).
205 Luther, *Formula*, *WA*, vol. 12, 220; Clemen 2, 440–1.
206 Luther, *Ursach und Antwort, daß Jungfrauen Klöster göttlich verlassen mögen* (1523), *WA*, vol. 11, 387–400; the biblical verse seems to be Cochlaeus's comment, as original editions lack it.
207 Addition by Cochlaeus.
208 Luther, *Ursach und Antwort*, *WA*, vol. 11, 394–5.
209 Translator's note: literally, 'a little work worth the cooking-pot'.
210 1 Tim. 5: 12.
211 Luther, *Resolutiones disputationum de indulgentiarum virtute* (1518), *WA*, vol. 1, 555–6; Clemen vol. 1, 54.
212 This is from a sermon by Luther on the Ten Commandments that Cochlaeus excerpted in his *Septiceps Lutherus* (Leipzig, Valentin Schumann, 1529); the passage quoted appears on sig. L4.
213 Luther, *The Adoration of the Sacrament*, *LW*, vol. 36, 275.
214 Luther, *The Adoration of the Sacrament*, *LW*, vol. 36, 291.
215 Luther, *The Adoration of the Sacrament*, *LW*, vol. 36, 300.
216 Luther, *The Adoration of the Sacrament*, *LW*, vol. 36, 300.

217 Luther, *The Adoration of the Sacrament*, *LW*, vol. 36, 304.

218 Luther, *Lectures on Galatians* (1519), *LW*, vol. 27, 391–2.

219 Luther, *Lectures on Galatians*, *LW*, vol. 36, 392.

220 Luther, *Concerning the Ministry*, *LW*, vol. 40, 8.

221 Luther, *Concerning the Ministry*, *LW*, vol. 40, 8–9.

222 Luther, *Concerning the Ministry*, *LW*, vol. 40, 11.

223 Luther, *Concerning the Ministry*, *LW*, vol. 40, 15–16.

224 Luther, *That a Christian Assembly or Congregation has the Right and Power to Judge All Teaching and to Call, Appoint, and Dismiss Teachers, Established and Proven by Scripture*, *LW*, vol. 39, 306.

225 Translator's note: presumably holy water.

226 Luther, *That a Christian Assembly*, *LW*, vol. 39, 306–07.

227 Luther, *That a Christian Assembly*, *LW*, vol. 39, 312–13.

228 See Luther, *Ordinance of a Common Chest* (1523), Preface, *LW*, vol. 45, 169–94.

229 Luther, *Wider die Verkehrer und Fälscher kaiserlichs Mandats* (1523), *WA*, vol. 12, 62–7.

230 Luther, *Wider den neuen Abgott und alten Teufel, der zu Meissen soll erhoben werden* (1523), *WA*, vol. 15, 183–98.

231 Luther, *Wider den neuen Abgott* (1524), *WA*, vol. 15, 187.

232 Emser's response to Luther is *Antwort auff das lesterliche buch wider Bischoff Benno* (Leipzig: Wolfgang Stöckel, 1524).

233 Luther, *Zwei Keyserliche uneynige und wydderwertige gepott den Luther betreffend* (1524), *WA*, vol. 15, 254–78.

234 Luther, *Zwei gepott*, *WA*, vol. 15, 254.

235 Luther, *Zwei gepott*, *WA*, vol. 15, 255.

236 Luther, *Zwei gepott*, *WA*, vol. 15, 255.

237 Luther, *Zwei gepott*, *WA*, vol. 15, 255.

238 Luther, *Zwei gepott*, *WA*, vol. 15, 277–8; Luther uses 'Christian' where Cochlaeus has 'Catholic'.

239 Luther, *Zwei gepott*, *WA*, vol. 15, 278.

240 *Articuli .cccc. Martini Lutheri. ex sermonibus eius sex & triginta* (Cologne, Peter Quentell, 1525).

241 Translator's note: literally, 'souls and humans'.

242 Charles V, *Das kayserl. Edict wider den Nürnbergishen Reichs Abschied, aus der Stadt Burgos in Castilien an die Stände des Reichs. Karl von Gots gnaden Römischer Kayser zu allen Zeiten Merer des Reichs. Burgos*, 15 July 1524. See Herte, *Lutherkommentare*, 69, n. 5.

243 Charles V, *Das kayserl. Edict*.

244 Caspar Tauber, in *Sententia lata contra Casparum Thauber ciuem Viennen. olim Lutheranae sectae imitatorem. Widerrueff etlicher verdambter yertung mit vrtayl vnd recht auffgelegt vnd erkant zu Wien in Oesterreych* (Vienna, 1524), sigs Av4-B1.

245 Luther, *Trade and Usury*, *LW*, vol. 45, 271–2.

246 Luther, *Eine Geschichte, wie Gott einer Klosterjungfrau ausgeholfen hat. Mit einen Sendbrief M. Luthers* (1524), *WA*, vol. 15, 86–88, with a postscript 89–94.

247 Luther's letter to the Counts of Mansfeld is in fact the body of *Eine Geschichte*, *WA*, vol. 15, 86–88

248 Luther, *Eine Geschichte*, *WA*, vol. 15, 88.

249 Luther, *To the Councilmen of All Cities in Germany, that They Establish and Maintain Christian Schools* (1524), *LW*, vol. 45, 348.

250 Luther, *To the Councilmen*, *LW*, vol. 45, 351–2.

251 Luther, *To the Councilmen*, *LW*, vol. 45, 252.

252 Luther, *To the Councilmen*, *LW*, vol. 45, 365–6.

253 Luther, *Exposition of Psalm 127, for the Christians at Riga in Livonia* (1524), *LW*, vol. 45, 319–20.

254 Luther, *The Burning of Brother Henry*, *LW*, vol. 32, 272.

255 *Missa de nuptiis Andreae Carolotadii, et sacerdotibus matrimonium contrahentibus* (Ausgsburg, Sigmund Grimm and Marx Wirsung, 1522).

256 On Karlstadt's career after leaving Wittenberg see George H. Williams, *The Radical Reformation*, 3rd edn (Kirksville, 1992), 109–20.

257 Luther, *Was sich Dr Andreas Bodenstein von Karlstadt mit Dr Martino Luther beredet zu Jena, und wie sie wider einander zu schreiben sich entschlossen haben* (1524), *WA*, vol. 15, 323–47.

258 Luther, *Against the Heavenly Prophets*, *LW*, vol. 40, 105.

259 Luther, *Against the Heavenly Prophets*, *LW*, vol. 40, 106.

260 Luther, *Against the Heavenly Prophets*, *LW*, vol. 40, 108–9.

261 Luther, *Letter to the Christians at Strassburg in Opposition to the Fanatic Spirit*, *LW*, vol. 40: 69.

262 Thomas Müntzer, *Ein gloubvirdig, vnd warhafftig vnderricht wie die Dhoringischen Pawern von Franckenhawsen vmb yhr misshandlung gestrafft, vnd beyde Stett, Franken-hawsen vnd Mollhawsen erobert worden* (Dresden, 1525).

263 For Cochlaeus's use of unpublished documents by Müntzer, see Herte, *Lutherkommentare*, 99.

264 Luther, *Eine schreckliche Geschichte und ein Gericht Gottes über Thomas Müntzer* (1525), *WA*, vol. 18: 367.

265 Luther, *A Sincere Admonition by Martin Luther to all Christians to Guard Against Insurrection and Rebellion* (1522), *LW*, vol. 45, 58.

266 Luther, *A Sincere Admonition*, *LW*, vol. 45, 67–8.

267 Luther, *Zwo Predigt auff die Epistel S. Pauli 1 Thess. 4. D. Martini Luther gethan vber der Leich des Chürfursten Hertzog Friderichs zu Sachsen* (1525), *WA*, vol. 17/1: 200.

268 Luther, *Admonition to Peace: A Reply to the Twelve Articles of the Peasants in Swabia* (1525), *LW*, vol. 46, 19.

269 Luther, *Admonition*, *LW*, vol. 46, 19.

270 Luther, *Admonition*, *LW*, vol. 46, 20.

271 Luther, *Against the Robbing and Murdering Hordes of Peasants* (1525), *LW*, vol. 46, 50.

272 Luther, *Against the … Peasants*, *LW*, vol. 46, 51–2.

273 Luther, *Against the … Peasants*, *LW*, vol. 46, 52.

274 Luther, *Against the … Peasants*, *LW*, vol. 46, 54.

275 Cochlaeus, *Wider die Reubischen und Mordischen rotten der Bawren die unter dem scheyn des heiligen Evangelions felschlichen wider alle Oberkeit sich setzen und empören Martinus Luther. Antwort Johannis Coclei von Wendelstein* (Cologne, Peter Quentell, 1525).

276 Luther, *An Open Letter on the Harsh Book against the Peasants* (1525), *LW*, vol. 46, 66.

277 Luther, *An Open Letter*, *LW*, vol. 46, 84–5.

278 Cochlaeus, *De Petro et Roma adversus Velenum Lutheranum* (Cologne, Peter Quentell, 1525); *Articuli CCCCC Martini Lutheri ex sermonibus eius sex et triginta* (Cologne,

Peter Quentell, 1525); *Wider die Reubischen und Mordischen rotten der Bawren ...
Antwort Johannis Coclei von Wendelstein* (Cologne, Peter Quentell, 1525); *Adversus
latrocinantes et raptorias cohortes rusticorum Mar. Lutherus Responsio Johannis Cochlaei
Wendelstini. Cathalogus tumultuum et praeliorum in superiori Germania nuper gestorum*
(Cologne, Peter Quentell, 1525).

279   Translator's note: Io, Io, Io, Io!

280   Hieronymus Emser, *Epithalamia Martini Lutheri Vuittenbergensis, Ioannis Hessi Vratislauiensis, ac id genus nuptiatorum* (n.p., 1525).

281   Andreas Krzycki (Critias), *Eucomia lutheri. Andree Cricij Episcopi Premislien. in
Lutherum Oratio. In imaginem eiusdem Lutheri. Conditiones boni Lutherani. Ingressus
Lutheri in Vuormatiam. Decij philomusi ac aliorum in Polonia varia de eodem Lutero
Epigrammata* (Cracow, 1524).

282   These poems are all from Krzycki's *Eucomia lutheri.*

283   Tomasso Radini (1488–1527), author of a notable oration against the Lutherans
(*In Martinum Lutherum ... Oratio* [Leipzig, Lotter, 1520]), to which Melanchthon
replied in his 1521 *Didymi Faventini adversus Thomam Placentinum pro Martino
Luthero theologo oratio* (1521), StA, vol. 1, 56–140. In response Radini issued *In
Philippum Melanchthonem Lutheranae haereseos defensorem oratio* (Rome, 1522; ed.
Giuseppe Berti, *Orazione contro Filippo Melantone* [Brescia, Paideia, 1973]).

284   Luther, *The Abomination of the Secret Mass* (1525), *LW*, vol. 36, 311.

285   Luther, *Abomination, LW*, vol. 36, 313.

286   Luther, *Vom Grevel der Stillmesse* (1524), *WA*, vol. 18, 25.

287   Luther, *Vom Grevel der Stillmesse, WA*, vol. 18, 25.

288   See Hieronymus Emser, *Missae Christianorum contra Luteranan missandi formulam
assertio* (Dresden, Emser, 1524); *Canonis missae contra Huldricum Zuinglium defensio*
(Strasbourg, Gruninger, 1524); *Hieronymi Emseri Praesbyteri Apologeticon in Vldrici
Zuinglij antibolon* (Dresden, Emser, 1525); *Wyder der ztweier Pröbst zu Nirmberg
Falschen grund und ursachen* (Dresden, Emser, 1525), ed. T. Freudenberger, Corpus
Catholicorum, 28 (Münster, 1959), 112–47.

289   These lines by Johannes Witz, known as Sapidus, seem not to have survived in
any other form.

290   This adaptation by Arnold Haldrein, known as Weselius or Besalius from his
home town of Wesel, also seems not to have survived. Cochlaeus knew him
personally and may have had a manuscript.

291   Johann Bugenhagen, *Epistola ad Anglos* (n.p., 1525).

292   Cochlaeus, *Responsio ad Johannem Bugenhagium Pomeranum*, ed. Ralph Keen (Nieuwkoop, 1988).

293   Luther, Letter to Duke Charles III of Savoy, Wittenberg, 7 September 1523
(Zurich 1524), *WA*, vol. Briefwechsel vol. 3, 150.

294   For background see Walter Friedensburg, *Der Reichstag zu Speier 1526* (Berlin,
1887, rpt Nieuwkoop, 1970).

295   Luther, Ein *Sendbrieff Dr Martini Luthers, an Hertzog Georg zu Sachssen, Landgraff
in Döringen, vnd Marggraffe zu Meichssen, darin er in freüntlich ermant, zu dem wort
Gottes zu tretten. Ein Antwort Hertzog Georgen zu Sachssen, Landgraff in Döringen,
Marggraff zu Meichssen, an Do. Marti* (Nuremberg, 1526).

296   Duke George's letter is printed after Luther's in *Ein Sendbrieff.*

297   Luther, *Sendschreiben an den Erzbischof Albrecht von Mainz und Magdeburg, sich in
den ehelich Stand zu begeben* (1525), *WA*, vol. 18, 408–10. Cochlaeus's quotation
comprises all but the last two paragraphs of this letter.

298 Luther's letter to Henry VIII of England, dated Wittenberg, 1 September 1525, is in *Literarum, quibus invictissimus princeps Henricus VIII. Rex Angliae, & Franciae, dominus Hyberniae, ac fidei defensor respondit ad quandam epistolam Martini Lutheri ad se missam, & ipsius lutheranae quoque epistolae exemplum* (n.p., 1526), sigs a3–4ᵛ.

299 See Rupert of Deutz, *De Victoria verbi Dei*, ed. Hraban Haacke (Weimar, 1970).

300 Rupert of Deutz, *Commentariorum, in Evangelium Iohannis libri XIIII* (Cologne: Franz Birckmann, 1526); *Commentariorum in Ioannis Apocalypsin, libri XII* (Nuremberg: Johann Petreius, 1526); *De divinis officiis libri XII* (Cologne: Franz Birckmann, 1526).

301 See Rupert of Deutz, *De sancta Trinitate et operibus eius*, ed. Hraban Haacke (Turnholt, 1971–2).

302 Luther's letter to Henry, with a translation, is available at Cochlaeus, *Responsio ad Johannem Bugenhagium Pomeranum*, 166–71.

303 Henry, in *Literarum*, sigs b2–b2ᵛ.

304 Henry, in *Literarum*, sigs b3–3ᵛ.

305 Henry, in *Literarum*, sigs c1–1ᵛ.

306 Henry, in *Literarum*, sigs f2–3.

307 From the anonymous prologue to *Literarum*, sigs a2–2ᵛ.

308 From *Epistola Martini Lutheri, Ad illustrisimum principem ac dominum Henricum ... Admonitio Johannis Cochlaei in utranque epistolam* (Cologne: Peter Quentell, 1525).

309 Translator's note: literally, 'you Cacuses'. Cacus was a giant son of Vulcan, the god of the forge and of volcanoes.

310 Cochlaeus, *Responsio*, 61–3.

311 Erasmus, *A Discussion of Free Will* (1525), *Collected Works of Erasmus*, (Toronto, 1947), hereafter *CWE*, vol. 76, 6–7.

312 Erasmus, *A Discussion of Free Will*, *CWE*, vol. 76, 14–15.

313 Erasmus, *A Discussion of Free Will*, *CWE*, vol. 76, 16–17.

314 Translator's note: or, 'the Evangelical spirit'.

315 Erasmus, *A Discussion of Free Will*, *CWE*, vol. 76, 18–19.

316 Luther, *Bondage of the Will* (1525), *LW*, vol. 33, 15–16.

317 Luther, *Bondage of the Will*, *LW*, vol. 33, 23–4.

318 Translator's note: this statement is in German; 'das ist zu viel'.

319 Luther, *Bondage of the Will*, *LW*, vol. 33, 29.

320 Erasmus, *Hyperaspistes diatribae adversus servum arbitrium Martini Lutheri*, in *Ausgewählte Schriften*, hereafter *AS*, vol. 4, 198; *CWE*, vol. 76, 93.

321 Translator's note: literally, 'to consume a considerable portion of my water', perhaps a reference to the water-clock used to time speeches in Athenian courts.

322 Erasmus, *Hyperaspistes, AS*, vol. 4, 202–4; *CWE*, vol. 76, 97–8.

323 Translator's note: the marginal note says the person meant here is Wilhelm Nesen.

324 Translator's note: characters from Terence.

325 Erasmus, *Hyperaspistes, AS*, vol. 4, 204–8; *CWE*, vol. 76, 99–100.

326 Erasmus, *Hyperaspistes, AS*, vol. 4, 228; *CWE*, vol. 76, 108.

327 Erasmus, *Hyperaspistes, AS*, vol. 4, 240; *CWE*, vol. 76, 114.

328 Erasmus, *Hyperaspistes, AS*, vol. 4, 264–6; *CWE*, vol. 76, 125.

329 Erasmus, *Hyperaspistes, AS*, vol. 4, 672–4; *CWE*, vol. 76, 296–7.

330 Translator's note: *Verbum Domini Manet In Aeternum*.

331 This is the sermon on Luke 19 for 13 August 1525; *WA*, vol. 17/1, 380–99.

332 This is from G. Schatzmeister, *Getrew Ermanung, So etlich christlich personen, auff*

yetz gehalten Reychstag zu Speyer den Fursten Teutschs Landts zugeschriben haben (n.p., 1526). Schatzmeister indeed seems to be a pseudonym.

333   Luther, Sermon for 13 August 1525, *WA*, vol. 17/1, 387–8.

334   Luther, Sermon for 13 August 1525, *WA*, vol. 17/1, 390–1.

335   On Cochlaeus's knowledge of the Baden Disputation see Herte, *Lutherkommentare*, 180–83; on the disputation in general, see Leonhard von Muralt, *Die Badener Disputation 1526*, Quellen und Abhandlungen zur Schweizerischen Reformationsgeschichte, vol. 6 (Leipzig, 1926).

336   This work by Thomas Murner does not seem to have survived.

337   In *Eyn Sendbrieff Martin Luthers, an den Konig zu Engelland Heynrichen dis namens den achten ...* (Zwickau, Gabriel Kantz, 1527).

338   Translator's note: *Suermeros*, Luther's 'swarmers'.

339   Translator's note: according to the marginalia, *Trotz* is a syllable expressing contempt.

340   Luther, *Auf des Königs zu England Lästerschrift Titel Martin Luthers Antwort* (1527), *WA*, vol. 23, 26–7.

341   Luther, *Auf des Königs Lästerschrift Antwort*, *WA*, vol. 23, 27.

342   Luther, *Auf des Königs Lästerschrift Antwort*, *WA*, vol. 23, 29.

343   Translator's note: the word for bubbles is *bullae*, a pun on Papal bulls.

344   Luther, *Auf des Königs Lästerschrift Antwort*, *WA*, vol. 23, 34.

345   Luther, *Auf des Königs Lästerschrift Antwort*, *WA*, vol. 23, 34

346   Luther, *Auf des Königs Lästerschrift Antwort*, *WA*, vol. 23, 35.

347   The 'Responsio Lutheri contra Regis epistolam, cum eiusdem Johannis Coclaei annotationibus', as well as a 'Brevis discussio responsionis Lutheri', are in the edition of *Epistola Martini Lutheri ...* (Cologne, Peter Quentell, 1527).

348   Luther, *Auf des Königs Lästerschrift Antwort*, *WA*, vol. 23, 31–2.

349   From Cochlaeus's contribution to *Epistola Martini Lutheri* (Cologne, Peter Quentell, 1527).

350   Translator's note: the famous oracle of Zeus, whose prophecies were given by the rustling leaves of the oak trees.

351   Erasmus, *Hyperaspistes II*, in *Desiderii Erasmi Opera Omnia*, ed. Joannes Clericus (Leiden 1706; rpt Hildesheim, 1962), vol. 10, col. 1422.

352   Erasmus, *Hyperaspistes II*, *Opera Omnia*, vol. 10, 1424.

353   Erasmus, *Hyperaspistes II*, *Opera Omnia*, vol. 10, 1482.

354   Erasmus, *Hyperaspistes II*, *Opera Omnia*, vol. 10, 1483–4.

355   From Duke George's preface to *Das New Testament, so durch L. Emser saligen verteuscht, vnd des Durchlewchten Hochgebornen Furstenn herren Georgen hertzogen zu Sachssen* (Leipzig, 1528).

356   Cochlaeus, *Auff Martin Luthers Schandbüchlin, An die Christen von Halle geschriben, Antwort Jo. Cocleus Dr* (n.p., 1528).

357   Translator's note: the Latin literally says 'the Leonine city, which is called the Burg'. It is clear from the context that this means Vatican City.

358   Translator's note: *Landknecht*.

359   Translator's note: 'Valid or pleasing': *ratum aut gratum*.

360   Translator's note: or perhaps 'to great acclaim'.

361   Translator's note: literally, 'was lying under a bench'.

362   Luther, *That These Words of Christ, 'This Is My Body', etc., Still Stand Firm against the Fanatics* (1527), *LW*, vol. 37, 15–16.

363   Luther, *That These Words ... Still Stand*, *LW*, vol. 37, 19.

364 Luther, *That These Words ... Still Stand, LW*, vol. 37, 67–8.

365 Translator's note: this takes *adversabantur ei* as meaning they were opposed to *him*, i.e. Luther. But it could also mean 'they were opposed to *it*', i.e. the Sacrament.

366 Cochlaeus seems to be quoting an unpublished speech; on his knowledge of Kautz, see Herte, *Lutherkommentare*, 199–203.

367 Jacob Kautz, *Syben Artickel zu Wormbs von Jacob Kautzen angeschlagen vnnd gepredigt* (n.p., 1527), sig. a2ᵛ.

368 Kautz, *Syben Artickel*, sigs a2ᵛ–3.

369 Cochlaeus's *Antwort D. Johannis Cochlei vff die diben zwyspaltigen artickeln der predicanten zu Wormbs* is printed as an appendix to Kautz's *Syben Artickel*; the passage quoted appears on sigs c1ᵛ–2.

370 Cochlaeus's address to the Senate of Worms is found in *Syben Artickel*; the passage quotes appears on sigs b3ᵛ–4.

371 This is from the preface to Cochlaeus, *Articuli aliquot, a Jacopo Kautio Oecolampadiano, ad populum nuper Wormaciae aediti, partim a Lutheranis, partim a Johanne Cochlaeo doctore praestantissimo, reprobati* (n.p., 1527).

372 Translator's note: literally, 'into ears'.

373 Nothing else is known of this lapsed Premonstratensian or his theses; see Herte, *Lutherkommentare*, 203–4.

374 On Sattler's martyrdom see *The Legacy of Michael Sattler*, tr. and ed. by John H. Yoder, *Classics of the Radical Reformation*, vol. 1 (Scottdale, PA, 1973), 66–85.

375 Translator's note: 'counterfeit and conceal' translates *simulabunt item ac dissimulabunt*.

376 Translator's note: 'by deceit and smoke' translates *per fucum et fumum*.

377 Translator's note: there is an underlying play on words here. The word translated as 'Fanatics' is *Suermeri* (a Latinization of Luther's word for fanatics, *Schwaermer*), which literally means 'swarmers'.

378 The text from which this is taken does not seem to have survived; see Herte, *Lutherkommentare*, 76 n. 24.

379 Luther, *Von der Widdertauffe an zween Pfarherrn* (1528), *WA*, vol. 26, 144–74.

380 Luther, *Von der Widdertauffe*, *WA*, vol. 26, 147.

381 Luther, *Von der Widdertauffe*, *WA*, vol. 26, 167–8.

382 Cochlaeus is taking this passage from *Septiceps Lutherus: vbique sibi, suis scriptis, contrarius, in Visitatione Saxonica* (Leipzig, Valentin Schumann, 1529), sig. G3.

383 Cochlaeus is drawing this quotation, and the one that follows, from *Septiceps Lutherus*, sig. G2ᵛ.

384 Luther, *Von der Widdertauffe*, *WA*, vol. 26, 165–66; *Septiceps Lutherus*, sig. G2ᵛ.

385 Melanchthon, *Articuli de quibus egerunt per visitatores in regione Saxoniae* (1527), CR, vol. 26, 9.

386 Melanchthon, *Articuli*, CR, vol. 26, 15.

387 Melanchthon, *Articuli*, CR, vol. 26, 26–7.

388 Luther's *Instructions for the Visitors of Parish Pastors in Electoral Saxony* (1528), *LW*, vol. 40, 269–320.

389 Cochlaeus's *Septiceps Lutherus: vbique sibi, suis scriptis, contrarius, in Visitatione Saxonica* (Leipzig, Valentin Schumann, 1529), and its German abridgment, *Sieben Köpffe Martin Luthers, von acht hohen sachen des christlichen glaubens* (Dresden, Wolfgang Stöckel, 1529).

390 Translator's note: in Greek mythology, Thyestes unknowingly ate the cooked flesh of his own sons, served to him by his brother Atreus.

391 Translator's note: the text reads *tandem urgente merito*, which means 'with the service urging at length'. This seems almost certainly to be a misprint for *marito*, in which case the last clause of the sentence means, as translated here, 'when her husband had pressed her for a long time'.

392 Translator's note: it is unclear what the proverb in question is.

393 Translator's note: literally, 'slipped away from himself'.

394 This remarkable story, dated 1532 according to other evidence, was apparently sent by Erasmus to a few of his correspondents; see P. S. Allen, ed., *Opus Epistolarum Des. Erasmi Roterodami*, vol. 10 (Oxford, 1941), pp. 76–8.

395 On the Pack Affair see OER vol. 3, 194 and the works cited there. Translator's note: *Luthericus*.

396 See Philip of Hesse, *Ein freuntlichs schreyben oder Sendtbrieff des hochgepornen Fürsten vnd Herren, herrn Philips Landgraffen zu Hessen +c. Vnd des hochgepornen Fursten Hertzog Georgen zu Sachssen antwort oder entschuldigung an den obgenanten Philips Landgraffen zu Hessen +c.* (Wittenberg, 1529).

397 *Sacrae Romanae Ecclesiae*, i.e. of the Holy Roman Church.

398 Translator's note: there is an anacolouthon in the original here; the sentence is not complete.

399 Duke Ferdinand of Austria, Mandate of 20 August 1527; see Herte, *Lutherkommentare*, 71.

400 Translator's note: literally 'I, knowing, know'.

401 Translator's note: the words 'most foolish of fools' are in Greek; *morotaton moron*.

402 Luther's letter to Wenceslaus Linck, Wittenberg, 14 June 1528, *WA*, vol. Briefwechsel vol. 4, 483–4.

403 Translator's note: *Ohe* or *Vae*

404 Translator's note: literally, 'the disguise'.

405 Cochlaeus, *An die Herrenn, Schulteis vnnd Radt zu Bern, wider yhre vermainte Reformation* (Dresden, Wolfgang Stöckel, 1528).

406 Luther, *Confession concerning Christ's Supper* (1528), *LW*, vol. 37, 362–3.

407 Cf. Luther, *Confession, LW*, vol. 37, 363–4; Cochlaeus is either paraphrasing Luther or drawing from a different source.

408 Cochlaeus, *Fasciculus calumniarum, sannarum et illusionum Martini Lutheri, in Episcopos & Clericos, ex vno eius libello Teuthonico, contra Episcopi Misnensis Mandatum aedito, collectarum* (Leipzig, Valentin Schumann, 1529), sigs A2ᵛ–3.

409 Luther's *Von heimlichen und gestohlenen Briefen* is found in *Welcher Gestalt wir Georg von Gottes Gnaden Hertzog zu Sachssen Landtgraff in Duringen vnnd Marggraff zu Meyssen von Martino Luther der gedichten Bundtnus halben inn schriften vnerfindtlich angegeben: vnd darauff vnsere antwort* (Augsburg: Alexander Weissenhorn, 1528); this volume also contains George's letter and is the source for the quotation that follows.

410 Translator's note: or 'this evangelical man'.

411 Translator's note: or 'debaters'.

412 Cochlaeus, *Septiceps Lutherus*, sigs 2–2ᵛ.

413 Melanchthon, prefatory letter to Archduke Ferdinand in *Danielis enarratio* (1529), CR, vol. 1, 1054.

414 Melanchthon, *Epistola de Coena Domini* (1529), CR, vol. 1, 1050.

415 See Luther, *Explanation of the Ninety-Five Theses* (1518), *LW*, vol. 31, 92; and *On War against the Turk* (1529), *LW*, vol. 46, 162.

416 Luther, *On War against the Turk, LW*, vol. 46, 166–7.

417 Luther, *On War against the Turk, LW*, vol. 46, 196–8, abridged.
418 Translator's note: i.e., someone who recants.
419 Cochlaeus's response to Luther's treatise is his *Dialogus de bello contra Turcas, in Antologian Lutheri* (Leipzig, Valentin Schumann, 1529).
420 Translator's note: the text reads *milleuos*, an apparently non-existent word. The printer has mistakenly used u instead of n, or has set the n upside down, a fairly common printing error. This would give *millenos*, which means 'one thousand each'.
421 Translator's note: literally, 'all Italy having been left aside'.
422 Luther's 'Large Catechism' actually first appeared in April 1529, but the 1530 edition contains an expanded preface. See *The Book of Concord*, tr. Theodore G. Tappert (Philadelphia, 1959), 357–461.
423 Translator's note: literally, a 'four-pointed torch'.
424 Translator's note: literally, 'four-pronged torches, burning in white wax'.
425 Translator's note: reading *capita* here as 'placards' (cf. its use to mean 'chapters' in a book.) Alternatively, this clause could read 'and published [it] through all the heads of the streets', but that seems to make less sense.
426 The Augsburg Confession is found at *The Book of Concord*, 23–96.
427 Augsburg Confession, Art. 24, 1–2 (*The Book of Concord*, 56). Cochlaeus is quoting the Latin directly, not translating the German version.
428 Augsburg Confession, Art. 25, 1 (*The Book of Concord*, 61).
429 The initial confutation of the Augsburg Confession, composed by Cochlaeus and others, was rejected for its severity.
430 Luther, *Brief an den Kardinal Erzbischof zu Mainz* (1530), *WA*, vol. 30/2, 397–412.
431 Luther, *Brief ... Mainz, WA*, vol. 30/2, 412.
432 Luther, *Exhortation to all Clergy Assembled at Augsburg* (1530), *LW*, vol. 34, 19–21.
433 Cochlaeus, *Septiceps Lutherus*, sig. L1.
434 Translator's note: i.e., the soles of shoes.
435 Translator's note: taking the nonsense syllables *Ika, Ika* as onomatopoeia for the sound of a donkey's bray, to continue the metaphor begun by 'ears that are too long'.
436 Translator's note: a nonsense syllable, perhaps indicating scorn or bewilderment.
437 Translator's note: 'Thus I wish it, thus I judge it, let my will take the place of reason' translates *Sic volo, sic jubeo, sit pro ratione voluntas*.
438 Luther, *On Translating: An Open Letter* (1530), *LW*, vol. 35, 182–3.
439 The Tetrapolitan Confession may be found in Martin Bucer, *Confessio Tetrapolitana und die Schriften des Jahres 1531*, ed. Robert Stupperich (Gütersloh, 1969).
440 See *LW*, vol. 34, 67–104.
441 See *LW*, vol. 47, 11–55.
442 The work from which this is taken did not appear separately, nor is is clear what the original German title was.
443 Translator's note: the word *protestatio* normally means 'protest', but here and in the next sentence the context seems to demand 'preface' or perhaps even 'abstract'.
444 Luther, *Commentary on the Alleged Imperial Edict* (1531), *LW*, vol. 34, 82.
445 Luther, *Commentary, LW*, vol. 34, 83–4 (abridged). Translator's note: *Altius quam inter Gallinas sederunt*–'they have sat higher than among the hens'–appears to be a proverb, but its meaning is obscure.
446 Luther, *Commentary, LW*, vol. 34, 86.
447 Translator's note: 'peasants' jam under the hedges' seems to be another proverb or figure of speech; once again, the meaning is obscure.

448 Luther, *Commentary, LW,* vol. 34, 88.

449 Luther, *Commentary, LW,* vol. 34, 90–1.

450 Luther, *Commentary, LW,* vol. 34, 103–4.

451 Luther, *Warning to his Dear German People* (1531), *LW,* vol. 47, 19.

452 From Cochlaeus, *Ein getrewe wolmeinende warnung D. Jo. Cocleus, wider die untrewen auffrürischen warnung M. Luthers ad die lieben Teutschen* (Leipzig: Michael Blum, 1531).

453 Luther, *Warning, LW,* vol. 47, 30.

454 Cochlaeus, *Vermanung zu frid vnd einikeit durch D. Johann Coclaeum, an den Achtbarn vnd hochgelarten Herrn Doctorn Gregorium Brück, de Churfürsten von Sachssen Rath +c. auff Martin Luthers Rathschlag,* in *Innhalt dieses Buchleins* (Dresden: Wolfgang Stöckel, 1531).

455 Luther, *Warning, LW,* vol. 47, 35–6.

456 Luther, *Warning, LW,* vol. 47, 36.

457 Luther, *Warning, LW,* vol. 47, 50.

458 Luther, *Warning, LW,* vol. 47, 52.

459 Luther, *Warning, LW,* vol. 47, 53.

460 Luther, *Warning, LW,* vol. 47, 21–2.

461 Translator's note: literally, 'on top of their backs'.

462 Luther, *Warning, LW,* vol. 47, 15.

463 The Dresden layman was no less than Johann, the crown Prince of Saxony; the work is *Widder des Luthers Warnung an die Teutschen* (Dresden: Wolfgang Stöckel, 1531); the work was reprinted in *WA,* vol. 30/3, 416–24, and the passage quoted appears on p. 416.

464 Luther, *Wider den Meuchler zu Dresden* (1531), *WA,* vol. 30/3: 447.

465 Luther, *Wider den Meuchler, WA,* vol. 30/3: 448.

466 Luther, *Wider den Meuchler, WA,* vol. 30/3: 469–70.

467 Luther, *Wider den Meuchler, WA,* vol. 30/3: 470.

468 Translator's note: or 'our confederation of the faithful'.

469 For Cochlaeus and the 1531 Swiss religious war, see Herte, *Lutherkommentare,* 118–22.

470 Translator's note: this is a guess at the sense of *ponebant carnem brachium suum;* literally, 'were placing (to) flesh their arm'. Alternatively, it could mean something like 'were taking their lives in their own hands' ('were placing [their] flesh [in] their arm'). The two accusative nouns and the lack of a preposition governing either one of them make the phrase very obscure.

471 Witzel (1501–73), one of the more colorful and enigmatic figures of the Reformation, was an ordained and married Lutheran pastor before returning, still married, to the Roman church, where he devoted the rest of his life to polemics against the Reformers and to proposals for reform within the church. See Barbara Henze, *Aus Liebe der Kirche Reform: Die Bemühungen Georg Witzels (1501–1573) um die Kircheneinheit,* Reformationsgeschichtliche Studien und Texte, vol. 133 (Münster, 1995).

472 Johannes Campanus (*c.*1500–*c.*1574), a Wittenberg-trained theologian, was with Witzel at the Marburg Colloquy, but became notorious for his denial of the traditional doctrine of the Trinity.

473 Georg Witzel, *Apologia: das ist, ein vertedigs rede Georgij Wicelij widder seine affterreder die Luteristen, mit sampt kurtzer abconterseyung Lutherischer secten, vnd preis alter Romischen Kirchen nutzlich zu lesen* (Leipzig: Nickel Schmidt, 1533); *Confutatio*

calumniosissimae Responsionis Justi Jonae, id est, Jodoci Koch, una cum assertione bonorum operum (Leipzig: Nicolaus Faber, 1533); *Von der Christlichen Kyrchen: wider Jodocum Koch / der sich nennet / Justum Jonam* (Leipzig, Nickel Schmidt, 1534).

474 From Michael Servetus, *Dialogorum de Trinitate libri duo* (Hagenau: Johann Setzer, 1532; rpt Frankfurt, 1965); tr. by Earl Morse Wilbur in *The Two Treatises of Servetus on the Trinity*, Harvard Theological Studies, 16 (Cambridge, MA; rpt New York, 1969), p. 188.

475 James 1: 8.

476 Luther, *Against Latomus* (1521), *LW*, vol. 32, 243–44 (abridged).

477 Translator's note: I have translated *virtus* here first as 'valor' and second as 'constancy'. It has a whole range of meanings–manliness, excellence, courage, valor, strength, constancy, firmness, virtue–all of which I think are at play in this description, which is one long sentence in the Latin.

478 Johann Bugenhagen, *Wider die kelch Diebe* (Wittenberg, Hans Lufft, 1532).

479 Michael Vehe, *Erretung der beschuldigtem Kelchdyeb von newen Bugenhagischen galgen* (Leipzig: Michael Lotter, 1535).

480 Luther, *Sermon at the Funeral of the Elector, Duke John of Saxony* (1532), *LW*, vol. 51, 234.

481 These 'postillae' of Cochlaeus remained unpublished; they are listed among the works 'not yet issued' in the 1549 catalogue of his writings (*Catalogus brevis*, sig. B4^v: 'Postilla in duas orationes funebres Lutheri translata').

482 Luther, *Sermon, LW*, vol. 51, 235.

483 Luther, *Sermon, LW*, vol. 51, 237.

484 Luther, *Sermon, LW*, vol. 51, 237.

485 Luther, *Sermon, LW*, vol. 51, 237.

486 From Luther's sermon on the Ten Commandments as excerpted in Cochlaeus's *Septiceps Lutherus*, sigs L4–4^v.

487 Luther, *Ein Sermon von der Bereitung zum Sterben* (1519), *WA*, vol. 2, 685–97, esp. 696–7; Clemen vol. 1, 172–73.

488 Luther, letter to the evangelical Christians in Leipzig, Wittenberg, 11 April 1533; *WA*, vol. Briefwechsel vol. 6, 449–50.

489 This letter is found in Cochlaeus's edition of *Hertzog Georgens zu Sachssen Ehrlich und grundtliche entschuldigung, wider Martin Luthers Auffruerisch und verlogenne brieff und Verantwortung* (Leipzig, Michael Blum, 1533), sigs B2^v–3.

490 *Hertzog Georgens ... entschuldigung*, sig. B4.

491 Luther, letter to Wolf Wiedemann, Wittenberg, 27 April 1533, *WA*, vol. Briefwechsel 6: 457.

492 Luther, *Verantwortung der auffgelegten Auffrur von Hertzog Georgen D. Mart. Luther* (1533), *WA*, vol. 38: 96–7.

493 Translator's note: assuming that *vendico* (to offer for sale, to barter) here is a misprint for *vindico* (to claim or acknowledge).

494 Luther, *Verantwortung, WA*, vol. 38, 97.

495 Translator's note: Cochlaeus normally uses *libellus* in its literal meaning of 'little book' or 'pamphlet'. Here, however, the meaning clearly must be 'libel', a sense which was already present in legal Latin of the 16th century.

496 Luther, *Verantwortung, WA*, vol. 38, 98.

497 Cochlaeus, *Hertzog Georgens zu Sachssen Ehrlich vnd grundtliche entschuldigung, wider Martin Luthers Aufrüerisch vnd verlongenne, Brieff vnd Verantwortung* (Leipzig: Michael Blum, 1533).

498 Luther, *Verantwortung, WA,* vol. 38, 103.
499 Cochlaeus, *Auff Luthers kleine Antwort ein kurtze widerrede Hertzog zu Sachssen betreffend* (Dresden: Wolfgang Stöckel, 1533).
500 Luther's 'Trostbrief' or consolation letter to the Evangelicals driven out of Leipzig is printed as an appendix to the *Verantwortung;* the passage quoted is found at *WA,* vol. 38, 113.
501 Translator's note: literally, 'licking' or 'lapping'.
502 Translator's note: 'Rue-crown': the Latin refers to the *corona rutea,* a translation of the German *Rautenkranz,* the emblem of the Dukes of Saxony. Cochlaeus apparently coined the adjective *rutea* for this context. I am grateful to Dr Ulrich Schmitzer and Dr E. Christian Kopff for providing me with information about the *Rautenkranz.*
503 Luther, *Kleine Antwort auf Herzog Georgen nächstes Buch* (1533), *WA,* vol. 38, 167.
504 Cochlaeus, *Auff Luthers kleine antwort ein kurtze widerrede Hertzog Georgen zu Sachssen betreffend* (Dresden, Wolfgang Stöckel, 1533).
505 Witzel, *Confutatio calumniosissimae responsionis Iusti Ionae, id est, Iodoci Koch, vna cum assertione bonorum operum* (Leipzig, Nicolaus Faber, 1533).
506 Translator's note: the reference to Thracians is explained by the mythic horses of Diomedes, who ate human beings; Heracles's eighth labor was to capture these horses. The Scordisci were a Celtic tribe who intermingled with the Thracians and were known for their raids on Macedonia in the second and first centuries BC.
507 Luther, Preface to Balthasar Raida's *Widder das lester vnd lügen büchlin Agricole Phagi, genant Georg Witzel. Antwort Balthassar Raida pfarherr zu Hirsfeld* (Wittenberg, Nickel Schirlentz, 1533), *WA,* vol. 38, 84.
508 From Cochlaeus, *De futuro concilio rite celebrando ... Epistola Johannis Cochlei ad Archiepiscopum S. Andree in Scotia* (Dresden, Wolfgang Stöckel, 1534). The letter to the archbishop is dated Dresden, 12 March 1534; Cochlaeus either is mistaken about when he wrote this letter or, like many of his contemporaries, sees the new year beginning on 25 March.
509 Cochlaeus, *An expediat laicis, legere noui testamenti libros lingua vernacula? Ad serenissimum Scotiae Regem Iacobum V. Disputatio inder Alexandrum Alesium Scotum, & Iohannem Cochlaeum Germanum* (Augsburg, Alexander Weissenhorn, 1533), sigs E7–8.
510 Cochlaeus, *Was von Kayser Sigmunds Reformation zu halten sei, ain disputation Johannis Coclei. Was auch von der newen Chroniken Sebastiani Franck zu halten sey?* (Dresden, 1533).
511 This text by Cochlaeus does not appear to have been printed.
512 From Cochlaeus, *Von ankunfft der Mess unnd der wandlung brots unnd weins in hochwürdigen Sacrament des Altars. Ain disputation Sebastiani Francken, mit Antwort Johannis Coclei auf 88. artickeln auss der newen Chronica* (Dresden, 1533).
513 Luther, *The Private Mass and the Consecration of Priests* (1533), *LW,* vol. 38, 147.
514 Luther, *The Private Mass, LW,* vol. 38, 149.
515 *Innocent III, Innocentij Papae, hoc nomine tertij, libri sex, de sacro altaris mysterio ex uetusto codice nuper exscripti & nunc per typographos excusi* (Leipzig, Nicolaus Faber, 1534).
516 *Innocent III, Liber de contemptu mundi, sive de miseria conditionis humanae* (Leipzig, Michael Blum, 1534).
517 *Isidore, Beati Isidori Hispaliensis quondam archiepiscopi De officiis ecclesiasticis libri*

duo, ante annos DCCCC. *ab eo editi, et nunc ex vetusto codice in lucem restitui* (Leipzig, Michael Blum, 1534).

518 Cochlaeus, *Von der heyligen Mess und Priesterweyhe Christlicher Bericht D.Jo. Cocleus* (Leipzig, Michael Blum, 1534).

519 Georg Witzel, *Von der Pusse, Beichte vnd Bann* (Leipzig, Valentin Schumann, 1534).

520 Witzel, *Von der heiligen Eucharisty odder Mess, nach anweisunge der Schrifft, vnd der Eltisten schrifftuerstendigen heiligen Lerern* (Leipzig: Valentin Schumann, 1534).

521 Witzel, *Vom Beten, Fastenn, vnnd Almosen, Schrifftlich zeugknusz* (Leipzig, Melchior Lotter, 1535; expanded ed., Leipzig, Nicolaus Wolrab, 1538).

522 Nicholas Amsdorff, letter to Luther, Magdeburg, 28 January 1534, *WA*, vol. Briefwechsel 7, 17. The letter was printed (Wittenberg: Hans Lufft, 1534), hence Cochlaeus's and Erasmus's knowledge of the judgment.

523 Translator's note: 'defense' here translates *purgatio*, which literally means 'clearance by ordeal'.

524 Erasmus, *Purgatio adversus epistolam non sobriam Martini Lutheri* (1534), *Opera Omnia*, vol. 9/1 (Amsterdam, 1982), p. 445.

525 Erasmus, Purgatio, *Opera Omnia* 9, 1, 476–8.

526 Translator's note: literally, 'coral'.

527 Translator's note: the translation 'through the unrelenting siege of hunger' takes *fama* as an unusual synonym for *fames*, hunger. This usage is attested, but is very, very unusual. The common sense of *fama* is 'reputation'; taking it in that sense, the text reads 'so that through the unrelenting siege, that city might be forced to the surrender of its reputation, at least'.

528 Cochlaeus, *XXI Articuli Anabaptistarum Monasteriensium* (Leipzig, Nicolaus Faber, 1534).

529 Cochlaeus, *XXI Articuli.*

530 Luther, *A Letter of Dr Martin Luther concerning His Book on the Private Mass* (1534), *LW*, vol. 38, 226.

531 Luther, *A Letter*, *LW*, vol. 38, 227.

532 Translator's note: literally, 'sealed'.

533 Luther, *A Letter*, *LW*, vol. 38, 232.

534 Cochlaeus, *Auf Luthers brieff von dem Buch der winkelmess zehen Fragstucke Dr Johan Cocleus an er. Just Jonas Probst zu Wittenberg. Sampt ainem Auszug XXVIII Artickeln* (Dresden, Wolfgang Stöckel, 1534)

535 Translator's note: Aeolus was the king of the winds in Greek and Roman mythology.

536 Translator's note: 'Dabit Deus his quoque finem', an exact quotation of *Aeneid* I, 119.

537 The judgment of Cochlaeus's and Witzel's teaching by Conrad Cordatus (1476–1546) is found in the preface to Michael Caelius, *Newer Jrthumb vnd Schwermerey vom Sacrament* (Wittenberg, Georg Rhau, 1534).

538 Cochlaeus, *Von newen Schwermereyen sechs Capitel, den Christen und Ketzern beyden nötig zu lesen, und höchlich zu bedencken der Seelen seligkeit betreffende* (Leipzig: Michael Blum, 1534).

539 Cochlaeus, *Von newen Schwermereyen.*

540 Paul Bachmann, *Lobgesang auff des Luthers Winckel Messe. Mit vnderricht von Christlicher Messe gemeyner Apostolischer Kirchen* (Leipzig, Michael Blum, 1534).

541 Cochlaeus, *Pro Scotiae Regno Apologia Iohannis Cochlaei* (Leipzig, Michael Blum, 1534), sig. A4.

542 Translator's note: 'beaten in the race' translates *pedibus vinci*, which literally means 'to have been conquered in or with the feet'.

543 Translator's note: 'Historical studies' here is a guess for *disciplinis Cyclicis*. 'Cyclicus' means cyclical, or in cycles; it may here be used to refer to the cycles of time, i.e. to history, but the phrase is obscure.

544 Cochlaeus, *Pro Scotiae Regno Apologia*, sig. B4ᵛ.

545 Translator's note: Phalaris was a tyrant who roasted his victims alive in a bronze bull. The Cyclopes ate human beings; the most famous example, of course, was the Cyclops Polyphemus who ate several of Odysseus' men.

546 Cochlaeus, *Pro Scotiae Regno Apologia*, sigs B4ᵛ-C1ᵛ (abridged).

547 Cochlaeus, *Pro Scotiae Regno Apologia*, sig. D4.

548 Translator's note: 'Good studies' translates *bonas literas*, which *may* be a technical term here meaning something like humanities or liberal arts. Three sentences later, in the reference to Melanchthon, *bonas literas* seems to mean 'great learning'.

549 For further information on the Edict of King Sigismund dated 4 February 1535, see *Acta Tomiciana*, ed. V. Pochiecha, vol. 17 (Wroclaw, 1966), p. 102, no. 77. Cochlaeus printed the Edict in *In Lutheri adversus Cardinalem et Episcopum Moguntinum et Magdeburgensem ... Responsum* (Dresden, Wolfgang Stöckel, 1535), sig. C3ᵛ–4.

550 Cochlaeus's surviving correspondence tells a different story: he had difficulty finding printers willing to be associated with his campaign against the Reformers.

551 Isaiah 56: 10.

552 Cochlaeus, *De Matrimonio serenissimi Regis Angliae, Henrici octavi, congratulatio disputatoria Johannis Cochlei Germani, ad Paulum Tertium Pont. Max.* (Leipzig, Michael Blum, 1535).

553 Translator's note: or 'his character'; *ingenium* means both.

554 Erasmus, *Ecclesiastes, Opera omnia* (Amsterdam, 1991), 5/4, 32.

555 Luther, sermon for 8 November 1534, *WA*, vol. 37, 593.

556 Luther, sermon for 8 November 1534, *WA*, vol. 37, 593.

557 Luther, sermon for 8 November 1534, *WA*, vol. 37, 593.

558 Luther, sermon for 8 November 1534, *WA*, vol. 37, 594

559 Luther, sermon for 8 November 1534, *WA*, vol. 37, 594.

560 Cochlaeus, *Auf Luthers newe lesterschrifft wider den Cardinal und Ertzbischoff von Mentz und Magdeburg ... Antwort Johann Cochlei* (Leipzig, Michael Blum, 1535).

561 Casper Querhammer, *Tabula contradictionum Lutheri xxxvi. super vno articulo, de communione eucharistiae* (Dresden, Wolfgang Stöckel, 1535).

562 Cochlaeus, preface (delicated to Sigmund von Lindenau, Bishop of Merseburg), to *Prognosticon futuri seculi a sancto Juliano, Episcopo Toletano, ante annos DCC scriptum, in Hispaniis* (Leipzig, Michael Blum, 1536). St Julian of Toledo died in 690.

563 Cochlaeus, 'Defensio Joannis Episcopi Roffensis et Thome Mori, adversus Richardum samsonem Anglum', in *Antiqua et insignis epistola Nicolae Papae I ...* (Leipzig: Melchior Lotter, 1536); cf. the life of Fisher at *Analecta Bollandiana* vol. 12 (1893) 97–278.

564 Cochlaeus, *Vom vermögen und Gewalt eines gemeinen Concilii. XXX bewerte und unverwerffliche Gezeucknüsse, in funferley unterschied. Widerlegung der XXX Artickeln, zu Wittenberg disputirt. LXX Sprüche zu disputiren, für ein gemeyn Concilio* (Leipzig: Nicolaus Wolrab, 1537).; *Quatuor Excusationum Lutheranorum Confutatio una, pro Concilio Generali ad Mantuam indicto* (Leipzig, Nicolaus Wolrab, 1537).

565 Translator's note: I have not found 'Pasquillos' in any Latin dictionary. However,

Spanish, French, Italian (and obsolete English) all have a word *pasquin-* or *pasquil-*, meaning lampoon, so I assume that it was a late Latin word as well.

566 See the anonymous *Pasquilli de Concilio Mantuano iudicium: querimonia Papistarum ad legatum pontificium in comicijs Schmalcaldianis Mantuanae miseris nimium vicina Papistis* ('Rome', no printer [possibly Wittenberg, Nickel Schirlentz], 1537); also Luther's *Die Lugend von S.Johanne Chrysostomo, an die heiligen Veter inn dem vermeinten Concilio zu Mantua* (Wittenberg, Hans Lufft, 1537) and Cochlaeus's *Bericht der warheit auff die unwaren Lügend S. Joannis Chrysostomi, welche M. Luther an das Concilium zu Mantua hat lassen aussgehen* (Leipzig, Nicolaus Wolrab, 1537). The reference to letters by Beelzebub remains obscure.

567 Luther provided prefaces to Jan Hus, *Etliche Brieue Johannis Huss des heiligen Merterers, aus dem gefengnis zu Costentz, an den Behemen geschrieben* (Wittenberg, Joseph Klug, 1537) and, the edition Cochlaeus is probably thinking of, *Vier christliche briefe, so Johan Hus der heylig marterer aus dem gefengknus zu Costentz im Concilio, an die Behem geschriben hat, verteutscht, sampt einer vorrede D. Mart. Luthers, das zukunfftig Concilium betreffend* (Nuremberg, Johann Petreius, 1536); he also translated *Einer aus den hohen Artikeln des Allerheiligesten Bepstlichen glaubens, genant, Donatio Constantini* (Wittenberg, Hans Lufft, 1537).

568 Cochlaeus published his *Warhafftige Historia von Magister Johan Hussen, von anfang seiner newer Sect, biss zum Ende seines Lebens ym Concilio zu Costnitz, auss alten Original beschrieben* (Leipzig, Nicolaus Wolrab, 1537), and *Von der Donation des Keysers Constantini, und von Bepstlichem gewalt, Grundtlicher Bericht aus alten bewerten Lerern und Historien* (n.p. 1537).

569 This work seems to have been unpublished; see Spahn, p. 360, no. 126.

570 This work does not survive under this title.

571 Cochlaeus, *De Immensa Dei misericordia erga Germanos: ex collatione sermonum Joannis Hus ad unum sermonem Martini Lutheri, quem in festo Epiphaniae habuit. X tituli et LXX propositiones tum Joannis Hus, tum Martini Lutheri* (Leipzig, Nicolaus Wolrab, 1537).

572 Translator's note: this sentence is very elliptical and rather unclear. The subjects of the verbs *diceret* and *obiceret* are not expressed, but apparently cannot be Hus, the main subject of the sentence. I have guessed 'someone' and 'another'.

573 This work, listed *as Cesnura Ioan. Cochlaei in disputationem quintam Lutheri contra Antinomos* in the *Catalogus brevis* (sig. B1), does not seem to have survived.

574 Richard Morison, *Apomaxis calumniarum, conuitiorumque, quibus Ioannes Cocleus, homo theologus exiguus artium professor, scurra procax, Henrici octavi, serenissimi regis Angliae famam impetere, nomen obscurare, rerum gestarum gloriam faedare nuper edita, non tam in regem, quam in regis inuidam, epistola studuit* (London, 1537).

575 From Cochlaeus, *Scopa Ioannis Cochlaei Germani, in araneas Richardi Morysini Angli* (Leipzig, Nicolaus Wolrab, 1538).

576 Augsburg Confession, Art. 24.10 (*Book of Concord*, 56).

577 Schmalkald Articles, Art. 2.1 (*Book of Concord*, 293).

578 Translator's note: the text alludes to seven men but names nine.

579 The Latin text of the '*Consilium de emendanda ecclesiae*' (with a different ending from what Cochlaeus provides here) may be found in Karl Mirbt, ed., *Quellen zur Geschichte des Papsttums und des Römischen Katholizismus*, 4th edn (Tübingen, 1924), pp. 267–70.

580 Luther, *Counsel of a Committee of Several Cardinals with Luther's Preface* (1538), *LW*, vol. 34: 235–67.

581 Johann Sturm, *Consilium delectorum cardinalium et aliorum prelatorum, de emend-anda ecclesia, epistola* (Strasbourg: Crato Mylius, 1538); Cochlaeus's response is the *Aequitatis discussio super consilio delectorum cardinalium* (Leipzig: Nicolaus Wolrab, 1538); ed. Hilarius Walter, Corpus Catholicorum, vol. 17 (Münster, 1931).

582 Cochlaeus, *Aequitatis discussio*, ed. Walter, pp. 2–4.

583 Translator's note: or 'in your character' or 'your intellect'; *ingenium* can mean all three of these things.

584 From Jacopo Sadoleto, *Epistolae de dissidiis religionis* (Strasbourg: Crato Mylius, 1539).

585 For the history of this letter see Herte, *Lutherkommentare*, p. 55, n. 12.

586 Cochlaeus, *De ordinatione episcoporum atque presbyterorum et de eucharistiae consecra-tione, quaestio hoc tempore pernecessaria* (Mainz, Franz Behem, 1541).

587 The prince in question was Philip of Hesse (about whom see Hans Hillerbrand, *Landgrave Philipp of Hesse, 1504–1567: Religion and Politics in the Reformation* [St Louis, Foundation for Reformation Research, 1967]); Cochlaeus's 'short pamphlet' may be *De matrimonio X. quaestiones contra Lutherum & Brentzium*, indicated as an unpublished German work in the 1549 *Catalogus brevis* (sig. B5ᵛ).

588 Cochlaeus, *De vera Christi ecclesia quaestio necessaria super septimo confessionis Augus-tanae articulo ad Caesarem Maiestatem ut Ratisponae in conventu imperiali discutiatur* (Mainz, Franz Behem, 1541); the German translation either was not published or has not survived.

589 Cochlaeus, *Philippica quinta Joannis Cochlaei, in tres libros Philippi Melanchthonis* (Ingolstadt: Alexander Weissenhorn, 1540, rpt 1543); in *Philippicae I–VII*, ed. R. Keen, vol. 1 (Nieuwkoop, DeGraaf, 1995), pp. 203–74. The encounter with Melanchthon at Worms is not documented elsewhere.

590 Translator's note: literally, 'whose life [singular] responds equally'. A roundabout way of referring to those who are well-to-do and able to finance their own private masses.

591 The Six Articles of 1539 (reprinted in part in Henry Bettenson, ed., *Documents of the Christian Church* [Oxford, 1943], pp. 328–29); see OER vol. 4: 65–66.

592 Charles V, *Ordnung, Statuten vnd Edict, Keiser Carols des fünfften, publicirt in der namhafften Stat Brüssel, in beysein irer Mayestet Schwester vnd Königin, Gubernant vnd Regent seiner Niderland, den 4. Octobris, anno Christi 1540* (Nuremberg, Johann Petreius, 1540).

593 Translator's note: the first time Cochlaeus has used this term.

594 The *Response* of the princes and estates of the Augsburg Confession to the Regensburg Book is found in CR, vol. 4, 477–91 in the Latin and 491–505 in the German version. The passage here appears at 4, 480.

595 *Response*, CR, vol. 4: 482.

596 *Response*, CR, vol. 4: 482.

597 *Response*, CR, vol. 4: 483.

598 The Lutheran theologians' response to Contarini judgment of the Regensburg proceedings, dated 20 July 1541, is found at CR, vol. 4: 559–61; the passage quoted is at 560.

599 Eck, *Apologia pro reverendis. et illustris. principibus Catholicis: ac alijs ordinibus Imperij aduersus mucores & calumnias Buceri, super actis Comiciorum Ratisponae* (Cologne, Melchior Neuss, 1542).

600 Translator's note: literally, 'now wanting, now not wanting'.

601 Albertus Pighius, *Apologia Alberti Pighii Campensis aduersus Martini Buceri calumnias, quas & solidis argumentis, & clarissimis rationibus confutat* (Mainz, Franz Behem, 1543).

602 See Cochlaeus, *Philippicae I–VII*, ed. Keen, vol. 1, xiii.

603 Cochlaeus, *Philippicae I–VII*, vol. 1, 204.

604 Cochlaeus, *Philippicae I–VII*, vol. 1, 206.

605 Cochlaeus, *De Canonicae scripturae & Catholicae ecclesiae autoritate, ad Henricum Bullingerum Iohannis Cochlaei libellus* (Ingolstadt, Alexander Weissenhorn, 1543), sig. A2.

606 Cochlaeus, *De animarum purgatorio igne epitome, contra novas sectas quae Purgatorium negant* (Ingolstadt, Alexander Weissenhorn, 1543); the German translation mentioned is *Zwey kurtze Tractätlein vom Fegfewr der Seelen, wider die newen Secten, so dasselbe verneinen. Erstlich beschriben durch weylandt den Gottseligen und Hochgelehrten Johannem Cochleum der H. Schrifft Doctorn, und jetzo mit dolmetschung dess ersten auffs new widerumb in Truck gefertigt: durch Johann Christoff Hueber* (Ingolstadt, David Sartorius, 1543).

607 Eberhard Billick, *Iudicium deputatorum vniuersitatis & secundarij cleri Coloniensis de doctrina & vocatione Martini Buceri ad Bonnam* (Cologne, Melchior Neuss, 1543).

608 Paul III, *Admonitio paterna Pauli III. Romani Pontificis ad inuictiss. Caesarem Carolum V.* (n.p., 1545); for Cochlaeus's knowledge of this document see Herte, *Lutherkommentare*, 70 n. 12.

609 Cochlaeus, *Philippica sexta* (Ingolstadt, Alexander Weissenhorn, 1544).

610 Cochlaeus, *Defensio ceremoniarum ecclesiae adversus errores et calumnias trium librorum* (Ingolstadt, Alexander Weissenhorn, 1543).

611 Cochlaeus, *De novis ex Hebraeo translationibus sacrae scripturae, disceptatio Iohannis Cochlaei* (Ingolstadt, Alexander Weissenhorn, 1544).

612 Cochlaeus, *Quadruplex Concordiae ratio et consyderatio super confessione Augustana protestantium quorundam sacri Romani Imperii Principum ac statuum, Caes. Maiestati Augustae exhibita* (Ingolstadt, Alexander Weissenhorn, 1544).

613 Cochlaeus, *De Sanctorum invocatione et intercessione dequam imaginibus et reliquiis eorum pie riteque colendis. Liber unus* (Ingolstadt, Alexander Weissenhorn, 1544).

614 Cochlaeus, *Replica brevis Johannis Cochlaei adversus prolixam Responsionem Henrici Bullingeri De scripturae et ecclesiae autoritate* (Ingolstadt, Alexander Weissenhorn, 1544).

615 Cochlaeus, *Sacerdotii ac sacrificii novae legis defensio, adversus Wolfgangi Musculi, Augustae concionantis arrosiones* (Ingolstadt, Alexander Weissenhorn, 1544).

616 Cochlaeus, *Vita Theoderici Regis quondam Ostrogothorum et Italiae* (Ingolstadt, Alexander Weissenhorn, 1544).

617 Cochlaeus, *Von alten gebrauch des Bettens in Christlicher Kirchen zehen Unterschaid* (Ingolstadt, Alexander Weissenhorn, 1544).

618 Of these the most important is Martin Bucer, *Ein Christliche Erinnerung, an die Keis. vnd Kon. Maiestaten, sampt Churfursten, Fursten vnd Stende des H. Reichs Teutscher Nation, jetzund zu Wurms versamlet* (Strasbourg, Crato Mylius, 1545).

619 This work does not seem to have been printed; Cochlaeus lists it among the unpublished German works in his *Catalogus brevis* (sig. B5ᵛ).

620 Cochlaeus, *In XVIII Articulos Mar. Buceri excerptos ex novissimo libro eius ad principes et status sacri Ro. Imperii latine scripto. Responsio Jo. Cochlaei* (Ingolstadt, Alexander Weissenhorn, 1546).

621 Translator's note: *magna fama, seu infamia potius.*

622   On Joris (1501–56) see Gary Waite, *David Joris and Dutch Anabaptism 1524–1543* (Waterloo, Ont., 1990).

623   *Articuli orthodoxam religionem, sanctamque fidem nostram respicientes* (Louvain, Reynier Valpen van Diest, 1545; rpt n.p., 1787); translated as *Zwen vnd dreissig Artickel, die allgemeinen Religion vnd Glauben belangend* (Nuremberg, Johann Petreius, 1545).

624   See the last two items in *Ordenung und Mandat Keiser Caroli V.: vernewert im April Anno 1550: zu ausrotten und zu vertilgen die Secten und spaltung: welche entstanden sind: widder unsern heiligen Christlichen glauben und wider die ordenung unser Mutter der heiligen Christlichen Kirchen: Item ein Register der verworffenen und verbottenen Buchern: auch von guten Buchern welche man inn der Schulen lesen mag: item eine vermanung des Rectors der Universitet zu Louen: item ein ander Keisers Mandat von des selbigen handel im 40. jar aus gangen* (n.p., 1550).

625   See Martin Bucer, *Der newe glaub, von den Doctoren zu Louen, die sich Doctoren der Gottheit rhumen, in xxxij Articulen furgegeben: Mit Christlicher verwarnung dagegen, durch die Prediger zu Strasbourg* (Frankfurt, Hermann Gulfferich, 1545); Luther, *Contra XXXII. Articulos Lovaniensium Theologistarum* (Frankfurt, Hermann Gulfferich, 1546), a translation of *Wider die XXXII. Artikel der Teologisten von Louen* (Wittenberg: Nickel Schirlentz, 1545).

626   Translator's note: 'our little Louvain friends' is my rendering of *Nostrollorum Louaniensium.* I cannot find *Nostrolli* in any dictionary, but it looks like a diminutive of *nostri,* 'our people', used scornfully here.

627   Translator's note: 'our little friends' again translates *Nostrolli*; see previous note. The reference to 'the mirror of Marcolfus' is obscure; presumably it refers to some proverb or folktale.

628   Luther, *Against the Thirty-Two Articles of the Louvain Theologists, LW,* vol. 34: 354–55. Translator's note: 'Little Masters' *Magistrolli*; cf. *nostrolli.* 'The Church of Evil' is my rendering of *Cacolyca* (assuming the element *caco-* is from the Greek *kakos,* evil), which is clearly a pun on *Catholica.*

629   Heinrich Bullinger was the author of the *Warhaffte Bekantnuss der Dieneren der kilchen zu Zyrich* (Zurich, Christoffel Froschauer, 1545).

630   Cochlaeus, *In Causae religionis Miscellaneorum libri tres in diversos tractatus antea non aeditos, ac diversis temporibus, locisque scriptos digesti* (Ingolstadt, Alexander Weissenhorn, 1545).

631   Cochlaeus, *Necessaria et Catholica Consyderatio super Lutheri Articulis, quos velit Concilio Generali proponi* (Ingolstadt, Alexander Weissenhorn, 1546).

632   Cochlaeus, *In quatuor Andreae Osiandri coniecturas de fine mundi, velitatio Johannis Cochlaei* (Ingolstadt, Alexander Weissenhorn, 1545).

633   Cochlaeus, *In primum Musculi Anticochlaeum replica Johannis Cochlaei, pro sacerdotii et sacrificii novae legis assertione. In epilogo adiecta est brevis responsio in Antibolen Bullingeri. Addita est appendix gemina in librum Buceri, quem in Bart Latomum edidit* (Ingolstadt, Alexander Weissenhorn, 1545).

634   Cochlaeus, *Nycticorax Evangelii Novi in Germania* (Ingolstadt, Alexander Weissenhorn, 1545).

635   Eberhard Billick, *Iudicii vniuersitatis et cleri Coloniensis: aduersus calumnias Philippi Melanthonis, Martini Buceri, Oldendorpij, & eorum asseclarum, defensio: cum diligenti explicatione materiarum controuersarum* (Paris, Nicolas Boucher, 1545).

636   Translator's note: a very awkward construction; literally, 'by the work of whom there was advice to the Church'.

637   Charles V, *Mandat Karls V. an die säumigen Reichsstände, sich umgehend auf dem*

Reichstag in Regensburg einzufinden (n.p., 1545); see Herte, *Lutherkommentare*, 69–70, n. 10.

638 Jn. 8: 51.

639 Cochlaeus, *Necessaria et Catholica Consyderatio super Lutheri Articulis, quos velit Concilio Generali proponi* (Ingolstadt, Alexander Weissenhorn, 1546); he seems to have forgotten counting this title among the previous year's publications.

640 Cochlaeus, *In XVIII Articulos Mar. Buceri excerptos ex novissimo libro eius ad principes et status Sacri Ro. Imperii latine scripto* (Ingolstadt, Alexander Weissenhorn, 1546).

641 This may refer to Cochlaeus, *Annotationes et antitheses Joannis Cochlaei, in quaedam scripta et propositiones collocutorum Wittenbergensium* (Ingolstadt, Alexander Weissenhorn, 1546).

642 Cochlaeus, *Epitome Apostolicarum constitutionum, in Creta insula, per Carolum Capellium Venetum repertarum, et e Greco in Latinum translatarum* (Ingolstadt, Alexander Weissenhorn, 1546).

Index